Pat Speer
105 Pierce Ave.
Bridgeport, CT 06604-1650

D0847747

"One cannot help but react to Leon Podles' book with a mixture of outrage, shock and, for Catholics at least, profound shame. The author's formidable investigative skills are brought to bear in his detailed accounts of several of the most outrageous Catholic clergy abuse cases, including that of Gilbert Gauthe, whose case broke the centuries' old cover of the hierarchy.

"*Sacrilege* is unique and invaluable as a one-volume source of the hard facts about clergy sex abuse and the variety of underlying causes. It is also invaluable as a source of comprehending the complex scope of the issue, because it provides highly insightful analyses into the ecclesiastical cover-up.

"There have been dozens of books written about clergy sex abuse, but this book is a 'must-have.' It captures the horror in searing detail, but it goes much deeper, delving into the often elusive causes of the horror. In so doing, *Sacrilege* is not just a story about the most devastating betrayal of trust in the history of Catholicism. It is a thoughtful inquiry into the never-ending 'why' that will not bring comfort to any decent person but will at least provide plausible and factually accurate explanations."

—THOMAS DOYLE, J.C.D., C.A.C.D.
coauthor of *Sex, Priests, and Secret Codes: The Catholic Church's 2,000-Year Paper Trail of Sexual Abuse*

"*Sacrilege* is a relentless examination of the clergy sex abuse crisis in the Roman Catholic Church with great compassion for the victims. Leon J. Podles stands apart from other investigators by virtue of his orthodoxy. That won't sit well with some church officials and ideologues of the left. All the more reason why this book deserves to be read."

—JASON BERRY
author of *Lead Us Not into Temptation: Catholic Priests and the Sexual Abuse of Children*

"*Sacrilege* is the most extensive inquiry to date into sexual abuse in the Catholic Church. Thoroughly documented and eminently readable, it is a harrowing journey into the darkest moment of the Catholic Church in modern times. Agree or not with its conclusions, you cannot fail to be provoked by this work."

—JOHN ZUCCHI
Professor of History, McGill University, Montreal

"Leon Podles is a scholar and an intent and committed Christian. His earlier book, *The Church Impotent: the Feminization of Christianity*, firmly establishes his credentials. He uses them exquisitely to consider the history and dynamic of sexual abuse of children by Catholic priests in the United States. He pulls no punches in calling the situation a sacrilege—the desecration or theft of something sacred. Certainly the sexual violation of thousands of boys and girls by the priests and bishops they trusted is profanity of the basest order. Podles' investigative skills make the book indispensable for anyone seriously concerned about sexual abuse of minors by priests and bishops, or anyone. His writing style makes for easy reading of a difficult and painful subject."

—A. W. Richard Sipe
author of *Sex, Priests, and Power: The Anatomy of a Crisis*

"Dr. Podles' book, *Sacrilege: Sexual Abuse in the Catholic Church*, is an informative, forcefully written, trenchant investigation of the extent and nature of the sexual abuse of children and adolescents in the Catholic Church. Although Dr. Podles' primary focus is the Catholic Church in the United States, his comparative examples suggest the historical, geographical and ecumenical persistence and magnitude of this abuse. His fearless pursuit of the predators and their accomplices, his disciplined deconstruction of the 'psycho-gab' used to justify and defend the abusers casts a harsh light on what appears to be systematic abuse. As a committed Catholic, stepped in its history, theology and governance, Dr. Podles suggests ways and means to address this tragic offense squarely and honestly, rejecting facile analysis and solutions. *Sacrilege* is a passionate plea for justice, recognition, repentance, restitution and responsibility."

—Carman Miller
Professor of History, McGill University, Montreal

# SACRILEGE

## SEXUAL ABUSE IN THE CATHOLIC CHURCH

LEON J. PODLES

CROSSLAND PRESS
2008

WARNING: THIS BOOK CONTAINS
EXPLICIT TESTIMONY OF ABUSE VICTIMS

Leon Podles can be contacted at podles@CrosslandFoundation.org.
His website, podles.org, carries updated information on cases in the book.



Published in the United States by
Crossland Press
P.O. Box 26290
Baltimore, MD 21210

ISBN-13: 978-0-9790279-9-4
ISBN-10: 0-9790279-9-3

Library of Congress Control Number: 2007922867

Printed in the United States of America

*To all the children*
*who were abused by priests*
*and who then committed suicide.*

IN MEMORIAM ÆTERNAM

# CONTENTS

# INTRODUCTION

UNDER THE PONTIFICATE OF JOHN PAUL II, the almost one billion members of the Roman Catholic Church faced challenges from the outside: the materialism and secularism of the West eroded faith and practice and led to a decline in the numbers of priests and even in the numbers of laity in most developed countries; extreme poverty afflicted many Catholics in South America and Africa; harassment, persecution, and even martyrdom were inflicted on Christians who lived on the bloody fringes of militant Islam. These external troubles are painful, but were hardly unexpected. The Founder had warned that the faith of some would be choked by the cares and pleasures of life, that the poor would be always present, and that his followers could expect persecution, as He himself was persecuted to death on a cross.

But the Founder's warnings about wolves coming into the sheepfold went largely unheeded. It was a warning that leaders of the Church did not want to call attention to, because it might apply to them. The Church in 2002 had a harsh light cast upon its internal operations, as revelation after revelation about the sexual abuse of minors by priests and about the failure of bishops to protect children shook the church, culminating (so far) in the resignation of Cardinal Bernard Law of Boston, in the bankruptcy of several America dioceses, and in the payment of hundreds of millions of dollars in damages to victims. Wolves in the guise of shepherds had been loose in the sheepfold, rending and tearing and destroying the souls of young

Catholics. The shepherds had failed to protect the sheep. The Church, as the heavenly Bride of Christ, may be without spot or wrinkle, but the earthly institution of the clergy was deformed by its failure to remove clerical molesters from its ranks. Even anti-clericalists were disappointed in the Church; even they expected its faults to be less sordid.

The flood of scandals in 2002 should not have surprised anyone because there were numerous warnings, which the public ignored and which the hierarchy was therefore able to treat as petty annoyances. But something happened to heighten the anxiety of the American public: September 11, 2001. Parents realized that American society was vulnerable to massive attack, and that our government had spent trillions of dollars in defense but could not protect us from nineteen determined men. Then came the revelations about the bizarre sexual hungers of John Geoghan and Paul Shanley in Boston, and the public was shocked at what certain priests had done to children and, perhaps even more, what bishops had allowed priests to do.

The Internet served to spread and magnify the news. What previously had been confined to local papers was now available worldwide. It was possible to get an overview of the problem while sitting at home in front of a computer. The long suppression of scandals, like the suppression of forest fires, made the resulting explosion all the worse. Fifteen years ago it would have been impossible to write this book without thousands of miles of travel and years of research in newspaper archives. But most of the news is now on the Internet. It is harder and harder to suppress or control the flow of information. There is no Index of Forbidden Websites.

I have confined myself almost entirely to using publicly available sources—newspaper and magazine articles, court documents, books—rather than conducting personal interviews. I have sought not to uncover new data but to interpret the data that is already in the public sphere but has often been ignored. I have cited only a small fraction of the material I have consulted, which in turn is only a small fraction of the material that is available (especially in court documents[1] ), and that in turn represents only a small fraction of cases of abuse, only a few of which have been documented in detail. But I am confident that further material will only confirm the patterns I have discerned.

The bishops made excuses, but the excuses did not excuse. Bishops claimed they were only following the advice of psychologists, but they put abusive priests in parishes even when the psychologists warned against it. Why hadn't bishops ever gotten angry at abusers? Why were abusers treated so gently, when men who left the priesthood to marry were treated so harshly? Why had bishops lied to parents? Why hadn't they disciplined their clergy, when they seemed so eager to micromanage everything else in America, from what married couples did in bed to what the government did about immigration?

The dismay and revulsion caused by the scandals did not divide along liberal / conservative lines, although the analysis of the causes tended to divide along the usual fault lines in the Church.[2] Some liberals, such as Robert Bennett, were horrified and devoted months of their time to trying to excise this cancer from the Church; others, like Andrew Greeley, Peter Steinfels, and the editors of *America* magazine, tried to minimize the problem, placing it "in context." They claimed Philip Jenkins, author of *Pedophiles and Priests*,[3] as a supporter, but his point (despite the misleading title of his book) was that a moral panic was growing up around clerical *pedophilia*, when the real problem was clerical *homosexual* molestation of teenagers.[4] Some conservatives followed the minimizing approach: Farley Clinton, a columnist for *The Wanderer*, a conservative Catholic newspaper, and also initially Cardinal Joseph Ratzinger (now Pope Benedict XVI). But other conservatives, such as Rod Dreher and Deal Hudson, were livid at the failures of the hierarchy. At *The Wanderer*, Paul Likoudis for years had broadcast the sins of abusive priests, sins which he identified with homosexuality.[5] Among those who reacted strongly to the news of abuse, liberal or conservative mindsets did, however, lead to different diagnoses of the cause of the scandals: celibacy and clericalism on the one hand, homosexuality and dissent on the other.

A book such as this one is inevitably something of an essay, the reaction of a person with a particular background to the events he is describing.

Readers will ask about my background, and wonder whether I have an ax to grind in writing this book.

I was raised in a generally non-practicing household (my parents had marital difficulties) but we children were sent to Mass and Catholic school. I liked the Catholic elementary school I went to. We had a round of First Friday Masses, May crownings, rosaries, spiritual bouquets, and all the popular devotions of the 1950s. My teachers were pleasant and competent; they occasionally showed irritation, but I now marvel at how they kept order in classes of fifty active children, taught them useful skills, and maintained their own sanity. I was not close to any of the priests of the parish, which was just as well, because one of them, Ross LaPorta, was listed by the Archdiocese of Baltimore as accused of abuse.[6] I remember being very uncomfortable about some of the questions a priest, perhaps LaPorta, asked me in confession; they may have been a preliminary to abuse, or the questions may have been innocently intended.

I won a full academic scholarship to Calvert Hall College High School which was run by the Christian Brothers founded in France by St. John Baptiste de la Salle. I underwent a religious conversion when I discovered G. K. Chesterton, C. S. Lewis, and J. R. R. Tolkien. I did extremely well in the liberal arts, and less well in trigonometry and mechanical drawing. In my senior year, my homeroom teacher and religion teacher was a Brother James, who became my nemesis.

He did not get along with the class, which dared to argue with him. Among other things, he was a strong proponent of contraception and small families, and I disagreed with him. In early fall I came down with a severe fever and was absent for ten days. My classmates gave me the religion assignments; I wrote them and put them on his desk the day I returned. When I received my report card I was surprised by the failing grade in religion, and feared for my scholarship. I asked him why I had received the grade, and he replied that since I had not put the assignments in his hand, he had never received them officially. I was infuriated, and returned to my seat and refused to make eye contact with him. He walked to my desk and slugged me so hard on the face that he broke my glasses. I left the classroom (after voicing my opinion of his stupidity and brutality), and reported what had happened to the principal. I was expelled.

Physical abuse sometimes prepares victims for sexual abuse. Boys are intimidated by the physical abuse, and then do not object when they are sexually abused. Such were the tactics several Christian Brothers of Ireland used on the boys at Mount Cashel in Newfoundland and the Christian Brothers of LaSalle used on boys in the reform schools in Ontario. I observed several incidents of physical abuse during my years at Calvert Hall. After I was expelled, the other boys in the school told me they had been intimidated by my fate: if the school could expel one of the best students, what would it do to them? I later heard rumors that that a violent brother had also been sexually interested in or involved with students. It would fit one pattern, although most abusers rely on persuasion and deception rather than force.

A chaplain at Calvert Hall, Lawrence Brett, a priest of the diocese of Bridgeport, was later accused of sexual abuse (see pp. 189–192). Jerome "Jeff" Toohey, who was a student in my year at Calvert Hall, was ordained, returned to the school as chaplain and advisor to the swim team, and fled to Las Vegas when he was accused. He has since returned to Baltimore and pleaded guilty to abuse (see pp. 199–200). I received a letter from Calvert Hall (which considers me an alumnus and still asks for money) informing the alumni that "in 2002, an alumnus wrote to us claiming that he had been sexually molested by Brother . . . Xavier," who had died in 1985. The school then got another letter from an alumnus claiming that this brother had molested him. The school announced that the special education program that had been named after Brother Xavier Langan was being renamed the La Salle Program. An atmosphere of physical abuse had prepared the way for sexual abuse.

I graduated from a public high school and thought I might have a vocation to the priesthood, mostly because of my interest in Thomas Aquinas and medieval philosophy. I therefore entered Guzman Hall at Providence College, a dormitory for college students who were thinking about the priesthood. I grew more and more uncomfortable there, and decided that I could not live in an institution the rest of my life, because I wanted to have a family. One source of my discomfort (although I was not aware of it) was the strong undercurrent of homosexuality at Guzman Hall. My roommate, Jeffrey Tacy, made a sexually aggressive move on me in my sleep. I thought he had gone insane. At dawn I reported the incident to the rector, Father Morris, whose response was, alas, typical of almost all the responses: "Why me, why me?" He focused not on my obvious distress, but on the inconvenience he faced.

I left Guzman Hall within hours and completed my education in the college. Tacy also left, but to my astonishment he was accepted the following year as a novice by the Dominicans. What had happened? Did the rector fail to report the incident? I suspect this was the case. Or did he report it and it was not believed? But no one ever questioned me. Or did he report it and the behavior was accepted as something normal for the priesthood? The rector left to marry. My abuser was eventually asked to leave the Dominicans because he spent his leisure time in gay bars. He got a law degree and entered another religious order. He was asked to leave that order because he developed AIDS. He used the last of his money to fly in a medical plane to his small hometown, and died. I pray every day for his soul. But he never asked me for forgiveness.

After college, I eventually went to the University of Virginia and studied medieval literature, with an emphasis on Old Icelandic and Old English. I taught middle school at the Heights, an Opus Dei school in Washington, D.C., where my future brother-in-law was stationed. To make it possible to marry, I took a federal personnel job in Baltimore, which shortly transmuted into a position as a federal investigator in the Office of Federal Investigations, which mostly performed background investigations for security clearances.

As an investigator I talked to thousands of people and read thousands of pages of legal documents. Some cases involved lying, alcoholism, homosexuality, adultery, violence, blackmail, extortion, suicidal tendencies, incest, and the full range of misbehavior that otherwise responsible adults engage in and the emotional problems they suffer from. (However, people also surprised me with their goodness.) I became moderately proficient at detecting liars and confidence artists. I was always surprised at the ease with which confidence artists fabricated résumés and were hired on the basis of non-existent experience. They were small imposters rather than Great Imposters, but they exploited the same weaknesses in employers: laziness about verifying work, desire to avoid confrontation, and reluctance to admit they had made a mistake in hiring someone.

My family rapidly grew to six children in eight years (twins helped), and when the time came, my wife and I decided to send them to our parish school. Our oldest grew increasingly bored, and I began having grave doubts about the school, doubts which crystallized when the eighth-grade students wrote letters to the Baltimore *Catholic Review* in which they opined that it was unreasonable to expect middle school students to refrain from sex, and that Catholics schools should distribute condoms. I was astonished that the teacher who collected the letters and forwarded them to the *Catholic Review* should consider them evidence about how well Catholic education was working, and I was even more astonished that the *Catholic Review* should print them as evidence of the success of Catholic education. It was not an environment in which I wanted to leave my children, so my wife and I homeschooled them through high school. I also became an assistant scoutmaster, camped many nights with my sons, and organized a trip for the whole troop to Germany.

Although I was not able to pursue my scholarly interests, I took up writing occasional pieces which were published in periodicals ranging from *America* and *The Antioch Review* to *Crisis* and *The Wanderer* (I may be the only person to have written for all four). The editors of *Touchstone,* an ecumenical venture of conservative Orthodox, Catholics, and Protestants, liked my articles and asked me to become a senior editor. My articles on male-female relationships in Christianity led to my book, *The Church Impotent: The Feminization of Christianity.* I had been puzzled by the lack of men in Catholic activities, and I was surprised that my circle of acquaintances included a large number of homosexuals. I realized that I had met these men through Catholic activities, through Mass and the charismatic renewal. My research soon revealed that men had stayed away from all the branches of Western Christianity for centuries. Men had doubts about the masculinity of those men who were closely involved with the Church (such as the clergy) and sometimes those doubts were justified. I decided there was a centuries-old misunderstanding of masculinity and femininity, a misunderstanding that led men to distance themselves from the Church and that relegated women to a role of passive obedience. My book was noticed; a few hated it, but most reviewers said I had called attention to an important problem, even if they did not agree with my analysis.

I first met Cardinal Law when we had dinner together in November 2001 to discuss someone whose services we both wanted for charities we sponsored. My wife and I were going to inform Cardinal Law that the person in question was not Law's indentured servant, and that if the person wanted to work mostly for another charity, Law had to let him go graciously.

The famous episcopal residence on Commonwealth Avenue was a cross between a bank and a train station: impressive but cold, and neither elegant nor comfortable. A nun cooked our dinner, and Law himself humbly served it and cleared the table. My wife and I kept trying to bring up the subject we all knew I wanted to discuss, and Law and his secretary managed to steer the conversation away from it every time the danger of actually discussing it loomed. It was rather like watching a good basketball team keeping possession of the ball. After dinner Law took us up to the roof patio and showed us the night scene. He pointed out the seminary, and said he wanted to establish a graduate theological school there. I asked why, since there were already so many Catholic colleges and universities in Boston. He replied that none of the others was orthodox. This is of course true, but it was rather odd for him to share this opinion with me the first time we met. He knew my theological opinions, and the remark was obviously manipulative, giving the appearance that he was taking me into his confidence. When we left the roof we took the elevator and his secretary could not fit into it. My wife and I had Law alone and she launched into the real subject of the evening, that he had to let our friend work elsewhere if our friend wanted to. Law mock cowered with his hands held up, saying no, no, he couldn't and wouldn't hear such things. That, alas, was also his response when infinitely more serious problems were brought up to him in the Boston archdiocese.

Shortly after my November 2001 meeting with Law, the secrecy in Boston began to end. In 2002, after the Boston newspapers began printing the stores about abuse, I wrote a *Touchstone* article pointing out that celibacy was not the source of the abuse. The editors at Spence Publishing, which had done my first book, asked me to expand the article to a book, but I was soon overwhelmed, horrified, and disturbed by the stream of revelations. I realized that problems I had experienced over the years were the result of the abuse I had suffered, because other victims had the same reactions. In some ways this was a relief, but it also increased my determination to get to the truth of what had gone wrong with my Church that had allowed such corruption to exist and spread.

The truth is important, and I am very dubious about those who want to use the revelations of abuse to push for a favorite reform, whether married priests or women priests or power sharing or the Latin Mass or purging homosexuals from the clergy. It would be immoral to use the sufferings of the victims to advance an agenda, unless that agenda were based in a convincing analysis of the problem. I would like Catholics to look at themselves in the mirror and see the truth about themselves and their failures. Priests have done terrible things, and much of the rest of the Church—bishops, popes, even the laity—has been complicit.

The first part of the book tells a partial history of the abuse. The abuse is far more widespread, goes back farther, and is far worse than any outsider could have imagined when the revelations in Boston began in 2002. I hesitated long about including explicit descriptions of the abuse. But the newspaper reports, which often use the word "fondling," have misled the public which wonders why the victims can't get over it and why the priests have to be punished so harshly. So I decided to include them. Spence Publishing refused to publish the book they had commissioned, because while they realized the descriptions of abuse were essential to the book, they could not bring themselves to publish them.

The descriptions of abuse, mostly taken from affidavits of victims, are deeply disturbing for the normal reader, and may be too much for someone who has himself or herself been abused, so I advise caution in reading the first two chapters in particular. But the reader should remember that the pain of reading about abuse is far less than the pain of experiencing abuse. It is painful to contemplate suffering, especially if we have been in any way complicit in it, if only by our failure to act. The German public is only beginning to face the horrors that the German civilians went through at the end of World War II. Not only were its cities bombed and its women and children incinerated, the women of Berlin had to submit to mass rape by the Soviet Army, rape which was not simply forcible intercourse but was made as degrading as possible. *A Woman in Berlin: Eight Weeks in a Conquered City*[7] was not published in Germany until 2003. It is the diary of an anonymous woman who lived through the rapes and described them in explicit detail. The American government in World War II tried to prepare the public for the carnage of the Pacific theatre by publishing uncensored pictures of the battlefield, with severed heads and limbs bobbing in the water. The public could not stand to see what it was putting American soldiers through and all subsequent pictures were sanitized. Films of the devastation of Hiroshima were suppressed for decades. Americans don't like to see the sufferings of their soldiers, or contemplate the even greater degradation that killing other human beings does to the human soul. But if we are willing to tolerate evils, we should not flinch from looking at those evils. Some may be inescapable, but many are the results of laziness and complacency.

The toleration of abuse was not necessary. It was and is convenient. A canonized saint tolerated abuse. Rings of abusers go back at least to the 1940s in America, and abuse involved sacrilege, orgies, and probably murder (and perhaps even worse).[8] Bishops knew about the abuse and sometimes took part in it. Those who complained were ignored or threatened, and the police refused to investigate crimes committed by clergy.

There are also those who might enjoy the descriptions of abuse. BishopAccountability.org maintains a website that contains articles and legal documents on abuse. It discovered that some legal documents containing descriptions of abuse were being linked to homosexual pornography websites. However, I doubt that persons who would be stimulated by the descriptions are likely to buy this book.

As hard as it may be to believe, I have also practiced restraint in using documents. As horrifying and disgusting as the abuse described in the book is, I have even worse things in my files. Psychologists also generally agree that victims usually cannot bring themselves to describe the worst abuse they experienced. A boy will admit that he was masturbated, but not admit that he was penetrated. There are therefore two levels of evil beyond the evil of the abuse described in this book: the descriptions of abuse I have not used, and beyond that the abuse that victims have not been able to bring themselves to describe.

At the center and heart of the book is the chapter on the victims, how they were chosen, how they were groomed, what was done to them, how the abuse affected them. It is painful to read; it was even more painful to write. But it is important to read details of the abuse to see why victims found the abuse so traumatic. The victims experienced traumas like those of combat soldiers. War may be a dreadful necessity at times, but the civilians who send young men to the hell of combat should not turn their faces away from the horror. Those whose complicity (and that included many besides the bishops) enabled the abusers should see what their silence led the victims to suffer.

The abuse and the toleration of the abuse have many causes; some were proximate, others distant. Different wings of the Church have looked at the causes that fit in with their particular agendas.

> The conservatives were blaming the era of post-Vatican II permissiveness, hedonism, widespread laxity, and the infiltration of homosexuals into the priesthood. The progressives or liberals were arguing that the decisions of Vatican II had not been applied; that the bishops and the

> laity had been rendered immature and irresponsible by an authoritarian, highly centralized Holy See; this, in turn, they charged, had encouraged a generation of clerics in arrested development at a time when permissiveness was prevalent in society at large.[9]

These explanations are not exclusive; there is plenty of blame to go around. Abuse increased in the 1970s and 1980s, but some of the worst abuse (verging on diabolism) occurred before Vatican II and the change in sexual attitudes in the 1960s.

The distortions in Catholic life that allowed the abuse to continue with little rebuke are, I think, of long standing; Catholic attitudes, in fact Western attitudes, to morality have been distorted for centuries by seeing morality as essentially obedience to an external law rather than an expression of the inner structure of reality. This creates resentment against the law as a restriction of human freedom, a resentment which, as we will see, can take the form of sexual abuse of children, and a failure to see that abuse does not simply violate an external law, but does real harm to victims. Forgiveness becomes cheap grace, since the sinner forgets that he has done real harm which must somehow be addressed before he can be forgiven.

The Vatican helped set the stage for the abuse by cultivating a clericalist mentality that saw the clergy as the real church, and making the purpose of canon law the protection of the rights and reputation of the clergy, not the protection of children from abuse. The Vatican had also carefully chosen and appointed bishops who would not rock the boat, who would not discipline the clergy and perhaps create a schism. The Vatican—and this means Pope Paul VI and Pope John Paul II—sought to maintain a façade of institutional unity by tolerating heresy, dissent, and immorality, and got a Church (at least in the United States) in which the laity mistrusted priests, bishops, and popes; the priests mistrusted the laity and bishops; the bishops mistrusted the laity, priests, and the Vatican. In fact, it is hard to explain why bishops almost always followed the same policy of transferring rather than punishing abusive priests unless they had been so instructed by the Vatican—the pope must have either let the situation develop or set the policy himself.

The abusers are the primary villains, and the Catholic bishops of the United States have belatedly joined in condemning them and removing them from the priesthood. However, the charter to protect children, zero-tolerance policies, fingerprinting of church volunteers, Good Touch-Bad Touch programs, all effectively direct public attention solely to the abusers and away from the complicity of bishops and church officials in the abuse. The abusers were sexually vicious and exploitative but the bishops coolly and deliberately ignored victims and constructed elaborate schemes to keep abusers in the priesthood where they had the opportunity to abuse again. The hard-heartedness and manipulativeness of seemingly rational men in responsible positions are perhaps in an objective view even more disturbing than the lust for sex and control that the abusers displayed.

Some have asked me how I can remain a Catholic after I have discovered the corruption in the Church. I am grieved by what I have found, but I also realize that we have been warned that such things will occur. Jesus' diatribe against the Pharisees in Matthew was directed not simply at them. He agreed with them doctrinally, and he told his followers to respect their authority. But the Pharisees used their religious authority to maintain a façade of righteousness and to demand obeisance from pious Jews, when all the while they were filled with avarice and corruption. The dynamics of corruption were present in the religious communities of Judaism and of the early Church that sprang from it, and the first believers in Jesus were given solemn warnings to beware of corruptions in their leaders.

Any religion can become corrupt.

> Religions can also make it harder for man to be good. This can happen even in Christianity because of false ways of living the Christian reality, sectarian deformations, and so forth. In this sense, in the history and universe of religions, there is always a great necessity to purify religion so that it does not become an obstacle to the right relation to God but in fact puts man on the right path.[10]

Martin Luther was not the only one to argue that the Church is *semper reformanda*, always to be reformed. The above quotation is from a 1996 interview with Cardinal Joseph Ratzinger, now Pope Benedict XVI.

A doctor can diagnose cancer without being able to cure it. I offer a few suggestions for reforms, but Catholics will have to examine their consciences to discern the failures that allowed such terrible things to happen in their Church. Acknowledging the truth is the first step to repentance. I hope that this book will help Catholics face the painful realities in their Church and discern what has allowed these affronts to God and man to go on so long, unchecked and unrebuked. Nor is abuse confined to the Catholic Church or to other churches, and all institutions that deal with children—Scouts, schools, Big Brothers—have to understand the conditions that set the stage for abuse so that they can prevent it.

That is why I have written this book. Attacking sexual abuse is not attacking the Catholic Church, but is seeking to hold it to its own standards of justice and mercy and love. Tom Paciorek, the All-Star major league baseball player, finally revealed that even he had been sexually abused by a seminarian and had been deeply wounded by the abuse. He spoke to the newspapers and appeared on television to discuss his abuse (and imagine how humiliating that felt) for the sake of children. He said, "This is no conspiracy. This is truth. I'm going to live in this truth, and we're going to do the right thing. I start thinking about children, and I just don't want anybody to have to go through what we did, my brothers and I."[11]

## *The Structure of the Catholic Church*

Even reporters in Catholic countries like Ireland are confused about the structure of the Roman Catholic Church, and readers of this book who are not Catholics may need a guide to the organization.

The Catholic Church recognizes the Sacrament of Holy Orders. It, like baptism, impresses an indelible mark on the soul. Once a priest is ordained by a bishop, he is always a priest, even if he cannot function as one. Bishops have the fullness of the priesthood. The pope, as far as his sacramental powers go, is one bishop among all the others.

The bishop rules a diocese; he is the ordinary of that diocese. He is appointed by the pope (although in the past bishops were elected by the people or priests or appointed by secular political authorities). Only the pope can remove him (again, it was different in the past). Each bishop is independent in his diocese and is responsible only to the pope.

Archbishops and cardinals have no legal authority over other bishops, although they have prestige, and can use that prestige to influence other bishops.

A bishop is responsible for his priests. He ordains them and assigns them and is responsible for their maintenance until their deaths. His relationship with them is governed by canon law, which in turn is promulgated by the pope. The pope also claims immediate jurisdiction over every Catholic, including every priest. A priest can appeal the actions of his bishop to the pope, that is, to a court in the Vatican.

Parallel to and outside the structure of the diocese are religious orders. They operate largely (although not entirely) independently of the local bishops and report to their own elected superiors. A bishop has little direct authority over a member of a religious order in his diocese. The pope theoretically exercises jurisdiction over these orders, although they are in practice almost entirely self-governing.

The Vatican itself is composed of various organizations. The pope appoints their heads and they report to him, but they are largely independent of one another and sometimes act at cross-purposes. There is not always a unanimity of opinion and policy throughout the Vatican.

For an American's perception of how the Vatican works (or sometimes doesn't work) John Allen's *All the Pope's Men* is invaluable, although he attributes the failure to address sexual abuse effectively to ordinary human and bureaucratic failings, an explanation which seems inadequate to explain the depth and extent of the evil.

CHAPTER ONE

# THE RECTORY BOYS OF EL PASO

Under conditions of privacy and confidentiality, Catholic priests and religious have access to people who are emotionally and spiritually vulnerable. The men (and occasionally the women) occupying these positions of trust are sometimes tempted to use their privileged access to satisfy their own desires, whether for power or money or sex. The powerful commit crimes, and the innocent and weak suffer; such abuse has gone on for centuries. The Catholic Church has created safeguards against this abuse, but the safeguards are not always adequate. Even worse, those in charge of administering the safeguards all too often do not take seriously their obligations to protect the innocent and weak. Other priorities—comfort, ease, reputation, money—determine what actions they take; they want the victims to be invisible.

The Fathers of the Church warned about the dangers of too-close association with handsome boys. Abba Isaac, a fourth-century Egyptian monk, wrote, "Do not bring young boys here."[1] Abba Carion, another Egyptian monk, wrote that "a monk who lives with a boy falls, he is not stable."[2] Benedict, the founder of Western monasticism, specified in his Rule that a light must be kept burning in the dormitory at night.[3] Basil, who gave the monastic rule to the East, said that "any cleric or monk who seduces young men or boys, or who is apprehended in kissing or in any shameful situation, shall be publicly flogged and shall lose his clerical tonsure."[4] The early church recognized human failings and took steps to guard against them and to punish criminals.[5]

In the eleventh century St. Peter Damian in his Letter 31, also known as *The Book of Gomorrah*, wrote to Pope Leo IX of the corruption of the clergy. Peter Damian was concerned with homosexual intercourse among clerics, the abuse of boys, and the degradation of the priesthood. Then as now authorities turned a blind eye to problems: "Listen you do-nothing superiors of clerics and priests. Listen and, even though you feel sure of yourselves, tremble at the thought that you are partners in the guilt of others; those, I mean, who wink at the sins of their subjects that need correction and who by ill-considered silence allow them license to sin."[6] Leo thanked Peter Damian for his efforts but did not follow his advice, setting a bad precedent of papal inaction.[7]

During the Catholic Counter-Reformation, bishops tried to raise the general level of morality and spiritual fervor among Catholics by insisting that serious sins be confessed to a priest. This practice brought dangers, especially as penitents were often women. In Spain, for example, women were restricted in their movements, and one of the few opportunities priests had to speak with women privately was in the confessional, which some priests used to solicit women. The Church required penitents to inform the Inquisition about such solicitation, and priests were severely punished. Homosexual priests had many opportunities to solicit males and did not need the confessional (which men tended not to frequent in any case).

Children, however, were vulnerable. In 1612 a ten-year-old Spanish girl, Catalina de la Cruz, testified to the Inquisition that her confessor, Gaspar de Nájera, had abused her. The Inquisitor "was extremely reluctant to take her testimony seriously even though he reported that Nájera had such a bad reputation that the children of Granadilla had made up a little ditty about him beginning with 'boys and girls watch out for Father Nájera.' When little Catalina presented herself, the Inquisitor warned her not to tell any lies 'because liars go to hell,' and after he finished taking her deposition, he expressed doubts about accepting it as valid because she was so young and unsophisticated."[8] Victims then as now were subject to closer scrutiny than priests were. Clericalism and disdain for the laity have a long and dishonorable history in the Catholic Church.[9]

A cover-up of sexual abuse was ordered by "the patron saint of all Christian schools,"[10] St. Joseph Calasanctius. He was himself pious and ascetic, as were most of his followers. The order he founded in 1621 expanded too rapidly and accepted questionable members. One was Stefano Cherubini. When Cherubini's abuse of students in the Piarist school in Naples was reported to him, Calasanctius wrote to the investigator "that Your Reverence's sole aim is to cover up [*cuprir*] this great shame in order that it does not come to the notice of our superiors, otherwise our organization, which has enjoyed a good reputation until now, would lose greatly."[11] Calasanctius took Stefano out of the Naples school where he was abusing boys and promoted him to an administrative position in the Piarist headquarters in Rome to keep an eye on him. There Stefano plotted.

In 1643 the authorities of the Roman Catholic Church appointed the influential and well-connected Stefano Cherubini, "a known child abuser"[12] to be the "universal superior of a Catholic teaching order," the Piarists, with the "full complicity of the Inquisition and the pope," Innocent X, over the protests of Piarists from all over Europe. Too late, Calasanctius then wrote to the cardinals that "I was frequently informed of the wicked practices [*cattiva practica*] that Father Stefano degli Angeli [Cherubini] . . . did with some pupils, and to avoid the scandal . . . I took him away from Naples and brought him to Rome with an honorable title out of respect for his family."[13] The cardinals were unmoved, and Cherubini remained in charge of the Piarists.

One Piarist complained that Cherubini and his fellow abusers tried to remake the Piarists after their own image, "blackening the purity and candor of the Order and of so many pure and holy souls with their fetid and infamous filth."[14] The order dissolved into chaos and in 1646 was suppressed, not to be restored for twenty years. Calasanctius died with his order in ruins and in disgrace. The conventional history books say the Piarists were suppressed because of the jealousy of the Jesuits; the true story of the sexual abuse and suppression came to light only in 2004 with the publication of Karen Liebreich's *Fallen Order: A History*.

The Catholic Church knew that priests sometimes abused their position to obtain sex from the laity and it therefore had procedures to punish such priests. But these procedures rarely have been rigorously followed, whether in the seventeenth century or the twentieth. Church authorities have been remiss for centuries in their protection of children, but it was not until the start of the twenty-first century that some light has been shone in the dark corners of the Church, partially revealing the extent and depth of the abuse.

## *El Paso*

St. Pius X parish in El Paso, according to author Paul Wilkes, "is considered not only one of the most outstanding Hispanic parishes in America, but one of the best, period."[15] It has a new Spanish Revival church building and a creative and active Hispanic congregation. There are fiestas in the plazas outside the church, "Tamales and Menudos" breakfasts after Mass, an outreach to AIDS patients, cooperation with poor parishes across the Rio Grande in Juarez, Mexico, and a five-hundred-fifty-student school with a gym that used to be the old church building, which was built by the founder of the parish, Msgr. Lawrence E. Gaynor. The current pastor, Father Arturo J. Bañuelos, from all accounts leads a parish that is serious about Catholic faith and service. Few if any of the current parishioners know what went on in the rectory in the 1950s and 1960s. Those who remember it are mostly no longer Catholics.

The diocese of El Paso, Texas, was not established until 1914, but it has churches that have been used continuously since 1680. In the nineteenth century the predominantly Mexican population was supplemented by Anglos (as all non-Hispanic persons of European descent are called) and the first cathedral church was therefore named St. Patrick's. El Paso was a poor border area and was always in desperate need of money and priests.

The bishop who presided over one of the earliest known abuse cover-ups in the United States was Sydney Matthew Metzger of Fredericksburg, Texas. He entered the seminary when he was thirteen years old, studied in Rome, was ordained in 1926, taught at St. John's Seminary in San Antonio, and became an auxiliary bishop in San Antonio. In 1942 Pope Pius XII appointed Metzger the second bishop of El Paso. Metzger traveled the United States, begging for money for his diocese. He also accepted priests who found a need for a sudden change of scene. Metzger's career was intertwined with the careers of a group of some of the worst known abusive clerics.

Lawrence E. Gaynor of New York attended several colleges, (including my alma mater, Providence College) before studying at St. Meinrad's Seminary and at St. Francis Seminary in Loreto, Pennsylvania. In 1941 he was ordained for the El Paso diocese and was stationed with two other transplanted New York priests at St. Genevieve in Las Cruces, New Mexico. People there remember him as being always active with the children of the parish. Gaynor also began visiting Holy Family parish in Deming, New Mexico, where the Rev. William J. Ulzheimer, the first director of the El Paso Catholic Youth Organization,[16] was pastor. In New Mexico Gaynor picked up two Hispanic boys whom he sexually abused. He had them enter the seminary and be ordained, and they served as priests in the El Paso diocese until around the time Gaynor died, when they broke away, left the priesthood, and married.[17] In 1946 Gaynor was transferred to St. Patrick's Cathedral in El Paso where he became a close friend of Bishop Metzger, who made him pastor of Holy Family Church, El Paso, from 1949 to 1954, in which year he founded a new parish, St. Pius X.[18] A parish booklet praised him as "a man of God, dedicated to the highest standards," who told everyone "the little children of the school and parish are his 'most precious possessions.'"[19]

Around 1958 Gaynor did something that got him sent to Via Coeli in Jemez Springs, New Mexico, a treatment center run by the Servants of the Paraclete. This was an institution founded by Father Gerald Fitzgerald (see pp. 89ff.) to treat alcoholic and depressive priests but which soon started receiving priests who were sexual abusers of minors. One member of the order, Father Wilfred Savard, met Gaynor there and did not like him. Savard placed him in the category of an "All Hallows type." (All Hallows is a seminary in Ireland that trains missionary priests.) In Savard's opinion, it produced a group of smooth talkers who were interested in sex and money.[20] After his stay at Jemez Springs, Gaynor returned to St. Pius X.

In El Paso Gaynor's path intersected that of Irving F. Klister. Klister was born in Rib Lake, Wisconsin, in 1915. The Catholic parish in Rib Lake, St. John the Baptist, was staffed by the Stigmatine Fathers, who later stationed an accused priest, Louis A. Telegdy,[21] there as pastor from 1961 to 1962. Rib Lake either had bad luck or perhaps this small town was used to hide abusers (and produce pornography, as we shall see). Klister entered the University of Notre Dame in 1937 and graduated in 1939.

While he was at Notre Dame Klister began to prey on youths, as he boasted in a 1987 handwritten letter to what he thought was a pornography dealer but was in fact a postal inspector. The boy was fourteen and Klister was twenty-two years old.[22]

> I lived in the Midwest area. Alone in a comfortable apartment. In the next block lived a family with two boys. One [—] was 14, streetwise, & had a reputation for having sticky fingers. He was big for his age; of Swedish descent, therefore blond, had a fine sculptured face and frame like an athlete. In other words, he was a doll and I hoped to be able to make it some day with him. I made him a friend[,] gave him money for errands, and had him in for treats of candy, pop, etc. He got to know the apartment and often saw money laying around. One day when I arrived home unexpectedly I found him in the act of breaking into the apartment thru a bathroom window (I often left partially open) with the intent of robbing me.
>
> Now I really had him. I told him I would not turn him in to the police or tell his parents if he would become my "special" friend. From then on it was "easy" to entertain him in the privacy of my apartment in quite a different way....
>
> For about the next year he would come to see me two or three times a week, fully knowing what would happen.[23]

Klister described in great detail how he abused the boy. I will spare the reader that.[24]

Church authorities apparently did not know about his proclivities when Klister was accepted at Mount St. Mary's Seminary in Emmitsburg, Maryland, and was ordained for the diocese of Superior, Wisconsin, in 1944. He was immediately assigned to the Cathedral of Christ the King and rose quickly: secretary and head of the Society of the Propagation of the Faith (1946), vice chancellor (1947), director of Catholic Boy Scouts (1948), and founder and first editor of the *Catholic Herald* (1955). His career flourished under Bishop Albert Gregory Meyer. Klister said he had met Msgr. Lawrence Gaynor at national meetings of the Society for the Propagation of the Faith and found him a kindred soul.[25] In Superior Klister was stationed at a French parish, St. Louis, and at the St. Joseph's Children's Home (1954) and the Motherhouse of the Sisters of St. Joseph. Around this time he did something that got him sent to Via Coeli. He probably earned his ticket to warmer climes because of alcohol abuse or his acting on his sexual compulsions.

Soon, though, in a pattern many abusive priests would follow, Klister left New Mexico and the Paracletes for a parish assignment in Texas. When Klister arrived in Texas he was first stationed at Holy Family parish in El Paso for one year (1956) until Gaynor could clear the Pius X rectory to provide a suitable environment for like-minded priests. In 1956 Gaynor and Bishop Metzger attended the golden anniversary of Holy Family parish in Deming. Gaynor said of the late Ulzheimer that he "was so loved by the young people of Holy Family parish that when the time came for him to leave they begged the Bishop to allow him to stay in Deming" and "he planted good seeds and he planted well."[26] The possible double entendre of the remarks will become clearer as the victims describe how Gaynor, the founder of the Catholic Youth Center, worked with young people.

A circle of abusive priests had been forming in the El Paso diocese. Arthur F. O'Sullivan was ordained for the Kansas City archdiocese in 1948. He was stationed at various parishes, the last one Holy Cross in Emmett, Kansas. In 1958 O'Sullivan also headed for the El Paso diocese. He was stationed with Gaynor and Klister at Pius X, and then became pastor of Holy Family church in Deming. He invited Gaynor, Klister, and Joseph E. Flanagan to a special Thanksgiving celebration.[27] They may have known one another before O'Sullivan came to El Paso, but in any case they soon discovered that they shared sexual interests. A Las Cruces resident who was a young man when O'Sullivan was pastor there remembered that O'Sullivan had the reputation for being homosexual and had a series of young men living in his rectory. O'Sullivan also held weekly drinking parties in the rectory, to which he invited the young man from Las Cruces, who saw Bishop Metzger there, but no sign of sexual activity at the parties. From 1963 to 1967 O'Sullivan was pastor of St. Matthew's in El Paso.

Joseph Flanagan, like O'Sullivan, was from the Kansas City archdiocese. He was ordained in 1948 and assigned to the Cathedral of St. Peter the Apostle. He was at Sacred Heart Church in Mound City, Kansas, from 1954 to 1958, and then transferred to St. Pius X in El Paso, where he joined Gaynor for three years. He then went to Immaculate Heart of Mary parish in Las Cruces (1961–62) and St. Catherine's parish in Pecos, Texas (1962–67), in the far eastern section of the diocese, as far from Las Cruces as is possible to go and remain in the diocese.

Two Anglo boys were growing up in El Paso. They were members of the baby boom that filled Catholic schools after World War II. Like many Catholic boys, they became altar boys and were taught to respect priests. One of these boys, whom I shall call "Mike," was eleven when he became an altar boy and served Mass for Klister. Mike later explained that Klister for him "was an authority figure that was at God's right hand."[28] Mike, like other Catholics, had been taught to obey priests unquestioningly: "Certainly you never questioned a [p]riest or his conduct or asked why when requested to do anything." Unfortunately for these two boys (and at least several others) the priests were not the men that they appeared to be.

Mike liked Father Klister, whom he found "a funny man" who was always joking and did everything to make the boy feel important. Klister told Mike to wear only underwear under the servers' robes; Klister explained it was hot, and he wore only boxers under his vestments. After Mass Klister asked Mike "to join him in drinking wine that was the blood and body of Jesus Christ." Mike was dubious. Father Klister insisted, "Come on [Mike] join me, it's good, it's fun, it won't hurt. Look at me it doesn't hurt me." The first time Mike said no, but later he drank and in fact became drunk. Then, "Father Klister unexpectedly stuck his hands into my robe and beneath my underwear and grabbed my penis." This act did not lead to anything else immediately and Mike tried to forget it. Klister was biding his time, seeing how the boy reacted.

About two years later Mike was given the great honor of being invited to dine with Msgr. Gaynor, the pastor of St. Pius X. They met at the Pius X rectory and then Gaynor's chauffeur drove them to St. Matthew's rectory, where Father Arthur O'Sullivan was waiting for them. O'Sullivan brought the thirteen-year-old boy a steak and a bourbon and Coke, and let the boy eat alone. Mike recalled being nervous as he heard the priests laughing and arguing in the next room; he couldn't eat much. O'Sullivan brought him another bourbon and Coke.

O'Sullivan asked Mike if he would like to live at St. Matthew's to be O'Sullivan's "rectory boy" and be paid $600 a month. Mike said he would have to ask his mother. O'Sullivan called Mike's mother, who said she would think about it. O'Sullivan assured Mike that he wouldn't have to do any chores that he didn't want to do and that O'Sullivan would take him to school and help him with his homework. O'Sullivan did want one thing from Mike. He led Mike into a dark room and then, as Mike later recounted,

> He began to put both of his arms around my neck as he stood at my back. His embraces seemed friendly and earnest. I felt his stomach on my back. He then ran his hands down from my neck and shoulder area to my stomach.... [He] then pulled up a chair behind me and began rubbing my sides and my hips up and down on each side with both of his hands. Then with a hand on my inner knee, he moved that hand up swiftly toward my groin and hurt my left testicle. He apologized and began rubbing my groin and penis apparently to comfort that pain. I was terrified but Father O'Sullivan acted as if nothing was wrong, as if it was all normal.

In a fit of jealousy, Gaynor interrupted this scene and took Mike back to St. Pius X rectory. Gaynor then answered the phone and argued with O'Sullivan. Gaynor told Mike that O'Sullivan and other priests were bad priests, that he would protect Mike from them. Gaynor gave Mike a drink, took a drink himself, and then gave Mike another drink. Gaynor then called Mike's mother and told her it was late and it would be best if he spent the night at the rectory. She agreed. It was then time for bed.

Mike recounted that

> Monsignor Gaynor then asked me if I had ever had sex with a woman. I told him that I had not. Monsignor Gaynor then told me that having sex with a woman was evil. He told me that if I put my penis in a woman that I would be destroyed forever and that I could never trust a woman. He then told me that if I put my penis in a mouth it is much more pleasurable than a vagina. Monsignor Gaynor then told me to remove my pants. My underwear remained on. He repeatedly spoke to me that I needed to learn these things that he spoke of. He told me "they were pleasurable, that they were not wrong, not to be afraid, and that it was ok."
>
> Monsignor Gaynor came to me continuing to talk of the pleasures of a man's penis in a mouth and how it was important that I learn this, that he wanted my penis in his mouth and that I needed to learn these things. He rubbed my inner thigh and penis and began talking about erections and told me he wanted me to get an erection. He pulled down my underwear, rubbing my penis directly on the skin and I began to gain an erection. Monsignor Gaynor then put his mouth over the head of my penis. I pulled away and ran into the bathroom. Although Monsignor Gaynor did not seem to object, he harshly yelled at me a few minutes later that I was taking too long in the bathroom and to come out. When I returned to his combination room and office, Monsignor Gaynor was completely naked laying in his bed. He requested that I approach his bed, he grabbed me and he kissed me, inserting his tongue in my mouth. The most powerful man that I knew again repeatedly told me that this

> pleasure was ok, that I needed to learn these things, not to be afraid, that it was not wrong.
>
> Monsignor Gaynor then told me he wanted me to suck his penis with my mouth. He sucked my penis with his mouth. With his demands, I went through the process with my mouth and face at his penis, but only touching the sides. Monsignor Gaynor became very mad at this. I la[y]ed face down on his bed with my face under my arms. Monsignor Gaynor came to me and began rubbing my back and my buttocks, again explaining that "it's ok". "Don't be afraid". "You need to learn this and the important pleasures it brings and it is not wrong and there are other pleasures that are important also". As Monsignor Gaynor rubbed my buttocks, he inserted something in my anus. I am unsure whether it was his finger, or an object. I do not believe it was his penis. He continued to talk to me the entire time. He stated "you need to learn these things. They are not wrong. Don't be afraid. I will protect you." He also told me that I am trusting you [Mike] that you will not tell what is happening here. He stated "that you are a special and privileged boy to hear and share these many things from me." He kissed me again and asked me to try to suck his penis again with my mouth. I did. But I did so again barely on the side of the penis and again [h]e got mad at me and yelled at me and criticized me that I was wrong and that I was not doing a good job. With this reprimand, he powerfully asserted that he had to arise early for the 6:00 a.m. mass and that I should be sure and wake him. He went to sleep. I dressed and snuck out of his home.

Mike's friend, whom I shall call "Bob," was also targeted by this circle of priests. Gaynor began by touching Bob's genitals and fondling them. Gaynor explained to Bob that he was a priest and that therefore "it was God's will what he and I did."[29] If Bob told anyone, Gaynor and O'Sullivan would get into trouble and Bob would go to hell. O'Sullivan repeated the warning. Bob, around twelve years old, was thoroughly intimidated. Gaynor also lavished money on Bob and helped him get a job, keeping Bob off balance by alternating kindnesses and threats.

Gaynor then began the serious abuse. Bob later recounted that Gaynor

> would suck my penis in his mouth and eventually convinced me that it was ok that I do the same to him. At one point, I believe it was Monsignor Gaynor's houseboy that was also brought in to these abuse acts by Monsignor Gaynor. This houseboy would suck my penis in his mouth, as well as Monsignor Gaynor's. On one occasion, Monsignor Gaynor's houseboy penetrated my anus with his penis while Monsignor Gaynor sucked my penis in his mouth and masturbated himself.

Gaynor passed Bob around to other priests in his circle. Bob recounted that

> Father Flannigan [sic] [Rev. Joseph Flanagan], at the St. Pius Rectory, rubbed and kissed my testicles, and sucked my penis in his mouth. He began rubbing my anus with his finger and I exploded in his mouth. As did Monsignor Gaynor, Father Flannigan told me it was ok and brought me a bottle of scotch whiskey. I believe I drank approximately one-half...of that bottle and then Father Flannigan began to lick my anus. Father Flannigan then sucked my penis in his mouth again.

The abusers were not after just sexual pleasure, but wanted to degrade the victims as much as possible. The Marquis de Sade had discovered how experience is heightened by a mixture of pleasure, pain, degradation, and cruelty. These priests were his disciples.

The abuse escalated. One of O'Sullivan's houseboys drove Bob to a house near Fort Bliss.

> They started showing dirty movies involving men and women making love which gave me an erection. Then Father O'Sullivan and his houseboy began sucking each others' penis [sic]. One of them gave me a deck of cards showing men sucking each others' penis [sic]. One of Father O'Sullivan's houseboys began masturbating himself while the other

> houseboy sucked my penis in his mouth. Then the houseboy sucking my penis began sucking the penis of the other houseboy until he ejaculated in his mouth. The driver who had brought me to this house then sucked my penis in his mouth until I ejaculated. Then he wanted me to suck his penis in my mouth and I told him no and another driver for the [p]riest came in a[nd] beat me with a stick and made me suck the other driver's penis in my mouth. They then turned me over and spread the cheeks of my buttocks and entered my anus with their penis. Following this, they made me fondle with my own penis and me get on my knees while one of them sucked my penis in his mouth. I was ashamed and scared.

After a similar incident, Bob said, "I bled from my anus for about three months."

## *The Aftermath*

The boys were thrown into emotional turmoil. Just after his experience with Gaynor, Mike was at a friend's house across the street from the St. Pius rectory. Mike spotted Gaynor and the chauffeur. Mike remembered that "I completely went out of control, yelling, screaming, lying on the couch and repeatedly hitting my head on the arm of the couch. I lost control, jumping up and down inside the house. I then ran outside of the house and R[—] tackled me and I intentionally pounded my head on the concrete driveway. Finally, R[—] and his mother overpowered me and I don't remember anything after that. I remember seeing doctors and going through tests."

Mike then told his mother what had happened with Gaynor. Mike's mother took him to see Bishop Metzger. The bishop kept them waiting and then defended his men. Mike remembered that Metzger "immediately began intimidating me and making me feel like 'dirt.' He asked me if I or Monsignor Gaynor or O'Sullivan had been drinking. He loudly and powerfully admonished me that 'did I know that drinking would make people do things they didn't really mean.'" Metzger asked Mike if he had "seduced Monsignor Gaynor." Mike began thinking that "all of the matters above were my fault." Metzger thundered that Mike and his mother "were going to hell if anything I told him was not absolutely truthful." Metzger, a narcissist (see pp. 340ff.), made himself out to be the real victim by telling Mike that his own mother had just died and "wasn't I ashamed to assert these things at his time of sadness," recalled Mike. Metzger told Mike and his mother that they would hear from him. They never did.

"I felt so dirty, so worthless. . . . I felt I was the one who had done wrong," Mike recalled on leaving the meeting. Mike went downhill during his high school years. He went to seven high schools and got 150 traffic citations. "It was . . . a black time in my life." Around 1965 Mike's mother told Father Austin Parks at the Jesuit High School what had happened and sought his advice. Parks told Mike, "You need to get in good with God again and you will not get in good with God again unless these experiences die." That was because, Parks implied, Mike was the one who had done wrong. Mike remembered that "Father Parks never told me it was wrong what was done to me. He glossed over it and even supported it, leading me to believe that it was normal and that [p]riests could never be wrong."

Metzger had one final humiliation for Mike. When Mike graduated from Cathedral High School in 1966, he was told he would have to kiss Metzger's ring. Mike refused. At the graduation ceremony Mike was given only a piece of paper, and "forced to attend religious classes at Cathedral High School during the summer of 1966."[30] Only then could he receive his diploma. Despite his experiences with several priests of the diocese of El Paso, Mike remained an active Catholic and became an important financial supporter of the diocese. Such behavior is a typical result of the traumatic bond, which I will discuss at length in a later chapter.

Bob's reaction to the abuse showed an even stronger form of the traumatic bond: "I recall that during these abuse episodes, I went to Father Robert Bangert and asked him if he would see what I would have to do to become a Catholic [p]riest." Bob showed the identification with the aggressor that victims often develop.

Metzger was not overly disturbed by the actions of the abusive priests in his diocese. Klister abused an eleven-year-old boy, who finally told his mother when she suggested getting his brother involved in the altar boy program under Klister. She met with Bishop Metzger and told him about the abuse. Sitting behind his mahogany desk in his impressive office, he explained to her that "in old times it was the custom to keep boys and that Klister was so brilliant it would be a loss to the Church." She also went to the police, who told her that they could do nothing, that the Church was a world unto itself. Klister had threatened to kill the boy, and the bishop implied that it would not be good for her husband's business for them to pursue the matter.[31]

Klister abused the son of a wealthy family and in 1965 had to disappear from El Paso. He went to Mexico for a few months, then (in unknown order) to Via Coeli (the treatment center in Jemez Springs, New Mexico), to Chicago (where he was said to have worked for a bishop[32]), and to St. Vincent's Hospital in St. Louis. He was at Cristo Rey parish in Santa Fe (1969–70) and then for fifteen years pastor at St. Joseph's parish in Springer, New Mexico, until around 1985, where he also had the pastoral care of the New Mexico Boys School for abused and neglected youth. It was a perfect arrangement. If Klister wanted to satisfy himself, he could abuse boys whom no one cared about and whose complaints no one would believe.

He then retired, served as a relief priest in various parishes—and devoted himself to child pornography. When he was arrested and his apartment searched, the postal inspectors found, along with *Brother Sun, Sister Moon* and *Damian the Leper*, about 120 pornography films with titles such as *Orgies*, *Rock Hard*, *Rim Big Kiss*, *Oral Sex in Young Boys*, *Anal Piss*, and, mysteriously, *Rib Lake*. These were paid for with the retirement money he received from the archdiocese of Santa Fe. Klister pleaded guilty to using the mails to receive "an obscene, lascivious, indecent, filthy, and vile film" showing boys committing sexual acts. He received probation (despite confessing child molestation). The archdiocese of Santa Fe claimed that Klister "had developed the problems since he retired" and had never been a teacher.[33] He was sued by a victim in 1996, but denied ever abusing anyone and died on April 19, 1997, during the lawsuit.

His obituary suggested memorial donations to the Servants of the Paraclete or to the Society for the Propagation of the Faith.[34] Gaynor and

Klister had met through the Society. Klister's only punishment was probation; Gaynor received none apart from early retirement and perhaps a limitation on his sacramental duties.

In 1964 Gaynor retired and moved to Las Cruces, where he abused a teenager, Gary Pineau, from 1968 to 1972.[35] Pineau was not a Catholic; he was introduced to Gaynor by a Catholic friend. Gaynor was living in an apartment in Las Cruces, where he said the old Latin Mass to the fascination of the teenage Pineau. After saying Mass Gaynor would take Pineau into the bedroom and perform oral sex on him. He also took Pineau and a friend of his to El Paso and then to Mexico, where he introduced them to whorehouses. Pineau even as a teenager thought of himself as a homosexual and wasn't interested in sex with women, but Gaynor encouraged the boys to have sex with women while he watched.[36]

O'Sullivan retired in 1968 and moved to San Diego. Joseph E. Flanagan was "Absent on Leave" from his home diocese after 1968. In 1973 Metzger accepted into his diocese the Rev. Bruce MacArthur, a priest of the diocese of Sioux Falls, South Dakota. MacArthur admitted abusing thirty girls, some as young as eight years old, beginning in the 1950s.[37] After complaints about his behavior, in 1963 MacArthur was sent to the Paraclete treatment center, Via Coeli, in New Mexico. He returned to South Dakota, and abused again. In 1965 he was sent to the Milwaukee, Wisconsin, archdiocese for further treatment and soon started a five-year molestation of the ten-year-old Judy DeLonga, who had been admitted to the St. Joseph Hospital in Beaver Dam, where MacArthur was chaplain from 1965 to 1970.[38] After returning to South Dakota and abusing again, MacArthur asked to be transferred to El Paso, where from 1974 to 1977 he resided at St. Patrick's Cathedral with Bishop Metzger. In 1978 MacArthur attempted to rape a 54-year-old patient at a nursing home. She must have seemed like an ideal target, because she "had a congenital disease that left her unable to speak or control her motor functions."[39] But MacArthur was discovered by a nurse's aide, arrested, indicted, pleaded guilty, and jailed after this "unfortunate incident," as the Rev. John F. Peters, the vicar general of the diocese of El Paso, put it.[40] MacArthur was released in 1981 and left El Paso (perhaps because

Metzger's successor was not as understanding); he returned to South Dakota and continued to work as a priest until 1992.[41]

During 1973, Metzger became involved in a unionizing controversy; in 1976 Pope Paul VI praised him for his "unwavering defense of the rights of working people."[42] Metzger retired on March 17, 1978, and died on April 12, 1986.

Gary Pineau said that because of issues of sacramental validity Vatican representatives were involved in the settlement of the suit that he filed against the diocese of El Paso in 1995, so in all probability the Vatican was also aware of the lawsuit filed by another victim, John Doe I against El Paso in 1996 and therefore would have been aware of the affidavits quoted above. The surprise that Vatican officials expressed at the flood of revelations that began at the beginning of 2002 was therefore somewhat feigned. Although it is true that the Vatican is not a unified entity and sometimes the right hand does not know what the left is doing, there were officials in the Vatican (such as the one who was involved in the Pineau lawsuit) who knew that terrible abuse had been going on in the United States for decades and that it was tolerated by bishops. In 2004 the diocese, which knew that victims had indicated that they had reported their abuse to Bishop Metzger in the 1960s, claimed that in the 1960s it had received "zero" reports of abuse.[43]

Not all the abuse was as cruel and degrading as the abuse described in the affidavits, but even if it had been, bishops would have tolerated it. They knew the Vatican did not want them to turn criminals over to the police and they knew that the Vatican made it extraordinarily difficult to laicize even criminal priests against their wills. Perhaps prelates in the Vatican were traditionalists and shared Bishop Metzger's attitude, that it was an old custom for priests to keep boys, as Stefano Cherubini had done in the seventeenth century when the pope had appointed him head of the Piarists.

## CHAPTER TWO

# THE HEART OF DARKNESS IN THE HEARTLAND: DAVENPORT, IOWA

SMALL DIOCESES IN QUIET CORNERS of the United States have seen some of the worst abuse. Troubled priests like Irving Klister may have gravitated to the border town of El Paso, where they would be as far as possible from the scenes of their original crimes and where they could slip over into Mexico, but even Midwestern cities where the priests were locally raised produced rings of abusers. Iowa claimed to have a lower than average rate of abusive priests,[1] but the documents of the diocese of Davenport that the court has forced it to release (and not all have been released and not all those released have been made public) portray one of the deeper circles of hell amid the cornfields of the Midwest.

In 1948 James Janssen, Francis Bass, Theodore Anthony Geerts, and James W. Murphy[2] all graduated from Kenrick Seminary in St. Louis. Janssen, Bass, and Geerts worked in the Davenport diocese, where they molested boys, and Murphy went to Memphis. According to the boys' affidavits, from which these accounts are drawn, the priests introduced the boys to nude swimming, shoplifting, mutual masturbation, fellatio, group sex, sacrilege, and the refined pleasures of viewing decayed bodies in morgues.

The bishop of Davenport, Ralph Lee Hayes, was warned in 1948 that something was wrong with Janssen; he knew at least as early as 1954 that

Janssen was molesting boys, and Janssen even confessed to him. But Hayes did nothing effective to stop the molestation, which continued under the next bishop, Gerald Francis O'Keefe (1966–93). O'Keefe even made Janssen, with his extensive history of accusations, the diocesan Boy Scout chaplain, and did not begin to remove him from contact with the public until Janssen's own nephew, by then a man, came forward with accusations that could not be ignored.

As bad news about abuse in the Catholic Church began to pour out in the late 1990s and early 2000s, Davenport's next bishop, William E. Franklin, thanked God and told the media that his diocese was not like other dioceses, that with one or two minor exceptions, Davenport was free of abusive priests, a claim that he got away with until the courts forced him to hand over some of the diocesan documents about abuse. All the evils present in other dioceses are concentrated and encapsulated in Davenport: abusive priests in a pedophile ring with links to a larger network, bishops who make disapproving noises but never discipline effectively, perjuring bishops and chancellors, deceived psychologists, police who do not pursue cases, and a laity who blame the boys for revealing the abuse and disturbing the comfortable illusions upon which Catholics base their view of the world.

## *Janssen*

James Janssen was born in Davenport in 1923, and his father died when he was six. He attended local Catholic schools and St. Ambrose University, which was run by the diocese of Davenport, studied at Kenrick Seminary in St. Louis, and was ordained in 1948. Immediately after Janssen's ordination, Father Marion L. Gibbons, the director of students at Kenrick Seminary, warned Bishop Hayes that something was wrong with Janssen. He was isolated; he had "no close friend." He was immature; he had "something of the juvenile in his character." He was heedless; he "did not have a grasp of possible consequences of some of his actions." He could never admit that he was at fault but instead put on an air of aggrieved innocence when accused of wrongdoing and then he feigned repentance: "On occasions of admonition, he, in so many words, expressed himself of being unaware of any fault having been committed—innocence personified—and also expressed a 'sincere' desire for correction." Gibbons judged that what he had at first thought was "simplicity" might in fact be "a dangerous spirit of duplicity." Gibbons recognized that Janssen was a confidence man. Gibbons alluded to something in which Janssen was involved and which could bring disgrace on the students of the seminary: "One such action, made known to me only after his departure, if known beforehand, could have had decidedly serious consequences for the person himself. It was reported to me since his leaving, and I intend to verify it thoroughly before determining my action in relation to the student body. If it is verified and the student body suffers, then Father Janssen can take the credit!"[3] Gibbons's indirection suggests that the matter was sexual.

Janssen baptized his nephew and namesake James Wells in 1948 and molested him at the home of the boy's parents in Lagrange Park, Illinois, on Thanksgiving Day, 1953. Wells remembered that "after dinner in our family home . . . he took me with him to take a nap. He fondled me while he masturbated. He told me it was our secret."[4] Janssen abused Wells about six to eight times a year when Wells lived in Illinois. Wells moved to Davenport in 1958 and Janssen abused him, now ten years old, more frequently (two or three times a week for several years) until he was thirteen. Janssen told his sister and brother-in-law that he needed to go upstairs to hear his nephew's confession; he would then take Wells into a bedroom and abuse him. He tried to get Wells to perform oral sex on him, but Wells refused.

When Janssen was assigned to St. Irenaeus parish in Clinton, Iowa (1950–53), he frequented the Clinton YMCA. There he was caught in sexual activity with two boys. The secretary of the Newton YMCA wrote in a 1956 letter that "several years ago" the general secretary of the Clinton YMCA "had found Father Janssen in the handball court with two boys in a very improper activity" and banned him from the building.[5] The Clinton YMCA was also aware that Janssen had been transferred from that town in 1953 by the diocese because of "homosexual tendencies."[6] However, a 1955 letter to

Hayes indicated that Janssen "frequents the YMCA at Newton" and that the police were making inquiries involving a "morals charge,"[7] but the police did not carry through an investigation that could have led to an arrest, a prosecution, and an abrupt end to Janssen's career as an abuser. It is not clear whether Janssen was still using the Newton YMCA after his 1953 transfer from Clinton to Newton. It is odd that Janssen was eventually transferred to the city in which he was supposed to be abusing boys at the YMCA.

In his brief assignment in the rural parish of St. Joseph's, East Pleasant Plain, Iowa (1953), between his assignments in Clinton and Newton, Janssen was deeply unhappy, on the point of a "nervous breakdown," because there were no boys around. Janssen conveyed the cause for his unhappiness to the chancery, which noted that "his primary interest, he says, is youth. He wants to be with them; he wants them around."[8] Despite the suspicion of the Vicar General Maurice J. Dingman that "there must be something going on,"[9] no one thought to question Janssen about why he was desperate to be around teenage boys. This is especially unusual if Janssen had been transferred from Clinton to St. Joseph's precisely because of the interest in boys he had demonstrated by his activities at the YMCA. Janssen lasted only one month at St. Joseph's and then took a four-month leave of absence before Hayes transferred him to Sacred Heart Church in Newton in 1953, where he was happier because he had access to more boys.

The first recorded complaint about Janssen was made in 1954. Bishop Hayes wrote a cryptic memo: "August 1954—his home—solicited to acts of impurity—was first attempt and has not been repeated—has no knowledge that other boys were solicited—the attempt has nothing to do with the sacrament of penance."[10] This occurred at St. Ambrose Academy, which was then the high school of St. Ambrose College. The file contains no indication that Hayes did anything to discipline Janssen or to help the victim. Hayes probably made the final remark about the "sacrament of penance" to make it clear that the solicitation did not occur during the sacrament of penance, because there is a canon law about solicitation in the confessional. Even abusive priests in Davenport were occasionally concerned about the finer points of church discipline, as we shall see.

An unsigned, undated memo (which seems to be in Hayes's handwriting and is on Bishop's House stationery) listed Janssen's offenses. Hayes was aware that Janssen was arrested in Des Moines for shoplifting with boys, that Janssen was going to midnight shows, that "Y. M. = serious charges," that Janssen was "forbidden to go to the Y," and cryptically noted "Guard = Pool."[11] After he got the November 2, 1956, letter from the Newton YMCA about Janssen's homosexual activities there, Hayes, on November 9, removed Janssen from Sacred Heart, put him on indefinite leave of absence, and told him to leave town. Janssen was ordered to Chicago, where he took classes at Loyola University. When Hayes sent Janssen for psychotherapy to Father William Devlin, S.J., M.D., Hayes wrote Devlin that he wanted to salvage Janssen, "but sometimes I wonder whether my approach has been the proper one."[12] Devlin referred Janssen to J. V. P. Stewart, a clinical psychologist, for a course of psychotherapy. Janssen demonstrated his intelligence by doing very well in the courses he took at Loyola and by manipulating the psychologist. Janssen couldn't deny sexual activity, but he knew the categories in which the psychologist thought and told his story in such a way that the psychologist concluded that Janssen wanted to be celibate, but needed help, especially the help of a good psychologist. Stewart concluded that Janssen was "very naïve" and had an "almost total lack of information regarding the nature and purpose of the sex drive." The psychologist recognized that there was "a disturbance in the sexual area" and traced it back to Janssen's lack of a father and to a mother who never mentioned sex. Stewart recognized Janssen's "emotional immaturity" and that Janssen had "some concern about his own masculinity." Janssen said that he had confessed to priests that he masturbated and had "some relationship with a male" but that the priests to whom he confessed gave him no advice.[13]

While he was studying theology, receiving therapy, and telling the therapist what he wanted to hear, Janssen was molesting a twelve-year-old boy in Chicago. Janssen was living at St. Isaac Jogues parish in Hinsdale, Illinois, where, according to the pastor, he did "excellent work, I thought, among the [B]oy [S]couts and teenagers."[14] There Janssen met a Boy Scout whose father also was a Scout leader. Janssen evaluated the boy's weaknesses. The victim later wrote, "I was a quiet boy who did not do well in school and was attending Catholic school when Father Janssen took an interest in me. I can remember that being a good feeling, as he was popular with the kids in school and my association with him made me feel accepted." He took the boy for a ride in his car and "quickly put his hand in my pants. When he did this, I would get an erection, although I was so naïve that I didn't know what was happening." Janssen took the boy to the rectory, "where he took my pants down and masturbated me. I had never ejaculated before and the first time it happened I thought something had broke." Janssen was pleased with the boy, and "would use every excuse to get me alone and do the same thing again."[15]

Janssen's therapist Stewart was deceived by a confidence man and perhaps also by his own desire to believe that his therapeutic skills had helped change Janssen. He thought that Janssen was salvageable and told the bishop that "it is my belief that Father Janssen can become a very understanding and acceptable pastor and that the insight he has developed over a considerable period of therapy is such that he is not likely to fall into his past errors." Stewart, suspecting the lack of a strong male figure was the source of Janssen's homosexuality, "strongly emphasized, it is urgent and essential that he have assigned to him particularly, a mature, understanding, spiritual director; one who can act almost one would say, as a father figure. Also that he have regular and frequent contact with this director."[16] Bishop Hayes liked the first part of the prognosis but disregarded the advice about the necessity of a spiritual director. Stewart was anxious about Janssen and wrote a year later to Hayes to make sure that Janssen had a director. Hayes replied, "I haven't assigned any particular priest as his spiritual director, although we discussed that matter in a general sort of way."[17]

After Janssen returned to the Davenport diocese and was assigned to St. Michael's parish in Holbrook, Iowa, the mother of the boy from St. Isaac Jogues parish in Hinsdale, Illinois, found a letter that her fourteen-year-old son had written to Janssen. It began, "Hi big dick hows your prick mines grate I have jacked off 3 times sofar. I can't wate until we jack off agun it's so much funn. Rember keep it sliding your dick that is."[18] Janssen replied less explicitly but signed his letter, "L. S., P. L., J. O., C. S. [abbreviations for vulgar expressions], your pal FJ."[19] The boy's mother told her pastor, the Rev. M. A. Henehan, who told both the bishop of Joliet, Illinois, and Hayes. Hayes wrote to Henehan expressing shock at the boy's letter but relief that "no general notoriety has arisen."[20] On October 3, 1958, Hayes suspended Janssen after he was confronted with this incriminating letter and confessed. Hayes recommended (but did not require) that Janssen go for treatment to Via Coeli, the Paraclete's center in New Mexico. Instead Janssen went to the Cistercian Abbey of Our Lady of New Melleray outside Dubuque. Janssen wrote to Hayes feigning repentance: "First of all, I am truly repentant for my past sins. Again, I am sorry for those relapses into sin which I admitted to you at your home. Only God knows how sorry I am."[21] The last sentence may be a deliberate double entendre: God knew that Janssen was not at all sorry. In January 1959, Abbot Philip O'Connor wrote to Hayes expressing confidence that Janssen had learned his lesson. Janssen laughed when he later told one of his victims that Hayes had said, "Janssen, what is going on?" and merely told Janssen to say the daily office of prayers, which he did briefly.[22]

In January 1959, three months after Janssen's suspension, Hayes appointed him as administrator of St. Patrick's Church in Delmar for six months. Hayes ordered him to have no contact with the boy he had molested in Illinois and not to go to Clinton or to Newton, the scenes of his previous crimes. Then in June 1959 Hayes appointed Janssen assistant at St. Mary's in Davenport, three blocks from St. Joseph's, where Father Francis Bass was staying. In September 1959 Janssen admitted to Hayes that he had been picking up boys and taking them swimming and to drive-in movies. Hayes ordered Janssen "never again at any time, under any circumstances to pick up boys in his auto" or Janssen would suffer "severe punishment."[23] In December 1959 the vicar general, Dingman, wrote Hayes that a professor of St. Ambrose College had seen Janssen with two boys, and Janssen was holding one boy and "rubbing the front part of the boy's body."[24] There were other witnesses. An unsigned, undated memo from approximately this period listed charges: "frequent swimming at

Fejerary Park wrestling with boys," "he picks kids up in his car for swimming," "telling boys he will organize smoking parties for the 7 and 8 grades," "wrestling and hugging boys (scouts) borderline acting, and other strange behavior."[25] Nothing was done.

In September 1960 Dingman again wrote Hayes about a mother who was worried that her son was spending too much time with Janssen and that on a hot day Janssen insisted that the boy sit on his lap in a car.[26] Hayes called Janssen in but Janssen maintained he never had boys in his car unless the parents were present and that he never took boys to a cabin unless parents were along. Hayes was dubious, writing "*an sit verum*" ("is it true?"), after Janssen's claims, but never questioned the boys, merely handing Janssen a letter of warning, in which he informed him: "You are hereby placed under obedience as follows: (1.) You are strictly forbidden to have boys ride with you in your automobile at any time for any reason whatever. (2.) You are strictly forbidden to take boys or to accompany boys to any cabin or cottage" and warned that he would make Janssen sell his automobile and "impose appropriate canonical penalties."[27] Janssen had reason to understand this as an empty threat.

Just before Christmas 1960 Hayes wrote a memo about what a mother had told him: Janssen and her fourteen-year-old son were "wrestling" and "closely embracing," that after Janssen visited she found a "dirty note" which was not in her son's handwriting, and that Janssen took her son for frequent rides and had taken him to Chicago.[28] Hayes called Janssen in; Janssen denied any improper conduct, feigning "offended innocence, claiming he was falsely accused," but "admitted disobeying my orders not to take boys in his auto—his excuse—he did not think the order was fair as other priests are not given similar orders." Hayes again was dubious, observing that "his past record is against him,"[29] but did nothing to enforce his orders, thereby letting Janssen know that all his threats of punishment were meaningless.

In February 1961 another irate mother threatened to go to the police, but Dingman reassured Hayes that "Father Hopkins [Janssen's pastor at St. Mary's] thinks the police would find it difficult to make the boys talk. Father Janssen has them intimidated." Dingman informed Hayes that

Janssen was continuing to take boys to a cabin.[30] Hayes did nothing, and the diocese was happy to use Janssen's intimidation of the boys to keep the matter quiet. The intimidation may have involved, as we shall see, visits to a morgue.

Bishop Hayes, like other bishops, showed no interest in the effect all this was having on the victims. Hayes also demonstrated the firm belief that is deeply imbedded in Catholic clerical culture that words are equivalent to deeds. That is, Hayes thought he had done enough when he forbade Janssen to associate with boys. Janssen ignored these repeated orders and admitted to Hayes that he was ignoring them. Hayes threatened the direst consequences and did almost nothing, leaving Janssen free to continue abusing boys. After two years and many complaints, Hayes transferred Janssen away from the cathedral city to St. Joseph's in Fort Madison. There Janssen's behavior apparently worsened.

Hayes died in 1967 and the new bishop, Gerald O'Keefe, took over the diocese, inheriting both Janssen and his file. Despite the complaints and despite Janssen's confession to Bishop Hayes, O'Keefe put him on the Priests' Personnel Board (1976–89) and made him diocesan chaplain of the Boy Scouts (1980–90). Unlike Hayes, O'Keefe did not like to keep written records of problems in the diocese, and complaints about Janssen went unrecorded. Bobbi R. Martin, a parishioner of Ss. Philip and James in Grand Mound, Iowa, learned in the spring of 1983 that Janssen had been arrested for shoplifting (at least his second arrest), that he had permitted boys "to smoke marijuana at the rectory," and also had shown them "pornographic movies." Martin and two others met with Msgr. Michael J. Morrissey, the vicar general of the Davenport diocese, in 1983 to inform him about what Janssen was doing, "but he did not appear interested in what we had to say."[31] No record was kept of this meeting, in line with O'Keefe's general policy of not keeping records about anything unpleasant. O'Keefe kept no records of complaints about Janssen—until Janssen's nephew, James Wells, began to seek help and recompense.

In 1987 Wells began confronting his memories of the abuse. In February Wells wrote to Janssen that a psychologist had diagnosed that he was depressed, and told him that "my problems were a direct result of the sexual abuse I was subjected to by you while I was a child."[32] The psychologist had urged Wells to report the abuse to the police, but Wells couldn't bring himself to do that for fear of hurting his mother, Janssen's sister. Janssen's lawyer wrote back that Janssen "denies the stated allegations," that the allegations are "slanderous" and that Janssen would "sue you for the ensuing damages to Fr. Janssen's reputation and standing in the community."[33] In January 1988 Wells went to see Msgr. Morrissey; his mother wrote to ask that the results of the investigation be sent to her son. Morrissey wrote Wells, "I am not really sure of what investigation I will make."[34]

On July 23, 1990, O'Keefe received a letter from the Rev. Robert T. McAleer about a man who had been hospitalized at the Iowa City Veterans Administration hospital. This patient revealed his problems to two priests who were chaplains there, the Rev. Dennis C. Martin and the Rev. David F. Hitch (whose brother Janssen had abused). At first the patient talked to his father about his "preference of homosexuality which was instrumental in his being dismissed from the seminary." The diocese had continued to send bills for his seminary education to his parents even after he had been dismissed. The parents did not appreciate that, especially after they had learned about Father Janssen's role in their son's troubles, which had been caused by sexual abuse. They had been away from the sacraments because they confessed their attitude toward Father Janssen to a priest, who refused them absolution because they couldn't forgive Janssen (who was and is completely unrepentant). Another man had come to McAleer because of marital problems, especially the "lack of ability to trust anyone including his wife." The man had been abused by Janssen and told McAleer that "he knew priests would 'take care of their own' and would cover up."[35]

O'Keefe fired Janssen as diocesan chaplain of scouting in July 1990 and put him on an indefinite leave of absence "for health reasons."[36] As of 1990 Janssen was still in contact with members of the "Tru Blu" club (a group of boys he had organized) and had a "stable of boys"[37] available. But on June 23, 1993, a woman wrote to O'Keefe that Janssen was bringing boys from Davenport for weekends, that the boys were talking about it, and it was "shocking."[38] O'Keefe, as far as is known, did nothing. When further allegations were made, Morrissey, the vicar general of Bishop Franklin, in April 1996 ordered Janssen "to withdraw from any kind of public ministry" and reminded Janssen that "both you and the Church are fortunate that this is not being pursued in a more public forum." Morrissey also informed all priests that Janssen was not available for any service of any nature. Franklin wrote Janssen in February 1997 listing the "restrictions on ministry,"[39] a solution that "allows Father Janssen to function as a priest [and] protects his reputation." Janssen, forgetting his earlier admissions to Bishop Hayes,[40] to this day denies ever abusing a boy.

Janssen also demonstrates that abusers do not always, or perhaps even often, fit into the neat categories that psychologists have constructed—pedophile, ephebophile, homosexual. Janssen had sex with boys at least as young as five and he had sex with other adult priests, but his preference was for boys who were undergoing puberty but did not yet have secondary male sex characteristics; he asked them to shave their pubic hair. When they were in their late teens he mostly lost interest in them.

## *The Pedophile Ring*

Janssen was not alone in the diocese of Davenport nor did he act in isolation. Three other abusers were in Janssen's class: Bass, Geerts, and Murphy. The four knew that they were all abusers; this would have been an extremely dangerous secret to reveal to anyone of whom one was not completely certain. The most probable way that they knew one another's criminal tendencies was that each one had been corrupted by the same priest at the seminary, who had put them in touch with one another. The abusers also had sex with one another during their orgies with the boys, an action that strongly suggests that they had started having sex with one another even at the seminary.

Janssen decided to share the Hinsdale boy (whom he had met while in Chicago [1957–58]) with his friends Bass and Murphy, who abused the boy. Janssen thought the boy had a great future as a male prostitute. The boy reported that "he also told me that I could make money letting older men perform oral sex on me and that he would show me how to make those connections in Chicago."[41] He took two boys to visit Father Murphy in Memphis, and each had to sleep with Murphy, who forced the boys to masturbate him.[42] Another boy reported that "in 1964, Janssen pimped me one final time" when Bass visited Janssen's rectory in Fort Madison and asked the boy to carry something from Janssen's bedroom. Bass "locked the door and made me disrobe. This scared me, but I complied. He fondled me on the bed and then took down his pants and had me masturbate him. When he was done, he took out a Polaroid camera and took a picture of me naked."[43] Janssen took the Hinsdale boy to his mother's house in Davenport, where he shared the boy with Bass and Murphy.[44]

Boys were not simply passed from abuser to abuser. Janssen gathered a group of boys whom he named the "Rod Knockers,"[45] (that is, masturbators) and introduced one boy to the pleasures of group sex, at first with Janssen and other boys. One victim remembered that "many times it was group sex like mutual masturbation or fellatio, or a combination of masturbation and fellatio involving the four of us." Janssen also took this boy to visit Geerts at St. Boniface Church in Farmington, Iowa. The first session in the rectory involved Janssen, Geerts, and three boys. Geerts showed them pornographic movies from his collection kept in the locked cabinet in the rectory basement. Geerts then "fondled me (my genitalia) and inserted his finger into my anus during this weekend."[46]

Another weekend the boy saw "Janssen and Geerts perform mutual fellatio on one another" and "one of the boys performing fellatio on Geerts while Geerts was kissing another boy on the lips with his finger in the anus of the boy he was kissing."[47] One weekend Janssen went with Bass, Geerts, and seven boys from St. Joseph's school; one boy remembered that "the weekend consisted of the usual group and couple fellatio / masturbation in the cabin and on [——]'s docked houseboat. During this weekend, Father Bass masturbated me while he performed fellatio on another boy."

The ring extended beyond the four who had attended Kenrick Seminary together. Janssen molested another boy from the time the boy was twelve until he went to St. Ambrose University. There, the victim recounted, Rev. William F. Wiebler (who later admitted to Bishop Franklin that he had abused twelve boys) "came into my dorm room and pulled my pants down. He told me Father Janssen had told him that I would not mind if he did this to me."[48] The abusers had a tight network and communicated with one another so that they would know which boys could be safely abused. Janssen was supposed to take care of Geerts's locked pornography collection in the basement of St. Boniface rectory if something happened to Geerts. However, Wiebler succeeded Geerts as pastor of St. Boniface in 1968. This arrangement occurred when another abuser, Bass, served on the personnel board of the diocese from 1958 to 1973.

The ring extended to Chicago and was therefore part of a larger network. Janssen offered to introduce one victim to other abusers in Chicago, who would pay to have sex with the boy. He and Bass also knew someone at the Cook County Hospital Morgue, a connection they exploited, as we shall see, in a gruesome manner. Father Andrew Greeley of Chicago has claimed in writing that he has evidence of a ring of pedophile priests in Chicago, a ring that was involved in murder (see pp. 521–522, note 8). Is this the ring that Janssen knew?

Janssen remained in touch with his fellow seminary classmates. His seminary classmate, fellow abuser, and sex partner Geerts wrote to O'Keefe in 1969 and asked him to put Geerts and Janssen together in a rectory. But Geerts decided to take a twenty-year leave of absence from the priesthood. He spent most of this time in San Diego, but ended up in Las Vegas, where his embarrassing "lifestyle" led a priest to write about him.[49] Geerts asked Janssen to communicate his desire to have permission to celebrate Mass; the bishop gave him permission, but Geerts was arrested (on unspecified charges). He died on September 4, 2004.

The diocese sent William Wiebler, who had retired in 1991, to the St. John Vianney Renewal Center in 2002 for treatment after he admitted to Bishop Franklin that he had abused twelve boys, but Wiebler left the center and moved into an apartment 750 feet from an elementary school in University City, Missouri. The diocese claimed that Wiebler was still receiving outpatient treatment, but Rev. Peter Lechner, a member of the Servants of the Paraclete and director of the center, has stated that the center does not offer outpatient treatment and cannot prevent patients from leaving.[50] Janssen and Bass, as we shall see, for a long while continued in daily association.

Janssen, while engaged in stomach-churning activities with boys, pretended sometimes to observe the canon law that forbids priests to absolve their accomplices in sexual sins. The pedophiles absolved each other but kept track of who had had sex with which boy during their orgies so that they would not absolve a boy with whom they had had sex during this particular orgy. Janssen took one victim to his parents' home and gave him to Murphy and Bass. The victim reported that "one time when Father Bass had told him I had committed a sin with him, I couldn't confess it to Father Bass. They debated this for awhile and decided that as long as I was not confessing something I had not done with both of them, that I could confess with the other that I had committed a sin."[51] After he abused boys, Janssen took them to a seafood restaurant that specialized in shrimp, and "he was always certain to remind the boys that they should abstain from eating meat on Fridays."[52] Legalism survived after morality died.

## *Facilis descensus Averno*

Janssen sought out vulnerable boys. Some were vulnerable simply because they were young and had no idea that what he was doing was beyond the pale of normal sexual development. Others had family problems. One boy's father had died; Janssen smelled blood and moved in, getting some money along with the sex. The victim remembered that "my mother paid him to babysit me during the time he abused me."[53]

Janssen, like other abusers, exploited the best and worst qualities of the boys. He used their faith, their loyalty, their physical desires, their fears. He broke down their inhibitions and created the transgressive spirit that is so prized by modern academicians, for whom the Marquis de Sade is a cultural hero. Janssen used cigarettes, marijuana, alcohol, nudity, and pornography to destroy inhibitions, all the while reminding the boys that priests were to be trusted and slowly leading them into more and more sexual activity, for which the priests gave the boys "absolution." Janssen and his friends could get the boys to do almost anything.

The boys were all taught in Catholic schools. An important text for religious education was the *Baltimore Catechism*, in which an illustration entitled "The Priest on Earth Another Christ" explained that "Catholics should show reverence and honor to the priest because he is the representative of Christ himself and the dispenser of His mysteries." The *Catechism* then quoted Pope Pius XI: "The priest is indeed another Christ, or in some way he is himself a continuation of Christ."[54] One victim explained, "I received my religious training in the Catholic [s]chool and I was trained that the priest was the equivalent of God or Christ on earth and that they should be obeyed."[55]

Janssen appealed to this trust that the boys had in priests. Janssen always told the boys the sex was a proof of trust. One victim remembered that "he started by touching me in the genital region outside of my pants and would tell me 'This is how we build trust.'"[56] Another victim said Janssen "would unzip my pants and start touching my penis—again saying, 'This is how we build trust.'"[57] Janssen took a twelve-year-old boy into his office in the parish and asked him repeatedly, "Trust me?" as he moved his hand closer and closer to the boy's genitals. He masturbated the boy and taught him how to masturbate him in turn. Janssen asked the boy to give him a "blow job." The sexually inexperienced boy pretended he understood what Janssen meant and blew on Janssen's penis. Janssen, the boy reported, instructed him in proper techniques: "Janssen said to suck and move my head up and down which I did." Janssen then fellated the boy and then they mutually masturbated each other to ejaculation. Janssen told the victim that this was "our secret."[58] He got one boy alone and masturbated him. The boy was dubious about this sexual activity. He explained his reaction at the time: "But since a priest was doing it, I assumed it was okay."[59]

Boys were introduced to masturbation and then to other sexual acts. Janssen slowly introduced one boy to sex by touching his genitals when he was eleven years old, by masturbating him when he was twelve years old, and by teaching him about oral sex when he was sixteen years old. The boy said that "he then put my penis in his mouth and performed oral sex on me. When he was done, Janssen forced me to perform oral sex on him. I did for awhile. I could not continue and lifted my head up. Janssen forced my head back down to finish. It made me sick. I ran to the bathroom and threw up and washed my mouth out."[60]

Janssen knew that boys desired to be initiated into the secrets of adult life, and therefore he set up a club, the "Tru Blu," that "created a devious mentality that certain things were not wrong." He encouraged club members to shoplift: "It was fun and a simple way to break down [a boy's] moral code."[61] Janssen began by teaching the boys to commit minor infractions; they would "jump fences in movies, steal from pop machines."[62] He did the same thing to the Scouts when he was a Scout leader. Janssen played Fagin to the altar boys, who remembered that

> Janssen encouraged us to steal things he could use. He was big into coin collecting and sponsored several coin shows in the gym at St. Joseph's School. He would go around and find out what different collectors had for sale and then tell us boys to steal those and give them to him. An especially easy target was an old man from Missouri nicknamed Kahoka Joe. He was in a wheelchair and easy to distract. We (the boys) stole many coins from him and gave them to Janssen.

The victim continued by explaining that, after Sunday Mass, Janssen and the boys opened the offering envelopes: "Many times there was loose money and often Janssen pocketed it and usually gave us some too."[63] John Doe II recounted that Janssen "would also take us to a store called Paul's in Clinton where I tried on some boots and Father Janssen told me to walk out with them on and not pay, so I did. Another time in Knoxville, Tennessee, Father Janssen took other minor boys and myself to an open flea market and gave us plastic bags and told us to take shirts or whatever we wanted."[64] Theft was an introduction to transgression for the boys. He taught the boys how to shoplift and was himself apparently arrested at least twice, once in Des Moines, as Bishop Hayes was aware,[65] and once in Clinton in the 1980s, as Bishop O'Keefe was no doubt informed by Vicar General Morrissey.[66]

Swimming in the nude was another step in breaking down inhibitions.[67] Janssen liked to masturbate boys while they were swimming. Bishop Hayes in a 1953 letter raised "the matter of going swimming"[68] but did not explain why he regarded swimming as suspicious. A victim from St. Irenaeus in Clinton, where Janssen was stationed 1950–53 remembered swimming in a spillway in the Mississippi with Janssen: "While we were swimming naked, Father Janssen came up behind me, grabbed my penis[,] and began to masturbate me."[69] John Doe II reported that "numerous times, Father Janssen would take us swimming at the YMCA in Clinton, Iowa. He would touch my penis while we were in the water."[70] In 1960 Janssen took a group of boys camping and swimming nude in the Mississippi. A fourteen-year-old who was along on the trip recounted that "he put his arms around me and vigorously fondled my genitals under the water, I was totally shocked and scared."[71] Janssen also "suggested that everyone float on their backs and while floating, arch their backs and expose their genitals out of the water. When this happened, the priest would laugh and say 'weenie on a plate.'"[72]

In 1963 Janssen took a boy to St. Ambrose College to go swimming. He had a key to the pool and the two swam naked. "He played with me as we both swam naked by throwing me into the air." Then the boy accidentally scratched Janssen. The boy remembered Janssen's reaction: "He grabbed me and shoved and held me under water in front of him as he shoved his erect penis in my mouth. He held me until my lungs were empty. I thought he was trying to kill me."[73] After his forced retirement Janssen worked as a teacher and lifeguard at the Davenport Outing Club and the Scott County Family YMCA. He was celebrated when he tried to be recognized as the world's oldest lifeguard. "He's a scream to be around," one woman said about the retired priest who played Jerry Lee Lewis and Chuck Berry on his cassette player at the pool.[74]

The YMCA in Clinton had apparently not notified other YMCAs about Janssen. Even if the Y's knew about Janssen, he still gained access to them and used them for nude swimming sessions with boys. On the way to the YMCA, he stopped at a bookstore to get the boys in the mood by showing them pornographic magazines. The boys were interested in "*Playboy*, *Sir*, *Gent*, *Cavalier*," but Janssen preferred the nudist magazines *Sun and Health* and *Sunshine* because, as one victim realized later, "there were always pictures of naked boys and young family members."[75]

Janssen showed the boys pornographic movies in the rectory, but he also took them to commercial movies. When he took a fourteen-year-old boy to see *Elmer Gantry* at a drive-in, he asked the boy to notice a scene in which it was implied that Gantry was about to have sex with a woman. The boy recounted that "Janssen grabbed my penis and asked me what I thought they were going to do now." Janssen then unzipped himself and started masturbating. He told the boy that "it was a perfectly normal reaction and said there was nothing to be embarrassed about. He then guided my hand to his penis and asked if I would 'finish him off.' He soon ejaculated at which time he asked me to reach around to the back seat of his car to get a box of Puffs. I realized after that I had never seen his car without a box of Kleenex in it."[76] Janssen was very active in this car (in which his bishop had forbidden him to drive boys). One victim recounted that "in 1962, he would abuse me in the back seat of his car. He masturbated me and I him. The semen got on the seat of his car and he commented as he wiped it up that he wished semen came in powder form." He later took this boy swimming and as the boy sat in his wet trunks in the back seat "a horrible odor came and wouldn't leave.... I later realized that the odor came from dried semen getting wet."[77]

Boys learned to overcome their disgust at unnatural acts. Janssen also involved the boys in degrading and disgusting "jokes." Once the parish bazaar left a pot of chili in the kitchen overnight to cook. "Janssen and the other boy ejaculated into the pot and laughed about it next day while watching parishioners eat."[78] This disgusting prank desensitized the boys for the next step—sacrilege. In addition to masturbating boys in the sacristy immediately before and after Mass,[79] Janssen was "brazen about his sexual activities"[80] and on at least one occasion had sex while standing at the altar in front of the congregation. According to psychiatrist Mark K. Schwartz, one victim reported that at St. Joseph's in Fort Madison, "Janssen had a boy sit underneath the altar hidden from the congregation's view. When Fr. Janssen approached the altar the boy reached underneath Fr. Janssen's robe and masturbated him."[81] Janssen made a charade of the sacraments; he abused a boy and then heard the victim's confession, ignoring the canon law against absolving an accomplice in a sexual sin. The boy confessed "that I blew someone [which was Janssen]. He would giggle and forgive me for my sins. He made a point of having the altar boys confess their 'sins' of sexual abuse by him before he would clear them for serving [M]ass." This victim also "witnessed Janssen, Bass[,] and Geerts confessing their sins to each other face to face."[82]

By involving the boys in such actions, Janssen made the boys compromise themselves to such an extent that they would find it impossible to accuse him without also accusing themselves. One boy was afraid that "I would be beaten if I ever told anyone."[83] If the boys showed reluctance or seemed they might expose him he played upon their fears. No one would believe them. "Janssen told me that I could never tell anybody, ever, because if I did no one would believe me." Janssen told the boys that if anyone learned what they were doing with Janssen they could never get married. The victim recounted that Janssen "also told me that if I told, I would never get married (because a woman wouldn't marry me)."[84] If a victim got married and had children, his wife would always suspect that he was having sex with his son.

In the most sinister tactic of all, Janssen and his friends used the morgue to unsettle the boys. His nephew James Wells reported: "He would also take me and several other Boy Scouts from Iowa to the morgue in Cook County. I was under 10 [before 1955] and was shown horribly disfigured, decayed bodies, including children."[85]

Bass also had a contact at the Cook County Hospital. In 1960 Bass took a group of boys to Chicago. One of them, Ed Thomas, had gotten into trouble with the law and been ordered by the judge to start attending church, where he met Bass, who promised to guide him to "a moral life."

Thomas, fourteen at the time, remembered this trip to the hospital:

> Somebody he knew met us. All had been arranged. As we moved deeper into the maze of dark passages, the smell of death grew thicker. There were bodies on carts parked along the walls. Father Bass had arranged for a guided tour.
>
> The morgue was being renovated. We arrived at a temporary wall with two doors about eight feet apart. "Take your pick," Father Bass said to me. I opened the door on the right. A yellow light immediately flooded the room, and I stood facing a gauntlet straight from hell. The room was stark, long, and narrow. Bunks end-to-end lined the outside walls and a double row of bunks filled the center, producing a U-shaped trail of horror ending at the door to my left on the other side of the room. The bottom bunks hit me at about the waist, and I was just tall enough to be eye-to-eye with the bodies on the top bunks. They were lying on what looked like large cookie sheets.
>
> Each corpse seemed more horrible than the last. Some were decomposed. Others were frozen in bizarre and terrifying postures with their eyes and mouths wide open. Our guide stopped us often and provided details. He showed me some babies.[86]

Janssen and Bass were accustoming the boys to transgression by seeing forbidden and horrible things. They also wanted to disturb them emotionally, so that the boys would seek emotional comfort in the physical contact that even abusive sex offers. They may also have been making, as one victim suspected, an implicit threat; the boys or their families would end up like the bodies in the morgue if they told anyone about the abuse.

Janssen played upon the boys' desire to protect others. Wells told a psychologist "that one of the reasons he cooperated was to keep his brother from being molested. He threatened he would tell if the priest molested his brother."[87] Wells kept silent, but Janssen molested the brother anyway. Another boy was silent about the abuse because "I knew if I told my father he would kill Father Janssen and I would lose my father."[88]

One of the strangest phenomena connected with sexual abuse is the traumatic bond (see pp. 271ff.). The abuser and his victim form a bond that prevents the victim from exposing the abuser. One victim helped cover for Janssen. As an adult, he truthfully wrote to the diocese of Davenport, "I was not involved in secret sex clubs with Father Janssen and had not participated in group sex."[89] The man had only individual, not group, sex with Janssen. This victim also wrote a letter supporting Janssen's attempt to become the world's oldest lifeguard. A Janssen victim married when he was thirty-four and had Janssen witness the ceremony.

Victims and their families show a weaker form of the bond when they do not want to admit that an evil man has done something criminal to them. Instead, they want to regard the perpetrator as "sick" and ask only that he be treated. Janssen molested Don Green at Ss. Philip and James parish; his family asked that Janssen be sent for "counseling."[90]

Another family wanted Janssen to "acknowledge he has a problem" and to "seek treatment."[91] Another mother "is not bitter against Father Janssen; she pities him and thinks he is not responsible for his acts."[92] The diocese had carefully concealed from the families that Janssen abused scores of boys for almost fifty years. The families might well have felt different if they knew about the other victims. The diocese knew about the traumatic bond and cultivated it. The diocese knew that victims wanted to think the abuser was sick and not a criminal and the diocese exploited that desire. The diocese manipulated the victims the same way the abuser did—doing small acts of kindness while cynically getting what it really wanted: silence. The victims and their families developed a traumatic bond with the diocese; the laity as a whole seems caught in such a bond, not wanting to admit that their church may have been run for decades by cynical and evil men, abusers and manipulators.

The boys did not consider the sexual activity to be homosexual. One victim explained that a neighbor of the cabin where the orgies took place yelled at them that they were "queers." He was surprised because "I never considered myself homosexual and we [the boys] even laughed at queer jokes."[93] The boys were young adolescents and did not think in categories of heterosexuality and homosexuality. They simply felt they were being initiated into adult masculinity. Janssen helped one young boy masturbate until he had his first orgasm. "Janssen made a comment that he was glad I was entering into manhood."[94] Janssen used heterosexual pornography to coax the boys into homosexual acts, deliberately confusing them about sexual categories. One victim married at twenty and quickly divorced; the young man later realized that this early marriage "in part was my wanting to prove to Father Janssen that I was heterosexual and not interested in any of his ongoing sexual advances."[95] He invited Janssen to the wedding.

The victims have suffered post-traumatic stress for decades, including fears of homosexuality, depression, and paranoia. One victim "heard voices" that said he was "gay" and fled to the mountains, ending up in a psychiatric hospital. Another victim says that to escape the nights filled with nightmares, "I tried to kill myself by taking a handful of Percodan and drinking a fifth of whiskey."[96] Dissociation, a split in a mind that is attempting to deal with horrors, is a common result of abuse (see pp. 266–268). One victim remembered that "I participated in and witnessed mutual masturbation and mutual fellatio. Two times at Geerts's rectory I sort of 'checked-out.' One of those times was while watching Janssen and Geerts perform mutual fellatio on one another. The other time was when I witnessed one of the boys performing fellatio on Geerts while Geerts was kissing another boy on the lips with his finger in the anus of the boy he was kissing." Another time what this victim saw was even worse, and his brain short-circuited to block it: "I checked-out this time by completely dissociating from my body by floating outside the cabin." The only memories the victim has of that night are in nightmares, and "always crying and screaming are in the dreams."[97]

Above all, the victims, having had their trust and bodies so abused, could no longer trust anyone. They couldn't trust the Church, they couldn't trust their employers, they couldn't trust their wives, they couldn't trust themselves. Janssen knew that sexuality implies trust: being physically intimate with someone implies a deep trust in that person. The boys intuited that sexuality and trust were closely connected, and Janssen manipulated this intuition to get what he wanted: sex and control. The control was used with callous disregard for the boys' developing sexuality (whether heterosexual or homosexual), introducing them to premature and intense experiences such as most adults never have (e.g., group sex). Their lives were scarred permanently. One victim realized that "if I hadn't been born into the Catholic religion, how different, better[,] and healthy my life would have been."[98]

But not only did Janssen manipulate the trust of the boys and of their parents, the bishops and other priests also manipulated the trust that the laity had in the clergy. The Catholic clergy in Europe had sometimes been heroic in accepting persecution from Protestants and revolutionaries to minister to the laity, and the laity responded with trust. A later generation misused this trust to create a false atmosphere of holiness around priests, who are men with normal—and sometimes abnormal—failings. The protection from exposure and just punishment has attracted and enabled abusers. The laity who reported the abuse to the bishop trusted that the bishop would do the right thing. The bishops in Davenport and elsewhere almost never did the right thing, but the trust the laity placed in the bishops enabled the bishops to tolerate abuse for decade after decade.

## *Lies*

Gerald Francis O'Keefe was bishop of Davenport from 1967 to 1993. He continued to receive complaints about abuse by priests, but he knew that a paper trail creates liability, so he kept few records. The diocese's own attorney, Rand Wonio, claimed that O'Keefe "didn't put a lot of things on paper."[99] This avoidance of documents enabled the diocese to claim later that there were no records of allegations from 1966 to 1988. But O'Keefe had access to all the previous records and complaints about Janssen and other abusive priests in the diocese. He also had the testimony of Ed Thomas about Father Bass, testimony that Thomas had given several times, beginning in 1974.

Bass, as has been related, had taken Thomas and other boys to the Cook County Hospital Morgue to soften them up. Ed Thomas had told that story and its sequels to the diocese several times. After leaving the morgue, Bass then took the boys to dinner and to his uncle's house. He persuaded Thomas to put on a purity string under his underwear, to protect the boy from sexual sins (this is an old Catholic custom). Thomas had begun to doubt the value of confession, but Bass persuaded him to go to confession, and Bass "would always want to dwell on sexual issues." Bass made Thomas get in his bed and tried to molest him; Thomas responded with a sharp elbow and ran downstairs.

After returning home, Thomas told his mother what Bass had done, and all she told her son was "to stay away from him." He went to St. Mary's to tell a priest: but the priest was Janssen, and he told the boy that his "suspicions were not correct."[100] Thomas grew up and left the Catholic Church.

In 1974 Thomas called an official of the diocese of Davenport to repeat this information: "the conversation was brief and the person was not interested."[101] By 1992 Thomas had become an assistant professor at Northern Illinois University; he saw a television show on child abuse, and again called the bishop's house to repeat the information. He heard nothing, called back, spoke to Msgr. Morrissey, and told him what Bass had done. This contact led to the only known record in the diocesan files of Thomas's numerous attempts to warn about Bass. Morrissey wrote in a 1992 memo to O'Keefe that "I believe no action needs to be taken, but this memo should be sealed and put into Father Bass's file. If something else comes up, I don't think we can deny this telephone call."[102] Clearly the implication is that the diocese liked to deny receiving allegations, but could not in this case.

In 2001 Thomas held a responsible position in the Iowa Department of Education. He called the diocese again to warn them about Bass. "I was shifted to a couple of unresponsive people and, finally, spoke with someone who apologized and assured me that Father Bass would not be around children any more."[103] A year later, Thomas called again and spoke with Vicar General Shafer.

In 1990 O'Keefe received a long letter from Father McAleer. It was mostly about Janssen's masturbating boys and the card games in which the losers had to get involved in oral sex, but McAleer also mentions the names Geerts and Bass as connected with abuse.[104] Hayes had known of the connection. The day after receiving a copy of Janssen's letter to a victim in which Bass was mentioned, Hayes appointed Bass to the newly created position of director of vocations.

In June 1992 O'Keefe was deposed in the civil trial when the Kasper family sued Father James Elmer Leu, the diocese of Davenport, and officials of the diocese. Leu had already been convicted criminally of abusing the two Kasper boys.[105]

O'Keefe was asked whether any other priests apart from Leu had been accused of sexual misconduct. O'Keefe responded that there was only one who had ever been accused, and that was a year before Leu was accused. O'Keefe was asked again, "And before that time, a year before Father Leu was accused, any other priest accused while you've been bishop?" To which O'Keefe replied, "No."[106]

O'Keefe was also asked, "So that every document that has been either generated or preserved about a priest of the diocese of Davenport would be, if it has been preserved, in the file of the priest. Is that right?" To which O'Keefe responded, "That's right."[107] O'Keefe was also asked about the secret archives, and he denied that they existed: "Is there a process or procedure where certain kinds of documents about a priest of the diocese of Davenport, because they are of a sensitive nature or a personal nature, that they are not maintained in the priest file and placed in the archive, for example." O'Keefe responded, "No. We don't do that."[108]

But O'Keefe knew of other abusive priests, and he had secret archives; he lied under oath.

Msgr. Michael Morrissey, vicar general of the Davenport diocese, was also deposed for the Leu case. He indicated that he had been working in various capacities in the bishop's office since 1967. Morrissey was asked, "Since that point in time, have you been aware of any claims made, other than this one, of any sexual misconduct on the part of any priest or any other diocesan employee?" to which he answered, "Yes, one," and named him, "Frank Martinez."[109] The attorney wanted to be sure that Morrissey was giving a complete answer:

> Q. So that we are clear, besides the claim that's been made against Father Martinez and the claim made here against Father Leu, you are not aware of any other claims—I use the word "claims," by the way Monsignor, so that I avoid the use of the term lawsuit, because a claim can be made by someone that does not necessarily lead to a lawsuit. Do you understand that?
>
> A. Yes I do.
>
> Q. So when I use the term "claim" asking you if you are aware of any complaint or claim made by anyone alleging sexual misconduct by a priest. Am I to understand that the only ones that you are aware of are the one that's with Father Martinez, which you've related to me, and the one with Father Leu that's the reason we are here for?
>
> A. That's the only claims [sic] that I am aware of.

But Morrissey also was not telling the truth. When asked in 2004 why he had said this, all Morrissey could say was, "I can't explain that answer."[110] If Morrissey were honest, which perjurers are not, he might have replied that he and Bishop O'Keefe had coordinated their testimony to deceive the court, the plaintiff, and the public about what had really happened in the diocese. As the attorney in the 2004 deposition continued,

> Q. Actually, at that time, Monsignor, you were aware of Jim Wells's complaints about Father Janssen, about the complaints of Father Wiebler that occurred before 1992, and specifically about the McAleer memo of 1990, weren't you, there were indications that Bass, Janssen, and Geerts had all molested multiple boys on multiple occasions.
>
> A. Yes, I was aware of that.[111]

Leu's second assignment was to Sacred Heart church in Newton, where Bass was pastor (1973–78). Bishop O'Keefe observed, "Father Leu got along very well with Father Bass and would have liked to have been his assistant at St. Patrick's [in Iowa City, Bass's next assignment]."[112] But after Bass moved, Leu served for a few weeks as administrator of Sacred Heart and was then assistant to the next pastor there, Rev. Joseph P. Denning, for half a year. Through Bass, Leu had a close connection with the pedophile ring. After the Newton assignment, Leu was an assistant for six and a half years at Our Lady of Victory in Davenport; his pastor, Rev. William O. Meyer, began a decade-long appointment as dean of Davenport while Leu was his curate.[113]

It was in Leu's next assignment, as pastor of St. Mary's in Lone Tree, that he systematically abused two brothers who were minors. Their mother reported the abuse to the diocese when she learned of it, but O'Keefe did not report Leu to the civil authorities. Instead he sent him to W. David McEchron, Ph.D., for evaluation. McEchron was, however, a mandated reporter and turned Leu over to the authorities. This was not what O'Keefe expected. O'Keefe was asked, "If you had known that he [McEchron] perceived himself to be a mandatory reporter, one obliged to report the information received by him to law enforcement authorities, would you have sent him [Leu] to Dr. McEchron?" To which O'Keefe, in a moment of honesty, responded, "No."[114]

Franklin inherited the problems when he became bishop in 1993 but took minimal action until the facts became public; he then created a smokescreen of lies to hide the reality of corruption in the diocese. In July 1996 Franklin received a letter from a victim: "I was sexually molested by Fathers Janssen, Geerts, and Bass at St. Joseph's Church in Fort Madison and in Farmington. This abuse occurred over a long period of time during the 60s and involved several boys."[115] Franklin wrote Janssen in 1997 to restrict his ministry in accord with the guidelines in "Restoring Trust," published by the National Conference of Catholic Bishops. Franklin allowed Janssen to function as a priest in a limited way and hoped that the policy "protects his reputation," still Franklin's first concern.[116]

In August 1998, "both the Davenport and Peoria dioceses stressed that there have been no incidents in the Quad-City region such as those that have occurred elsewhere in the Midwest."[117] This was not true, as the bishop and other officials of Davenport knew. In 2002 after the bad news began flowing from Boston, the pastor of Sacred Heart Cathedral in Davenport, Msgr. Marvin A. Mottet, was able to maintain that "I think Catholic people have a lot of common sense. They know this is happening, but they know it isn't happening here,"[118] because the diocese was successful in concealing abuse longer than Boston was. When Father William Wiebler was accused in 2004 of molesting a boy, "Jack Doe," in the 1970s, court documents revealed that he had met with Jack Doe, Bishop Franklin, and Chancellor Irene Loftus in May 2002 and had admitted abusing twelve other children. It is not clear whether Wiebler did or did not deny Jack Doe's particular accusations during this meeting.[119] Even after this admission and after lawsuits had been filed against Janssen and Bass, the diocesan newspaper listed Bass, Janssen, and Wiebler as retired priests in residence at the chancery "so that friends may remember them with personal greetings for Christmas"[120]—although Wiebler was not even at the chancery. He was in a treatment center outside of St. Louis, which he would soon leave without permission to live in an apartment in St. Louis.

Bishop Franklin feigned a conversion on Ash Wednesday 2004, and promised openness and transparency, but in the very document that pretended to come clean about Janssen the bishop misrepresented what had happened. The bishop quoted the first part of the therapist's comments about Janssen, but omitted the therapist's strong recommendations that Janssen be supervised. Franklin also neglected to mention that the diocese had not done this, even after the therapist had written to Bishop Hayes a second time to make sure that Janssen was being closely supervised. Franklin claimed he was making a full confession of the diocese's failures, but what he offered was in political terms a modified limited hang-out. Franklin mostly told the truth, but not the whole truth, especially the part of the truth that would reveal how badly the diocese had failed.[122]

## *Moral and Financial Bankruptcy*

There is no indication in the files that Hayes was an abuser or sexually corrupt, nor did he seem to have any psychological block that prevented him from thinking about sexual depravity (that would be unusual for a priest who was used to hearing confessions). Hayes recognized that what Janssen was doing was wrong, and ordered him to stop. Janssen refused, and Hayes, like almost all other bishops, took no further action to carry out his threats of punishment. Janssen knew there would be few or no consequences of his abuse, because he knew that Hayes would not carry through on his threats. Hayes tried to get Janssen to stop the abuse, but he was not willing either to initiate canonical proceedings against Janssen or to go to the police. Hayes knew that he would get nowhere if he tried to discipline Janssen canonically, because Rome would put endless procedural obstacles in the way of effective discipline (see pp. 407–409). Janssen knew that too.

The evidence is strong that O'Keefe (who died in 2000) himself was compromised in some way.[123] He himself had been sued for abuse, a suit that was withdrawn because it was based on a victim's recovered memory (which without corroborating evidence is insufficient proof).[124] O'Keefe did not keep records of the complaints against Janssen. Despite all that was in the files from Hayes's time, including a confession of guilt from Janssen, O'Keefe put Janssen on the personnel board, made him diocesan chaplain of Scouts, and recommended that he receive the St. George Medal, the highest national Catholic Scouting award for adults. Either O'Keefe was incompetent to the point of being mentally ill (and there is no evidence of that) or he deliberately and maliciously put Janssen in a position in which he could influence the careers of fellow abusers, put him in another position in which he could have even easier access to boys to abuse them, and with supreme perversity made sure that Janssen was publicly honored for his Scouting "activities," the true nature of which O'Keefe knew from Janssen's file. O'Keefe looks as if he were an accessory before the fact to felonious child abuse. It appears he consciously wanted to help Janssen abuse boys, and that is why he made him Scout chaplain. Both his failing to keep records and his appointing of Janssen to two sensitive positions provide serious circumstantial evidence for O'Keefe's criminality, as does his perjury during the 1990 deposition in the Leu case. O'Keefe also appointed as his vicar general (the most important person in a diocese after the bishop) Msgr. Thomas J. Feeney, who held that post from 1968 to 1981. Feeney, who died in 1985, has been accused of molesting a boy from 1957 onward.[125] O'Keefe was forced only by the threat of public exposure to take limited action against Janssen.

Although the motives for inaction of both Hayes and O'Keefe may have differed, the effect was the same: they both allowed Janssen and the other abusers to go unchecked. O'Keefe was forced by Wells's revelations to take some action, but Janssen was still treated with gentleness. Because of fear of adverse publicity and lawsuits, Bishop Franklin began to rein Janssen in a little, but his main concern was still preserving Janssen's reputation.

The diocese asked Rome to laicize Janssen, Geerts, and three other priests. On September 20, 2004, the diocese announced that the pope had dismissed James Janssen from the priesthood, without trial, without right of appeal. At eighty-two Janssen maintains his innocence, forgetting that he had admitted the abuse to Bishop Hayes.

Janssen was defrocked on July 28, 2004, but for a while continued to live in the chancery of the diocese, at 2706 N. Gaines St., Davenport, where Bass and Martinez also continued to live. Bass, who took boys to the morgue, never admitted abusing boys, and received as his punishment from the Vatican (that is, Cardinal Ratzinger, now Pope Benedict XVI) an order to say Mass once a week for his victims, and a few minor restrictions.[126] In their cases and in the cases of William Wiebler and Richard Poster (former director of liturgy for the diocese who is in federal prison for the possession of child pornography[127]), disgrace has been made as comfortable as possible, possibly because they might otherwise be inclined to reveal further embarrassing information. Janssen had no criminal convictions and planned a new career. On October 2, 2004, he attended a training session given by the Iowa Foster and Adoptive Parents Association, of which he is a member. Janssen was addressed as "Rev." by the teacher.[128]

The parishioners of Ss. Philip and James in Grand Mound tried to erase Janssen's name from a stained glass memorial window but found they had to remove the window and replace the glass to rid themselves of Janssen's name. The damage that Janssen caused in the lives of the parishioners is not so easily removed. After the abuse by Janssen became public, the diocese ignored the parish. The parishioners then complained that "at no time did diocesan officials contact us as parish council members. At no time were we offered a parish meeting with diocesan officials or otherwise for a more complete discussion of the complaint. And, at no time were any follow-up procedures established to assess the ongoing impact of the disclosures in our parish."[129] Bishop Franklin then unexpectedly attended a Mass at the parish and listened to the parishioners, and later held a news conference, in which he promised to come clean—but didn't.

The diocese continues to try to escape lawsuits. After Franklin pledged transparency, he has continued to fight repeated court orders to turn over all records. He has invoked the statute of limitations, arguing in effect that the diocese successfully concealed the abuse until after the statute of limitations had expired and was therefore untouchable. As the plaintiff's attorney said, "The wrongdoer is attempting to benefit by its secret wrongdoing."[130] The diocese of Davenport has steadfastly maintained that "it had no legal duty to inform parishes of past sexual misconduct by priests"[131] and that for a court to punish the diocese for assigning abusive priests to parishes interferes with the free exercise of religion. The diocese maintained that it has no duties to lay Catholics: "The diocese of Davenport, which is comparatively large and bureaucratic, simply cannot be reasonably expected to have a fiduciary relationship with each one of its churches' parishioners. The [d]iocese cannot be held to a standard of personal trust and confidence with each and every parishioner." The diocese repeated this assertion: that "no fiduciary relationship exists between a diocese and its parishioners," that "the [d]iocese has no duty to warn of misconduct," and that "a minor is not obligated to attend church, or interact with a parish priest."[132] In dealing with their diocese, let lay Catholics beware; a diocese acknowledges no duties that it owes to lay Catholics.

The diocese filed for bankruptcy on October 10, 2006. Franklin has claimed, "It is also important to bring closure to this tragedy—for the victims and for the [d]iocese. Bringing closure may be impossible in the context of present and future litigation."[133] Bankruptcy ends all legal action; the bankruptcy judge decides the cases. There will be no more discovery of embarrassing documents, no more questions about the failures of diocesan officials, no more questions about why bishops tolerated abuse for so many decades, and above all no cross-examination of the abusive priests about the origin of their pedophile club. The diocese has to accomplish these legal maneuvers without the aid of its vicar general, Msgr. Drake R. Shafer. Shafer was accused privately, and then himself went public in the summer of 2003 to deny the accusation. However, in March 2004 it was revealed in court that Shafer had sent an e-mail to the victim on April 5, 2002, admitting to the incident in the 1970s, which "was the only time in my priesthood when anything remotely like it happened." Shafer wrote, "I did not intend to abuse you that night or any other. I hope you know that our friendship at that time meant a lot to me and I would never have wanted to hurt you in any way and I am so sorry I did." Shafer offered two excuses: he was drunk and he himself had been abused by a priest—"it went on from nine- to twelve-years old. I never told anyone then that it happened and that priest is dead now for many years."[134] Shafer settled the lawsuit against him.[135]

The diocese used the threat of bankruptcy to bring the victims to settle. It paid out $9,000,000, about $250,000 to each victim. The settlement also protects the diocese. David Clohessy, the head of SNAP (Survivors' Network of those Abused by Priests), explained that as a result of the settlement "church leaders don't take the witness stand, and secret documents aren't disclosed, and the true extent of the cover-up is hard to determine and spell out for the public."[136] The diocese has resumed its annual appeal and anticipates no difficulty in replacing the money paid out to victims.

Janssen was sued by his nephew James Wells and in May 2005 came to trial. Janssen had denied under oath in sworn statements that he had molested James Wells. At first Janssen missed a court date; he then appeared and admitted the abuse. The next day in court he retracted his testimony. He had lied under oath, he said, because "I was overwhelmed by pressure."[137] The jury decided against Janssen and awarded $1.89 million to his nephew. But Janssen's erratic behavior at the trial may have been calculated. His admission to lying was carefully timed to avoid a perjury charge under Iowa law.[138] Bass settled with his accusers out of court[139] and gave a carefully worded apology that avoided an admission of guilt. He then took up the penance that Cardinal Ratzinger had assigned him: saying Mass.

When Janssen was at St. Joseph's in Fort Madison he was a modern priest, "Father Jazz"[140]; he quoted popular songs in his sermons.[141] Some parishioners in Fort Madison, where Janssen served and victimized boys, are upset that anyone should criticize him: "I wonder if it's even true," said Bernice Holtkamp. "Father Janssen was priest at St. Joseph when we moved out there in '58. He would get up there and preach off the cuff. He was great at that." Her daughter, Cathy Holtkamp, added, "Maybe it has happened, but it's been blown all out of proportion." Tom Stellern, president of the local Knights of Columbus, saw greed as the motivation of the victims: "I've never been for this handing out of cash. You can ruin someone's reputation based on an accusation. If you pay out, he's guilty. They need to guard against that."[142]

Janssen was at St. Joseph's Church in Sugar Creek in the 1960s, and left a trail of victims, some of whom are suing Janssen and the diocese anonymously. Jim Roling, a member of that parish, who remembered "spending many evenings playing cards and hanging out with" Janssen, is reportedly worried that "allegations left neighbors suspecting each other and outsiders pointing fingers at the community for hurting the Church this way." The parish members suspect each other of being behind the lawsuit, and fear that the lawsuit may hurt the Church. Roling continued, "We are shocked they don't put their names on the lawsuit. Not publicizing the names behind these lawsuits really bothers me."[143]

Kay Johnson of Delmar, where Bass was stationed 1981–92, was "appalled" when she heard that Bass was being sued. He was "such a kind man"; maybe the priests were wrong to abuse boys, "but now that they're old men, why are they doing this to them now?" One woman remembered that as a girl she knew one of Bass's alleged victims and that it was "common knowledge among the kids that Bass was allegedly abusing many of the boys he befriended." She tried to tell her mother, who reportedly "slapped her face and told her not to speak about priests that way."[144]

According to the Davenport diocese, parents were not always upset that Janssen had molested their children. The victim's mother who intercepted the letter to Janssen was distressed; according to a diocesan summary, the father was not: "Bishop Hayes also received a letter from the boy's father, who stated that his son had already experimented 'this act,' felt that Father Janssen had benefited their family overall and hoped that Father Janssen would be a stronger and wiser priest."[145] Janssen worked with the son's Scout troop in which the father was a Scout leader.

The mildness of the reaction of almost all those who learned about Janssen's molestation of boys demonstrates that American society was not dominated by "homophobia," an extreme and disproportionate hatred of homosexuals. Only a few mothers showed anything like anger about Janssen's sexual acts with their sons. Bishops, priests, psychologists, police, parishioners, and even a father thought it at worst a minor annoyance. The bishops who supervised Janssen and the other abusers may not have liked the abuse (although O'Keefe's attitude is unclear), but they regarded it as a small fault in a priest, objectionable chiefly because it might lead to bad publicity. A large segment of the laity were content that priests were allowed to abuse boys, as were the bishops of Davenport, as was the Vatican, which made it almost impossible to defrock a priest. Exposing and punishing the abusers would disturb the normal routine of the Church; the suffering of the victims was the price that Catholics were willing to pay to maintain the belief that no priest was criminal and that all priests could be trusted. Everyone found the alternative, a close scrutiny of priests' lives, too dangerous to the fiction that the Catholic Church, clergy and laity, had constructed to further Catholic self-satisfaction.

Especially unimaginable is that there is a centuries-old underground in the Church that perpetrates a tradition of abuse, an abuse that was tolerated even by a canonized saint (see pp. 19–20). The abuse increased during the 1960s and 1970s, but it did not begin then, although Janssen explained his actions to one victim by claiming "it was the 60s with 'free love.'"[146] A boy who has been molested by a priest may react violently and self-destructively or he may think that abuse is simply a normal part of life, like masturbation, that is not publicly talked about. William Manseau, just before he entered the seminary, was kissed erotically by his mentor, the Rev. Thomas Sennott, and felt he had been initiated sexually.[147] Such a man can become a priest himself and molest boys himself. The process is analogous to multigenerational incest that perpetuates itself over centuries. The Vicar General Shafer explained to his victim that he himself had been molested. Janssen, Bass, Geerts, and Murphy were all at Kenrick Seminary in the 1940s. They all became pedophiles and they all knew one another and collaborated in committing crimes. Janssen was involved in some unnamed scandal at the seminary. The suspicion is that they themselves were abused by an official in the seminary, who may have introduced them to perverted sexuality and introduced them to one another. It would have been very dangerous for any of the abusers fully to reveal himself to someone he did not know was a fellow abuser, so they must have known somehow about each other's willingness to engage in perversion. As priests they shared boys among themselves and sent them to other molesters.

The abusers knew that bishops, even if not themselves corrupt, hated confrontation and bad publicity even more than they disliked child abuse—a dislike that in any case did not seem to be very strong in any of the bishops or officials in the Davenport diocese. Bishops believed in the possibility of true repentance and change (a hope at the heart of Christianity) and the abusers exploited this belief by feigning repentance. But bishops continued to believe in the possibility of repentance even after the abusers had demonstrated over decades that they were not really repentant and did not want to change. The next step the bishops would have to take was confronting and punishing the abusers. Most bishops are men who hate confrontation—that is one reason the Vatican made them bishops. The Vatican had sent clear signals that it did not want bishops to punish any priest by laicizing him, no matter what crime he had committed. Almost all the laity were happy with this arrangement, and police and courts went along with it too. The only ones to suffer were the victims.

The victims were invisible to everyone. The abusers were narcissists who had no empathy for the sufferings of their victims. The priests, officials, and bishops of the Davenport diocese were all caught up in a clerical narcissism, in which only repercussions that affected them had any meaning. The laity too were afflicted by a Catholic narcissism that idolized the clergy. Governor Frank Keating, appointed and then fired by the bishops as head of the national review board on sexual abuse, concluded that the bishops "cared more for the steady stream of financial support from the laity and the reputation of the [C]hurch than for the ravaged and frightened souls of children."[148] It was not only the bishops who stopped their ears to the cry of the oppressed and abused—almost all priests and laity did.

The Davenport documents that have been made public are horrifying enough. Two groups of documents have not been made public. One is in the hands of the attorney for the plaintiffs. He has held them back as a bargaining chip with the diocese. The other is a group of personnel records which the diocese has been fighting not to release. Both groups of documents must contain information even more damaging than that revealed by the documents already filed in the court, documents cited in this chapter. What could be worse than the pedophile ring, the group sex, the morgue visits? The still-secret information may contain information about the extent or nature of the abuse. Perhaps many more priests and diocesan officials were involved either as abusers or as agents of a scheme to conceal the abuse. But the nature of the abuse may be what the diocese is trying to conceal. The transgressive spirit that inflamed the abuse that Janssen, Bass, Geerts, and the others committed led them to molesting children and to sacrilege. Beyond that lies only diabolism.

# CHAPTER THREE

# DISTANT THUNDER

A RING OF ABUSERS took over the Piarist order in the seventeenth century with the connivance of the papacy and the Inquisition, but the facts remained hidden until 2004. The ring of abusers in El Paso went back to the early 1940s, but has not been publicized until this book. The ring of abusers in Davenport went back to the early 1950s, but did not become public knowledge until late 2002. Abuse, however horrendous, was kept out of the public eye by a tacit agreement of bishops, police, prosecutors, and newspapers. However, a mounting series of events, culminating in the resignation of Cardinal Bernard Law, forced the American bishops and the Vatican to make some gestures toward protecting children. The storm that swept Law from the archdiocese of Boston really began in another backwater of North America: Newfoundland. Canada was alerted that children were being abused by Catholic priests and religious, and then the United States was alerted by the legal turmoil that roiled the small diocese of Lafayette, Louisiana.

## *News from Newfoundland*

The first rumblings of the sexual scandals that were to engulf the Catholic Church in North America and throughout the world began on the far fringes of the New World, in Newfoundland. Newfoundland has always been poor.

Its only resource was fish, and they swam away. Nevertheless, it was a refuge to Irish fleeing from famine. Poor and Irish in the middle of the North Atlantic: not a happy fate. Few people were interested in helping these people, except for the Christian Brothers of Ireland. This group was founded by Edmund Ignatius Rice at the beginning of the nineteenth century to educate poor boys. The Catholics of Newfoundland begged the Brothers to come, which they finally did in 1875. They started Mount Cashel orphanage in 1892, but as mortality declined there were fewer and fewer orphans at Mount Cashel and more and more boys from disturbed families. Government funding became dominant, and by 1975 all but one of its ninety-one boys were wards of the state.

Boys can be difficult to deal with. Boys from poor backgrounds, fatherless boys, boys who have been brutalized are even harder to control. The orphanages and industrial schools founded in the Victorian era had as their first purpose the protection of society from these rough boys.[1] Life was hard in the nineteenth century and hard in the Ireland and Newfoundland of the mid-twentieth century. The boys were reasonably well taken care of in the institutions; at least they were better off than they had been as vagabonds or members of abusive families. But corporal punishment combined with casual nudity (common in boys' schools) created a situation in which sexual abuse could be overlooked. This happened not just among the poor but in the English public (i.e., private) schools which upper-class boys attended.

When the Christian Brothers of Ireland first came to Newfoundland, discipline was firm but loving, but by the 1950s the Christian Brothers brutalized the boys with "excessive, if not savage, punishment."[2] Brother Edward English "would fly into rages during which he would pummel the boys with his fists or lash them with his belt or a special leather strap."[3] Physical abuse glided over easily into sexual abuse. The Brothers addressed the boys in their charge as "you little motherless bastard" and "you little motherless fucker."[4] Having thoroughly intimidated the boys, several Christian Brothers began using them for sex. Dereck O'Brien reported that "I heard a noise and looked up to see a young fellow performing oral sex on

Brother English."[5] A nine-year-old boy reported that Brother English "feels me up all the time and puts his hands inside my pants. He tells me to play doctor with him and when I do, he puts my hand inside his pants and makes me play with his bird. He tells me to fool with the hairs and to move my fingers on the thing. I does this for him because I'm afraid he will hit me if I don't do it."[6] A boy reported that when he was thirteen Brother English "asked me to give him a blow. He forced my head down on his penis and I took it in my mouth."[7]

Brother Alan Ralph and the superintendent of the school, Brother Douglas Kenny, also abused boys physically and sexually. The brothers had a variety of ways of having sex with their charges: "forced mutual fellatio, buggery, forced mutual masturbation, fondling of the students' genitalia, 'inappropriate' kissing, and insertion of fingers in rectum."[8] Mount Cashel was ideal for men who liked to have sex with adolescent boys. The boys were the perfect victims; they often had minor problems with the law; their families were poor or broken or nonexistent. Who would believe the victims if they complained? To whom could they turn? They were the offscourings of a poor society.

In 1975 Detective Robert Hillier of the Newfoundland Constabulary began his investigation of complaints and quickly assembled enough information to justify arresting several brothers. Brother English admitted to sexual involvement with a number of boys; Brother Ralph gave a written partial confession. The detective was "astonished that the Brothers would so matter-of–factly admit to the allegations."[9] They were not worried because they knew Church and state would protect them. Chief-of-Police John Lawlor ordered Hillier to halt the investigation and to remove from the report any mention of sexual crimes. The Christian Brothers Council protected the accused brothers by spiriting them out of the province. The Ministry of Justice agreed not to take action if the abusers left the province.[10] They neglected to tell much about the sexual abuse to Alphonsus J. Penney, archbishop of St. John's, Newfoundland. A reporter, Bill Kelly of the *St. John's Evening Telegram*, got wind of the story, but Brother Gabriel McHugh, superior general of the Christian Brothers, while admitting the truth of the allegations against English and Ralph, asked Kelly not to harm Mount Cashel by reporting on the abuse. The publisher told the reporter to kill the story.[11]

The Provincial Department of Justice refused to allow the Department of Social Services access to the detective's report. Brother Ralph was sent to Southdown, a treatment facility in Aurora, Ontario (see p. 306), and Brother English to the House of Affirmation in Whitinsville, Massachusetts (see pp. 311–314). No one tried to locate and treat the victims. In 1982 more reports of sexual abuse reached the authorities; this time the boys were doing to each other what they had learned from the brothers. Brother David Burton was accused and tried for child molestation in 1982. The vicar general of the diocese of St. John's, Raymond Lahey, who was subsequently appointed bishop of St. George's, Newfoundland, testified for Brother Burton and against the victim. Brother Henry Bucher also testified in support of Brother Burton, who had admitted to having sex with his victim fifty times.[12]

Brother Gordon Bellows, the provincial of the Canadian province of the Irish Christian Brothers, also had a high opinion of Brother Burton, who, he told the court, "is an extraordinary human being who tragically fell.... He is a beautiful person."[13] Bellows said that Brother Burton would be treated at Southdown (which had great hiking trails for its "bio-energetic therapy"[14]) and that he should not have a criminal conviction for the child abuse because "I feel it would destroy his credibility, destroy his authenticity, make it difficult for him to continue in a teaching career....It would simply crush him as a human being. For that reason, I would find it absolutely appalling."[15] As to the victim, defense counsel William English claimed that "I don't think that there has been any firm evidence before you that this boy has been devastated as a result of this,"[16] which echoed Brother Bucher's remarks about the victim: "The assumption that this person has been destroyed is something that I find hard to accept and deal with."[17] The judge, despite these character references, sentenced Brother Burton to four months in jail.

The sentence was immediately appealed, and the appellate court took only twelve days not only to uphold the conviction but also to reduce Brother

Burton's sentence to those twelve days that he had already served in jail. The justices focused on the high reputation of the Christian Brothers. Crown Prosecutor Ronald Richards, who was at the hearing, said that "absolutely no consideration was given to the child and every consideration was given to the Christian Brothers."[18] Brother Burton was sent to Southdown and then assigned to a Christian Brothers' school in British Columbia, where he served under the principal Brother Kevin Short, who had been accused of abuse in the suppressed 1975 report.

In 1989 a telephone call to a Newfoundland talk show set off an investigation that revealed the mishandling of the 1975 allegations of abuse at Mount Cashel. A victim, Shane Earle, went to the *St. John's Sunday Express* and told of the abuse he had suffered at Mount Cashel beginning when he was six years old. Public officials could not ignore the story and abusers immediately started feeling consequences. Brother Burton lost his teaching job, as did Brother Ralph. His principal, Brother Short, was arrested, as were Brother Stephen Rooney, Brother Joseph Burke, vice principal of Vancouver College, Brother Kenny, and Brother Edward French.[19]

The Canadian government was asked why the institutions that were supposed to protect children had for decades failed to protect them. The government set up a Royal Commission under Samuel Hughes, retired justice of the Ontario Supreme Court.[20] The mandate of the Hughes Inquiry allowed it to examine the abuse only insofar as it was germane to the miscarriage of justice (a fact of which the Newfoundland government reminded Judge Hughes). Judge Hughes let the victims testify and the testimony was televised. Several of the victims had tried to commit suicide. Why hadn't the boys told someone? Robert Connors, one of the victims, knew his social worker was Peggy Cosine, but he only saw her once, by chance, in the thirteen years he was at Mount Cashel.[21] Connors and Earle told social worker Robert Bradbury about the abuse.[22] The report was given to Brother Kenny, the superintendent of Mount Cashel. Kenny, on crutches from a hockey injury, called Connors in after supper. Kenny accused Connors of talking to the police. Then "he made a swing with the crutch and he just managed to…[catch] me on the shoulder with the crutch and he broke the top of the crutch off on my shoulder."[23] The boys learned not to say anything to the authorities because the authorities were in league with their abusers. A couple wanted to adopt Shane Earle; Kenny discouraged them.

John Lawlor, who according to Detective Hillier had ordered the suppression of the report of sexual abuse, developed large memory lapses when he testified before the Hughes Inquiry, as did other officials. Newfoundland suffered from a sudden epidemic of amnesia. Other important witnesses were dead. Brother Gabriel McHugh, superior general of the Christian Brothers after 1978, claimed that the deceased minister of justice, Vincent McCarthy, had in 1975 ordered the expulsion from the province of Brothers English and Ralph. Brother McHugh visited Mount Cashel in 1975 after the allegations of abuse, but made no attempt to contact victims, much less to help them. The Hughes Commission reluctantly decided not to question the abusers for fear that their criminal trials would be tainted and that they would get off on a technicality.

Eventually eleven Christian Brothers were convicted of abuse, and the congregation was ordered to pay $70 million to the hundreds of abuse victims. The Mount Cashel orphanage was demolished, the land sold, and the money put in a fund for the victims. The courts ordered the Christian Brothers to sell two schools that they owned in Vancouver in order to make the payments. The parents at the schools had to raise $19 million to contribute to the judgments so that the schools would not be closed and sold. One school was Vancouver College, where abuser Brother Burke had served as vice-principal and abuser Brother Kenny as supervisor of the boys' dormitory.[24]

The archdiocese also investigated the abuse of children and issued *The Report of the Archdiocesan Commission of Inquiry into Sexual Abuse of Children*, also known as the "Winter Report." It said that Archbishop Penney was in part to blame. On July 18, 1990, Penney resigned because of his mishandling of this and other sexual abuse scandals, saying, "I apologize and express my sincere regrets for failing the victims and their families in their moment of acute pain and desolation. I take full responsibility and have submitted my resignation."[25] Penney's example of acceptance of responsibility has not been imitated by other bishops who have allowed sexual abuse in their dioceses.

Priests of the diocese of St. George in Newfoundland were also guilty of the abuse of minors. In 1979 a young man complained to Penney, the metropolitan archbishop of the province that included St. George's, that he had been abused by the Rev. Kevin Bennett, who in 1989 pleaded guilty to molesting thirty-six boys.[26] Apart from telling Bennett's bishop in 1979, Penney did nothing in response to the complaint against Bennett, which was the way he handled complaints in his own diocese of St. John's.

The Rev. James Hickey, ordained in 1970, had an outstanding career in the archdiocese of St. John's. He founded the Basilica Youth Choir and became vocations director, director of communications, editor of *The Monitor*, and pastor of many churches. Hickey had a great interest in youth and was considered "charismatic," as offenders often are. In 1975 the archdiocese had started hearing complaints about his abuse of altar boys, more than a decade before Hickey's crimes became public. In 1979, Archbishop Penney assigned seminarian Randy Barnes to work at Hickey's parish. Barnes protested this assignment because of the "stories" circulating about Hickey. Penney did not inquire as to what the stories were. Barnes saw boys spending the night in Hickey's bedroom, and one time Hickey had a male friend in and asked Barnes "to make it a threesome."[27]

One boy who had been sexually assaulted by a man was distressed and went to confession to Father James Hickey, who lured him into his bed. Hickey had tastes perverse even for a pedophile; he liked to have oral sex immediately after anal sex. As youth director for the archdiocese, Hickey stood next to the pope when John Paul II visited Newfoundland. He also took the pope to visit the parish of the Rev. John Corrigan, who was later convicted of child abuse.[28] The boy whom Hickey had molested himself became a priest, saw a psychologist in 1987, and told Archbishop Penney what had happened. The victim also told social services, who turned the report over to the police. In 1988 Hickey was charged with thirty-two counts of criminal sexual behavior. Twenty men testified about what

Hickey had done to them; the priest pleaded guilty. Seven more priests were charged in the following months because Canada has no statute of limitations for serious crimes.

The Canadian bishops learned from the bad publicity. They issued a series of protocols, *From Pain to Hope*, which specified that bishops must give prompt attention to complaints, cooperate with the civil authorities, and aid victims. But the Canadian report still has a strong note of tenderness toward convicted abusers. It holds out the possibility of return to ministry upon recommendation from the treatment center and cautions those who are angered by child abuse: "One must strive to maintain an attitude of charity toward those accused and even those found guilty. Our legitimate desire to protect children to the utmost must not lead us to be unjust toward the adults who have inflicted such serious wrongs upon them, not to decide summarily that such individuals must bear the scarlet mark of shame for the rest of their lives."[29] Such words are no doubt intended as a rebuke to the harsh judgmentalism of people who would say of priests who abuse children "whoever causes one of these little ones who believe in Me to sin, it would be better for him to have a great millstone fastened round his neck and to be drowned in the depths of the sea." The report had little to say about sin and repentance, and its confidence in the treatment centers is misplaced.

And a few Canadian bishops still had no comprehension of what was going on. Bishop Colin Campbell of Antigonish, Nova Scotia, suggested the victims were old enough to know better and should have stopped the assaults. "What I am suggesting is that maybe some—a few, a few of them, many of them, most of them, who knows—had some kind of inkling that this was wrong and could have said, 'No, thank you very much.'"[30] The Christian Brothers stated their disagreement with Campbell, but his fellow bishops voiced no criticism of his statement.

In 1979, the Rev. Ronald Hubert Kelly of Newfoundland pleaded guilty to ten counts of drunkenly abusing teenage boys.[31] He was given a suspended sentence, ordered to a very brief stay in Southdown, and in 1985 got a full pardon, removing his criminal conviction. By 1990 he was vice chancellor for temporal affairs for the archdiocese of Toronto and a key aide to Cardinal G. Emmett Carter.[32] When his name was raised at the Hughes Inquiry, he took a leave of absence and dived into the pension fund of the United Food and Commercial Workers Union of Canada, speculating in real estate ventures whose losses ended up with the union and whose profits ended in Kelly's pockets. Kelly was last reported in Panama.[33]

A new round of charges of physical abuse was made in 1989 by men who had been boys at Mount Cashel from 1950 to 1964. The allegations led to a seven-year investigation, arrest warrants, and extradition requests for Christian Brothers who had been transferred to the United States.[34] Former Brother Gerard Kevin Barry was convicted of sexual assault that he had committed in the 1950s. The judge who sentenced Barry had a stronger sense of the evil of the abusive acts than the Catholic bishops have had; he wrote, "The humiliation and pain was enough to bear but on top of everything else the victim was a religious boy who believed in the teachings of the Church. He believed the acts committed against him were mortal sins and he had to live with the fact that he believed he was committing a mortal sin."[35]

In 1996 Pope John Paul II canonized the founder of the Christian Brothers, Edmund Ignatius Rice. Rice's collateral descendent Leo Gerald Rice told the police that the Christian Brothers had sexually abused him after he was orphaned and placed in the Mount Cashel orphanage in 1966 when he was eight years old. Brother English soon noticed him, took him into his room, and then undressed him. Rice said that "he got on top of me. I was face up. He had his penis between my legs, he was going in and out. He then took it out and put it on my stomach and 'came' on my stomach."[36] The Vatican has not concerned itself with the internal affairs of the Christian Brothers, who are largely exempt from supervision by the bishops because they are under papal jurisdiction. The Christian Brothers of Ireland govern themselves, and presumably the Vatican is satisfied with the governance, because it does not interfere.

The Christian Brothers of Ireland were a prestigious and powerful international order, enjoying the support of the Vatican and ministering to destitute orphans and abandoned children who had no one to protect them. Mount Cashel was organizationally independent of St. John's archdiocese, but the archdiocese harbored its own abusive priests, and the abuse at Mount Cashel occurred in an atmosphere in which abuse was tacitly accepted or at least tolerated. In this situation everyone failed the victims at Mount Cashel, including the secular authorities who colluded with the Christian Brothers. The 1975 report was sanitized on someone's order, the newspaper story was suppressed, and the abusers sent away.

The dynamics of abuse in Newfoundland were also at work in other Canadian and U. S. dioceses, and probably many dioceses throughout the world: sexual abuse, neglect by the Vatican and senior prelates, and secular collusion. When the Newfoundland situation—both the abuse and the cover-up by church and state—finally came to light in 1985, it could have been a warning that the time of reckoning had come, and that benign neglect was not the proper response to the sexual abuse of minors. But the terrible warning of Mount Cashel was not heeded. Far to the south, in Louisiana, an area of the United States that was closely linked to Canada by the Acadian dispersion, the lessons of Mount Cashel would be taught again. Again the Church would pay no heed. When they observed the unfolding of the scandal in Boston and the downfall of Cardinal Law in 2002, Canadians had one message for U. S. Catholics: "We told you so."[37] But no one, least of all the American bishops, was listening.

## *Gauthé in the Bayous*

Vermilion Parish in Louisiana is 65% Catholic, Cajun, peopled by descendants of French Canadians driven into exile. It is in the diocese of Lafayette. The county seat is Abbeville, "Priests' Town." In 1971 Gilbert Gauthé was ordained a priest and thereafter molested children as young as six years old at every parish in which he served. In one parish he would molest a child, parents complained, and the bishop transferred him. At the next parish he molested a child, parents complained, and the bishop transferred him; and so on. In 1984 he was charged with eleven counts of child abuse; he pleaded guilty and was sentenced to twenty years in prison. He was released after nine years and went to Texas, where he was accused of molesting a three-year-old. He received only probation and later showed up as a bus driver for a senior citizens' group. How did all this happen?

Gilbert Gauthé was born in Napoleonville, Louisiana. There he had the good fortune to grow up near Henry Politz, ten years his senior, who became a federal judge and gave Gauthé a get-out-of-jail-free card. Gauthé claimed to have been molested when he was in the fifth grade. An unidentified older boy, a neighbor, "took off my pants and underwear and began to feel me. I can't say he forced me but he was a very threatening person and I knew I'd get beat up. This happened maybe twice as best I can remember and the third time he did oral sex on me—forcing me to do the same thing to him."[38]

Even before entering the seminary Gauthé had been a pedophile. As a young man, "he and his younger brother, Richard, a Boy Scout leader, had molested scores of children."[39] Richard married a woman with three children and molested them, and was thrown out of the Air Force and, in 1970, out of the Boy Scouts for molesting other boys.[40]

After Gauthé's ordination his molestations continued without pause. In 1972 two parents confronted Gauthé and he agreed to go for psychiatric treatment.[41] He did not tell the bishop about this event. In his parishes Gauthé was a popular priest; he was neither reserved nor pious. He charmed little old ladies and came to dinner with an open-necked shirt. He had a camper with a TV and wore hunting boots under his cassock; he was a hip priest and an outdoorsman who took kids on hunting trips. "The charismatic Gauthé got along with the kids famously, and spent thousands of the parish's dollars on a treasure trove of goodies for his youthful parishioners. The haul included a van equipped with television and a video recorder, a large-scale television and video game equipment for the parish rectory, a black Chevrolet Camaro and even a hunting camp in the marshes of south Louisiana, where Gauthé kept numerous shotguns."[42] At that camp and back at the church he did things to the boys: "Repeated acts of sodomy; oral sex; instigation of sexual acts between boys; taking photographs of kids in sexual acts; showing pornographic videotapes; fondling boys' sexual organs in the confessional, in the sacristy, in the rectory, on Saturday trips to the marsh."[43]

A parent, Roy Robichaux (pseudonym), learned that Gauthé had molested his sons and went to the chancery in January 1983 to see Msgr. Henri Alexandre Larroque, the vicar general, second in charge of the diocese. Larroque told the father that "we've known that Father Gauthé had a problem for some time, but we thought it had been resolved." Larroque's main focus was Gauthé: "We're talking about ruining a man's career."[44] After all, in Larroque's mind, "this is very minimal."[45] The psychologist who talked to the Robichaux boys estimated at least 30 boys were involved. Msgr. Richard V. P. Mouton, pastor and one of Lafayette's deans, was very concerned: "Imagine how Gauthé's mother would feel."[46] Mouton dismissed the boys' problems, "They would bounce back and get over these things."[47]

Bishop Gerald Louis Frey admitted during the civil trial that in 1974 he had known of Gauthé's molestations because Gauthé had admitted to them, but the priest promised not to abuse again.[48] Frey transferred Gauthé to New Iberia and in 1975 named him diocesan Boy Scout chaplain—a position to which several bishops named accused abusers, as we shall see. From 1975 to 1976 Gauthé shared a rectory with Rev. Ronald Lane Fontenot and they also shared boys. Fontenot was suspended in 1983 because of child abuse. He then moved to Seattle, became a counselor, stayed with the Jesuits, and molested boys in a hospital.[49] He then went to the Servants of the Paraclete in New Mexico for treatment, and from there to nearby Albuquerque, where he took the name of Jean-Paul Fontenot (in honor of the pope?), worked for a law office (he was later sued for "propositioning and mauling male coworkers and clients" there), set up shop as a counselor and advertised: "Gay/Bi male survivors of Abuse: Options Counseling is forming a new therapeutic group to gay/bi males who have been physically and/or sexually abused as a child, adolescent[,] or adult." When he treated one client (who later sued him), he recited a brutal homosexual fantasy with a man matching the patient's description, "hugged and kissed the man in an 'unprofessional and suggestive' nature," and "touched the man's body in a 'suggestive, unexpected, and unpermitted way.'"[50]

Meanwhile Gauthé was next sent in 1976 to St. Mary Magdalene in Abbeville, where parents complained to Msgr. Richard Mouton, the pastor, about Gauthé's kissing their boys. Later in court Mouton explained to the plaintiffs' attorney how he had reacted or rather not reacted:

> Attorney: And you never made any inquiry as to this potential for sexual misbehavior either by talking to Gauthé, or by talking to the lay people, the parents, or even to the altar boys?
> Mouton: That is correct, sir. I tend, just personally, not to remember these things about people, I don't gossip.[51]

Mouton did, however, tell Gauthé to see a psychiatrist. Bishop Frey promoted Gauthé in 1977 to pastor of St. John's in Henry, Louisiana. In 1980 Frey received a letter complaining of Gauthé's over-familiarity with boys but did nothing in response to the complaint.

In 1980 Richard Gauthé's wife caught him molesting her children from a previous marriage. She reported, "Richard told me both he and Gilbert had been doing this for years. I knew Gilbert was a priest and had access to all those kids and I tried to turn him in, but the police didn't believe me. They said that, even if it was true, what I knew was hearsay and they couldn't arrest him."[52] The police could have conducted their own investigation, or they could have gone to the bishop, but they too did nothing to protect children.

Finally, in June 1983, some parents went to a lawyer, Paul Hebert, about Gauthé, and Hebert asked Msgr. Larroque to contact families of altar boys to see if anyone else had been molested and needed help. Larroque did not do this, but he realized that a lawsuit impended and that money was at stake. Gauthé suddenly had to leave Louisiana. The House of Affirmation in Massachusetts, run by the fraudulent Rev. Thomas Kane (see pp. 311–314), was Gauthé's home from August 1983 until October 1984 when he was indicted and sent to the Institute of Living in Connecticut.

Gauthé liked to have sex with males as old as fifteen years, but he preferred younger males, and tended to lose interest in boys when they approached puberty. Young boys' bodies are small. One eight-year-old boy had to go to the hospital in 1983 with rectal bleeding after Gauthé sodomized him.[53] The boy's mother testified at the civil trial; when asked what he thought of when he saw Mouton and Frey (who were both in the courtroom): "When I look at Monsignor Mouton and Bishop Frey, I think of Gauthé *sticking* his penis in my child's mouth, ejaculating into his mouth, putting his penis into his rectum—that is what I think about!"[54] If Frey and Mouton had done their duty, if they had acted on what they had known since at least 1974, the boy would never have been abused.

Why did Frey tolerate pedophilia? According to someone who worked with him, "Frey hates confrontations."[55] This is an important clue to understanding the mind of the bishops. Very typically they hate confrontation more than they dislike child molestation. Jason Berry, the journalist who broke the Gauthé story, thought that homosexuality was at the root of the diocese's problem, because a toleration of adult sexual misbehavior among homosexual priests had extended to pedophiles. Plaintiff attorney J. Minos Simon was denied church documents on twenty priests he accused of sexual misconduct; Berry after a long investigation estimated fifty out of the 205 were active homosexuals. He sized up the situation in this way: "The cleric who suffered most from the constellation of clergy child abusers was Bishop Frey, who was surrounded by gays in the chancery, yet I am convinced was not one himself."[56]

In the fall of 1985 Gauthé was tried; he was represented by the attorney Ray Mouton, who agreed to a plea bargain which, Mouton thought, would guarantee that Gauthé would get psychiatric treatment and spend at least twenty years in jail. Gauthé pleaded guilty to eleven counts and admitted molesting thirty-seven boys. But even before the trial ended, Mouton's plans to keep Gauthé out of circulation began to go wrong.

Gauthé had a friend in a very high place: his old neighbor Federal Judge Henry Politz of the Fifth Circuit U. S. Court of Appeals, one step below the Supreme Court. Politz, ten years older than Gauthé, was a longtime friend of the Gauthé family: the father of Judge Politz and the grandfather of Gilbert Gauthé had been sharecroppers together in Napoleonville.

This distant connection does not seem to explain the extraordinary level of interest that Politz displayed in Gauthé. During the trial Gauthé kept asking Mouton to call Politz, whom Gauthé said could help him. Mouton refused to do this for ethical reasons. Politz offered Mouton unspecified help because of his acquaintance with three important men: "Edwin Edwards, who was governor at the time; the Rev. Philip Hannan, who was archbishop of New Orleans; and C. Paul Phelps, then corrections secretary."[57] Politz asked for the file of the trial and began discussing with Nathan Stansbury, the district attorney, the possibility of claiming that Mouton was incompetent counsel. Mouton resigned from the case. He explained that "the very idea of this prominent judge reaching out to help him gave me a very uneasy feeling, ethically and morally."[58]

Gauthé was not sent for psychiatric treatment; instead he was kept at Wade Correctional Institution, whose warden, Richard Stadler, was a self-described protégé of Judge Politz.[59] The judge visited Gauthé in prison, and Gauthé proclaimed Politz was his "legal and moral counselor."[60] Politz was accompanied on these visits by Msgr. Murray Clayton of Shreveport, Louisiana. Gauthé did not have to take Depo-Provera, the drug that reduces the sex drive, a treatment that his own attorney, Mouton, had hoped he would get. Instead he was given a private, air-conditioned office (off-limits to guards) and had young male assistants. Gauthé used his office to store his pornographic drawings and to meet with young prisoners. He shaved them and kept their pubic hair in a bag; Gauthé did not like the secondary sex characteristics of adult males. To Mouton's horror, "Gauthé actually served his time in a facility where juveniles were also housed and he continued to have sex with young men."[61] He was furloughed for weeks at a time to see his mother and was seen attending society functions in Louisiana with Judge Politz. Despite the agreement that Mouton thought would prevent parole, Gauthé was released after nine years, in 1995, for good behavior. Richard Stadler, by then corrections secretary, had asked for a review, and the review board had done some creative accounting of time served to let Gauthé out as soon as possible. Upon his release Gauthé collected $15,000 "retirement pay" from the Catholic Church.

Gauthé moved to Polk County, Texas, and posed as a retired paramedic. A neighbor remembers that when he talked, "It was constantly about children. Gil told me that he was good friends with a federal judge… He told me this friend could get him out of jams."[62] In July 1996 Karen Munson accused Gauthé of molesting her three-year-old son. The court twice asked Louisiana for Gauthé's criminal record. The state of Louisiana "forgot" to send this record to the Texas court,[63] and Gauthé was allowed to plead no contest to a nonsexual charge—injury to a child—and received only probation. He is therefore not registered as a sex-offender. One of Gauthé's legal counsels at his trial had been Judge Politz's law clerk; another was Robert Bennett, former head of Harris County district attorney's special-crimes bureau and one of Houston's best defense attorneys. A probation officer at the court house jokingly asked Bennett why he was representing a "kiddie diddler." Bennett responded that "when a federal judge calls and asks you a favor, you do it."[64]

Karen Munson knew that she was up against powerful people determined to protect Gauthé: "A judge and a priest and whoever else want to protect him. The little innocent kids don't have a chance."[65] Msgr. Clayton, a friend of Gauthé, was indignant about the treatment that Gauthé was getting from the press. He lamented that "no good, only evil has been generated by those responsible for the tragedy of this recent media feeding frenzy. A quiet, mild-mannered man struggling to redeem his life has been smashed down."[66]

In March 1997 Gauthé moved to Waskom, Texas, a town just across the border from Shreveport, Louisiana. In fact he was living in Shreveport, in a house owned by Msgr. Clayton. Gauthé worked in the Shreveport jail as a paid counselor for sex offenders. He stopped by Politz's office frequently to visit. Gauthé denied there was any sexual relationship between him and Politz.

In 1997 Politz hosted a lunch at the Shreveport Petroleum Club for the chief of the prison system, several attorneys, and Gauthé. Gauthé also accompanied Politz to the opening of a new prison; the judge seems to have had a sense of humor. Local television began airing stories about

Gauthé, and the police told him to leave the city. Judge Politz called the police chief and told him that "this is not the Wild West. You can't order people out of town."[67]

But later that year the district attorney in Louisiana returned Gauthé to jail because a sister of an altar-boy victim claimed that Gauthé had raped her when she was twelve years old. Unfortunately, the original plea bargain included an agreement that the state would never prosecute Gauthé for crimes committed before 1985. Therefore in February 2002 Gauthé was set free. A newspaper tracked down Gauthé; he was working as a bus driver in a senior center until the center was informed he had a felony conviction. He lost that job and now works as a groundskeeper in a Houston suburb.

Very important people were determined to protect Gauthé at all stages in his career, both before and after his conviction. Bishop Frey protected him from exposure and transferred him and allowed the molestation to continue. Judge Politz used the full influence of his office to protect a convicted child molester, to get his sentence shortened, and to get him out of jail in Texas. Politz was skating on extremely thin ethical ice. Rules were bent and legal procedures ignored to let Gauthé have sex when he was in prison and to get him out of prison as soon as possible. What was going on? Jason Berry detects a hidden world of homosexuals in the Church who are determined to protect their own, and the Gauthé case would seem to indicate that these connections extended into the secular world. Did the judge use his political influence to pull strings, or were there other people in high places with skeletons in their closets that they did not want rattled? The FBI started an investigation of Politz's actions, but he died on May 25, 2002, when he was sixty-six. Now only Gauthé knows, and who can believe anything he might say?

Two prominent, widely publicized cases had warned the Catholic Church in North America that some priests and religious were using their positions to prey sexually upon minors, but the warnings were not taken with full seriousness. Bishops had tolerated this vice as a minor peccadillo, something on the order of mild intoxication at the parish picnic, and they could feel no sense of urgency in dealing with the problem. They jealously guarded their independence and would not cooperate in a uniform national policy. Predators almost always went unpunished, and bishops allowed them to continue their clerical careers after, at worst, a mild rebuke or a short treatment. The victims remained invisible to clerical eyes, and their shame and their fear of not being believed kept almost all of them locked in silence for decades.

## CHAPTER FOUR

# STORM WARNINGS

THE DISASTERS at Mount Cashel in Newfoundland and in Lafayette, Louisiana, should have warned the American bishops that they needed to exercise extreme caution in handling cases of sexual abuse. Since the 1950s they had also received warnings from priests and psychologists that sexual abuse was a grave evil which would harm the Church in many ways and that the problem was one which the bishops could not ignore. The correspondence of bishops in the 1950s shows that they knew some of their priests were sexually abusive, and that they realized other bishops would stoop to deception to get rid of a troublesome priest. When principals of public schools get rid of their problem teachers in this way, it is called "passing the trash." The bishops were warned this way of dealing with abusers was irresponsible, but they still used transfer, either within a diocese or between dioceses, as the easiest method of keeping sexual abuse secret.

### *Father Gerald Fitzgerald*

The Rev. Gerald Fitzgerald in 1947 established a treatment center, Via Coeli, in Jemez Springs, New Mexico, for priests suffering from alcoholism and depression. He also founded a new congregation of religious, the Servants of the Paraclete, to help these priests, and he eventually established houses in other states and other countries. But he discovered that bishops were referring priests with a different type of problem to him.

By 1952 Fitzgerald had had experience with a "handful of men" who were abusers and he had penetrating insights into their character and behavior. Fitzgerald found it "quite universal that they seem to be lacking in appreciation of the serious situation." Fitzgerald warned one bishop, "I myself would be inclined to favor laicization for any priest…for tampering with the virtue of the young, my argument being, from this point onward the charity to the Mystical Body should take precedence over the charity of the individual." At most the best should be confined to a monastery and allowed only to say a private Mass. Fitzgerald was dubious about abusers who, having been caught, professed repentance: "In practice, real conversions will be found to be extremely rare."[1]

One abuser treated in the first years of the Servants of the Paraclete was Rev. John Sullivan. After studying at Mount St. Mary's Seminary in Emmitsburg, Maryland, and St. Mary's Seminary in Baltimore, Sullivan was ordained in 1942. He soon started to offend. In 1949 he had sexual intercourse with a teenage girl and impregnated her; she tried to abort the child and ended up in a hospital. His bishop, Matthew F. Brady of Manchester, New Hampshire, merely transferred Sullivan, who soon began to harass a female college student. When he was caught, Sullivan tried to commit suicide. He was then caught with a prostitute, and parishioners started complaining about his behavior.

Brady was at his wits' end as to what to do with Sullivan, and in 1957 wrote to Fitzgerald that "at times, I have considered him insane, diabolically cunning, and again, as at present, sincerely remorseful. . . . The solution of his problems seems to be a fresh start in some diocese where he is not known."[2] Fitzgerald said not to transfer Sullivan: "A new diocese means only greener pastures." Fitzgerald gave a piercingly accurate and prophetic analysis of this type of clerical offender, "Most of the men would be clinically classified as schizophrenic. Their repentance and amendment is superficial and, if not formally at least sub-consciously, is motivated by a desire to be again in a position where they can continue their wonted activity."

Fitzgerald would never recommend such priests for a new position, "even presuming the sincerity of their conversion. We feel that the protection of our glorious priesthood will demand, in time, the establishment of a uniform code of discipline and of penalties." In 1957 there was no such code; in 2007 there is still none. Fitzgerald continued, "We are amazed to find how often a man who would be behind bars if he were not a priest is entrusted with the *cura animarum* [the care of souls]." Already in 1957, there were enough cases so that Fitzgerald could use the word "often" to refer to them. Fitzgerald pointed out that punishment, if it is certain, has a deterrent effect on crime: "If the discipline were more uniform and certain, priests before ordination could be instructed and duly warned, and this would be a deterrent to the initiation of these vicious habits."[3]

Fitzgerald was willing to help Sullivan on condition he become a "permanent guest" because Fitzgerald wanted to "help him save his immortal soul." Fitzgerald was concerned about the sinner and the criminal, but his concern was to lead the sinner to repentance so that he might escape eternal punishment, not to gloss over his sins to keep him functioning as a priest. Fitzgerald said that this severity was also for his own sake, because, "I have my own soul to save, and I do not dare recommend such men for the *cura animarum*."[4] This was an implicit warning to the bishop: if the bishop were to recommend Sullivan to another bishop, he would endanger his own soul and face damnation. Such frankness and directness strengthened Brady's resolve.

When Sullivan applied to other dioceses and the bishops inquired about him, Brady replied, "My conscience will not allow me to recommend him to any bishop, and I feel that every inquiring [b]ishop should know some of the circumstances that range from parenthood, through violation of the Mann Act [against female prostitution], attempted suicide and abortion."[5] Brady can be criticized for not disciplining Sullivan faster or for not reporting possible criminal activity to the police (the Mann Act violation), but at least he had a normal human reaction to such behavior, and he was convinced by Fitzgerald's arguments against passing the trash. The bishops all thanked Brady for his "candid report." One chancellor added that "it is our sad experience that we get excellent recommendations for gentlemen of the cloth who do not deserve them!"[6] A bishop remarked, "I have had my own share of problems of this kind during the twelve years of my episcopate and am not looking for additional trouble."[7] American bishops in the 1950s were aware that priests committed sexual abuse and that bishops often got rid of their problem priests by passing them on to other unsuspecting bishops.

But even when Fitzgerald was still in control, not everyone in his order seemed to agree with him. Father John Lee, superior of the Servants of the Paraclete in Nevis, Minnesota, although he had been informed both by Sullivan and by the diocese of Manchester of Sullivan's record,[8] helped Sullivan get a parish assignment. In June 1961 Sullivan had shown up again at Via Coeli, but Fitzgerald's opinion remained the same: Sullivan would have to remain at Via Coeli for life or else be laicized. Fitzgerald had observed that Sullivan had "a generic lack of comprehension of the damage done by his past." Fitzgerald's only hesitancy to recommend laicization was that Church "leaves these men in the world but still under the obligation of celibacy." To Fitzgerald "it seems like telling a man to go to hell to expect him to observe priestly chastity in the world when he obviously is not capable of observing it. I feel that these men should be laicized, but I do wish that this laicization would leave open for them a plank on which to walk to salvation, the prospect of the Sacrament of Matrimony."[9] Fitzgerald hoped that the Vatican Council would change the discipline of the Church and allow laicized priests to marry.

From Fitzgerald's remarks we can deduce several things:

- At that time church law provided for both voluntary and involuntary laicization, but laicization did not usually grant priests the right to marry. This discipline has been changed and normally priests who are laicized are also given permission to marry.
- Fitzgerald initially thought that the main problem was heterosexual priests who could not be continent but who could live chastely within marriage.

- Fitzgerald thought that unchaste behavior seriously endangered the salvation of the sinner.
- Fitzgerald stressed to bishops that the abuser refused to realize "the greatness of his offense." He could not understand how the abusers always took their crimes so lightly: "Personally, I would want to spend the rest of my life on my knees asking for God's Mercy, for I know no more terrible threat than the words of Our Lord, those who tamper with the innocence of the innocents—it were better if they had never been born."[10] Fitzgerald realized the futility of trying to rehabilitate abusers. Their hearts were hardened, like that of Pharaoh. Despite Fitzgerald's advice, bishops for decades continued to give abusers chance after chance at vast cost in the wreckage of human lives and souls.
- Fitzgerald was a strict, old-fashioned priest who took his duties seriously because he thought his work was concerned with the eternal destinies of souls, the souls both of innocent children and of vicious sinners. He was concerned for both the good and the bad, but he did not treat them in the same way, or pretend that the bad were not bad.

## *Psychologists*

When psychologists began studying American priests, they were not happy with what they found. In 1948 William Bier discovered that seminarians varied greatly from the average male in that they answered questions on a personality test the way women answered them.[11] Charles A. Weisberger found that they tended to answer questions on his personality test the way a psychopath would answer them (see p. 297). In 1968 other psychologists determined that a group of male candidates for religious life manifested sociopathic symptoms in that "70% were described as psychosexually immature, exhibiting traits of heterosexual retardation, confusion concerning sexual role, fear of sexuality, effeminacy and potentially homosexual dispositions." In fact eight percent were "sexually deviant."[12]

While he was still an active priest, Eugene Kennedy did a large-scale psychological investigation of American priests. In 1972 he warned the

American bishops about his findings. He discovered that (like many other American men) a large proportion of priests were "undeveloped persons."[13] That is, "these priests have reached a level of overall personal growth that is not equal to that which is expected of them at their age and in view of their careful selection and lengthy training." Priests are supposed to be *presbyteroi*, elders, noted for their wisdom and maturity. Underdeveloped priests have a great deal of trouble with personal relationships, which tend to be "distant, highly stylized, and frequently unrewarding."[14] They have trouble achieving responsible closeness, which can be achieved only by "a person who has worked through the adolescent challenge of securing his own identity."[15] Most importantly, these underdeveloped priests "have not resolved the problems which are ordinarily worked through during the time of adolescence. Sexual feelings are a source of conflict and difficulty and much energy goes into suppressing them or the effort to distract themselves from them. They find it difficult to place sexuality into an easy and manageable perspective in their lives. Sexuality is, in other words, non-integrated in the lives of undeveloped priests and many of them function at a pre-adolescent or adolescent level of psychosexual growth."[16] Kennedy thought optional celibacy would help priests achieve maturity, and he himself resigned from the priesthood to marry.

His description of underdeveloped priests could have led an observer to predict the sexual abuse crisis. A large segment of priests had not gone through adolescence; they were devoting much of their energy to coping with sexual feelings; they had trouble relating to adults. Adolescent males have a homosocial phase in which they fear women and relate to males as they learn what it is to be men. Heterosexual adolescents occasionally engage in homosexual behavior. A homosexual adolescent often cannot admit his sexuality to himself until he is an adult, at which time he engages in irresponsible adolescent sexual behavior. Psychological tests showed tendencies to deviance and homosexuality among many seminarians. When church discipline collapsed after the Vatican Council, most victims of priests were therefore male teenagers.

## *Conrad Baars*

Conrad W. Baars and Anna A. Terruwe presented a paper entitled "Human Growth in the Priesthood" at a meeting sponsored by members of the 1971 Synod of Bishops. Baars said that "we also discussed this paper in person with other members of the Synod who could not attend this presentation, and had it distributed in English and French to every Synod participant."[17] Karol Wojtyla, the future Pope John Paul II, was at this synod. This paper was revised and republished as *The Role of the Church in the Causation, Treatment and Prevention of the Crisis in the Priesthood.* In this pamphlet Dr. Baars stated, "Everyone agrees that there exists a crisis in the priesthood. Not everyone realizes that this crisis, as the title of this paper suggests, amounts to an illness, severe in some, moderate to slight in others." From his clinical practice, Baars estimated that "20–25% have serious psychiatric difficulties" and that "60–70% suffer from a degree of emotional immaturity." Baars also observed that "psychosexual immaturity expressed in heterosexual or homosexual activity was encountered often."[18]

Underlying Baars's assessment of the priesthood and its difficulties is an analysis of a faulty understanding of the role of emotions, a misunderstanding that has seriously distorted Catholic life, especially among the clergy. We will return to this theme in Chapter Sixteen. Baars made ten recommendations, including better vetting of applicants to the priesthood. None was implemented, but Baars's language of affirmation and unconditional love was popularized and misapplied.

Baars did not explicitly mention pedophilia or child molestation, and this delicacy deprived his report of the force and effect it could have had. But Baars knew that psychobabble had replaced prophetic language as the *koine* of the clergy. Everything was seen in psychological terms; old-fashioned jeremiads were passé. According to Father Thomas Doyle, whose work we shall consider next, Baars's paper "was hugely prophetic. The description it gives of underdeveloped priests closely resembles the profile of priests who have sexually abused children and adolescents. Unfortunately those to whom it was presented did not heed it at all."[19]

## *Doyle-Mouton-Peterson Manual*

Father Thomas Doyle, O.P.; F. Ray Mouton, Gauthé's defense attorney; and Father Michael Peterson, head of the St. Luke Institute in Maryland, wrote a ninety-two page report entitled "The Problem of Sexual Molestation by Roman Catholic Clergy: Meeting the Problem in a Comprehensive and Responsible Manner."[20] The report, completed by May 1985, was the result of their collaboration on the Gauthé case. As a canon lawyer at the Vatican embassy in Washington, D.C., Doyle had been instrumental in convincing Archbishop Pio Laghi, the Vatican's apostolic pro-nuncio to the United States, that Bishop Frey had to be replaced. As Doyle, Mouton, and Peterson discussed the Gauthé case, Mouton had crafted his ultimately fruitless strategy for treating Gauthé and keeping him away from additional victims. Out of their discussions and experiences, the three very different men drafted their unsolicited report for the bishops. James Quinn, archbishop of Cleveland and William Levada, then a Los Angeles auxiliary bishop and later archbishop of Portland and San Francisco, reviewed drafts and offered advice. At first it seemed that Bernard Law, Boston's new archbishop, who was created cardinal in May 1985, would lead a committee to consider the report. Then Levada informed Doyle that the issue would be dealt with at the bishops' gathering in June, but not by Law's committee. But when the bishops met in Collegeville, Minnesota, the session on sexual abuse was closed to the press and the authors of the report were not involved at all. In December 1985 Peterson wrote an executive summary[21] and sent it to every bishop in the United States, who mostly ignored it. Almost no priest was even aware of the report's existence.

Peterson's summary pointed out that the problem of abuse among priests was not really pedophilia, which is sexual attraction to children who have not reached the age of puberty, but sexual activity with teenagers. Legally, however, sexual activity with minors, even those well over the age of puberty, is pedophilia and raises "the same legal liabilities and questions." Peterson also points out the homosexual nature of the problem: "Most of the pedophiliac clerics I have seen and my colleagues have dealt with are homosexual pedophiles and not heterosexual pedophiles; this is surprising since the greater percentage in the general population is the opposite." This type of sexual deviation is difficult to eradicate: "The recidivism (relapse) rate for pedophilia is second only to exhibitionism, particularly for homosexual pedophilia." Peterson suspects that the source of pedophilia (remembering here that he includes interest in adolescents) may be "biological, with a strong contribution of premature, early childhood introductions to sexual behavior."

The executive summary pointed out that the Church had previously been shielded from the consequences of its actions and inactions, but "our dependence in the past on Roman Catholic judges and attorneys protecting the [d]ioceses and clerics is GONE." Mouton and Doyle warned against proposals to escape liability by hiding evidence:

> The idea of sanitizing or purging files of potentially damaging material has been brought up. This would be in contempt of court and an obstruction of justice if the files had already been subpoenaed by the courts. Even if there has been no such subpoena, such actions could be construed as a violation of the law in the event of a class action suit. On a canonical level, to sanitize the personnel files could pose a problem of continuity from one diocesan administration to another.
>
> One other suggestion regarding files has been to move them to the Apostolic Nunciature where it is believed they would remain secure, in immune territory. In all likelihood such action would ensure that the immunity of the Nunciature would be damaged or destroyed by the civil courts.

The executive summary estimates possible damages at one billion dollars and warns that bishops might end up in jail.

Doyle discussed how bishops should conduct investigations, and noted that canon law, while allowing for clerics to be punished by dismissal from the clerical state for sexual sins, also specified that "the penalty prescribed by law or precept must be diminished if the culprit had only imperfect use of reason; lacked use of reason because of culpable drunkenness or other mental disturbances of a similar kind; acted in the heat of passion." Almost all cases of sexual abuse would be mitigated by these factors, and canon law would therefore not allow the priest to receive the ultimate punishment of dismissal from the clerical state. The summary outlined the bad consequences of sexual abuse for the victims and the Church. The victims suffer "long and short term traumatic injury" including "a devastating effect on the child's short and long term perception of the [C]hurch and its clergy." Peterson continued that "the abused child's faith in the sacraments as sources of grace and communications with Christ, through the ministry of a priest, will be seriously weakened" and the Church will be seen "as a haven for homosexuals and sexual perverts." The authors advised the bishops that the welfare "of the victims is most important and should be given a priority by Ordinaries."

The executive summary proposed immediate evaluation and treatment after an allegation is made, because "the priest must clearly be seen as one suffering from a psychiatric disorder that is beyond his ability to control" and therefore the priest must be immediately removed from contact with possible victims. To begin to deal with sexual abuse, a committee of the National Conference of Catholic Bishops was advised to hire two groups of consultants. One would be a Crisis Control Team, consisting of a trial lawyer, a canon lawyer, and a psychiatrist to assist bishops in dealing with the different types of issues that allegations of abuse raise. The second would be a Policy and Planning Group, made up of bishops and the Crisis Control Team, as well as others, such as directors of seminaries, on an as-needed basis. This group would develop guidelines and national policies.

The bishops rejected the proposal to set up the Crisis Control Team and the Policy and Planning Group because, as their staff report explained, "dioceses prefer to respond through their own expert personnel."[22] The bishops said they would set up their own committee to study the problem, but they waited until 1993 to do so. They were suspicious that Doyle, Peterson, and Mouton wanted to milk the bishops for money. Doyle said that "the bishops called us a SWAT team looking for gain."[23] In any case, the bishops were smug about the dangers. As one bishop told Doyle, "No one's going to sue the Catholic Church. The faithful won't sue the Church."[24]

The strain of dealing with the abuse and the indifference of the bishops sorely tried Mouton, Doyle, and Peterson. Mouton took to drink, his marriage broke up, and he left the Church. He has recovered to some extent but is not a Catholic.[25] Doyle's career was destroyed. He had been a secretary at the Nunciature; he was being groomed for a diplomatic career and possibly a bishopric. But he wouldn't play the clerical game. He lost his job at the Nunciature and his job teaching at Catholic University. He entered the Air Force as a chaplain. This protected him from the bishops to some extent, but he was initially assigned to Thule, Greenland. Doyle became an expert witness in many cases of clerical sexual abuse. In 2004 at the very end of his career as a military chaplain (he served in Iraq during the war), Doyle was suspended by the bishop in charge of military chaplains because of an obscure dispute over the interpretation of the canon law about daily Mass. Peterson's story is the most troubling one, as we shall see when we examine the treatment centers for sexual abuse (see pp. 315–316).

The Doyle-Mouton-Peterson report is not perfect. It praised Dr. John Money, a defender of pedophilia, for his success in treating sexual disorders.[26] The bulk of the report focused on medical, canonical, and civil issues, with only a half-page on spiritual matters. It concentrated on legal difficulties and on the financial losses that the sexual abuse of minors would cause to the bishops. The report lacked any extensive coverage of the moral and spiritual issues that sexual abuse and the toleration of sexual abuse raise, any sense of outrage at the evil that is done to children by the abuse and by the failure to respond to it properly, and any warnings about the danger of eternal damnation, such as one might expect from Catholic observers, for the criminals who corrupt children, or for the victims corrupted as innocent children and led into lives of sin, or for the bishops who tolerate the corruption and often create the conditions in which it occurs.

This objectifying tone exemplifies what Dr. Conrad Baars diagnosed: a lack of proper emotional response. Would an approach that was not clinical and that manifested moral indignation have guaranteed that the bishops ignored the authors? Perhaps. The bishops ignored them in any case. That the bishops would probably ignore a plea centered on moral and spiritual (as opposed to financial and legal) consequences is itself a sign that the bishops were lacking in proper emotional response. The flaw runs very deep, and has roots in a distorted idea of the moral and spiritual life, as we shall see in Chapter Sixteen.

Would the bishops in the 1970s and 1980s have heeded denunciations such as Fitzgerald's? Some bishops in the 1950s did. Their response to the Sullivan case, although not perfect (they should have both reported him to the police and asked Rome to laicize him), was that of decent human beings who saw a grave evil and did not want to facilitate it. But as cases of molestation of adolescents became more numerous, according to the *John Jay Report*, and as the rape of little children came more and more to the bishops' attention, two peculiar things happened. The priests and therapists who staffed the treatment centers stopped giving tough advice such as Brady had heard from Fitzgerald, and the bishops became more willing to accept sexual offenders from other dioceses. As we shall see, both of these developments coincided with a therapeutic trend in which the church unwisely participated. It is also likely that as the percentage of offenders in ministry grew, the opportunities for blackmail and the inducements to silence increased as well. And so from the 1960s to the 1990s the bishops allowed the molestation of hundreds of small boys and girls by a handful of pedophiles, the abuse of hundreds (at least) of teenage girls, and the abuse of thousands of teenage boys, all of whom were damaged and some of whom committed suicide, by priests who were fixated themselves in adolescence. Further, an unknown number of adult women and men also suffered in relationships with priests, relationships which, if not criminal, were nonetheless immoral and abusive of the pastoral office.

The response to Peterson's distribution of the executive summary to the bishops was a deafening silence. Msgr. Robert Rehkemper, during the trial of Rudy Kos in Dallas, denied ever having received it,[27] as did the attorney for the diocese, Randal Mathis: "Our position has always been, we never got any such report."[28] But in fact the Dallas diocese had received the summary. The report was filed and disregarded, but not forgotten.[29]

The bishops were satisfied with their handling of abusers, and responded only to external pressure, especially to financial pressure from court settlements and to bad publicity. They continued to disregard the harm done to the victims. This may have been the result of blindness, or it may have been a careful balancing of goods and evils: the damage done to the victims as opposed to the preservation of the reputation of the clergy and the continuation of policies with which the bishops were satisfied and with which they presumed Rome was satisfied. They did not feel the urgency that the Doyle-Moulton-Peterson report tried to convey. They thought they could make some minor corrections, end the bad publicity, and manipulate victims into settling out of court so that the extent and depth of the problem could be concealed. The stage was set for disaster.

CHAPTER FIVE

# THE GATHERING STORM

The report written by Peterson, Doyle, and Mouton had been shelved, but the bishops had discussed the issue of sexual abuse by priests at their June 1985 meeting. Did any concerted effort to deal with the problem emerge from their discussions? If the bishops disagreed with the approach that Peterson promoted, did they implement another approach? Unfortunately inertia among the bishops was vast and deep. Going through their files and getting them in order, or opening a file and reading it was too much trouble, despite the fact that it might have saved children from trauma or even death. The bishops found it easier to let the abusers continue on their way until the law or, more often, the newspapers exposed the abuse. The abusers were confidence artists of varying degrees of cleverness who knew how to exploit episcopal lassitude, and some went very far indeed before their activities in bed made headlines.

### *Bruce Ritter of Times Square*

John Ritter was born in 1927 into a middle-class family on the outskirts of Trenton, New Jersey.[1] His soon-widowed and impoverished mother raised him during the Depression. At the height of his celebrity he was Franciscan

Father Bruce Ritter, founder of Covenant House, which took in $85 million a year in donations (the third largest amount of public support in the United States), played host to former President Ronald Reagan, who had named him an "unsung hero" in the 1984 State of the Union Address; to President George H. W. Bush, who announced his "Thousand Points of Light" initiative at Covenant House; and to Mother Teresa, in whose presence Ritter felt anxious. But at the time of his death he lived alone and in disgrace, after he was accused of sexually abusing over a dozen boys and young men, some of whom had sought refuge with him at Covenant House.

He went into the navy in 1945, and after his discharge in 1947 worked as a loader of freight cars. Seeking an outlet for his intellectual abilities he entered the Franciscans, where he changed his name to Bruce.[2] Bruce is an unusual name for a priest; it is English for Brutus. There is no saint named Brutus, and the classical Brutus, Caesar's assassin, is not usually regarded as a hero. However, Bruce is a stereotypical name for a homosexual.[3] *New York* magazine once printed "The Last Lines of Plays That Never Made It to Broadway." One was, "I see it now, Bruce, gay *is* good." Ritter liked to signal his intentions slyly but clearly to those in the know.

Ritter left the Franciscans briefly to try out the Trappists, but returned to the Franciscans and in 1954 studied in Italy, where something suspicious happened with an altar boy. Franciscan Georgi Eldarov, who was a friend of Ritter's at the Franciscan seminary in Rome, remembered an odd story that occurred when Ritter was working at a local church and supervising altar boys in a seaside town near Rome: "Bruce had said that a child twelve or thirteen had tried to touch him in a sexual way. The child was told not to come around anymore. But it was Bruce who made the complaint against the child. At least, that is the way it was brought to us. It was all quite puzzling." Eldarov remembered that another Franciscan did not like this story: "He was very unhappy about it. He said why would Bruce complain? It does not seem natural that a child would attack a grown-up instead of the opposite unless a child felt that they had been made to do this, to make the adult happy or comply."[4] While he was in Italy Ritter also angrily complained that a sixteen-year-old boy had made a pass at him at the beach. Nothing was done to investigate these stories.

After his ordination in 1956, Ritter was eventually assigned to teach philosophy at St. Anthony-on-Hudson, the Franciscan seminary in Rensselaer, New York, but he grew bored. When he switched to a job teaching at Manhattan College life became more interesting. He lived alone in a cottage on campus with an expensive stereo and with beer to attract students. He told the tale of the events that led to his famous work one way; the people who were there told it another way. In his account of the beginnings of Covenant House, Ritter claimed that he preached to the college students at Mass:

> "How long will it be before you guys sell out? To money, power, ambition....Will you sell out by the time you're twenty-five?"
>
> I finished my sermon on that note and turned back to the altar to continue the celebration of Mass. I was proud that almost four hundred students had come to church that brilliant Saturday afternoon in October 1966.
>
> It was a good sermon. I liked that sermon. I had worked hard on it. It was all about zeal and commitment and how the students at Manhattan College should be more involved in the life and work of the Church.
>
> One of the students, Hughie O'Neill, stood up in church and said, "Wait a minute, Bruce." He happened to be president of the student body and captain of the track team.
>
> "Bruce," he said, "you're making two mistakes. The first mistake you're making is that we are not going to sell out by the time we're twenty-five; we'll undoubtedly do it by the time we're twenty-one. Your second mistake, and your bigger one, is that you're standing up there telling us this and not leading us by your example and life-style not to.
>
> "We all think that you're a pretty good teacher, Bruce, but we don't like your sermons. We think that you should practice what you preach."
>
> That's a pretty heavy shot to take from your students on a Saturday afternoon. (There was a general murmur of agreement from the other kids in the church.)

> I thought about it a lot over the next few days and realized, of course, that Hughie O'Neill was correct. The next Sunday, at all the Masses on campus, I apologized to the student body—for not edifying them—and asked my superiors and archbishop for a new assignment to live and work among the poor on the Lower East Side of Manhattan." [5]

And so Covenant House was born. A wonderful story, but is it true?

Hughie O'Neill told it differently. O'Neill wasn't captain of the track team. There were not 400 people, but forty. The exchange occurred not at Mass, but during an informal discussion. It was not a few days, but a few months later that Ritter started talking to his superiors, and he didn't leave Manhattan College for two years.[6] Franciscans require friars who set up a new work to go out in a group of three. Ritter found Father James Seraphin Fitzgibbon, who worked with him in the street ministry for a few years and lived with him in the Greenwich Village apartment that was Ritter's home and base of operations, but whose name never appeared in Ritter's stories. Ritter never found a third friar. Fitzgibbon went on to other work in 1970, left the priesthood in 1971, and married, and the Franciscans seem to have mostly forgotten about Ritter.

Ritter's work with runaways supposedly started in an equally dramatic fashion. Ritter claimed it was a dark and stormy night in February 1969. Suddenly,

> six kids knocked at my door....
>
> It was snowing outside and cold. What would you have done? I invited them inside, gave them some food and blankets, and the kids bedded down on my living-room floor. One of the boys looked at me. "We know you're a priest," he said, "and you don't have to worry. We'll be good and stay away from the girls." I thanked him for that courtesy!
>
> The next morning it was still very cold and still snowing very hard. The kids obviously did not want to leave. They had no place to go. The girls got up and cooked my breakfast and burned it; the boys cleaned my apartment and cased it.

> One boy went outside for just a few minutes and brought back four more kids. "This is the rest of us," he said, "the rest of our family. They were afraid to come last night. They wanted us to check you out first. I told them that you didn't come on to us last night so that it was probably okay."
>
> These kids had been living down the block in one of the abandoned buildings with a bunch of junkies who were pimping them. The junkies had just forced the kids to make a porn film before they would give them some food. The kids hated that. They really hated that. In disgust and a kind of horror at the direction their lives were taking, they fled the junkies and came down the street to my place.[7]

Another touching story. It appeals to an elemental fear of the cold, to the reader's fears about the safety of children, to a voyeuristic interest in teen sexuality. It makes the reader feel warm and fuzzy while surreptitiously tickling his sexual appetite. It is an improbable story: could junkies make a movie? It alludes to the possibility that Ritter might be the sort of person to have a sexual interest in the children. No one else remembers anything like this incident happening. Fitzgibbon remembered an endless stream of people knocking on the door and asking for help. Two of the girls whom Ritter helped, Mary Lane and Jane Myers, were grateful for the food and shelter he gave them, but said there were problems. Ritter was mean to the girls, "but to the boys he was warm and compassionate."[8] Ritter kicked the girls out during the day but let the boys stay. One of the boys told Mary that Ritter "had made a sexual advance to him."[9] Another boy said the same. Fitzgibbons never saw any indication of this, but he was soon off the scene, leaving Ritter alone with the kids in Covenant House.

Quite alone. Effectively, no one was supervising Ritter: not the Franciscans, not the archdiocese of New York, not the city or the state of New York. Social work is always underfunded and caseworkers have too much to do. Ritter knew this, and claimed "that he was under the aegis of the Franciscan Order as one way to keep the archdiocese, and Catholic Charities in particular, at bay. Then he would turn around and lead state officials to believe that he was under the supervision of his 'Church superiors.'"[10] He could therefore run his refuge for kids, Covenant House, just as he pleased, and he had no supervisor to take complaints about him.

The kids and the charity workers in Greenwich Village suspected something was wrong with Ritter.[11] They were right. Fourteen-year-old Darryl Bassile, handsome, thin, blonde, had a hard life. His mother was an alcoholic, his stepfather raped him. He ended up in an abusive residential school, and fled into the open arms of Bruce Ritter. The priest spent time with him, talking about the sexual abuse the boy had suffered. They were watching television together. "But as Darryl remembers, Father Bruce lay down on the couch and put his feet up in Darryl's lap. Still staring at the television, Ritter then sat up and moved slowly over toward Darryl. Then he began rubbing his back. It was the only signal that a young kid with a history of sexual abuse needed. 'I just knew what to do. I knew exactly what to do,' said Bassile. 'We had sex. There were no words. There wasn't any discussion about it. It just happened.'"[12] This was Ritter's *modus operandi* when he wanted sex, and his victims, who had no contact with one another, all told the same story. They were messed-up kids and could have been lying, but they could not all independently have come up with the same lie.

Ritter went from success to success and moved his operations from Greenwich Village to Times Square, where it would be more visible. A "charismatic" speaker, he raised money at suburban churches by telling sad stories about the fates of runaway suburban kids. He also discovered a talent for writing newsletters that grabbed at the heartstrings and purse strings. Like the Music Man visiting River City, Ritter found trouble among the youth wherever he went. "The Houston police tell us that 5,000 teenagers in that city ran away last year. Nationwide the estimates run about a million." Ritter sounded the same alarm in Miami, Fort Lauderdale, New Orleans, and Toronto.[13]

Ritter also liked to talk about teen sexuality. He described Peter: "He was wearing skin- and muscle-tight brief cut-offs and a body shirt unbuttoned to the waist." Peter explained to Ritter that "I'm a go-go boy, Bruce, in this bar on Second Avenue. I dance there. If the johns like me they stick a five-dollar bill in my jockstrap."[14] Ritter became a big opponent of smut and served on the Meese Commission, denouncing the pornographers and pimps, while his staff screened the black and Puerto Rican drug addicts—most of the clients of Covenant House—for the occasional handsome blonde boy who would be referred to Father Ritter for "special treatment." The treatment was supposedly intense rehabilitation and reintegration into the middle-class world, but Ritter had his own ideas about what the treatment should include.

This secret sexual life was going on just outside the spotlight of public recognition. Movers and shakers on the right liked Ritter. They thought he was helping kids, but they also thought they could use him. Paul Simon and Peter Grace and Charles Keating cozied up to him and he was inducted into the Knights of Malta. Charles Sennott suspected that they were using the Covenant House in Nicaragua to funnel arms to the anticommunist contras.[15] Perhaps this was the case, but they were definitely using him to make their political conservatism look compassionate. They too had mixed motives. Ritter was helping distressed kids, but he was also helping to take the focus off of state welfare programs and put it onto voluntary programs. Rivers of money were also flowing through Covenant House, and that too was useful.

The money poured in. Ritter paid himself a large secret salary, dabbled in the stock market, and had a nice apartment with blonde boys in his bed. It was a good life, and Ritter reveled in it. Then President Reagan mentioned Ritter and Covenant House in a speech; Bush came to Covenant House to announce his "Thousand Points of Light" initiative. Ritter reflected that "a lot of people asked me what it felt like, what it meant to me to be mentioned by the [p]resident in the State of the Union Address. I was amazed and delighted. I was really proud that Covenant House was singled out for praise by the [p]resident. It was a very special moment for me. To move from the status of maverick, renegade, instigator, and agitator to that of unsung hero was quite a trip—even if the journey did take fifteen years!"[16]

The spotlight grew more and more intense, and the danger that the secret sexual life and financial shenanigans might be revealed grew greater. Ritter kept giving signals that all was not well. In one letter he wrote about a brothel owner who tithed to his church and tried to give money to Covenant House. Ritter didn't see him as a hypocrite, because "I know a lot about mixed motives. I'm the world's expert on mixed motives—my own—trying to disentangle the good from the evil, to unravel the knotted skein of my better self…the weeds growing with the wheat…and suddenly I am overwhelmed by my kinship with this man, for we are both sinners hoping in the mercy of God and his forgiveness."[17] When Mother Teresa came to visit Covenant House, Ritter wrote, "I had never met Mother Teresa before. In fact I've managed to avoid meeting her—it makes me very nervous to be around holy people. It always seems to me that they can size me up in a wink and nail me for the sinner I am."[18]

Ritter saw the lost innocence in a kid's face. He wrote, "It got me thinking: Did I want to be innocent again? I'm not really sure. Could I even stand it? What would happen to all my hard and painfully won knowledge—about myself, my kids, the world in general, the healthy ingrained suspicion of my motives?"[19] Were these just the remarks of an ordinary sinner who has some self-knowledge? Or were they something else? His Franciscan superior should have sat him down and asked, "Bruce, what are your mixed motives? Let's talk about them. Are you tempted by the sea of sexuality that swirls around Covenant House in Times Square?" Ritter's mother had visited Covenant House and was very dubious. She kept warning him that "he who touches pitch will be defiled by it."[20] He (like Archbishop Weakland) should have listened to his mother (see p. 594, note 17).

But Ritter seemed to enjoy the danger. His near-revelations of his true self may have been a form of exhibitionism. Danger increases sexual pleasure for many people: why do people have sex in public places, why do they commit adultery when the consequences could be catastrophic? Adrenalin and testosterone are a heady mix.

Ritter's downfall came in 1989 when a handsome boy he had picked up at the New Orleans Covenant House decided to go straight and to tell the truth to a reporter, Charles Sennott, at the *New York Post.* Other victims had gone to reporters before, but the editors hadn't trusted the tales of street kids who were accusing a respected priest of child molestation. The district attorney became involved and had the boy wear a mike. It all came out. Ritter flailed for a while, but he was doomed. He had to give up Covenant House, which was reorganized and put under Catholic Charities. The Franciscans wanted him to move back to a friary to discuss things, but he refused. He tried to get a bishop in India to take him, but the *New York Post* squelched that plan when they got wind of it and came out with the headline, "HE'S BAACK." Ritter was never prosecuted for his sexual involvement with minors. He had played tricks with money but did not steal outright any of the tens of millions that came through Covenant House.[21] He escaped the law, left the Franciscans in 1990, and retired to a farmhouse in upstate New York supported by a few loyal friends.[22]

What was Ritter after? If it was simply sex, he could have gotten it more easily without having to deal with a lot of sad, disgusting, and dangerous people, although the danger in Greenwich Village and later in Times Square may have acted as an aphrodisiac. He also wanted to be famous, a poor boy who made good. Covenant House gave him fame, and he was courted by the wealthy and powerful. But when he began his work with runaways he could never have guessed that Covenant House would open the door of the White House to him. He desired some of the kids sexually, but he also desired to help the young down-and-outers in some way. He misrepresented the nature of his clients to raise money. Middle-class Americans would not empty their pockets for black and Puerto Rican drug addicts; so Ritter told them woeful tales of blonde fourteen-year-olds from Minnesota,[23] the type he liked to take to bed. The youthful beauty of these kids appealed to him, and he know it would appeal to other people, if not in exactly the same way. The blonde kids looked like the kids of the middle-class donors, and the donors could identify with them, in a way that they could not identify with blacks and Puerto Ricans, who are also human, young, and in even greater need. The middle-class donors were not exercising *caritas*, which is not limited by race or class. Ritter was willing to work to help the unpopular poor; but he may also have been saying to himself that this work in some way made him a superior person and outweighed his crimes, his sexual sins, and his violation of his vows.

Ritter's downfall in 1989 should have sent a warning to American Catholics that it was possible that a popular, charismatic priest who was doing a lot of good work also could be sexually involved with minors and destroy young lives. Ritter should have been prosecuted. Many people, even those who had some professional contact with him, still mistakenly think that he was involved with a single young man. They don't know about the fourteen year old who sought refuge with Ritter from a stepfather who raped him; the boy ended up as Ritter's catamite. A criminal prosecution would have alerted people to the evils that Ritter had done and that other priests were capable of doing. When the state could not discover any prosecutable financial offenses, it lost interest in Ritter. Fooling around with money would have been a far worse offense, in their view, than fooling around with the throw-away children of the poor.

Ritter always preached that "kids should not be sold. They should not be exploited."[24] He had many perceptive things to say about the corrupting influence of prostitution, pornography, and the drug trade. But like many other human beings, he refused to follow his own good advice. Ritter died without making a public confession and explaining all that he had done. He may have had connections with other priests who liked to violate their vows with teenage boys. In 1985 a fifteen-year-old male prostitute was beaten and taken to Covenant House to be helped. "He had a chilling allegation that he had engaged in many illicit sexual relations through a pedophile-priest ring on the East Coast." But the police felt that Covenant House discouraged the boy from cooperating, and "that Ritter was trying to cover for his fellow priests."[25] Ritter's case may not be just a model for the scandals revealed in 2002; he may have had connections to the priests whose crimes filled the courts and newspapers.[26] That is only one of the many unanswered questions about his life.

## *James Porter of Fall River*

The son of an oil company chemist, James R. Porter was born in 1935 in Revere, Massachusetts. In 1956 he graduated from Boston College and worked at the Cathedral Camp in East Freetown, Massachusetts, which was in the Fall River diocese. There he molested a ten-year-old, John Doherty, and another twelve-year-old boy who grew up to become an FBI agent. Porter was in charge of a dormitory, and on two or three occasions the second boy was awakened by Porter who "climbed on top" of him and straddled him from behind.[27] The boy told the Rev. William J. McMahon, the head of the camp, and the abuse stopped, but Porter went on to St. Mary's Seminary in Baltimore to study for the priesthood. In 1960 he was incardinated in the Fall River diocese and got his first assignment at St. Mary's Church in North Attleboro, Massachusetts. He came recommended by the seminary rector as "manly, a genuine young man."[28]

He was no elderly, reserved priest, no sourpuss, no curmudgeon. St. Mary's parishioners couldn't have been more delighted with this vigorous new curate, who was a refreshing contrast to the more aloof priests in the parish. Chain-smoking, restless, eager to take on responsibilities, he lost no time organizing the Little League All-Stars, coaching CYO basketball, and supervising the altar boys.[29] He was athletic and a great bowler. Porter was popular among kids because he was one of them: "frivolous to the point of immaturity," as a psychologist later characterized him.[30] That is why he got along with boys; he was still an adolescent himself.

> [The] boys of St. Mary's Parish thought he alone among priests could speak their language. He kidded around with them, knew their favorite TV shows, and was always showing off his athletic talents—boasting that he had been a Golden Gloves boxer and tackling them on the ground and wrestling with them. To this day, men who knew Porter when they were children can still call to mind a vivid picture of the way he stood on the porch of St. Mary's rectory, hooked one arm around the railing, and

> performed a dazzling one-arm pull-up. They speak with one voice about his impact on them.[31]

He was, like so many abusers, "very charismatic." [32] Porter was not effeminate in any way; he was an immature male adolescent, and both adults and children liked this in a priest, because religion has long been viewed as suitable only for women and children and not a serious matter for responsible male adults.[33]

Porter also had a strong adolescent interest in sex. He molested his first child within a week of his arrival in the parish: Paul Merry, a fifth-grade student and prospective altar boy who lived next door to St. Mary's. Luring Merry into his quarters with an offer of cake and soda, Porter then requested a massage, complaining that he was "stiff from moving furniture." Moments later, he dropped his pants and placed Merry's hand on his groin while fondling the boy's genitals—a ritual that continued at least once a week for the next three years.[34] Merry claimed the pastor knew what was going on. In April 1960, Porter took Merry into the rectory office and allegedly began molesting him. Suddenly, Rev. Edward B. Booth, Porter's superior and the pastor there (who has since died), walked in. "Father Porter jumped right up," Merry said. "First Father Booth looked at Father Porter, and then back at me, and then at Father Porter, who was zipping up his fly. Then Father Booth shook his head and walked out the door. He didn't say a word."[35] Father Booth really wished that Porter would not create problems for either for himself or for Booth. The victim was invisible. A mother found out that Porter had molested her twelve-year-old son. She went to the rectory to report this and to demand action. She said Father Booth informed her that Father Porter was receiving "treatment" for his problem, and there would be no need to remove him from the church. She said Father Booth demanded, "What are you trying to do, crucify the man?"[36]

A girl from the parish was in the hospital because she had been in an accident in which her uncle had been killed. Her parents asked Porter to break the news of her uncle's death to her. He did this, and then molested her. Judy Millet says Porter raped her when she was ten years old. "He did it everywhere. At the kids' homes. At the church. In the rectory. He fondled people openly everywhere. At church dances. In the halls. He came to the pool. He was always patting people's fannies."[37] The current editor of the *Revere Journal*, Richard Powers, was in the parish school. He remembered Porter: "We frantically rebuked his clumsy attempts to grab our crotches . . . a sixth grade friend told me Porter had acted with him like a dog straddling a friendly leg. The only innocent one left in the Catholic school building after a basketball game, my friend escaped by hiding under a desk on the second floor while Porter stalked him."[38] Porter molested boys in groups: one victim remembered "doggie humping. He'd get everyone wrestling—twelve-year-old boys like to wrestle. . . . When we'd look over, he'd be ejaculating."[39] In 1960 Porter molested the twelve-year-old Tom Fulchino. In 1990 Tom's son, Chris, was molested by the Rev. John Geoghan.[40]

Porter assaulted boys and girls (but mostly boys) between the ages of six and fifteen, but most were between ten and thirteen. He fondled their genitals, received and gave oral sex, dry humped, and anally sodomized both boys and girls. He abused children singly or in groups, in public or in private. He would isolate an individual in his office at the rectory, on a float in a swimming area, in the child's own bedroom, in the vestibule of the church. Groups of children would be fondled through their pants in the basement of the church rectory under the pretext of wrestling, or while boys waited in line for Little League batting practice, or on a roller coaster at an amusement park.[41] Victims reported that Porter, evidently titillated by the risk of discovery, sexually molested boys and girls in their own homes, on the beach, on the church property, and even on the church altar. He liked the church as a venue for sex. One male victim recalled being molested beneath an outdoor statue of the Virgin Mary. A woman told of being fondled by Porter inside the confessional booth.[42] Porter raped Fred Paine on Holy Saturday in 1961.[43]

The pastor was not the only priest at St. Mary's who knew what was going on. Rev. Armando Annunziato, the number two priest at St. Mary's, also, according to children and parents, knew what was happening. Stephen Johnson said that Annunziato walked in while Porter was raping him but then "just shut the door and walked out."[44] John Robitaille said that Annunziato walked into the church basement while Porter was raping him. Robitaille remembered that Annunziato "saw me, he looked me in the eye, and he turned around and walked back upstairs."[45] A girl saw Porter in the church, standing at the altar with two boys and with his pants undone; she ran to the rectory to report that "a stranger" was in the church. Annunziato yelled at her to "stop stirring up trouble" and slammed the door in her face.[46] A boy tried to resist Porter and struck him; he was sent to Annunziato, who told him that he was possessed by Satan. One mother said Annunziato told her that "you have to understand that Father Porter is only human."[47] In 1964 Annunziato finally told Bishop James L. Connolly, the bishop of Fall River, that Porter had been sexually involved with nine altar boys.[48]

Why didn't parents or victims complain or raise a big fuss? One mother explained, "My husband said, 'Who would believe you? It's his word against yours.'" Another, who remembers telling "ten or twenty" other mothers that Porter had touched her son improperly, said not one would believe her. Boys who were sexually initiated by the priest said they kept it to themselves because they were scared they would be called homosexual. Catholic guilt kept the girls quiet. Girls who normally told their best friends all their secrets say they didn't divulge what Porter had done to them because they were sure it must have been their own fault.[49] How could a priest have done something wrong? Wasn't he next to God? If anything happened, it couldn't have been the priest's fault. That would be like saying God was the Devil.

The complaints kept coming to the chancery of the diocese of Fall River, where Msgr. Humberto Medeiros, later archbishop of Boston and a cardinal, was the chancellor. In 1963 Henry Viens twice told Msgr. Medeiros that Viens' nephew had been molested. Medeiros promised that Porter would be "taken care of immediately" and that he would be removed from St. Mary's Church and sent for "rehabilitation."[50] Instead Medeiros transferred Porter to Sacred Heart in Fall River, another parish with a large school. Bishop Connolly soon knew what was going on. In 1964 Medeiros, the chancellor, told Connolly that he had heard that Porter had molested thirty or forty boys. Connolly wrote in a memo "at Feehan [a school] they call him the horn."[51] Medeiros told Connolly that the students would ask one another, "Has the horn tackled you yet?"[52] In the summer of 1964 the New Hampshire state police picked up Porter and accused him of molesting a youth. Connolly noted that the boy was "non-Cath." Why was this important? Was it a bigger or lesser problem that Porter was molesting children who weren't Catholic? Bishops were often able to persuade or intimidate Catholic parents into not pressing charges, but their power over non-Catholics was far less.

In 1964 Bishop Connolly sent Porter home to Revere for a week. Porter wrote to Connolly about a talk with his family doctor, who "pulled no punches with me [and] had no sympathy....It was during those talks that I began to realize what it was to be a priest...and to admit I was a complete selfish, immoral disgrace to God, myself, and all concerned."[53]

Medeiros sent Porter to Wiswall House in Wellesley, Massachusetts, for electroshock treatments. His doctor thought that Porter had "simmered down."[54] Porter wrote to Bishop Connolly, "I am feeling much better and doing very well, positively. There have been many temptations as you can imagine, but thank God, with His grace, I have handled them well."[55] The next day he molested two children. While assigned to St. Luke's Hospital in New Bedford, he said Mass at nearby St. James, although priests had been warned to keep him away from children because of his "problem with boys." In this church he raped one boy, who reported the abuse to Msgr. Hugh A. Gallagher, the pastor of St. James and dean of New Bedford, and Porter never said Mass at this church again.[56]

Porter started trolling Little League games and beaches, where Joe, a twelve-year-old, met him, and felt Porter put his hand down his bathing suit. Three more incidents followed: once when Porter invited Joe into the basement of St. James' Church, undressed him and ejaculated against his buttocks; once when he forced the boy to perform oral sex on him in his car; and once when he came to Joe's home to visit his family, asked to see Joe in his bedroom, and forced the boy to massage him even as his parents sat in the kitchen of their small bungalow.[57]

In 1966 police in Revere informed the Rev. James D. Bono of Immaculate Heart Church that Porter had molested the son of an officer. Bono confronted Porter and called Medeiros, who responded, "Yes, we know."[58] Medeiros said that he had sent Porter home in hopes he would receive treatment. Bono was working at St. Patrick's in Stoneham, in the Boston archdiocese. Porter's father saw Bono the following day, and said that he had paid $10,000 for psychiatric treatment for Porter. The diocese of Fall River was doing nothing for him.

In the spring of 1967 Porter raped eleven-year-old Christine Hickey in the sacristy of St. Patrick's in Stoneham. A priest there reported it, the Rev. Paul Shanley, of all people, who arranged for Porter to be sent to the Servants of the Paraclete center in New Mexico.[59] Shanley knew about child molestation: he had allegedly abused a teenage boy at this church in 1966.[60] Connolly ordered Porter to make a retreat at St. Joseph's, a Trappist abbey in Spencer, Massachusetts. Porter wrote Connolly in May 1967, "For once, I've faced reality and can't feel pity for myself. I've caused great spiritual harm to others and must do all I can to reconcile myself with God and pray for those whom I've hurt."[61] Whether Connolly believed this is not recorded.

In 1967 Porter arrived at Jemez Springs, New Mexico, a center run by the Servants of the Paraclete, an order founded to help troubled priests (see p. 308–311). The center was not a medical facility and offered only a program of rest and prayer. How did the order decide priests were cured, since they did not receive medical treatment? A Paraclete priest, William Foley, explained that "we just get an intuition that they're going to work out."[62] Porter knew what words would open the doors and give him the freedom to go out and molest. He wrote to Connolly, "I am sure now that for the first time in my life that I am facing my problem as I should.... I realize ... that the temptation will always be there, but I am resolute that I not only have the ability, with God's grace, but I do have the will and drive to control it...now."[63]

Porter was supervised in New Mexico by Rev. John B. Feit. Feit was a member of the Servants of the Paraclete because he had himself been sent to Jemez Springs for treatment. He had a criminal conviction and was a suspect in a murder (see pp. 310, 436–437). Feit sent Porter out to parishes in New Mexico, where Porter molested boys and had to be returned to the center four times. On one occasion, when he was assigned to Truth or Consequences, New Mexico, Porter was caught sodomizing a boy in a body cast. His victims were mostly Hispanic boys, seven to ten years old. In July 1969 Feit sent Porter to Houston where he molested boys, and Feit reported to Connolly that Porter had "lapsed into former failings."[64]

Immediately after this relapse the Servants of the Paraclete recommended Porter for a position at a parish in Minnesota, where the order ran Our Lady of the Snows, a clergy retreat house. The priest who had recently been named the new head of the retreat house, Peter Burwell, wrote in a letter that Porter had experienced a "nervous breakdown" and "some moral problems"[65] but that he "gives every sign of having former problems under control."[66] Lawrence A. Glenn, bishop of Crookston, Minnesota, didn't ask what the "problems" were, and from August 1969 to September 1970 Porter was assigned to St. Philip's in Bemidji, a parish with a school. Porter's home diocese, Fall River, was supposed to approve Porter's transfer to Minnesota, but no one ever informed Fall River of Porter's assignment, as far as anyone in the Crookston diocese can tell.[67]

Porter used his usual charm and enthusiasm to get access to boys. He coached basketball and took the team to the town championship in 1969. Dan Dow was an altar boy at the parish. He knew what would happen after Mass: "Caught. Then pinned by this man in the basement of the rectory. The whispers, the touching, the force of it, the threats to never tell or God would get him. Then being set free only to have it happen again."[68] James Grimm reported that when he was twelve years old, Porter did "everything you can imagine," to him, including oral sex and sodomy, at least three times a week, and more often during baseball season, when Porter was the school's coach.[69] Porter liked to court danger. He molested boys under the table when he was the guest of a family; he molested one victim on the roof of the parish school.[70]

Bishop Kenneth Povish, who had just assumed control of the Crookston diocese in September 1970, was told that parents had complained to the pastor of St. Philip's, Rev. W. F. Leman (who initially denied that any abuse had occurred) that Porter had molested their sons on a trip to a baseball game in the Twin Cities and were threatening to go to the police. Povish immediately removed Porter from the parish and sent him for more evaluation.[71] The result of the evaluation was not encouraging. Frederick Bennett, a priest-psychologist at St. Michael's Community in Sunset Hills, a Servants of the Paraclete residence near St. Louis, wrote to Daniel A. Cronin, the new bishop of Fall River in November 1970, stating that Porter should be removed from the priesthood. Porter had become adept at seducing young boys while performing his priestly duties, and seemed unaware of the psychological harm he may have caused his victims. Bennett advised that "I believe, quite strongly, that he should apply for laicization and should never again function as a priest." His priesthood gave him "easy access to boys," an access which Porter was able to exploit because of "the lack of surveillance by parents who instinctively trust priests, his athletic abilities which are attractive to boys, and, especially, a pattern of behavior over many years in which he has learned how to appeal to boys and to seduce them while functioning as a priest."[72] "He is . . . a basically immature person," a further report by Bennett stated. "He does not seem to be aware of the psychological harm that he may have caused the youths. Moreover, when he is entangled in these sexual situations, he apparently fails to see the inevitability of discovery of such a large number of youths involved."[73]

The focus was still on Porter, with little or no mention of his victims. In 1971 Feit wrote to Cronin about Porter, "I think that your present position of understanding without condoning any of the mistakes of the past is the best position. In this way, Father Porter will continue to have the support and the encouragement of the [C]hurch to make a rational and mature decision in regard to his future."[74] How after fifteen years of sexual involvement with children and sacrilege anyone could expect Porter to be "rational and mature" is incomprehensible. But perhaps Feit and the bishop had different standards of rationality and maturity than most adults have.

Still, under pressure from bishops and therapists, Porter decided to ask for laicization. A lengthy file was sent to Pope Paul VI in 1973. It contained statements from bishops, priests, and Porter. The pope probably did not read the whole file, but a high official read it and certainly gave the pope a summary. Former Bishop Connolly wrote to the pope about Porter's "constant victimization of young boys" and depicted Porter as morally weak and resistant to rehabilitation. He summarized Porter's character: "I would simply say that he presents a character of acute weakness from a moral standpoint. He is stubborn, persistent in his evil conduct. His promises mean nothing."[75] Porter abused perhaps forty boys, Connolly told the pope. An unnamed archbishop-coadjutor of St. Paul and Minneapolis wrote that "it is my conviction that every possible means toward the salvation of this vocation has been taken and to no avail," and that "there seems to be no prospect whatsoever of a change of mind on the part of the petitioner."[76] This archbishop-coadjutor probably became involved because the diocese of Crookston is a suffragan (dependent) see of the archdiocese of St. Paul and Minneapolis.

Porter himself wrote to the pope that "it became known and reported to [Fall River] Bishop [James] Connolly that I had become homosexually involved with some of the youth of the parish. Bishop Connolly decided to send me home to my family for a short while until the scandal of this affair died down. . . . A short time later Bishop Connolly gave me another chance and assigned me to Sacred Heart Parish in Fall River. I can't recollect much about my stay there except that after a short time I again fell into the same situation that plagued me in North Attleboro."[77] Porter acknowledged he had used his priesthood as a cover: "I know in the past I used to hide behind a Roman collar, thinking that it would be a shield for me. Now there is no shield. I know that if I become familiar with children, people would immediately become suspicious."[78] He admitted he would always use the priesthood "as a protection and means to feed my sickness and trouble."[79]

Msgr. Humberto Medeiros's role in Porter's career was spelled out in this report to the pope. As chancellor of the diocese of Fall River he had made the decisions to transfer Porter from parish to parish after numerous reports that Porter molested children. He had not notified any parish or parent and had made no effort to help any child. Paul VI then made him a cardinal, Cardinal Humberto Medeiros, predecessor of Cardinal Bernard Law of Boston. Medeiros had followed a policy that was fully acceptable to the Vatican. There is no indication that the pope or any Vatican official who read Porter's file ever inquired whether any of the child victims had been hurt, whether they needed help, whether anyone had helped them. The children were invisible.

On January 5, 1974, James Porter was released from the priesthood.

In 1975 Porter met Verlayne Bartlett in Minnesota. She was shy and from a difficult family situation. He courted her and asked her to marry him. He had told her he had been a priest but had left because "he and the higher-up's didn't get along."[80] Therefore when he said that they couldn't get married in the Church unless they both took a psychological test, she thought it a little odd but assumed it was because he had been a priest. The archdiocese of St. Paul and Minneapolis saw "no foreseeable insurmountable problems" and offered "every encouragement."[81] The chancellor, the Rev. John F. Kinney, sent Verlayne his best wishes. No one in the archdiocese told her that Porter had been released from the priesthood because he had molested dozens of children. Porter and Bartlett married in 1976. She soon discovered that he was irresponsible about keeping jobs and that he had a bad temper.

In December 1989 the FBI questioned Porter about a missing youth; he had an alibi, but he told the agents that he had molested "forty to fifty boys" when he was a priest in Massachusetts: "He said he would rub his penis against the boys while wrestling with them. Porter states he only disrobed about five (boys). . . . There was no anal penetration, but he received and performed oral sex with a few of the boys."[82] The FBI turned over the report to the Oakdale, Minnesota, police department, which is not saying what it did with the report.

Back in Massachusetts Frank Fitzpatrick had grown up and married and worked as a private investigator. Something really bothered him in his life, but he could not remember what it was. In September 1989, after years of pain, he finally remembered: "Emotions and sounds were the things to flood back on that first occasion. I felt an immense, monstrous betrayal by someone that I loved. I relived the part of the sexual assault that had occurred when my eyes were shut. There were sounds of rhythmic, heavy sexual breathing in my ears and some kind of crumpling sound."[83] Porter had fed him mincemeat pie laced with sedatives and then raped him.

Fitzpatrick tried to track down Porter and called Annunziato, who declined to help with words that revealed his knowledge of the abuse: "I've been praying for you and others for many years now, but I think it best to leave this in the hands of God."[84] The chancellor of the Fall River diocese, Msgr. John J. Oliveira, said that he had no information about Porter, not his middle initial, not his date of birth, not his Social Security number. Oliveira did not want to help and echoed Annunziato's words: "Maybe it would be best to leave it in the hands of the Lord."[85] But Fitzpatrick was an insurance investigator who knew how to find people. He tracked Porter down and called him. Porter admitted that he had molested children, maybe fifty, maybe a hundred. "I'm surprised nobody spotted it," Porter confessed to Fitzpatrick at one point; "when it finally came out, naturally I was hiding behind the cloth."[86]

Fitzpatrick found other victims through an advertisement. He contacted the Bristol County district attorney's office, which refused to prosecute Porter despite Porter's admission and the testimony of the victims. Fitzpatrick went on WBZ-TV in Boston on May 7, 1992. The district attorney still refused to prosecute, but the *Boston Globe* picked up the story and kept it alive. Cardinal Law was unhappy. What was all the fuss about, wondered Cardinal Law: "The papers like to focus on the faults of a few. We deplore that. By all means we call down God's power on the media, particularly the *Globe*."[87] Law's prayer was answered, although not in the way he expected, when the *Globe*'s exposés forced his resignation ten years later.

In July 1992 twenty-five of Porter's victims appeared on national TV. On September 23, Minnesota indicted Porter for molesting his children's babysitter. At the same time Massachusetts indicted him on forty-six felony counts of child molestation. Porter complained that people were making his life miserable: "Since the accusations against me became public earlier this year, I and my family have been repeatedly pursued and harassed, both by the news media and by people who appear to have other intentions." Porter continued that "several of my neighbors have also let it be known to me that they do not want to talk to me or be seen talking to me."[88] He would soon have problems more serious than unfriendly neighbors.

Porter was tried and convicted in Minnesota in December 1992. In October 1993 he was found guilty in Massachusetts of forty-one counts of child molestation. He blamed the Church: "It was the Church that sent me from one parish to another."[89] He complained that the Church had let him down. In New Mexico twenty-one Porter victims sued the diocese of Santa Fe and the Servants of the Paraclete and settled for $17 million in 1994.

In 1999 Porter was denied parole. Porter wrote to his ex-wife Verlayne Bartlett: "The more I participate and focus in therapy I become painfully aware of the hurt, pain & harm I inflicted on you and the family."[90] In prison, now divorced from Verlayne, he became engaged to Annie Milner of Providence, a sixty-nine-year-old former nun, who had known him forty years. Milner became the recipient of his reports about his spiritual progress: "He has said to me, 'I want my victims to know that I realize what I've done to their lives.'" Milner added, "If the victims can only see he has changed, they would change their hearts a little bit."[91] In May 2004 they married in prison while he awaited a hearing on whether he should be committed indefinitely as a dangerous sex offender.

The Church in Fall River needed help. Bishop Cronin had been transferred to Hartford in 1991 when Archbishop John F. Whealon had died, shortly before the Porter crisis broke. When Fitzpatrick appeared on television in May 1992, the see of Fall River was still vacant. The Vatican in desperation turned to a Franciscan, Seán O'Malley, who was appointed bishop of Fall River in June 1992. He was at first unable to comprehend the situation but quickly gained trust and tried to repair the damage.

Was Porter an aberration? Were the officials in Fall River simply flummoxed in dealing with child molestation, something totally unknown to them? On September 26, 2002, the Bristol County district attorney's office, whose jurisdiction comprises part of the Fall River diocese, released the names of twenty-one priests about whom the diocese of Fall River had received complaints. These cases are almost all beyond the statute of limitations because the bishops and the officials of the diocese of Fall River did not report them to the police when the allegations were made. The officials tried to protect Porter in the same way by not reporting his crimes to the police, and Massachusetts was able to prosecute Porter only because of the tolling provisions in the statute of limitations law—he had moved out of state, and the clock was stopped. In February 2004 the Fall River diocese revealed it had received allegations about an additional ten priests, whom it did not name. So Porter was not an aberration or an exception, and the diocesan staff had ample experience in dealing with abusers, going back to the 1950s and earlier. Porter captured the horrified imagination of the public only because the details of his case became known; the details of the other cases remain hidden.

Father Booth, the pastor at Porter's first assignment at St. Mary's in North Attleboro, is dead. Father Annunziato, who worked with Porter at that parish, died in 1993. He refused to be interviewed about Porter or to answer questions about his knowledge of Porter's sexual activity with children. O'Malley made Annunziato a monsignor in March 1993; Annunziato had served for years as director of the diocese's two orphanages, St. Mary's in New Bedford and St. Vincent's in Fall River. O'Malley said Annunziato needed encouragement because he was old and sick, and O'Malley thought Annunziato was innocent of failing to report Porter, although ten children had said that he had witnessed Porter molesting them. The bishop didn't believe the children because they "may have been confused."[92] But why did O'Malley believe what the children said about Porter and not what they said about Annunziato? O'Malley, having salvaged the diocese of Fall River, was sent to Palm Beach, where two bishops in a row had to resign when their past sexual involvement with adolescent boys became public, and then to Boston in 2003, where he negotiated a settlement and avoided a trial with publicity that would have further damaged the Church there.

Porter confessed to his wife Verlayne Bartlett that he had molested her twenty-three-year-old sister. The Porter family is in ruins. Bartlett asked to meet with Harry Flynn, the archbishop of St. Paul and Minneapolis, whose words had misled her into the marriage. Flynn at first agreed, but the night before the meeting his office called her to say he was busy with his new duties and would not be able to meet with her "in the foreseeable future."[93] The archdiocese of St. Paul disclaimed any responsibility: "No one here consciously knew that a pedophile priest had applied to get married in this archdiocese" and "in no way, shape[,] or form would we have permitted a marriage to go forward with someone of that background in our church."[94] But why had they ordered the psychological test before allowing the marriage? Either the archdiocesan staff is lying, or they were negligent in determining why Porter had left the priesthood.

The victims remain invisible to the hierarchy until newspaper stories or court cases force the hierarchy to act. The focus of the hierarchy was and remains on the clergy; they are stuck in a narcissistic mode in which the whole story is about *them*, about their rights and privileges, about their importance, about how all of this is affecting *them*. Porter was not the only narcissist. Why was Annunziato made a monsignor? To soothe his feelings, although it was a slap in the face of the victims who had witnessed his indifference to their sufferings. One victim's response: "Isn't it sad that Porter was continuously given consideration by the Church, and that we were offered nothing?"[95] But then the victims were mere laity and children, totally invisible to the pastors, to the bishops, to the pope. The evil continues, generation after generation. Porter molested his own children, according to his ex-wife. His son, Sean Porter, died in July 2003 after spiraling downward into "alcohol, gambling, and drugs."[96] Porter himself died of cancer in February 2005.

"It all goes back to Rome," said Steve Johnson, one of Porter's victims. "Ultimately the Vatican and the pope are responsible. My healing process has been one of forgiving James Porter. I cannot, until Rome decides to mandate specific reactions to remove these priests, embrace my religion—the religion I was raised in. I'm too angry."[97] The pope and the officials in the Vatican knew how bishops were handling the cases: transferring priests without warning parishes, offering every consideration to priests to protect them from the consequences of their actions, and totally ignoring victims. Porter, like many others, was a manipulator. He knew how to make the right noises when he was caught. But confidence men succeed over the long run only because their adult victims prefer to be conned, and the Catholic hierarchy willingly allowed itself to be manipulated rather than face the depth of evil in the Church and begin the painful process of repentance and purgation.

## *Rudy Kos in Dallas*

Born in 1945, Rudolph Kos had a sad background: when he was five, he saw his father attack and nearly kill his mother; he didn't see her again for decades. His parents divorced. He was molested by an uncle,[98] and then he sexually abused his brothers and when he was seventeen years old he spent a year in a juvenile detention center for sexually molesting a fifteen-year-old neighbor.[99] In 1966, while on leave from the Air Force, he married, but his marriage was annulled because of nonconsummation. His wife said the marriage was a front; he was interested only in boys: "It was a just a shield to make his life look normal so he could molest boys without any suspicion."[100] Rev. Leon Deusman, nephew of Bishop Thomas Tschoepe of Dallas, was on the tribunal that handled this annulment. He wrote in the annulment file that "she implies that the petitioner has some problems. For her to comment might have civil consequences. Something is fishy—perhaps should get petitioner to level with me."[101] When she was deposed, the ex-wife said that she had informed Deusman that Kos "was gay and was attracted to boys."[102] Deusman denied that she said this to him. Kos worked from 1968 to 1977 as the coordinator of pulmonary rehabilitation at Methodist Medical Center in Dallas. There he met a ten-year-old who was being treated for asthma. He began abusing him and later visited him in Fort Worth, where he introduced the boy to beer and marijuana at the age of twelve.

With this background, someone must have thought that Kos was obviously a perfect candidate for the priesthood, because obstacles to his ordination kept disappearing. Windle Turley, the attorney for Kos's victims, said that "it appeared Rudy Kos had friends in high places who bent the rules, broke their own policies, helped him get an annulment of his marriage, rushed him into seminary, and then when all of the things started to happen, the same people turned their backs on the complaints."[103] Turley suspected not simply ignorance, but toleration, or even approval of Kos by church officials.

Msgr. Gerald A. Hughes, rector until 1975 of Holy Trinity Seminary in Irving, Texas, rejected Kos and wrote on his file that "there is a certain amount of instability here that I do not like."[104] The Rev. Michael J. Sheehan, the next rector (a former aide of Cardinal Bernardin who was later made archbishop of Santa Fe to clean up the mess left by Robert F. Sanchez and then temporarily made administrator of Phoenix when Bishop Thomas J. O'Brien was arrested on a hit-and-run charge and resigned) admitted, "Father Don Fischer, a top diocesan official, had pressed for acceptance of Kos despite his previous rejection."[105] Fischer was vocations director of the Dallas diocese. Sheehan never checked the annulment records and never saw Deusman's intriguing comment. In 1977 Kos entered Holy Trinity Seminary, where Sheehan was living as rector. During the trial Turley asked, "Father Sheehan liked Rudy Kos a lot, didn't he?" In fact, "Father Sheehan liked Rudy Kos so much, that he arranged his room to be either adjacent to or across the hall from his own room?"[106] The implications of Turley's line of questioning are clear: there was between Sheehan the rector and Kos the seminarian a close, perhaps a too close, relationship that led Sheehan to overlook Kos's failings.

At Holy Trinity, Kos met an eighteen-year-old seminarian who quickly became his best friend. This man testified that Kos, who was thirty-three at the time, bought him gifts, including a gold cross, and gave him alcohol and Valium. He said he allowed Kos to use his feet to masturbate and claimed not to have realized the activity was sexual. Kos told him it helped a prostate problem, he said. "It was not something I wanted to happen," the man explained. "It was something I let happen. I thought he had a foot fetish."[107]

Kos directed his attentions to other seminarians as well. In Kos's senior year James Harris told Msgr. Robert C. Rehkemper, the vicar general of the diocese, that Kos was making sexual advances to another student. Rehkemper was surprised but did nothing. "When he hit me with this I said, 'This is really strange because Rudy had been here for four years, and was regularly evaluated,' the white-haired Msgr. recalled. Here we are at the very end and we get this information. I said, 'It's quite unusual, and it comes at a bad time, naturally.'" Father Rehkemper said he passed the information to the head of the seminary and told the informant to do the same.[108] They told Sheehan, who did nothing and claimed to have forgotten that they ever told him.

Father Joseph F. Wilson was at Holy Trinity Seminary (1984–86) when Bishop Tschoepe visited to hear Paul Shanley, advocate of man-boy love, instruct the seminarians and priests (including Kos). Wilson remembered that "the lecture he [Shanley] gave was for the priests of the Dallas diocese and for the 3rd- and 4th-year seminarians—I was sitting directly behind the then-Bishop of Dallas, Thomas Tschoepe, who laughed and joked his way through a truly vile presentation."[109] Mark D. Jordan also taught Kos. A self-proclaimed Thomist and homosexual, Jordan later wrote *The Silence of Sodom*, in which he claims that the Roman Catholic priesthood has long been a queer institution.

Michael J. Hartwig was Kos's professor of moral theology and later became rector of the seminary. He left to live with Donald Baker, president of the Dallas Gay Political Caucus. Hartwig's thesis about celibacy was that "long-term sexual abstinence is harmful and if not warranted by concerns about equally serious harms, is immoral. The practice of sexual abstinence leaves young adults ill equipped to make informed and sustainable sexual commitments. The assumption that it is not harmful legitimizes inhumane church expectations that certain individuals practice long-term or life-long abstinence, most notably gay men, lesbians, divorcees, and single adults."[110] The seminarians at Holy Trinity were taught moral theology by a homosexual who believed that sexual abstinence was harmful and immoral.

Another text the seminaries used[111] was *The Sexual Language* by the Rev. André Guindon (see p. xxx), which taught them "that most recent studies tend to disprove that lasting harm results from pedophiliac contact itself. Rather, the trauma comes from the familial panic which is the usual response to the incident." The parents are the ones who cause all the trouble by complaining that an adult is having sex with their child; the parents, to Guindon's astonishment, consider such harmless activity "molestation."[112]

Kos graduated and was ordained in 1981 and assigned as an assistant at All Saints parish, whose pastor, Msgr. Rafael Kamel (also chancellor of the diocese) "hated confrontation," as Msgr. Rehkemper and everyone else knew, according to Turley.[113] He would therefore not make a fuss about the peculiar behavior of his assistants,[114] one of whom was the Rev. William Hughes, who was later accused of molesting a thirteen-year-old girl.[115] The mother of the girl found the love letters Hughes had written to her daughter. She gave them to a trusted priest at Holy Trinity Seminary and the letters disappeared. She met with Bishop Tschoepe and Rehkemper, who didn't offer to help. Rehkemper told her that "all girls have crushes on parish priests."[116] Tschoepe later appointed Hughes to the diocesan personnel board in which he could influence the assignment of other priests; Hughes left the priesthood in 1992.

Another priest with Kos at All Saints was Robert R. Peebles.[117] Kos noticed how the diocese treated Peebles and deduced that he could expect help and money from the diocese if he molested children. Peebles was ordained in 1977 and in the early 1980s he was the diocesan priest in charge of the Boy Scouts. Peebles molested boys, perhaps twenty, he admitted, at his parishes.[118] His conscience bothered him. In 1982 he told another priest that he was molesting children, but the priest merely told him "not to be overly worried" and that the boys "could bounce back."[119] But the problems were too much for the diocese to ignore and it got rid of him by ordering him to join the army. In 1984 Peebles invited a fourteen-year-old boy, a former parishioner from All Saints, whose confirmation advisor he had been, to Fort Benning, where Peebles was chaplain. Peebles got the boy drunk and tried forcibly to rape him. The boy complained to base military police, who arrested Peebles.[120] Unbeknownst to the parents, Kos had already abused this victim's younger brother. The diocese got Peebles off by promising he would receive treatment. The boy received in compensation $5,000,000 from the archdiocese, but he has constant nightmares and physical scars from the incident—forcible penetration of the anus can easily tear it. Rev. David E. Fellhauer, juridical vicar of Dallas and later bishop of Victoria, Texas, told the parents that if they prosecuted "it would bring great scandal on the [C]hurch and controversy and conflict within the church parish."[121] He also promised the parents that Peebles would no longer be a priest and would receive extensive treatment: "We take care of our own."[122] The diocese immediately made Peebles pastor of another parish, St. Augustine's in Dallas, where he again abused boys.[123]

Dr. Lee Emory treated Peebles; she told the diocese that "there is a lot of vulnerability for recurrences,"[124] as his conduct at St. Augustine's indeed demonstrated. It was his last assignment. In 1986 Peebles wrote to the Vatican that "I have a loathsome sexual perversion which I never asked for and never wanted. I am a pedophile, sexually attracted to young adolescent boys."[125] Three years later Pope John Paul II laicized him, but did not suggest that the diocese find the boys Peebles had molested and offer them help. In 1987 the Dallas diocese gave Peebles $22,000 for tuition at Tulane Law School and $800 a month living expenses for two years. In 1990 Peebles applied to the Louisiana bar and asked Lee Emory not to tell the full truth. Emory wrote to the bar admission committee that Peebles "has an excellent prognosis"[126] and recommended him, but did not mention anything about molestation.

Kos, Hughes's and Peebles's rectory mate at All Saints, was another "charismatic personality." Someone who knew him at the seminary said, "He had this charm about him. He was generally cheerful, optimistic, confident. He was also a person who seemed very trustworthy. You could talk to him and get good advice. He had a lot of common sense."[127] Kos was popular at his first assignment at All Saints; a parent later called him "a Pied Piper to the young boys of the church."[128] The parents were happy to see their boys involved with him as they entered their teen years when they would face so many temptations. He was macho in a fourteen-year-old way; boys loved him, because he was one of them. He attracted them with "candy, gifts, video games, alcohol and drugs,"[129] and he found that liquor worked best. One victim was reported as saying that "on a trip to see Mr. Kos's mother when the boy was thirteen, Mr. Kos bought him a bottle of Everclear, a beverage with an extremely high alcohol content. He then watched as the boy became so drunk that he passed out into a toilet."[130] He took boys to Disney World and Six Flags. He entertained them and palled around with them to the applause of anxious parents who were happy to see their sons associating with a priest. Kos claimed, "I'm another John Bosco."[131] Catholic pedophiles often have pictures of Don Bosco, the patron saint of youth.

Kos borrowed some money from the diocese to buy a computer and never repaid it. He stole money from the parish to buy gifts for his victims, including "$350 pairs of tennis shoes,"[132] an extravagance with sexual significance for Kos. The Rev. Robert Williams, Kos's curate in a later assignment, told Msgr. Rehkemper that the theft amounted to "a few thousand every month,"[133] which allowed Kos to spend as if he had a $100,000 per year income, as victims later estimated. The theft allowed Kos to accumulate possessions such as a new Cougar with the vanity plates, "Father Rudy." The theft also financed drug purchases, not for Kos, but for his victims. Kos drank very little but gave the boys alcohol and drugs, including Darvocet, Valium, and codeine (all controlled substances). Kos had hepatitis A, B, and C, diseases that are often sexually transmitted. The diocese knew that Kos was sick but never inquired how he contracted the illnesses.[134]

Kos liked feet. The victims said the episodes would begin with the priest massaging their feet and escalate into rubbing their feet against his crotch. One boy, whom Kos began abusing at age ten, said the abuse even happened once in his own home while he and Mr. Kos lay under a blanket watching TV with the boy's family. With some boys Kos had oral and anal sex. He told one ten year old, after he had oral sex with him, that "you're in God's hands" and then led him to a church shower and sexually abused him after telling him he would "cleanse" him with holy water.[135] After he spent the night in Kos's bed the boy would join the other two priests at the breakfast table and hold hands in prayer. Kos liked young males before and after puberty. He molested nine year olds, but continued abusing boys after they reached adulthood—one until he was twenty-two. Kos had kept in touch with the boy whom he had abused at the Methodist Medical Center. When the boy was sixteen, Kos invited him to live in his room at All Saints for two years and told everyone he had adopted the boy. The *Texas Catholic*, the Dallas diocesan newspaper, wrote a glowing article about this wonderful arrangement.[136] The boy was in fact being victimized by Kos.

Did the boys have suspicions something was wrong? They were nine or ten years old when Kos started abusing them. One of them later said that "I knew he wasn't doing anything wrong because he couldn't, because he was a priest. That would be like saying God was doing something wrong," and that "he was not just a priest, he's my priest. He's my buddy. He's my best friend at the time."[137] Kos did not have much time for God. Dr. Richard Jaeckle, a psychiatrist who later evaluated Kos, said that "he had no prayer life as a priest, which I thought unusual."[138]

But Kos claimed powers above those of ordinary priests. A victim testified that "Rudy had the power to heal people. If you came to him with cancer, he would pray over you, and—and there were stories that he had healed people in that way."[139] At healing Masses, Kos would "slay" people in the spirit. This charismatic practice involves touching people gently on the forehead; they then relax totally and fall to the ground. Once, a six-year-old boy came up to Kos to be prayed over, but

> Father Rudy fell over. And I think everybody in the church jumped up and ran up there to help him. And he kind of was real shaken. And I think that just after that he spoke to the church about it and said that sometimes the soul of a child is so pure and so innocent that when he is praying over them, as the Holy Spirit moves through him into the child, it just basically bounces right off the child and back. And it hit him and knocked him out.[140]

That night Kos used a victim's feet to masturbate. All these fireworks were very impressive to adolescent boys and convinced them that "he had a special relationship with God and God was using him in a certain way to minister to his people."[141] How could a man who worked miracles ask a boy to do anything wrong?

The priests at Kos's next assignment, St. Luke's parish in Irving (1985–88), were less tolerant of his behavior. The principal of St. Luke's school, a deacon, and several parishioners quickly complained about the amount of time Kos was spending with boys. In January 1986 the pastor, Daniel J. Clayton, began keeping detailed logs of the comings and goings of boys from Kos's bedroom. He sent them to Msgr. Rehkemper with a letter: "I present this to you out of concern for Rudy Kos, for myself and for any danger that may come to the Church at large or here at St. Luke's."[142] There is no mention of protecting potential victims. In January 1986 Rehkemper wrote a memo for Kos's file: "Suspicious as to his behavior as to whether he is either a homosexual or a child abuser."[143]

Later in 1986 Clayton wrote to Kos, "I find the boys and young men staying overnight in your room inappropriate . . . .I ask you that it come to an end."[144] Clayton pleaded with Bishop Tschoepe to help: "I will not play psychologist, but I feel anxious about the situation….You are the only one I have to turn to. My instincts tell me to do nothing is not a solution."[145] But Tschoepe did not get to be bishop by doing things, making waves, and "causing scandal," i.e., bad publicity.

The personnel board asked Bishop Tschoepe to write Kos ordering him to cease the overnight stays. Tschoepe did not. Instead Rehkemper spoke with Kos. He wrote a note to himself for the file: "I told Father Kos that if anyone other than his mother or father or adopted son stayed the night in the rectory in the future he would be running the risk of being suspended. I had him understand that we were not accusing him of any wrongdoing but that it was imprudent and the diocese could be jeopardized by a legal suit if anybody wanted to make an issue of it."[146] Rehkemper does not mention any concern for children. Priests in Dallas have since 1988 been forbidden by diocesan policy to have anyone but close relatives or other priests stay overnight with them in the rectory. But parishioners were never told about this policy, even up to the date of the civil trial against the diocese in 1997. Why not? "I haven't found a reason to,"[147] testified Bishop Charles V. Grahmann, Tschoepe's successor, and this after the diocese had had to deal with several cases of molestation.

During the trial Rehkemper was questioned about how the diocese handled accusations against priests. The newspaper storyrecounts the exchange between Sylvia Demarest, attorney for the plaintiffs, and Msgr. Rehkemper:

> "Are you telling me, in order to deal with Father Kos, you had to have actual proof he was molesting children?" Ms. Demarest asked Msgr. Rehkemper.
>
> "Yes," the silver-haired cleric replied.
>
> "All this conduct over all those years didn't make any difference?" Ms. Demarest asked.
>
> "If you don't have evidence, you cannot remove a pastor," he replied.
>
> "Yes, you can."
>
> "You have to have evidence, my dear lady."
>
> Ms. Demarest asked him about the diocese's personnel manual, adopted in 1988, that discusses procedures for handling complaints against priests.
>
> It says no anonymous calls or letters will be acknowledged. If a letter is signed and the writer is not willing to let his or her name be known to the priest, the letter ordinarily "will be destroyed and it will not be a matter of record for the priest's personnel file," the manual states.
>
> "You could get ten anonymous phone calls a day and five letters a week, and you would not look into the situation?" Ms. Demarest asked Msgr. Rehkemper.
>
> "That's right," he replied.[148]

Rehkemper said he never asked Kos whether Kos was abusing children because "I didn't see any reason to." Rehkemper also testified that he did not know of the existence of this 1989 policy statement by the Catholic bishops of the United States: "Church leaders are advised to investigate immediately, to remove a priest rapidly where the evidence warrants it, to seek appropriate treatment for the offender and to extend pastoral help to the victim of such a tragedy and to the victim's family."[149] Rehkemper claimed not to know of the existence of a special diocesan commission that was supposed to investigate allegations of child abuse. There were many things in the diocese that the number two man did not know, claimed not to know, or did not want to know.

In 1988 Bishop Tschoepe made Kos the pastor of St. John Nepomocene in Ennis, at first with Ernesto Torres, a Filipino priest, and then with the recently ordained Robert Williams as an assistant. The parish had an elementary school, a high school, and a large program to teach children the fundamentals of their faith. The complaints continued. In December 1991 Williams told Rehkemper that boys were staying overnight with Kos. In late 1991 Bishop Grahmann himself began hearing complaints about Kos and boys. He met with Kos and told him to stop the sleepovers but Kos ignored him. Williams reported in early 1992 that the sleepovers were continuing. Grahmann told Kos to stop and Kos again ignored him, and two months later Williams wrote a twelve-page letter detailing the problems. He wrote that he saw a boy in bed with Kos. "One boy was the favorite and would sleep over five nights a week," he wrote.

> Rudy did not hide the boys' presence. He would cook for them and give them free run of the rectory. I could see that the staff did not like it but were reluctant to say anything. Rudy was constantly buying them [the boys] presents and lots of food. . . . He was always very physical with the boys. When he hugged them, he would hold them tightly against him and then rub them against him, almost like they were a towel with which he was drying himself. Other times he would hold them up against him and tickle them."[150]

Grahmann claimed never to have read the letter. Rehkemper later testified that he didn't remember reading Williams's eyewitness account of Kos in bed under the covers with a boy. "That's the most important piece of evidence in the case," Turley said. "You were waiting for someone to see him sleeping in the bed with someone, and you just let it get by you?" "Yes," Msgr. Rehkemper replied.[151] Rehkemper did not think the matter of alleged child molestation important enough to read carefully a letter from an eyewitness. Or the monsignor lied under oath.

Although Rehkemper never asked Kos if he abused boys, Grahmann asked Kos whether he was a pedophile, and Kos said no. Grahmann claimed never to have looked at Kos's personnel file, which contained complaints from two priests in letters that named at least twenty boys who stayed overnight with Kos and who could have been questioned. Why didn't Grahmann look at the file? "There was no reason for me to look in the file."[152] Williams met with diocesan officials eight times about Kos. Why? "I was concerned about the children."[153] He was not getting the clear message that the officials were sending him: they did not share his concern.

In January 1992 the diocese sent Kos to a psychiatrist, Dr. Richard Jaeckle, whose comment about Kos's nonexistent prayer life has already been mentioned. Jaeckle, a specialist in childhood allergies, treated Kos until September. Jaeckle felt that Rehkemper had misled him. "He led me to believe there were these complaints and they were later resolved and that was it." As Jaeckle understood it, "They were never able to pin anything on him."[154] While the psychiatrist was trying to avoid blame by shifting it back to the diocese, diocesan officials like Rehkemper made it clear that they didn't want to act before they had proof that no one, including Kos, could deny, because they didn't want Kos to sue the diocese. Meanwhile the children were left with their secrets, without help, in the darkness of their souls.

In February 1992 Kos said the funeral Mass for Jay Lemberger, a young parishioner of All Saints. Jay was twelve when he met Kos in 1981. When the boy spent nights at the rectory, Kos taught him how to use a computer and talked to him about becoming a priest—one just like Kos. His parents have a photograph of Jay in his altar boy clothes, standing next to Kos, with a picture of Pope John Paul II in the background. Lemberger's father had to travel a lot on business, and Kos was always willing to help with Jay and his friends. Mrs. Lemberger said that "he wrestled with them, took them places, bought them pizzas. He was really likable." Around 1990 Jay began to suffer from manic-depressive states. He curled up on the floor at a swim meet and started crying. He saw a psychiatrist and was hospitalized. He did drawings as part of his therapy. One was "Treads," showing a single tennis shoe. "Once, Pat [Jay's father] and I gave Jay a pair of tennis shoes to wear while he was in the hospital," recalled Nancy Lemberger. "I couldn't understand why Jay tore those shoes to shreds."[155]

They understood at the trial after they heard what Kos did with boys' feet. Jay drew a picture of Jesus carrying the cross, and of a figure throwing stones at Him. On the figure's eye Jay wrote "Rudy." Kos was the only person permitted to see Jay privately in the hospital; he brought Jay communion and talked to him. Jay's journal kept referring to death as "the other side." "He wanted to go to the other side because of the guilt," a psychiatrist, Dr. Kliman, said. "He couldn't resolve it except to kill himself."[156] A few days before Kos was going to visit him in Colorado for a ski trip, Jay shot himself. Kos was the first person outside the family to hear of Jay's death. He drove back to All Saints and preached the funeral Mass. "Blessed are they that mourn," read Kos from the Book of Matthew, "for they shall be comforted."

In April 1992 a social worker consulted by the diocese had said that Kos was a "classic, textbook pedophile."[157] The diocese sent Kos to St. Luke Institute in Suitland, Maryland, for an evaluation in June 1992. The assessment was inconclusive. "We believe it's in everybody's interest to gather more information,"[158] Dr. Stephen Montana wrote to Grahmann. Grahmann did not send Kos for further examination.

In September 1992 the first victim met with Msgr. Glenn D. Gardner, who had just succeeded Rehkemper as vicar general. Gardner gave the victim a list of people to call; no one from the diocese ever called the victim, who reflected, "I thought for sure I'd at least have a meeting with the bishop or an apology. It was like they didn't care."[159] After getting the run-around for four months, the victim contacted a lawyer and decided to sue. At this time Kos admitted molestation; he told Jaeckle that "this is different than the previous administration, which tried to hide this."[160] The diocese sent Kos to the Servants of the Paraclete treatment center in New Mexico and had Father Williams read a letter from the pulpit that Kos had left because of stress. Williams was asked at the trial: "The diocese asked you to read the parish a lie?" Williams answered, "Yes."[161] The lie had serious consequences. Kos asked a parishioner if he could store his belongings at the parishioner's house. The parishioner, feeling sorry for Kos and his supposed illness, agreed. Kos wrote letters to the parishioner's son from the center, and when he was back in Texas at Christmas on leave from the treatment center, he abused the boy.

Kos was disappointed in the diocese. He told a friend who visited him in New Mexico that "he felt like the diocese cut him off. He was angry at them. He thought they had a chance to keep it quiet. He thought that's what they were going to do."[162] The diocese did not exactly cut Kos off. It paid off $75,000 in credit cards and loans and paid his living expenses, medical treatment, and training as a paralegal under an assumed name. The diocese spent $200,000 on Kos after he left because, Msgr. Gardner claimed, canon law obliged the diocese to help Kos. However, the diocese never used this financial leverage to get information from Kos about the boys he had molested. "I never thought of doing that to someone who was sick,"[163] Gardner explained.

In his concluding remarks, plaintiff attorney Turley said sometimes a jury must help an institution "that has become lost to find its way."[164] The plaintiffs had sought $476 million in damages. On July 25, 1997, the jurors found against the diocese and awarded $101.6 million in actual damages and $18 million in punitive damages. At the civil trial jurors also found that sexual abuse by Kos and the diocese's negligence were the "proximate cause" of the suicide of a young man. At the end of the trial, the judge did something unusual. She removed her judicial robes and sat in the jury box and said to the victims and church leaders, "I've been so close to your tragedy, it just breaks my heart....Everybody in this courtroom has been grieving. If anything like this can ever be positive, then let there be healing and let there be hope."[165] Unusual behavior for a judge; but the whole trial was unusual, and not everyone in the courtroom had hearts of stone. Some did care about the children.

After the verdict Rehkemper, who was now pastor of All Saints where Kos had abused children, could not contain himself. He had nearly been cited for contempt of court for refusing to answer questions during the trial.[166] His associate at All Saints, according to Turley, reported that Rehkemper had said, "I would rather go to jail than tell the truth."[167] Rehkemper called a reporter in for an interview. Why hadn't he acted: "You can't act on suspicions," he said. "You have to prove it before you move in on somebody. Otherwise, you'll get another legal suit—defamation of character." Rehkemper claimed that "I acted as responsibly as I could. I couldn't hide under his bed. I couldn't hide in his closet. I couldn't put a camera in his room. I couldn't break down the door. If I had known there was sexual abuse going on, I would have done something." The fact that boys were spending night after night in Kos's room didn't mean anything immoral was occurring, he said. In any case the children were also at fault: "They [the victims] knew what was right and what was wrong. . . . Anybody who reaches the age of reason shares responsibility for what they do. So that makes all of us responsible after we reach the age of six or seven."[168] Rehkemper was number two man in the diocese, the vicar general, when the abuse occurred. A priest and a number of lay people had tried to get him to act. But he wasn't responsible; the nine-years-olds who had been anally raped were. The diocese decided to move Rehkemper from the Dallas area, but it found a nice retirement job for him, as pastor of Our Lady of Good Hope parish in Hope, Arkansas, President Clinton's hometown.

Bishop Tschoepe did not appear at the trial to explain his actions. The diocese told the judge that the eighty-one-year-old retired bishop had Alzheimer's disease and could not testify. After the trial a reporter went looking for Tschoepe. He found him serving as assistant pastor at St. Joseph's church in Waxahachie, Texas. The bishop, supposedly disabled with Alzheimer's, said Mass ten times a week, drove a car, and went shopping. He spoke with the reporter: "My memory's not good," he said before turning away from the reporter and later driving off. "That's going way back. I don't have anything to say. I stayed out of it [the trial]. I told them I wasn't going to [testify]. Whatever you heard [during the trial], half of it isn't true." Asked later whether he had Alzheimer's, Bishop Tschoepe laughed and declined to comment.[169] Tschoepe was asked if there was sexual abuse in the diocese. He responded, "A little bit. It's all blown out of proportion."[170]

In San Diego Kos had set up a new life with funds from the Dallas diocese. He had changed his name and undergone therapy. He was now a satisfied homosexual who realized he had needlessly been turning his affection to males under the age of consent. He claimed to be celibate but lived across the street from a school with a thirty-eight-year-old man he called his lover. Kos considered himself a priest, and a key point of being a priest was that "they have an obligation to me to take care of me for life."[171] Dignity, the Catholic organization for gays and lesbians, had asked Kos to say Mass for them, but he hadn't done it yet. This idyllic existence was interrupted when Kos was arrested in October 1997 while he was drinking at the Loft, a gay bar in San Diego, on a Dallas warrant and returned to Dallas for trial, where he eventually pleaded guilty to one count of sexual assault of a child and two counts of sexual indecency with a child. Kos was sentenced to life with eligibility for parole in fifteen years.[172]

Grahmann had the settlement negotiated down to $31 million—$11 million from the diocese, $20 million from insurance companies. Grahmann met with top lay Catholics to hammer out a deal. They said that he agreed to retire after a decent interval. In January 2000 the Vatican sent Bishop Joseph A. Galante from Beaumont, Texas, to be coadjutor bishop with right of succession, a clear signal to Grahmann that he was expected to retire. He didn't. Instead he refused to discipline a priest, Ramon Alvarez, the number three man in the diocese, who was accused of grabbing a man's genitals during a blessing.[173] Grahmann and Galante got into a public fight about it; the lay group then went public and accused Grahmann of welshing on his promise to resign. Grahmann denied he had ever made such a promise—but his memory, as was clear from his testimony at the civil trial, is not very good. Grahmann refused to budge from his episcopal throne, despite the clear indication that the pope wanted him to retire, and Pope John Paul II backed down and transferred Galante to another see, leaving Grahmann in triumphant possession of Dallas.[174]

Michael Hartwig, Kos's dean and teacher of moral theology at the Dallas seminary, invited the seminarians to his "wedding" with Don Baker, former president of the Dallas Gay and Lesbian Activists' Alliance.[175] They moved to Connecticut where Hartwig got a job teaching at Albertus Magnus College, a Dominican college that gets substantial support from the Knights of Columbus. Hartwig and his partner attended college social events, and Hartwig worked on his book on the immorality of sexual abstinence. *The Wanderer* put two and two together, however, and wrote about Hartwig, who therefore became known to donors who thought they were supporting a Catholic school. The president found an excuse in a slight misrepresentation to terminate Hartwig. Baker died in 2000 of cancer, the obituary said, and was buried from Our Lady Help of Christians in Newton, Massachusetts. Hartwig wrote his book, *The Poetics of Intimacy*, about "the *immorality* [emphasis in original] of sexual abstinence"[176] which is "harmful"[177] and "a serious risk to Christian life."[178] Rudy Kos took this advice to heart.

CHAPTER SIX

# HURRICANE HITS BOSTON

Boston has been the storm center of the scandals. The *Boston Globe* never forgot that Cardinal Law had called the power of God down upon them for printing the history of Porter's abuse. Law had violated a fundamental rule of life: *Never pick a fight with someone who buys ink by the barrel.* The courts in Boston also refused the archdiocese's request to seal records. The records of the diocese of Bridgeport remain sealed, although courts have recognized the standing of newspapers to sue to get access to them, and they may become public. But as I write, Cardinal Egan of New York does not have to face public scrutiny of his actions for his handling of abuse cases when he was bishop of Bridgeport. Cardinal Mahony has so far kept the Los Angeles files away from the courts and the press, although there too cases are making their way through the court system and at least some of the records may become public. The Philadelphia grand jury report portrays an archdiocese with almost unbelievable perversions.[1] Boston and Cardinal Law had the misfortune of having the records of its horrors revealed before the public was desensitized by a flood of revelations.

In this book I will not give an account of all the abusive priests in Boston (there are sixty large binders that contain the personnel records that were released in the Boston trials), nor will I attempt to follow the career of every abuser from beginning to end, but I hope to give the reader an idea of both the scope of the problem and the nature of the abuse that was tolerated. Not only individuals were corrupt; the ecclesiastical system had adapted to corruption as the normal state of affairs.

## *Geoghan's Thirty-Six Years of Pedophilia*

John J. Geoghan's childhood was not a disaster like Rudy Kos's, but it had its tragedies. His father died in 1940 when John was only five. He vividly remembered the funeral as a happy event—his reaction was not necessarily bizarre, because his family was devout and had confidence that their father was happy in heaven. Geoghan became fascinated with the idea of heaven and decided to become a priest. He was fortunate to have his mother's brother, Msgr. Mark Keohane, as a substitute father.

Geoghan reported that his first sexual feelings were frightening, but that he thought of himself as a heterosexual and that he fantasized about women. This is not unusual for pedophiles, that is, men who are attracted to pre-pubescent children, not to adolescent or adult males. Such abusers are not sexually attracted by mature male sexual characteristics (as homosexuals are). Their attraction to children is often a perverted variation of an attraction to the female, because even boys, if young enough, lack secondary male sex characteristics. Geoghan molested both boys and girls, but his main attraction was to boys, which is why doctors classified him as a homosexual pedophile (although there is no indication he was attracted to adult men).

He graduated from Holy Cross High School in 1952 and entered Cardinal O'Connell Seminary. In 1954 its rector, John J. Murray, wrote, "Geoghan has given the faculty of this seminary cause for concern in the past two years. . . . He has a very pronounced immaturity . . . a little feminine in his manner of speech and approach. Scholastically he is a problem . . . I still have serious doubts about his ability to do satisfactory work."[2] Murray suspected that Geoghan was a loser. When Geoghan did not show up for summer seminary camp in summer 1955, the rector of St. John's Seminary, which he had entered from O'Connell Seminary, was unhappy, and Msgr. Keohane had to intervene, explaining that Geoghan "has been treating with a physician since he left Brighton because of a nervous and depressed state."[3] Geoghan left the seminary and went to Holy Cross College in Worcester from which he graduated in 1957. Then he returned to St. John's, where he met John McCormack, Paul Shanley, and Joseph Birmingham. He was ordained in 1962.

From 1962 to 1966 Geoghan was stationed in Saugus, Massachusetts, at Blessed Sacrament church, where his crimes began. In 1995 he admitted to abusing boys while he was in this parish. His *modus operandi* continued to be the same for over thirty years: he sought out boys without fathers or with absent fathers and offered to be a father to them. He took them out, became close to them, put them to bed, masturbated them, and performed oral sex on them.

Did his seeking out fatherless boys have something to do with the loss of his own father? Probably. Someone who has lost his father when he was a child would tend to identify with fatherless boys. But why the sexual interest, and why almost always in boys? Geoghan later explained that he "avoided girls" and that "I picked the boys because in some way they were the safest, the girls and the mothers would have been more dangerous."[4] What does that mean? That parents would be less outraged at the abuse of boys? Geoghan had a preference for boys and didn't want to admit it even to himself, because he did not want to think of himself in any way as a homosexual. Geoghan never indicated that he himself had been sexually abused as a child, but Geoghan was an accomplished dissembler and rationalizer. It would explain a lot if he had been. He was diagnosed with "congenital right-hemisphere brain impairment."[5] But this did not affect his ability as a confidence man to locate hurting families, to insinuate himself into them, and to manipulate people's weaknesses to get what he wanted: sex with children and a cushy career as a priest.

Did the diocese have any idea of what was going on at Blessed Sacrament? Rev. Anthony Benzevich, who had been stationed at that parish with Geoghan, at first told Mitchell Garabedian, attorney for the plaintiffs, that he had reported to the archdiocese that Geoghan was taking boys to his bedroom, but he (Benzevich) was threatened with assignment to South America if he opened his mouth. But after he consulted with Wilson Rogers III, the son of Law's attorney, Benzevich could no longer remember that he had told this information to the archdiocese.[6]

After an abbreviated and therefore suspect seven-month stay at St. Bernard's parish in Concord, Massachusetts, Geoghan was at St. Paul's parish in Hingham, Massachusetts, from 1967 to 1974, and soon abused someone. It came to the notice of the archdiocese, and Geoghan, around 1968, was sent to Seton Institute in Baltimore, which treated priests and religious with psychiatric disorders. Cardinal Cushing supervised the first part of Geoghan's career until 1970, when Cushing died and Cardinal Medeiros, who as chancellor in Fall River had enabled James Porter to move from parish to parish molesting children, took over the governance of the archdiocese of Boston.

In the early 1970s Geoghan entered the life of the Mueller family. He babysat the small boys (seven, ten, and twelve), took them out for ice cream, and helped with their baths. The smallest complained that Geoghan was "touching my wee-wee." The older ones confirmed it and said Geoghan had told them not to tell their mother, "because Father said it was confessional."[7] Geoghan used the mystique of the sacraments to commit abuse. Joanne Mueller says he molested her sons and that she told Rev. Paul Miceli, who asked her to keep quiet. (He now says he recalls nothing about this.) In 1973 Geoghan disappeared from St. Paul's for eight months. In 1974 Cardinal Medeiros wrote to Geoghan about his transfer from St. Paul's, "I am confident that you will render fine priestly service to the people of God in St. Andrew parish."[8]

St. Andrew's church in Jamaica Plain was Geoghan's next assignment from 1974 to 1984. He was made Scout chaplain and put in charge of altar boys. In 1974 Frank Leary was thirteen, the fifth of six children of a single mother on welfare. He helped around the church. Geoghan brought him into the rectory to show him his stamp collection and prayed with him. As the boy prayed, Geoghan pulled down his pants and started performing oral sex on him. Leary remembers a priest yelling, "Jack, we told you not to do this up here! What the hell are you doing? Are you nuts?"[9] The real question is why the other priest didn't call the police – but it was extremely rare that any cleric sought to protect children.

In 1979 a Miss Coveny told the Rev. William Francis, chaplain of the Boston police, that Geoghan had done something immoral (archdiocesan records do not have details). Bishop Daily wrote to Rev. Francis Delaney, Geoghan's superior at St. Andrew's, that "the charges were quickly proven to be completely unfounded and totally irresponsible. One phone call accomplished that." Daily was able to do a complete investigation and exonerate Geoghan with one phone call. Daily continued, that to console Geoghan, "I have written to ask him to drop by at the Chancery . . . to personally assure him of his good record and his good name and priestly reputation."[10] Neither Daily nor any of the other bishops ever showed any interest in consoling the victims until lawyers became involved.

Maryetta Dussourd was rearing her three boys and a girl as well as her niece's four boys in 1977,[11] when Geoghan, whom she perceived as "charming, youthful-looking, and charismatic,"[12] met them. The boys ranged from four to twelve. He became very close to them. An archdiocesan memo said that Geoghan stayed in their house even when he was on retreat because he missed the boys so much. He would "touch them while they were sleeping and waken them by playing with their penises."[13] He performed oral sex on them, fondled them, or forced them to fondle his penis as he prayed. One boy later explained to his mother that Geoghan persuaded him not to tell by saying, "You'd [the mother] hate me and that you'd never love me again because you love the Church more than you love me."[14] In 1980 Dussourd discovered what was going on because her great-nephews returned home and told their aunt (her sister), Margaret Gallant, who complained to Rev. John Thomas. He confronted Geoghan, who casually admitted, "Yes, it's all true."[15] Thomas told Bishop Daily, who sent Geoghan home that day. Thomas was horrified that Geoghan might suffer consequences. Dussourd reports that Thomas pleaded with her not to go public, not to hurt Geoghan: "Do you realize what you are taking from him?"[15] Dussourd did not know what to do. Other parishioners shunned her as a troublemaker, causing scandal about poor dear Father Geoghan.

When Geoghan was confronted with the charges concerning the Dussourds, he casually admitted "homosexual activity with seven boys ages six to eleven,"[17] but excused his behavior because "it was only two families."[18] The archdiocese was aware that Geoghan "admits the activity but does not feel it is serious or a pastoral problem."[19] The archdiocese apparently concurred with Geoghan's judgment of the abuse. Bishop Daily didn't act to prevent further abuse. He explained later that "I am not a policeman, I am a shepherd."[20] But a shepherd only for priests; damage to the laity, especially to the weak and helpless, did not concern Daily.

In 1980 Geoghan took a year's sick leave and saw Dr. Robert W. Mullins, who knew Geoghan well. Mullins was a neighbor of the Geoghan family in West Roxbury and a family physician without any expertise in psychiatry or sexual disorders. Dr. John H. Brennan, whom Geoghan also saw during this year off, was a psychiatrist, who wrote to the archdiocese that Geoghan "was now able to resume his priestly duties."[21] But Brennan had no experience in treating sexual disorders; his experience was more personal. In 1977, three years before he treated Geoghan, Brennan was sued by a patient who said he had sexually molested her and who settled for $100,000. (Another suit by another patient was filed in 1992.[22]) But Brennan had other qualifications: he was director of psychiatric education at St. Elizabeth's Hospital in Brighton and received referrals for many patients from a priest-psychologist, the Boston Franciscan Fulgence Buonanno. Brennan was solidly in the old boys' network in Boston and could be expected to deliver what the archdiocese wanted to hear.

Geoghan knew what the doctors would say. He wrote to Cardinal Medeiros, "I have been receiving excellent care on direction from two wonderful Catholic physicians, Dr. John Brennan and Dr. Robert Mullins. They assure me that within a relatively short time I shall be able to return for fruitful years of priestly ministry. I am eager to return."[23] Cardinal Medeiros put him into St. Brendan's parish in Dorchester but neglected to tell the pastor, the Rev. James H. Lane, that Geoghan had a history of sexual abuse.

At St. Brendan's, Geoghan prepared children for First Communion and then took them to his summer house, where he abused them. Geoghan spent so much time with children that some people in the parish began to get suspicious. Geoghan's past continued to haunt the archdiocese. On July 24, 1982, Mr. and Mrs. Ralph Dussourd, Margaret Gallant (the sister of Mrs. Dussourd), and Fran Dussourd met with Bishop Daily to demand that Geoghan be removed from ministry. They told Daily that Geoghan met one of the boys he had molested and took him out again for ice cream. Daily's response was to send Geoghan to Rome for a two-month sabbatical with $2,000 expense money.

In August 1982 Margaret Gallant wrote to Cardinal Medeiros to report that she had been asked to keep silent so as not to hurt the boys—which she points out is "absurd" since the names of minors are protected by law. She pointed out that a layman who has abused children would be confined and exposed so as to warn parents and children. Abuse by Geoghan is worse than abuse by a layman because it "hits the very core of our being in our love for the Church." Gallant, a better diagnostician than the family doctor and the psychiatrist, continued, "I do not believe he is cured; his actions strongly suggest he is not, and there is no guarantee that persons with these obsessions are ever cured." She expressed compassion for Geoghan but sought action for "the children in the [C]hurch." The child victims were invisible to Medeiros and the other bishops: "My two sisters and my niece have never as much as received an apology from the [C]hurch, much less any offer of counseling for the boys. It embarrasses me that the Church is so negligent." Gallant remembered that Father Damien of Molokai, the leper saint, "went after a child molester and beat him up." She, alas, suffered from an illusion: "We . . . have the right to expect service from the Ordained."[24] Medeiros replied to Gallant that he was worried about scandal and pleaded for Christian forgiveness.

Geoghan returned from Rome refreshed and ready for more action. His pastor, Lane, eventually found out about the abuse, and Geoghan lost access to the children at St. Brendan's. Cardinal Law came to Boston in March 1984. Despite Geoghan's 1980 admission of sexual abuse and further complaints from St. Brendan's parish, in November 1984, after lunching with Geoghan's uncle and patron Msgr. Keohane, Law assigned

Geoghan to St. Julia's parish in Weston and a month later persuaded doctors to sign off on a statement that Geoghan was medically cleared. According to Dr. Robert W. Mullins, after the "unfortunate traumatic experience" (that is, getting caught), Geoghan has had "a brief, but beneficial, respite," and "is able to resume full pastoral activities without any need for specific restrictions."[25]

Msgr. Francis Rossiter at St. Julia's was told of Geoghan's past and he promptly put Geoghan in charge of three youth groups. Bishop John M. D'Arcy was not happy and wrote to Law, asking him whether this assignment was a good idea, in view of Geoghan's "history [note the word and its implications] of homosexual involvement with young boys."[26] D'Arcy was shortly (February 1985) sent off to South Bend, Indiana, although he had to leave his dying mother behind. He has claimed it had nothing to do with this protest, but obviously D'Arcy did not fit into the clerical culture of Boston. He did not *understand,* the way the other bishops did.

In 1986, two years after his supposed full recovery, Geoghan demonstrated why he was so eager to return to ministry. He heard that the father of a family he had known at St. Andrew's had committed suicide. Geoghan went right over to offer help and to help himself to the boys. Geoghan took twelve-year-old Patrick McSorley out for ice cream. Then Geoghan "patted his [Patrick's] upper leg and slid his hand up toward his crotch. 'I froze up,' McSorley said, 'I didn't know what to think. Then he put his hands on my genitals and started masturbating. I was petrified.' McSorley added that Geoghan then began masturbating himself."[27]

In the mid-1980s Geoghan spent a lot of time around the Boys' and Girls' Club in Waltham. There he met Mark Keane, with whom he talked about his swimming, and then, according to Keane, pushed him under a staircase and performed oral sex on him.[28] More allegations were made to the archdiocese and Bishop Daily began to be worried.

Dr. Brennan was not sanguine about Geoghan's state in April 1989. He told Bishop Daily that "you better clip his wings before there is an explosion....You can't afford to have him in a parish."[29] Law sent Geoghan to St. Luke Institute in Suitland, Maryland, for an evaluation; the diagnosis was "homosexual pedophilia."[30] Auxiliary Bishop Banks told Geoghan he had to leave the ministry, but instead Geoghan was put on sick leave, and in August 1989 Law sent Geoghan to the Institute of Living in Hartford, Connecticut. Dr. Robert Swords and Dr. Vincent Stephens said that tests indicated that Geoghan "showed an immature and impulsive nature" and "could be a high risk taker." Their diagnosis was "atypical pedophilia, in remission" and "mixed personality disorder with obsessive-compulsive, histrionic, and narcissistic features."[31] The doctors were perceptive, except about the "in remission." Geoghan had freely lied to them about the extent of the abuse, and the archdiocese had not bothered to tell the Institute everything that was in its records.

Even after the archdiocese had withheld pertinent information from the Institute and allowed Geoghan to get away with his lies, the diagnosis was still not what Bishop Banks wanted to hear and what he had paid to hear. Banks wrote to the doctors that he was "disappointed and disturbed by the report," because he had been assured that "it would be all right to reassign Father Geoghan to pastoral ministry and that he would not present a risk for the parishioners whom he would serve." Swords then gave Banks what he wanted to hear: "We judge Father Geoghan to be clinically quite safe to resume his pastoral ministry," and later added Geoghan was "fit for pastoral work in general including children."[32] In December 1990 Dr. Brennan had again changed his opinion of Geoghan and this time was upbeat. He wrote to Bishop Banks that "there is no psychiatric contraindication to Fr. Geoghan's pastoral work at this time."[33] Law sent Geoghan back to the boys of St. Julia's.

More complaints came in, and Cardinal Law removed Geoghan from parish work in January 1993. St. Luke Institute again evaluated Geoghan in January 1995, and the diagnosis was the worst yet: "It is our clinical judgment that Father Geoghan has a longstanding and continuing problem with sexual attraction to prepubescent males. His recognition of the problem and his insight into it is limited."[34] In July 1995 Law sent Geoghan to an Ontario treatment center, Southdown, which also was pessimistic about him.

In 1995, Geoghan, facing a barrage of civil suits from his victims, sold to his sister his interest in the houses he had inherited from his mother, houses worth about $1 million, for one dollar. He thereby made himself judgment-proof and indigent. His defense was paid by the state of Massachusetts, and therefore by the taxes paid by the families of the boys he had molested.[35] He wallowed in self-pity, writing to Rev. William Murphy, "I have been falsely accused and feel alienated from my ministry and fellowship with my brother priests. I cannot believe that one would be considered guilty on an accusation based on speculation but I have experienced this. Where is the justice or due process? . . . I will do all in my power to maintain my innocence."[36] Geoghan seemed to have forgotten that in 1980 he had admitted abusing the Dussourd boys.

Against the advice of his assistants, at the end of 1996 Law granted Geoghan early retirement and wrote to him, "Yours has been an effective life of ministry, sadly impaired by illness. On behalf of those who you served well, and in my own name, I would like to thank you."[37] Law thanked a man who had, his victims claimed, molested over 130 boys, poisoned scores of families, destroyed people's faith, and would cost the archdiocese of Boston $30 million and Law his job. Even after his forced retirement, Geoghan continued to function as a priest, which allowed him to pursue his other interests. He agreed to baptize a child; the infant's brother served as altar boy. Before the baptism, the boy claimed, Geoghan helped him put on a pair of dress pants and masturbated him while pretending to help with the zipper.

In 1997 the climate was uncomfortable for Geoghan, and the archdiocese of Boston found his continued presence in the state of Massachusetts a source of legal complications. They tried to get him out of sight; Rev. William Murphy wrote in a memo for the file: "I spoke to Father Geoghan today regarding the proposal he make a visit to Alma, Michigan, and the Sisters of Mercy. Father Geoghan has concluded that he lacks sufficient emotional strength for a move to Michigan."[38] Paul Shanley, as we shall see, had offered Bishop McCormack to set up a safe house for priests such as Geoghan, where they could hide from publicity and the law.

The law was closing in on Geoghan, and the archdiocese of Boston began reconsidering its thirty-year support for him and his misdeeds. Rev. Brian M. Flatley, handling the Geoghan case, wrote to Law, who was sympathetic to Geoghan's request not to be sent to a residential treatment center, that Geoghan "was not totally honest" and he was not convinced that Geoghan was "not lying again" when he denied molesting yet another group of boys.[39] It was beginning to dawn on Flatley that Geoghan was a confidence man.

On February 17, 1998, the Vatican, that is, Pope John Paul II, having reviewed Geoghan's dossier and having expressed no known interest in what had happened to his victims, removed Geoghan from the priesthood.

On January 18, 2002, Geoghan was found guilty of indecently touching a ten-year-old boy. It was one of his lesser offenses, but it was one that the archdiocese of Boston had not managed to conceal until the statute of limitations protected Geoghan from prosecution. The boy testified that he was at the Waltham Boys' and Girls' Club; "he was trying to teach himself to dive from the deep end of the swimming pool, he said, when a familiar man asked if he wanted help. 'Yes,' answered the boy, and he dove some more, coached by the priest he had seen a few times around his Waltham housing project. But about fifteen minutes later, as he floated in the pool near the priest, the boy was startled by an unexpected touch: a hand that slid up his leg, beneath his bathing suit, and squeezed his buttocks."[40]

Judge Sandra Hamlin gave Geoghan the maximum sentence, ten years, because "this defendant hid behind his [priest's] collar and under the sanctity of the Roman Catholic Church engaged in what this court can only describe as depraved and reprehensible behavior."[41]

Child abusers, called "skinners," are targeted in prison. Prisoners need someone to look down upon in order to maintain some self-respect. Murderers can at least console themselves with the thought that "I am not a child raper." Geoghan was sent to a medium security prison, MCI-McCord. There the guards and other prisoners did not treat him with the tenderness that he had grown accustomed to receiving from the archbishops of Boston. Guards called him Satan and Lucifer. He said his bed was urinated on and defecated on. He complained, was marked down as a troublesome prisoner, and was sent to a high security prison, Souza-Baranowski.

Joseph L. Druse (born Darin Ernest Smiledge) was, according to his father, physically and sexually abused as a child. When he was eight years old, a school psychiatrist wrote of him that he "has a very accurate detailed knowledge of both sexual behavior and anatomy."[42] Like many children who are abused, he grew up hating gays, and in 1988 a homosexual made the mistake of touching Druse's crotch. Druse beat him and wrapped a rope around his neck, pulling it tight and yelling, "You're dead. You deserve to die. You're a faggot. All fags should die."[43] Druse hated Jews and gays; he therefore joined the Aryan Nation, a group of losers whose only badge of superiority is their white Gentile skin. He ended up in Souza-Baranowski. Druse had lots of time on his hands in the high security prison. In 2002 he amused himself by sending letters filled with fake anthrax to lawyers and organizations with Jewish-sounding names and his own excrement to the Massachusetts attorney general.

Massachusetts decided the perfect place to place John Geoghan, convicted pedophile, was in a unit with the homophobic, neo-Nazi murderer, Joseph Druse. Geoghan was unrepentant in prison; he told his fellow prisoners that "his accusers had come out of the woodwork to make money."[44] Druse decided to avenge the 150 children that Geoghan molested. On August 23, 2003, during the five minutes that prisoners were allowed out of their cells to return their lunch trays, Druse followed Geoghan into Geoghan's cell. Druse had a cut-up book and stuffed it into the closed door so that it could not be opened from the outside. He tied Geoghan's hands behind his back with a T-shirt and tied stretched socks around Geoghan's neck. He used a shoe as a garrote to strangle the sixty-eight-year-old, 130-pound Geoghan. As Geoghan lay on the floor, Druse repeatedly jumped on him, breaking his ribs and puncturing his lungs. Druse also had a razor and apparently intended to make sure that Geoghan would never be able to have sex with a child again even if he survived the assault. But the guards forced the door open and took Geoghan to the hospital, where he died.

Druse considered himself a hero. He told the guards that "I just saved your kids from being raped,"[45] and shouted to the other prisoners as he was taken away, "Let's keep the kids safe." They responded, "Druse, Druse, Druse."[46] He was following his own conscience in these matters instead of being hemmed in by the archaic traditions that reserved executing criminals to the state (a power Massachusetts had renounced, so Druse can be punished no more than he is already being punished). What Druse did was to make it harder to expose the malefactors in the Boston archdiocese.[47] Druse also inadvertently gave a "gift" to Geoghan's victims. Geoghan had been convicted of only one count of child molestation. At the time of his death, he was appealing his conviction. If an appellant dies during an appeal, the conviction is vacated. The court has therefore declared John Geoghan an innocent man.

And Geoghan's eternal fate, and his victims' fate, and his murderer's fate? Not to worry. According to Msgr. John Jenik of the South Bronx, "I mentioned him [Geoghan] in my homily at Mass Sunday and used the word 'horrific' to describe him. But I also said that forgiveness is extended to one and all including Hitler and Stalin because it is the church position that all will be saved."[48] Easy forgiveness is a topic to which I shall return; the consequences of automatic universal salvation I have discussed elsewhere.[49]

## *Paul Shanley: Every Parent's Nightmare*

Shanley at one time was the darling of liberal Boston. He was a street priest who defended homosexuality. He liked to have sex with males of all ages, starting around six. He also generously shared boys with other priests and with the general public, all the while announcing his rejection of church moral teaching to the applause of his admirers. He also said he had sex with women, and is accused of abusing small girls.[50] He was completely liberated from all the restraints that Christianity has put on the sexual appetite.

Paul R. Shanley came from a modest background: his father owned a bowling alley and a poolroom; his mother was a legal secretary. Paul Shanley worked as a linotype operator for two years, but then he took aptitude tests at the YMCA which showed his aptitude for "boys' work," and went to

Boston University and then to St. John's Seminary. His fellow students included John McCormack, who would become a bishop and would be so kind to him in his troubles, and other members of his class who would be accused of sexual abuse: Joseph E. Birmingham (see p. 174), James D. Foley (see p. 173), John M. Cotter, Eugene M. O'Sullivan, and Bernard J. Lane.[51] He also, he later claimed, met a cardinal who took a personal interest in him: "I have abided by my promise not to mention to anyone the fact that I too had been sexually abused as a teenager, and later as a seminarian by a priest, a faculty member, a pastor, and ironically by the predecessor of one of the two Cardinals [Law and O'Connor] who now debate my fate."[52] In Boston the predecessors were Cardinals Medeiros (against whom an accusation has been made)[53] and Cushing; in New York Cardinals Cooke and Spellman (whom New York gays have longed claimed as one of their own[54]). The timeframe suggests that Shanley was referring either to Spellman or Cushing. The archdiocese did not express any surprise at Shanley's accusation; did they already know about it?

Shanley was ordained in 1960 and his problems immediately started in 1961 at St. Patrick's church in Stoneham. A father reported to Stoneham police chief Bernie Vacon that Shanley had sexually abused the father's thirteen-year-old son, Thomas Peter Devlin. Shanley denied it, and the father didn't want to go public because he was embarrassed and also didn't want to get in a fight with the Boston hierarchy. The boy's mother wrote to the pastor of St. Patrick's, Msgr. John Sexton,[55] and to Cardinal Cushing, but nothing happened. Vacon got more calls about Shanley but could do nothing.[56] Marjory Mahoney said that in 1962 Shanley abused her twelve-year-old brother, Bill O'Toole. The boy's father and grandfather were policemen but that did not stop Shanley from taking Bill on retreats to a cabin in the woods. Somehow there would always be just one bed too few, and Bill ended up in Shanley's bed and arms. Shanley told Bill "he was doing the Lord's work by finding out who the homosexuals were. . . . Shanley also warned him that if he told anyone, he would burn in hell."[57] Bill went into a downward spiral of drug use and died in 1998 of AIDS. On his deathbed he told his mother the whole story.

Another boy reported he was only seven years old in 1963 when Shanley, while explaining about Holy Communion, started touching the boy's genitals. The next year Shanley had this boy sit on his lap during confession, massaged the boy's genitals, and had the boy massage his genitals. Shanley called it "exchanging." He also told the fatherless boy that he would have to teach the boy about the "birds and bees and also molested the boy at Camp Fatima."[58] According to another parishioner of St. Patrick's, he was eleven years old when Shanley took him on a trip and molested him.

When he was fourteen years old, Patrick Brennan, who had no father and a sick mother, met Shanley at St. Patrick's. Shanley, according to Brennan, chatted with him and suddenly asked if he could check him for a hernia; he then, according to Brennan, "pulled down my pants and fondled me."[59] At St. Patrick's Shanley called boys in for "sessions." During one of these he interrogated a twelve year old about "sex, masturbation, genital development, pubic hair, wet dreams: and then asked him to expose his genitals."[60] Shanley had gotten off to a good start in his "boys' work," and found little opposition from his superiors in the archdiocese of Boston.

In 1966 a boy who is now a CEO in a Boston corporation encountered Shanley. In his affidavit he wrote that Shanley called him (then sixteen years old) to the rectory in the summer of 1966 and explained the "theory of the lesser of two evils....He said I should consider spending the night with him there and if I felt the need to seek out sexual relief from girls, I should contact him and that the lesser of two evils would be for him to masturbate me and for me to masturbate him. He said he had put himself at risk and would take responsibility for that, in order to 'save my soul.'" Later that summer Shanley took him to a cabin in the Blue Hills and again had oral sex with him. He told his parents, who reported it to a priest they trusted, who told the archdiocese.[61]

This led to the first recorded accusation in the archdiocesan files, in 1967 (during Cushing's tenure as archbishop): Rev. Arthur Chabot claimed that "during the summer months (July or August) said priest [Shanley] masturbated the boy."[62] But Shanley denied the accusation, and Msgr. John S. Sexton, the pastor of St. Patrick's, without talking to the boy, accepted

Shanley's denial.[63] In the same year Shanley advised Medeiros, who was then bishop of Fall River, to send James Porter to the Servants of the Paraclete in New Mexico.

At Stoneham Shanley immersed himself in the youth culture. For six years he ran "a discotheque with psychedelic lighting and big name bands."[64] He won the Mayor's Citizenship Award in Boston and Stoneham's Outstanding Young Man of the Year. After a minor controversy at the parish where he was stationed, in May 1969 Shanley was assigned to campus ministry at Boston State College. In 1968 Shanley started a retreat center, Rivendell, in Weston, Vermont, where, some visitors claimed, they "were invited to participate in orgies under a big teepee."[65] Cushing in 1970 assigned Shanley full time to an apostolate to alienated youth, a ministry based at Warwick House in Roxbury, where he worked with the Rev. John J. White, who soon was living with a gay roommate, "a black queen who painted his toenails."[66]

Shanley continued to sound the tocsin about Trouble in River City: "There were one million teenagers on the road last Summer. Father Shanley said the number is expected to triple by this Summer." Shanley was concerned "that hustlers, and psychotics who prey on young people"[67] would get to these kids first. Marijuana, heroin, bombings, blood in the streets—all these threatened Boston if people didn't cough up money for Shanley's youth work. Only Shanley, the hippie priest, stood between Boston and catastrophe.

Shanley continued to keep in touch with boys he had known at St. Patrick's in Stoneham. One reported that, now fifteen years old, he visited Shanley for counseling from 1967 to 1970 and Shanley "sexually abused me by performing oral and anal sex, masturbating, asking me to masturbate him" and suggested "sado-masochistic sex" but the boy drew the line there.[68] A fourteen-year-old boy went for a walk on a summer evening in 1968. Shanley saw him and offered a ride. The boy went along. Shanley drove to the Blue Hills Reservation and there, the boy said, tried to force the boy to receive and give oral sex. The boy refused and bit Shanley. Then Shanley "pushed my face to the right and he stuck his penis in my anus. It hurt so bad

I said please stop hurting me and he pushed harder. I was crying."[69]

In the same year Shanley was gentler with another boy, whose grandmother had given Shanley the money to buy "Terrible Mountain," his cabin in Maine, where Shanley stashed runaways and fugitives from the FBI. Shanley counseled the boy at an apartment on Beacon Street. First, the boy recounted, Shanley had him strip naked to get comfortable with his body. One time the boy arrived at the apartment, was buzzed in, and found Shanley "taking a bubble bath in the bathtub, with candles lit around the room and Gregorian chants playing." The boy, although very dubious, climbed into the bathtub with Shanley. After getting into bed with the boy, the boy remembered that Shanley performed "manual masturbation and oral sex" on him, and at a later similar session, "put his finger in" the boy's anus. Shanley also gave the boy marijuana, beer, and wine.[70]

In 1970 Shanley was active in the gay scene in Boston. In 1970 one boy allegedly was abused ("mutual masturbation, mutual oral sex, and anal rape") by Father Thomas Curran of St. Mary's of the Annunciation in Cambridge.[71] Curran took the thirteen-year-old boy to meet Shanley. In a wooded area, the boy remembered, "I was forced to engage in mutual masturbation and performed oral sex on both priests. While being abused by one priest, the other would watch." In 1974 Shanley frequently took the boy to Warwick House and they had oral and anal sex. Shanley also took the boy to St. Gabriel Monastery in Brighton where, the boy claimed, "he would have me perform various sexual acts on men who lived at the monastery." Once, the boy remembered, "Shanley watched as … [a] man performed oral sex on me in the man's bedroom."[72]

Shanley met the boy's cousin and was generous in sharing them with men in the Fenway. The boy remembered that Shanley "would observe me and my cousin engaging in oral and anal sex with each other, and with other men, that Father Shanley prostituted my cousin and me out to." Under Shanley's directions, the boy and his cousin picked up customers at the Copley Square Greyhound station. Shanley let the boys keep the money "but in return we had to give him detailed descriptions of our sexual encounters" while he masturbated.[73] Shanley took the boy to the Carnival

Lounge, a gay strip club in the Combat Zone (Boston's adult amusement district), had the boy dress in a G-string and dance, and then go into the back room to have sex with a customer.

In this same year, 1974, when Massachusetts considered making discrimination against homosexuals illegal, Shanley and Barney Frank strongly supported the bill. When the Catholic bishops of the United States restated traditional moral teaching on homosexuality, Shanley protested it. He was miffed that Medeiros "has forbidden me to perform gay marriages or even found a gay parish."[74] In 1976 he tried to buy a country inn where his counselees, "homosexuals, bisexuals, asexuals [?], transvestites" could come for "meals, sports, wine-drinking."[75] He eventually had this dream fulfilled when he bought and ran a gay resort in Palm Springs.

In 1974 one fourteen-year-old Latino was used by a friend of Shanley's to transport something clandestinely. The friend taped a large manila envelope to the boy's chest. They then drove from Lowell to Boston to give the envelope to Shanley. The friend then got the envelope back from Shanley, now full of money. This went on for months. Later, when the boy was seventeen, Shanley tried to convince the boy that the boy was gay by taking him to a gay bar, where, the boy reported, "he would get me drunk and have sex with me in the parking lot outside the bar. He also started engaging in sex acts with others, mostly older men."[76]

Cardinal Medeiros was aware of Shanley's sexual activities. In 1974 a mother discovered her son's diary, which detailed his sexual relationship with Shanley which began when the boy was fourteen years old. Shanley also shared the boy with other men. The mother gave Medeiros the diary; Medeiros threatened Shanley, but did nothing.[77]

Shanley told many of his victims that sex between men and boys was normal. He also said it publicly, as Medeiros was aware. An October 1977 letter in Shanley's file in the chancery reported a speech Shanley had given to Dignity-Integrity at St. Luke's Episcopal Church in Rochester, New York. Dignity is the Catholic organization that holds that homosexual behavior is not deviant or immoral; Integrity is the Episcopal counterpart. Shanley is reported to have said that

> Homosexual acts are not sinful, sick, a crime, nor are they immoral...straight people cannot tell the truth about sex....He stated that celibacy is impossible, therefore the only alternative is for gays to have sex with different persons whenever they want to. He spoke of pedophilia (which is a non-coerced sexual manipulation of sexual organs including oral-genital sex between an adult and a child). He stated that the adult is not the seducer—the "kid" is the seducer and further the kid is not traumatized by the act per se, the kid is traumatized when the police and authorities "drag" the kid in for questioning. He states that he can think of *no* sexual act that causes psychic damage—"not even incest or bestiality...." "Homosexuality is a gift from God and should be celebrated.[78]

When he gave this speech, Shanley represented "sexual minorities" for the archdiocese of Boston to the Young Adult Ministry Board of the United States Catholic Conference (the national organization of Catholic bishops). Shanley was consistent in his rejection of Catholic morality; the homosexuals who heard him in 1977 (expressing no disagreement and taking him as their spokesman) are now embarrassed and want to put some distance between themselves and Shanley.

Mean-spirited conservatives must have written to the Vatican about the updated morality that Shanley was espousing at gatherings of homosexuals (and in the pages of the liberal *National Catholic Reporter*) because Medeiros found it necessary to write a long letter in response to a 1979 inquiry from Cardinal Franjo Seper, Cardinal Ratzinger's predecessor at the Sacred Congregation for the Doctrine of the Faith. In it he discussed the homosexual movement and its effect on the seminaries.

Shanley may have studied moral theology from the books of André Guindon (see p. 457). Presumably because his views were known, Shanley was invited to speak at a gay conference in Boston on intergenerational sex, after which a caucus met and organized NAMBLA, the North American Man-Boy Love Association. Shanley's ideas echoed Guindon's assessment of pedophilia. A gay newspaper reported that Shanley

> told the story of a boy who was rejected by family and society, but helped by a boy-lover. When his parents found out about the relationship, however, the man was arrested, convicted, and sentenced to prison. "And there began the psychic demise of that kid," Shanley commented. "He had loved that man . . . it was only a brief and passing thing as far as the sex was concerned, but the love was deep and the gratitude for the man was deep, and when he realized that the indiscretion in the eyes of society and of the law had cost this man perhaps 20 years . . . the boy began to fall apart." Shanley concluded, "We have our convictions upside down if we are truly concerned with boys . . . the 'cure' does far more damage."[79]

Although his friends claim Shanley was not involved with NAMBLA, one of his accusers said that when he was sixteen in 1974 Shanley introduced him to "Socrates," one of the founders of NAMBLA. After Shanley was accused of pedophilia, "Socrates" defended him by saying he couldn't imagine Shanley having sex "with anyone under the age of twelve."[80] Socrates used a narrow definition of pedophilia, which did not include boys over twelve.

The Vatican expressed concern about such sentiments, and Medeiros admitted Shanley had a problem. Medeiros's solution in 1979 was to take Shanley out of the street ministry to runaways and homosexuals and to put him into a parish. Shanley was unhappy. He claimed the archdiocese was abandoning the outcast sexual minorities, and in any case whatever Shanley said about the positive value of homosexuality was mild compared to what was being said in the Boston seminaries: "I have been given a list of the theological 'updating' which occurs at St. John's Seminary and the St. William's Hall programs. Were I to release this to the press you would have to fire another half-dozen of your top priests since what they are saying is far more shocking than my poor offerings."[81] André Guindon's ideas seem to have been in general circulation (see pp. 457–458).

Medeiros refused to be blackmailed: "I shall pass over in amazed but laughable silence the threats you invoke against me concerning further public pronouncements—this time about our Seminary." Was Medeiros calling Shanley's bluff because he knew there was nothing shocking at the seminary, or because he knew that Shanley wouldn't go public? Medeiros then defended himself against the accusation that he was hurting homosexuals by transferring Shanley: "I reject completely your accusation that I am inflicting punishment on homosexuals and their families. In fact, if I continue to leave you in this work that is the worst damage that I could inflict on them in the long run."[82] Medeiros is correct: Shanley's distorted moral teachings (and his equally distorted actions) would harm homosexuals by encouraging them to continue in sinful and physically destructive behavior. But why did Medeiros think that parishioners would not also be harmed by Shanley? Why was being in a parish supposed to work a magical transformation of someone he knew to be a troubled priest? Why did Medeiros share the blindness that has almost universally afflicted clerics when it comes to dangers to children? Medeiros sent Paul Shanley, apologist for man-boy love, to the unsuspecting parishioners of St. John's/St. Jean in Newton.

According to an article in the *Boston Globe*, around 1980 Jackie Gauvreau, a choir member at St. John's, made the mistake of asking Shanley, her parish priest, to drive a troubled boy to the Department of Youth Services. When they got on the expressway, Shanley grabbed the boy's genitals and assured him that having sex with a man or a woman was no sin. The boy told Gauvreau, and Gauvreau tried to tell the chancery. They refused to listen. Bishop Thomas Daily told the receptionist to put her on hold for hours until she gave up. Gauvreau called forty times and was ignored. Gauvreau told three priests, Michael Doocey, Arthur Calter, and Joseph McGlone, all of whom did nothing. She told Cardinal Law twice. Once after a televised Mass, she told him face to face, "Paul Shanley, the priest at St. John's in Newton, molested a fifteen-year-old boy," and gave him her name and parish. Law said he would look into it but did nothing. She met him after another Mass and asked him: "Excuse me, but do you remember I told you that Paul Shanley molested a fifteen-year-old boy?" Law told her to call his bishops. She called and eventually met with Bishop John Mulcahy, who did nothing. She confronted Shanley and told him, "You're a child molester." He ignored her, and warned parishioners that someone was out to destroy him. She told parishioners, who were angry at her for attacking popular, charismatic Paul Shanley, and they made life miserable for her until she left the parish. Kathryn D'Agostino heard Gauvreau's warnings and explained that "I didn't believe her. I didn't think she was lying, but I thought she was deluded. From what I knew of this guy, I thought it was impossible." D'Agostino was a friend of the Fords, whose son Greg has accused Shanley of molesting him.[83]

As Gauvreau later said of Medeiros and "his cronies," "They dared to ignore me when all the while they knew this malicious man, this sadistic whore, was abusing and sodomizing children."[84] Allegations that Shanley was involved in NAMBLA were made publicly. In his 1981 book *The Homosexual Network: Private Lives and Public Policy*, Enrique T. Rueda reported that Shanley was among the religious leaders who, according to the *Gaysweek* article, "voiced their endorsement of love between man and boy."[85]

Shanley continued his heroic struggle against the repressive Catholic establishment. A seventeen-year-old boy, weak and recovering from a grave illness and surgery, had read the Bible during his convalescence. He came to Shanley to ask about the Holy Spirit. Shanley gave him a curt answer, and turned to a more interesting topic: sex. Shanley railed against Pope John Paul II, who was "out of touch with current theologians, and was morosely conservative particularly with regard to sexual ethics." Shanley got the boy upstairs in the rectory, and explained "that there were Catholic theologians, copies of whose books he had there, that were teaching that homosexual activity was not a sin." The boy slept at the rectory, and woke up, he reported, to discover Shanley "inserting his penis into my rectum."[86] Shanley claimed he was "a worker of God" and that the acts of abuse were sanctioned by God.

At St. John's/St. Jean the 1984 CCD class included Gregory Ford, Paul Busa, Anthony Driscoll (who sued the archdiocese), and another seven-year-old boy. This boy remembered Shanley taking him out of CCD class, and playing a game in which the boy would have to "taste" Shanley, that is, have oral sex with him. Shanley also penetrated the boy's anus with his finger, an action that Shanley usually performed while having sex. I have not referred to the statements by the three victims who sued, because they all based their claims on recovered memory. But the other alleged victims had not forgotten. Most of them did not know one another, and their statements all describe the same type of behavior that the victims who sued also described.

The archdiocese in 1990 took Shanley out of parish work, and his old classmate, now Bishop John McCormack, was in charge of him until McCormack left for New Hampshire in 1998. St. Anne's church in San Bernardino, California, was Shanley's next post. Bishop Banks (who later claimed to know nothing about the allegations against Shanley[87]) wrote to Philip Behan, the bishop of San Bernardino (whose current attitude toward his brother bishop Bernard Law might be called frosty) about Paul Shanley, "a priest in good standing": "I can assure you that Father Shanley has no problem that would be of concern to your diocese."[88] Shanley acted like a conservative; his parishioners said "he would often tackle difficult issues such as abortion from the pulpit and would always espouse standard church positions."[89] Shanley always knew what kind of image he needed to cultivate.

While he was working at St. Anne's, Shanley also said Mass at ski resorts. At one resort at Easter, 1990, he met Kevin English, tall, seventeen, and sexually confused, who thought he was homosexual and who (therefore?) wanted to be a priest. English sought advice; Shanley offered to help him. English remembered that "he said my body was for experimentation and that he was helping me discover myself. He was mentoring me."[90] The sex continued, according to English, for three years. English drove to Palm Springs and had sex with men from all over the world. English now suspects that Shanley was paid for this.

Shanley told English that he stayed in the priesthood for the money. Shanley was always pleading poverty to extract more and more money from the Boston archdiocese. He was getting about $1,500 monthly from Boston but English remembered that "he always had $500 bills in his pocket, took limousines[,] and drove a Lincoln Town Car." In December 1990 Shanley and his old friend the Rev. John J. White bought a gay guest house, Cabana Club Resort in Palm Springs (fifty miles from St. Anne's), where

White owned the Whispering Palms, "one of the friskier resorts," where "nude sunbathing was encouraged, and sex by the pool was permitted."[91] On weekends Shanley said Mass and conducted youth retreats at St. Anne's; on weekdays he immersed himself in the clothing-optional gay resort. White was also on disability retirement from Boston. He spent his time around the Greyhound bus station, trying to pick up black Marines (and occasionally getting beat up).[92] Jack Prey, a real estate agent in Palm Springs, said that Shanley and White had company: "There are the two priests who met at a seminary, fell in love, and bought a local condo. Other priests have bought homes together, vacationed, and secretly retired there."[93]

The bishops of Boston continued to hold Shanley's hand and defend him. They sent him (and White) monthly checks for disability. Bishop McCormack claimed to have no idea about their double life in California. Shanley was at the parish to which he was assigned only a few hours a week and stayed there only once or twice during the years he was stationed there.[94] The pastor at St. Anne's said Bishop McCormack didn't show any curiosity about where Shanley was the other ninety-five percent of his time. McCormack came to visit Shanley in 1991. McCormack claimed he stayed at the rectory; the pastor of St. Anne's said McCormack and Shanley went off together, and the only other place that we know of where Shanley had to stay was the gay resort he owned.

After this visit, Shanley wrote McCormack, portraying himself as an heroic dissenter, and reiterating that he could not take the Vatican-required oath that he would uphold Church teaching. His dissent from Catholic teaching on sexuality was well known to McCormack. He also made a curious remark: "Thank you for acting as go-between with Fred Ryan. Here's the latest batch." The Rev. Frederick Ryan, one-time vice-chancellor for the archdiocese of Boston, had an office covered with photos of male athletes. Ryan was twice accused of photographing male teenagers in the nude, and then molesting them.[95] Ryan was defrocked by the Vatican in March 2006. What did the "batch" consist of? There were other batches; this was the "latest." Why were they sent to McCormack and not directly to Ryan? Did McCormack also have an interest in the contents of this "batch?"

In 1993 someone who complained that Shanley had abused him in the 1960s phoned McCormack. McCormack found the call distressing: "He was mean to me. . . . He made me scared to death of him"; the caller, perhaps with a prophetic charism, "told me I would burn in hell for what just happened."[96] But McCormack was not going to let the fear of hell deter him from supporting Shanley, who was sinking deeper and deeper into the homosexual scene in California and who thought it an ideal place for Boston priests who needed a refuge from the law. Here is one of the exchanges: Shanley to McCormack: "I am anxious that public charges may be brought against me. Have you heard any more from the victims [note, not 'alleged victims' or 'accusers'] or lawyers?...I've heard no more from anyone about my proposal to offer a safe house for 'warehoused' priests."[97] McCormack to Shanley in a letter sent to the Cabana Club: "Regarding your idea of a safe house, it is an idea that I have been thinking about for some time. We even have a place in mind."[98] What were they hoping to keep abusive priests safe from: irate parents, publicity, subpoenas, arrests?

In late 1993 Shanley was sent to the Institute of Living in Hartford, Connecticut, for evaluation. The Boston archdiocese has refused to release this evaluation, but other released files show that Shanley admitted to nine sexual encounters, of which four involved boys, and that he was diagnosed as "narcissistic" and "histrionic."[99] Shanley admitted that he was "attracted to adolescents" and on the basis of this confession the Boston archdiocese secretly settled several lawsuits against Shanley.[100] The archdiocese of Boston in 1993 had to admit to the diocese of San Bernardino part of the truth about Shanley, and the bishop of San Bernardino (not having been to seminary with Shanley) immediately dismissed him.

McCormack sent Shanley (and other abusive priests), or to be more exact, Shanley's partial file, to Rev. Dr. Edwin Cassem (see pp. 317ff.). Cassem wanted to examine Shanley, but McCormack warned him that Shanley would be "terribly threatened by this and uncooperative with the effort."[101] Cassem seemed to be the perfect psychiatrist: he was a Jesuit and former chief of psychiatry at Massachusetts General Hospital. What McCormack did not send to Cassem was all the pertinent background information about Shanley, such as his speech before the formative meeting of the North American Man-Boy Love Association. Cassem later said he was "appalled" that the Boston archdiocese had not sent him that information. If he had known it, he would have recommended that Shanley be "laicized and jailed." Having learned more about Shanley, Cassem did not like him: "He was a notorious, dangerous pedophile." Cassem continued that Shanley "was a predator. He was a scumbag . . . castration was too good for him."[102] This was not what McCormack wanted to hear about his old classmate Shanley, so he thought Cassem should not know about Shanley's interesting background.

In 1995, Francis Pilecki invited Shanley to work at Leo House in New York. Pilecki had this job at a Catholic Charities-supported hotel because he had lost his former job as president of Westfield State College. He had to resign that position because two male students there accused him of molesting them.[103] Pilecki had met Shanley at McLean Hospital in the 1980s, where Pilecki was a psychiatric patient being treated for depression after being charged with sexually assaulting male college students; Shanley was a chaplain. They had a lot in common. Pilecki had been a friend of Bruce Ritter of Covenant House, with whom he shared an interest in young males. Pilecki later pleaded guilty to molesting a thirteen-year-old boy.[104] Shanley was looking for a place to hide, but an accuser tracked him down and called Sister Karlin at Leo House, who in December 1995 wrote to Law: the caller "openly said Fr. Paul Shanley was a child molester and we had better be aware. Here am I with this time bomb. Would you be so kind as to clarify Fr. Paul's integrity and reputation and character?"[105] Shanley denied the accusations, and Rev. Brian Flatley of the Boston archdiocese called Sister Karlin and soothed her fears. Flatley also tried to soothe Shanley: he told him that Leo House was "a good placement" for him, but there are "concerns, notably about the nature of Father Shanley's relationship with a young man who is his roommate," and fears that an openly gay employee (Dale Legace, "very small and pretty," was "obsessed with Judy Garland and Liza Minnelli"[106]) might give the impression that Leo House might become known as "a gay hotel."[107] Flatley had told the vice chancellor of

New York, Msgr. Edward D. O'Donnell, that in 1993 "it became known...that Father Shanley had a past history of aberrant sexual involvements,"[108] but the two priests did not share this information with the nuns who ran Leo House.[109]

When Shanley finally had to retire in 1996, Law wrote: "For thirty years in assigned ministry you brought God's word and his love to his people, and I know that continues to be your goal despite some difficult limitations. This is an impressive record and all of us are truly grateful for your priestly care and ministry to all whom you have served during those years. Without a doubt over all of these years of generous and zealous care, the lives and hearts of many people have been touched by your sharing of the Lord's spirit. You are truly appreciated for all that you have done."[110]

Pilecki retired in 1997, and Shanley wanted to succeed him as director of Leo House. Law drafted a letter in June 1997 to Cardinal O'Connor, referring to "some controversy from his past," but concluded that "if you decide to allow Father Shanley to accept this position, I would not object."[111] But O'Connor was afraid of bad publicity (not of harm to children) and Shanley did not get the job. He began to lament "my days here are numbered. Shortly I will be without a job or a place to live."[112] Of course he had his pension, paid for by the donations of the families whose children he had allegedly molested in Boston and he also had the proceeds from the sale of his gay resort in Palm Springs. Shanley complained to Cardinal Law about the trouble his victims were causing him: "As you know, I continue to be stalked and harassed, a predicament that could ultimately undermine my ability to function here. Your letter of encouragement came like a bolt out of the blue, entirely unexpected, bringing tears to my eyes."[113] Cardinal Law never wrote to any of the victims; his solicitude was reserved for abusive priests.

Shanley and his longtime companion, Dale Legace (twenty-one years his junior), moved to San Diego at the start of 1998 and rented an apartment on Albatross Street in Hillcrest, a gay section, where he introduced his neighbors to opera and worked as a volunteer for the police (the Boston archdiocese is not the only clueless organization). In March 2002, Shanley and White decided to take a vacation in Thailand, internationally known for its child prostitution.[114] Shanley had been there before.

Shanley's victim Paul Busa, by 2002 an Air Force policeman in Colorado, went to the police, and a warrant was issued for Shanley. The police in San Diego, acting on a fugitive warrant, arrested Shanley on May 2, 2002. Shanley was indicted on sixteen counts of child abuse involving four boys. On July 10, he pleaded not guilty. The archdiocese of Boston announced in May 2004 that Paul Shanley had been removed from the priesthood by Pope John Paul II forty-four years after he was ordained and forty-three years after the first alleged abuse. Sister Jeannine Gramick, whose ministry to homosexuals had attracted the scrutiny of the Vatican, called his removal "grossly unfair."[115] Shanley's other accusers dropped out of the trial, leaving Busa as Shanley's sole accuser, and his accusations were based on recovered memory. Nevertheless, the jury found Busa's testimony convincing, and on February 7, 2005, Shanley was convicted of sexual abuse.

Priests in the archdiocese of Boston repeatedly abused children and adolescents with the full knowledge of the bishops of Boston. The bishops usually did nothing except transfer the abusive priests; the bishops occasionally sent a priest for treatment but usually neglected to tell the therapist all the facts; they ignored complaints from the laity, whom they obviously regarded as interlopers. The mystery is why sexual abuse was regarded by the bishops as such a trivial matter. Massachusetts Attorney General Thomas F. Reilly concluded that the bishops "didn't seem to recognize the wrongfulness of it."[116] Boston set the tone for the entire New England province, which has a lengthy history of abusive priests and remarkably patient bishops.

CHAPTER SEVEN

# THE SCOPE OF DESTRUCTION: NEW ENGLAND

SEXUAL ABUSE BY CLERGY is not confined to a few cities or states or even countries; however, New England stands out as a major hub of abuse. Perhaps this is an illusion created by the diligence of the *Boston Globe* and by the successful concealment of cases in other cities. Perhaps Irish alcoholism and clericalism created the conditions in which a priest could abuse with impunity, because everyone understood that Father had problems and no one would accuse Father publicly of diddling with children, lest the Prots attack the Church. The corruption in the dioceses of New England is breathtaking: every clerical vice, up to and including vehicular homicide and perhaps murder, was known about, "understood," and tolerated. Geoghan and Shanley were not unique. The New England Province had scores of priest-malefactors, some of whose behavior bordered on madness.

## *Boston*

The candidate for the most certifiable is Rev. Robert V. Meffan, who styled himself the "second coming of Christ." He was, he said, "Christ," and the young women aspiring to enter the convent were the "brides of Christ"; he reminded them of what brides were supposed to do. He explained to a reporter that "what I was trying to show them is that Christ is human and you should love him as a human being. Don't think he's up there and he's spiritual and he's not human and physical. He's human, he's physical, that's what I was trying to point out to them. I felt by having this little bit of intimacy with them that this is what it would be like with Christ. . . . It was a very beautiful, I thought, beautiful spiritual relationship that was physical and sexual."[1] Bishop John M. D'Arcy thought Meffan was mad. Meffan wrote to Cardinal Bernard Law to protest his eventual suspension, claiming that he was "a prisoner of love in a sea of allegations." Law responded that these comments were "a beautiful testament to the depth of your faith and the courage of your heart."[2]

In 1975 a Dominican warned that Rev. Thomas P. Forry's housekeeper lived in fear of her life. Bishop D'Arcy wrote a letter in 1978 also warning about Forry's temper. It was ignored. D'Arcy wrote another letter to Cardinal Humberto Medeiros, complaining that he had been ignored, and that the parishioners had a priest with "severe emotional problems."[3] Forry admitted that he had a fight with his housekeeper in 1979 during which he bruised her, cut her, and tore the hair from her scalp. He then tried to keep her quiet by threatening "to come back some night from his home in South Boston, assault her again, and then get people in South Boston to say he never left South Boston."[4] D'Arcy warned Law, but Law transferred Forry to another parish.

In 1984 a woman who said she was sexually involved with Forry claimed that Forry had abused her son. Her estranged husband also accused Forry of abusing the boy but backed off when Forry threatened to have his friends kill the husband. In 1988 Law allowed Forry to join the army as a paratrooper chaplain, neglecting to bring up any of the incidents and allegations, at least in writing. There his aggression was put to good use when he served in the Gulf War; one day he "fearlessly faced down and disarmed a distraught soldier,"[5] but unfortunately for Cardinal Law Forry survived and in 1992 returned to Boston. A woman complained Forry had beaten her son, that he had abandoned her, and that she was dying of AIDS. Forry had to pay $10,000 toward a settlement with the woman but in 1995 was back in ministry. In 1999 Forry was a prison chaplain, engaged in "screaming and shouting and exhibiting emotional and behavioral problems"[6] such as shoving a piece of food into a nun's mouth.

The Rev. James D. Foley, a classmate of Bishop John B. McCormack, was undoubtedly heterosexual: he had two children. Rita Perry, a married woman suffering from depression, came to him in the early 1960s; he counseled her in bed, as he had counseled other women. An annoyed Cardinal Richard Cushing exiled Foley to Calgary, where he had, as McCormack put it, "growing up issues,"[7] including an affair with a nineteen-year-old woman and visits from Rita Perry. Irate Canadian husbands forced Foley to return to Boston in 1968, where he took up again with Rita Perry, who was separated on and off from her husband. At first Perry did not recognize Foley because she had had a lobotomy. She cannot give her side of the story; she is dead. A later archdiocesan memo summarized what was revealed in a 1993 meeting between Foley and Law with McCormack attending: "[Foley] [h]ad two children in '65 and relationships married woman—overdosed while he was present—started to faint—he clothed—left came back—called 911—she died—a sister knows—Needham."[8] That is, Foley went to bed with the woman; she overdosed on barbiturates and passed out. He got dressed and left her with a three-year-old girl. He returned, found her dead, called 911 anonymously, and left.[9] The policeman who responded found the woman's body and the crying baby. The children Foley had fathered were raised by the woman's husband; they had no suspicions about Foley until they saw his story on television and later a court-ordered DNA test proved he was the father of two of the four children of Rita Perry.[10]

In 1993 after the new sexual abuse policy (prompted by the Porter scandal) was put into place, Law and McCormack finally reviewed Foley's past when Foley applied for renewal of his position as pastor. Law at first was horrified and wanted Foley to spend the rest of his life in a monastery "doing penance."[11] Foley complained, "But why am I being asked to resign? Is it because at sixty-one years old, I am now being considered an unstable womanizer who is a threat to my parishioners? I have never been a womanizer to begin with, and it is inconceivable that I should ever be seduced again into an unhealthy relationship of any kind."[12] McCormack persuaded Law to put Foley back in a parish. Foley knew he was above the law, like the other criminous clerics in Boston. In 1996 police stopped him for driving the wrong way on one-way streets. "He was running red lights thinking they were red only for other people."[13] Foley was not suspended until 2002, when his name hit the newspapers.

Bishop John McCormack and Rev. Joseph E. Birmingham served together in the 1960s as priests at St. James' parish in Salem. There, Birmingham molested James Hogan. According to Hogan, Birmingham called him out of class at the parish school into a conference room and fondled him. Hogan also said that he is certain that McCormack "knew he was a frequent visitor to Birmingham's bedroom upstairs at the rectory,"[14] where Birmingham and the boy had oral sex. McCormack said he had no memory of such incidents. In 1968 the boys at the parish school wrote a letter to Cardinal Cushing complaining that they were tired of Birmingham "sticking his hands down their pants."[15] He would take the boys for rides to get ice cream; the last one to be dropped off would have to pay for the favor. After Birmingham molested him, he would ask the boy, "Does that feel good? Don't you think you might like boys?"[16] The boys made up a chant, "Father B.s a queer, that is what we hear."[17] Parents later complained about Birmingham to McCormack, who told them to take it up with the pastor.

In 1970, Mary McGee and four other mothers met with Rev. John J. Jennings, director of priests' personnel for the archdiocese, to complain about Birmingham. His closing comment was, "Ladies, you have to be very careful of slander."[18] When the principal of St. James' school complained about Birmingham, Jennings called her "a meddlesome female."[19] The Rev. Patrick Kelly wrote to the archdiocesan personnel office in 1970 about Birmingham. He confronted Birmingham with the "rumor of possible homosexuality."[20] Birmingham denied it, but Kelly and the principal suspected it was true. All Kelly recommended was that Birmingham be transferred. In Lowell, where he was stationed after 1970, Birmingham was questioned by the police about a rape case. He admitted to molesting boys in the past, but insisted he was "cured," although he had never been treated.[21]

In 1985, despite all the complaints, Law made Birmingham pastor of St. Ann's church in Gloucester, where he again molested boys. In April 1987 Birmingham was in treatment for pedophilia at the Institute of Living. McCormack had just received a letter about him and had also received a complaint from a parent. McCormack wrote to the father that he had met with Birmingham and "there is absolutely no factual basis to your concern regarding your son and him. From my knowledge of Father Birmingham and my relationship with him, I feel he would tell me the truth."[22] When asked in his deposition to explain why he had said that to the father, despite his knowledge that Birmingham had been accused of abuse, McCormack replied, "I just can't explain it."[23]

In 1989 Birmingham died. Thomas Blanchette had reconciled with Birmingham before his death (see p. 486) and approached Cardinal Law, who was saying the funeral Mass, and told him that Birmingham had abused him. Law invoked the seal of the confessional over Blanchette in an attempt to keep the abuse secret. Law has only vague memories of the meeting (as of so much else).

Ronald H. Paquin was born in 1942 and raised in a poor French Canadian community. At age eleven he was raped by three boys. After the death of his father when he was thirteen years old, Paquin sought consolation with the Rev. Bernard St. Hilaire, junior priest in the French parish of St. John the Baptist in Lynn, north of Boston. When Paquin was fifteen years old (in another version Paquin said twenty years old) they began a sexual relationship that lasted nine years (or perhaps thirty, in another version that Paquin told). They knew each other's vices. Paquin was once in a car with St. Hilaire while St. Hilaire was abusing a boy.[24] St. Hilaire died in 1977. While Paquin was still in the seminary he began molesting boys.[25] He was ordained in 1973 and went to St. Monica's church in Methuen, a parish with a large school, where he was put in charge of the altar boys, the Catholic Youth Organization, and the Boy Scouts. A victim there, Robert Bartlett, reminisced of Paquin that "he was so young. He was so cool."[26] Paquin drove a sports car which he let underage boys drive; he also gave them beer and marijuana. He wanted something from them in return. He invited them into his room, talked about girls, watched television, and slowly progressed to mutual masturbation and oral sex. Boys sometimes balked, but Paquin frequently quoted his favorite Bible verse: "You should not favor one body part over another."[27] Catholics can often be a little vague on the Bible, and the boys did not recognize this verse was a complete fabrication.

Bishop McCormack in a memo in 1991 described Paquin's approach: "At around age twelve or thirteen, Father Paquin would gather around a group of boys who would be friendly with him.... He would invite them down to the rectory frequently. Often they would be encouraged to sleep overnight.... The boys he surrounded himself with were vulnerable boys whose folks were separated, divorced, or as in [one] instance, his father was in prison. When they slept overnight he would ask different boys to sleep with him in bed."[28] The boys had been raised to do whatever Father told them to do, and couldn't imagine he would ask them to do anything wrong.

In 1976 John J. Facella told the Rev. Allan E. Roche, the pastor of St. Monica's, that Paquin had molested his son Tony. Roche told Facella that "I shouldn't report it to the police, that it would come down to Tony's word against a priest, and that with my wife dying at home, I already had too much on my plate."[29] Roche said he would take care of it; he didn't. Robert Bartlett remembered having sex with Paquin in 1978. Two eighth-grade boys knocked on the door and Paquin asked Bartlett to stay and join in the fun. That was too much for Bartlett, who ran downstairs and told Roche, who ran upstairs to stop the orgy. The only consequence for Paquin was that he couldn't have boys in his room any longer. Roche was aware of the abuse but did not stop it because he was near retirement, and it would have caused too much trouble to intervene, he explained in 1995.[30] Paquin began a relationship with another preteen boy at St. Monica's church, and it continued after the boy entered St. John's Seminary in Boston.[31]

In 1981 Paquin was transferred to St. John the Baptist parish in Haverhill, where Rev. Francis J. O'Neill had recently become pastor, and that November Paquin took four boys to New Hampshire. After a night of sex and alcohol Paquin drove the boys home; he fell asleep at the wheel and the car overturned, crushing and killing sixteen-year-old James Francis.[32] Paquin continued as the associate pastor of St. John the Baptist. His old pastor O'Neill died in 1988 and the replacement, Rev. Garrett J. Barry, was almost immediately demoted and sent to another parish. Rev. Frederick Sweeney arrived in 1990 as the new pastor. Judge James Sweeney (Frederick Sweeney's brother) and the Rev. Dennis T. Nason persuaded the archdiocese to remove Paquin. In 1990 Law took Paquin out of the parish and sent him to St. Luke Institute in Suitland for treatment. In 1998 Law assigned Paquin as chaplain to the Youville Hospital, although someone had already complained that Paquin had abused him when the victim was a patient at another hospital. Paquin was living at Our Lady's Hall, an archdiocesan priests' residence, and bringing a boy there for sex (see p. 306).

Paquin admitted to the newspapers only the incidents of abuse that fell outside the statute of limitations. But a boy whom he befriended and abused hundreds of times went to the police; Paquin was criminally charged, pleaded guilty in 2002, and was sentenced to twelve to fifteen years for raping the boy.[33] In court the victim told Paquin that "you created a world for me where I believed that 'it's normal for boys to shower with their fathers,' a world where 'fathers and sons' are supposed to share these sexual acts."[34] Paquin had told him that these sexual experiences were part of a psychological study of the sexuality of boys. The victim continued, "You don't deserve to ever call yourself father or priest. I'm ashamed that I allowed you to marry my wife [and me] and I am ashamed that I let you continue to be my friend after all that happened. You manipulated my parents, my friends, and me. You did this to me for so long. May my prayers be answered that you and people like you rot in hell."[35] This victim saw justice done.

But not all of Paquin's victims lived long enough to see this justice. In 1999 John Wain's body was found on the grounds of St. Basil's Seminary in Methuen.[36] John and Joseph Wain had settled a civil suit against Paquin but the mental torture remained, and John had committed suicide; James Francis had been crushed to death. Two victims were dead because of Paquin—at least two.

Unmarried clerics were not the only abusers of boys in the Boston archdiocese. Christopher Reardon grew up in St. Agnes parish in Middleton, Massachusetts, twenty miles north of Boston. He got his bachelor's degree from Franklin Pierce College in 1994 and his master's degree from Springfield College, both in recreation. He was married in 1999 (but never consummated the marriage), worked at St. Agnes parish and the YMCA, where he taught swimming and ran a summer camp with his wife, and volunteered with the Boy Scouts.

Reardon won the confidence of boys and parents. The parents invited him to dinner, attended his wedding, and sent their sons to him for swimming or religious instruction. He led the boys on slowly. He gave them his cell phone number, the key to his house, and the code to his home security system. He first showed "his young 'friends' pornographic magazines and videotapes he lugged around in a blue L. L. Bean backpack." Then he "convinced the boys to experiment with sex toys and engage in mutual masturbation." Finally he was "able to convince some of the boys into sexual contact."[37] He told them, "Don't worry, it's natural. It's what guys do to get ready for girls in college."[38] He threatened uncooperative boys with banishment from the YMCA and also showed them lists of other boys who had cooperated. He persuaded them to keep quiet or else he would get them into trouble. The boys said they were embarrassed to tell their parents.

Reardon had control issues, like many pedophiles, and was a compulsive recordkeeper. He kept a list, with sexually explicit details about their bodies, of 250 boys. Using a camera hidden in the rectory ceiling he made a videotape of himself and a twelve-year-old boy masturbating while watching a pornographic film. In his closet at home, he had "photographs of nude children, inflatable dolls, electric sex toys[,] and lubricants."[39] Police also found "cups of semen," "instructions . . . on how to have sex with young boys and how to overcome their reluctance."[40] He had notes about the North American Man-Boy Love Association (NAMBLA). Reardon justified the abuse by claiming he was "simply acting as a sex teacher."[41]

In 1999 some boys walked by Reardon's house and screamed, "Child molester!" A neighbor's child asked her mother why they did that; the mother told the child Reardon was not a molester but just worked with boys at church.[42] At his house, Reardon tossed an eleven-year-old on the bed and raped him. In August 1999 the Rev. Richard A. Driscoll told Rev. Jon C. Martin, the pastor at St. Agnes, that Reardon was behaving suspiciously with boys.[43]

At the beginning of 2000 a female worker notified James Flanagan, an official of the archdiocese's Youth Ministry, that she was concerned about Reardon's behavior around boys. Flanagan told her to talk to Martin. She did, but he dismissed her concerns "as gossip."[44] But Martin said he told Vicar General Bishop Francis X. Irwin in the chancery about Reardon. On June 9, 2000, a boy went to the police. On June 10, at a church picnic he had organized, Reardon was arrested and was led away in handcuffs.

In August 2002 Reardon pleaded guilty to seventy-five charges of child rape, indecent assault, and giving pornography to a child. He was sentenced to forty to fifty years in prison. The victims testified how he had hurt them. One was unforgiving: "My hope is you are gang-raped [in prison] so you know how we all feel and my other wish is that you spend the rest of your life in jail."[45] Even after the conviction some of his victims still liked him. One said that "we sent cards. He's still my friend, but I don't respect him as much anymore."[46] Traumatic bonding is one of the mysterious effects of abuse (see pp. 271ff.).

Reardon was supervised by the pastor of St. Agnes, the Rev. Jon C. Martin. At the Sunday Mass after the arrest, Martin told the parish children that "people we love sometimes do hurt us, and we have to forgive them."[47] "'We love you Father,' one man shouted as the congregation rose to its feet in a standing ovation."[48]

Martin had problems of his own. He claimed that he had been abused as a child. Someone had told the archdiocese that Martin had molested a fourteen-tear-old boy in 1965; Martin denied the allegation.[49] Reardon abused boys a few feet from Martin's study and bedroom, while Martin, the chaplain of the Middletown jail, was busy demonstrating the proper use of condoms to the young male ex-prisoners who slept over in his bed at the rectory. One of the men had followed Martin from parish to parish for a decade. One victim reported that he heard Martin and Reardon discussing sex in late 1999. Martin "grabbed his crotch and told Reardon that he was going to the prison to 'get some,' referring to sex with inmates."[50] Martin admitted that the housekeepers found used condoms in his bed, but said they were from private study. The Rogers Law Firm, the archdiocesan house attorneys, came around two weeks after Reardon was arrested to discourage the staff and parishioners from saying anything: "They seemed most concerned about the condom. [One lawyer] asked us not even to speak among ourselves, not to talk even to each other."[51] The Rogers Law Firm also tried to dissuade the Essex County district attorney from investigating Martin, who resigned from St. Agnes and made himself scarce, but who was eventually found at Cardinal Law's compound in Brighton.

## *Manchester*

At least forty priests, about ten percent of the clergy who have served in the diocese of Manchester, New Hampshire (which comprises the entire state), have sexually abused minors.

In 1970 Paul L. Aube was ordained. At his first parish he had sex with three boys who were between the ages of sixteen and eighteen; one relationship began within days of the priest's arrival. Aube disliked his own behavior, and he asked for advice from his pastor (now deceased). The pastor consoled him: "Well, Paul, we're all human, you know. We have weaknesses."[52] One widowed mother asked Aube to help her twelve-year-old son; Aube taught him to masturbate and then taught him how to perform oral sex. The boy eventually complained to his mother, who slapped him and told him not to lie.

At his next parish Aube had sex with five boys between the ages of sixteen and eighteen. One altar boy was impressed by Aube's ability to read minds (Aube used information he had learned through confession). He cultivated the boy, and they began having oral sex in the rectory. Aube had a stable of victims, to whom he gave a special cross to wear to demonstrate that they had gone through a "rite of passage" and had the "favor of a priest."[53]

In 1975 the Nashua police department found Aube with his pants down in a car with an eighteen-year-old, John Doe LII, whom Aube knew from his church youth group. Bishop Odore J. Gendron learned of this and referred Aube for counseling; the bishop also made sure that no record of the incident appeared in police records. Dr. J. Edward Connors, a psychologist the diocese used for consultations, had grave doubts about Aube: "His past and present history seems to predict episodic difficulties and there may be deep defects in the basic personality structure which are not amenable to psychiatric treatment with any great hope for a change."[54] Aube himself also said that he no longer wanted to work in a parish or with youth, but over his objections the diocese assigned him to youth ministry, where he assaulted seven boys. In 1981 the diocese learned that Aube was having sex with a sixteen-year-old boy (this time in the rectory rather than in a car).

Aube and the boys identified their relationships as homosexual. These were warm, affectionate relationships with a religious tinge. Aube told one boy that he had a "'Christ-like' love for him" and that Aube, like Christ, would die for him.[55] Aube used Bible passages to convince another boy to have sex.

In 1981 Aube again went to Bishop Gendron and asked for help in controlling himself. Gendron referred him to a psychiatrist but did not put any restrictions on his ministry. The psychiatrist recommended that Aube be transferred to hospital ministry and wrote the bishop that "it should be firmly pointed out to Father Aube, that sexual intimacies of any type with a minor in the State of New Hampshire, is considered a felony, and can result in a significant prison term."[56] But no one reported these felonies to the state, as required by state law. The diocese instead assigned Aube to hospitals, where he assaulted boys.

When a victim contacted the diocese in 1983, they responded that the first allegation against Aube was in 1981. This was not true; the diocese knew of the police incident in 1975. Aube's faculties were finally revoked in 1994. He cooperated, claiming that he had asked his bishop for help in controlling his abusive urges and that he had paid for his psychological treatment. He acknowledged his guilt: "I know what my Lord stands for, I know what my church stands for, and I know what I want to stand for, and I betrayed that. But I did whatever I could to rectify it. And I'm proud of that."[57] Former Manchester bishops Gendron and Francis J. Christian refused to cooperate with investigators unless they were given immunity from criminal prosecution.[58]

In 1952, in the pre-Vatican II era, Gerard F. Chalifour was ordained. About ten years later, he started having sex with adolescent boys. The diocese knew this, but it did not try to control him in any way. Chalifour once took a boy on a trip and tried to molest him in a hotel room. The boy fled to the lobby and called his parents, telling them, "Chalifour is 'gay and he's after me.'"[59] The parents called the police, who picked up the boy from the hotel. This police report, like the initial one on Aube, is missing from police files. The parents met with Bishop Gendron, who asked them what they wanted him to do about it. They left it up to the bishop, who spoke with Chalifour and sent him to therapy. Nothing else was done. The abuse continued, and the diocese threatened Chalifour with more therapy. Only after a victim filed a lawsuit did the diocese send Chalifour to the Servants of the Paraclete in New Mexico.

Although a member of his family had approached the diocese to warn them that he was an active homosexual, Roger A. Fortier was ordained in 1980. By 1984 the police were suspicious and questioned Fortier. Fortier told the police that he was a homosexual, that he had showed boys pornographic movies, and that he had given them beer. Fortier was assigned to another parish and began working with youth. In February 1993 Fortier was appointed a pastor, and in June of the same year sent to the Servants of the Paraclete in St. Louis because of his homosexual activities. Fortier continued having sex with boys (and others). Fortier was arrested, tried, and convicted, but the diocese continued to lie in an attempt to help him. Bishop Christian wrote to the parole and probation office that the diocese had no knowledge of any sexual problems with youth.[60]

When Gordon J. MacRae was at St. Mary's Seminary in Baltimore in 1978, the rector received a therapist's assessment that he should not accept MacRae, but he shopped around for another therapist and bought a better assessment. In 1983 MacRae began sexual play with a thirteen-year-old boy. A priest once came into the rectory room and saw MacRae and the boy kissing; the priest left and said nothing. The boy told another priest what was going on. The priest told the boy to "go home and reconsider" this claim.[61] The boy told a social worker from Catholic Charities, Judith Patterson, about the sex play; she decided this was "clear-cut sexual abuse."[62] Patterson talked to her superior and to Father John Quinn, who was head of Catholic Charities, and told him that these incidents would be reported to the state. Quinn tried to convince Patterson the boy was lying.

Quinn claimed there was a special way of handling this: first the bishop would be told, and he would tell the state. Quinn spoke with Bishop Gendron, who met with Sylvio Dupuis, the commissioner of the department of welfare, who in turn referred it to the division of children and family services. But Msgr. (later Bishop) Christian swore under oath that Gendron never met with Dupuis. The authorities did not conduct an investigation and concluded that the therapy to which MacRae had been sent was enough to resolve the situation.

MacRae shared one victim with other men in the rectory. The victim went into the army and after he was discharged moved in with MacRae in 1988. He told MacRae that he needed money and MacRae told him he could make some money by just lying flat. The young man moved out and told a police detective about MacRae's suggestion.

MacRae befriended a boy whose parents were separated and started having sex with him. The boy began abusing drugs and alcohol. MacRae arranged for him to go to the Derby Lodge, a treatment facility, where the boy told a counselor about MacRae. The counselor could not believe it and told MacRae, who threatened to kill the boy if he told anyone again.

MacRae worked as a counselor at Spofford Hall, another drug and alcohol treatment facility. In 1988 a patient told the state police that MacRae had fondled him during counseling. The diocese suspended MacRae's faculties. At this time MacRae told a fourteen-year-old boy about an easy way to make money and about a friend "who earned $600 an hour acting as a male prostitute."[63] The boy was not interested, but later in the year the boy needed money, and allowed MacRae to take nude photos of him for twenty dollars. The police found out, and MacRae was convicted of a misdemeanor, sexual solicitation. He was sent to the House of Affirmation, which warned that he "has little awareness of the impact of the behavior upon the adolescents."[64] The diocese then sent MacRae to the Servants of the Paraclete in New Mexico, where strange things happened.

MacRae stayed there one year, 1989–90. The director, Rev. Dr. Peter Lechner, sent Bishop Gendron the reports on MacRae in April 1989, and Bishop Gendron responded, "I will, as you request, destroy the various psychological reports you included."[65] Dr. Lechner rejected the assessments that the psychiatrists in the East had made; he thought MacRae showed "a depth of conscientiousness and sensitivity to others, and a very high degree of ethical concern."[66] In fact, the Servants of the Paraclete were so impressed by MacRae that they hired him as an assistant director. This was in line with their habit of employing criminals (see Feit, p. 310). Even after MacRae was convicted, the Paracletes offered Bishop McCormack money to help MacRae fight the conviction. At the trial the Servants of the Paraclete sent the Rev. David Deibel[67] to assist MacRae. At the end of the trial, the judge thanked everyone, both friend and foe of MacRae, but singled out Deibel for some pointed comments: "I found, with the exception of Father David Deibel, the priest and lawyer, that you all spoke in good faith, whether I agreed with what you said or not. I believe that Father Deibel attempted to mislead the Court, that he intentionally minimized the behavior of Gordon MacRae, and that he is not a credible witness. I hope and trust he is not representative of the attitudes of the governing body of the Catholic [C]hurch concerning sexual predators within its clergy."[68]

Full of self-pity for his sentence, in 1999 MacRae wrote the Vatican and complained that the diocese of Manchester had not helped him enough. Bishop McCormack wrote to the Vatican to explain that the "extent of the guilt or the innocence of Gordon MacRae is difficult to establish, even though the civil court found him guilty." McCormack explained that public opinion prevented the diocese from offering MacRae open support, but it "supported him privately with funds." McCormack worried about the punishment this poor man was suffering: "Some believe his prison sentence is unduly harsh and lengthy," and "his lengthy jail sentence is even more inappropriate given his rehabilitation."[69] Bishop Christian in a memo chimed in with his sympathy: "The sentencing . . . was not proportionate to the sentencing in similar cases."[70] Gordon MacRae is serving a sentence of sixty-seven years for his abuse.

McCormack in September 2002 told the parishioners that the man he had appointed their pastor in June 2002, Rev. Roland P. Cote, had a homosexual relationship with a teenager, but not to worry: the boy was over eighteen years old (probably). As Cote explained, "It did not involve a minor or a parishioner."[71] (The "Officer, he *said* he was 18" defense.)

In December 2002 the diocese of Manchester admitted it may have violated the criminal law when it failed to protect children from abusive priests. Bishop John McCormack signed an agreement that the attorney general had enough evidence to convict: "evidence likely to sustain a conviction of a charge...against the diocese."[72] The possible offenses were endangering a child, contributing to the delinquency of a minor, failing to report child abuse, perjury, and compounding felonies. Until 2007 the diocese must submit its personnel records to the attorney general for an audit. By the end of 2003 the diocese of Manchester had paid out $18.8 million to victims of sexual abuse by its priests. Bishop McCormack has refused to heed numerous calls to resign.

## *Springfield*

The diocese of Springfield, Massachusetts, has the distinction of long paying a pension to a registered sex offender, Rev. Richard R. Lavigne, who is strongly suspected of murdering one of his victims.[73] In the Springfield parishes where he worked after his 1966 ordination, many people found him "outstanding" and "inspirational."[74] But the father of an abuse victim has given a succinct characterization of this priest: "He's a creature from hell."[75]

Bishop Christopher J. Weldon started getting complaints about Lavigne's behavior in the late 1960s.[76] Lavigne invited boys to his rectory or his parents' house, plied them with liquor, and molested them. As victim Kenneth Chevalier describes what happened to him in the late 1960s, "I remember going to the parish rectory . . . and we slept in his room. My brother and I weren't there at the same time. He [Lavigne] would give us a large T-shirt to sleep in and he would sleep in the same bed. . . . He would scratch our backs and tickle us real soft with his hands and fondle me . . . on my private parts."[77] He also had the boys steal antiques for him from farms and barns in the area.[78]

Lavigne molested the boys in the Croteau family. On April 12, 1972, thirteen-year-old Danny Croteau spent the night at the rectory, and the next day he went out at 3 P.M. and was never seen alive again. At 2:30 A.M. his parents reported him missing; at 8:30 A.M. the police called and said his body had been found in a stream. His head had been bashed in with a rock. There were signs of a violent struggle. Lavigne went with Danny's father to identify the body and said the funeral Mass for him. The police quickly identified Lavigne as a suspect for the following reasons:[79]

- Three years earlier Lavigne had taken boys on a camping trip to molest them and then joined with the boys in teasing the then-ten-year-old Croteau, who twice said, "I'll tell."
- Croteau's best friend remembered that "we played street hockey a lot. I can remember very clearly that on many occasions, we would be in the middle of a game . . . everybody would be having a good time, all of a sudden I would see Danny crying and I would look up to Prouty Street, which was about five houses away, and see Father Lavigne parked in the big four-door car."
- Lavigne at first claimed he was never alone with Croteau, but then admitted that the week before the murder Croteau had spent the night with Lavigne at Lavigne's parents' house.
- Danny had twice the level of alcohol that qualifies as legal drunkenness. Lavigne regularly gave his victims alcohol, and then lied to the

parents that the boys had gotten into the liquor cabinet.

- Lavigne told investigators that he never gave Croteau any alcohol, but a friend of Croteau said that he gave the boys consecrated wine from the chalice after Mass and then, "Father Lavigne would always tell us to chew gum."
- Danny's stomach was full of wads of chewing gum.
- The police went to the rectory to examine Lavigne's clothes, but the priest at the rectory would not let them in, and the police did not try to get a search warrant.
- Lavigne knew the spot on the river where Danny was found. He had taken Joe, Danny's brother, fishing there. The day after the murder police found Lavigne walking by the murder site. The police interviewed him, and he asked them, "If a stone was used and thrown in the river, would the blood still be on it?"[80] But the police had made no public announcement about how Danny had been killed. The rock was found, and forensic specialists decided that Danny had been killed by a left-handed assailant. Lavigne is left-handed.
- Lavigne told the funeral home to keep the coffin closed because Danny's face was mangled. But it wasn't, as Lavigne knew, because he had seen the body and identified it.
- At the funeral home a Franciscan priest came in and wept loudly in front of the casket. He did not know Danny, but he was from the Franciscan house in Springfield, where Lavigne used to take his victims to confession. The Franciscan denied hearing the confession of the murderer; but what else could he do, and still preserve the seal of confession?
- Lavigne took a polygraph test about the murder; it was inconclusive but it revealed that "Lavigne was a homosexual."[81]
- The blood tests were inconclusive.

The district attorney at the time, Matthew Ryan, a close friend of Bishop Weldon, decided not to prosecute Lavigne because he "didn't think he could win a case against a priest."[82] The evidence for either the murder or the molestation was not strong enough to get an indictment, Ryan claimed. He later learned that Lavigne had molested two of his nephews, and now he thinks that Lavigne was the murderer.[83]

In 1991 Lavigne was arrested and in 1992 pleaded guilty to molesting two boys. He had to spend seven months at St. Luke Institute and was on probation for ten years. In 1994 the diocese paid $1.4 million to settle lawsuits stemming from Lavigne's abuse. He was not removed from the priesthood by the then-bishop, John A. Marshall, because it was thought that the process was "too cumbersome and time-consuming."[84] The Vatican finally removed Lavigne from the priesthood in November 2003, but he continued receiving his monthly stipend of $1,030 and his health benefits of $8,800 a year until May 2004.

The Rev. James J. Scahill said, "I think that Lavigne has gotten away with murder for more than thirty years. But the people who have enabled him are worse than him."[85] Bishop Dupré met with priests and told them, according to Scahill, that Bishop Weldon (now deceased) in the 1970s destroyed records of allegations of sexual abuse. Dupré denied having said that, and has used the diocesan newspaper to attack Scahill's reputation.[86] For about two years beginning in June 2002, Scahill, pastor of the most affluent parish in the diocese, withheld the percentage of the collection that he is required to send to the diocese as a protest against the bishop's failure to defrock Lavigne and the payment of Lavigne's stipend. Dupré was furious with Scahill because Scahill had cost him money (similar anger has never been shown toward child abusers). Lavigne's victim Danny Croteau is dead—murder. Another victim, David Bessone, is dead—suicide.[87]

Hours after he learned that the *Springfield Republican* knew that he had been accused of sexual abuse, on February 10, 2004, Bishop Dupré fled to St. Luke Institute, the psychiatric center in Maryland (see pp. xxx), and resigned as bishop of Springfield.[88] In searching church records for evidence against Dupré, investigators found mention of an anonymous letter to Lavigne that accused Lavigne of Croteau's murder. Lavigne had also given a copy of this letter to his lawyer. Police suspect that Lavigne himself wrote the letter to confuse the investigation.[89]

Dupré was indicted for child rape in September 2004 but escaped because of the statute of limitations.[90] The two accusers had supplied not only their own testimony but extensive corroborating evidence in the form of witnesses, credit card receipts, phone bills, etc. In 1976 the then-Father Dupré befriended one refugee boy whose father was unable to come to the United States. According to the press release of the alleged victim's attorney, Dupré masturbated himself with the twelve-year-old boy's hand, and then "proceeded to other forms of abuse, including the penetration of our client's mouth and anus."[91] Dupré plied the boys with wine, cognac, and gay pornography. This continued until the first boy was in high school and started dating girls. Dupré started abusing the second alleged victim (whose father died while the boy was in a sexual relationship with Dupré) in 1979; he had group sexual sessions with the boys. Dupré was concerned for his own health. He showed them pictures of people dying of AIDS, and warned them that if they had sex with other men he could get AIDS and die.

Dupré convinced the boys that God teaches love and that their relationship was a logical expression of love. He told one victim that the boy was his "godson," and the other boy that he was "in love" with him. When he became a bishop in 1990 Dupré asked the boys to be quiet to avoid embarrassing him. He sent them cards and money.

One of the men became actively gay. Dupré denounced gay marriage, and the man began to see their relationship in a different light after pondering the things that Dupré was publicly saying about homosexuality. Dupré fled the day the Massachusetts legislature voted on gay marriage. He remains a bishop, but has taken the Fifth Amendment and refused to answer any questions in a civil suit filed by his alleged victims.[92]

## *Bridgeport*

The Rev. Lawrence F. X. Brett, a "charismatic young priest"[93] at St. Cecilia's Church in Stamford, Connecticut, in the diocese of Bridgeport, organized a group called Brett's Mavericks. "He let them drive his car, a red '62 Pontiac Tempest with red vinyl seats, even though they were too young to drive....

He swore like a sailor and smoked a pipe and took them to dirty movies in the city. Some of the boys say he even took them to Manhattan to find hookers."[94] He molested Frank Martinelli when Frank was about fourteen years old. Brett performed fellatio on the boy after confession and told him it was a way to receive Communion.[95] Brett liked the combination of sacraments and sex.

Tony Cardone remembered serving Brett's Mass, going to the sacristy, where "amid the priests' robes, the chalice and the faint smell of incense, Cardone recalled, Brett explained that performing fellatio on each other was 'the way Christian men receive communion.' 'He would unzip himself and then unzip me,' Cardone said. 'I remember him telling me one time I had the body of a Greek god.'"[96] He took the boys to St. Mary's Seminary in Baltimore (known familiarly as "The Pink Palace") and slept in the room reserved for the archbishop and other dignitaries. There, under the crucifix, he had sex with the boys.

Brett was spiritual director at Sacred Heart University. He left suddenly in 1964 after he admitted biting a teenager's penis during oral sex. (But he had an explanation: he was trying to keep the teenager from ejaculating.) When asked years later whether such behavior would be cause for suspicion, Bishop Edward M. Egan responded, "I would have to know all the details."[97] Bishop Walter W. Curtis, Egan's predecessor in Bridgeport, decided to send Brett out of state but to keep him on the books as a priest of the Bridgeport diocese. The diocese put out a memo instructing officials to say "hepatitis was to be feigned"[98] if anyone asked what had happened to Brett. In fact, he went to the Servants of the Paraclete in New Mexico for treatment. Father Gerald Fitzgerald was still in charge, and Brett did not like him. Despite Father Fitzgerald's opinions about child molesters (see p. 93), Brett was sent out to work in parishes and to teach in middle school, where he met Raymond Romero. He took him to the rectory and talked about sex. Brett then performed fellatio on Romero, and persuaded Romero to do it to him. He warned Romero that no one would believe him if he complained.[99] In Nevada City he befriended the Berliner family and watched their children when the parents were away. He told Hal Berliner Jr. that his parents had asked Brett to give Hal sex instruction: "Brett, the younger Berliner said recently, described physical love, spiritual love, platonic love, and 'a special kind of love in which a priest relates to a young boy.' He lighted candles and said prayers, wrapping his act in the symbols and rituals of the Church. 'It was a test of my love of God to allow him to perform fellatio on me,' Berliner said."[100]

Despite these sexual crimes, Father Brett had a successful career. He was a writer (*Guardian Angels, Redeemed Creation: Sacramentals Today*) and in 1969 became chaplain at Calvert Hall, the boys' school in Towson, Maryland, which I attended for three years (1960–63). According to students there, Brett did not engage in lengthy seductions. Once, Father Brett told fourteen-year-old Frank Vonasek "that he'd heard from some of the other boys that Vonasek was gay, and that one way to prove that he wasn't, was to allow Brett to perform oral sex on him to see if he became aroused. Afterward, Brett told the boy he couldn't tell anyone what occurred because 'that will prove that you're gay.'"[101] A teacher became suspicious, and in October 1973 Brett was fired. Students were told he had "hepatitis."

Brett led retreats, wrote *Share the Word* for Paulist Press, and kept in touch with Wayne Ruth, a student from Calvert Hall days and a friend of Cardinal William Keeler of Baltimore. Bishop Egan of Bridgeport met with Brett in 1990 and wrote that "all things considered, he made a good impression. In the course of our conversation, the particulars of his case came out in detail and with grace."[102] In 1992 Brett confessed to several more incidents. In 1993 Frank Martinelli, whom Brett had molested in Stamford, Connecticut, filed a lawsuit, and Bishop Egan of Bridgeport called Brett in for a meeting. Brett decided it was time to disappear. Ruth sold Brett's house, and later visited him in St. Maarten, where Brett had a villa and was president of the condo association. Brett's Johns Hopkins psychologist, Gregory Lehne, also visited there, as did two priests of the Bridgeport diocese. They neglected to tell the police or the courts or the bishops (all of whom were looking for him) where Brett was. According to neighbors, Brett had many teenage boys visit him at his condo. After the FBI, private investigators, and the Roman Catholic Church had failed, a reporter from the

*Hartford Courant* succeeded; he found Brett,[103] who decided it was again time to disappear (and he has as of late-2006 not reappeared).

Bridgeport had numerous accused priests in addition to Brett.[104] Rev. Gavin O'Connor molested three boys in the same family from 1977 to 1985. One boy tried to commit suicide in 1986, thereby revealing the abuse. In 1988 O'Connor was made a pastor. The family sued. Egan paid defrocked abuser Gavin O'Connor $17,000 in 1989 but fought the victim's family until 1998, when the last case was settled.[105]

Egan received and investigated an allegation about the Rev. Walter Phillip Coleman. Coleman was allowed to keep working for a year during the investigation, and then he retired to work at a parish in Milford in the archdiocese of Hartford until the local paper discovered him.[106] Egan had claimed that he had a policy in Bridgeport that "any clergy accused of sexual misconduct with minors was, after a preliminary diocesan investigation, to be sent immediately to one of the most prominent psychiatric institutions in the nation for evaluation."[107] Except when Egan decided not to do this.

Egan said he wasn't interested in allegations, only "realities."[108] Bishop Curtis admitted he had transferred pedophiles to give them a fresh start, and had destroyed records of accusations. By May 1990 Egan had received accusations against Rev. Charles T. Carr, but did not suspend him until 1995 when a lawsuit was filed.

Allegations of abuse by Carr go back at least to 1982.[109] A mother had told a pastor that Charles Carr, his assistant at the parish, had put his hand down her son's pants, but the pastor did not consider this a sexual move. Carr spent a few months at a high school before parents complained about him. In 1984 Carr met thirteen-year-old Jon Fleetwood. He became friendly with the Fleetwood family and invited Jon to watch movies at the rectory, where he put his hand down Jon's pants. Carr asked Bishop Curtis to appoint him to a boys' high school. Curtis did, on the advice of the psychiatrist who was treating Carr for self-esteem problems. As the plaintiff's attorney asked Curtis, "Isn't that like sending Dracula to guard the blood bank?" Curtis then appointed Carr to be spiritual director at another boys' high school. The mother of the boy whom Carr had abused in 1982 wrote to

Egan, but Egan refused to meet with her. He instead sent Carr to the Institute of Living, where the doctors could not decide whether Carr was telling the truth, so Egan sent Carr back to the high school and then to a parish. The diocese tried to collect back tuition from a family who had accused Carr of fondling their son in 1984, even though the father had lost his job.

The diocese of Bridgeport began receiving complaints about Rev. Raymond Pcolka in 1966, during his first assignment.[110] A 1983 letter (which later disappeared) accused Pcolka of molesting a young woman. A 1989 allegation claimed that James Krug had been molested. In 1976 a woman complained that Pcolka was involved with her daughter-in-law. Nothing was done about these allegations. In 1993 the victims of Pcolka filed suit, and the diocese promptly asked for a gag order to prevent the public from having access to information about the abuse. At least twelve people accused Pcolka of oral and anal sex, beatings, violence, and sadistic language. When Egan was asked about this, he responded that "the twelve have never been proved to be telling the truth."[111] Rev. Chris Walsh, director of communications for the diocese, told the *Connecticut Post* that the diocese had never had any complaints about any priest.[112] But many people had already complained about Pcolka.

Egan never met with victims or apologized to them. By the end of 2003, the diocese of Bridgeport had agreed to pay out $40 million in damages. Some damage was irreparable. Rev. Alfred J. Bietighofer had committed suicide.[113] Bill Slossar, who had been assaulted by Pcolka in the 1970s, could never overcome his depression and committed suicide on Mother's Day 2002.[114]

## *The Bishops*

In the New England province Bishop McCormack stands out as the bishop most associated with the child abusers. He knew many of them personally from his seminary days and made every effort to keep them in the priesthood where they continued abusing. Cardinal Cushing and Cardinal Medeiros are dead; Cardinal Law's memory does not function when it comes to abuse cases.[115] Bishop D'Arcy, the only bishop to show any common sense, is in South Bend. William F. Murphy is bishop of Rockville Center, New York, Robert J. Banks was bishop of Green Bay, Wisconsin, until 2003, and Alfred C. Hughes is archbishop of New Orleans. Their handling of sexual abuse in Boston certainly did not hurt their careers. The pope has not asked any of them to resign. McCormack is in Manchester, New Hampshire, a diocese that narrowly escaped a criminal charge by allowing the state's attorney general to set some of the diocesan policies on the handling of sex abuse.

The priests and bishops of Boston generally seem incapable of admitting that a bishop has ever made a mistake. The doctrine of infallibility, which covers the traditions handed down from the apostles and papal and conciliar clarifications thereof, has apparently been extended to assignments of parish priests. Cardinal Law simply assumed that Medeiros had never made a mistake, and that it was not necessary to look into personnel folders before making an assignment. This refusal to admit the possibility of mistakes is arrogant, and continues to be the dominant attitude among bishops. Everything they have done to protect children has been done with the greatest unwillingness and only in response to public and media pressure. Again, public relations is their dominant concern.

The tolerance of sinning priests was also encouraged in New England by the old boys' network. The priests and bishops went to seminary together and sometimes worked together in parishes; they were related by ties of kinship and mutual friendship; they were therefore sympathetic to one another's faults. Law, if he was telling the truth, was in part a victim himself of the old boys' network. His auxiliaries knew which priests had severe problems but did not call Law's attention to them. He assumed that they knew the diocese and would handle problems. But sometimes Law was informed, yet he now claims that he has no memory of conversations he had and letters he signed. If he is telling the truth, he may have mental problems of his own. How could anyone forget the allegations of child molestation? Is there something in Law's background that makes him unable to deal with difficult personal situations? Does he simply repress the memories of the allegations, as some of the youngest victims repressed their sexual abuse? If the cardinal archbishop of Boston himself had psychological damage because of some early trauma or difficulties, how did he ever get put in such a position of responsibility in a diocese with such problems? Like other bishops, Law could not look evil in the face and confront it. This was the type of man that Rome favored for bishops, and the type that was recommended by Americans. No one wanted a bishop with hard edges, one who would look for problems and seek to confront them even at the cost of massive public controversy.

The priests of Boston and of New England shared a professional bond. Like policemen reluctant to turn in other policemen, like doctors unwilling to testify against other doctors in malpractice suits, they protected one another, and tended to see outsiders, including the Catholic laity, as aliens, or even as the enemy. The Irish have long had a notorious problem with drinking, and the priests of the New England province are mostly of Irish descent (although a few French Canadian names are sprinkled among the offenders). If the New England Province is worse than other regions of the country (which seems more and more unlikely as more diocesan documents are released) it may be because widespread clerical alcoholism, a problem long-excused by a sympathetic laity, distorts priests' judgments and lessens their inhibitions. However, similar abuse by the Germans of St. John's Abbey, which we will see in the next chapter, makes this a less likely explanation of the problems of the New England province.

# CHAPTER EIGHT

# THE SCOPE OF DESTRUCTION: AMERICA AND THE WORLD

ALTHOUGH BOSTON WAS THE FIRST CENTER of the storm, reporters in other cities realized that there were local stories, both old and new, of sexual abuse by priests. Victims also realized that after the revelations in Boston their stories would be believed and they therefore came forward with fresh accusations. The abuse, it soon became clear, was not confined to the United States or to the English-speaking countries, although some Vatican officials suspected it was. Priests (like the rest of mankind) are sinners everywhere. The incidence of abuse seems to vary around the world. Clerical culture may be corrupt to different degrees in different countries. Or more probably the common law system and tort law gave lawyers both the motivation and the means to ferret out abusers, motivation and means that were lacking in countries of the civil law (this is, whose systems descend from Roman law). But throughout the world, more and more reports of abuse began to surface in the press, if not in the courts.

## *Baltimore*

The *Baltimore Sun* has gone fairly easy on the Catholic Church; it has printed the cases that ended in court, but has not done investigative reporting the way the *Boston Globe* has. I lived in Baltimore for decades and was on the fringes of several cases of abuse. I also observed many things that never made it into the press.

The Rev. Thomas W. Smith did not like the glare of publicity on his parish when his associate, the Rev. Marion Helowicz, in 1988 pleaded guilty to child abuse in a Towson courtroom, because Smith was also guilty of abusing numerous minors in the 1960s, and the archdiocese of Baltimore knew it.[1] In 1993 another accuser came forward with an accusation against Smith from the early 1980s. The archdiocese decided to send Smith away for an evaluation, and Smith realized he could not hide the accusations any longer. He borrowed a 12-gauge shotgun from a friend and, on August 21, 1993, shot himself. Since then, the archdiocese indicated that "numerous individuals have reported sexual abuse by Smith in the 1960s to early 1980s."[2] During the time that the archdiocese knew of Smith's abuse, its supervision that was intended to prevent further abuse consisted of a single monthly telephone call from Auxiliary Bishop William Newman.

The Rev. William Q. Simms, who came to St. Andrew-by-the-Bay with a boy in tow, was into sadomasochistic sacrilege. Two boys filed suits in 1988, saying that when they were thirteen-year-old altar boys at his parish, he had them dress up as saints and martyrs before they had sex. They engaged in "ritualistic sexual fantasies" that included "imitations of torture inflicted on Christ and certain saints,"[3] including St. Isaac Jogues, whose tortures at the hands of Indians are legendary among Catholic schoolchildren. The lawsuits were settled out of court, but not until after the Baltimore archdiocese tried to make the boys' names public.

I was on a talk show around 1990 when several people called in to say that Simms had been saying Mass at different churches in the suburbs. I contacted the archdiocese of Baltimore which referred me to the lawyer of the insurance company who represented the archdiocese in the lawsuit. The lawyer was interested in hearing what the talk show had produced. He said that the archdiocese's defense was that Simms was a compulsive pedophile and that the archdiocese was not responsible for his actions when he abused children in parishes. I was then called in by the archdiocese to speak with two officials who had been in charge of investigating Simms, Msgr. G.

Michael Schleupner, later the chancellor, who occasionally said Mass for Dignity, a Catholic gay apologist group, and Msgr. W. Francis Malooly, later chancellor and now auxiliary bishop of Baltimore. Malooly said he never listened to gossip about priests' sexual misbehavior. They asked me why I had spoken to the insurance company lawyer. Because the archdiocese (specifically Msgr. Malooly) sent me to him, I replied. Schleupner and Malooly explained to me that Simms was a homosexual; he could control his impulses and say Mass in parishes without endangering children. I advised them to consult their insurance company's lawyer and to make sure their explanations agreed with his before they went to court about the allegations about Simms. I also said that Baltimore looked as if it were following the pattern of Lafayette, Louisiana, where Jason Berry thought that a chancery dominated by homosexuals had turned a blind eye to child abuse. Schleupner said that Baltimore was not like that.

Simms quietly worked for the archdiocesan marriage tribunal for many years and resided at St. Thomas Aquinas parish in Hampden. Unfortunately for Simms, the spotlight of public attention was turned on this parish when a fifth-grade teacher, David Czajkowski, was convicted of molesting girls at the school and at his home.[4] The memory of Simms' misdeeds was revived by this and other scandals and Cardinal William Keeler decided to retire him.

I went to a boys' high school, Calvert Hall, from 1960 to 1963 with Jerome F. "Jeff"Toohey Jr. He was ordained and later assigned to his alma mater as a chaplain from 1984 to 1993. He developed a sudden interest in sports and served as moderator of the swim team. The yearbook had a picture of him with the Speedo-clad boys. Archbishop William D. Borders referred a boy to Toohey because the boy feared he was homosexual; the boy in December 1993 said that Toohey abused him;[5] Toohey fled to Las Vegas, denying everything. Toohey eventually returned to the state and took up real estate. A civil lawsuit against him which tried to escape the statute of limitations by alleging repressed memory was dropped after the Maryland Court of Appeals ruled that recovered memories could not be used to extend the statute of limitations.[6] However, in January 2005 another former

Calvert Hall student, Thomas Roberts, accused Toohey of abusing him during the late 1980s and early 1990s.[7] His mother sent Roberts to Toohey for counseling. After counseling, Roberts spent the night at Toohey's house and had sex with him. Roberts also kept a contemporaneous journal of all the sexual encounters. In November 2004 Toohey pleaded guilty.[8]

Priests were not alone in abusing children. John Joseph Merzbacher molested dozens of children when he was a teacher at a Catholic elementary school in South Baltimore. He came from a sleazy background. His adoptive father, his mother, and his stepfather all operated bars and strip joints in the decaying working-class areas of east Baltimore.[9] Merzbacher had only a few college credits, but in its desperation to find teachers, Baltimore City hired him as a teacher. He had problems at the public schools in which he taught. The school administration of Baltimore City did not mention these problems when Merzbacher was hired to teach by a school of the archdiocese of Baltimore.[10] Irresponsibility about the safety of children is not confined to the Catholic Church.

One alleged victim of Merzbacher said that he saw Merzbacher having intercourse on a table with Sister Eileen Weisman, the principal of the Catholic Community Middle School at which he taught from 1972 to 1979.[11] Several plaintiffs said that Merzbacher bragged about it: "Privately he would say he had to fuck her so he could do what he wanted in the school."[12] His former students said that Merzbacher had a gun in his desk; he once held it to a victim's head when he molested her. He had sex, according to the plaintiffs, with many boys and girls during and after school. Sister Eileen, the students said, saw the molestation and did nothing.[13] The students were terrified into silence after Merzbacher convinced them that he had Mafia connections. Gary Homberg, who taught at the school with Merzbacher, gave an affidavit in which he said, "I personally observed John Merzbacher sexually touching, molesting, and fondling both male and female students." After one student came to Homberg to tell him that Merzbacher "was raping him and threatening to kill him if he ever told anyone," Homberg called a meeting at his house with Sister Eileen, the Rev. Herbert Derwart, and another priest, and told them what had happened. These three archdiocesan employees met privately, and then told Homberg "that they would like me to continue as a teacher in the school, but only under the condition I made no mention to anyone of my observations of John Merzbacher's sexual misconduct."[14] Homberg resigned his teaching position, but did not tell anyone else of Merzbacher's conduct because he was afraid of him.

Sister Eileen Weisman later became principal of the school of the Cathedral of Mary Our Queen. When the Merzbacher story broke, she spoke to the assembled parents at the Cathedral school and said only, "My conscience is clear." The parents applauded her. Weisman never said what she knew about what was going on in her former school.[15] Neither the prosecution nor the defense called her as a witness, although the defense attorney had said in his opening statement that Weisman would be called. The trial was terminated abruptly when both sides unexpectedly agreed to stop calling witnesses, even though the defense had not developed the arguments it had laid out in the opening statement.[16] Merzbacher was convicted on one charge, but all other charges were dismissed, which means that if his conviction is overturned on appeal on a technicality, he cannot easily be retried on the other charges.[17] Therefore, Weisman faces little possibility of being called to testify (and in any case she moved to Rome in 2003).

At the Cathedral school of which Weisman was later principal, a recently (1998) ordained assistant priest, the Rev. Thomas A. Rydzewski, spent a great deal of time during the year 2000 with the lower grades, but Weisman noticed nothing unusual, although Rydzewski had Star Wars toys and other attractions for children. He also had a stash of child pornography. His purchases through eBay brought about his downfall:

> The seller, Marla Willette, became suspicious after talking to other doll sellers who said they also had sold lifelike, high-priced "My Twin" dolls to Rydzewski, who traded on eBay as "skywalker-198," according to the affidavit.
>
> When Willette checked Rydzewski's seller profile, she later told police she found a "very disturbing" list of items—more than $6,000 in

> purchases that included boys' clothing, vintage advertising depicting children, and videotapes about homosexual encounters involving young boys, police reported.
>
> Using an Internet search engine, Willette also discovered that Rydzewski was a Catholic priest and that his eBay shipping address of 5200 N. Charles St. in Baltimore was the address of the Cathedral of Mary Our Queen.
>
> "Willette said that she felt the items Rydzewski was purchasing online were completely inappropriate for a priest, thus resulting in her telephone call to the Baltimore City police and U.S. Postal Inspection Service," FBI Special Agent Michael W. DuBois said in the affidavit.[18]

No one at the Cathedral had noticed anything—not Cardinal Keeler, who occasionally visited his cathedral (he lives downtown), nor the other priests, nor (most surprisingly) the housekeeper. Rydzewski had already attracted the attention of the FBI in the Candyman sting which tried to identify child pornographers. The FBI arrested him at the Cathedral rectory on December 12, 2001. He pleaded guilty to a charge of receiving child pornography on his computer at the Cathedral and was imprisoned.[19]

The case that received international attention was that of the Rev. Maurice J. Blackwell. In 1964 Blackwell was Outstanding Catholic Youth of the Year. He entered St. Mary's Seminary, and there, during the late 1960s, as two men said in 1992, Blackwell had sexual relationships with them when they were teenagers. One boy was being physically abused at home; he moved in with Blackwell at the seminary and various rectories, and the sexual relationship (which progressed from "kissing to fondling, masturbation, oral sex, and attempted anal sex"[20]) lasted until he was twenty-six years old. Another boy, whose parents were going through a divorce, moved in with Blackwell when he was fifteen years old, and the cost of room and board was sex. In 1974 Blackwell was only the second black priest ever ordained by the archdiocese of Baltimore, and perhaps the archdiocese was not anxious to lose him. Blackwell made St. Edward's a lively African-American parish; there he baptized Dontee Stokes.

At St. Edward's Blackwell had a dozen young men take refuge from family problems with him at various times. The 1993 police report indicated that Dontee Stokes had come to the Bible study class at St. Edward's when he was fourteen years old. Blackwell called him into his office to talk; the hugs became longer and more intimate each time. Stokes later informed his doctor "that the suspect had been touching and fondling the complainant over the past three years."[21] (The only part of the lie detector test that Stokes failed was when he denied that Blackwell had penetrated him; there were some accusations he could not bring himself to make.)

The city prosecutor failed to charge Blackwell. Then Archbishop Keeler suspended Blackwell, sent him to therapy for three months at the Institute of Living (which decided that Blackwell was not a pedophile), but reinstated him when the parishioners at St. Edward's demanded to have him back. They "criticized the archdiocese for suspending the priest on the basis of a single allegation."[22] The spokesman who had been hired to spin for the archdiocese announced that "the archdiocese is satisfied that the accusation is groundless."[23] But in 2002 Keeler admitted that "we acknowledge...Father Maurice Blackwell was credibly accused of abuse" and "the victim was offered counseling and treatment."[24] The family denied there had been any such offer.

In 1993, the archdiocesan review board criticized Keeler and said that Blackwell should be suspended because the archdiocesan report had found the accusations against Blackwell "consistent and credible," and Stokes had passed two polygraph tests. The board concluded that "we believe the return of Father Blackwell to the parish—even under protective constraints—constitutes an unacceptable risk."[25] The board did not fulfill its duty as a rubber stamp. It could not conduct an investigation on its own; it could not speak with the accused and with the accusers; it had to rely on a report of an archdiocesan team composed of priests; it often met only after the archdiocese had decided what to do.[26] But it would not agree that Blackwell should be returned to his parish.

In 1998 the Baltimore archdiocese removed Blackwell after another report of a five-year homosexual relationship in the 1970s, and this time

Keeler, by now a cardinal, did not cave in to the parishioners' demands that Blackwell be reinstated.[27] The archdiocese said it sent letters to the state's attorney about a boy's allegation that in the 1960s, when he was in the fifth grade, he had had a sexual relationship with Blackwell that lasted several years. The state's attorney's office "lost" the letters.[28]

As the years passed Stokes obsessed over the abuse and his betrayal by church and state. In 2002 as the papers filled with stories of abuse by priests, Stokes became depressed and suicidal. Baltimore is a violent city, and there are tens of thousands of handguns circulating. Stokes put his .357 Magnum in a duffel bag and drove down to Blackwell's house. He saw Blackwell and demanded an apology; Blackwell sneered and turned away; Stokes pulled the gun out and shot him three times.[29]

After the shooting Stokes went to his aunt's Baptist church, answered an altar call for sinners, confessed to the pastor, and turned himself in to the police. Keeler's first reaction was, "I am appalled that another act of violence has occurred in the city of Baltimore and that tragedy touches a person I have known personally."[30] He visited Blackwell in the hospital. Keeler later apologized for his decision to reinstate Blackwell, claiming that he had offered Stokes counseling. The Stokes family said they had never received any such offer. At that point Keeler had "no plans to apologize personally to Stokes or his family"[31] and only slowly and reluctantly decided to meet with them to apologize.

Stokes was indicted on charges of attempted murder. He testified that he had been in a dissociative state, an out-of-body experience (see p. 266). Black jurors in Baltimore are reluctant to convict any young black man, because so many are in prison. The jurors who tried Stokes found him not guilty of attempted murder, but guilty of handgun charges. The jury recommended leniency.[32]

Keeler had to sit through the meeting of the bishops in Dallas in which he and the other bishops were excoriated for their toleration of abuse and heard the victims describe their suffering; he also learned that a member of his family had been sexually abused by a relative. In September 2002 the archdiocese of Baltimore released a list of all priests who had credible accusations of abuse and an accounting of the $5.6 million spent in settlements and other expenses.

In February 2005 Blackwell was found guilty of assaulting Stokes, but was granted a new trial because two detectives and Stokes, while testifying at the trial, had made remarks about there being other victims. The state decided not to pursue a new trial, so Blackwell remains innocent in the eyes of the state and does not face imprisonment.[33]

## Louisville

The Rev. Louis E. Miller is the prime known offender in the Louisville archdiocese. He was eventually indicted on scores of counts of sexual misconduct with boys and girls in different counties and was named in fifty of the 133 lawsuits filed against the diocese of Louisville. He claimed that he was the victim of sex play when he was four or five years old and that he was accosted in a movie theater when he was fourteen years old. A niece and a cousin of Miller both said he molested them, along with four other members of his family, and Miller told a psychiatrist that he admitted "'to periodically acting out sexual impulses in this manner his entire adult life,' mostly involving boys ten to fifteen."[34] He would talk about sex and ask about their "development under guise of sex instruction."[35] Miller pleaded guilty to all counts on which he was charged, admitting that "I remember these children very well. I remember fondling these children."[36]

Miller had a long career of molesting even before his 1956 ordination. One lawsuit accused him of molesting a boy when Miller worked as a camp counselor in the early 1950s. He confessed it in 1960 to an unnamed superior (according to a later psychiatric report). He left Holy Spirit parish in 1961 after parents complained (he had molested fourteen members of a single class, a total of twenty-four students at Holy Spirit parish alone). He was transferred to another parish. At one parish he kept a student after the last class on Friday to molest him, telling him it was sex education. When parents complained, he was transferred to St. Athanasius' church, where he victimized six children. Parents complained. He was transferred to St.

Aloysius' church, where he victimized twelve more until parents complained. Then he became pastor of St. Elizabeth of Hungary church, where he molested nine victims. One had been molested by another priest and then further molested by Miller when he sought counseling. Parents complained again, and eventually Miller was assigned to a home for the elderly, until he retired in 2002.

Archbishop Thomas Cajetan Kelly claimed that no one in the archdiocese had heard any allegations about Miller before 1989 and that as soon as it heard of abuse the archdiocese then moved Miller into positions where he did not have contact with children. But Miller wrote in the journal that he kept as part of his therapy "that as early as 1961, he offered, in the wake of molestation complaints, to leave the priesthood. But then-Archbishop John Floersh said 'no' and that '[I] would be a good priest.'"[37] Retired auxiliary bishop Charles G. Maloney wavered on whether he had been told about Miller as early as the 1960s. In 1975 Sister Mary Fulgence Logsdon told the diocese that an eighth-grader in the parish school claimed that Miller had molested him. The diocese moved Miller to another parish. Mary Miller accused Archbishop Kelly of perjury. When she had sued Miller, Kelly had testified under oath that "no other lawsuits have been filed against Father Miller."[38] But there had been, and Kelly knew it; both Miller and the archdiocese had been sued in 1990.[39] Kelly proudly claimed to have the amnesia that seems to be an occupational hazard of bishops: "I have a wonderful gift that I hardly ever recall details of those conversations about abuse."[40]

Kentucky has no statute of limitations for felonies, and therefore Miller was indicted. He pleaded guilty, and at seventy-two years of age was sentenced to twenty years, although Kentucky has something called "shock probation" which spares first-time offenders from long terms, and in December 2003 he sought it, but withdrew his request after massive public outcry.

In 1983 the Rev. Thomas P. Creagh, another abuser, masturbated a boy at the rectory of St. Albert's in Louisville, where Creagh was pastor. The victim's parents, the Halls, then complained to Bishop Kelly. In a March 9, 1993, memo, Kelly recorded what he had done in response to this accusation: "I told Father Creagh that I had to view this incident in what I regard is an excellent pastoral ministry at St. Albert's, and that it would not be my indication to remove him from office there. The parents could, of course, destroy his ministry and harm the parish greatly if they make public accusations. In that case, Tom would have to go."[41] In a memo written on June 14, 1983, Kelly said that while "Father Creagh did not express remorse over the incident, he was clearly embarrassed at having to confess the incident."[42]

Kelly wrote that the Halls and their attorney came to the archdiocesan offices on March 18 and "demanded $150,000 in damages, the removal of Father Creagh from his parish, and absolute assurance that such an incident would not occur again in the archdiocese. . . . I found the demands extortionary, and the attitudes hostile and vindictive."[43] In the bishop's eyes, the parents, not the abuser, were in the wrong for demanding that Creagh be denied access to children. Creagh was sued for molesting a boy at St. Albert's later in 1983, after Kelly left him in his position there. Creagh is also accused of molesting boys in the 1970s. Since 1964 Kentucky law has required all citizens to report suspected child abuse; Kelly never reported any abuse. On June 10, 2003, the archdiocese of Louisville settled with 243 victims of abuse for $25.7 million.

J. Kendrick Williams had served as a priest in Louisville before becoming bishop of Covington and then founder and first bishop of the Lexington, Kentucky, diocese in 1988. After four people accused him of sexual and emotional abuse, Williams resigned on June 11, 2002, denying everything,[44] and receiving a standing ovation from the meeting of priests at which he announced his resignation.

## *St. John's Abbey*

St. John's Abbey in Collegeville, Minnesota, has for several decades been a center of liturgical renewal and sexual molestation. Not only did some monks have sex with children, teenagers, and each other, but they also went to gay bars in Minneapolis. Discipline was so lax at the abbey that a senior monk was reported to have banged on the bedroom doors of another monk begging to be let in, crying, "I love you, I need you."[45] The monks also lived the good life; one collected Waterford crystal.

The Benedictine monks preyed on boys and girls and on each other. When the novices entered the dining room, the predators "would descend like vultures."[46] The corruption went to the top. The abbot, John Eidenschink, led the pack. In 1962 a young novice asked to speak with Eidenschink (also a canon lawyer) about his doubts regarding celibacy. Eidenschink told the monk to "take off your clothes."[47] The novice stripped and lay down on the bed. "Eidenschink asked him about his sexual fantasies, his fears and whether he felt adequate with women. As the monk became aroused, Eidenschink began to touch him and examine his genitals. This happened frequently for the next three years. The novice asked the rector of the seminary about this odd counseling. The rector yelled at him and told him to leave the room."[48]

As long as they were in the six-to-eleven age range, Father Richard Eckroth liked both boys and girls. Living up to the profile of a pedophile, he kept a careful log of all the children he took to a cabin and sauna that the abbey owned. The children claim he had them strip and then raped and sodomized them. They say he threatened to kill them if they told their parents. One girl who was taken to the cabin when she was between the ages of seven and eleven remembers that Eckroth stripped her naked. Then "he started cussing at me in my ear, calling me horrible names—he said I was a little bitch, a whore, that my daddy wanted him to do this and if I told anyone he would kill me or my mom….I remember he had a knife to my throat and penetrated me with his hand."[49] John Vogel said that he was eight when Eckroth climbed on top of him and raped him. Then Eckroth washed the mess of anal rape off him and spoke of religion. He threatened to kill Vogel if he told anyone.[50] Eckroth denied abusing anyone, but he was sent to St. Luke Institute where the psychologists concluded that "there is substantial evidence that Eckroth has been sexually inappropriate with minors."[51] Eckroth is also an on-again off–again suspect in a murder case.[52] Mary and Susanne Recker, whom Eckroth had hosted at his cabin, were stabbed to death in 1974. Eckroth passed a lie detector test, but the investigative report has disappeared, and police are trying DNA tests.

Father Brennan Maiers molested Joe Johnson; he also had sexual relationships with women and men in New York in the 1970s and was cited for indecent conduct in a Minneapolis adult theater in 1984.[53] Brother Andre Bennett ran the infirmary; he gave students sleeping pills and molested them when they were in a drugged sleep.[54] When John Arendt went to talk with Father Allen Tarlton, Tarlton said: "Take off your clothes," and then molested him.[55] Tarlton liked to talk with one student at the prep school about homosexual sex. The student described what ensued: "He then proceeded to fondle me, caress my body, and then performed oral sex on me.... He then rimmed [kissing and licking of the anus] me. I recall masturbating and ejaculating at this time."[56] Ray Vogel often volunteered to help at St. John's Abbey. Father Cosmas R. Dahlheimer befriended him and molested his sons. Allen Vogel was taught to revere priests, and when Dahlheimer abused him, he said, "I wondered whether this was part of religion. I remember thinking of priests as being God to me at the time."[57]

Bill Quenroe was a sophomore at the prep school of St. John's Abbey when he needed help with theology from a priest, who gave him help by drinking whiskey with him and then ordering him to perform oral sex. Quenroe later attempted suicide.[58] When a student at St. John's prep died, one of his friends sought out Father Dunstan Moorse for counseling. After developing a relationship with the boy, Moorse told him that "I had an outmoded and provincial mindset when it came to sexual matters and that I should adopt a new one." Moorse proposed a "man-on-man bonding experience," so he "took out a condom to further enhance this educational experience. I recall him placing the condom on his penis and then he masturbated until he ejaculated. He encouraged me to do the same."[59]

In 1985 the National Conference of Catholic Bishops met at St. John's about sexual abuse by clergy. In 1994 the abbey helped set up the Interfaith Sexual Trauma Institute, but, as Richard Sipe pointed out, an alleged abuser was included on the staff.[60] Thirteen monks are on restriction at the abbey. They are under close supervision and have limited contacts while they are at the abbey but they are allowed to travel without supervision. Abbot John Klassen had generally tried to do the right thing. The abbey, unlike many dioceses, no longer hides behind the statute of limitations. It has apologized to all the victims and has set up an external review board to handle allegations.[61] SNAP (The Survivors Network of those Abused by Priests) will help decide the composition of the board. Ray Vogel, the father of several abused boys, said, "I pray for Abbot John. There's a lot of good men at the abbey, and Father John is one. I think he's doing right by people now, and I pray he has a long life, that he gets done all the things on that agreement."[62] Whether the Vatican will allow laity to judge religious is still not known.

## *Arizona*

The two dioceses of Arizona, Tucson and Phoenix, have intertwined stories of abuse. Robert C. Trupia,[63] known as the "chicken hawk" to his fellow priests,[64] studied at St. John's Seminary in Camarillo, California. After his ordination he was at St. Francis church in Yuma in the Tucson diocese from 1973 to 1976. Ted Oswald, a former policeman who was then a Franciscan lay brother and who is now a priest, was talking to some boys at St. Francis of Assisi when they asked him if Trupia was queer; he asked what they meant. They told him that Trupia had been sodomizing them after Mass every week for two years. The brother had them write down their statement and sent it to the bishop. The chancellor of the diocese rebuked Oswald because "the statements could get priests into trouble."[65] Someone removed the boys' statements from the Tucson diocesan file.[66] Trupia was immediately transferred from Yuma to Tucson, and Bishop Francis J. Green made him vice chancellor, head of the marriage tribunal, and a monsignor.

Trupia hosted a diocesan program called "Come and See" for young men with an interest in the priesthood, often taking the teenagers on trips to St. John's Seminary. The title of the program was the subject of vulgar puns. In 1982 Trupia was caught at the seminary in bed with a student, and Cardinal Timothy Manning of Los Angeles reported the incident to

Bishop Manuel D. Moreno of Tucson. Not until 1988 was Trupia was banned from the campus, after he had sex in the bell tower with a young drug addict.[67] Trupia, like Bruce Ritter, may have enjoyed planting public clues to his homosexuality. The titles of hymns that Trupia wrote are double entendres: "Gift of Love," "Resucitó" ("I Will Rise"), and "Lord, You Have Come."

In 1989–91 Bishop Moreno, who knew Trupia's abuse background, gave him a scholarship of $15,000 to Catholic University to get a degree in canon law. In 1992 Moreno confronted Trupia with an accusation and Trupia admitted he was a "loose cannon," unfit for the priesthood. But Trupia threatened to tell the public about the sex life of the archbishop of Phoenix, James S. Rausch, if Moreno did not change the suspension into a retirement as a priest in good standing.[68] Richard Sipe knew Rausch and said that

> I have interviewed at length a man who was a sexual partner of Bishop James Rausch. This was particularly painful for me since Rausch and I were young priests together in Minnesota in the early 60s. He went on to get his social work degree and succeeded Bernardin as Secretary of the Bishops' National Conference in DC. He became Bishop of Phoenix. It is patently clear that he had an active sexual life. It did involve at least one minor. He was well acquainted with priests who were sexually active with minors (priests who had at least thirty minor victims each). He referred at least one of his own victims to these priests.[69]

Bishops and priests passed boys around like party favors.

Were Rausch's problems purely personal? Investigative reporters at the *Arizona Republic* have found that the policies he established in the Phoenix diocese were not good:

> Court records and interviews with victims indicate Rausch and O'Brien [then vicar-general and later bishop] worked closely with the diocese's attorneys to keep many allegations from becoming public by negotiating

> confidential settlements, appealing to families to protect the image of the [C]hurch and promising to remove child molesters.
>
> "Bishop Rausch was certainly a good man, and he did many very good things," Sipe said. "But he was also sexually active, which sets the tone for the diocese through easy forgiveness and understanding and too great an acceptance of violations by other priests."[70]

An affidavit filed in a lawsuit that the Tucson diocese settled for an estimated $14 million alleged that "Rausch, Trupia, and the late Rev. William T. Byrne all had sex with a Tucson teenager who was later given a chancery job to ensure his silence."[71] The alleged victim, Brian F. O'Connor, says that Bishop James Rausch picked him up in 1979 when O'Connor was seventeen years old. Rausch was cruising under the name "Paul." After several encounters O'Connor discovered that Paul was in fact Bishop Rausch. After O'Connor became addicted to heroin, Rausch turned him over to Trupia, who referred him to William T. Byrne for treatment (which included sex). When O'Connor got off heroin he was more attractive to Trupia and the two began having sex. Trupia gave him a job in the chancery. O'Connor was bothered by the whole situation, and went to Bishop Green of Tucson, who gave him a promotion in the chancery in return for his silence. Trupia was vice chancellor in charge of the marriage tribunal; O'Connor was the *apparitor*, representative of the bishop on this tribunal, until 1988.

Despite Trupia's 1992 confession, Bishop Moreno wrote to the victim's family that Trupia had denied the allegations.[72] In 1995, three years after the confession, Moreno got around to writing the required report to the Vatican about the threat of exposure that Trupia had made. In 1995 Trupia had written to Moreno, "I informed you of my direct knowledge regarding another bishop's activities, which knowledge was potentially of a highly explosive and damaging nature to the Church in Arizona. Let me assure you again that I would not want to be put into a position to be subpoenaed and have to testify under oath as to what I know about this other bishop. At the same time, I am growing weary of trying to stand between the Church in Arizona and a torrent of bad publicity that your attempted actions continue to make ever more likely."[73] The "attempted actions" were Moreno's feeble attempts to discipline Trupia.

Trupia appealed to the Vatican. In 1997, Cardinal Dario Castillón Hoyos, prefect of the Vatican Congregation for the Clergy, decided for Trupia and ordered Moreno to retire Trupia as a priest in good standing and to pay Trupia's legal expenses. Hoyos knew about the blackmail and the threatened exposure of Rausch.[74] Moreno protested, but because of the Vatican's order, the diocese of Tucson had to continue to provide Trupia $1475 a month and health insurance. Trupia also had other friends who could help him, including the Rev. Charles G. Fatooh, the vicar general of the diocese of Monterey, California.[75] Fatooh gave Trupia work and rented him a condo in Maryland, where, according to neighbors, Trupia's young male friends visited him. Trupia drove a Mercedes C320 with a rosary dangling from the rearview mirror. In 2001 he was arrested for abuse but got off because the alleged molestations were outside of the statute of limitations.[76]

In the summer of 2004 Pope John Paul II ended Trupia's manipulation of the canon law process by removing him from the priesthood, and there is no appeal from a personal decision of a pope. In the period between his suspension and his removal, the Tucson diocese had paid him at least $177,000[77] and $14,000,000 to his more than thirty known victims.[78]

The *Arizona Republic*'s Nena Baker reported that Moreno's deposition was not sealed. She wrote that "the deposition and other records show that diocese officials protected one another, lied to a victim's family, failed to counsel victims, destroyed statements, did not notify child protective authorities, and were uncooperative with police." On March 7, 2003, Moreno resigned as bishop of the diocese of Tucson, which in September 2004 filed for bankruptcy because of the sex abuse lawsuits.

Thomas J. O'Brien succeeded Rausch as bishop of the Phoenix diocese in 1982. At least forty-two of the eighty-eight parishes of the Phoenix diocese had abusive priests in them; ten of the twelve large Hispanic parishes had abusive priests in them. As chancery official under Rausch and as bishop, O'Brien had refused to offer any consolation or comfort to families of victims, because, he explained, "I was advised by legal counsel that to do so could be construed by the authorities as trying to put pressure on the families to drop the charges."[79] When Doris Kenney met with O'Brien (then the chancellor under Rausch) he asked her if she had told anyone. When she said she had, "he pointed his finger across the desk and thundered at her, 'You shouldn't have done that.'"[80]

Immediately after the Rev. John Maurice Giandelone was ordained in 1979, he was assigned as youth minister and assistant pastor of St. Joseph's parish in Phoenix. He became friends with the Kulina family, who were strict Catholics, and took an intense interest in their son Benjamin, to whom he gave marijuana and beer to loosen his inhibitions.[81] His parents discovered the sexual relationship. The Rev. Joseph C. Ladensack, director of religious education, arranged for the parents to meet with O'Brien, who was then a vicar general of the diocese under Rausch (who was frequenting male prostitutes at this time). O'Brien told Ladensack that the parents did not want to press charges. The Kulinas had misplaced faith: "We had been taught all of our lives to respect and trust the [C]hurch and that if everyone else fails you, the Catholic Church would not fail you and would help you."[82] O'Brien told the Kulinas to keep quiet, because going public would "do harm to young Benjamin, that it would hurt the Church and that nobody would believe them."[83] O'Brien later claimed to have no memory of this meeting.[84]

When O'Brien became bishop, he transferred the known abuser Giandelone to a high school.[85] Ladensack, who by this time was vicar of Christian formation and had responsibility for the high schools, told O'Brien he thought this was a bad idea. O'Brien replied: "That's my decision," and, "as a matter of fact, Joe, I think you're a little bit too obsessed with this gay pedophile issue. I think, Joe, you have some kind of problem. Maybe you need to go get some counseling and deal with the problem."[86] O'Brien thought that anyone who objected to a priest giving oral sex to a teenage boy must clearly be mentally disturbed. O'Brien ended the screening that Ladensack had set up to keep erratic homosexuals out of the seminary. Ladensack resigned as vicar of Christian formation.

After Giandelone was transferred to the mainly Hispanic St. Mary's parish in Chandler (a parish that has had four abusers as associate pastors), he molested Henry Takata. Ladensack had served in this parish, and the parents called him. The father of Henry Takata had a gun and wanted to kill Giandelone, because he had gone into his fifteen-year-old son's bedroom and found Giandelone performing oral sex on the boy. Giandelone later explained, "I was lonely and all I wanted to do was love on him and lay my head on his stomach."[87]

Ladensack told them to call the police and then he called Bishop O'Brien. O'Brien, according to Ladensack, exploded, "He said why did you go out there? Why did you call the police? You have to come to me with this immediately and to me first and only to me. He said you owe me obedience, you took a vow of obedience and you need to—must I remind you young man—that you need to keep your vow of obedience."[88] Then O'Brien entered into the area of obstruction of justice, giving the state grounds to prosecute and almost certainly convict him: O'Brien told Ladensack to "tell the family to take back the complaint."[89] But Ladensack was not easily intimidated. He was a decorated Vietnam veteran (two Silver Stars, six Bronze Stars, a Purple Heart), who knew the code of military justice and the Nuremberg Trials, and who knew he could not obey an unlawful order. In 1986 after Ladensack told O'Brien he had "severe problems" with the way O'Brien was handling abusive priests, O'Brien suspended Ladensack and had his successor in the parish read a letter from the pulpit implying that Ladensack had had a nervous breakdown. Ladensack left the priesthood and married.

In 1984 Giandelone pleaded guilty to molesting a teenager in St. Joseph's parish in Phoenix in 1979.[90] After completing his probation, he worked as a priest in a nursing home for three years before he left the priesthood, moved to Fort Myers, Florida, and married. In 2002 Benjamin Kulina, now a police lieutenant, contacted Giandelone on the phone and got him to admit the abuse.[91] Giandelone was indicted, pleaded guilty, and was sentenced to jail.[92]

On May 3, 2003, Bishop O'Brien, in order to receive a guarantee of immunity from criminal prosecution for obstruction of justice, failure to report crimes, intimidation of witnesses, and extortion, signed an agreement with the county attorney, admitting that he had concealed sex-abuse allegations from the police: "I acknowledge that I allowed Roman Catholic priests under my supervision to work with minors after becoming aware of allegations of sexual misconduct. I further acknowledge that priests who had allegations of sexual misconduct made against them were transferred to ministries without full disclosure to their supervisor or to the community in which they were assigned."[93]

As part of the agreement with the state, O'Brien was required to appoint new officials to handle sex abuse allegations. If he or his successors interfere with the complaints, the bishop can be prosecuted.[94] O'Brien had offered to resign, but the Vatican refused to let him resign and refused to appoint a co-adjutor, fearing that it would look like caving in to lay interference. On Saturday night, June 14, 2003, Jim Reed, (who had been drinking that night), a Navajo, a father of four, crossed the street in front of Bishop O'Brien's car. O'Brien hit him, shattering the car's windshield, but didn't stop, and left the man in the street, where he died. O'Brien drove home, and then went to a Father's Day party at his sister's. He left the car there with a shattered windshield which had clothing and flesh embedded in it, and tried to find a glass repairer to fix it. He never called the police. But a witness to the accident copied down the license number, and the police traced the car to O'Brien.[95]

O'Brien was charged with felony hit and run; only then did the Vatican let him resign.[96] O'Brien was convicted and sentenced to probation: he had to perform forty hours of community service a month by visiting the sick and dying. He said this was far too much work, and the forty hours should include travel time (he has a chauffeur; no one is letting him near the wheel of a car). The judge, who had not given O'Brien any jail time for obstruction of justice, said that O'Brien would have to work the forty hours a month, excluding travel time.[97]

## *California*

Bishop George Patrick Ziemann is a friend of Cardinal Roger M. Mahony, with whom he had attended seminary. Ziemann began his career as a priest in the Los Angeles diocese. An accuser, Richard, has sued Ziemann, alleging that, when Ziemann was a priest at St. Matthew's parish in Huntingdon Park in the Los Angeles archdiocese in the late 1960s, the priest began having sex with the boy, who was then eleven years old. Ziemann would give Richard fifty to hundred dollars, tell him not to worry about it, then hear his confession and give him ten Our Fathers and ten Hail Marys as penance. This sexual relationship continued until 1986. Ziemann denied committing any abuse but admitted he continued to give Richard money that belonged to the Church.[98]

Mahony made Ziemann head of a junior seminary. There, in 1980, a seminarian, Richard Nason, asked Ziemann, his spiritual advisor, for help because a priest-instructor at the seminary, a friend of Ziemann's, was pressuring students to have sex.[99] Ziemann did nothing. In 1986 Mahony made Ziemann an auxiliary bishop in Los Angeles. In 1992 Ziemann became bishop of Santa Rosa, which had had major problems with sex abuse. In 1993 Ziemann ordained Jorge Hume Salas, a Costa Rican, who had never been to seminary and had been a deacon for only fifteen months. Salas had one overwhelming qualification: he gave Ziemann his body. Salas stole money from his parish and showed a strong interest in teenage boys. Sister Jane Kelly spoke with the Rev. Thomas Keys, vicar general of the diocese, to protest Salas's thefts and his sexual involvement with Latino youths. Kelly recounted how Keys promised that he would get back to her and that he would "have Father Jorge Hume Salas removed from priestly ministry. How gullible we were. It would be weeks before I discovered that Tom Keys had lied to us."[100]

In 1996 Ziemann sent Salas off to a treatment center because of the allegations of theft and homosexuality. Salas claimed that before he left Ziemann called him for a private interview and then undressed him. "Salas said that Ziemann then masturbated him, and he, in turn, masturbated

Ziemann. During this incident, Ziemann asked Salas to suck his nipples. Ziemann also asked Salas to orally copulate him. Salas said he refused, and that the bishop orally copulated him. Salas then returned the act."[101] Ziemann visited Salas at the treatment center where they had sex again. After Salas returned to Santa Rosa, Ziemann gave him a beeper so that Ziemann could summon him when he wanted sex.

Salas was a confidence artist and liar. Before he was ordained he had pretended to be a priest and heard confessions and said Mass. Such pretense should have permanently barred him from the priesthood. Salas knew that his dubious background meant that he was not a convincing witness in the lawsuit he was planning against Ziemann, so he decided to get evidence that Ziemann was pressuring him into a sexual relationship by using the threat of reporting the 1996 theft to the police and to the immigration authorities. Salas collected some of Ziemann's semen on a tissue and preserved it. He also wired himself with a tape recorder and steered the conversation around to sex: "all the time [you say], 'This the last time, the last time, the last time.' Never it came the last time. All the time I came with you you have sex and sex and sex and sex. It's not good for me, not good for me . . . all the times when I had to sleep with you." Ziemann responded: "I know, it's been my fault. And I'm sorry for that. Because I don't think you wanted to do that."[102] Hume Salas also went on to accuse Ziemann of giving him a venereal disease—Ziemann again apologized. But where did Ziemann get the disease? Salas sued Ziemann and subpoenaed a blood sample. Ziemann realized it was all over, resigned in 1999, and confessed. Ziemann settled with Salas for $535,000. The settlement funds came from the money the laity had given the diocese for religious purposes.[103]

Ziemann's financial mismanagement lost the diocese of Santa Rosa $31 million. All the money that parishes had deposited with the diocese was gone—all the building funds, all the money to cover teachers' salaries, all the Boy Scout dues—gone. Ziemann had wanted to be loved and therefore spent money recklessly whenever someone asked for it. Under Ziemann Santa Rosa was supporting more ministries than Los Angeles was. Keys, the supposed financial genius, had invested $5 million in a Luxembourg scheme that promised a 400 percent return. It was, of course, a fraud.[104]

Ziemann retired to a Benedictine monastery near Tucson where he was not supposed to say Mass publicly. He did anyway. The Vatican heard of it and forbade Ziemann to say Mass at all. Ryan DiMaria sued the Los Angeles diocese because Msgr. Michael A. Harris had molested him and Ziemann had failed to act on the seminarian's 1979 complaint. In 2002 Ziemann had been deposed for a civil trial and was scheduled for another deposition; Mahony was also scheduled to be deposed in this trial. To avoid these depositions, Mahony and Bishop Tod D. Brown of the Orange diocese together ended the case by settling with DiMaria for $5.2 million.

When he was auxiliary bishop of Fresno, Mahony was also a licensed social worker and was therefore required by law to report child abuse. When he became bishop of Stockton, California, in 1980, Mahony surrendered this license and removed himself from the reporting requirements. He inherited from Bishop Merlin J. Guilfoyle the case of the omnivorously abusive priest Oliver F. O'Grady. "O'Grady was an equal opportunity pedophile, targeting males and females, with whom he variously engaged in oral and anal sex, masturbation, digital penetration, groping, and fondling. This, while having illicit affairs with at least two of the children's mothers."[105] Pedophiles often have sexual interest in both adult women and in both male and female small children because their bodies are feminine.

In the early 1970s, according to a 2003 lawsuit, O'Grady assaulted two altar boys (one eleven years old, the other twelve) at St. Anne's parish in Lodi[106] (the case was settled in March 2005 for $3.6 million). In 1976, during his appointment in Lodi, O'Grady wrote a letter, now in his personnel file, to Nancy Sloan apologizing for abusing her. O'Grady later said that Guilfoyle didn't send him to counseling and that the bishop was angry with him for having written the letter. From the late 1970s to the early 1980s, O'Grady abused Cristin Perez and her brother, Daniel Howard, at Sacred Heart parish, Turlock, California.[107]

In 1982 Mahony transferred O'Grady to Stockton, and in 1984 for reasons that are unclear, the diocese sent O'Grady to William Guttieri, a psychiatric social worker. O'Grady admitted abusing a boy (it turned out to be James Howard), and Guttieri notified both child protective services and Tom Shepherd, the lawyer for the diocese. A detective interviewed the mother, Ann Howard, but could not get any information from the nine-year-old James. The detective then got a call from Shepherd, who "assured him that O'Grady would get counseling through the church and that he would be transferred to a new assignment where he would be working with adults away from any children."[108] Mahony hired Dr. William Morris to evaluate O'Grady. Morris concluded: "Father O'Grady reveals a severe defect in maturation, not only in the matter of sex, but more importantly in the matter of social relationships. Perhaps Oliver is not truly called to the priesthood."[109]

Just before he became archbishop of Los Angeles in 1985, Mahony appointed O'Grady pastor of St. Andrew's parish in San Andreas—despite the information in the file about abuse by O'Grady, including the 1976 confession (information which, at the civil trial, Mahoney denied ever seeing). Mahony's successor as bishop of Stockton made O'Grady associate pastor of Sacred Heart in Turlock, where he met the Doe family (who wish their name not to appear in the records). He molested their son, who became suicidal, and he molested their nine-month-old daughter leaving her with vaginal scarring from digital penetration. In spring 1993 O'Grady had traveled to San Diego to officiate at the marriage of one of the Howards' relatives; there had been a scene at the wedding. A victim later telephoned Jane Doe, and told her how O'Grady had molested her and her siblings, and that he might be going after the Doe children.

They decided to confront O'Grady. Jane Doe, Ann Howard, the grown Howard daughter, and the daughter's boyfriend all drove to O'Grady's rectory. The boyfriend got there first and was beating up O'Grady when O'Grady picked up the phone and dialed 911. Suddenly realizing that a complaint to the police about being beaten up for being a child molester was probably not a good idea, he put the phone down immediately, but the 911 system had registered his address, and the police arrived, and everything started coming out. James and John Howard then pressed charges. The now-jailed O'Grady confessed the molestation to an Episcopal priest, the Rev. Deborah Warwick Fabino, who reported the confession to the police. O'Grady pleaded guilty, and remained in prison until 2002, when he was released and deported to his native Ireland.

In 1994 Jane Doe tried to meet with Mahony by using Fabino as an intermediary. "I just wanted to understand from him how he could have allowed this man to have continued as a priest and how he could have sent him [to San Andreas] knowing what I'm convinced he knew," says Doe. Mahony refused to meet with her. "I got a cursory letter back from one of his representatives saying it wasn't possible," Fabino said. "That was it."[110]

In 1995 the Doe family settled with the diocese of Stockton. In 1998 the Howards sued and Mahony, now archbishop of Los Angeles and a cardinal, had to testify. He did not make a convincing witness. During a break in the trial, he told reporters he had done everything humanly possible to prevent abuse. Anderson, the attorney for the plaintiffs, took that point up when the questioning resumed.

> "At the time, Cardinal, did you talk to the police?"
>
> "No," Mahony said.
>
> "You could have."
>
> "Well, I'm not sure I could have. But...."
>
> "What was restraining you?" Anderson asked.
>
> It went on like this for several minutes, Anderson knocking down Mahony's claim that everything humanly possible had been done to prevent future abuse.
>
> Did you send O'Grady to a doctor specializing in sex offense? he asked.
>
> "At the time, I was really unaware that there were such specialists," Mahony said.
>
> Did you check O'Grady's file?
>
> No, Mahony said.
>
> Did you conduct an investigation of your own?
>
> Sending him to a psychiatrist seemed appropriate enough, Mahony answered.

Did you interview witnesses? Anderson asked.

No, Mahony said.[111]

The jury thought that Mahony was lying. One said, "I found Mahony to be utterly unbelievable."[112] Either that, or he demonstrated breathtaking incompetence by not even opening the personnel folder of an abusive priest to see what was in it.

Mahony's troubles with Stockton are not over. He gave another deposition on November 23, 2004.[113] In his 1998 sworn testimony he had said that while he was bishop of Stockton the only priest about whom allegations of sexual abuse were made was O'Grady, an Irish citizen whose mother Mahony had visited in Ireland.[114] This was not true: Mahony had handled three other cases of sexual abuse by priests. Two of them involved Mexican priests, Antonio Munoz (1981) and Antonio Camacho (1984). Mahony had himself written memos (one of them five pages long); he had suspended the priests the day he received the allegations, had contacted the police and immigration authorities, and in Camacho's case had written to all of the bishops in the western United States to warn them about him.[115] In 2004 Mahony explained his earlier testimony as a memory lapse: "We had had many events in the archdiocese of Los Angeles, and I was very preoccupied. We had the visit of the Holy Father. We had the earthquakes. We had riots. We had everything. And I simply did not remember everything that happened many years ago in Stockton."[116] The jury's intuition in 1998 that Mahony was lying seems to have been correct. A victims' group has asked the district attorney to consider bringing perjury charges against Mahony.[117]

In 1979 Msgr. Michael A. Harris was principal of the Orange diocese's Mater Dei High School in Santa Ana. Richard Nason, a seminarian at Our Lady of the Angels (see above) informed Ziemann that Harris had molested a student at Mater Dei, a friend of Nason.[118] Ziemann did nothing. Harris, known as the "Hollywood priest" because of his good looks and charisma, was a wildly popular money raiser. At the 1987 opening of the Orange diocese's new high school, "to a roar of applause from the audience, he ripped open his black clerical shirt to reveal a Superman logo. The 'S' stood for Santa Margarita High. Harris was the guiding force behind the new school and its first principal."[119] He had raised $26 million for the school, where he found several good candidates for his bed.

When he was teaching at Mater Dei, Harris assaulted Vincent Colice from 1977 to 1979. On his deathbed with AIDS in 1993, Colice gave his mother permission to go public with a secret he had told her two years earlier: that Harris had sexually assaulted him. Lenora Colice wrote Harris and accused him of molesting her son. Harris replied that "through counseling and other resources I have endeavored to work through many things. Hard work and prayer have helped. It may not be any consolation, but I am very sorry."[120] Harris later denied this was an admission of guilt.

By 1991 Harris was principal of Santa Margarita High School. The parents of Marcus Ryan DiMaria, a seventeen-year-old student at the school, asked Harris to counsel DiMaria who was depressed because a friend had committed suicide. DiMaria, a vulnerable boy, ended up in Harris's bed. DiMaria struggled for years with the emotions the seduction had brought on, and, as we have seen, he finally sued the diocese of Orange and the archdiocese of Los Angeles, which as the metropolitan see had responsibility for the Orange diocese. In 1994 Harris had resigned from the priesthood and with the help of his wealthy backers he became head of a low-income housing foundation, for which he received $91,000 a year.[121]

Since Ziemann and Mahony both faced having to testify, the two dioceses offered DiMaria $5.2 million. One line of questioning that would have been extremely uncomfortable related to sexual activity at St. John's Seminary in Camarillo, Mahony's alma mater. St. John's "may be one of the country's gayest facilities for higher education. Depending on whom you ask, gay and bisexual men make up anywhere from thirty percent to seventy percent of the student body at the college and graduate levels." The rector Rt. Rev. Helmut Hefner thinks the percentage of gays in the student body may be fifty percent, but "that hasn't caused any discomfort to heterosexuals."[122] However, some homosexuals have a very elastic definition of celibacy and chastity which does not necessarily exclude sexual activity, and the revelation of a gay culture at the main California seminary would not go over well in the midst of all the scandals of priests having sex with seventeen-year-old boys.

Even more than the money, DiMaria wanted other children to be protected. As part of the settlement, Mahony had to agree to the following:

- The archdiocese had to institute a zero tolerance policy for sexual abuse;
- The archdiocese had to require every priest to sign an agreement not to molest children;
- The archdiocese had to insert a green page in the personnel folder of every priest about whom incriminating information existed so that anyone who saw the folder would be alerted;
- The archdiocese had to establish a toll-free victim hotline;
- The archdiocese had to distribute materials about sex abuse to parishes and schools;
- The archdiocese had to "conduct exit interviews to query graduating students about abuses they may have observed at St. John's Seminary College."[123]

DiMaria, although he had no direct connection with the seminary, had presumably heard enough about sexual misbehavior there to suspect that the gay culture of the seminary was contributing to a general atmosphere of sexual license in the archdiocese.[124]

Having been forced into these reforms as a condition for not having to testify, Mahony then put himself forward as a pioneer in child protection after the Boston scandals broke at the beginning of 2002.

After Mahony became archbishop of Los Angeles, he met with his priests in the summer of 1986 and told them that if they had any sexual difficulties they should come to him to talk about them. In late 1986 the "gregarious and charismatic" Rev. Michael Stephen Baker admitted to Mahony that he was molesting boys. Mahony was deeply concerned for the priest; "he was very solicitous and understanding,"[125] Baker later said. The next day Baker met with Mahony and John P. McNicholas, the archdiocesan attorney. McNicholas asked, "'Should we call the police now?' Baker said he recalled Mahony's response: 'No, no, no. . . .'"[126] Mahony did not ask for information or order an investigation. Baker was sent to therapy and given a series of temporary assignments in parishes, assignments which Mahony claimed he knew nothing about, although he had signed off on some of them. No one in the parishes was told of Baker's admission. In 2000 an attorney representing the two boys whom Baker had admitted molesting in 1986 informed Mahony that Baker had continued the molestation for thirteen years. The boys had remained silent because Baker had threatened them and had made their mother financially dependent on him. Baker had even paid for the family to move to Arizona, where he would go to molest the boys. Accompanying Baker on trips to Arizona was Msgr. Timothy Dyer, a classmate of Baker's from St. John's Seminary and the vicar of clergy for the archdiocese of Los Angeles.[127]

The two Mexican boys whom Baker had molested hired Lynne Cadigan, a lawyer from Tucson. She contacted Baker, who offered her $1 million (there has been no indication of the source of this money) and asked her, "Just don't tell Roger [Mahony]. I'm supposed to be staying out of trouble but I'm still doing things I shouldn't do. Roger will be mad if he finds out."[128] Roger did find out; whether he got mad we don't know, but Roger immediately (to Cadigan's surprise) gave the boys $1.3 million (of which Baker paid about $600,000), but did not tell the police. He let Baker retire in December 2002 with $100,000 severance pay. The next month the archdiocese learned that Baker had molested ten more boys, but did not tell the police or parishes.

It was not until the Boston scandals broke and the *Los Angeles Times* began putting pressure on Mahony that he decided to tell the police, and then only after a debate detailed in e-mails that someone had intercepted and supplied to the media. Mahony wrote a letter of apology to his priests (omitting small details like the $1.3 million settlement) and expressed astonishment that the admitted child molester had not been telling the full truth. In a moment of candor, Mahony said, "I have to be honest with you. There is absolutely nothing good about the Baker case. Just absolutely nothing."[129]

## *Ontario*

Although the abuse at Mount Cashel in Newfoundland is mentioned in books and articles, abuse on an even greater scale was going on in Ontario at St. John's and St. Joseph's training schools, run by the Brothers of the Christian Schools (F.S.C), the group founded in France by St. John Baptist de la Salle. Boys were committed to these Ontario schools for a variety of offenses, including being incorrigible, stealing a candy bar, and taking a car for a joy ride. David McCann went there in 1958 at the age of twelve. There "he saw Brothers beat the children. He saw them kick them. He saw them punch them in the face so hard that blood spattered on the school's cinderblock walls."[130] Several boys died of neglect.

As at Mount Cashel in Newfoundland, the physical abuse was a prelude to sexual abuse. One boy was beaten unconscious by a brother; he awoke "as the [b]rother cut open his jeans to sodomize him."[131] Another boy witnessed "a sexual assault in which a [b]rother attempted to shove a tree branch up a child's anus."[132] Brother André Charbonneau sexually abused one boy and then "urinated over him, wrapped him up in the soaking sheets and made him stand that way for several hours."[133] Brother Joseph (Lucien Dagenais) had lost his hand in an industrial accident and had a hook. He rammed it up a boy's rectum.[134]

David McCann (who had been sexually abused at St. Joseph's school) in 1990 watched the news about Mount Cashel and thought his story might at last be believed. He organized a handful of other victims to press for justice. Eventually over 1,600 victims of physical and sexual abuse at these schools came forward. Twenty Christian Brothers were prosecuted; most were convicted. One confessed and excused himself: "It's a weakness. We're not perfect. God can accept a weakness. The good Lord will forgive us like anybody else."[135] The victims were compensated with a few thousand dollars each from a $16,000,000 (Canadian) negotiated settlement. In the summer of 2004 Ontario premier Dalton McGuinty finally apologized: "I say directly to the victims: you were failed when you needed us most. And that your government is, and always will be, very sorry."[136] Not all victims heard the apology. Several had committed suicide because of the delays in the trials and restitution. Others were in prison; they had committed sexual crimes themselves, imitating what they had been taught by the Christian Brothers.

## *Ireland*

English-speaking lands have so far provided most of the scandals involving priests and minors. Richard Sipe suspects that Ireland (and the lands dominated by Irish clergy) was so traumatized by the massive deaths of the potato famine that it developed a rigid form of Catholicism that over-idealized clergy and religious and allowed sexual abuse to flourish.[137] But Spain and the United States seem to have roughly the same percentage of priests who are sexually involved with minors—in Spain about seven to ten percent[138]—and the names of the priests in the United States are not just Irish: Polish, German, and Spanish names occur in the accusations. However, Ireland has had some major scandals.

In 1994 the case of Father Brendan Smyth led to the fall of the Irish government. It was a long and sad story. He joined the Norbertines in 1945 and was stationed at Kilnacrott Abbey most of his life (when he was not hiding from the police) and it was there, shortly after his ordination, that Smyth's "problem with children surfaced"[139] (according to Abbot Smith of Kilnacrott Abbey). Smyth liked both boys and girls, mostly very young. He was "the Pied Piper or Santa Claus"[140] who would tickle children in front of their parents; the children knew what it meant, but the parents saw only a priest who was good with children. He masturbated one young girl until her hymen broke; he had two boys masturbate each other while he watched. A boy was placed in a Catholic institution which had a sideline of supplying children for priests' sexual needs. Father Smyth would come and ask to see the boy in a private room; he would French kiss him; "then the priest would open his trousers and place the boy's hand on his penis, making the boy masturbate him until he ejaculated."[141]

When Ireland began to grow uncomfortable for Smyth, he was sent to Fargo, North Dakota, and then to Providence, Rhode Island, without any indication, the Americans claim, that he had any sexual problems. In both places he molested boys before he returned to Ireland. Like most pedophiles and abusers, Smyth showed "no remorse"[142] for his actions.

The border between Northern Ireland and the Republic gives protection to criminals. Abbot Smith said he was unable to control Smyth's movements, and the priest went north to escape the Garda and south to escape the Royal Irish Constabulary. The hierarchy generated the usual fog of lies. Cardinal Daly disclaimed any jurisdiction over the abbey and any ability to deal with Smyth, who was totally under the jurisdiction of the Norbertine abbot. But Daly suddenly discovered his ability to forbid that same abbot from appearing on television to answer questions about the case.

The Irish government scrutinized the diocese of Ferns and issued a report that shocked Ireland.[143] The worst offender was the Rev. Sean Fortune, who left a train of ravaged lives and corpses over twenty years. He was brutal, but manipulated the victims, the laity, the bishops, and the government, to get what he wanted: money and sex.

At the end of his life, when the justice system was closing in on him, he claimed to have been molested himself by a religious.[144] He also seems to have molested boys before he entered the seminary.[145] He first studied for the Christian Brothers, and then when he was twenty years old in 1973, he entered the seminary of the diocese of Ferns, St. Peter's College, which had a secondary school attached. There he met a thirteen-year-old boy, whom he first engaged in sexually explicit conversation, which escalated rapidly to touching, masturbation, oral sex, and anal rape. The victim told the principal of St. Peter's, who "reacted violently to what Stephen [a pseudonym] said and refused to believe him, telling him that Sean Fortune was going to be a good priest and that if he persists in saying these things, he would be thrown out of the college."[146] Victims were often punished for reporting Fortune's abuse.

Fortune was also involved with the Boy Scouts; he both molested the boys and propositioned the leaders. One adult leader made a full report of the molestation to the headquarters of the Boy Scouts of Ireland, and Scout officials met with Bishop Donald Herlihy of Ferns to discuss Fortune.

Herlihy then ordained Fortune in 1979 and sent him to Belfast with an order to keep away from the Boy Scouts.[147]

Fortune ignored the order, and soon did something that got him summarily dismissed from the Belfast diocese and sent back to Ferns. Herlihy sent Fortune to be evaluated by a psychology professor, Feichin O'Doherty, who reported to the bishop that Fortune dismissed his molestation of the scouts as "just messing" but it was in fact "homosexual behavior, and might even be classified as indecent assault in Civil Law."[148]

Like other abusers, Fortune was a narcissist and sociopath. O'Doherty noted Fortune's "apparent lack of real feelings about the reality of his position,"[149] and that he did not take his actions and situation "seriously enough."[150] O'Doherty concluded that he needed "a radical and fundamental change in his personality,"[151] what Catholics call repentance and conversion. Instead Herlihy and his successor as bishop of Ferns, Brian Comiskey, shifted Fortune from parish to parish.[152]

As a priest Fortune had a special position in rural Irish society. Some laity were superstitious and had apparently never heard of the sin of simony; they tried to buy blessings and healings from Fortune. Fortune told boys that "because he was a priest and could not get married what he was doing was not wrong."[153] It was, after all, "natural,"[154] as he tried to convince the boys. Fortune was always greedy for money, but he was even greedier for sex.

Fortune was a big, powerful man, and brutal with his victims. He picked up one teenage hitchhiker who had a scar on his face. Fortune masturbated and smeared his semen on the boy's face, telling him "it would heal his face."[155] He cornered one boy and raped him, leaving him "in a mess on the floor, bleeding heavily."[156] Boys came back from visits with Fortune "unable to walk properly" and with "a great deal of blood" on their clothes."[157] He hunted boys through a ruined castle and raped them.

Fortune made the victims swear on the Bible not to tell anyone of the abuse. It did little good if the boys did. One victim told his mother; she "dismissed the suggestion outright and physically attacked" him.[158] Another told a priest, who wanted to reenact the abuse.[159] For some boys the only escape was death. At least two of Fortune's victims committed suicide. Others tried and failed.

Bishop Comiskey inherited Fortune when he took over the Ferns diocese. Comiskey played the role of the responsible progressive. He said all the right things about protecting children from abuse and then gave Fortune a parish after several accusations of child abuse. He asked for a public discussion of priestly celibacy as he was brushing off numerous complaints about Fortune's erratic behavior. He had the report from O'Doherty; he sent Fortune for treatment, but Fortune did not attend the treatment center that Comiskey had told him to attend. Counselors and doctors who saw Fortune (even though Comiskey did not fill them in on the history) kept warning Comiskey that something was wrong; Fortune did not like these assessments so Comiskey let him find his own psychiatrist, Ingo Fischer, who told Comiskey that he was stable, heterosexual, and "fit for parish work"[160] if he continued to see Fischer. In fact Fischer said it was essential to Fortune's progress that he be "restored to some ministry."[161]

Comiskey claimed he never acted canonically against Fortune "because of warnings from the Vatican that bishops had to proceed very carefully and make sure that they had hard evidence before removing a priest."[162] The board of inquiry concluded there was "no adequate explanation for the failure of Bishop Comiskey to deal rigorously and effectively with [Father] Fortune."[163] There may have been other reasons for Comiskey's lack of action, which the reasons that some complainants suspected were "sinister."[164] The report hints at them.

Comiskey was a self-acknowledged alcoholic.[165] He sought treatment at a center for alcoholism and his memory lapses and major errors of judgment may be a result of his alcoholism.

The board of inquiry claimed to find no evidence of a pedophile ring, which it narrowly defined as abusers sharing victims with one other. But the board discovered several abusers had been at St. Peter's College both as seminarians and staff, including the principal. Some who were at the college remembered "a relatively high level of sexual activity both with adults and children."[166] One boy saw Fortune abusing a young teenager while "two other adults were there."[167]

When the law began closing in on Fortune, he told people that if he went down, he would "bring Bishop Comiskey with him."[168] Those who heard it thought he was referring to Bishop Comiskey's alcoholism. Immediately before his trial, facing sixty-six charges of sexual abuse and knowing he would be found guilty, Fortune committed suicide. In his suicide note Fortune denied abusing boys and claimed that Bishop Comiskey was "responsible for all this as he had raped me and buggered me."[169] Comiskey denied this, and the board of inquiry said it did not believe it. But Comiskey liked to vacation in Thailand, a big destination for sex tourists.[170]

The parents of a girl who was over sixteen made a complaint to the South Eastern Health Board about "inappropriate behavior"[171] of Bishop Comiskey with their daughter. Comiskey denied doing anything. The chancellor of the archdiocese of Dublin investigated and reported to the Vatican that "a delict [crime] had not been committed as regards the behavior alleged but the fact that under the influence of alcohol Bishop Comiskey was alleged to have acted in such a manner was something that needed to be addressed to ensure that no repetition of such behaviour could take place."[172] It seems that under the influence Comiskey had done something which, if not criminal, was unbecoming of a bishop. Like many alcoholics, Comiskey may not even have remembered what he had done in this case, and there may have been others of which Fortune was aware.

The diocese of Ferns in Ireland has produced another priest whose story is little known outside Ireland, but whose career indicates that the troubles in the Catholic Church go far deeper than garden-variety sexual immorality. The Rev. Micaél Ledwith taught systematic theology at Maynooth, the national seminary of Ireland. In 1984 he was being considered for the position of bishop of Ferns (with Dublin a possibility in the future) but then some seminarians raised awkward questions with the bishops who were the trustees of the college about Ledwith's sexual harassment of the younger seminarians,[173] so Comiskey became bishop of Ferns instead. These older seminarians were told to "go home and say your prayers,"[174] and Ledwith tried to keep them from being ordained.

The dean at Maynooth, the Rev. Gerard McGinnity, was "demoted and humiliated for attempting" to help these seminarians.[175] When Dr. Gaetano Alibrandi, the apostolic nuncio to Ireland from 1969 to 1989, asked for information from McGinnity about Ledwith, McGinnity told him about the accusations the seminarians had made. This is not what the Vatican wanted to hear. McGinnity was sent on a sabbatical to Rome and then stationed in a remote rural parish for three years. He was then sent to be dean of discipline at a high school seminary and did not even receive a state salary for teaching, although he had a doctorate in patristic theology from Trinity College in Dublin. In 1987, although he knew about the allegations that Ledwith had sexually abused seminarians, Alibrandi put Ledwith's name on the list of three candidates that was sent to the pope to choose among for the position of archbishop of Dublin.[176]

Meanwhile, having lost his chance at the bishopric of Ferns, Ledwith became in 1985 the head of Maynooth and also a member of the Pontifical International Theological Commission, a group that advises the pope on sensitive theological issues. The Commission's head was Cardinal Ratzinger, now Pope Benedict XVI. In 1991, Ledwith served as an assistant under Bishop Walter Kasper at the Synod of Bishops. His career proceeded smoothly until 1994, when he privately settled an accusation of a minor (which he denied). The trustees of Maynooth wanted him to go away and therefore set up a retirement fund of 77,000 Irish pounds plus a gratuity of six months salary. Ledwith also receives a pension from the Irish state. So far it was but the dreary, oft-told tale of pederasty, homosexuality, and cover-ups.

Ledwith left Ireland and quickly surfaced in the United States, where he is teaching in Washington state at the Ramtha School of Enlightenment, a gnostic university. The foundress, JZ Knight, born in Roswell, New Mexico (of UFO fame), has become the channeler of Ramtha, the "Enlightened One," a Cro-Magnon Lemurian warrior who 35,000 years ago fought against Atlantis and is now an ascended master, who teaches (with an acknowledgment to second-century gnosticism):

1. A transcendent, ineffable deity from whom the known world emanated in increasingly dense and less spiritual layers;
2. Human beings as sparks of divinity fallen into matter; and
3. The necessity for humans to return to their origin through the acquisition of knowledge, or gnosis.[177]

Shirley MacLaine is a disciple of Knight. Some adherents (like the second-century gnostics whom the Fathers of the Church attacked) get the distinct impression "that they are above morality due to their divine status."[178] It is the usual New Age folderol with trappings of classical gnosticism. This is the gospel that Ledwith is traveling around the world proclaiming—and he remained a priest in good standing of the diocese of Ferns until he was defrocked in 2005.

There are two main interpretations of the Ledwith case. The first is that Ledwith has been a confidence artist and a fraud all along. He has never been a Christian believer but has manipulated the Catholic Church to obtain prestige, money, and sex. This means that a confidence man was president of the national seminary of Ireland, a candidate for the see of Dublin, and a principal theological adviser to the pope. The second possibility is that Ledwith converted from Christianity to gnosticism. This means that a president of the national seminary of Ireland, a candidate for the see of Dublin, and a principal theological adviser to the pope became a subscriber to the ancient heresy that parts of the New Testament were written to combat. Gnosticism is currently *in* among pop theological liberals like Elaine Pagels, who promotes the gnostic gospels as an alternative source of Christianity. Did Ledwith actually convert to this intellectual fad? Or was he so shallow he did not see any incompatibility between gnosticism and Christianity? One does not jettison orthodox Christianity overnight; what was he teaching at Maynooth and what was he telling the bishops and the pope? Did the ancient heresy of gnosticism have a voice in the highest councils of the Roman Catholic Church? If so, didn't anyone notice? Or is it considered impolite (i.e., noncollegial) in the Vatican to point out to a theologian that he has ceased to be a Christian?

## *Austria*

Hans Hermann Groër was an obscure Benedictine monk known only for his devotion to Our Lady of Fatima.[179] In 1952 he became the prefect of students in a boys' seminary at Hollabrunn and spent forty-four years of his life in such environments. On Ash Wednesday 1964 a student at Hollabrunn, Johannes K., committed suicide by throwing himself in front of a train. A fellow student was found reading the dead boy's diary. The seminary rector Johannes Kurz ordered him to be silent: "if he talked, he would go to hell."[180] Groër abused Udo Fischer and Josef Hartmann at the seminary during the early 1970s. Groër became head of the Legion of Mary and gathered disciples who promised total obedience and secrecy (see p. 477–479). Groër entered Göttweig as a monk in 1974, bringing (eventually) seventeen young men with him; later seven of them said they were sexually abused by Groër.[181]

In the early 1980s two auxiliary bishops of Vienna investigated accusations of sexual abuse against Groër.[182] In 1985 Udo Fischer accused Groër of sexual abuse to Abbot Clemens Lashofer and Father Ildefons Fux, who warned Fischer: "Think on the end of Judas!"[183] In January 1986 Placidus Kubalek, a monk and a member of the Legion of Mary, committed suicide by throwing himself from a tower at Göttweig. He was depressed because of guilt feelings.

Thirteen months after Fischer had accused Groër, in July 1986, Groër was appointed by Pope John Paul II as archbishop of Vienna; immediately rumors that he was an abuser began circulating through Vienna. In September 1987 Groër invited the young pilgrim Wolfgang Kimmel into his bedroom and abused him. In May 1988 the pope made Groër a cardinal. Provoked by Groër's 1995 declaration that pederasts would not inherit the Kingdom of God, Josef Hartmann, in an interview in the April 3, 1995, edition of the Austrian news magazine *Profil*, announced that Groër had abused him in 1971, when he was fourteen years old and studying at Hollabrunn. After Hartmann went public, other former students revealed that Groër had abused them when they were around thirteen years of age.

After Groër was publicly accused, the Austrian bishops, remembering the calumnies of the Nazis,[184] initially attacked the accusers, but one of them, Christoph Schönborn, later apologized to the victims for his attack on them.[185] However, Groër remained in office until he stepped down at the normal retirement age and was succeeded by his auxiliary bishop, Schönborn. The pope received Groër socially (to Schönborn's surprise and disgruntlement[186]) at the convocation at which Schönborn was made a cardinal. In 1998 more former seminarians came forward and accused Groër of abuse committed in the 1970s.

Groër returned to Maria Roggendorf as prior; more accusations surfaced. A novice there admitted having sexual activity with Groër in the confessional, but excused it: "we weren't under age."[187] The Vatican sent the head of the Benedictines, Abbot Marcel Rooney, to investigate. After receiving a report of this investigation, in February 1998 Schönborn and other Austrian bishops said that "we have arrived at a moral conviction that the allegations made against the former archbishop Cardinal Groër are essentially true. . . . I hope that Cardinal Groër will say a few words that will clarify matters and liberate. . . ."[188] Schönborn also said, "As bishop of this diocese, I apologize for everything by which my predecessor, and other church dignitaries, have wronged people entrusted to them" and offered help to anyone harmed by Groër.[189] All Groër said was "I ask pardon of God and man, *if* [my emphasis] I am guilty."[190] Bishop Kurt Krenn of Sankt Pölten continued to denounce Groër's victims as "Lausbuben"[191] (pranksters) and denied that Groër's statement was a confession of guilt but only a contribution to peace in the Church. Groër went into exile at Marienfeld near Dresden and died in 2003. At his death John Paul II wrote that Groër had served "with great love for Christ and his Church."[192] The Austrians, already unhappy with papal policies, continue to leave the church en masse.

The abrasive and alcoholic former boxer Bishop Kurt Krenn (who is an argument for appointing conciliatory bishops) has continued to roil the waters. He called Schönborn a liar during the controversy,[193] and after Groër's death said that the Austrian bishops who had said Groër was guilty had made a "grave mistake" and should apologize.[194] On his website Krenn has a eulogy of Groër by Ildefons Fux, who said that the fate of Groër reminded him of the Passion of Christ. As a result, Hartmann, who had wanted to forget the whole affair, decided to sue the Austrian Church. Msgr. Helmut Schüller, in charge of handling sexual abuse cases in the archdiocese of Vienna, was unhappy with these developments: "There has never been an official report, nothing's cleared up, and now a number of Austrian bishops [i.e., Kurt Krenn] are even trying to rehabilitate Groër."[195]

In July 2003 *Profil* published pictures of the regent and subregent of the large seminary[196] of Sankt Pölten at a lively Christmas party. Austrians saw Subregent Wolfgang Rothe French-kissing a seminarian under the mistletoe and the Regent Ulrich Küchl with his hand on a seminarian's crotch. Krenn dismissed this as *Bubendummheiten*, *Bubenstreiche*, "frat-boys' pranks," and told the Austrian bishops that what he did in his diocese was "none of their bloody business."[197] But more serious allegations followed: someone at the seminary had downloaded pornographic pictures, including child pornography and bestiality. The regent was rumored to have conducted a "marriage" ceremony for two seminarians at a local bar. Another seminarian was accused of putting sexual pressure on local schoolchildren.[198] When the police searched the seminary, they found a computer with child pornography (17,000 images) belonging to a Polish seminarian; they also discovered a digital camera with incriminating pictures. Klaus Küng, doctor, member of Opus Dei, and bishop of Feldkirch, was sent by the Vatican as a visitator with authority to reform the diocese. He forbade Krenn to speak publicly and closed the seminary, announcing that the allegations of homosexual relationships and pornography use were true, and that there were "other difficulties." These other difficulties may include a "suicide" by drowning of a seminarian in October 2003.

The Austrian bishops were not happy with the Vatican, which had known about the allegations concerning the seminary months before they became public. Schönborn's vicar for sexual abuse victims, Msgr. Helmut Schüller, said that the Vatican had taken from the local bishops' synod the power to discipline member bishops who were harming the Church and had reserved all disciplinary authority to itself, and then did nothing. Schüller said this stabbed the local church in the back.[199] Austrians were more and more unhappy with the Vatican's policy of neglecting problems in the hope that they would solve themselves without Vatican bureaucrats having to do anything, especially not confront an erring bishop. Although Küng replaced Krenn in July 2004, resignations of laity from the Church in Austria swelled with every new revelation of corruption.

## *Poland*

Juliusz Paetz worked at the Vatican for the Synod of Bishops from 1967 to 1976. He then began working in the papal household, where in 1978, as one of the few Poles in the Vatican, he attracted the attention of the newly elected Karol Wojtyla. He continued working in the papal household until 1982, when the pope appointed him bishop of Lomza and in 1996 archbishop of Poznan, Paetz's hometown.

In 2002 he was publicly accused of sexually harassing seminarians. He had visited the seminary using a tunnel between his palace and the seminary and had been overly familiar with seminarians, showing up unannounced at night in their bedrooms, to the point that in 2000 the seminary rector, Rev. Tadeus Karkosz, had banned him from entering the seminary.[200] Seminarians tried to handle the matter privately but were rebuffed, and eventually had to make their accusations public in a respected national conservative newspaper, *Rzeczpospolita*, one that could not be accused of anticlericalism.[201] Paetz resigned, protesting his innocence and claiming his gestures had been misunderstood.

But Paetz's failings may have had even more serious consequences. He was a descendent of a German family (hence the name) who had emigrated to Poland in the seventeenth century. Because of his mixed German-Polish heritage, he worked in the Synod of Bishops in a delicate area of German-Polish relations. The secret police of Communist Poland therefore had an eye on him, and they may have discovered his homosexual proclivities (which some claim were also known to Cardinal Jozef Glemp).[202] The election of a Polish pope would make such information about him even more useful to the communists. Jerzy Urban, who had been the last government spokesman for Communist Poland, in 1996 named an "Archbishop P." as the spy that the Communists had in the Vatican.[203] Paetz's homosexuality may well have had consequences for international politics and for the safety of patriotic Catholics in Poland. The Church in Poland knew that some priests were blackmailed into collaborating with the Communists; was Paetz, an archbishop, the highest ranking of them? Did high officials in the Vatican have sexual secrets that made them reluctant to discipline child abusers out of a fear of retaliatory exposure?

Throughout the world abusive priests left victims, who were ignored or regarded as a nuisance by the authorities of the Church, whose first concern was to preserve the reputation of the clergy and whose second concern was to put abusive priests back into ministry. Secular authorities too demonstrated little concern for victims. How did the abusers choose and cultivate victims? How do the victims react to the abuse? The hardness of heart of the authorities who let abuse continue had severe consequences in the lives of the victims, as we shall see in the next chapter.

## CHAPTER NINE

# VICTIMS

SINCE 1950 tens of thousands of boys and girls were molested by priests in the United States. The victims were chosen because they were vulnerable, and the vulnerability was often the misplaced faith they or their parents had in the trustworthiness of the Catholic Church. The victims suffered the immediate horror and degradation of sexual abuse; they and their families endured decades of pain, which sometimes ended only in death by suicide for the victims, and unending grief for the families.

### *The Number and Sex of Victims*

How many victims of abusive priests were there in the United States? According to all experts, only a portion, perhaps a very small portion, of sexual abuse is ever reported. As the *John Jay Report* states, "All researchers acknowledge that those who are arrested represent only a fraction of all sex offenders."[1] David Finkelhor concurs: "All researchers believe that there is a vast number of unreported cases for every reported one."[2] Because the crime of sexual abuse is committed in private, it is difficult to determine how many victims priests abused. The true number is somewhere between base figure of 10,677 alleged victims of abuse in the *John Jay Report* (raised to 12,257 by later additional reports)[3] and the millions of victims in the Unites States claimed by some victims' organizations.

Any reasonable projection of the number of victims also depends upon an estimate of the true number of abusers. The *John Jay Report* counted

4,392 accused abusers between 1950 and 2002. Further reports up to the end of 2005 raised the number of accused priests to 4,977.[4]

There are indications of discrepancies within the *John Jay Report* itself. The first is the difference between diocesan priests and religious priests. Approximately 100,000 priests of both types were in ministry in the United States between 1950 and 2002. The *John Jay Report* indicated that of diocesan priests, 4.27 percent were accused of abuse, and of religious priests, 2.7 percent were accused of abuse.[5] This discrepancy requires an explanation. Unless religious priests were of higher moral and spiritual caliber, the lower figure probably indicates that fewer abusers among their ranks were reported. Religious priests often use only their religious names rather than their given names, and after the Second Vatican Council went back to their given names. They were also transferred around the United States and internationally far more frequently than diocesan priests were. In all probability, they offended at about the same rate, but were not reported at the same rate. Reports also may have been sent to international headquarters rather than kept in the United States.

The second major discrepancy is in the percentage of abusers among dioceses. It seems there was an attempt to structure or present the information to conceal an important fact. The John Jay analysis "revealed little variability in the rates of alleged abuse across regions of the Catholic Church in the U. S.—the range was 3% to 6% of priests."[6] Here the key word is *region.* Dioceses were grouped into regions, thereby concealing a vast difference among accused abusers from diocese to diocese.

The numbers that dioceses reported showed a wide divergence in the percentage of priests accused of abuse. Several dioceses reported minimal percentages: Miami, .9 percent; Denver, 1.1 percent; San Francisco, 1.6 percent; San Antonio, .9 percent. Other dioceses reported much higher percentages: Boston, 7 percent; Belleville 7.1 percent; Albany, 8.2 percent; Covington, 9.6 percent.[7] The first group of dioceses with low percentages is almost certainly greatly understated; even the second group is probably somewhat understated.[8] Further revelations have only increased the percentage of abusive priests in these dioceses.

These differences may mean that the dioceses with low percentages are severely underreporting the number of alleged abusers, and that the overall national percentage is closer to the 9% of the dioceses with the highest percentage of abusers. Or it may mean that some dioceses have a corrupt clerical culture and therefore have a higher percentage of abusers. The question demands further investigation.

The number of abusers is probably in the 5,000–10,000 range. The *John Jay Report* claims that the average number of victims per abuser was two. But other studies show that pedophiles have 150-250 victims on the average. Why the discrepancy?

The *John Jay Report* summarized its findings: "The majority of priests (56%) were alleged to have abused one victim, nearly 27% were alleged to have abused two or three victims, nearly 14% were alleged to have abused four to nine victims and 3.4% were alleged to have abused more than ten victims."[9]

Most of the victims (80.9 percent, according to the *John Jay Report*) were male,[10] in fact post-pubescent males,[11] and male victims report abuse less often than female victims do.[12] David Finkelhor concluded that "boys appear less likely to report the experience to anyone."[13] Abusers who target males have larger numbers of victims than other types of abusers. One study showed that an average of 150 male children was molested by each homosexual (that is, male-oriented) pedophile.[14] "Alan," for example, a pedophile who restricted himself to boys, had perhaps a thousand victims (see p. 333).

Serial pedophiles like John Geoghan accounted for most of the cases of abuse. Such abusers are true pedophiles, targeting pre-adolescent children. Among abusive priests, the percentage accused of abuse of pre-pubescent children was small and declined over the decades after 1960.[15] Most abusive priests instead targeted boys at or a few years after the age of puberty.

The abusers were therefore closer to homosexuals than to pedophiles. Although I am not aware of any study that has attempted to determine the average number of victims of men who target early adolescent boys, in all probability such abusers have an average number of victims somewhere between the hundreds of victims that pedophiles have and the smaller number of sexual partners that homosexuals have (see p. 331). However, it must be more than the two that the John Jay study shows. If most of the priest-abusers were sexually interested in boys between the ages of twelve to sixteen (before strong secondary male sex characteristics appear), then the victims were always growing too old and had to be replaced by fresh victims.

Stephen Rossetti wrote that in his experience, priest-abusers had eight or nine victims[16]; this estimate agrees with that of Thomas Plante, who thought that priest-abusers have about eight victims on average,[17] but this only means the abusers *admit* to eight to nine victims. Paul Isely points out that in one study when offenders were interrogated under circumstances that increased the likelihood they were telling the truth, they confessed "six times as many victims" as they had initially reported.[18]

Even using the average number of victims that Rossetti and Plante estimated, the number of victims of priests is probably closer to 40,000. Using the multiple that Isely thought had been validated by an experiment, the numbers swiftly mount into the hundreds of thousands. Very conservatively, one can estimate that 100,000 to 200,000 victims, the vast majority being adolescent boys, were abused by priests. Few victims have reported their abuse because they are ashamed,[19] because they still feel connected to their abusers (see pp. 271ff.), and because the statute of limitations prevents any civil or criminal action against most abusers. Lawyers sometimes warn clients that they can themselves be sued for defamation if they accuse a priest. Therefore, once an abuser is exposed, there is little motivation for his other victims to come forward

Moreover, these are figures from the United States, which has only six percent of the Roman Catholics in the world and about eleven percent of the priests in the world. To arrive at estimates of abusers and victims in the universal church (and there is no reason to think Americans are uniquely sinful), one must multiply the American figures to arrive at an estimate of perhaps 45,000–100,000 abusive priests since 1950 and anywhere from 100,000 to 2,000,000 victims, most in countries which have had nothing like the American reforms that have led to a decline in sexual abuse both in the general population and in the Church. Millions of Catholics worldwide are affected because a priest has sexually abused them or someone in their immediate family.

## *How Victims Were Vulnerable*

The priest-abusers were narcissists who had no feeling for the pain they were inflicting; they were confidence artists who could exploit the weaknesses of those with whom they were dealing, whether victims, bishops, fellow priests, or laity. The adults who enabled the abuse were usually culpably weak, and I shall discuss their complicity in the abuse in following chapters. The victims had a variety of innocent weaknesses which the abusers exploited: the sexual ignorance of the very young; the emotional turmoil of adolescence; sickness or injury; family problems, such as divorce or death or poverty; the absence of a father; or most dangerous of all, piety. The parents were often "good Catholics," who placed priests on a pedestal and considered it a privilege to be allowed to associate with priests. Such parents wanted their sons to be pious and to associate with priests and would hear nothing bad spoken of them, as the children well knew.

### YOUTH

Some victims were small children, but most were adolescent boys. Small children have very little idea of what is going on when they are molested. Their chief weakness is their ignorance. But most of the victims were boys at or beyond the age of puberty. They knew something about sex, but they had extensive weaknesses. Boys can have adolescent questions: Am I gay? What is sex all about? Will drugs or alcohol soothe the pain I feel? They see the priest honored and deferred to; they are told to pay attention to Father. Father can use their ignorance to misinform and exploit them.

## FAMILY PROBLEMS AND FATHERLESSNESS

Although some victims were from intact middle-class families, most of the victims were poor. Their family problems often contributed to the poverty: divorce, single motherhood, alcoholism. Because the boys were poor the small attentions that priests gave them meant a lot: an ice cream cone, a trip to a game. The boys who, if not poor, came from limited circumstances were often dazzled by the adult toys that priests had, toys often paid for by money stolen from the parish.

John Geoghan specialized in preying on "dysfunctional" families. These had poor, disadvantaged children and overwhelmed mothers. "There were fathers who were alcoholics, or working out of town five or six days a week."[20] The Lambert brothers said that the Rev. Joseph Burns of the Brooklyn diocese "was a surrogate father for them, filling the void left by an alcoholic and absentee father"[21] before he abused them. The victims of the layman John Merzbacher in a Baltimore Catholic school were poor and did not know where to turn for help.

When the bishop and chancery protected the abusive priest against a family that was poor, isolated, and without influential friends or knowledge of the legal system, the conflict often took on aspects of class warfare. The bishops had millions to pay for the best lawyers; the victims and their families had few or no resources. The class warfare continues. Having learned from Boston that a full exposure of what they have done will force them to resign, bishops are fighting the release of documents to the public, and will pay victims more if the documents are not put in the public realm. The victims need the money, the lawyers want the money (and have staff to pay), and the bishops have bottomless resources to keep themselves in office and out of jail.

## EMOTIONAL TURMOIL

Adolescence is a difficult time for boys, and some boys have it rougher than others. "Lonely boys, looking for affection and attention, are the preferred targets of third-party aggressors."[22] But all adolescents have problems, and priests have access to adolescents at times of particular emotional vulnerability. Victims said that priests abused them when they were visiting a dying father in the hospital, when they were themselves in the hospital, or when they went for counseling after the death of a relative.[23]

David Prunty, a high school sophomore, was in a psychiatric hospital when the Rev. Michael Allen came to visit him. They struck up a friendship, which progressed to sex. Prunty had lost a father, and he said that Allen filled that gap—and more: "He was a needed presence in my life and I came to almost idolize the man."[24] The relationship tapered off after Prunty entered the seminary (victims of abusive priests sometimes themselves become priests). Prunty wrote to Evansville bishop Francis Shea, who did not respond. Later he wrote to Shea's successor, Gerald A. Gettelfinger, who arranged a meeting between Prunty and the vicar general, but they did not resolve the situation. Through an attorney Prunty then demanded $150,000 damages. The diocese claimed that Prunty had not suffered any harm because of his relationship with Allen; Prunty was already damaged goods when Allen started using him. The attorney for the Evansville diocese, David V. Miller, wrote, "Prunty had already been having 'psychological and emotional struggles' before he met Allen at the age of [fifteen], citing the death of his father, a family history of depression and Prunty's ongoing confusion about his sexual identity." Miller also wrote that the diocese would offer a "vigorous defense" and warned, "David should be aware that if that defense is successful, he will then be in harm's way, again by his own conduct, because he will have maliciously ended the career of a very fine man"[25]—of Allen, a man who preyed upon depressed teenagers. Prunty was intimidated by the "in harm's way." This Mafia-like threat dissuaded him from going public for several more years. In April 2002 Gettelfinger again tried to keep Prunty silent, but Prunty went to the press.[26]

## PHYSICAL AND MENTAL WEAKNESS

Paul Downey of Manchester, New Hampshire, claimed that Rev. Paul Osgood "sexually manipulated him while taking his confession as Downey, then about thirteen years old, lay in his hospital bed, shaved for surgery and about to be wheeled to the operating room to have his appendix removed."[27] James Porter molested an injured twelve-year-old girl in the hospital when he was asked to tell her that her uncle, the driver, had been killed in the same accident;[28] when he was a chaplain in New Mexico, he "was caught sodomizing a child in a body cast."[29]

The Jesuits used Sacred Heart Center in Los Gatos, California, for priests they wanted to keep out of trouble. Unfortunately, some of them discovered the perfect victims, or so it seemed: two dishwashers who were developmentally disabled, i.e., mentally retarded. Father Edward Thomas Burke, S. J., lured the victim James Doe into his room with videos of trains. The Jesuit then locked the door and had sex with the victim. The victim in 1989 made friends with a dress shop owner, Holly Ilse, in Los Gatos and complained about what the priest was doing. Ilse began a crusade to protect these victims. The victims were difficult witnesses because they were afraid of the Jesuits, and they initially denied that anything had happened. One abuser confessed to his superior that he had had sex with a victim. The superior, since he was not compelled by law to report it, did nothing.[30] Burke was charged and pleaded guilty.[31] Brother Charles Leonard Connor, S. J., was convicted in 2001 of a lewd act against a disabled person, John Doe.[32]

Camp Fatima in New Hampshire was a source of victims for alleged pedophiles —the Rev. Paul Shanley, the Rev. Bernard J. Lane,[33] the Rev. Ronald H. Paquin (see pp. 175–177), the Rev. Edward T. Kelley (see p. 306), the Rev. Ernest E. Tourigney,[34] the Rev. Eugene Sullivan (director of schools for the archdiocese of Boston), Brother Guy Beaulieu, and the camp director, Rev. Karl E. Dowd[35]—especially during "the weeks reserved at the camp for those with mental disabilities."[36] In Louisiana Chris Fontaine was seventeen and borderline mentally retarded when he met the Rev. Dino Cinel. Cinel photographed him and sold (Cinel says gave) the pictures to Dreamboy U.S.A., which had an entire issue devoted to Fontaine. In one photo Fontaine "is watching a Smurf cartoon on television while Cinel performs oral sex on him."[37]

## SENSITIVITY AND PIETY

Boys who are intelligent, precocious, bookish, sensitive, and pious are at risk from the type of abuser who is not an arrested adolescent like Rudy Kos, Gilbert Gauthé, or James Porter, but a more adult, "normal" personality, the type of homosexual whom women find attractive because they are refined and sensitive. Boys who are uncomfortable in the rough and coarse world of their peers and who want to live in the adult world are especially vulnerable when a priest offers them an entrée into this world at the price of a sexual relationship. One group of victims described themselves as "quiet young men who craved the attention of a priest,"[38] another group described themselves as "adolescents who were shy around peers and preferred spiritual and aesthetic pursuits."[39]

This type of victim is "the devout child raised never to question the clergy's authority."[40] In Philadelphia, "Timmy" was taught that "priests are never wrong; it was always the child who was wrong."[41] Therefore when Father Stanley Gana abused him, Timmy thought that Gana's behavior "had to be proper because he was a priest."[42] "Sean," a victim of the Rev. James J. Brzyski of Philadelphia, believed that "to say anything bad about a priest was a mortal sin and that he would go to hell if he told."[43] Sean, while being abused by Brzyski, was chosen to serve the Mass of Pope John Paul II when the pope visited Philadelphia.

Such relationships often look like the classic mentoring relationship that pederasts dream of, in which a mature man initiates a boy into the adult world. Psychoanalyst Richard B. Gartner described the case of Julian, who for three years beginning when he was twelve years old was "mentored, loved, and molested" by a priest identified as "Father Scott," who "made Julian his special altar boy, invited him to visit him in his rooms, and undertook to educate him in classical texts, languages, and music." Scott persuaded Julian that "the male relationships in classical Greek texts" described an ideal. The relationship of Scott and Julian, which progressed to anal intercourse and mutual masturbation and group sex with a third boy, was held up to the boy as the highest possible relationship, because it included all types of love, "love of beauty, love of thought, love of logic, love of art, and love of one another that was intellectual, sensual, and emotional." Julian was made to feel complicit in the sex, which he both disliked and found satisfying.[44]

Abusers often describe their relationships as consensual friendships. The Rev. Robert Burkholder of the Detroit archdiocese started molesting boys soon after he was ordained in 1947. His victims ranged in age from seven to fourteen years old. Burkholder described his sexual actions as "affection" and insisted that the sex was consensual: "it takes two to tango; it was always a two-way thing." It developed naturally: "The boys work in the rectory with the priest and you get friendly." Of the thirteen-year-old boy he molested, Burkholder said, "He might have been lonely. And priests are people too. We need friendships and kids love priests."[45] Burkholder engaged in group sex with his victims, telling them "their bodies were gifts from God and, therefore, to be shared with priests."[46]

Some victims came from stable, intact middle-class families who had a fatal weakness: they were pious and bought into the clericalism that viewed the priest as a sinless channel of divine grace.[47] In one group of victims, almost every one "came from Catholic families in which at least one parent was very religious and observant."[48] A pious father was especially dangerous to his son because he would encourage the boy to associate with priests, and the son knew that his father idolized priests and did not want to hear anything bad about them. Jim Parker remembered that his father's "faith and commitment to the Catholic Church appeared to be the greatest passion in life."[49] The parents of one victim said that "we had been taught all our lives to respect and trust the Church. That if everyone else fails you, the Catholic Church would not fail you and would help you."[50] The father of a victim in Santa Barbara realized that "the closer a family is to the Church, to the priest, those are the families that put their children at the highest risk."[51] The child of such a family thought that anything the priest said came from God—anything.

The psychologists who interviewed the Gauthé victims reported, "Consider, if you will, the impact on the child [who] is sexually abused during the week, and on Sundays witnesses his parents bowing, kneeling, genuflecting, praying, receiving the sacraments and graciously thanking the priest for his involvement in their lives. Such events [make] him believe that such sexual activities have been sanctioned by their parents."[52]

To an eight-year-old boy, a priest said:

> "Now, look," he said, "Do you love God?"
>
> Boy: "Of course I love God."
>
> Priest: "If you love God, there are certain things you have to do. Are you sure you love God, because he wants you to do some very difficult things. You know when you were born, you were born without clothes. Now, I want you to show your love for God by taking your clothes off, so God will know you're here like when you were born."[53]

Small children might be slightly uncomfortable with these requests, but they had seen their parents hanging upon every word a priest said, and could not imagine disobeying a priest.

Adolescents are also vulnerable. They may hear and even believe some of the teachings of the Church about restricting sexual actions to marriage, but they also know that this advice is generally ignored. The desire for sexual experience is powerful during adolescence, and an adolescent is always ready to listen to arguments that justify having sex. Priests would target those who were having difficulties with sex. Boys in Catholic schools were addressed by priests on sexual morality. "The priest explained that masturbation was considered sinful by the Church and encouraged anyone who was struggling with these issues to bring them up in confession. These lectures were used by certain priests as a means of selecting victims."[54] Boys with strong sexual urges and sensitive consciences were the most likely to reveal their condition to priests, and some priests took advantage of these revelations.[55]

Sometimes the priests decided that arguments were not enough and that stronger measures had to be taken to convince their victims to give in. The Rev. Rudy Kos convinced boys he could work miracles (pp. 133–134).

Whether he was engaged in his usual fakery or whether he had tapped into the power of spirits other than the Holy Spirit is not clear. The Rev. Paul Aube also claimed miraculous powers, especially the "gift of knowledge." "He implied he could read people's minds, and knowing their thoughts, feelings, and aspirations. He even claimed to be aware of events that had happened to us and others, and sometimes prophesied about our or other's futures. This absolutely amazed and captivated me and my brothers,"[56] one victim wrote to Bishop O'Neil of Manchester. Aube had picked up bits of information from associates of his victims, knew adolescent psychology, and appealed to boys caught up in vaguely New Age, Star Wars ideas about "The Force" (Aube's nickname was "Aube Wan-Kenobi"). This confidence artistry shaded off into appeals to darker spirits: "Aube spoke about seeing Satan in flames above his bed, and recounted seeing a vision of Satan."[57] Adolescent boys, who feel mysterious powers awakening in their own bodies, are fascinated with magic and evil spirits. Was Aube simply appealing to this fascination or was there something deeper and far worse at work? Aube's bishops never showed any interest in his alleged spiritual powers. Priests' involvement in pederasty and possibly even in Satanism did not disturb the bishops' serenity.

Aube used the Catholic traditions of erotic mysticism[58] as part of his seduction techniques. Aube embraced the boy who wrote the above letter, kissing him on the mouth, and running his fingers through his hair, telling him, "I love you like the Lord loves you" and, "God loves you so much that if you were the last person on earth, he would still send Jesus down to die for you, and I also would die for you!"[59] For a fourteen year old this was a heady and poisonous cocktail of hormones and (allegedly) the Holy Spirit.

The Rev. Robert V. Meffan (see pp. 171–172) in Boston was deeply influenced by erotic mysticism, the idea that the Christian is the bride of Christ. In the 1980s, he took under his wing some teenage girls who were considering the convent. He encouraged them to "be brides of Christ" and described himself as "the second coming of Christ." They claimed Meffan "regularly invited them to his bedroom or visited them in their religious houses, where he would invite them to undress and 'link spiritual stages with sexual acts,' including fondling, kissing of genitals, and encouraging them to 'mentally masturbate.'" Meffan is unrepentant. In 2002 he claimed his sexual relationships with teenage girls were "beautiful, spiritual experiences" intended to bring young people closer to God.[60]

The Paciorek of Detroit are a well-known athletic family. They had handsome athletic boys and were deeply respectful of priests, and they therefore provided a perfect target for the Rev. Gerard Shirilla, who molested four of the five boys. Bob Paciorek, one of the victims, explained that "we came from a strict Catholic family, and anybody in the priesthood, who's a priest, we look at him as Jesus on earth, Lord on earth, you know. And so, my God, this isn't wrong. He's God."[61] Tom Paciorek explained, "The way we were brought up, in the Catholic faith, anybody that represented the Church, a nun or a priest, represented God on earth."[62] The boys kept quiet for years to avoid hurting their devout parents' feelings.

Many other victims had problems or weaknesses, but Tom Paciorek's only weakness was his faith. He was a star athlete at St. Ladislaus High School in Hamtramck, Michigan, where Shirilla was teaching and leading the glee club, of which Tom and John were members. When he was fifteen Shirilla was teaching Tom to drive when the teacher put his hands on the boy's genitals, causing an erection and telling him, "That's OK, John liked it."[63] Then in 1962 Shirilla entered Sacred Heart Seminary and the Pacioreks sent Tom to live with Shirilla for a weekend while they were out of town. Shirilla molested Tom all weekend, scarcely letting him sleep, and until Tom went to college molested him about one hundred times. Shirilla took the boy into a private room at the seminary, gave him a back rub, massaged his genitals, and ended by putting his finger in the boy's rectum. Tom kept quiet from despair and humiliation, knowing that "anybody who wore a cloak or habit represented Jesus on earth,"[64] not realizing that Shirilla was also molesting his brothers who were then eight and twelve years old. Tom Paciorek had a long and successful career in major league baseball, playing for the Dodgers, Braves, Mariners, White Sox, Mets, and Rangers and in the 1981 All-Star Game and the 1974 World Series. He had a degree of physical strength, mastery, and self-confidence that few boys or men ever attain; yet he was molested, trapped in a traumatic bond with his abuser, and wounded in his deepest relationships with his family, all because his parents and Church taught him to idolize priests.

A priest knew everything and could do no wrong. "Father says . . ." ended all arguments in a Catholic parish. One victim protested to the Rev. Louis Miller: "This is not right." Miller responded, "I'm a priest. I wouldn't do anything that is not right." The victim's response was, "How do you argue with that."[65] When thirteen-year-old James Boklage was in the hospital, Miller was the chaplain and molested him; Boklage explained that "if it had been anybody except a priest, I would have told somebody at the time. Because it was a priest, that automatically told me I was the one that was wrong."[66] In New Mexico David Frances was one of the altar boys, ages ten to thirteen, whom the Rev. David Holley molested.[67] Holley told the boys he was teaching them "how to be men." He molested them before Mass and then told them to keep quiet because he "had the power to send us to hell."[68]

## *What Victims Suffered*

What did the priests do to children, especially to the boys? The press often glosses over the actions with the word "fondling," a word with positive, affectionate overtones. Mark Serrano, a victim, does not like the word: "It's not fondling to strip a child naked, after manipulating him emotionally and mentally, and then perform sexual acts on the child."[69] As one victim said, "You read media coverage and hear a word like 'fondling.' People need to know the details, the sensation of semen in my pants and having to flee from that rectory—but not being able to tell my parents."[70] The abusers often added to their sexual pleasure by surrounding it with the trappings of Catholicism, adding the frisson of sacrilege to the evil pleasures of abusing a child, on a downward path that leads to diabolism.

## GROOMING AND INITIATION

What were the strategies that abusers used to get access to children, especially boys? First of all, by offering "help." Who doesn't need help with an adolescent boy? That gave the priests access to the children, and gave the parents a motivation to overlook any signs that all might not be well between the priest and the child. The abusers used gifts, drugs, alcohol, and pornography to break down resistance. Freda Briggs, an Australian child protection expert, describes the process of grooming: "Offenders often carefully plan their targeting strategy. They may give longed-for physical tenderness, or flatter their chosen target by giving them access to the secret sexuality of male adults: sharing alcohol, cigarettes, drugs, pornography. This latter ensures the offender's safety: boys dare not disclose forbidden activities to parents."[71] The boys are made complicit in illegal and immoral actions, and their sense of guilt and shame ensures their silence.

Priests sometimes pretended they were giving their victims sex education. In many Catholic schools priests spoke to groups of boys who were twelve or thirteen years old about sex (I experienced this at St. Matthew's school in Baltimore around 1959). The priests concentrated on the moral aspects of sex. They "explained that masturbation was considered sinful by the Church and encouraged anyone who was struggling with these issues to bring them up in confession. These lectures were used by certain priests as a means of selecting victims. Those who complied were invited to special 'counseling sessions.'"[72] Many abusers, including Cardinal Groër, used the anxiety that Catholic adolescents and young men feel about masturbation to lead them into sexually charged situations that opened them to abuse.

Explicit sex education, which has become prevalent even in Catholic schools, is often quasi-pornographic; some classes demonstrate the proper use of a condom by using a model of male genitals and by using street language to make sure that children know what the teacher is talking about. Boys therefore did not detect any strong discontinuity between what they heard and saw in sex education class and what priests were showing them. It is dangerous for a parent to allow another adult to discuss sex with his children. When I pointed this out at the parish meeting on sex education at the Cathedral of Mary Our Queen in Baltimore, I was booed by the parents. The parents soon heard that the wonderful young assistant priest at the parish, Father Tom Rydzewski (see pp. 201–202), who was spending so much time in the school, was a child pornographer who was busily grooming their children.

We moved to Naples, Florida, and discovered our house was in St. Ann's parish. We do not go to this church because my teenage children have aesthetic objections to priests' wearing clown wigs during Mass. In this parish in the 1970s the Rev. William Romero took over the youth group—and the youth. He taught catechism. As one former student described it: "He used to lock the door and distribute sex education material. He'd count the pages before handing them out and then count the pages when he got them back. I just remember the ripples of embarrassment. It was obviously stuff we weren't supposed to see. . . . We were instructed that he was progressive and the school was behind the times."[73] Romero preyed upon the students.[74]

Instead of attending St. Ann's, we went to St. William's in Naples, where the former pastor, a close friend of Bishop John Nevins, was the Rev. Neil Fleming, who had an independent "medical" practice at Boystown, a Miami orphanage. Fleming told a fourteen-year-old boy that "he needed a sperm sample because one of the boy's testicles had not descended. He then performed oral sex on the youth."[75] Fleming's brother Jim, who later became a priest, tutored the boy and joined in the molestation, according to the boy.[76]

The Rev. Thomas Sebastian Schaefer of the Washington, D.C., archdiocese had an altar boy to whom he gave a job at the rectory. The duties were answering phones—and other things. Schaefer told the boy, "Let me teach you about your body." He showed the boy *Penthouse* and *Playboy*, had mutual masturbation and oral sex with him, and took pictures of him. He also gave him money. Schaefer left the parish and the boy had the same duties with the new pastor, the Rev. Alphonse Michael Smith. The boy assumed this was just part of what priests and altar boys did: "It was just more of the same.

I thought it was normal."[77] Both abusers eventually confessed.[78]

Abusers isolate their victims from their peers and from their parents, making them more emotionally dependent on the abuser and reducing the risk of the victim's revealing the abuse. Priests hired boys to work in their rectories, physically isolating the victims, or took boys to isolated cabins or vacation houses. The predator would cut off a vulnerable boy from the crowd. In 1948 the Rev. Joseph Gausch of Philadelphia wrote to another abuser, the Rev. Charles L. G. Knapp, about how he culled a class of eighth-grade boys and "kept the crowd small . . . purposefully,"[79] "rounding up a few of the desirables and making off somewhere."[80] Priests used confession to convince boys that masturbation and heterosexual sex were sinful but that homosexual sex was acceptable. Abusers sought to place barriers between victims and parents. They would threaten to reveal minor infractions to the parents. Father James J. Brzyski of Philadelphia told one victim that "your parents know what goes on. We have a deal."[81] Their insistence that the boy keep associating with the priest (whom they thought was a good influence) despite his protests convinced the boy for twenty years that his mother had sold him to the abuser.

Priests plied boys with liquor to loosen up their inhibitions and then told them that sex, including boy-priest sex, was natural. In Massachusetts, the Rev. Robert A. Shauris owned a house with several other priests in Fitchburg.[82] There, according to Jim Kane, he gave the fourteen-year-old Kane Black Russians and showed him pornographic films.[83] Another Worcester priest owned a house on Cape Cod; there he took young teenage boys and, according to one of them, Joseph P. Cote, gave them liquor, showed them pornographic movies, and "organized an event called 'the Greek Olympics' which involved boys running naked through the neighborhood at night."[84] The Rev. Eugene Vollmer on Long Island gave his altar boys marijuana, communion wine, and pornographic videos. He and the boys masturbated each other and gave each other oral sex. The boys were not comfortable, but he told them that "this is what guys do. It's a natural part of life. It's no big deal."[85] The boys eventually reported it to the diocese, one in a formal petition for annulment of marriage. Nothing was done.[86]

Priests convinced their victims that the sexual experiences were part of initiation into adult masculinity. James Porter told his victims in Minnesota that the abuse "was part of becoming a man."[87] Boys yearn for initiation, and our society lacks any clear road map to guide them into becoming men. Priests are logical initiators of Catholic boys, who are then told that the initiation must remain secret—a common feature of initiation in all societies. Boys sense the necessity of secrecy and feel it is a sign of the reality and validity of the initiation.

## SEXUAL ABUSE

Sometimes the abuse boys suffer is horrendous: Michel Dorais describes that the boys he studied experienced "being torn during anal penetration, being obliged to practice fellatio despite repeated vomiting, being severely beaten, being sprayed with urine or covered with excrement."[88] The abuse reported by the victims of priests sometimes reached this level, as we have seen in El Paso and Davenport, but more often included mutual masturbation, oral and anal sex, and group sex. Priests did not often have to resort to violence, but their softer methods made the victims feel complicit and induced a greater degree of guilt and self-destructiveness.

When the Rev. Dino Cinel came to New Orleans he looked up the age of consent and tried to confine himself to legal boys (like many abusers he liked to keep records of his activities, in his case photographs and videos). A priest in the rectory did not seem to notice or to object that teenage boys were sleeping in Cinel's bed, but he did call Archbishop Hannan when he discovered "160 hours of homemade pornographic videotapes in which the handsome priest performed anal sex, oral sex, group sex, and a dizzying array of other diversions (often including his fluffy white lapdog) with at least seven different teenage boys."[89] Cinel liked to film brothers having sex with each other, and he also tried to get their mothers and sisters involved. Archbishop Hannan held the tapes for three months before turning them over to the district attorney with the politest suggestion that nothing be done to Cinel.[90]

Father Brendan Smyth had a victim, Danny, an eleven-year-old orphan in a Catholic institution (where sexual abuse seems to have been common). "As soon as he was alone with the priest the kissing would begin, not the fatherly peck on the cheek: French kissing with the priest's tongue probing the boy's mouth. The priest would then open his trousers and place the boy's hand on his penis, making the boy masturbate him until he ejaculated."[91] For a boy of eleven years of age, this was not only disgusting behavior but it simply was not in keeping with the teachings of the Church: "Masturbation was a sin," said Danny. "At least that is what we were told—although it seemed to be permitted if you were doing it to or with a priest."[92] Smyth would also take several boys on a trip together. Danny remembered, "I was on trips where he got me and another boy together in a room at [a] hotel or boardinghouse." The other boy recalled that "he would force us to lie together on a bed while he watched us masturbate each other."[93]

In Newfoundland the boys of Mount Cashel were abused by the Christian Brothers of Ireland. The Newfoundland Court of Appeals described the abuse one brother, E. E., inflicted: "While the boy was in his bunk in the dorm E. E. fondled his genitals and placed his penis between the boy's legs, ejaculating after motion simulating intercourse. The other incident involved Brother E. E. grabbing the boy by the neck and hair and attempting to have anal intercourse . . . and oral sex on the Brother in a parked car at the Basilica after a religious service."[94] The brothers also liked the combination of sex and religion.

When he was thirteen, in 1975, Scot Edgerton served Mass at a church in Milwaukee. He wrote a letter to Archbishop Weakland in 1980 describing what happened: Father Richard W. Nichols first dressed him in his server's vestments. Edgerton thought it odd to be dressed rather than dressing himself. In the sacristy after Mass the priest grabbed him from behind, "the priest's grip was getting tighter and Edgerton remembered feeling as if he couldn't breathe. . . . Nicols [sic] managed to push his hands down the boy's pants and grab his penis. 'I can see funerals really excite you,' Edgerton said the priest told him."[95] Edgerton broke away and ran, and the priest harassed him for months. Edgerton did not know where to turn for help.[96]

In Louisville, Father Louis Miller pulled John Thornberry out of class to run an errand. Thornberry said that "the priest brought him to the rectory basement, pulled down his own pants, then put the boy's hand on his penis and forced him to masturbate the priest until he ejaculated."[97] At St. John's Abbey, according to a statement given by a student at the prep school, Father Allen Tarlton liked to talk about homosexual sex with a student. In his office, the student recounted, Tarlton "asked if he could see me naked, and I replied yes. He then proceeded to fondle me, caress my body and perform oral sex on me. . . . He then rimmed [kissing and licking of the anus] me. I recall masturbating and ejaculating at this time."[98]

Scott Gastal was a victim of Gilbert Gauthé. Gauthé started abusing him a week after he made his First Communion. Gauthé enjoyed degrading the boys. He photographed them giving oral sex to each other. Gastal, when he was ten years old, described what Gauthé had done to him: "he put his mouth on my pee-pee and he made me put [my] mouth on his pee-pee, and he would kiss us and make us put our tongue in his mouth and he would lick our behinds. He would make us put our mouth on his balls and he would put his mouth on our balls . . . when he would make us put our mouth on his pee-pee and put some juice in our mouths."[99] Then Gauthé anally penetrated Gastal, who bled rectally. He told his mother of the bleeding; she took him to the hospital. Neither his parents nor the doctor asked why he was bleeding; they may have suspected and didn't want to know the truth. Rectal trauma frequently occurs when an adult's penis penetrates a child's anus. "Edward" of Philadelphia had to have "eighteen inches of bowel removed due to a perforation."[100]

Younger victims were targets for physical coercion. Gary Bergeron was twelve years old when he served Mass for Father Joseph Birmingham. After Mass when Birmingham and Bergeron were in the sacristy, Birmingham offered to wrestle:

> We were on the floor. His legs were wrapping around me. Then he was behind me. I was sweating as he started to kneel behind me. I wasn't having fun and it seemed the harder I tried to get away, the more he was

> grunting as pushing against me. My pants were pulled down now. How did he do that, what's going on. I felt a sharp pain and tried to scream, but he had one of his big hairy hands on my mouth. "Shhhhhhhh," he said. "It's okay. You know you're one of my favorites."[101]

Bergeron had to throw away his underpants because they were soaked in blood.

Birmingham could also be violent during oral sex. Olan Horne was in a store when some people made fun of his abuse by Birmingham. He told them what had happened:

> Let me explain something to you. . . . You're grabbing an eleven-year-old kid. You pull him to the floor. You grab him by the back of the head and you take your cock, and you stick it down his fucking throat. Got him by the back of the head doing it. Kid's fucking having a panic attack. And then this guy puts me on the floor with his knee in my back, you know, the guy's ejaculating all over my back. He's beating the shit out of me because I'm trying to get away. . . .[102]

This was not a good introduction to sexuality. Porter anally raped his victims; when one boy tried to scream from the pain, he remembered that Porter "put his hand over my mouth so no one would hear me."[103] No one wanted to hear the victims: not the police, not the district attorneys, not the parishioners, especially not the bishops, and sometimes not even their own parents.

The sadism in this abuse sometimes becomes unmistakable. A seventeen-year-old victim was being sexually abused by a priest just before she entered a convent. She told him she had a toothache. He took her to a dentist who pulled out all of her upper teeth.[104] Father James H. Mulholland of Philadelphia wrote letters to his victims. With delight he described what was done to a boy at St. Patrick's in Kennett Square:

> POOR BOY! He was stripped by the loving brothers, hung by his ankles by his hands tied up tight with a light rope or heavy cord going from his

> wrists and under his crotch and ending in a loop around his well known-privates [sic] (struggling could be painful). He was pulled up high and a low charcoal fire was shoveled under him, then wet leaves put on the fire—heat and smoke right up his body—an old Apache torture. . . . Little brother now obeys.[105]

Mulholland had "some sort of private Masses in the church basement with only his 'special boys.'"[106] The Philadelphia archdiocese has a file of his letters to boys, letters "illustrated with pictures of chains, nooses, and people hanging from chains in prison cells. The words 'burning,' 'torture,' and 'killing' are triple-sized."[107] Cardinal Bevilacqua kept Mulholland in parishes despite the letters; even the Philadelphia Review Board decided in 2004 that, in spite of these sadomasochistic letters and reports of similar behavior, Father Mulholland was *not* covered by the Bishops' Charter and was *not* to be removed for sexual abuse.

## SACRILEGE

Abusive priests often added the pleasures of sacrilege to the pleasures of abuse. Catholicism has external rites, customs, and objects that provide an opening for abuse or add a religious air to the abuse. Priests invoked God while abusing children. James Porter violently sodomized an eleven-year-old girl while, she reported, "He told me he was stronger than me and that he had the power of God."[108] (Remember that Pope Paul VI read Porter's file and never asked about the victims.)

The Catholic practice of confession is fraught with dangers for any priest, as the Church has long recognized. Richard Sipe observed that "confession is supposed to be a complete revelation of yourself. In order to be forgiven, you have to tell all of your sins without reservation. For the devout it opens them up to a tremendous amount of vulnerability,"[109] a vulnerability that abusers exploited. For a celibate to hear the endless stream of small and large sexual sins that the laity commits can endanger even a sincere commitment to chastity, and some priests are not sincere. The files of the

Church in Spain are full of trials of confessors who seduced women during confession. The confessional grille and anonymity were instituted to reduce temptation, but these were abandoned in mindless optimism after Vatican II. At one time (thankfully no longer), priests were also told to ask penitents for all details of sexual sins: with whom, how often, what position, etc., because of an obsession with the precise nature of a sexual act. This was highly imprudent and multiplied the dangers to both priest and penitent.

The eighteen-year-old freshman and seminary candidate Gary Belkot went to confession to Augustinian priest Arthur Chappell at Villanova University. Belkot says that "we would pray together. He would hear my confession and being vulnerable he would initiate the sexual abuse. He would say this was the way Jesus and the beloved disciple John were close."[110] The story of the erotic relationship between Jesus and John is standard in Catholic homosexual circles and a very useful seduction tool, as Chappell discovered. When Martin Robertson was molested by a stranger, he felt frightened, and made the mistake of going to confession to the Rev. Louis Miller; "Miller sexually gratified himself in the confessional while asking the boy explicit questions about how the attacker had abused him."[111] Rev. Lawrence Brett of the Bridgeport diocese heard the confession of a boy when he was fourteen. Brett then performed fellatio on the boy and had the boy perform fellatio on him "by telling the child that the act was a way to receive Holy Communion."[112]

Msgr. Francis A. Giliberti of Philadelphia told a sophomore high school class that "any sex outside of marriage is a mortal sin." One student in the class, "Jay" took this to heart and thought that he, fifteen years old, was "doomed to hell"[113] because of masturbation. Giliberti told students he would help anyone who had this problem, and Jay sought him out for confession. Giliberti took him to a beach house and molested him.

Girls were also abused through confession. When Karen Pederson was eight, she went to confession. She alleged that "she was told by Rev. Robert E. Kelley that he intended to 'absolve' her sins through what Mr. Shea [Pedersen's attorney] described as a ritual bath. She was given three soap and water baths by Rev. Kelley. On the fourth occasion, according to the suit, she was taken to an ice cream stand where she was digitally penetrated."[114] Another girl said that Kelley threatened to throw her into an open grave if she ever told anyone what he was doing to her. The bishop sent Kelley to the House of Affirmation in Louisville. After Father Nicholas V. Cudemo of Philadelphia raped an eleven-year-old girl, he heard her confession and told her "the only way to connect to God was through him."[115] With others he gang raped another victim, and then put the consecrated Host, which Catholics believe to be the very body of Christ, into her vagina, telling her she had "fucked God" or "fucked Jesus," after which he heard her confession.[116]

A female victim, Jane Doe, in the La Crosse, Wisconsin, diocese was unable to sue her abuser the Rev. Thomas Garthwaite because of a peculiarity in Wisconsin law. In an interview she alleged that she was abused when she was fourteen years old: "Tom Garthwaite abused me in the confessional. We were having sex on the altar of the church. He was putting the host inside my vagina, and eating it out. . . . [He] made me come to the confessional and tell him how sorry [I] was that I took a man of God and caused him to sin. Then he made me suck him off. He would hold my head to his penis—to his belly—and he would ejaculate in my mouth and say 'Swallow it, bitch.'" In 1995 Doe told Raymond L. Burke, then bishop of La Crosse and now archbishop of St. Louis, about the abuse. He removed Garthwaite and later told Doe, "I do not question your veracity." But the abuse had unusual effects on the victim. Her psychologist, Joseph F. Roe, wrote to Burke that Jane Doe "has shown symptoms that I cannot explain on a purely psychological basis," and that "I would like to be able to refer her to someone who would be qualified to discern whether or not she is possessed."[117] Burke seriously considered the request for an exorcism. This is one of several chilling hints of diabolism scattered throughout the histories of abuse.

The sacrament of the Eucharist was used in the abuse to give the abusers a special frisson. Gauthé "was a priest who seduces a child in the sacristy then celebrates Mass, giving the boy's mother [H]oly [C]ommunion as the child holds a plate under her chin."[118] William Romero in Naples, Florida, gave the children consecrated bread and wine (which Catholics believe are the Body and Blood of Christ) as he molested them[119]; Irving Klister in El Paso got his victims drunk on wine he had consecrated as the Blood of Christ before he molested them (see p. 25). In Davenport a priest had a boy masturbate him during Mass (see pp. 52–53).

Perhaps one of the reasons so many victims (81%) were male was that the priest-abuser was attempting to defile Christ, whose male sex the boy victims had the misfortune to share. According to a lawsuit, the Rev. Frederick Lenczycki dressed up an altar boy "like a baby Jesus and molested him."[120] The Rev. Anthony Corbin dressed up an eighth-grade boy in a loincloth like the crucified Christ and had sex with him.[121] The archdiocese of Boston gave $150,000 to a man who alleged that the Rev. Denis A. Conte had "provided him with pornographic books and pictures, tied him to a rectory bed, and performed oral sex on him while telling him that he was 'being crucified like Christ.'"[122] The Rev. William Q. Simms of the Baltimore archdiocese, when he arrived as the new pastor of St. Andrew-by-the-Bay, came with an adolescent boy. He supplemented this boy with a boy from the parish whom he dressed in skimpy women's clothes and also had him "act out sexual and religious fantasies in which he was told that St. Isaac Jogues had been similarly tortured before his martyrdom."[123] James Porter had sex on the altar with two boys.[124]

Charles Bailey has accused the Rev. Thomas Neary of the Syracuse diocese of raping him about one hundred times (the diocese calls it "inappropriate touching"). Neary promised the ten-year-old boy that "sex would make him more holy." Neary wore his clerical garb while he had sex with Bailey, telling Bailey that "he was doing God's will." During the rape Neary said the Our Father. Anal penetration is painful for a small boy, so when Bailey "cried in pain" Neary "told him to be quiet because his suffering was nothing compared to the pain of Jesus' crucifixion."[125] Neary was not only destroying the boy's innocence, he was identifying the abuse with God, trying to place a barrier that would keep the boy from God.

Leslie Lothstein at the Institute of Living, where many abusive priests were treated, explained that "parishioners know that a priest has these magical functions to bring Christ's presence to them. When you're abused by someone like that, it's not just abuse of the body, it's abuse of the soul. Victims live a life of tremendous shame, thinking that they've had sex with God."[126] The victims became like the mentally disturbed girl in Ingmar Bergman's film *Through a Glass, Darkly.* She announces that God is going to walk through the door, and what comes through is a spider—she screams and goes mad. God is the Devil.

## SILENCING THE VICTIMS

Abusers had various ways to assure their victims' silence. James Porter told his small victim to keep quiet or "God would get him."[127] The Rev. Daniel C. Clark[128] kept two boys, eleven and twelve, quiet by telling them that "he would stop taking his medicine and he would kill himself."[129] When the victims threatened to tell, the abusers told them that they wouldn't be believed. Paul Aube was hurting a twelve-year-old boy who said he was going to tell his mother. Aube "laughed and said, well, who do you think they'll believe? You know, you or me. I'm a priest."[130] One girl reported that a priest told her that if she told anyone about the abuse, "her mother would no longer want her" and that she would be "taken away."[131] Victims knew that they would not be believed if they complained. Of his parents one victim said, "there is no way in hell my parents would have believed it. They were very religious and I might as well have told them a Martian landed in my backyard."[132]

The victims rarely told for years; only a very small fraction of victims ever comes forward. Mark V. Talley, who was abused by the Rev. Louis Miller, explained, "I dared not say anything; I thought God would punish me in some ways for ratting out one of his priests."[133] Paul Barrett, a victim of Daniel Clark of Louisville, explained that "if I spoke out, who would believe . . . my word against a priest's? In the Church you are raised to worship the men God sent to spread his words. You are taught not to question the Church."[134] Douglas Dukes, molested at twelve by the Rev. Arthur L. Wood, said that "all he had to do was ask me not to tell my parents and I didn't tell my parents. I trusted everything he told me. He could have told me the moon was made of green cheese and I would have believed it."[135]

The victims also kept silent because of the traumatic bond they developed with their abusers (see below).

## *How Victims Were Affected*

Predators seek out vulnerable children and prey on them. Because the children, especially the boys, had problems before the abuse began, it is hard to gauge precisely how sexual abuse affected them. But it always hurts. A doctor may poison a patient who is already sick or dying, but that does not reduce the doctor's guilt. When the victims of James Porter finally met and discussed what had happened to their lives, it was "a litany of sexual confusion and broken marriages, depression, suicide attempts, and psychiatric institutionalization. Only a handful of survivors were on their first marriages. Drug abuse and alcoholism were nearly as common a bond as the terrible childhood guilt we had felt after Porter's predations."[136] Studies confirm that Porter's victims were typical in their reactions, that sexual abuse increases the risk of "posttraumatic sex disorder, major depression, anxiety disorders, borderline personality disorder, antisocial personality disorder, paranoia, dissociation, somatization, bulimia, anger, aggressive behavior, poor self-image, poor school performance, running away from home, and legal trouble."[137]

Victims often blamed themselves: "Porter was holy; we must be evil, we concluded in our individual silences."[138] Joe was twelve when James Porter forced him to have sex; Porter had to leave the parish and the parishioners were told he had had a nervous breakdown. Joe blamed himself as the sinner: "I not only had sex with a priest, but I caused him to have a nervous breakdown. This was the guilt, the shame, the fear I'd burn in hell. I thought I must deserve it. Why would God do this if I didn't deserve it?"[139] The guilt sometimes led to suicide.

## PSYCHOLOGICAL PROBLEMS

Boys who are abused are more suicidal than other boys, and are more likely to develop "major depression, bulimia, antisocial personality disorder, behavior problems, PTSD, and borderline personality disorder."[140] To escape the abuse, victims often split their personality, isolating the painful reality in a separate part of their personality: "They do this by focusing in another reality or by creating an unreality of fantasy."[141] This alternate reality can be induced by drugs; it can also be induced by religion and spirituality.

"Billy," a victim of the Rev. James J. Brzyski of Philadelphia, described how his personality split: "It just went from having one person inside me to having two people inside me. This nice [Billy] that used to live, and then this evil [Billy], this darkness that had to have no morals and no conscience in order to get by day by day and, you know, not to care about anything or have no feelings. . . ."[142]

The less severe forms of this splitting are called dissociation[143]: "Frequently a victimized person will report that he will 'leave' his body or 'check out' so that the abuse happens 'only to my body and not me.'"[144] This splitting of the personality allows the victim to experience extreme violation and pain while thinking it is not really happening to him. Sexual abuse is a trauma which, if sufficiently severe, leads to dissociative states similar to those experienced by those who have been in battle. The individual seeks to protect himself from the abuse by separating the real self from the body. John N. Briere defines dissociation as "a defensive disruption in the normally occurring connections among feelings, thoughts, behavior, and memories, consciously or unconsciously invoked in order to relieve psychological distress."[145] The body is suffering the abuse and pain, not the real self. This dissociation, which is widely recognized, was experienced by Dontee Stokes when he shot his abuser, the Rev. Maurice Blackwell, and was the basis for Stokes's acquittal.

Tom Paciorek was molested repeatedly when he was a teenage athlete: "I compartmentalized everything inside of me. . . . During the molestations, physically I was there, but mentally, I was not."[146] Eddie Francis remembers that when the priest molested him before Mass that he had "an out-of-the-body experience"; because he was mentally leaving his body behind he thought the priest was not really touching him.[147] The dissociation produced by any type of childhood abuse is made worse when the abuser is a spiritual mentor. As Gunthild Ritschl observed of Cardinal Groër's abuse of those who came to him as a confessor: "What has he suffered in these countless confessions, when he had repeatedly confessed a sin against the sixth commandment, and on the other hand the confessor himself lay in bed with him, the man must become schizophrenic if he takes it seriously."[148]

This dissociation also is the source of true recovered memories.[149] No one has instant recall of every event he has ever witnessed. Something, like Proust's madeleines, will trigger a memory. The memory of an event may be compartmentalized or dissociated from normal memory so that the event is recalled only when the individual is in a particular state of mind or a certain type of event happens. Dissociation caused by trauma may also cause amnesia, that is, repressed memory. The conscious self is split from the part that remembers the abuse. The existence of such repressed memory is bitterly controverted among psychiatrists and therapists. Feminist counselors claim to be able to elicit repressed memories of childhood incest, as Freud did with Anna O. Others claim that incest "remembered" by this technique never occurred, that the memories are elicited by leading questions. However, only a handful of the accusations against priests have been based on recovered memory (including Shanley's accusers). Most victims wish they could forget.

In some cases the victims of abuse may be suffering not from memory repressed by a psychological mechanism (a matter of controversy) but by recognized effects of drugs. Rohypnol, the date rape drug, is like Valium but more powerful. Rohypnol, according to the U. S. Office of National Drug Control Policy, "can mentally and physically paralyze an individual. Effects of the drug are of particular concern in combination with alcohol and can lead to anterograde amnesia, where events that occurred during the time the drug was in effect are forgotten." It also produces "headaches, memory impairment, dizziness, nightmares, confusion."[150] Rohypnol has been available from the 1970s, and it has effects similar to those of Valium, which has been long easily available. Rudy Kos gave his victims alcohol and Valium (see p. 132). A Davenport, Iowa, victim had only partial memories of what went on during the abuse (p. 56). In Philadelphia Father David C. Sicoli gave "Hugh" a margarita. Hugh could not remember what happened next, but recalled "vivid images from that night and added that he felt strongly that something happened that 'my brain's not letting me see.'"[151] Ryan's visions of Hell may have been an after-effect of some drug. The grand jury felt that "there were still some details of Ryan's abuse that were still 'put away.'"[152]

Frank Fitzpatrick seems to have an authentic case of repressed and recovered memory. James Porter gave him drugged mincemeat pie when Fitzpatrick was only twelve and then molested him. Fitzpatrick completely repressed the memory. As he matured, he kept being bothered by fears that he was homosexual or bisexual and by a chronic anger that would erupt over minor incidents. He sought therapy but couldn't resolve his feelings. Then one day he lay on his bed to explore what was bothering him: "Emotions and sounds were the things to flood back on that occasion. I felt an immense, monstrous betrayal by someone I loved. I relived the part of the sexual assault that had occurred when my eyes were shut. There were sounds of rhythmic, heavy, sexual breathing in my ears and some sort of crumpling sound. The feelings of being sexually assaulted were clear and unmistakable."[153] Over the next few weeks clear memories of Porter returned. Fitzpatrick's recovered memories were accurate and confirmed by the testimony of scores of victims who had never forgotten the abuse. Very few accusations have been based on such recovered memories, but it seems possible that a child can repress memories of trauma and remember them only as an adult. As Fitzpatrick explained his experience: "it is precisely because what my perpetrator did was so horrifying, so damaging, so emotionally traumatic to me that I put it all away into a remote corner of my mind until in middle age I became emotionally secure enough to handle it."[154]

The splitting may go so far as to produce multiple personalities: "In extreme instances, this condition may have the label multiple personality disorder, in which different 'personalities' are amnesic to each other's experiences."[155] Some psychologists deny that this phenomenon exists and think the symptoms are induced by faulty therapy, but I have been involved in a case of what looked like genuine multiple personality, induced by multigenerational incest. I think it real but extremely rare, and I do not know of any cases of accusers of priests having multiple personality disorder.

Sexual disorders are a more common result of abuse: "Sexual preoccupations and compulsions, precocious or aggressive sexual behavior, promiscuity, prostitution, fear of sexual interaction, and sexual dysfunctions"[156]—and abuse. When a boy is made to feel powerless by an abuser, the feeling leads to "anxiety, fear, a lowered sense of efficacy, a perception of oneself as a victim, a need to control, and identification with the aggressor."[157] This identification with the aggressor can take the form of traumatic bonding or of becoming an aggressor oneself, of repeating the abuse on young victims. Adults who were sexual abuse victims as children have as their primary self-identification "victim" because they still feel powerless. But if they abuse someone else, they now have the power. It is an evil circle that perpetuates abuse.

The victim fears that he too will become an abuser; sometimes he does abuse. When he was eleven, Robert Malo was orally and anally raped by the Rev. Victor Frobas (see p. 313), who was being treated by the House of Affirmation and was sent out to work at a parish. Malo turned to drugs and alcohol and crime, but eventually he put his life in sufficient order to marry. Then he abused his own children and was jailed. His wife was left with five children to care for; she had a nervous breakdown from the stress and feared losing custody of her children.[158] The Rev. Michael Hands of Rockville Centre says that when he was in high school he was abused by Msgr. Charles Ribaudo, and Hands later himself abused a boy (such allegations are often lies and are an attempt to win clemency, but sometimes they are true).[159] Two of James Porter's victims are themselves in jail for molesting children.[160]

The Rev. Peter Dunne of Philadelphia molested boys for forty years. He was diagnosed as an untreatable pedophile but remained an active priest until a lawsuit was filed against him by a man he he had abused when the victim was a thirteen-year-old Boy Scout. This boy, "Gordon," had confessed to him that he was attracted to boys. Gordon became an Eagle Scout and abused smaller Scouts. He continued abusing after he grew up, became a doctor, and married. His wife discovered that Gordon had "sexual inclinations" toward his own son. Gordon had internalized the lessons that Dunne taught him, and had "become fixated on the preadolescent and adolescent sexual arousal memories."[161]

Sometimes the victims of sexual abuse do not perceive it as abuse. The infamous study "A Meta-Analytic Examination of Assumed Properties of Child Sexual Abuse Using College Samples" (see p. 444) said that not all those engaged in adult-child sex experienced any harm or distress, and that therefore this type of activity should not be called child sexual abuse but adult-child sex. The researchers were right that not everyone *experiences* adult-child sex as abuse; some see it as neutral or pleasant, just a part of normal growing-up. Such were the sex offenders of the Australian study, all of whom had been abused as children (see p. 274). The "offenders had been seriously damaged by sexual abuse in childhood"[162] but did not realize it. The "perpetrators who discounted the effects of abuse on their own lives also discounted the damage they did to other children; they rationalized that the boys liked and wanted what they did to them."[163] The college age group in the first study may not have experienced or felt damage; but that does not mean that the damage was not there. Perhaps the worst damage is precisely experiencing adult-child sex as normal. Such people are more likely than those who were distressed by the abuse to have sex with children, because they feel sexual abuse is a harmless activity, just part of ordinary life. Those children in turn may experience the catastrophic effects of such abuse.

The feeling of powerlessness is made worse when the victim comes up against the massive resources and prestige of a Catholic Church determined to protect the abuser. A priest molested two sons of Juanita S. A psychologist reported to the court that Juanita suffers from "an acute psychotic episode, profound depression . . . [and] extremely acute feelings of betrayal and victimization," both because the priest was getting away with it and because his attorneys were harassing her family.[164] The families are also affected. A victim in Maryland told his wife of his abuse; they divorced.[165]

### INABILITY TO TRUST

Anthony Muzzi, one of Geoghan's victims, cannot bring himself to go into a church; he also "has had lifelong trouble trusting people: friends, colleagues in his construction and excavating business, even his wife."[166] In Louisville Ronald L. Snipp said that he was molested by Rev. Arthur L. Wood when he was twelve and that "it changed me. It made me totally untrusting of people."[167] A girl who was abused at twelve by a priest told her psychologist that "I think 50 percent of all men are child molesters. I know it's not true, but I still feel it. I sit in church and look at fathers with their kids and wonder which ones are."[168] Baseball star Tom Paciorek was molested; despite his successful career, the molestation hurt "his ability to maintain trust and intimacy in relationships."[169] He was not able to trust his wife; "I was never able to share any type of intimacy with her,"[170] he said, and he began a series of affairs that resulted in his being divorced. When she was ten, Judy Mullet was raped by James Porter. She now says, "I'm very confused about my faith. . . . I never went back to church after high school. It's a confusing thing when the person who is supposed to be so good—I mean, he's next to God when you're so little. . . . I didn't even know what sex was back then, then of all of sudden he does something like that. If you can't trust your priest, who can you trust?"[171] One psychiatrist who interviewed Porter's victims described their agony: "It was too much to bear. If God would betray you, who does one turn to?"[172]

### TRAUMATIC BONDING

Trauma is experienced by soldiers in combat. The horror of being showered with a buddy's gore and intestines never goes away. Rape victims also experience trauma because of the deep violation of personal integrity, which is often accompanied by threats of death. The memories of trauma are different from ordinary memories. Some theorize that the adrenalin rush of trauma imprints traumatic memories in a different way than normal memories.[173] The victim wishes that he could forget but cannot. The memory remains undigested. It occasionally may be totally repressed (whether this happens is controversial) but more often it remains painfully vivid. It does not fade like other memories and does not become integrated into the acceptable life story that a person tells to himself. Non-victims frequently tell victims of sexual abuse that they should forgive and forget, let go, find closure. This is not possible with traumatic memories. The trauma produces the devastating psychological effects discussed throughout this chapter.

Trauma is an intense experience, and like all intense experiences—sex, sports, adventure—it can create a bond among those who go through them together. Shared suffering often bonds people more strongly than shared pleasure does. Comradeship in war is sometimes the most intense experience of union that men have, more intense than marriage. Bonding in these situations is comprehensible to most of us who have experienced with others the sadness and tragedies of life. But a traumatic bond can also be created when one person is causing the suffering and the other person is victimized by it.

Even captors and captives can bond. In Stockholm, Sweden, a bank robbery in 1973 resulted in the criminals taking hostages in a bank. The criminals were alternately kind and abusive to the hostages, threatening to kill them. This situation rapidly produced an extreme form of traumatic bonding between criminal and hostage. The hostages were totally cooperative with their captors, they cared about their captors, they expressed rage and contempt for their rescuers; after serving ten years in jail, the criminals married women they had taken hostage. "All this was celebrated in a double wedding ceremony attended by many fellow hostages."[174] From this incident the Stockholm Syndrome was named; it is a vivid example of traumatic bonding.

The victim does not bond with the torturer, however, unless the torturer shows kindness in some way. The relationship has "exploitation, fear, and danger" as well as "elements of kindness, nobility and righteousness."[175] The victim begins to identify with the abuser who hurts and betrays him, and wishes to curry favor with the good side that the abuser shows, so that the pain might lessen. When an abuser exercises power to hurt a victim, he can create a situation in which he makes the victim participate in his own abuse. The abuser does this by a complex strategy that combines abuse and kindness.

When the abuse occurs in a relationship that has elements of what look like genuine affection and love, the traumatic bond can be extremely strong. Women, to the mystification of bystanders, return to abusive husbands and boyfriends. A priest cultivates his victim; he may even feel affection for him along with sexual desire and desire to control. The victim may feel horror and disgust at the abuse, but that paradoxically binds him to his abuser. "The repeated experience of terror and reprieve, especially within the isolated context of a love relationship, may result in the feeling of intense, almost worshipful dependence upon an all-powerful, godlike authority."[176] This is even more likely when the abuser is a priest already endowed with godlike powers, a man whom the boy has been told by his parents and by the community that he should obey in all things.[177] This image of the abuser is similar to that of God in an influential strain of Catholic moral theology (see p. 477).

The victim accepts this trauma because it lifts him out of everyday reality into a world in which both pleasure and pain are heightened. The pleasures look ordinary to outsiders, but the victim experiences them as wonderful in contrast to the pain the abuser inflicts. Ordinary mortals cannot understand the exalted, transcendent world in which the abuse and pleasure occur, and when they try to rescue the victim they are often rejected. The victim defends the abuser because the abuser rescued him from the tedium of everyday life and opened a magical fantasy world in which experiences out of the ordinary are possible. Perhaps traumatic bonding is so strong because it appeals to an underlying brain or personality structure. Experts "liken the helplessness of the hostage to that of an infant, and the dependence of the hostage on his captor to the dependence of an infant on a parent."[178] Parents—good parents—give their children both pain and pleasure. A child receives food and caresses, but also painful discipline from a parent. He enters into the mysterious world of adults only through his parents.

For males puberty is an extremely confusing time; a boy is suddenly flooded with intense and incomprehensible feelings, which he is not allowed to talk about. What is sex all about? It is the big semisecret of the adult world. An abusive priest initiates him into the mysteries of sex. How is the boy supposed to know that this is not part of the adult secret world? Official teachings and public pronouncements, children soon realize, have little to do with how people actually behave.

In the Australian study of prisoners who committed sex offences against children (discussed above) researchers found that all sex offenders had themselves been sexually abused as children,[179] but they mostly did not experience the sexual activity as abuse. They thought "that the sexual abuse had little or no impact on their lives and was comparatively unimportant."[180] They "bore no ill will to the pedophiles who abused them" (except for government caregivers) and they "remembered the positive aspects of relationships." In fact, "two-thirds of all prisoners liked the sexual experiences they had" and almost ninety percent "thought that sexual abuse was 'normal.'"[181]

The victims enjoyed fondling and receiving oral sex; but "anal sex caused excruciating pain, physical injury, and confusion."[182] The confusion was strong when the abuse was committed "by men in religious orders who subjected boys to appalling acts of violence and degradation in the name of God."[183] But despite the pain and degradation, the offenders remembered that "these were affectionate times"; "he played with me, talked to me, and listened to me"; "he hugged and cuddled me and told me he loved me"; "it was the only affectionate touching I'd ever received"; "I felt flattered. After all, the priest was God's representative"; "he made me feel special and said he loved me."[184] Such an alteration of pain and affection can easily create a traumatic bond.

Tom Paciorek, the above-mentioned high-school athlete, was abused by the Rev. Gerard Shirilla about a hundred times.[185] Paciorek hated it, but felt powerless against a priest who was an expert manipulator. Shirilla once took him to the seminary to have sex, and there Paciorek finally said, "Gerry, I've had enough of this shit," and threw him against a wall. Shirilla collapsed as if he were having a heart attack, and Paciorek gave in. Every time Tom tried to say no, "tears would well up and he'd start this unbelievable sobbing and wailing until he got what he wanted."[186] It stopped when Paciorek went off to college (Shirilla turned to the younger brothers) and Tom let Shirilla officiate at his wedding. Tom can't understand why he did it. All he can now say is that "it was just like a make-believe world."[187] Shirilla had manipulated his victims into entering into and acting out his own fantasies.

Springfield, Massachusetts, welcomed refugee families in the 1970s. Then Father, now retired Bishop, Thomas Dupré was there to help himself to the teenage boys. Two boys tell this story: one was twelve when he came to the United States with most of his family except his father. Dupré befriended him and taught him English and, according to the boy, took the boy's hand and masturbated himself with it. The sexual relationship progressed to sodomy, according to the alleged victim. The other boy lost his father during his relationship with Dupré and became even more vulnerable. Dupré plied them both with wine, cognac, and gay pornography and continued sex with them until one boy started dating girls in high school and the other was twenty.

The boys were in a classic relationship of traumatic bonding with Dupré. Dupré pretended to be their protector. One boy said that he expressed doubts about the sex, and that Dupré showed him pictures of people dying of AIDS, "stating that if [the boy] had sex with others, [Dupré] could become infected and die." According to the boys Dupré justified the sexual relationship by claiming it "was a logical expression of love, and that God teaches love." In 1990 Dupré was named auxiliary bishop. He then, according to the now-grown men, called them and said that he would not accept appointment as bishop unless they agreed to keep quiet; they agreed. Dupré kept on friendly terms with the men, as if they had a perfectly ordinary relationship, and he sent them holiday and birthday cards and sometimes money. According to their statement, the men "grew up believing Dupré cared for them, and only recently realized they had been preyed upon." One went to a therapist and realized he had been abused. He met with Dupré, who, according to the statement, said "that he was sorry and did not realize that our client did not want sexual relations. He stated that he wanted to remain friends with our clients for the rest of their lives." The mother of one victim wrote to Dupré in 2003 about the alleged abuse and, shortly after, he announced that he had health problems that might force him to retire soon. [188]

A weak form of traumatic bonding also explains why so many victims regard their abusers as sick rather than evil and ask that the abusers be treated rather than punished. The Rev. Gary Hayes, who says he was himself abused by two priests when he was young, says of abusers, "These are sick people. They are not evil people as the hierarchy has tried to portray them. They have a disease."[189] On the rarest occasions the abusers may exhibit such signs of mental illness that they may well have diminished responsibility, but most of the time the abusers are evil, coolly planning to exploit the weak to satisfy their desires for sex and control. Any rational evaluation of such men sees them as criminal and evil men, but the victims often have lingering attachments to them and want to think as well of them as they can, even when the victims recognize that they have been abused.

This lingering bond is harmful both to the victim and to society. The victim cannot see clearly the truth of the situation that he has been the victim of evil, not of sickness. He *should* feel anger at the abuser and the abuse. He should report the abuse to the authorities[190] and demand that the abuser be punished, not sent away for treatment. Since the victim often cannot do this, because of the lingering effects of the traumatic bond,[191] it is all the more important that others show proper anger at the evildoer and demand that he be punished. But abuse victims, like torture victims, make people uncomfortable. They turn their faces away and don't want to get involved. It is easier to ignore the evil than to confront it.

## FEAR OF HOMOSEXUALITY

Most (81%) of the victims of priests were boys, and sexual abuse "often precipitates crises about sexual orientation and gender identity."[192] It violates their status as men in three ways: A boy, to be a man, must convince himself and others that he is no longer a child (neither dependent nor vulnerable), that he is not a woman (neither passive nor effeminate), and that he is not a homosexual (and thus feels no attraction to other men).[193] Because the abuse attacks the boy's manhood, he is extremely reluctant to report it. Michel Dorais found that "almost all the respondents who took part in this study reported that they had been reluctant to disclose the abuse they had suffered. It took weeks, months, years, in some cases decades before they could overcome their fear and bring an end to their silence."[194] Boys who have been abused fear that they are homosexual. It is "almost universal for male survivors of childhood sexual abuse to have doubts and fears regarding their sexual orientation."[195]

Boys' fear that they would be thought to be homosexual was well based. In 1984, when "Daniel" was an altar boy at the church of the Incarnation of Our Lord in Philadelphia, he was anally raped by Father Martins, a Brazilian pediatrician and religious order priest. The boy cried in pain and bled. Daniel told his lay math teacher who was horrified and immediately told the pastor, Father John Shelley, who refused to help the boy. The boy told his mother and he called the police. When he returned to the parish school the next day Father Shelley "told him he was not welcome anymore." The children at the parish school called him "faggot" and a teacher, Sister Maria Loyola, "stated referring to him in class as 'Daniella,' prompting the class to laugh."[196] When he protested, she gave him a demerit.

The fact that an unusually large percentage of homosexuals have been abused as children[197] suggests that childhood sexual abuse is one cause of homosexuality. Perhaps the abusers were attracted to boys who were already homosexual; or perhaps the trauma of premature homosexual experience turned the boys to homosexuality. One study showed "that homosexual identification is seven times greater for victimized males and bisexual identification six times greater for victimized males than for a comparison group of nonabused adolescent boys."[198] In another study, boys who had been molested were almost four times as likely to identify themselves as homosexual or bisexual than those who had not been molested (7.4

percent as opposed to 2.0 percent).[199] If the boy responded to the abuse and felt pleasure in it, a pleasure which is a physiological reaction to sexual stimulus, he would tend to think that he was a homosexual.

Even if one accepts the theory that homosexuality is a normal variation of human sexuality and that some boys develop homosexually, the premature sexual initiation of a young boy is still as much a form of abuse as the statutory rape of a girl, and like the girl, the young homosexual is likely to think that he led the abuser on, that he is in some way responsible for the abuse.[200] When Shanley had sex with the homosexual young men who were distressed and came to him for counseling, it was as much a form of abuse as his molestation of teenagers.

Homosexual development is even more fraught with pitfalls than heterosexual development is, and homosexuals should be at the forefront of those who seek to protect boys from homosexual abuse, instead of campaigning for lowering the age of consent to homosexual acts. Julie Bindel, who has campaigned internationally for the protection of abused women and children, laments that "more gay men have attempted to explain the 'erotic nature' of intergenerational sex, or shown sympathy and understanding of 'boy lovers,' than have joined forces with those of us who wish to see an end to child sexual abuse."[201] Robert F. Miailovich was the president of Dignity/USA, the Catholic organization that does not accept traditional teaching on the wrongness of homosexual acts; he denounced "shrill voices of knee-jerk, vigilante enforcers, the money-grubbing of attorneys and clients who seem to feel that there is a cash price that somebody has to pay to offset everything bad in life," and asked why, "out of all the horrendous things like abandonment, hunger, homelessness, poverty, ignorance, physical violence, and war that can befall a youth, why does an inappropriate sexual encounter with an adult seem to rank alone at the unforgivable center circle of Hell?"[202] Miailovich should read the accounts of abuse and the effects it had on victims to learn that what he characterizes as "an inappropriate sexual encounter" is enough to make a victim's life a waking hell.

## LOSS OF FAITH

Eric Patterson was one of the Rev. Robert K. Larson's victims (see below). He was hospitalized for depression. He told his sister that God was a vindictive supreme being "that's out to get you." His sister spoke of God's mercy, but Patterson couldn't think of God that way, because "when I was age twelve, Father Larson practically raped me."[203] After he told his sister this he began pounding his head on the floor and had to be restrained and sedated. In his suicide note he wrote that he "tried to please God every day but I have always come up so short that he makes me feel guilty about my life."[204] A man who was abused when he was an altar boy said that "at first I was mad at the priest. Then I was mad at God. If priests are his word on earth, how could He let them do this."[205] Mark Serrano, victim of the Rev. James Hanley,[206] said that "in my twenties I couldn't go to Mass without seeing the image of the priest and thinking of Hanley's genitals."[207]

Wayne Sagrera was a lifelong Catholic who stopped going to church soon after he realized his diocese had knowingly given a child molester access to his sons, three of whom were abused as altar boys by Gilbert Gauthé. He lamented that "never once has one of these [church officials] come forward and asked how our children are, or how we are. Not one . . . ever had the courtesy to ask." "I hoped the Church could be the Church I thought it was, instead of the one I learned it is," Rose Sagrera said; "I had believed everything in the Bible and the *Baltimore Catechism*—I went to Catholic school and I believed the Church was supposed to be forgiving, loving, and caring. But I learned it can be very evil; that it has very little concern for individuals, and that it won't go after the lost sheep."[208]

The victims often cannot believe in the Church; they cannot even believe in God. They have "a long-term aversion to all organized religion."[209] "I went to a psychiatric hospital at age eleven, suffering from deep depression, and that built up my courage, so that over the years it has begun not to matter what other people think," victim Craig said. Abuse by a priest leads to a deep alienation from the Church and from God: "As a Catholic kid, a priest was just like God. I couldn't function anymore." "I have a whole different outlook on religion now. I question every religion out there. Before, I was a normal Christian who looked at it as a foundation for life. At one time, I had even thought about being a priest. Now, I see the Catholic Church as a joke because the hierarchy has allowed the abuse of children to continue."[210] "I felt that God has betrayed me for bringing Fr. Aube into my life."[211] The mystery of evil is made all the harder to bear when Satan wears a Roman collar.

## SUICIDE

Victims of abuse often blame and hate themselves to the point of killing themselves. A victim of a priest especially feels this way. The victim feels there must be something terribly wrong with him that had driven a person so close to God, a priest, to do something wrong. Because a boy's normal body feels involuntary pleasure in the abuse, he therefore feels that he is guilty of having done something wrong. When the priest-abuser hears his confession and absolves him, or, even worse, when another priest tells him he should confess the abuse, it reinforces the victim's belief that he, not the abuser, is guilty. "Perhaps because of their deeply inculcated self-loathing, survivors seem most disposed to direct their aggression against themselves."[212] Probably hundreds of victims of priests have committed suicide, sometimes quickly, sometimes "slowly with drugs, alcohol, and engaging in other risky behavior."[213]

Professor of sociology David Finkelhor believes that children who are sexually abused "are two to eight times more likely to commit suicide than the general population."[214] Dennis A. Gaboury, a law firm administrator in Baltimore and himself a victim of the Rev. James Porter, said that of the hundred or so victims of Porter, "Four committed suicide and another twelve attempted suicide."[215] The body that has been abused is defiled and is a source of pain to the victim. The victim hopes to escape the pain by getting rid of the body through suicide: "Boys who have lived through the enslavement of abuse are among those most inclined to self-mutilation or suicidal ideation: this body, used as an object by the aggressor, is superfluous and can be discarded."[216] In the Dorais study, a third of the victims had contemplated suicide; they explained "they just couldn't live with their memories and that the only way to get rid of the body that had provoked the abuse, and still bore the scars, was to kill it."[217] Some mutilate themselves. One boy said he was molested by the Rev. James Clark of Fremont, California; the boy later cut off his hand with a fishing knife. One victim could stand the shame no longer, "one day dousing his penis with lighter fluid and setting it on fire."[218] Many victims attempt suicide. Stephen Johnson, victim of James Porter, attempted suicide three times.[219]

The admitted abuser Rev. Robert Larson of Kansas left a trail of bodies in his wake. He was imperious and dashing (the grandiosity of the narcissist). His abuse was reported to the diocese of Wichita as early as the 1960s. In 1981 a victim complained to the chancery in Wichita and was told by a pastor that "we're well aware of the situation, and we're taking care of it."[220] The diocese kept sending Larson to treatment and reassigning him to parishes. He went to one clinic and was diagnosed as not a pedophile; he had brought an altar boy with him "and on the way back he would be feeling the guy up in the car."[221] Larson liked to tuck in boys' pants in the sacristy. He forced boys to perform oral sex on him. The boys did not respond well to sex with Larson: their families report that after they were molested their personalities changed; they became "introspective, sad, short-tempered, and—ultimately—dangerously desperate."[222]

Five of his victims committed suicide. David Romey was always hanging around with Larson. He shot himself in the head in 1978, when he was twenty-three. His sister found his body in a darkened basement stairway. When he was eight, Bobby Thompson was chosen by Larson for special attention and at eleven he began his downward spiral. In 1990 a psychologist evaluated Thompson and concluded that "previous suspicions of sexual abuse by a priest in Bobby's early years seems highly likely based on his concerns about masculinity, his attempts to avoid closeness particularly with his stepfather...his avoidance of sexuality, and his confused identity and depression." In 1996, when he was twenty-one, Thompson "walked into his mother's garage, started his car's engine, and sat down to die." In his suicide note Thompson said that "it has just become too much pain and trouble for me to continue." Larson molested two cousins, Gilbert Rodriguez and Paul Tafolla. Rodriguez in 1998 walked into a stand of trees at the edge of a field and killed himself with a shotgun. A year and a half later, Tafolla died of a drug overdose in a hotel room. Eric Patterson was abused and fell deeper and deeper into depression. In 1999, when he was twenty-nine years old, he shot himself in the head with a Colt 45. Larson, who pleaded guilty to sexual abuse and is in jail, disclaims any responsibility for the deaths.[223] The victims are in their graves; their molester was released from prison in April 2006 and will spend the rest of his life at a treatment center in St. Louis.[224]

John Brian Greenlaw was seven years old when he started talking about suicide. He hanged himself and almost died when he was seventeen; he finally killed himself when he was thirty-three by an overdose of drugs and alcohol. Only then did his mother discover what had gone wrong. He had been raped by Father John Geoghan when Geoghan had taken him out for ice cream. Geoghan had also molested his sister.[225] The Rev. Ronald Paquin of Boston had an appetite for young boys, as many parents complained to the archdiocese of Boston, which did nothing. In 1981 Paquin took Jimmy Francis and three other boys to New Hampshire. They drank heavily, and Paquin ended up in Francis's sleeping bag. They continued to drink, and Paquin drove the boys back to Massachusetts the next morning. Paquin fell asleep at the wheel; the car went off the road. Francis was pinned, asphyxiated, and died. Francis's friends mourned; Paquin said the funeral Mass, and put the grief to good use by luring a distraught boy into his bed at the rectory. Bishop McCormack was told all this. His response was, "How much are you looking for?"[226]

Kevin McDonough had told his friends but not his parents that he was abused by the Rev. Peter J. Frost in the 1970s in Boston. He had been a happy child, but at thirteen he became withdrawn and morose. He joined the Marines, but couldn't last. He came home and slashed his wrists. He went into therapy, found a job and a girlfriend, but on May 1, 2001, he died of an overdose of cocaine. Only then did his seventeen-year-old niece Tara tell Kevin's parents that he had been molested by a priest. His aunt, a nun, wrote to Cardinal Law, "Kevin is dead from an overdose in an attempt to relieve his pain. I believe that it was directly connected to the sexual abuse he endured. So in my estimation Peter Frost is a fraud, a perpetrator and a murderer. . . . I would hope that Peter Frost be defrocked and deprived of any financial support from the Archdiocese of Boston."[227] Law never responded. Frost admitted to Cardinal Law that he had abused boys and that one of his victims had committed suicide, but Law held out hope to Frost for future assignments.[228] Frost was not defrocked until 2005.[229] The Rev. Christopher Coyne of the Boston archdiocese explained that it was far too much trouble to defrock him: "It's a very long and involved process, and if a man cooperates, it moves forward much quicker. If a guy just doesn't get it. . . ."[230]

A twelve-year-old boy in Emerson, New Jersey, was victimized by a Franciscan brother. He wrote in his notebook, "It wasn't worth living," drank a bottle of wintergreen and died.[231] Dennis C. of Orlando was in high school when he was molested by a priest; when he was twenty-seven he hanged himself after telling his brother, "Contact Father S.—and tell him I forgive him."[23] Dennis Brown had sued the diocese of Brooklyn because of alleged abuse by the Rev. James Collins in 1970. Six others also complained about Collins. Brown had moved to Atlanta but battled alcoholism. In September 2002, just before the suit was filed Brown drank antifreeze and died.[233] Jim Kelly was abused by the Rev. James Hanley. Jim committed suicide on October 12, 2003.

Victim Doe XII[234] at the age of nine decided he wanted to be a priest. When he was thirteen, he became close to the Rev. Gordon MacRae of the Manchester diocese (see pp. 183–185) who bought him gifts, took him out for ice cream, and told him stories: How MacRae's father had abused him by holding a torch next to his face, making him color blind (not true); how MacRae had a gun (true); how MacRae used to be a police officer (not true) who "used to hunt for kidnapped kids and recover them so they could be returned to their parents"[235] (not true); and how MacRae "had something wrong with his brain and how he could potentially die at any time"[236] (not true). MacRae got closer and closer to the boy as the boy went through puberty and explained to him that "masturbation was good and that [Victim Doe XII] should feel good about it."[237] Having stirred all the emotions of a boy—admiration, fear, pity, sexual desire—he then started to kiss him mouth to mouth and played the "spider game," fondling the boy's genitals. The boy was frightened by this fondling, and never had an erection, and MacRae lost interest in him.

When the news about MacRae hit the newspapers, Victim Doe XII started vomiting, sleep walking, and having night terrors. He had

> recurrent and intrusive recollections of his abuse, dreams and flashbacks of his abuse, events that symbolize his abuse (seeing a priest), his attempts to avoid thoughts of his abuse (doesn't practice his religion), isolating himself from others, foreshortened future (doesn't want a child, doesn't feel he could be an appropriate parent), difficulty with sleep, hypervigilance, finds sex problematic, and some feelings of guilt because he did not report Father MacRae, and thus others were abused in Keene, New Hampshire.[238]

Victim Doe XII has had thoughts of suicide. He had all the newspaper articles about MacRae spread over his floor, and "thought about cutting his throat with a knife and letting the blood spurt onto the articles." This victim fantasized about killing his abuser. He concocted a punishment that would fit the crime; he has thought of "dressing up as a priest and taking communion wafers and coating them with poison. He would then place one in Father MacRae's mouth as he received communion. Father MacRae would then die and [Victim Doe XII] would commit suicide. [Victim Doe XII] explained that Father MacRae should die through the body of Christ for what he has done to him and others."[239] MacRae had used the bait of the priesthood to poison and kill the souls of New Hampshire boys; Catholicism, which claims to bring life and healing, brought corruption and death to the souls of this boy and so many other boys and girls.

CHAPTER TEN

# ABUSERS AND THEIR TREATMENT

ABUSERS WERE OFTEN SENT by their bishops for treatment. This implied that they were "sick," that they had an illness that needed treating, that it could be treated, and that there were experts who could give a diagnosis, prescribe and carry out treatment, and decide what the prognosis of the "illness" was.[1] However, even the definition of pedophilia is itself a subject of controversy, as is the question of whether it is a mental disease at all. Most psychiatrists (but not all) classify sexual attraction to pre-pubertal children as a mental illness or disorder, if only because acting on it will get the pedophile into trouble.[2] The priest-abusers who were involved with pre-pubertal children were a small and decreasing number throughout the second half of the twentieth century.

However, most of the abusers were sexually involved with teenage boys. It is difficult to classify a male's sexual attraction to sexually mature teenage boys as a mental illness or disorder without also classifying homosexuality as a mental disorder, and the American Psychiatric Association voted in 1974, after an intense and disruptive political campaign, to remove homosexuality from the category of mental disorder or illness. It is now simply another sexual orientation. So men who are attracted sexually to teenage boys, ephebophiles, no longer have a recognized psychiatric disorder. They may have other problems which lead them to act on this desire, but the desire itself is not recognized as a psychiatric disorder. Despite this, priests who were sexually involved with teenage boys were sent for treatment as if they were pedophiles.

## *Pedophilia: Orientation or Illness?*

Mental illness itself in most cases is an illness only in an analogical sense, and sometimes the analogy is very distant: compulsive shopping is classified as a disease. Are adults (almost always men) who are sometimes, or largely, or exclusively sexually attracted by prepubescent children suffering from a mental illness? Is pedophilia a mental disorder?

Psychiatrists have sought to make their diagnosis of mental diseases scientific, and have therefore based their classifications on biological "facts." Freud taught that "it is a characteristic common to all the [sexual] perversions that in them reproduction as an aim is put aside. This is actually the criterion by which we judge whether a sexual activity is perverse: if it departs from reproduction in its aims and pursues the attainment of gratification independently."[3] Robert L. Spitzer, the founder of the modern *Diagnostic and Statistical Manual*, the handbook that psychiatrists use to classify mental disorders, followed Freud in characterizing disorders as "a failure 'to adequately perform its biological "design" (naturally selected) function.'"[4] Fred S. Berlin classifies pedophilia as a disorder because "God or nature has put sexual desire into each and every one of us for a very important reason—the preservation of the human race."[5] Such psychiatrists judge sexual acts (and the desires for them) teleologically, by whether they fulfill or frustrate their biological purpose of reproduction.[6] They therefore arrive at conclusions similar to those of Aristotelians, who believe that natural processes have a *telos*, a purpose, and to those of Christians, who believe the universe is designed and that its purpose can be discovered in part by reason and more clearly by revelation from the Designer. Such an approach necessarily classifies homosexuality as a disorder, as critics of the teleological approach recognize and dislike.[7] It is intellectually incoherent to classify pedophilia as a mental illness because it frustrates a biological function without also classifying homosexuality as a mental illness.[8]

A brief survey of anthropology, history, and psychology shows that in many societies, including Western societies until very recently, children have been seen as legitimate objects of sexual desire. In many cultures very young girls are married to older men for economic or political reasons; men have power and use women in the service of that power. In England the age of consent was ten until the latter nineteenth century.[9] In Delaware it was once seven years of age (the traditional "age of reason" when a child can tell right from wrong). The idea that sexual interest in children is a sign of mental disorder is a very recent development.

Many men feel sexual desire for children; this desire is probably more common than homosexual desire, because men who are heterosexual in adult orientation can be involuntarily attracted to the relative femininity of children's bodies. One study of physical responses showed that over half the male subjects (twenty-eight of forty-eight young soldiers) were sexually aroused by pictures of children.[10] John Bierne and Marsh Runty discovered in their study that "21% of subjects reported sexual attraction to some small children, 9% described sexual fantasies involving children, 5% admitted to having masturbated to such fantasies, and 7% indicated some likelihood of having sex with a child if they could avoid detection and punishment."[11] Other studies reported similar percentages of men who admitted feeling sexual desire for children.[12] Sexual desire for children is common and was not stigmatized as a mental disorder until the nineteenth century. Of course, almost all men who feel such desire do not act on it because of religious, ethical, or social restraints; nor, surprisingly, do all child molesters feel such desire. They instead can be motivated by repressed anger, desire for control, or a desire to transgress.

This has important practical and forensic consequences. If a man is accused of abuse, and if he is tested to see if he is sexually attracted to children, the presence of sexual desire does not mean that he has acted on it. Nor is the converse true. A man accused of abuse may be tested and show no signs of sexual desire for children. This does not mean that he did not molest a child, because molesters sometimes do not feel sexual desire but have other motivations. Priests who did in fact abuse small children were sometimes diagnosed by psychiatrists as *not* having pedophilia, a sexual desire for small children. The diagnosis may have been correct; but desire, or at least sexual desire in the ordinary sense, may not have been the motivation for the abuse.

Most human beings sense that their sexual desires are disordered even though they are not mentally ill. By the strictest Christian definition, any sexual desire a man feels for anyone who is not his wife is disordered, and if the desire is consented to, it is a sin. All men may be disordered in this sense; but not all men have mental illness connected with sex. However, the greater the disorder, the more likely it is to affect the whole personality. Many pedophiles seem to have otherwise normal personalities, but some show signs of true mental abnormality. Abusers often keep detailed records of their sexual activity and of their victims, although they know that these records could be used to convict them in court. Choosing evil, as abusers do, darkens the intellect and destroys the good of reason. It is irrational to do something wrong, and the irrationality of a particular type of evil tends to infect the person and makes it hard for him to see the truth.

Some pedophiles are motivated by sexual desire, a desire that they do not choose and which is difficult or impossible to eradicate.[13] It is simply a fact that some men feel sexually attracted to children and some men are sexually attracted to other men. If heterosexuals and homosexuals can both act on their sexual desires without committing sins or crimes, why is it wrong to act on the attraction to children? Pedophiles therefore feel they are unfairly stigmatized, that society is narrow and repressive, that they can persuade society to change, as homosexuals have done. Regardless of whether or not society changes, pedophiles believe that sexual acts with children are not wrong, even if society may (unfairly, in the pedophile's view) punish them. But if a pedophile can escape punishment, he has no qualms of conscience about engaging in sex with children and sees the doctors who try to cure him as simply agents of a repressive society.

## *Psychiatry and Social Control*

Psychology is in fact often at the service of social control. Psychologists once recognized "drapetomania," "one of the 'diseases and physical peculiarities of the Negro race.'" The word "drapetomania" was created by the noted Louisiana surgeon and psychologist Dr. Samuel A. Cartwright by combining the Greek words for "runaway slave" and "mad" or "crazy." It was used to describe the mental disease that "induces the Negro to run away from service, [and] is as much a disease of the mind as any other species of mental alienation, and much more curable, as a general rule."[14] Dr. Cartwright opined that it could be cured by a sound thrashing.

Some condemn modern psychiatry as following this tradition of social control. Frederick Suppe claimed that "sexual paraphelias constitute conflicts between an individual and society" and by labeling them as mental illnesses "psychiatry has resorted to the codification of sexual mores while masquerading as objective science."[15] Soviet Russia shared Dr. Cartwright's approach to mental illness; anyone who disagreed with scientific socialism must by definition be out of contact with reality and was therefore treated by institutionalization and powerful psychotropic drugs. Other psychiatrists praise psychiatry as a means of social control and maintain that "we can only decide what is pathological with reference to the social and political."[16]

Thomas Szasz, skeptical of the whole psychiatric enterprise, rejects calling pedophilia an illness. Pedophilia is not in the same category as schizophrenia. Pedophiles are not delusional and they can control their actions. They do not abuse children on the street, but rationally and calculatedly get access to children. Szasz thinks the focus should be on the fact that sexual congress with children is a sin and crime. Pedophiles are almost excused by those who call them "sick," as if they cannot help themselves. When an abuser proceeds from desire to act, however, he leaves the realm of mental activity and can be judged by society.

Such an approach recognizes that abusers are responsible for their acts. They are not so much sick men in need of a cure as criminals who should be punished and sinners who need to repent. When the legal system looks at abuse and sees illness instead of crime, the abuser often escapes his just desserts. When Father Ronald Hubert Kelly pleaded guilty in 1979 to "serious offenses of indecent assault against young boys" in Newfoundland, Mr. Justice James Gushue of the Newfoundland Supreme Court of Appeal upheld Kelly's suspended sentence, lamenting "these unfortunate incidents" but saying that Kelly was "no criminal in the commonly understood meaning of the word, but in fact suffers from a type of mental illness aggravated by drink and drugs which could very well respond to proper treatment."[17] After four and a half months, the director of Southdown, the Rev. Canice Connors, pronounced Kelly cured, and Kelly soon became vice chancellor for secular affairs for the archdiocese of Toronto and also obtained a pardon for his crimes.

But why should sexual activity with minors be a crime at all?

## *Consensual Morality*

Under traditional Christian morality sexual acts with children outside of marriage (very young adolescents could marry) fell under the same condemnation as all sexual acts outside of marriage, whether the acts were heterosexual or homosexual. Those who wish to justify the social condemnation of child-adult sexual congress as more than the tyranny of the heterosexual and homosexual majority have sought a basis in modern consensual morality: that is, if two or more people agree to do something sexual, and if there is not a gross disparity of power among them, the act is moral in the eyes of society and should not be forbidden by law.[18]

This consensual approach has difficulties in pinpointing what is innately wrong with adult-child sex.[19] First of all, adults often force children to do things without their consent, such as taking a bath or going to school. This is done for the objective good of the child. Secondly, older minors can certainly consent to sexual activity with adults. Such activity may or may not cause harm to the minor, but it risks great harm, as we have seen in the chapter on victims. Adult-child sexual activity is therefore at the very least a type of child endangerment, as much as taking a child for a wild ride in a car with bad brakes or giving a child marijuana would be. The child may not be hurt, but he may well be. If he is not hurt he may as an adult feel free to engage in the same dangerous activity with children, and the chances of a child being seriously hurt are therefore increased. Adults are generally allowed to engage in dangerous activities if they wish to; children are generally not allowed to do so because society wants to protect them and its future, and children have a weak sense of the long-term consequences of their actions.

Children, like other people in a weak position, have historically been exploited by adult men. One of the fruits of the French Revolution was an insistence on the equality of the value of all human beings, an equality which was first confined to men and then only gradually extended to women and children. In the United States women reformers campaigned successfully through the latter part of the nineteenth century and the early twentieth century to raise the age of consent to the range of sixteen to eighteen years of age. One of the fruits of the Progressive era, age of consent laws are designed to prevent the exploitation of the weak by the strong, to protect children from adults who want to exploit their bodies. The Progressives saw that the power disparity was the key to understanding the abusive nature of intercourse between an adult and a child, even if the child is sexually mature and consents (that is, is not forced). Normally the law is not invoked unless the difference in age is greater than five years.

This Progressive approach avoids two difficulties: it does not have to prove that every child is necessarily harmed by a sexual approach by an adult,[20] nor does it have to prove that a child or minor is incapable of giving consent. Protection is therefore extended to teenagers, who may be sexually mature, but who are in a weak position vis-à-vis adults, especially adults in positions of authority, such as priests and teachers. Sexual activity, whether heterosexual or homosexual, with minors can therefore be logically condemned as a crime without identifying sexual desire for teenagers as a mental illness. Many heterosexuals desire teenage girls; this is the basis of modern American advertising. Many homosexuals desire teenage boys, as we shall see in the next chapter.

## *Transference and the Helping Professions*

Pedophilia, even if it is not a disease but an orientation like homosexuality and heterosexuality, is often found in men with undeniable mental disorders that affect how they approach sexuality. Abusers suffer from narcissism, sociopathy, lack of empathy, and repressed anger, all of which may motivate or facilitate their sexual abuse of children. Those who desire children and adolescents and who act on those desires are found in all occupations, but certain occupations make it easier for an abuser to abuse. Prominent among these are the helping professions—doctor, teacher, social worker, minister, and above all, priest.

Every profession (in the broadest sense) that puts a professional in contact with a vulnerable person contains the potential for abuse. All power tends to corrupt, and those who are placed in contact with people who are open, hurting, or vulnerable are sometimes tempted to use their position to get something they want—sex, money, or some other source of satisfaction. The helping professions include doctors, therapists, and religious leaders of all denominations. Doctors have physical intimacy with their patients, and the Hippocratic Oath contains a pledge to abstain "from abusing the bodies of man or woman, bond or free."[21] Benjamin Franklin headed a royal investigation in France about sexual abuse of patients by doctors. Several surveys have shown that one out of ten physicians has had sexual contact with a patient.[22] One Massachusetts study revealed perhaps "one third of all money awarded for medical malpractice is for damages for sexual misconduct."[23]

Sexual abuse of both minors and adults is often made easier by what Freud called transference. He noticed an erotic dynamism in his relationship with his patients. Analysts for decades were becoming sexually involved with their clients at an alarming rate. "When a person in need asks an authority figure for help, he or she often ascribes magic-like powers to the helping person. The feelings seem to be connected to our experience of childhood relationships to parental figures, particularly the all-embracing, absolute trust an infant has of his mother or other early caretakers." The emotions we felt toward our parents are transferred to this new figure from whom we seek help. "The greater the distress, the more power the person imbues on the authority figure."[24] Carl Jung became erotically involved with his patient Sabrina Spielrein, whom he started seeing when she was nineteen.[25] The human encounter movement popularized nude encounter groups, and some sex therapists began having sex with their patients as part of therapy (see Kaiser's experience, p. 452). One study of members of the Los Angeles County Psychological Association showed that "17% of the men in private practice indicated that they had engaged in therapist-client sexual intimacies"; 10 percent of the psychiatrists in this group admitted to erotic contact with patients.[26] States began criminalizing doctor-patient sex. Physicians of souls also abuse their positions, and not only in the Catholic Church. In the United Church of Christ, about 13 percent of pastors reported sexual contact with a church member. A 1988 survey showed that 12 percent of pastors had had intercourse with someone in their church (other than a spouse).[27] Among Southern Baptists a survey indicated about 10 percent of pastors had sexual contact with members of their congregations.[28] All Christian clergy have unsupervised contact with open, vulnerable, and wounded people, and about 10 percent of clergy in all denominations give in to the temptation to exploit these relationships for sexual gratification. The percentage of abusing clergy may be higher than the percentage in other helping professions.[29]

## *Manipulative Confidence Artists*

Transference can help lead astray even a sincere pastor, but it is exploited by the confidence artist. The role of religious leader is perfect for the abusive confidence artist. "The predator is typically charismatic and ingratiating, able to charm and disarm in order to achieve the exact, desired response. The precise skills used by the predator to groom victims also elicit trust and support from the larger community, creating an aura that makes discovery of perpetration unlikely."[30] Even if he is discovered, the confidence artist knows how to work the system. John C. Gonsiorek writes of the type found among abusive physicians and clergy:

> This group is adept at manipulating colleagues.... When caught, they mimic the healthy/neurotic therapist who is remorseful. They "confess" only to inappropriate behaviors they believe others already know about. However when their attempts to manipulate are not persuasive, they often become hostile and engage in counterattack. They do not hesitate to damage others to avoid consequences and are adept at outmaneuvering others.
>
> Occasionally, some may voluntarily seek therapy and appear to be deeply involved in a rehabilitation effort; however, they are adept at manipulating their way through programs, particularly structured programs that can be "figured out."[31]

Therapists and treatment centers should have assumed that any abuser might be a manipulative confidence artist who knew how to pretend to respond to the treatment; but therapists and treatment centers often allowed themselves to be deceived.

Confidence artists almost always possess charisma, "a special magical quality of personality by virtue of which the individual possessing it was set apart from ordinary men and women, and treated as if endowed with supernatural or superhuman powers. Such people have the capacity of immediately impressing and of attracting devoted followers."[32] The charismatic confidence artist half-believes his lies are true, and is therefore able to win over his dupes. The institutionalized charisma of the priesthood provides the confidence artist with additional advantages which his personal gifts can build on. "A successful confidence trickster requires a capacity to believe in his own fantasies which is beyond the reach of the ordinary person."[33] Because religious life is built upon faith, the trickster can use the language of faith and trust to inspire (mistaken) confidence in his sincerity even after he has been caught.

Priests and ministers are often called charismatic. What people mean is that the clergyman has qualities that somehow set him apart; such ministers "have the capacity of immediately impressing and influencing others and of attracting devoted followers. Charisma is closely linked with intensity of conviction. The ability to speak fluently in public and good looks are helpful additional assets."[34] Because he feels set apart, the charismatic person may feel entitled to special privileges, and they are often sexual.

The Rev. Paul Aube was a master at duping his superiors. In 1993 Aube wrote Bishop Leo O'Neil of Manchester and thanked him for his "compassionate letter." O'Neil wanted a full psychological evaluation of Aube and he agreed to it "if my doctor, my counsel, and I conclude it to be in my best interest and that of the Church." They of course did not conclude that. Aube expressed sympathy for O'Neil: "I have some insight of the anguish and concern these matters cause you. I am trying to be open and honest with you as to where I am in my efforts to become a better steward of the gift of my life from the Lord."[35]

Aube's 1994 letter to O'Neil is full of false notes, but the bishop, if he heard them, didn't seem to mind. Aube, like all the others, claimed, "I am innocent"[36] and protested undying devotion: "My loyalty to the Church and my obedience to you are obligations that I take very seriously." To Aube, his ordination was everything: "The priesthood of Jesus Christ which He has called me to share with Him, is my whole life. I would die for it and/or accept any cross that He wants me to carry because of it."[37] Real people do not talk this way. Aube had claimed the gift of knowledge (see p. 180), the ability to read men's (or, more often, teenage boys') minds and hearts. He made shrewd guesses and used knowledge gained through confession to impress people with this gift.

The New Hampshire attorney general offered Aube limited immunity in return for the information in an interview, so it might be reliable. Aube claimed to be heterosexual, but "homosexual curious, if you want to put it that way."[38] Aube had never fallen into theological error: "I've always been very orthodox as far as living up to the teachings of the Church," unlike his seminary professors.[39] He apparently missed the lecture on homosexuality (if there was one). He claimed to have had no sexual encounters or difficulties before his ordination and to have no homosexual feelings or temptations. In fact, he claimed, he disliked homosexuals. A teenage boy told Aube that he had been molested and had become involved in homosexual activities. Aube claimed that "I became extremely, extremely uptight at that point because that's when what happened to my brother hit me [apparently molestation, but this remark is not explained]. I didn't know if I wanted to jump over the table and choke him because I hated homosexuals."[40]

In his first assignment he admits to three sexual encounters, and the boys were seventeen and eighteen—in fact, the encounter occurred on one boy's eighteenth birthday. Aube claimed, "I would say that 95% of the people I had sexual contact with were people who ah, doubted their sexual identity or already had had ah, homosexual experiences."[41] Aube was unhappy about his sexual behavior and told his pastor (now deceased), who consoled him: "Well, Paul, we're all human you know. We all have weaknesses."[42] That was the extent of the pastor's reaction, according to Aube. Aube bought boys many gifts, but never, he said, in connection with sexual favors. He also gave them crosses "to get them closer to Christ."[43] Aube tried to approach Bishop Gendron about his problem, but never found the opportunity. At one parish Aube discovered the pastor was embezzling money, and the pastor in revenge accused him of all sorts of things, including "being homosexual."[44]

Aube was deeply pious, he said, far more pious than his bishops: "Ah, I hate to admit this. At every meeting I've had with any of my ordinaries, and of my [b]ishops, I'm the one that had to initiate, I'm the one that had to request for us to pray before we started the meeting. That was always depressing to me. I felt they are the ones who should initiate it, not me."[45] Bishop Gendron however did pray, and the memory of his piety led Aube to exclaim: "I would die for the Church, I would die for the priesthood."[46] Aube knew his own weaknesses, and pleaded not to be put back into parish work. However Gendron "asked me to go back to parish work. I said I did not want to go back to parish work. I really didn't want to do anymore [sic] youth work."[47] After Aube was discovered by the police in 1975 giving oral sex to a teenager, all Gendron said was that it was "most unfortunate"[48] and did not place any restrictions upon his ministry.[49]

How much truth was Aube telling? Some of his testimony was lies. He molested younger boys, thirteen-year-olds, as well as sixteen- to eighteen-year-olds. He taught a twelve-year-old how to masturbate.[50] What he said about the bishop's reaction rings true, but of course Aube was trying to shift part of the blame onto the bishop (where in fact some of it certainly belongs). However, his histrionics and silly rhetoric were equivalent to wearing a sign around his neck reading "phony." Why anyone took him seriously is hard to imagine, but he succeeded in manipulating not just his victims, but the diocesan officials, the police, the laity, and the psychologists who treated him.

## *Sociopathology and Lack of Sympathy*

A confidence artist hurts his victims and usually feels no distress at the damage he causes. The abusers, the bishops, and most priests showed an incomprehension of the pain of the victims. This lack of empathy is characteristic of sociopaths. They have no sense of the emotional damage abusers inflict on their victims. One would think that the clergy, a "helping profession," would not attract sociopaths.[51] But it does.

When a group of candidates for a clerical order was tested, they scored very high on the Mf scale (evincing feminine interests) and on the Pd scale, psychopathic deviance, of the Minnesota Multiphasic Personality Inventory.[52] Another study showed the same result, and the tester reluctantly concluded "a sizeable proportion of the seminarians have at least a tendency in common with the psychopathic deviate."[53] This type of person does not show emotion: "The psychopathic deviate…is one with apathy of emotional life. This connotes the fact that he lacks emotional responses suitable to a given situation, as well as the fact that he does not show emotion in all the situations in which one would normally expect him to do so."[54] In fact, the seminarians were not as psychopathic as the test showed; they were lying in their answers because they thought they *should not* feel or show emotion.[55] However, such standards can become internalized and make the personality truly psychopathic, with an absence of deep emotional response. Why did seminarians think they should be psychopathic? The answer to that lies in distortions of Catholic spirituality and doctrine which I will examine in Chapter Sixteen.

## *Narcissism and Self-Centeredness*

The narcissist lives in a fantasy world in which he is the center of the universe. The abusive Rev. Thomas Laughlin declared to his victims, "I am God."[56] Narcissism is disordered self-love. A person should have a proper amount of self-love; he can fail either by having too little or too much.[57] A narcissist has too much self-love, and it can either be a small excess or a great excess. Most people sin by excess; most people have an opinion of their abilities that is slightly higher than is justified by reality. However, some individuals have a vastly inflated notion of their own importance. This may come across as arrogance, but it may also come across as *charisma*, the word that has recurred so often in the discussion of abusers. Charisma can be positive or negative: "charismatic persons are those who 'charm' us in the sense that they appeal, through the impact of powerful personality, more to the emotions than to the intellect. The charismatic person makes us feel loved or appreciated, singled out for special affection."[58] Pope John Paul II, for example, had this ability to make all the individuals in a large crowd feel he was establishing rapport with each one individually.

The pathological narcissist, because of his high opinion of himself, has a sense of entitlement: "admiration is taken for granted rather than appreciated."[59] Such narcissists do not feel remorse, and their self-esteem is regulated by shame rather than guilt. Some of the characteristics of narcissists that have been prominent in the abusers are:

- Fantasies of or demands for specialness or greatness;
- Need for uncritical and continuous admiration;
- Exhibitionistic tendencies (the "show off");
- Affectations of mannerism, dress, and speech;
- Impaired capacity for love and empathy with consequent shallowness of object relations;
- Excessive self-preoccupation and feelings of entitlement and proportionate inability to appreciate and respect the needs of another;

- "Don Juanism" (i.e., compulsive sexual conquests without regard for the partner);
- Disproportionate anger and envy when supplies of admiration are inadequate;
- Self-destructive patterns of behavior.[60]

Not only the abusers show these characteristics. These characteristics are found in many Catholic bishops (and other clergymen) who are not abusers. But they are destructive characteristics even if they do not lead to abuse.

Within the class of the narcissist, there is a common and recognizable subtype, the erotic narcissist:

> These persons have an indifferent conscience and an aloofness to truth and social responsibility that, if brought to their attention, elicits an attitude of nonchalant innocence. Although these narcissistic individuals are totally self-oriented, they are facile in the ways of social seduction, often feign an air of dignity and confidence, and are rather skilled at deceiving others with their clever glibness. They are skillful in enticing, bewitching and tantalizing the needy and the naïve.[61]

This describes almost all the abusers, especially the abusers of adolescent boys. There is a close alliance between narcissism and at least one type of homosexuality. The homosexual who is attracted to another male because he sees in that male his idealized and usually younger self is a narcissist in this area of his life. This homosexual narcissism reinforces any other narcissistic tendencies the person may have.

Sociopaths also show narcissism: "A pattern of traits and behaviors which signify infatuation and obsession with one's self to the exclusion of all others and the egotistic and ruthless pursuit of one's gratification, dominance, and ambition."[62] The narcissist is grandiose, obsessed with fantasies of success, convinced he is unique, requires excessive admiration and adulation, feels entitled to priority treatment, exploits others for his own ends, lacks empathy for the feelings of others, is envious of others, and is arrogant and enraged when frustrated or contradicted.[63]

Narcissists are attracted to the ministry "because of the public and performing aspects of the position and the opportunity to foster a dependent group of admirers. Engaging in sexual liaisons is part of the larger and continuous pursuit of fulfilling their need for admiration, devotion, and unquestioned love."[64] The new Catholic liturgy places far more emphasis on the personality of the priest-presider than the old liturgy did. "Importance is attributed to the person of the priest; he must be able to handle things skillfully and to be able to present everything well. He is the real center of the celebration,"[65] as Cardinal Ratzinger observed (and disliked) in the new liturgy. The priest not only faces the people but also is supposed to preach at every Mass. Narcissists are "attracted to preaching and presiding roles in which they focus attention on themselves and 'work' the crowd."[66] The Catholic priest who behaves like an emcee during Mass is revealing his narcissism.

Despite their lack of empathy abusers are often excellent confidence artists. They are "very appealing to their congregations because they are often highly intelligent, forceful, and adept at telling people what they want to hear."[67] They sense others' desires and weaknesses in order to exploit them. It is this paradoxical combination of qualities that makes confidence artists so dangerous. They have a strong sense of how others react, but they do not suffer in any way when others are suffering. If they were cold and had no sense of what others were feeling, confidence artists would be less dangerous. But they give the impression that they participate in the feelings of their victims, who therefore think that no one so obviously sympathetic could deliberately inflict pain. The most dangerous confidence artist is the one who can assess what another person is feeling; we assume that he also participates in that feeling and place trust in him, but since he does not really feel what the other person is feeling, he can hurt another person without remorse. Donald Cozzens observed that "many of the clergy abusers show little genuine remorse and few signs of genuine concern for their victims."[68] Gauthé's main concern about his treatment center was that the food was not good enough.

A child is inevitably self-centered. He or she only gradually begins to realize the existence of other human beings—*incipe parve puer risu cognoscere matrem*, "begin little boy to greet your mother with a smile," as Virgil says. The child slowly realizes that other people have the same inner life and begins to feel empathy with the life of others, establishing the primary bonds of community and love that make us fully human. The narcissist never develops this empathy; his interest instead becomes totally directed at himself. He wants to be the center of love and attention, without giving any himself and he therefore arrests his development: "those who remain narcissistic in adult life retain this need to be loved and to be the center of attention together with the grandiosity which accompanies it."[69] Even if not all homosexuality is narcissistic, the regressive homosexuality found in abusers in the priesthood is characterized by narcissism, and clericalism feeds the grandiosity of the narcissistic priest.

I have used the term narcissism because we are accustomed to psychological terminology. A better term would be disordered self-love. A person should see and love himself as he really is. We should know our strengths and weaknesses; we should see ourselves as we are in reality and love and esteem ourselves accordingly. We should strive to do the same with other persons. It is hard to know how someone else feels, but we should strive to attain a knowledge of others, including how that person feels. An individual is not the center of the universe. A believer knows that God is the center; but even a person who does not believe in God can realize that he is not the most important person in the universe. But the narcissist suffers from disordered self-love. He imagines a universe of which he is the center and God, and he tries to control other people to make that fantasy a reality. The ministry exercises a fatal attraction for the narcissist, "who believes that the actual purpose of spiritual activity is 'worship' of themselves."[70]

The overwhelming concern that the Catholic clergy (and clergy in other churches) show for their reputation is a symptom of narcissism. Rev. Gianfranco Ghirlanda, dean of the canon law faculty of the Gregorian University in Rome, maintained, "If a priest is reassigned to parish work after molesting someone, his past shouldn't be revealed, since that violates his right under church law to good reputation."[71] The Rev. Francis P. Rogers of Philadelphia participated in the gang rape of a boy. He eventually admitted he had abused children but added, "I don't know why it has to come out now. . . . It will just ruin my reputation."[72]

## *Control and Repressed Anger*

The narcissist constantly bumps against reality and receives unwelcome reminders that he is not really the center of the universe, that it is not really under his control. Psychiatrists, as we have seen, often claim that abuse is not so much about sex as control. The imprisoned pedophile Alan revealed to his music therapist (who had also been abused as a child) the interior history of his abuse in circumstances that suggest he was telling the truth. When he was seven he was caught in sex play and his mother was horrified and punished him. He then felt that he was a misfit because he was "different," in fact "unique,"[73] that he was the "victim."[74] He felt that "through no fault of his own" he had been deprived of a "normal" life.[75] He explained to the therapist that "as I convinced myself that I had somehow been cheated by fate, I felt I had a license to do anything I chose to."[76] As a misfit he did not feel in control of his life, but "I could...make myself feel stronger and more in control of life by forcing some even more vulnerable child into submitting to my will."[77]

At an extremely early age, Alan's life became totally centered on sex. When he was six, he was already masturbating nightly and constructing elaborate fantasies involving younger boys. In these fantasies Alan was in control; he was no longer the victim of fate but the victimizer, and he "increasingly enjoyed the feelings of power."[78] He realized he would also have to manipulate adults, and was astonished that even in reality he could easily manipulate everyone. He said that "it suddenly felt as if I were living in a world that was under my control."[79] This feeling of power gave him a new high.

Abuse is often called "ritualistic." Alan explained, "I saw these abuses as rituals because by the time I actually acted them out, I had pictured them so vividly and so frequently in my imagination that their ultimate enactment had a distinctly ritualistic feeling for me."[80] Even when a boy realized what was going on and tried to skip directly to sex, Alan insisted that he enact all the stages of Alan's own fantasy. This is what therapists mean when they say that abusers *act out*: they are acting out their inner fantasies.

When he seduced a boy, Alan gradually began training him to keep secrets; they shared a guilty complicity about small things (Alan's swearing) which progressed to small crimes (drugs and marijuana) and eventually abuse. The boy was already implicated before he took the final step of participating in sexual abuse. Secrecy had ensnared the victim.

Before he was eight, Alan also discovered that there was something in abuse besides the physical pleasures of touch: control. When Alan finally persuaded a boy to do something, "the real high was once more when he submitted, and I saw he was defeated."[81] But he did not get the same thrill when he had the boy repeat that action, so he had to go further in the abuse. When he had made the boy act out every conceivable perversion, he lost interest in him and sought a new victim: "they no longer resisted, they gave me practically everything I wanted, except for the thrill I wanted most."[82] Alan went through a thousand boys before he was caught.

Alan thought he was manipulated by desires he did not wish for. He felt that *he* was a victim, and therefore had the right to control others to overcome his own sense of lack of control. Sexuality is very intimate, and Alan therefore wanted to control boys' sexuality to show that he could make them do anything he wanted. He fantasized elaborate scenarios of seduction and abuse and then manipulated boys and adults into making them become a reality. He was the puppet master; they were his puppets.

Alan's explanations help us understand why "power, control, personal reassurance, anger, and hostility"[83] are central issues for clerical abusers. A male in our culture who is interested in religion feels different, because religion is largely a feminine preserve. A homosexual male as he is developing feels different and feels that he is a victim of fate, which explains why males who develop homosexually are more likely to become abusers than heterosexuals are (see p. 335). The combination of religious and homosexual orientations increases the danger. A man who feels that he is not in control of his own life can become a clergyman and control others' lives, but he still resents his control by the denominational hierarchy or congregation, and Catholic priests and religious especially have their lives controlled by bishops or superiors. This deeper lack of control that Catholic (and to some extent Anglican) clergy experience may explain why they seem to have more minors among their victims than Protestant clergy have. The majority of priest-offenders are in the "passive/control/victim" group. The abuser adopts a "victim mentality" and is "typically angry, justifies his anger with self-righteousness, uses self-pity, and carries deep resentment, usually kept secret by a fixed smile."[84] A bishop characterized an abuser as having "a rather strange combination of subservience to authority and of resentment to authority."[85] He can become a liturgical expert and control the actions of hundreds or thousands or millions of people, who go through rituals the expert has imagined; they are his puppets (this is perhaps another reason why ritualistic churches like the Anglican and Catholic attract pederasts).[86]

## *Learned Abuse*

Stephen Rossetti said that two-thirds of the abusers he has treated have themselves been abused.[87] Richard Sipe concurred, "Seventy to eighty percent of priests who sexually abuse have themselves been abused as children, some by priests."[88] Priests sometimes abused boys because they had themselves been abused by priests or other adults when they were boys. The victim of this traumatic bond identifies himself with the abuser. Psychiatrists often see this and have named it identification with the aggressor.[89] If the abuser is a priest the victim may become a priest. He has experienced being under the control of an abuser, and he in turn wants to control a victim.

However, abusers sometimes falsely claim to have been abused in an attempt to arouse sympathy. When a group of abusers was subjected to proper interrogation the percentage of those who claimed to have been abused as children fell from 67% to 29%.[90] This is still much higher than the 8.6 percent abused in the general population (see p. 560, note 2). The *John Jay Report* discovered only a few cases in which priest-abusers themselves claimed to have been abused,[91] but this was not an issue that diocesan files of abuse complaints would ordinarily have addressed.

## Treatment

Thomas Szasz claims psychiatrists have been the accomplices of abusers because they are guilty of "medicalizing life"[92] and have treated abusers rather than punishing them. Pedophilia is a sexual desire for children, but when it crosses into the realm of act, it becomes a crime and calls for punishment. But punishment and treatment are not mutually exclusive. An abuser should be punished for his actions, but he may also (in rare cases) sincerely want to get rid of the desire for children or learn how he can lessen the chances of his acting on it—after he gets out of jail. Such misdirected sexual desire has a cause; it may even be organic; it probably can't be cured, but an abuser who is sincerely repentant needs to learn the self-disciplines that derail the thought processes that lead to abuse. Catholics call this avoiding the near occasions of sin; Jews call it respecting the fences around the Law. The abuser has to learn not just to avoid children but also to avoid the deeply entrenched habits of thought and emotion that lead the abuser to act on his desires. For this, therapy can sometimes help.

Some facilities for priests were mostly local institutions, like Our Lady's Hall outside Boston; others, like the houses run by the Servants of the Paraclete, the Houses of Affirmation, and St. Luke Institute, treated priests from many dioceses. Treatment varied in seriousness, from hiking to Depo-Provera, a drug that reduces sexual desire, also known as chemical castration. Some centers used a form of the twelve-step program that has been successful in treating addictions. Others used individual therapy or group therapy such as role playing. However, many of the abusers were also confidence men and knew how to convince therapists that they were cured, when in fact nothing had changed. Spiritual direction did not seem to play a prominent role. Severe spiritual disciplines—fasting, vigils, silence, ceaseless prayer—do not seem to have been prescribed.

## OUR LADY'S HALL

The director of Our Lady's Hall in Milton, Massachusetts, the Rev. Robert P. Beale, was suspended because he was credibly accused of abusing a minor. He has also had a career in show business as a member of the "The Singing Priests." A therapist at this center, the Rev. Edward T. Kelley, was reclassified as a client because he was accused of molesting children.[93] One of the clients, the Rev. Ronald H. Paquin (see p. 177), who was sent to Our Lady's Hall after he was removed from his parish following complaints that he was molesting children, had dozens of visits from a fifteen-year-old boy, who would sometimes stay in his room overnight. Paquin masturbated the boy or performed oral sex on him during these visits. The boy wondered about the place: "The facility did not require visitors to check in or out or have any apparent supervision, the [boy] said, and his presence there was never questioned by other priests."[94] Our Lady's Hall seems to have been at best a warehouse for abusive and other problem priests.

## SOUTHDOWN

Southdown in Ontario was founded in the 1960s as an independent center to treat chemically addicted priests but it also has treated sex offenders. It uses "cognitive-behavioral and 'relapse-prevention' strategies."[95] Bioenergetic analysis, yoga, and massage make the clients fully aware of their bodies in an attempt to circumvent the intellectual and verbal defenses that educated clerics can put up. For abusers of minors, Southdown claims only a 10% recidivism rate. The Rev. Canice Connors headed Southdown before moving to St. Luke Institute (see below). He had been abused himself when he was twelve.[96]

## INSTITUTE OF LIVING

Founded in 1824 as the Hartford Retreat for the Insane, the Institute of Living treated in a genteel atmosphere upper-class patients with mental problems. Its chief psychiatrist in the 1950s, Dr. Francis Braceland, was a Catholic who was determined to make psychiatry respectable among Catholics. After insurance companies grew impatient with the lack of results from expensive psychiatric treatment and that source of patients and funds dried up, in the mid-1980s the Institute branched out to treat the patients from an institution with deep pockets: the Catholic Church. Dr. James Gill, priest, psychiatrist, and Jesuit, was the Institute's liaison to the bishops. During their three-to-six-months' stay, priests were tested for organic brain abnormalities and then were treated by a combination of talk therapy and drugs.

Cardinal Egan, the one-time bishop of Bridgeport, Connecticut, blamed the Institute for telling bishops that abusive priests were cured and could be trusted with children. But the Institute in 1990 had warned that "we are in a weak position when we try to make predictions about future behavior."[97] The director of psychology, Leslie Lothstein, claimed that the bishops usually ignored reports: "I found they rarely followed our recommendations. They would put them [abusers] back into work where they still had access to vulnerable populations."[98] The chief of psychiatry at the Institute added that "in some cases, necessary and pertinent information related to prior sexual misconduct has been withheld from us. In some cases, it would appear that our evaluations have been misconstrued in order to return priests to ministry."[99] But the Institute's diagnosis of John Geoghan was "atypical pedophilia in remission"; they told Bishop Banks that "it is both reasonable and therapeutic for him to be reassigned back to his parish" and later said Geoghan was "psychologically fit" to work with children.[100] The discharge summary was sympathetic to Geoghan: "During certain stressful, vulnerable points in his priesthood, the patient did focus on immature sexual objects [this is how the Institute referred to children]. It was not a classical case of pedophilia, in that the abuse was sporadic and eventually did stop and had a playful, childlike quality to it. It was not sexually stimulating or eroticized, and it was not sadistic or without remorse."[101] How did the psychiatrist know this? Geoghan had told him.

The Institute often produced the paperwork that the bill-paying bishops wanted, knowing the bishops could take their business elsewhere. The Institute relied upon the abusers' accounts of what they had done. In 2002, after the flood of abuse stories, the Institute required bishops who sent abusive priests for treatment to give "the full facts and circumstances" that led to the request for treatment, including all "complaints, disciplinary actions, treatment records, and criminal and civil allegations."[102] After this information was required, bishops stopped sending priests to the Institute.

## THE SERVANTS OF THE PARACLETE

Father Gerald Fitzgerald did not intend to establish a center for treating priests with sexual disorders, but that is what Via Coeli at Jemez Springs became (see p. 90). In 1966 Father John Murphy, pastor of the church in Jemez Springs, complained in a letter to some U.S. bishops that the clients were making homosexual passes at local residents.[103] The letter warned that "homosexual solicitation in my parish is a matter of grave concern to me," and that "staff, superiors of the four separate houses [that] constitute Via Coeli almost without exception have serious unresolved behavior problems that necessitated their removal from the active ministry." It also contained allegations of drug and alcohol abuse. Father Fitzgerald, at that time still the head of the Paracletes, denied most of the allegations, and Murphy's complaint was dismissed by another priest as "a 'nut' letter, and I feel sure that most, if not all, the bishops will consider it as such."[104] They did, to their regret.

The Servants were careless about where they sent their patients. In 1967, when his bishop sent James Porter to the Servants, the bishop warned them that "his trouble was boys" and said, "I think he should be shielded from anyone, old or young, troubled with his weakness."[105] But the Servants sent him to parishes, where he molested children. John Salazar, the psychiatrist who treated pedophiles for the Servants, claimed that he warned Father Fitzgerald and Archbishop Davis, "Do not assign those kinds of priests to parishes or to grade schools or high schools for their ministerial duties because they will come into contact with youngsters."[106] The Paracletes denied Salazar had ever told them this.

Father Fitzgerald had a low opinion of abusers. In 1957 he advised Archbishop Edwin Byrne in writing *not* to offer "hospitality to men who have seduced or attempted to seduce little boys or girls," and continued that he thought "these men are devils, your Excellency, and the wrath of God is upon them, and if I were a Bishop I would tremble when I failed to report them to Rome for involuntary laicization." He expressed his anxiety about the children: "Experience has taught us these men are too dangerous to the children of the parish and neighborhood for us to be justified in receiving them here."[107] Fitzgerald did not want to risk the safety of children by putting these abusers in his treatment center in New Mexico, which makes their assignment to parishes all the more puzzling. But there were clearly disagreements among the officials of the Paracletes.

Fitzgerald wanted to put priests who abused children on an uninhabited island in the Caribbean he had purchased for $28,000: "It is for this class of rattlesnake I have always wished the island retreat—but even an island is too good for these vipers of whom the Gentle Master said—it were better they had not been born—this is an indirect way of saying damned is it not?"[108] Fitzgerald thereby identified the priest child molesters with Judas. Salazar recounted that "they had come to the conclusion there were problems they couldn't contain and those who did not respond to treatment were going to be banished for the rest of their lives as a means of preventing behavior that victimized other people."[109] But Salazar was opposed to the island solution, because he thought it would become an "organized den of iniquity" in which the strong pedophiles would prey upon the weaker,[110] and he did not think pedophilia was incurable. He advised instead a treatment program, the "Graduated Step Rehabilitation Program for Impaired Priests."[111] Salazar later claimed that he did not mean the program to include pedophiles, but he wanted it to replace the idea of an island for pedophiles, so he must have meant it to include pedophiles.

Fitzgerald told Archbishop Byrne that he intended to discuss these molesters with the pope and to say that they should automatically be removed from the priesthood. He met with John XXIII once and Paul VI twice.[112] Fitzgerald wanted the criminal abuser to repent and be saved, but he also wanted to save children from abuse. This was not to be. According to one newspaper report, the Vatican ordered Fitzgerald to sell the island. According to the Servants, for reasons unknown, Archbishop Byrne, who was then in Rome, ordered him to sell the island.[113] After apparently losing a battle within the order about devoting one of the several communal halls at the facility to pedophile treatment, Fitzgerald accepted a new assignment in Italy for the remaining four years of his life.[114] The Servants of the Paraclete in 1967 made an agreement with the archbishop of Santa Fe to send "rehabilitated priests" to parishes without even informing the pastors of their history.[115] The Paracletes then sent their patients into local, mostly Hispanic churches, sometimes with disastrous results. There the patients could abuse with less danger of being caught, protected both by the reverence Hispanics have for priests and by the language barrier which made it difficult for families to report abuse to the authorities.

The staff at the Paraclete center was itself sometimes questionable. John B. Feit arrived at a New Mexico center for troubled priests in the early 1960s, after his criminal problems in South Texas prompted his bosses to remove him from parish work. In 1962 he pleaded no contest to aggravated assault in the attempted rape of Maria America Guerra, a twenty-year-old college student. Ms. Guerra testified during his trial that the priest had attacked her inside Sacred Heart Catholic Church in Edinburgh, Texas. He had been tried the previous year on a more serious charge of assault with intent to rape, but jurors deadlocked and the judge declared a mistrial. Feit was and is a suspect in a murder. He heard Irene Garza's confession at Sacred Heart Church. People who were trying to go to confession that night remember that he had disappeared from the confessional box. Authorities later found her body in a canal,[116] where Feit's photographic slide viewer was also found. Feit changed his story to investigators and failed lie detector tests (see also pp. 436–437).[117]

Within a few years, Feit had joined the Paracletes and had become a top administrator supervising priests sent there for counseling. One priest he supervised was James Porter (see pp. 118–119). Once, in 1969, Feit failed to disclose to the priest's home diocese in Massachusetts that Porter had relapsed while on a probationary assignment in Houston. "Thus far, there has been no occurrence of the problem which plagued Fr. Porter in the past," Feit wrote to the diocese.[118] Porter was returned to the Paraclete Center in 1970 and that time the psychiatrist gave up on him and pronounced him hopeless, but Feit continued to have hope for Porter.

The Paracletes continued their policy of hiring their patients to run the center. When the abuser Gordon MacRae was sent to the Paraclete center (1989–1990), the staff there felt that MacRae was a kindred soul and hired him. The Rev. David Diebel, who was then working for Paracletes, was singled out by the New Hampshire judge at MacRae's trial as not "a credible witness" (see p. 184) because of the way he supported MacRae.

In the twelve years before they closed the New Mexico center in 1994 the Paracletes treated about 400 priests for "psychosexual issues"[119] with a twelve-step program, with Depo-Provera, and with hikes in the mountains. In 1986 Dr. Jay Feierman of the treatment center asserted that "our recidivism rate for behavior which would be considered criminal is 0% to the best of our knowledge."[120] Their knowledge was not very good: they destroyed their own records,[121] which shows a certain lack of interest in following cases to find out the long term results of treatment.

## THE HOUSE OF AFFIRMATION

In 1973 Dr. Conrad Baars (see p. 95), the Rev. Thomas Kane, and Sister Anna Polcino founded the House of Affirmation in Worcester, Massachusetts. Kane was a fraud and Baars soon became suspicious of Kane's financial dealings. Kane and Polcino fired Baars in 1975 and told everyone he was incompetent.[122] Four years later Baars wrote that "there are people who have been treated for years—at great expense—in institutions or homes that have the word 'affirmation' in their logo, who are unable to tell me in what way those places were different from those not claiming to offer affirmation therapy."[123] Baars's widow said that he died in 1981 of a broken heart.

Affirmation therapy, developed by Baars, is essentially unconditional love and acceptance. Baars admired the example of John XXIII, whose love for everyone he met was immediately apparent. When a person is affirmed, he can see that he is essentially good and can then become fully the person he was intended to be. Baars found this therapy especially useful in treating those who had totally repressed their sexuality and therefore distorted their personality. They had to realize that all the essential elements of the human person, including sexual feelings, were good (although they needed direction and control) and are not part of our "lower" or "sinful" nature, which should be rejected (see p. 468).

Kane claimed to have a doctorate in psychology from the University of Birmingham; he didn't. He claimed to be running a charitable institution; he pillaged its treasury to buy real estate.[124] He claimed to be helping child abusers; he was helping them to abuse children. His book *Intimacy* was closely examined after the scandals in Boston. It could have served as a primer *for* molestation of adolescents and adults by clergymen, according to psychotherapists who have studied sex abuse. Gary Schoener, a licensed psychotherapist and executive director of the Walk-in Counseling Center in Minneapolis, who has treated several former House of Affirmation residents, called the text "psychobabble." One passage, which Schoener called "nonsense," claims that "married lovers are not sexual and passionate enough. And what's more, neither are celibate lovers, who should at least be as sexual and passionate as married people. There is no other way to be a really great lover." "How can you possibly do that without having sex?" Schoener said, suggesting that, at best, the authors were advocating masturbation. "Masturbation is still a violation [in the Catholic Church], though it's a slightly different type of sin." On a more alarming note, he said the work could influence priests who abuse adolescents and adults. Unlike pedophiles who have almost total control over their victims, clergymen who abuse the post-pubescent often must conjure up a sexual-theological excuse for their actions to lure in their subjects. "The lines that we hear priests use could come from this," Schoener said. "There are lines in this I heard just last night, because last night I read the deposition of a woman who was sexually abused by her priest. It's almost identical."[125]

Kane lost control of the House of Affirmation in 1986, and the satellite house in Clearwater, Florida, also went under. "Spokesmen for the bishop's office in Worcester, Mass., acknowledged . . . that an investigation has been under way for nearly a year into charges that the Rev. Thomas A. Kane, a Catholic priest and co-founder of the chain, used House of Affirmation finances to support personal real estate investments in Massachusetts, Maine, and Florida, paid salaries from House of Affirmation funds to persons employed in his personal business enterprises, and misrepresented his academic credentials."[126] But these small personal problems, of which his bishop was aware, did not end Kane's career. In 1988, at the recommendation of Bishop Timothy Harrington, Kane was made the national director of the Guild of Catholic Psychiatrists, despite his fraudulent claim of having a Ph.D.[127] In 1992 he was breeding bulldogs and teaching a course in ethics at a Catholic college.

In 1993 Kane was stationed at Sacred Heart Church in Worcester. He was then accused by Mark Barry of assaulting him at St. Mary's Church in Uxbridge, starting in 1968 when Barry was nine years old. The abuse, Barry claimed, continued for eleven years and took place at the House of Affirmation while Kane was director there. Barry said Kane had a country house in Manchester, Vermont, where he took Barry and offered him to other priests. There Kane took pictures of Barry and the priests having sex.[128] A suit filed in 2002 claimed that Kane was running a sex ring in which John Geoghan, David Blizard, and Victor Frobas shared boys among themselves.[129]

Before filing for bankruptcy after a civil lawsuit involving boys, Kane transferred his real estate to Msgr. Brendan P. Riordan, a director of the House of Affirmation (as of mid-2007 he remains pastor of a church in the Rockville Centre diocese), and to Msgr. Alan J. Placa, the counsel for the House of Affirmation, "who is also a lawyer and a longtime friend of former

New York City mayor Rudolph W. Giuliani, [and who] was recently removed from his position in New York after a sexual misconduct allegation was made against him by a man living in that state."[130] This is one of many pieces of evidence for a network of those accused of both sexual and financial improprieties, a network that, according to *Salon* and *The Village Voice*, has friends in the highest offices of government.

Barry's lawsuit was settled out of court and the records sealed. However, someone leaked the file: the agreement provided that Barry would not sue the Rev. Thomas Teczar, the Rev. Robert Shauris, and the Rev. Msgr. Brendan Riordan.[131] Kane disappeared. He surfaced years later as Thomas A. Kane, Ph.D., head of World Wide Teaching Institute in Guadalajara, Mexico. The website there claims that he has "an American doctorate, a British diploma, and three honorary doctorates from American universities. It also notes that he is an appointed scholar at Harvard University and author of a book on teaching English around the world."[132] And, no doubt, the dauphin of France. Kane was tracked down by a Houston lawyer, Daniel Shea, who had met him in 1974. Shea was studying to be a priest at the time and was referred to Kane for counseling; Kane made a pass at him and Shea decided against entering the clergy. Shea now represents those sexually abused by priests.[133]

Kane remains on the books as a priest of the Worcester diocese. When an alleged victim sued Kane, Ray Delisle, diocesan spokesman, claimed that "[diocesan] officials had no idea where he was and he was not on the payroll." But as was pointed out to him, Kane said in a 1999 deposition that "the diocese gives me a little money because I've chosen to live a very private, priestly life,"[134] and the checks were sent to Mexico. Ah, said Delisle, I was mistaken, the diocese *is* paying Kane. The amount? It's a secret.

Some prominent people worked at the House of Affirmation. Sean Sammon, current head of the Marist Brothers, joined the staff in 1978 and became the organization's international clinical director in 1982. The director of education was the Rev. Stephen J. Rossetti, now director of St. Luke Institute. Neither noticed that Kane was a fraud, or if they did, they did not make an issue of it.[135]

## ST. LUKE INSTITUTE

Michael Peterson was raised a Mormon, converted to Catholicism, and then became a priest-psychiatrist. He showed little interest in the sacramental life of the Church; he had to be assisted in performing the baptismal rite. In 1977 he had converted the Marsilin, a house near Boston, into a treatment center for alcoholic clergy. Peterson's sexual proclivities already were clear. Michael Kennedy, director of operations at Marsilin, said, "Michael Peterson was clearly homosexual. Our concern was that he was abusing drugs. A private indulgence might not matter, but his behavior became erratic."[136] Kennedy claimed that Peterson wanted power, and that his knowledge of the sins of the clergy gave him power. When Kennedy told Peterson he needed help to deal with his own drinking, Peterson refused to seek it. When Kennedy insisted, Peterson fired him and nine others. They filed wrongful termination suits, and Marsilin declared bankruptcy.

Peterson opened St. Luke Institute in 1982 and bought up houses in the neighborhood for his patients, in violation of zoning regulations. The Institute offers more psychiatrically based treatment than the other American centers and is not fraudulent in the sense that some of the others were. But Father Peterson's homosexuality distorted the program at the center. His acceptance of the dubious theories of John Money (see pp. 442, 445) caused the Vatican to call the Institute's diagnoses into question.

Peterson drank more and more and frequently traveled to San Francisco, which was probably where he contracted AIDS.[137] He told Father Thomas Doyle he contracted it from a cut. He died and was given a magnificent funeral at St. Matthew's Cathedral in Washington, D.C, with Archbishop Hickey presiding. In the scramble for power after Peterson's death, Richard Sipe and others resigned from the board. One doctor who resigned wrote, "I have become progressively uncomfortable with the moral tone of the Institute and its therapeutic programs. In my opinion, the Institute has been used as an outlet for the psycho-pathology of its founder and . . . for other members of the staff from its inception."[138] One client claimed that

St. Luke did not treat homosexuality: "It was very clear that the idea of a homosexual monogamous relationship would be the preferable thing" to promiscuity.[139] Most would agree it is, but the patients are priests who have promised to be celibate.

The Rev. Paul J. Mahan, a patient at St. Luke, was quoted as saying, "Two of the priest residents . . . and one of their therapists, go out regularly to some sort of cross-dressing 'drag queen' revue."[140] Mahan is, however, not trustworthy. The therapists at St. Luke Institute accurately diagnosed him in 1995, informing the Boston archdiocese that Mahan was "untreatable," "sexually addicted," "at considerable risk for acting out," a "voyeur, frotteur, pedophile, and ephebophile," "an alcoholic, a liar, and a narcissist." Despite this, and the admissions by Mahan that he molested children, and the report by Bishop McCormack's deputy, the Rev. Brian Flatley, that Mahan "is a threat to adolescent males," the Boston archdiocese sent Mahan for further treatment to Southdown and put no controls on his movements. He molested more children.[141]

The Rev. Canice Connors, the director of St. Luke who had worked at Southdown, appointed Curtis Bryant as supervisor of therapists; Bryant had only just completed his internship in psychology. The staff soon complained about Bryant's erratic behavior, which seemed to be connected to alcohol.[142] Complaints were made to the American Psychological Association (it turned out Bryant was not a member) and to the state of Maryland, which placed Bryant's license on "inactive status" in 1996. In December of that year Connors left and was replaced by the Rev. Stephen Rossetti.

Rossetti seemed to think that the way to stop priests from molesting teenage boys was to get them involved with adult men. One of the goals of St. Luke is to have patients "develop satisfying relationships with age-appropriate peers."[143] Some Vatican officials disliked St. Luke. The Apostolic Signatura, in upholding a priest's appeal (this priest after further canonical action was eventually found guilty), opined: "St. Luke Institute, a clinic founded by a priest who is openly homosexual and based on a mixed doctrine of Freudian pan-sexualism and behaviorism, is surely not a suitable institution apt to judge rightly about the beliefs and the lifestyle of a Catholic Priest."[144] The American bishops who continue to send priests to St. Luke Institute think otherwise.

Treatment at the center begins with an evaluation by CAT scans and electro-encephalograms to detect any organic brain abnormalities, with aptitude tests, and with a device that has the unpronouncable name of the penile plethysmograph, known to the patients as the "peter meter." A band is placed around the patient's penis to measure the level of arousal. He is then shown pornography of various types to see how much he is aroused by men, women, boys, girls, and little children. The pictures of child pornography have been replaced by stories. The treatment includes drugs and psychotherapy.

Rossetti claimed that less than one per cent of the priests he has treated fall again and that therefore the treatment centers "work." He said Fred Berlin at Johns Hopkins reported a relapse rate of only 2.9% over a five-to-six year period, and a church facility reported only a 2.5% relapse rate.[145] Such results are so out of line with other recidivism data that they need to be carefully scrutinized and replicated by outside researchers. Studies have shown that for molesters of boys (including teenagers) the relapse rate is generally from 30 percent to 40 percent.[146] No one knows how well the treatment centers work. In fact at least one, the Paraclete Center has destroyed records, making such studies impossible. The criteria for pronouncing offenders cured are vague. Rev. Michael E. Foley, co-director of the Paraclete center, explained that "we just get an intuition that they're going to work out."[147] If the supposedly cured abusers molest again, the victims may not report the abuse for thirty years, during which time the "cured" abuser may be victimizing scores of children.

## THE REV. DOCTOR EDWIN CASSEM, S. J.

After 1992 Cardinal Law began tightening up the handling of problem priests in Boston and sent them (or sometimes just their partial files) to a treatment team at Massachusetts General Hospital, a team headed by Father Edwin "Ned" Cassem, S. J., who was also head of psychiatry there until 2000. No one on the team specialized in sexual offenders. When asked whether he had ever studied sexual offences, Cassem replied, "I try not to touch it with a ten-foot pole."[148] Often Cassem merely reviewed files and gave an opinion without ever seeing the patient, or the victim, or anyone else involved in the case except an archdiocesan official.

One problem priest was Paul Shanley. Cassem, after reviewing his file but not seeing him, said that Shanley had a "pathology [that] is beyond repair,"[149] an opinion which allowed Shanley to retire on medical disability. In a deposition, Cassem said he had never been told about Shanley's involvement with NAMBLA or that Shanley said that children seduced adults. After he learned these facts about Shanley, Cassem said that "castration was too good for him." Cassem claimed that he would have recommended that Shanley be laicized and jailed if he had seen all the documents in the archdiocesan file.[150]

Cassem knew that as a doctor he was required by law to report sexual abuse to the state, but neither he nor anyone else at Massachusetts General Hospital ever did so. Nor did he ever tell anyone in the archdiocese to do so. Nor did he ever suggest that parishes be warned that they had had a pedophile in their midst. Nor, except for once, did he suggest to the archdiocese that it help the victims. Nor could he find his notes about the priest-treaters' meetings, or about many of the abusers he evaluated and sent back into ministry where they abused again. He was as bad as Cardinal Law in keeping his files orderly.[151]

Paul Edwards accused Msgr. Michael Foster, the judicial vicar of the archdiocese of Boston, of abusing him.[152] Foster began a withering counterattack that centered on destroying Edwards's credibility. Cassem in an affidavit pronounced Edwards "a sociopath and a psychopath" and "a threat to the physical safety of Msgr. Foster"[153] *without ever having seen Edwards* but after having reviewed a file, provided by Foster's lawyers, that was full of falsities. When questioned by the Rev. Sean Connor, a church investigator, on how he could do this, implying that the affidavit was therefore fraudulent, Cassem angrily defended himself, and concluded, "You are stuck on the wrong issue here—what are the FACTS, not what is the down and dirty truth. You sounded like an enemy of Msgr. Foster. In fact you (by the music) resented it when I called him 'Msgr.'—you can't fool an old man here, Father. I strongly suggest that you read yesterday's gospel & Jesus's comments about lawyers."[154] Cassem still works in the psychiatry department of Massachusetts General Hospital.

Abusers of both children and teenagers were treated as if they had a mental illness. The treatment was often perfunctory and unprofessional; the aim was to get priests back into ministry—and it too often succeeded. Even if the abusers had received professional treatment of the highest standard, the therapists faced an almost impossible situation.

Whatever limitations therapists may have had, whatever faults they had, whatever mistakes they made, were almost irrelevant, because bishops who referred abusers to therapists were not acting in good faith. The Philadelphia grand jury examined the endless ways in which Cardinal Bevilacqua and his subordinates manipulated the treatment system to keep abusers in parishes where they abused children. Bevilacqua publicly promised never to give an assignment to a pedophile. He then made sure that no abuser was ever diagnosed as a pedophile.[155] Church officials withheld information from therapists and coached abusers on how to avoid a diagnosis of pedophilia.

In fact what Bevilacqua meant (he is trained as a lawyer) was that he would not assign a priest only if the priest was diagnosed as *only* a pedophile. Father Stanley Gana admitted abusing children, but he also admitted having sex with adults, being a drunk, and stealing church money. Therefore he could be assigned to a parish because, Msgr. Lynn explained, "He's not a pure pedophile."[156]

If a treatment center, such as St. Luke, insisted on diagnosing a priest as a pedophile, the Philadelphia archdiocese switched to St. John Vianney, which was under the control of the archdiocese and would come up with acceptable diagnoses.

Since celibate priests were getting their names in the newspaper for having sex with minors, and those minors were almost always teenage boys, celibacy and homosexuality were both blamed as sources of the abuse, but by different parties in the Church. As Andrew Greeley observed, "The Catholic left would have us believe that the most serious problem the church faces is clerical celibacy," and "the Catholic right...wants to blame everything on homosexuals."[157] Although both left and right are more interested in furthering their agendas than in attaining the truth about the sexual abuse crisis, sexual practices and orientations are indeed a logical place to look for sources of sexual disorder.

CHAPTER ELEVEN

# ABUSERS AND HOMOSEXUALITY

AT THE END OF 2005, the Congregation for Catholic Education at the Vatican issued an "Instruction Concerning the Criteria for the Discernment of Vocations with Regard to Persons with Homosexual Tendencies in View of Their Admission to the Seminary and Holy Orders." In this document it was asserted that the Church "cannot admit to the seminary or to holy orders those who practice homosexuality, present deep seated homosexual tendencies or support the so-called 'gay culture.'" The document said these norms were "made more urgent by the current situation" and alluded to "the negative consequences that can derive from the ordination of persons with deep-seated homosexual tendencies."[1]

The response was immediate and in fact preceded the official release of the document: the Vatican was condemned as homophobic, there was a denial that there was a "gay culture" in the seminaries, and most of all a furious denial that homosexual priests had anything to do with the sexual abuse of minors, an insinuation many detected in the mention of "current situation" and "negative consequences."

Americans seem not to have taken notice of the scandals involving homosexual behavior in the German-speaking lands, especially the allegations of abuse of seminarians (minors and adults) made against Cardinal Groër of Vienna (see pp. 234–235) and the homosexual orgies at the seminary at Sankt Pölten in Austria (see p. 236). However, the Vatican was well aware of them and the instruction was in part motivated by well-publicized problems in the German-speaking Church. Although the documents may have been provoked by specific events in Europe, the Vatican may also have had in mind the fact that the victims of sexual abuse in the United States were largely adolescent males, and may have thought that homosexuality was at least one source of the abuse.

## *Gay Seminarians*

A homosexual subculture in American (and foreign) seminaries seems to have flourished in the 1960s in the general chaos that followed Vatican II,[2] although the roots go back centuries, as we have seen in Chapter One. Howard P. Bleichner, a Sulpician who worked in seminaries in Baltimore, San Francisco, and Washington, D.C., observed that after the Second Vatican Council, "seminaries suddenly began to develop gay subcultures that encompassed faculty and students."[3] Cardinal Francis E. George of Chicago admitted that this subculture deters heterosexual men because they fear that they will be thought to be homosexual if they enter the seminary. George contended that "it is an ongoing struggle...to make sure the Catholic priesthood is not dominated by homosexual men."[4] Rev. Donald Cozzens, former head of the Cleveland seminary, wrote that "the need gay priests have for friendship with other gay men, and their shaping of a social life largely composed of other homosexually oriented men, has created a gay subculture in most of the U. S. dioceses. A similar subculture has occurred in many of our seminaries."[5] Cozzens and many others who have a liberal and progressive attitude to reform nevertheless do not like what they see in the seminaries. The Jesuit novitiate in California on its public website celebrated a Mardi Gras at which seminarians dressed as "Jabba the Slut" and "Pretty Boy."[6] Gay culture did not disappear from seminaries after the wide-open 1960s and 1970s.

Mark Brooks, an ex-Marine, was at the St. Francis Seminary at the University of San Diego[7] in 1981 where Rev. Vincent Dwyer was advising the seminarians "not to fear intimacy." Dwyer didn't fear it; he had seduced a sixteen-year-old girl at Santa Catalina, and her distress caused her to drop out of school. In 1995 Dwyer settled with her for $75,000[8]; in 1998 he received the National Federation of Priests' Councils Presidents Award; in 1999 he was sued by a man for abuse. Brooks was expelled from St. Francis in 1983 for protesting the "hot house atmosphere" and the disproportionate number of gay priests. Brooks asked, "Were many of these priests sexually manipulative and abusive? I am sorry to have to say yes again. I should point out that many of these priests often preyed upon young unsuspecting 'gay' seminarians who were sincere and devoted to their vocations."[9] Brooks wrote a report and sent it to John Paul II, but received no response. Brooks tried to pursue his vocation; in a psychological report commissioned by the Los Angeles archdiocese, he was diagnosed as having posttraumatic stress disorder. The report explained, "The primary source of stress was the sexual assault you experienced in seminary during an episode of alcohol intoxication. A secondary source of the stress we believe is being discredited and expelled from the seminary as a result of 'blowing the whistle.'"[10]

Although Michael Rose may not have been sufficiently alert to the agenda of those who told him what went on in seminaries, his book *Goodbye! Good Men*[11] rings true. American seminaries accepted bizarrely homosexual behavior for several decades, and the priests formed in those seminaries are now moving into positions of authority, including bishoprics. When I was at a lecture in St. Mary's Seminary in Baltimore in the 1980s, I heard the faculty behind me discussing in normal voices the absence of a priest faculty member who had slept with seminary students, had flaunted it too openly, and had been sent to rural Pennsylvania for a few months to cool off. A friend who taught at a seminary in the northeast United States had to break up a lover's quarrel involving a former hairdresser who had been recruited by an influential monsignor. The bishop of this diocese, who enjoyed sleeping (literally sleeping, no euphemism is meant) with seminarians, recruited an airline steward to the seminary.[12]

This atmosphere was common in seminaries and continued in some at least until very recently. Christopher Schiavone, who was in St. John's

Seminary in Boston in the 1980s, remembered that "some of us found refuge in a campy, secret subculture poor in genuine emotional intimacy but rich in the bitchy humor for which we gay men are 'Will & Grace' infamous. We had women's names for one another, and for some of our teachers. We trashed each other's style of dress and gossiped among ourselves about who was 'going out' with whom."[13] The Rev. Andrew Walker of Bridgeport says he was harassed and then asked to leave Baltimore's St. Mary's Seminary in 1997 because he was diagnosed as "homophobic."[14] Two seminarians, one straight, one gay, who entered Theological College (also known as T.C. or the "Theological Closet") at Catholic University in 1997 both left because of the intensity and weirdness of the gay subculture, whose existence was never openly acknowledged. Many students of that period witnessed sexual activity among fellow students.[15]

England also faces the prospect of the Catholic priesthood becoming "a gay profession." A paper prepared for the British bishops feared that "with a higher proportion of homosexually inclined entrants... very often the heterosexual can feel in the wrong place."[16] The rector of Allen Hall in the Westminster diocese admitted that "a sizeable number" of his seminarians are gay. Despite being forbidden to do so, seminarians at the English college refer to each other by girls' names: "Daisy, Phyllis, Mavis, and Big Shirl."[17] Catholic seminaries have the same campy subcultures as Anglican high-church seminaries, because they attract the same type of candidates. Such behavior is a sign of the psychosexual immaturity that is one of the main causes for the sexual abuse of boys.

David France, an openly gay editor of *Newsweek* who for some reason has an intense concern that homosexuals not be barred from the Catholic priesthood and who is an apologist for Paul Shanley, admitted that the abuse of minors was in fact committed by homosexuals. His explanation, which is a major theme of *Our Fathers*,[18] was that homosexual men who entered the seminary had totally repressed their sexual feelings because of the homophobia of the Catholic Church. After ordination when they were put under stress their sexual impulses did not turn to adult men but to teenage boys, he asserts. Now that seminaries have substantial gay minorities who can be open about their sexual orientation, gay seminarians do not have to repress their feelings but can talk about them and deal with them. Therefore celibacy is increasing and the molestation of teenagers is rapidly falling. There are more homosexual priests, but they are also more likely to be truly celibate and chaste in this new, open environment than they were in the enforced closet of the older seminaries.

Perhaps. But those who know the situation, A. W. Richard Sipe and Thomas Doyle, have said that the seminary environment remains full of predatory homosexuals, and that they would not advise a homosexual who sincerely intended to be celibate to enter a seminary—the pressure for sexual activity is too great.

## *A Gay Priesthood?*

What began in the seminaries continued in the dioceses. Attorneys in Springfield, Massachusetts, suspect that the bishop and many of his officials were sexually involved with teenage boys: The majority of the fourteen clergy recently accused of sexual abuse were in high positions in the diocese. Among the accused are: Bishop Dupré, who fled Springfield hours after being confronted with an accusation of abuse by the local newspaper, claiming to have heart problems, but showing up at St. Luke Institute in Suitland, Maryland (see p. 188); the Rev. E. Karl Huller, diocesan superintendent of schools; the Rev. Thomas F. Meehan, director of vocations and archivist; the Rev. Francis P. Lavelle, secretary to two bishops; the Rev. Edward M. Kennedy, head of the Spanish apostolate; Msgr. David P. Welch, editor of the Catholic newspaper and executor of Bishop Weldon's estate.[19] The Rev. James Scahill claimed that Bishop Dupré told a group of priests that files that might have had abuse allegations were destroyed after Weldon died. (Dupré denied saying this.[20])

Leroy T. Matthiesen, when he was bishop of Amarillo, Texas, from 1980 to 1997, recruited abusive priests who were being treated by the Servants of the Paraclete in New Mexico. In 2002 after the scandals broke, his successor, Bishop John W. Yanta, had to dismiss eight priests, 25 percent of the total priests in his small diocese. Matthiesen says he does not regret hiring them.[21] Matthiesen celebrated Mass for a New Ways Ministry conference in 2002 despite Vatican disapproval of the organization. New Ways pushes for the acceptance of homosexuals and homosexuality in the Catholic Church. To signal his loyalties, Matthiesen wore "a rainbow-colored alb," symbol of gay liberation.[22] This conference featured talks on the presence of heterosexism (a bad thing) in Catholic parishes, heterosexism manifested in such things as "Mother's Day and Father's Day celebrations, the absence of gay and lesbian members, and the sacrament of Baptism"[23] (I assume because infants, the normal recipients of baptism, are a public testimony to heterosexual behavior).

What percentage of Catholic priests are homosexual? Estimates range from 3 percent to 80 percent. Gays tend toward the highest estimates, but one should remember Edmund Burke's maxim: "He that accuses all mankind of corruption ought to remember that he is sure to convict only one." Seminary rectors, who are in the best position to know, estimate 50 percent of seminarians are homosexual, and that the percentage has increased in recent decades. Donald Cozzens, who was rector of the seminary in Cleveland, cites studies that about a third or a half of Catholic priests are homosexual (most are celibate).[24] Eugene Kennedy claims that "a substantial core of healthy men departed from the priesthood, altering the proportion of the mature to the immature among those who remained."[25] Others claim that the Roman Catholic ministry is becoming a gay profession,[26] just as the mainline Protestant ministry is becoming a female profession. A young Jesuit claims that "a majority of Jesuits under forty are not heterosexual."[27] In a *Los Angeles Times* poll in 2002, 15 percent of priests of all ages identified themselves as homosexual or mostly homosexual, but 23 percent of priests ordained twenty years or fewer identified themselves as homosexual or somewhat homosexual.[28] All these analyses remain guesses; researchers claim that the bishops have refused to cooperate with studies that seek to identify the extent of sexual problems among priests.

In 1989 Andrew Greeley was raising the alarm that "the Catholic [C]hurch in this country is developing a heavily homosexual priesthood" and that "lavender rectories and seminaries are tolerated. National networks of active homosexual priests (many of them in church administration) are tolerated."[29] But in 2004 he suddenly decided that all the alarm about the growing percentage of homosexuals in the priesthood was unnecessary and homophobic. Greeley now accuses those who arrive at high estimates of "charlatanry,"[30] and claims that a survey that meets professional sociological standards shows about 16 percent of priests are homosexually inclined[31] (and most are faithful to celibacy).[32] This is still several times the percentage of homosexuals in the general population (about 2 to 3 percent).

The departure of heterosexual priests to marry after Vatican II may have left homosexuals in control of large sections of the Church's middle management. When I worked as a federal investigator and investigated the background of applicants for sensitive employment, one of the areas we looked into (in pre–Clinton days) was homosexuality. I asked my supervisor why we bothered; homosexuals were not more likely than heterosexuals to be traitors. I was told that closeted homosexuals were subject to blackmail (which is true) and more importantly it had been observed that when a homosexual got into a position in the federal government in which he could hire other people, suddenly the entire section became homosexual, and what little work it did evaporated to nothing in the atmosphere of sexual competition, jealousies, and fights. I asked a Jesuit how some provinces had become so gay. He thought that once a provincial or novice master was gay, the candidates he attracted were often gay, and the organization changed character.[33]

The documents that have been issued by some Vatican officials who wanted to stop the ordination of homosexuals have become, like much else the Vatican puts out, dead letters and are openly ignored. The Chicago province of the Dominicans has accepted for ordination Patrick Baikauskas, the most prominent gay activist of Springfield, Illinois. Baikauskas is open about his background: "I'm forty-seven years old. I'm divorced. I'm a recovering alcoholic. I'm gay."[34] When a lay Catholic activist asked him to publicly renounce his gay activist background, Baikauskas replied: "I'm not sure what he wants me to denounce. My working for services for people living with AIDS? My working to secure equality in the workplace and housing for gay men and women? The [C]hurch is not against these things. Neither is the [C]hurch opposed to people being in love. So I cannot denounce any of those things."[35] He hopes to become "a college campus minister recruiting other men into the order" because gay priests "seem to be very successful—compassionate, pastoral."[36]

Baikauskas may be sincere in his desire to be celibate, but it is odd that his hopes focus on recruiting more gays into the Dominicans. He may think it best for the gays, he may think it best for the Dominicans, but does it serve the Church to have a gay clergy, who seem obsessed with gay issues? The Dominicans and the Vatican Congregation of Religious both see no problem with ordaining Baikauskas and only criticize him for his lack of "prudence,"[37] that is, openly declaring what he is and what he is about. A quiet, discreet conversion of the clergy into a homosexual club is acceptable.

Jason Berry suspects that homosexuality may have been a factor in the toleration of the abuse of minors. His sources indicated that about 25 percent of the clergy in Lafayette, Louisiana, site of the Gauthé trial, were homosexually active, and Berry concluded that "the root crisis in the diocese was a climate of secrecy and denial about sexual dynamics that permeated ecclesiastical governing."[38] Homosexual priests who themselves would not become sexually involved with boys do not feel the same revulsion and anger about the abuse that a heterosexual priest might feel. This revulsion against homosexuality, sometimes called homophobia, is not primarily moral but stems from the strong pressure that men feel, as they grow up, to conform to heterosexual standards of masculinity, whether in sexual behavior, displays of courage, or competitiveness. Homosexuals by definition have resisted this pressure to a greater or lesser extent, and therefore they do not feel the same revulsion that heterosexuals do. Berry noticed this lack of revulsion in Rev. Michael Peterson.[39] Of course heterosexuals too may lack moral outrage (see Archbishop Robert F. Sanchez's remarks, p. 402).

The homosexual priests who would never touch a minor but who are sexually involved with adults may create an atmosphere of tolerance for sexual irregularities, including pedophilia and pederasty. Rudy Kos studied in the Dallas seminary that has been the object of serious allegations. Any seminary that would invite Paul Shanley to speak on sexuality had no common sense—or worse, it knew very well what it was doing. One reporter who covered the Kos trial remembered that everyone was talking about "the cadre of militantly gay priests who had achieved influence in this area's Holy Trinity Seminary. Parents told me how their sons came back from seminary complaining about the verbal hammerings they had endured for being straight."[40] One priest reportedly came to work in the Dallas chancery on the condition that the diocese also hire his life partner.[41] Windle Turley, who represented some of Kos's victims, thought that the "underground nature of un-celibate behavior, both homosexual and heterosexual...has made possible a brand of adult dishonesty and manipulativeness in which pedophiles find convenient shelter."[42]

## *Homosexuality and the Abuse of Minors*

In addition to denying that there is any problem created by homosexual seminarians and priests, critics of the recent instruction suspect that the Vatican sees a connection between homosexuality and pedophilia. When the revelations of abuse began in 2002, defensive statements multiplied: Stephen Rossetti of St. Luke Institute denied any link between homosexuality and child abuse: "No mainstream researcher would suggest that there is any link between homosexuality and true pedophilia, that is, sexual attraction of an adult to prepubescent minors. In addition, most adults in society who sexually molest minors are not homosexually oriented."[43] Andrew Greeley claimed that "because some few abusers are homosexual, it does not follow that all homosexuals are abusers."[44] Gay writers Donald L. Boisvert and Robert E. Goss insist that "no rational evidence suggests that homosexuals are more prone to child molestation than heterosexuals."[45]

The defensive note in these statements was caused by the disturbing discoveries of the National Review Board, that among the victims of priests, despite the universally recognized tendency of boys to report their abuse less frequently than girls do,[46] "more than 80 percent of the abuse at issue was of a homosexual nature."[47] A recent survey of victims discovered that "93 percent of victims of priests under 18 years of age are male" as opposed to 20 percent of the victims of abusers in the general population.[48]

One way of denying that homosexuality is involved in the abuse has been to deny that the sexual abuse of males was in fact homosexual. The "sexual abuse of boys is not related to the issue of adult homosexuality. The majority of offenders are not homosexual in their adult orientation and to equate 'homosexuality' with child sexual abuse is a grave inaccuracy, even though the sexual contact is between males."[49] There is evidence for this. In the above-mentioned victim survey, when the victims were over twenty years of age, the profile of the victims of priests was overwhelmingly female (94.5 percent female and 5.5 percent male[50]), about the same as in the general population.

Because homosexuals do not want to be connected in the public mind with child abuse, the relationship of homosexuality and the abuse of minors has not been treated with full honesty. There has been some spin[51] and an occasional deliberately misleading statement.[52] All homosexuals are certainly not abusers, but most of the clerical abusers are homosexual in that they targeted males, and in fact sexually mature, post-pubescent adolescent males. Among adolescent victims of priests, 93 percent were male.[53] Most scandals were not about the rare condition of true pedophilia, the abuse of children before the age of puberty, but about sexual activity with sexually mature boys: "the vast majority of priests who sexually abuse minors choose adolescent boys—not young children—as their targets."[54] As Father Thomas Doyle explained, "Most pedophiles are heterosexual in their orientation. In the beginning, many years ago, most of the situations we were dealing with were pedophiles, but as more digging was done, it turned out that most of the offenders were not pedophiles, but ephebophiles, people that are compulsively attracted to young adolescents, and most of them happen to be homosexual in orientation."[55] This "happen to be" is a key phrase; is it sheer coincidence that so many clerical abusers prefer boys, or is there something about homosexuality in general or at least about clerical homosexuality that leads to the sexual abuse of adolescents?

Ephebophilia, unlike pedophilia, is not a psychiatric term[56]; it is simply a form of homosexuality, one that is characterized by sexual interest in the *ephebe*, the youth who has reached puberty but who does not yet have strong secondary male sex characteristics. The Greek word *ephebe* referred to a youth before the beard came in. The girl victims of abusive priests were often the victims of the handful of true pedophiles who were also attracted to adult women and eventually even married (as James Porter did). These pedophiles were not attracted by masculine sexual traits, but by the sexlessness or relative femininity of the bodies of prepubescent boys and girls. The boy victims on the other hand were mostly teenagers and were the victims of priests who were sexually attracted to teenage boys or to young men. If one defines a homosexual as a man who is sexually attracted only to adult men, then, of course, homosexual priests have committed none of the abuse, and such homosexuals may even be less likely than heterosexuals to be attracted to small children, or at least have less access to them. The clerical abusers seem to be attracted to the male at a specific stage of development: just at or after puberty, but before emotional maturity. This may be because the abusers themselves are immature, a subject to which we will return later.

## *The Profile of Victims*

Why were so many of the victims male? In part the greater promiscuity of homosexuals explains the disproportion. Even if the percentage of abusers among homosexually oriented and heterosexually oriented men is the same, homosexuals may have more victims.

Homosexuals who are active with adults have many more partners than heterosexuals have. A 1978 pre-AIDS study showed that 43 percent of white homosexuals had 500 or more partners, and another third had from 100 to 500 partners[57] (allowances must be made for boasting). Two-thirds of white male homosexuals had had more than ten sexual partners in the previous year.[58] A recent survey comes up with more believable figures: Men who have had sex with men have had a mean of 44.3 sexual partners since age eighteen; men who have never had sex with men have had a mean of 15.7 sexual partners since age eighteen.[59] Even after AIDS, Chicago gays in the Male Same Sex Market (MSSM; that is, gays who are looking for sex partners, as opposed to heterosexuals who are looking for sex partners) are far more promiscuous than nongays: "Well over half (61.3 percent) of the MSSM participants reported more than thirty adult sex partners, compared with just over 20 percent of their nonparticipant equivalents; a very large proportion (42.9 percent) of MSSM participants had more than sixty partners, compared with a very small fraction (3.8 percent) of the nonparticipants."[60]

Pedophiles oriented to males also show a greater number of victims. About 95 percent of the population is heterosexual, and 5 percent or less (probably closer to 2 percent) is homosexual.[61] But the ratio of female victims to male victims of pedophilia is not what one would expect from these figures, 20 (or more) to 1, but rather 2 to 1, in almost all studies. Although pedophiles are often heterosexual in their adult orientation, crimes against boys are committed almost entirely by men who self-identify as homosexuals or bisexuals (although self-deception may be involved by men who would prefer to think of themselves as homosexuals rather than pedophiles).[62] Therefore 5 percent (or less) of the population commits 30 percent (or more) of sexual crimes against children.[63] Some have generalized from this disproportion that "homosexuals molest children at a rate vastly higher than heterosexuals."[64] These statistics by themselves do not necessarily imply that men who develop homosexually are any more likely to become pedophiles than men who develop heterosexually.

Homosexual pedophiles have more victims than heterosexual pedophiles have, in line with the greater promiscuity of homosexuals in general. In one study, nonincestuous offenders against female children "had an average of 19.8 victims, while nonincestuous offenders against male children had an average of 150.2 victims."[65] The disproportion of male victims may be due not to a greater number of pedophiles who molest males (that is, who are homosexually oriented) but to the tendency of such homosexually oriented pedophiles to have far more victims than heterosexually oriented pedophiles have.

### *Sexual Development and Control Issues*

Of the males who develop heterosexually, some will be sexually attracted to prepubescent girls; that is, they will be heterosexual pedophiles. The others will not be attracted to prepubescent girls at all but will be attracted to sexually mature females, in accord with the biological purpose of sexuality, the reproduction of the species. Of the males who develop homosexually, some will be sexually attracted to pre-pubescent boys; that is, they will be homosexual pedophiles. The others will not be attracted by prepubescent boys at all but will be attracted by sexually mature males, including teenagers. Such homosexuals are called androphiles, from Greek *andros*, man, and this includes the recently invented category of ephebophile.

A study of sexual offenders against children (eleven years old and younger) used a penile plethysmograph to measure sexual arousal when the offender was shown nude pictures of boys and girls. Using various corrections, the researchers still estimated the ratio of homosexual offenders to heterosexual offenders as 11 to 1.[66] The ratio of heterosexuals to homosexuals in the general population is at least 20 to 1. The researchers concluded that males who develop homosexually are more likely to become pedophiles, or, as they indirectly put it, "A homosexual development notably often does not result in androphilia [sexual attraction to adult men] but in homosexual pedophilia."[67] They stress that this does *not* mean "that androphilic males have a greater propensity to offend against children."[68]

As they develop, androphiles (those attracted to adult men) and pedophiles both feel a strong sense of difference from the rest of society. One pedophile, "Alan," (for more of his story see pp. 302–303) explained why this sense of difference led him to a desire to control children sexually.

As a small boy, even before puberty, he was aware that he was different, that he was attracted to physical contact with boys (he didn't even know enough to realize that this was sexual desire). He thought of himself as a victim of this difference, and as a victim he was not bound by the rules of society. He also thought that this difference was in control of him. He felt that, although he couldn't control himself, he still didn't want to be a passive victim of his desires; therefore he wanted to be in control of others. He constructed elaborate fantasies every night and masturbated. Then he realized that he could "act out" his fantasies.

He learned to manipulate children and by doing this discovered two pleasures. One was simple sexual pleasure. The other was something mysterious and different, the pleasure of control. The first time he had a victim do something out of the ordinary, such as unbuckle his pants, he felt an electric thrill of control. It was this thrill he wanted even more than the sex. But Alan discovered that once he persuaded a victim to do an act, the next time the victim did the same act, he did not experience the same thrill. The thrill came only the first time. So to get the thrill with the same victim he had to go step by step into more and more intimate acts, ending in oral sex. Once he reached that stage, there were no more thrills, just sex, and he had to start over with another victim.

Psychologists describe abuse as a power issue. Abuse includes sex, but the real thrill is establishing control, which is why pedophiles have so many victims. The pedophile feels a deep need to control because he feels he is not in control of himself—that this mysterious difference is in control of him, through no fault of his own. In his mind, he is the real victim. To overcome a sense of victimhood and powerlessness, he establishes control over others.

This desire for control also explains why the word *ritualistic* is so often used to describe abuse. The abuser has constructed an elaborate fantasy and a scenario of the abuse; he is the playwright and the victims are the actors over whom he has total control. They are his puppets; he can pull strings and make them do anything he wants them to do. Even when the victim sees what is coming, the abuser doesn't want to skip over the stages he has envisioned and begin sex immediately.

The desire for control also explains the strong tendency that pedophiles have to keep detailed records, although the records increase the danger of discovery and conviction. Alan kept boxes of photographs of the boys; he had a sequence of photos of each victim in the same series of poses. This gave him a sense that he was the puppet master and they were his puppets under his absolute control. It also gave him further control over the boys, since they feared that he would show the pictures to others. Both heterosexuals and homosexuals sometimes have impulses that conflate sex and control and therefore engage in similar record keeping: Don Giovanni had his *Catalogue Aria* ("and in Spain one thousand and three"); the Rev. Wilputte Alanson Sherwood of Phoenix kept four binders of records of his 1,840 male sexual partners, rating each on a scale of 0 to 10 on face, body, personality, and sexual appearance.[69] Record keeping is even more prominent among pedophiles because control is more important to them.

This dynamic may also explain why homosexual development ends in pedophilia more often than heterosexual development does. The boy who is developing homosexually feels that he is different from other boys and that he is being controlled by something he does not like, and that other people also do not like. He therefore is more likely to seek to re-establish a sense of control over his own life by controlling others. He can manipulate adults, which is gratifying, but he cannot control them. It is easier to establish control over those who are younger; the ultimate control is sexual control. The process of initiating and carrying through abuse gives the abuser a strong sense that he is in control. He does not feel he is doing anything wrong, because *he* is the victim and is angry—at God, the world, society—for having made him different. This anger is diverted into establishing sexual control over others weaker than he is.

This anger, so prominent among abusive priests (see p. 466), explains why abuse is not simply sexual seduction, but often involves the degrading and sacrilegious actions we have seen in El Paso, Davenport, and so many other places. In fact, it seems that anger rather than sexual desire is the primary motive for the abuse. Boys may be chosen more often than girls not because, or at least not just because, the abuser's desires are often directed to males, but because the boys share maleness with Jesus. In the boy the abuser sees a vulnerable Jesus and seeks to defile him. But certainly homosexual desire is present in a good proportion of the abuse.

A homosexual whose desires are directed to sexually mature males and who also strongly desires control can manipulate adults but usually finds it is hard to control them. He can more easily control those younger than himself—teenage boys—and follows the same scenario as pedophiles follow in the process of establishing control. He establishes elaborate plans to prepare the victim—by getting to know the family, by getting the family to trust him, by getting the boy to feel that he has a special relationship with him. The abuser does something wrong in front of the boy, like cursing, and then excuses himself, saying it was a slip, and asks the boy to keep it a secret from his parents so that the parents won't break up the relationship. He then gives the boy gifts, and then alcohol, and then introduces the boy to other adult pleasures: drugs and pornography. At this point the boy feels implicated, at fault himself, and finds it impossible to tell his parents what he has done.

When both have been drinking, the abuser performs some sex act on the boy. A small boy is often horrified, but the abuser pretends repentance, says it won't happen again, it was the alcohol, calms the boy down, and gives him some big gift to make up for it. Gradually the abuser introduces the idea that although the boy doesn't enjoy this at first (although small boys are capable of climax even before they are able to ejaculate), in life you have to do things that you don't like to get things you do like—that is, the gifts the pedophile offers. An older, adolescent boy may enjoy the physical sensations even if he dislikes the abuse and he therefore feels complicit, a feeling his abuser carefully cultivates. At this point the boy cannot tell his parents that he has engaged in a perverted sex act, so the abuser is safe. After a while the abuser loses interest in this victim because the thrill of establishing control is gone and the boy breaks away. That is why pedophiles and pederasts have multiple victims. If it were only the sex, one victim would be enough, and would lessen the danger of discovery. The small boy who is the victim of a pedophile usually breaks away at puberty when the pedophile loses interest in him; the older boy who is the victim of a pederastic homosexual breaks away when he graduates from high school or goes to college or joins the military.

The stronger attraction to youth that is demonstrated by the higher proportion of homosexuals who develop pedophilia suggests that a higher proportion of homosexuals also develop an attraction to teenagers. One survey showed that 25 percent of homosexuals had sexual contact with males under the age of sixteen, when the homosexual was at least five years older than the youth.[70] A strong undercurrent of man-boy love exists in the homosexual movement, although they are busily trying to forget it.[71]

Gerald Hannon, a Canadian journalist, opera singer, professor, pornographic actor, and prostitute,[72] wrote an article for the Toronto gay publication *The Body Politic,* "Men Loving Boys Loving Men." Hannon described two pedophiles and what they did with boys, and said they "deserved 'our praise, our admiration and our support.'" *The Body Politic* maintained that "boy-lovers do suffer a special and vicious oppression in a society which has fabricated their own rigid notion of what they are," and celebrated the founding of NAMBLA, the North American Man-Boy Love Association.[73] Hannon is also very religious. His article, "Holy Hustling: Sex For-hire as a Spiritual Path," appeared in *Utne Reader* and he is a church composer. St. Basil's Catholic Church at St. Michael's College in Toronto featured a Kyrie he wrote; he sang in the choir and received warm applause afterwards.

The Toronto gay paper *Xtra* in the mid-1990s accepted ads from NAMBLA. A Canadian gay activist worried that "the fringe group that espouses man-boy love destroys the credibility of the gay rights movement."[74] The worry was unjustified. Canada has homosexual marriage, legal group sex clubs, and an age of consent of fourteen.[75]

The *Washington Blade* (a gay newspaper) admitted, "Some aspects of gay male culture do place a high value on youth, complete with terms like 'chicken' and 'twink' to describe desirable young men."[76] Paul Shanley was invited to a conference on intergenerational sex that led to the founding of NAMBLA, the North American Man-Boy Love Association, and this gathering was reported in the gay newspaper *Gaysweek* as a gay event. The ILGA (International Lesbian and Gay Association) was expelled from the UN and as of 2002 had not been readmitted as a nongovernmental organization, because it will not confirm that it has no ties with pedophiles.[77] The gay publication *XY,* aimed at twelve- to twenty-nine-year-old gays, interviews NAMBLA members and attacks the age of consent.[78] Homosexuals like Peter Tatchell of Outrage! constantly press for lowering the age of consent; in the Netherlands it is twelve. Tatchell condemns "abusive, exploitative relationships," but states that there are "many examples of societies where consenting intergenerational sex is considered normal, acceptable, beneficial, and enjoyable by old and young alike."[79]

*The Gay Report*,[80] written by Karla Jay, a lesbian activist who taught at Pace University, and by Allen Young, who wrote for many gay publications, was praised by Christopher Isherwood and Andrea Dworkin. The book surveyed the ambiguous 1970s' gay attitude to sex with children: "There were various perspectives on whether sexual contact with adults was helpful or not." Some gays thought that "forcing a child into sex is completely reprehensible"[81]; others were less condemnatory: "I would not encourage direct sexual involvement between an adult and minor; yet I do not think such involvement should be criminal either."[82] Still others felt that "relations between the ages should be free, as well as between the sexes and among the same sex. At any age…"[83] and that "all young guys should be urged to try homosexual sex."[84] Even those who were dubious about man-boy sex recognized that gays desired young males: "Homosexuals who accept positions of teaching or counseling of teenagers should understand that they're in a position of trust, and should try to control their lust for boys and not molest them sexually."[85] We also hear the cry of the oppressed pedophile: "How long will we boy-lovers have to wait? How long before we can walk honestly and proudly hand in hand with our young friends?"[86] The authors Jay and Young maintained a firmly noncommittal attitude: "Does a sexual relationship between a child and an adult harm the child?" and "Do the men who engage in sex with children deserve the harsh punishment and general opprobrium they now experience in this society? These are not questions that can be answered satisfactorily in this book."[87] The gay intellectual milieu out of which Paul Shanley came did not always condemn man-boy sex; for the most part, gays had qualms about it only because such activity led straights to regard gays as child molesters.[88]

Mainstream writers also have been sympathetic to pedophilia. Hanna Rosin in the *New Republic* gave a favorable review of a documentary on

NAMBLA, *Chickenhawk*.[89] Camille Paglia admired Allen Ginsberg's "pro-NAMBLA stand" because "male pedophilia is intricately intertwined with the cardinal moments of Western civilization."[90] Toby Johnson, writing in *White Crane: A Journal Exploring Gay Men's Spirituality*, admitted that gay priests should not have introduced heterosexual boys to sex, but "wasn't the psychological trauma caused less by the priest's advances than by society's and the Church's hysteria around sexuality and homosexuality?"[91] He echoed Paul Shanley's defense of pederasty (see p. 161). In general, gay publications like the transgressive aura of pederasty, the forbidden fruit that outrages society.[92] Andrea Dworkin celebrated the dissolution of taboos: "The incest taboo can be destroyed only by destroying the nuclear family as the primary institution of the culture....As for children, they too are erotic beings, closer to androgyny than the adults who oppress them. Children...have every right to live out their erotic impulses....The distinctions between 'children' and 'adults' and the social institutions which enforce those distinctions, would disappear as androgynous community develops."[93]

A stream of gay fiction, praised by the mainstream press such as the *Washington Post*, sympathetically portrays man-boy sex. In one novel the seducer is seven years old. Philip Jenkins notes the inconsistency in the media's description of sixteen-year-old boys as "victims of 'pedophilia,'" while the *Los Angeles Times* reviewer Eric Lax praised Gavin Lambert's *Mainly about Gavin Lambert*, saying that "since [Lambert's] sexual initiation at age eleven with a teacher at his preparatory school, he has felt only 'gratitude' for realizing his homosexuality."[94] Others make heroes of Oscar Wilde, who liked fourteen-year-old boys, Roman Polanski, who liked young girls, and Larry Flynt, who made a joke of child molestation.

Both literary critics for whom *transgressive* is a word of praise and whose hero is the Marquis de Sade, and psychologists who desire an ever-expanding field of sexual liberation put forward the idea that sex with boys is the next area to escape from repression. The media horror at the exposure of the sexual abuse of minors by Catholic priests has not been entirely convincing. Both advertisements and entertainment sexualize teenagers, and critics continue to praise Roman Polanski, who cannot reenter the United States because of an outstanding charge of child molestation against him[95] but who received the Palme d'Or at the Cannes Film Festival in 2002. Judith Levine won an award from the *Los Angeles Times* in 2003 for her book *Harmful to Minors: The Perils of Protecting Children from Sex* (see p. 440).

### *Homosexuality and Narcissism*

Freud thought that homosexuality originated in narcissism.[96] A male loves an image of himself, another male, rather than something different, a female. Narcissism alone would not lead an adult homosexual male to be sexually involved with someone significantly younger than himself. But a homosexual who loves not simply an image of himself but an idealized, youthful image of himself will seek out young males. In addition a homosexual male who is himself frozen at an adolescent state of maturity will seek out as a sexual partner someone who corresponds to this image of himself. Since his image of himself is an adolescent, he will seek out an adolescent.

Gay men, according to other gays, generally have a taste for very young men.[97] Philip Guichard, a young gay man, claimed (but is the article completely serious?) that "many gay men are embracing the pederast within" and "every gay man I know in a position of power has a 'boy' for a boyfriend. By *boy*, I mean a kid between the ages of, say fifteen and twenty-two, when your chicken card gets revoked."[98] The chicken hawk is a familiar type of gay; and fifteen- and twenty-two-year-old males are sometimes at the same stage of physical development. Kim Sue Lia Parkes, a lesbian who was Phoenix bishop Thomas O'Brien's spokesman, did not like the emphasis on youth she saw among gay men: "[For] gay guys, the ads in the personals you see often [say]: 'I'm twenty-one but I look sixteen.' The culture of gay men venerates youth."[99] The Rev. Daniel Robert Callahan of Baltimore left the priesthood because of his homosexuality. A young homosexual man met him through a 1993 personal advertisement and became a lover and friend, and put up a website to memorialize Callahan after his death. In one photo on the website, Callahan, ordained in 1951, is in his sixties, and looks older. His friend and lover looks around seventeen to twenty years old.[100]

The involvement of men in their forties and fifties with teenage boys suggests that one type of homosexuality is developmentally caused, that somehow these men never matured.[101] This type of immature homosexuality is prominent in cases involving priests.

Homosexuality and pederasty overlap because boys after fourteen or fifteen often look like youthful but sexually mature men. In Rockville Centre, New York, a thirteen-year-old boy thought he was homosexual. He told his mother, who sent him to Priest A. "To the initial surprise of the victim, when he disclosed to Priest A that he was gay, Priest A confided that he too was dealing with the same issues.... After one trip to Lincoln Center, when the victim was about fourteen, Priest A took him downtown to the West Village. They went to a gay nightclub called the Limelight. Ironically this club was located in an old church. That club was a warren of rooms that Priest A seemed to know his way around. The pair found themselves in a back room, where adult men were engaging in a variety of sexual acts. As the victim candidly explained to the grand jury, he was both terrified and excited by what he saw. He felt that Priest A had brought him to the club so that he could experience for himself what they had only previously discussed privately. Priest A quickly went off with other men and began engaging in sexual activity with them. The victim found himself surrounded by strangers who were undressing and touching him."[102] A fourteen-year-old boy was accepted into the world of homosexuality without hesitation.

Gays themselves have recognized that immaturity seems to be more characteristic of gays than of heterosexuals. They lament this immaturity and attribute it to the fact that many gays do not recognize their sexual orientation until they are in their twenties and thirties, and at that point start obsessing about sex and engaging in irresponsible, promiscuous behavior the way that heterosexuals, who have no inhibitions about recognizing their sexual orientation, do in their teens. This immaturity leads to the campiness of using girls' names and to general bitchiness, but also to the homosexual abuse of adolescents. This social phenomenon, caused, according to homosexuals, by a social non-acceptance of homosexuality, may simply reinforce the underlying dynamics in the type of homosexuality based upon the love of an idealized, youthful self.

Although estimates very widely, probably around 20 percent of Catholic clergy are homosexual, and many of them are at least trying to be celibate. Since at least 4 percent of priests have abused minors, almost all of them teenage boys, around 20 to 25 percent of homosexual Catholic clergy have been sexually involved with teenage boys, while only about 1 percent of heterosexual clergy has been involved with minors, including teenage girls. This includes true pedophiles, who have dozens or hundreds of female victims. Very, very few heterosexual Catholic priests are involved with teenage girls; if they break their vows of celibacy, they do it with adult women, which is wrong and almost always abusive, but not criminal. The minor victims of priests are almost always teenage boys.

Whether or not homosexuals in general are more likely than heterosexuals to molest teenagers is difficult to ascertain, but there is no question at all about homosexuals in the Catholic clergy. Among priests, 81 percent of reported abuse was of minor males (almost all teenage boys), as opposed to about 33 percent in the general population; only 19 percent of the reported abuse was that of minor females, as opposed to about 66 percent of reported abuse in the general population.[103] The situation is similar in the Anglican churches (see pp. 346ff.). Something about the clerical life seems to attract men who have a sexual interest in teenage boys, and whatever increases the risk is not specific to Roman Catholicism (celibacy, minor seminaries, etc).

## *Incidence and Type of Abuse*

The reported number of incidents in the John Jay study peaked in 1980, forming a bell curve from 1950 to 2000 (see Chart I). At the peak of the abuse the ratio of male to female victims also peaked (see Chart II). The

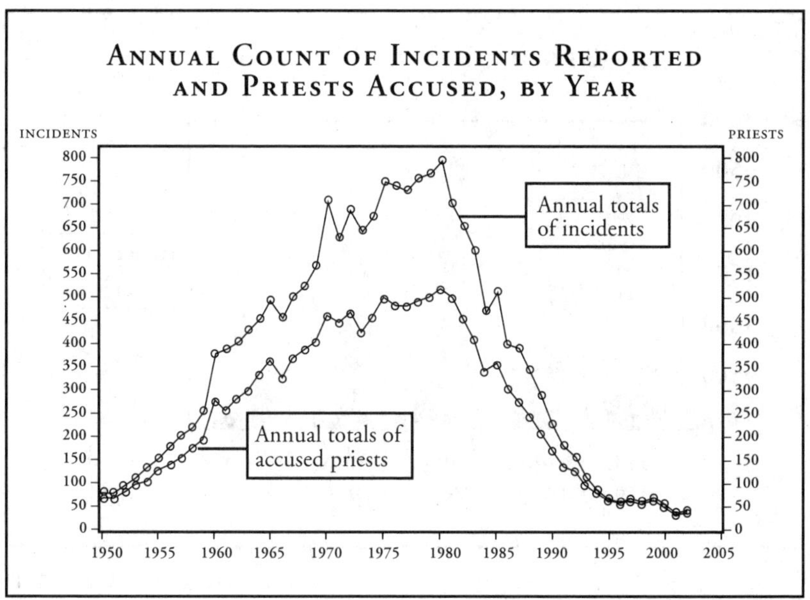


CHART I

proportion of victims who were small children slowly declined: Philip Jenkins is therefore correct when he says that the reaction to pedophilia bears all the marks of a moral panic. The problem of pedophilia is real, but it is small and actually decreasing. For example, 27.7 percent of male victims from 1950 to 1959 were under the age of ten, but only 9.7 percent of male victims from 1990 to 2002 were under the age of ten (and the absolute number of victims in this age group also decreased from 135 to thirty-nine). As Jenkins tried to emphasize in his misunderstood book *Pedophiles and Priests*, the abuse was in fact homosexual in nature, not pedophiliac. The victims have been mostly sexually mature boys, not prepubescent children. Of boys abused from 1950 to 1959, 17.8 percent were ages fifteen to seventeen, but from 1990 to 2002, 55.2 percent were in this age group (eighty-seven victims vs. 222 victims).[104] The victims now are older and the abuse is homosexual. The abusers are probably, in accord with therapy at St. Luke Institute, choosing more "age-appropriate partners" for homosexual relations, thereby not falling afoul of the law. The bell curve is therefore trailing off for several reasons: the number of

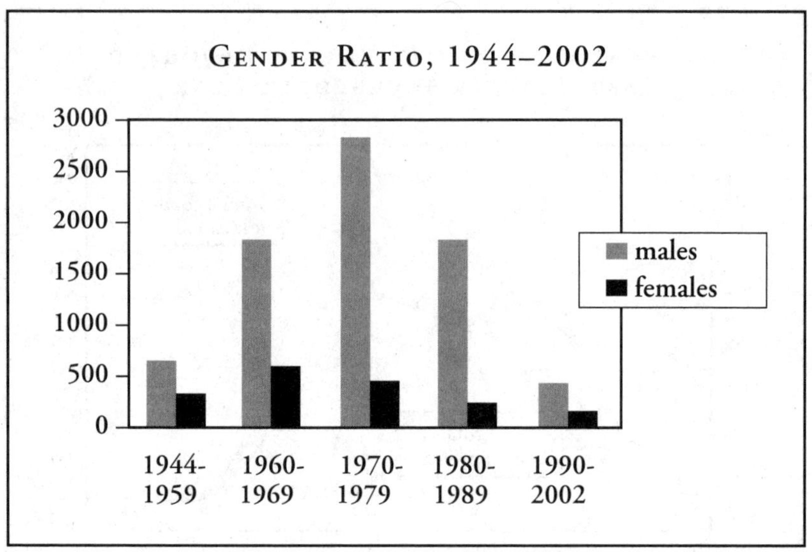


Chart II

priests is falling; their average age is rising and consequently their testosterone levels are falling; some discipline is being reasserted in the seminaries; the worst abusers have been suspended; and homosexual priests have finally learned to respect the age of consent.[105]

The decline in the reports of abuse by priests parallels the decline in reports in society as a whole (see Chart III). The question is whether these declines in reports of abuse represent a real decline in cases of abuse or some aspect of reporting.[106] The chief factor is the delay in reporting of childhood sexual abuse.[107] But the decline appears to be real. The actions of bishops after 1985, however inconsistent and unsatisfactory, seem to have led to a real decline in abuse. Similarly the American policy in this past generation of imprisoning criminals has led to a general overall decline of the crime rate, of which the decline in sexual abuse is a part. In 1986, 19,000 individuals were incarcerated for sex crimes against children; in 1991, 43,500 were incarcerated; in 1997, 60,700 were incarcerated. The more criminals there are in prison, the fewer crimes there are. The fewer abusers there are in priesthood, the less abuse of minors by priests occurs.

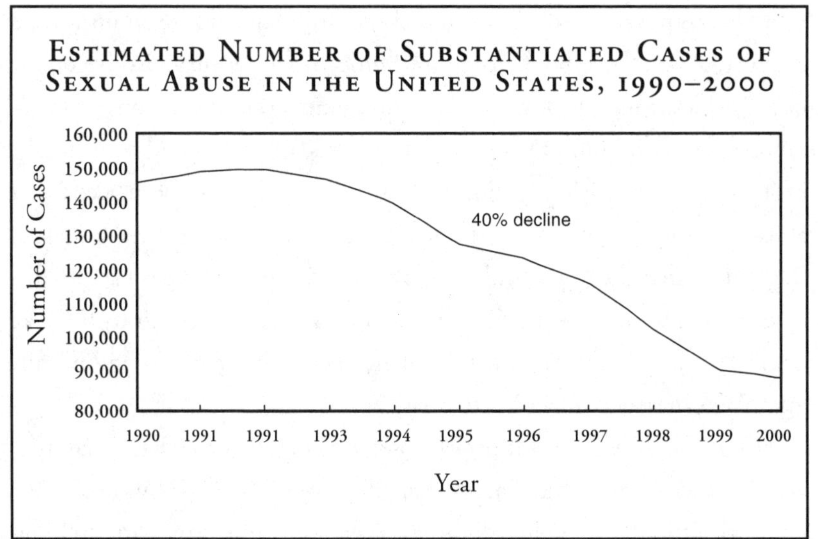


Source: David Finkelhor and Lisa M. Jones, "Explanations for the Decline in Child Sexual Abuse Cases," *Juvenile Justice Bulletin*, January 2004.

Chart III

## *Priests and Control*

The Catholic priesthood may present special risks. Many clerical abusers resembled the Rev. Peter Dumont of Philadelphia, whom therapists at Southdown characterized as "homosexual, extremely intelligent and narcissistic, with a tendency toward manipulation."[108] Males who are developing homosexually feel different, and they feel they are being controlled by something outside themselves and are therefore being victimized by mysterious forces. They therefore may seek to establish sexual control over others, and minors are more easily controlled than adults. The priesthood gives unparalleled access to and control of children; a priest is expected to discuss during the sacrament of confession the child's most intimate sexual thoughts and acts. The priest stands in the relationship of father and represents God to the child. Catholic and Anglican priests are also in charge of ritual, and children are accustomed to the priests enacting rituals and directing others to enact rituals.[109] The abusive priest has sexual fantasies and manipulates the victim to act them out in a stage play or ritual, thereby demonstrating his control.

The homosexual who fears loss of control may become an ultra-rigid ritualist, a familiar type of Anglican homosexual; he may also become a liturgist, satisfying his desire for control by directing the actions of thousands or even millions of people. This dynamic of fantasy and control may explain why a surprising number of liturgical experts have been accused of abuse. Liturgy is a way of controlling people and making them carry out the fantasy that the specialist has envisioned. Anyone who has tried to disagree with a liturgical expert has had an experience that confirms the joke among Catholics: "What is the difference between a terrorist and a liturgist? You can negotiate with a terrorist."

One abuser was a lay liturgist, Joseph Mangone of Dallas[110]; another was the Rev. Kenneth Martin, associate director of the U. S. bishops' secretariat for liturgy.[111] The Rev. Norman Page was arrested in April 2005 on charges of molesting boys between the ages of fourteen and eighteen; he had been the director of the office of liturgy for the archdiocese of Toronto.[112] Most prominently of all, Father John Huels, a Servite, who abused a fifteen-year-old boy, became provincial head of the Servites and then had to step down after the abuse became known, but was still hired to teach at St. Paul's University in Ottawa and to serve as a liturgical advisor to the Canadian and American bishops.[113] St. Paul's had also hired the known abuser the Rev. Barry Glendinning, who then became advisor to the archdiocese of Toronto's liturgy commission.[114]

## *Priests and Immaturity*

Immature homosexuality is involved in many of the Catholic abuse scandals. The sexual abuse of minors is perpetrated almost entirely by men: "on the whole, sexual victimization is a problem in the relations between men and children."[115] The children in the case of abusive priests were almost always teenage boys. A homosexual priest who has repressed any recognition of his homosexuality until after ordination may be especially prone to such behavior, and would seek the company of males who are at about the same stage of emotional development, that is, in their teens.

Clerical homosexuals have given some spectacular demonstrations of immaturity. Poor St. Sebastian, pierced with arrows, has become a religious icon for homosexuals.[116] A group of homosexual priests set up a website, St. Sebastian's Angels (David France claimed it was for mutual spiritual support),[117] which rapidly degenerated into the homosexual version of a frat house in its grosser moments. France blamed Bishop Reginald M. Cawcutt, the now-retired auxiliary bishop of Capetown, South Africa, but the other participants quickly joined in the antics. Stephen Brady of Roman Catholic Faithful was web-surfing when he discovered the website. He could scarcely believe what he was reading (and seeing). Bishop Cawcutt introduced himself in this way:

> Have you ever gone skinny dipping: gosh I have a pool right outside my bedroom and no one is allowed to wear a costume in it—well not guys anyhow!
>
> Do you make fun of people: not very often but lemme at uncle asshole Ratz

Cawcutt continued about the rumors that Ratzinger might be sending an order that would ban gays from ordination:

> kill him ? pray for him? why not just fuck him??? any volunteers - ugh!!! [DELETED] you told us ages ago about the possibility of a letter from him - can YOU give us any update? Certainly bishops of the world have not yet received anything like this - certainly not anything to do with gay students or whatever. I do not see how he can possibly do this - but... If he does, lemme repeat my statement earlier - that I will cause lotsa shit for him and the Vatican. And that is a promise MY intention would be simply to ask the question what he intends doing with those priests, bishops (possibly "like me") and cardinals (and I might as well put in popes) who are gay.

Another priest in the chat room chimed in:

> GUYS everyone has a skeleton in there closet and the rat has to have his. I have heard something that the rat has a child but again this is only rumor. Could it be possible? Well it is time the enemies of the rat find his Achilles heel...

Another commented on Ratzinger:

> NOW this asshole "romani" named ratzinger and his cronies want to cause a witch hunt. I have asked god to forgive me because i have never desired that god sends someone to his eternal rest as much as I want this man to.

This bishop and these priests reject Catholic moral teaching. One can be a heretic and a homosexual and still be mature. But these clerics are also highly immature, and such psychosexual immaturity, almost all agree, is one of the roots of the sexual abuse scandal in America. Bishop Cawcutt and the priests in this chat room were adolescent in their attitudes to sexuality. One commented that "I got my balls sucked out the end of my cock a few days ago. . . ." Another priest posted a picture of himself and a boy: "The little guy with me is not my current lover, but he was a guide 'äsuncion' 12 years old and a great little kid!" The source of the sexual scandals was homosexual priests who were stuck in adolescence themselves and sexually attracted to adolescent males. They were also deeply mired in adolescent anger.

After he found the website, Stephen Brady tried to deal with St. Sebastian's Angels privately: "Before RCF [Roman Catholic Faithful] ever made any of this material public, the Papal Nuncio and five U.S. Cardinals were contacted and offered the information RCF had obtained on St. Sebastian's Angels with the hope they would address the situation. They did not respond." He had a priest write this to the priests who were participating in the chat room:

> We are not accusing you personally of any crime or sin, however the chat room is a scandal and we have learned that the only response to such darkness is to draw it into the light. The existence of the Chatroom with

> recorded pictures and messages will be made available to the Church and to others. We do not do this for the sake of bringing scandal but because the Church itself has not shown itself to be capable of dealing with these issues. Given time, we poor weak human beings can come to accept almost anything, but the darkness still hates the light!
>
> We sincerely pray for you and encourage you, if the need is there, to seek God's mercy in the sacrament of Confession and counseling and the assistance of those in authority. You are a priest forever and like all priests, on the day of your ordination or religious profession you freely assumed the cross and the joy of celibacy. We pray that you and all priests may be faithful to that commitment.

A priest in the chat room responded: "Dear (Fr.) G. . . FUCK YOU, ASSHOLE!"

A few American bishops took the problem seriously and disciplined their priests, but most were content to let things continue.[118] The publicity eventually became too much for the Vatican to endure, and Cawcutt was removed from his post, but he remains a bishop, is unrepentant, and goes around preaching his peculiar version of chastity.

Something had gone wrong and these priests had never attained mature masculinity:

> Males, like females, start life in total symbiotic identification with their mothers. But in order to develop appropriate masculinity they, unlike females, must thrust aside this symbiosis, break off the identification with their mothers, and develop a new, positive identification with their fathers. This transition is treacherous, and in many males the process is not completed. They are left anxious about masculinity, fearful of again becoming fused in the primal symbiosis with mother, and hostile toward women and the male-female sexual complementarity. Out of these conflicts emerge the homosexual, fetishistic, and pedophilic deviations.[119]

Immaturity characterizes both homosexuals and pedophiles. Anticlericals have long suspected priests of being homosexual momma's boys, "muttersöhnchenhaften,"[120] and in many cases the suspicion is justified.

## *Too Close Identification with the Feminine*

Pepe Rodríguez interviewed abusive priests in Spain and concluded that in most cases both the abuse and the vocation stemmed from a bad relationship with castrating mothers. In Spain, as in much of the Western world, religion is a matter for women. Some mothers had kept their sons emotionally dependent on them and kept them in the feminized religious world of childhood. These sons feared both a mature sexual relationship with women and the antireligious world of adult men.[121] The priest formed in this milieu has, according to Rodríguez's analysis, sexual feelings but cannot direct them toward women. He therefore directs them to males, and since his own emotional state is frozen in childhood/adolescence, he directs them to immature males.

Christianity in the Western world has become the preserve of women: women constitute the majority of the laity, especially of the active laity, and have done so for centuries. I examined the causes and effects of this feminization of the Church in my book *The Church Impotent: The Feminization of Christianity*. Men who are attracted to a career in the Church may be attracted because they do not like the world of adult men. They may be immature and effeminate, never having broken the initial tie with the world of the mother. Mothers are often happy that their sons become priests because they will not lose their sons to another woman. Priests who have this personality structure identify with women and their interests. There are many priests of this type, and the Minnesota Multiphasic Personality Inventory shows that priests deviate most from the mean in the MF (Masculine / Feminine) scale, that is, they answer questions as a woman usually would answer them and not as a man usually would answer them.[122] Whenever they are sexually aberrant, they are also likely to be true pedophiles.

They may be more mature but still identify with the world of women rather than of men. Eugen Drewermann identified such clerics as "men . . .

who do not want to be men, but it is their latent homosexual aura that makes them appear to many women as the better, more cultivated, more sensitive and more considerate 'men.'"[123] An effeminate priest is no danger to most teenage boys, because boys will have nothing to do with such a man. A priest who is mildly feminine may simply appear as a refined adult and appeal to sensitive boys (see p. 247). Such a priest may have both the cultural interests and sexual interests of a woman: he is attracted to males. Such homosexual priests are a danger to sensitive boys who are attracted by the adult and cultivated world of the clergy.

## *Too Much Rejection of the Feminine*

Another type of homosexual is the arrested adolescent, who sometimes appears more masculine than heterosexual priests. A man may also be a homosexual because he is hypermasculine, rejecting the feminine totally. He is an adolescent, having all the charm and narcissism and sexual obsessiveness of adolescence, and is a danger to boys of average masculinity. He does not want to connect with adult women sexually. He is stuck in what is sometimes misleadingly called the homosocial phase of adolescence, the phase at which sexual desires are strong but the boy still wants to keep his distance from anything feminine for fear it will threaten his newly attained masculinity.

Stephen Rossetti of St. Luke Institute admitted,

> A significant number of priests who sexually molest minors are involved with post-pubescent adolescent males, about fifteen to seventeen years of age. It appears to be true that many in this subpopulation of priest child-molesters are homosexually oriented. But theirs is a particular kind of homosexuality, which one might call "regressed" or "stunted." These homosexual men are emotionally stuck in adolescence themselves, and so are at risk for being sexually active with teenage males. The issue is therefore not so much homosexuality but rather their stunted emotional development.[124]

A priest in this prolonged adolescence may look like a welcome relief from effeminate priests, and therefore strongly attract normal male adolescents, to the delight of their parents who have a hard time keeping such teenagers connected with the Church.

A former parishioner of Rudy Kos said, "Rudy came off as being very masculine, maybe a little bit macho. I looked at it as a faith-enrichening experience for the young boys to spend time with a young, physically fit, active priest."[125] A victim of Gauthé remembers Gauthé's use of masculine toys to lure teenagers: "The kind of entertaining toys he had were a powerful magnet for a kid from south Louisiana. Hey, you show a teenage boy from south Louisiana your collection of shotguns, tell him you are going to take him hunting and let him use those guns, and you've got a friend. Plus parents were encouraging their kids to spend more time with Gauthé."[126] Gauthé looked like a good old boy, not like the stereotype of the effeminate gay, and the parents could not imagine that he was sexually interested in their boys. Gauthé looked different from most priests who, even if they were heterosexual, behaved more like women than men.

## *Multigenerational Abuse*

If a teenager is abused sexually, he may freeze at that stage of sexual development himself. The abusers "tend to be those who are emotionally stunted, perhaps because they themselves were abused, and they might be fifteen years old themselves emotionally."[127] Their sexual desires therefore focus on male adolescents. These victims in turn may become abusers, and even become priests, perpetuating a type of multigenerational incest.

Paul Shanley claimed to have been abused as a child and as a seminarian. In Nashville, Tennessee, the Rev. Edward McKeown admitted molesting twenty boys. He told one victim that a priest had molested him.[128] One of the accusers of Marcial Maciel Degollado, the founder of the Legionaries of Christ who was disciplined by the Vatican in May 2006 (see pp. 517ff.), said that Maciel "had told other victims that he had been sexually abused as a child."[129] Juan Vaca, an accuser of Maciel, had taught at the Legionaries minor seminary at Ontaneda in Spain where, he said, the rector was dismissed for abusing boys. The rector, according to Vaca, "had himself been abused by Maciel as a boy."[130]

The Rev. Ron Voss of the diocese of Lafayette, Indiana, abused a boy who died young of a heart attack. The mother confronted Voss, who admitted the abuse, and he explained that he himself began a sexual relationship with a priest when he was fifteen or sixteen. Voss found that relationship "nurturing" because "the priest said he loved me." Voss claimed that when he in turn had sex with a boy, he didn't know that he "was doing anything wrong."[131] In the same diocese the Rev. Robert Moran counseled a nineteen-year-old parishioner who came to him because his father was dying and the mother had turned to drink. Moran turned out the lights and something happened. The boy said that Moran persuaded him to enter the seminary. He also persuaded the seminarian that "their affair was not wrong" but "no one else would understand."[132] The young man was eventually ordained, and even served on the diocesan review board for sexual abuse victims, but left the priesthood after receiving psychological counseling. The accuser of the Rev. Philip Mahalic, the "golden boy" of this diocese, admitted that he was the one who, in confession, suggested a sexual relationship to the priest. Mahalic eventually responded, and encouraged the young man to enter the seminary. Mahalic was director of vocations.[133]

Abusive priests have frequently been corrupted by their superiors. According to Richard Sipe, "A high percentage of those who later abuse children—whether or not they themselves were abused as children—were in effect given permission for such activity by a priest or religious superior who himself crossed the sexual boundary with the priest abuser during the time he was studying for ordination."[134] Sipe refers here to homosexual activity. When a seminarian is led into homosexual activity by his teachers or superiors, he naturally feels that the teaching of the Church on sexuality and celibacy is not to be taken seriously.

In their ministry, homosexual priests do not come into contact with many young adult men. Heterosexual priests have many opportunities to meet adult women, and counseling (as with married Protestant ministers) often leads to emotional involvement. But the males that priests are likely to come into contact with in their ministry are there because a woman (girlfriend, fiancée, wife) puts pressure on them to be there. In this case the adult males are heterosexual and will reject advances. Or the males are young, and are there because mothers put pressure on them to be involved with the Church. They may be heterosexual, but they are also going through a sexually charged and confused adolescence, and are interested in anything to do with sex. They are physically attractive and emotionally vulnerable. Most of the abusers are predatory; they usually do not just fall into a sexual infatuation with a young male (although this may happen). They instead carefully and maliciously plan opportunities to initiate sex and to degrade the victim.

The boys who are so abused include many who are interested in the priesthood, an interest that led them to associate with priests, and many who, because of the psychological phenomenon of the traumatic bond (see pp. 211ff.) and identification with the aggressor (see p. 269), decide that if the world is divided between powerful abusers and weak victims, they want to become one of the powerful abusers. They become priests and in turn abuse boys who are at the age that the priests themselves were abused as boys.[135]

### *Homosexuality as a Risk Factor*

The dynamics of homosexual development lead to a greater proportion of homosexuals as compared to heterosexuals who are attracted to minors. Homosexuals admit that they are more promiscuous than heterosexuals. Homosexual priests who are involved with minors have many more victims (and therefore do far more damage to the community) than a heterosexual priest who is involved with female minors will have. The heterosexual priest who is involved with adult women may be of the narcissist type who likes to collect conquests, but far more often the priest has an infatuation with a woman who is not his wife (a phenomenon also observed among married men) and either decides to leave to marry her or decides his ministry is more important to him than the woman is. If a homosexual priest, however, like other homosexuals, is promiscuous, he opens himself to more possibilities of blackmail.[136] If he discovers and disapproves of a homosexual priest who is involved with minors, and tries to stop the crime, he can be threatened with exposure himself. This is true of heterosexual priests as well (Archbishop Sanchez of Santa Fe is an outstanding example; see p. 402) but to a lesser extent. Heterosexuals have fewer affairs, and the affair is less disgraceful because it can lead to marriage.

Homosexuality is therefore a major risk factor in the sexual abuse crisis. Homosexuals tend to be attracted to teenagers more than heterosexuals are, and the type of homosexual who is likely to become a priest is precisely the immature type who is even more likely to be attracted to teenagers. No doubt there are mature, sincere homosexuals in the priesthood who fail no more than their heterosexual brothers fail. These priests, being mature, do not make a parade of their sexuality. The type of priest whose homosexuality is noticeable is almost always the immature, adolescent type, the type who ends up working with youth, and the type who ends up in court. Their immaturity alone should have put their superiors on notice that they were unsuited to the order of *presbyteroi*, the elders of the Church.

This immaturity stems not only from the psychological dynamics that I have examined in this chapter, but from distortions in Christian life in both theory and practice that I will examine in later chapters. Christians in general have been infantilized by two associated developments in the post-medieval church, a voluntarist moral philosophy that emphasized obedience to law rather than growth in moral and spiritual maturity, and an autocratic ecclesiastical government that created a clericalism which led Christians to believe that their primary duty was to obey, not to grow in the friendship that is charity. Those formed by such a conception of obedience were infantilized and denied moral and spiritual maturity, with disastrous consequences, of which sexual abuse was only one.

# CHAPTER TWELVE

# ABUSERS AND CELIBACY

Many have long suspected that celibacy places impossible burdens on human nature. Martin Luther claimed that the demand that priests be celibate led to "horrifying, horrid, and innumerable sins of impurity of every kind."[1] Henry C. Lea continued this line of argument: "When the desires of man are once tempted to seek through unlawful means the relief denied to them by artificial rules, it is not easy to set bounds to the unbridled passions which, irritated by the fruitless effort at repression, are no longer restrained by a law which has been broken or a conscience which has lost its power."[2] Lea chronicled the heterosexual irregularities of the medieval clergy, and he only barely alluded (in Latin quotes) to homosexual or pederastic sins. Very few men can be celibate, according to this analysis; if they cannot marry, they will commit some type of sexual crime. Such is Louise Haggett's thesis: she "connects the intense loneliness of mandatory celibacy with resulting clergy sexual abuse."[3]

The Latin Church insists that almost all its clergy be celibate. Why is celibacy so important to the Church? Even if it is important, does requiring priests to be celibate create more problems than benefits? When priests cannot have lawful sexual intercourse in marriage, does their desire turn toward teenage boys? Are the celibate clergy really chaste, or do priests fail so often that almost everyone has some skeletons rattling around in his closet, and therefore everyone turns a blind eye to the transgression of his neighbor, even when the victims are minors?

## *The Value of Celibacy*

Catholics, Protestants, and Orthodox all have a strong sense that the pastor should not be in the marriage market with his parishioners. The pastoral office has parental and paternal qualities, and a hint of incest therefore contaminates any sexual interest a pastor may have in a member of his flock, however legitimate such interest may otherwise be.[4] Liberal Protestants try to explain this suspicion of pastor-parishioner relationships by claiming there is a power imbalance between any pastor and any parishioner, but that is not always true. The status of the clergy has declined; many laymen and laywomen are rich and powerful. Not just a power imbalance, but a taint of spiritual incest makes pastor-parishioner relationships distasteful and wrong.

The three traditions deal with this situation in different ways: the Latin Church ordains a man who is unmarried and who says he is called to celibacy; the Eastern Churches (both the Orthodox and those in union with Rome) will ordain a married man, but if his wife dies he cannot remarry. Protestants prefer to ordain a married man but will ordain a bachelor who is therefore in the awkward position of not being able to seek a wife in his congregation without a great many contortions.

Celibacy, especially for Catholics, is a sign of the kingdom of God, and it helps make that kingdom present. Marriage, although a great good, is confined to the present age of the world. In the coming kingdom there will be neither marriage nor giving in marriage, and in all Christians' lives marriage (although not the love of the spouses) is a temporary condition, which death destroys. A celibate is a person who is called by Christ to witness to the coming kingdom. His choice not to marry makes no sense unless Christ is calling him to celibacy, and it is therefore a sign of the reality of Christ.

The celibacy of the priest also helps make the kingdom present because he can devote himself more directly to bringing about the kingdom. Celibacy is important because it allows a Christian to serve the Lord more directly and completely, without distractions: "The unmarried man is anxious about the affairs of the Lord, how to please the Lord; but the married man is anxious about worldly affairs, how to please his wife, and his interests are divided" (1 Cor 7: 32–33). The laity are properly involved in the affairs of the world, including marriage, but a priest (like the religious in a slightly different way) has been called to anticipate the kingdom by devoting all his energies to the advancement of the kingdom. Celibacy in that sense is more perfect, because it is the state to which all Christians are eventually called, a few sooner, the rest later.

To understand why the Church places such a strong emphasis on clerical celibacy, in spite of the difficulties it causes, it is necessary to consider the general Catholic attitude to sexuality. I myself do not have the gift of celibacy. I was called to be a father (I have six children) and I feel grateful to Abraham for having established the centrality of fatherhood in religion. In this above all Christians (like Muslims) are spiritually Semites. Judaism exalted the father, the family, and procreation. These were not peripheral matters in Judaism, but were close to the heart of the relationship between God and man, and especially between God and Israel. At the very beginning God created humanity male and female, and the first command he gave them was "increase and multiply." Procreation is a participation in God's work of creation. In fact, God is really the primary actor even in human procreation. When Eve conceives she proclaims that she has gotten a man child with the help of the Lord. God is beyond sex, he is not a male-female dyad, as in much of paganism; there is no *heiros gamos* in heaven that is imitated by human copulation on earth. Sexuality is a created reality, but its creativeness mirrors and participates in the divine creativeness.

God promised Abraham not eternal life or redemption or salvation, but descendants. Abraham believed this, although he and his wife were too old for children. When he offered the Lord hospitality at Mamre, he was in turn promised that Sarah would bear a child. Similar divine interventions brought fertility to barren women throughout the Bible. Therefore the virginal conception of Jesus, without the agency of a human father, was only the culmination of God's action within Judaism, not a break from it.

Fertility and children and family were the goal; sexual pleasure was the means to these higher goods. In intertestamental Judaism, virginity and celibacy were more and more valued. Priests were celibate during their time of service in the temple; soldiers were celibate while on campaign, and even when on leave—that is why David's plan for Uriah the Hittite failed (2 Sam: 11). The virginal fruitfulness of Mary combines these two themes in Judaism—celibacy and fruitfulness.

Jesus himself never married and commended those who were eunuchs for the kingdom. Paul went back and forth. He himself was unmarried and commended that state, because marriage, although good, distracted from the things of the Lord. Even married couples could refrain from intercourse for a while to devote themselves more intensely to prayer, just as they would fast from food. But they should not refrain from intercourse indefinitely, because, Paul realized, that would open them to temptation.

The time was short, the Lord was near, and all had the duty to preach the gospel before the end, and should try to avoid getting tangled up in worldly affairs, an entanglement that marriage inevitably brought. But the end did not come immediately, and Paul saw that human nature had not been abolished. It was dangerous for young people to be unmarried; celibacy opened them to temptations. Paul counseled young widows to remarry and not to enter into the order of widows who had apparently pledged celibacy. He knew that their desires would reawaken, that they would want to marry, and that they would go back on the pledge of celibacy and disgrace the Church by their instability.

Clerical celibacy is not explicitly mentioned in the New Testament, but there are many odd phrases that could be interpreted (but do not prove) that some of the preachers of the Gospel were celibate even while married. Peter, unlike Paul, had a sister as wife. This again is an unusual phrase and may imply that Peter lived in a brother-sister relationship with his wife. The New Testament Church apparently knew of the custom of spiritual marriage, in which a man and a woman would marry or enter a close relationship of betrothal, but refrain from sexual relations. This might explain the passage in which Paul counsels that marrying one's virgin or not marrying her are both good, but that the latter is better (I Cor: 7, 36).

After the persecutions, there are indications that a married man ordained to the priesthood was expected to refrain from intercourse with his wife. We know this chiefly because of the laws punishing those who did not refrain from intercourse.[5] We can deduce that at least in some churches the clergy were expected to refrain from intercourse with their wives (this is surprising); and that the clergy didn't always refrain (this is not surprising). Since in the ancient world almost everyone was married at an early age by parental arrangement, and the Church chose only mature men (elders, Greek *presbyteroi*) as priests and leaders of the Church, only married men were available. Why were married men expected to refrain from intercourse?

Various reasons which sometimes reflect classical suspicion of the body and sexuality (an early example of inculturation) were given by Fathers of the early Church,[6] but the main reason is the same as in the temple priesthood: sexuality is good, but it is a distraction from the main duty of the priests, to offer sacrifice and intercession for the people, first in the temple and then in the spiritual sacrifice, the Eucharist. Perhaps the priest was first expected to refrain from intercourse immediately before celebrating the Eucharist (as in modern Orthodox churches). As the custom of offering the Eucharist every day spread, the priest was therefore in effect celibate. Or perhaps he had to keep himself always ready to offer intercession, and therefore always had to refrain from intercourse. The Eastern Church either had a different discipline from the beginning or changed the ancient discipline, because after the Council of Trullo (692 A. D.) it accepted married priests (but not bishops), who were allowed intercourse with their wives.

Human nature and sexual problems go together. But has the Western, Latin tradition of celibacy made them worse? In the West after the fall of the Roman Empire, society and the Church were barbarized. Priests were ignorant and often lived in illegal marriages or concubinage. The monasteries preserved both learning and higher spiritual ideals, and the great monastic popes tried to reform the clergy along monastic lines. Peter Damian testified to the corruption of the clergy, which extended to homosexuality and pedophilia, and told Pope Leo IX that harsh remedies were necessary to restore discipline (see p. 18). Priests were expected to be learned, to be prayerful, and to be unmarried. Human nature being what it is, and the disciplinary power of the popes being severely limited by feudal arrangements, concubinage was still widespread when the Reformation started, and clerical celibacy was nonexistent in such fringe areas as Iceland.

Martin Luther thought that celibacy was a rare gift, and that almost everyone, including the clergy, should marry to prevent sexual corruption.[7] The Catholic reformer Erasmus, himself the illegitimate son of a priest, agreed, "I would like to see permission given to priests and monks to marry, especially when there is such a horde of priests among whom chastity is rare. How much better to make concubines into wives and openly acknowledge the partners now held in infamy."[8] At the Council of Trent the Catholic Church recognized the problem of a disorderly and corrupt clergy and set up a seminary system, which at times has worked. Where it hasn't worked very well, it has led to priests living in semi-clandestine marriages, especially in Latin America and Africa,[9] although hardly unknown in contemporary Germany, where bishops will not assume that a woman who is living with a priest and bearing children necessarily has any sexual relationship with the priest.

Andrew Greeley pointed out that "because some few abusing priests are celibates, it does not follow that all celibates are abusers."[10] Celibacy does not cause priests to abuse teenage boys, because the vast majority of priests (over ninety percent) have not been involved in such abuse. Heterosexual men, if they are unmarried, do not develop a sexual interest in teenage boys, much less in small children. They may have affairs with adult women, or they may even develop an interest in teenage girls, especially in our culture, which sexualizes youth, but they do not turn to men unless females are totally unavailable. Situational homosexuality occurs in prisons and on ships at sea, but not in places in which women are available. Women are not only available in Catholic parishes; they dominate numerically and are the laity with whom priests have the most interaction. Priests are constantly sought out as counselors by distressed and vulnerable women, with predictable results (Protestant ministers have the same temptations to which they sometimes succumb).

But are celibates more likely than other men to be abusers? In Ireland, yes, about five times more likely.[11] In Australia, a substantial portion of men who were abused as children were abused by the Catholic clergy, a portion far out of line with the number of clergy in the population. Among Australian incarcerated sexual offenders who were between the ages of eleven and fifteen when they were themselves abused, fifty percent had been abused by Christian Brothers and by Catholic priests; of the non-offenders who had been abused at that age, fifty-nine percent had been abused by religious figures ("29% by Roman Catholic priests, 10% by Christian Brothers, 10% by church youth leaders, 10% by ministers of religion in other denominations"[12]). Catholic priests and religious are only one-tenth of one percent of the Catholic population, and an even smaller proportion of the entire Australian population, which is about one-quarter Catholic, but they committed half the abuse. In Austria from one to three percent of the reported abuse against minors was committed by priests, who constitute only one-thousandth of the adult male Catholic population.[13] Priests therefore abuse from ten to thirty times as often as other Austrian men. Celibates do seem to commit abuse of minors disproportionately, at least in some societies. However, they commit abuse not because they are celibate, but because abusive personalities are attracted to the clerical and religious state.

A broader question is whether celibacy creates a culture in which abuse is tolerated, either by separating men from families or by creating a culture in which almost all supposed celibates are secretly sexually active. David Clohessey thinks that "in a group where nobody is allowed to have sex, then many priests have secrets....And that makes it tougher for them to report other priests involved in misconduct."[14] Richard Sipe thinks that only two percent of the Catholic clergy have attained spiritually mature celibacy[15]; about half are substantially celibate with occasional reversals; half at any given time are not celibate in any meaningful sense—they are in heterosexual relationships (thirty percent), homosexual relationships (fifteen percent), or engaging in "problematic sexual behavior" (five percent).[16] Celibate priests violate their vows, as married men do, but unlike married men, priests' continued employment is contingent upon a pretense of faithfulness to the vow of celibacy, and therefore all those who violate their vows, whether with women, men, or children, will have an implicit compact not to expose one another.

Celibacy may also attract those who have sexual difficulties and hope that celibacy is a way of resolving or avoiding them. Those who have trouble relating to women may see celibacy as a relief from the trials of courtship. Homosexuals may see celibacy as a way to escape constant questions about when they plan to marry. Pedophiles may see celibacy as a way to escape from the sexual feelings which frighten and horrify them by repressing sexuality altogether. All of these men will have difficulty maintaining celibacy, even if they are sincere, because they are unable to marry, rather than choosing to be celibate for the Lord in response to an inner call.

The Catholic system of seminary training established by the Council of Trent has also been blamed for many of the difficulties surrounding celibacy. The Council was aware of the low moral and educational standards of the parish clergy. It therefore recommended the establishment of seminaries which boys would enter at a young age, *a teneris annis*, as young as five in some cultures, so that they would be shielded from temptations and grow used to the idea and discipline of celibacy. The seminaries maintained a monastic discipline, and were often successful in maintaining celibacy among their charges as long as they were in the seminary. But these seminarians, not having gone through the normal social-sexual development of adolescence, may be frozen at the stage of adolescence, and, if they are homosexual, be attracted to teenage boys, who are at the same level of emotional development.

When newly ordained priests suddenly had much more freedom, especially in the prosperous atmosphere of post-World War II American Catholicism, they lost the monastic supports to celibacy. Some think that celibacy is not really possible outside monasticism or a monastic lifestyle. A priest who lives the upper-middle class American bachelor lifestyle of ease and comfort, with fast cars, electronic equipment, and vacations, will find it hard to be celibate (and most are not, according to Sipe). However, just as married people have an asceticism proper to marriage (getting up for 2 A. M. feedings, changing diapers, enduring noise and chaos patiently, coping with financial worries), so diocesan priests who are truly conscientious about fulfilling their duties will have enough ascetical disciplines to maintain their celibacy. They may not have midnight prayer in a cold chapel but they will have midnight calls to the hospital, pleas to deal with suicidal adolescents, interventions in dangerous and hopeless domestic violence, not to mention the political dangers that confront priests in much of the world, whether in South America, Africa, or Asia. Monastic discipline is only one way of asceticism; there are others proper to married people and to parish priests.

## *The Protestant Experience*

Sister Karol Jackowski has voiced a common but incorrect opinion: "no one but the Catholic Church protected priestly pedophilia as if it were just another sexual practice to be overlooked."[17] On the contrary, the Catholic Church has suffered from a universal dynamic in which a group seeks to protect its leaders and views any criticism of them as disturbances of group harmony and hates any critics as troublemakers. The weak are easily sacrificed to protect the ease of the powerful. Marie Fortune thought that all she had to do was educate the liberal Protestant churches with which she dealt about the harm that sexual abuse does and the ways to end it; she soon realized the protection of vulnerable church members from sexual abuse was not high on the agenda of church leaders and discovered "the lack of courage on the part of many who had responsibility to act."[18]

Celibacy or other characteristics unique to the Roman Catholic Church have been blamed for its sexual scandals. However, churches that do not require celibacy have similar or worse problems.[19] Anglicans in developed countries are what liberal Catholics would like the Roman Catholic Church to become: a church with a Catholic liturgy, but decentralized, with doctrinal freedom, women priests, and an acceptance of homosexuality and same-sex marriage, even for bishops. Still, Anglicans have not attained the expected state of mature sexual responsibility. Although unrepressed by a Cardinal Ratzinger, Anglicans have handled sexual scandals worse, if possible, than Catholics have.

## ANGLICANS — AUSTRALIA

In Anzac Parade, Australia, in 1966, the newly arrived Rev. Alan Sapsford was regarded as a "family man."[20] For thirty years he helped himself to the church's altar boys, some of whom committed suicide. One of them became an Anglican priest himself and told the Anglican hierarchy what had happened. Sapsford confessed his guilt and was fired, but the parish was told he was retiring because of "ill-health."[21] Then Archbishop Keith Raynor of Melbourne gave Sapsford a license to preach, thereby exposing other boys to danger. The Rev. Paul Walliker explained Raynor's action: "I've seen the Church deal with people on the basis of who they know and who their friends are in high places, and if you have the right friends, then you're safe."[22] Sapsford had the right friends in high places, and he also had friends in the parish. When the parents of abused boys demanded a church inquiry, the other parishioners turned on them. One mother explained, "I can't describe to you how it feels, for instance, to be yelled at, called names, called a slut, that my children deserve it, he was a good man."[23] When the parents asked the police to protect them, they were blocked by Detective Sergeant Lance Marke, a friend of Sapsford.[24] Sapsford died suddenly, and the bishop is dealing with victims through lawyers.

Police suspect that for over a generation a pedophile ring in the Australian Anglican church molested hundreds of boys. The Adelaide Pedophile Task Force quickly identified forty-seven suspects and 196 victims.[25] It was centered in the Church of England Boys' Society, with which the archbishop of Brisbane, Phillip Aspinall, was heavily involved for decades. Complaints against members of the society had been made for decades; in 1999 Aspinall wrote, "The church had to limit its liabilities and not be seen to elicit complaints."[26] Aspinall wrote a character reference for the Rev. Louis Victor Daniels before Daniels was sentenced in 1999 for four counts of indecent assault and two counts of oral sexual intercourse. Despite his "sexual relationship" with the boy, Daniels was lauded by the character witnesses for his "hard-working, self-sacrificing nature."[27] Daniels was sentenced to twelve months, three of which were suspended. Rev. Robert Brandenburg, a commissioner of the Society, committed suicide in 1999 by drowning himself in a reservoir in Paradise on the day he appeared in court on child molestation charges: giving boys alcohol and marijuana and showing them pornographic movies before assaulting them.[28]

The Rev. Garth Stephen Hawkins never passed his seminary exams or graduated but was ordained in 1972. He had a brief marriage but preferred boys. He found alcohol useful in persuading boys to have oral and anal sex with him; occasionally, he badly scratched their backs in his enthusiasm. Sometimes the alcohol backfired; he got one boy drunk, put him into bed, and was about to begin molesting him when the boy vomited.[29] Thirteen-year-olds can't hold their liquor. One boy, Steve Fisher, was vulnerable, because of a sick mother and absent father; he had a typical traumatic bond (see p. 271ff.) with Hawkins. After being abused, Fisher "parted on good terms"[30] with Hawkins, who later baptized him and presided over his marriage. Hawkins was eventually defrocked.

After abusing scores of children at Brisbane Grammar School, the Anglican layman Kevin Lynch was hired as a counselor at St. Paul's school. As counselor, he had boys who were distressed or in trouble, in complete privacy, as long as he wanted. It was a perfect arrangement. He had a routine of simple medical tests and psychological games (including hypnosis) which became more and more intimate as sessions proceeded. A boy got used to having less and less clothing on during the sessions until he was naked while being taught relaxation techniques. One boy remembered lying down, letting Lynch put baby oil on his penis, and then having Lynch observe (and help a little) while he masturbated. This was all done, Lynch explained to the boy, to demonstrate to the student that he was heterosexual and not homosexual. A student who had graduated went to the police, who wired him and had him go back to Lynch, who admitted the abuse: "You realize that I could have gotten seven years for it. You realize that it's a criminal offense of a major nature." Lynch also explained to the boy, "You were probably one of the most uptight kids" and, "Now what you have to understand, is that you had to let yourself go physically, sexually, without anger and without guilt."[31] For an Aussie, Lynch spoke fluent psychobabble. The police charged Lynch on January 22, 1997, and he committed suicide the next day. The headmaster of St. Paul's, Gilbert Case, was furious at the student, whose accusation he thought was "vexatious, vindictive, and entirely without foundation."[32]

A week later, four priests concelebrated a requiem Mass for Lynch, at which he was praised as "quite simply the most complete and skillful school counselor that I have known in forty years of teaching."[33] Many students in the congregation knew Lynch's skills. Of course no one, including the staff, was told the real reason why Lynch committed suicide, or even that he had committed suicide. In February 1997, Case eventually told the school council what had really happened and the school council did nothing—no investigation, no review of child protection policies. However, more students came forward with stories of abuse. Student Three was sent to Lynch for smoking marijuana. Lynch questioned the student about his masturbation techniques, and "talked about being gay and told him that a member of the staff was also being counseled because he was gay."[34] Student Four was puzzled how being hypnotized and waking to find his shorts undone was helping his dyslexia, and he asked a science teacher, who told him, "He's [Lynch] a counselor, you'll have to ask him."[35] After Lynch's suicide this boy told his parents about the abuse; their response was to do nothing. Lynch confused several students with psychological mumbo-jumbo. With one student the abuse progressed, beginning in grade eight, through masturbation, mutual masturbation, and oral sex, all of which continued after the student graduated, when he weekly went to Lynch's house, where he saw students from St. Paul's visiting. Headmaster Case had called Lynch at home and Student Eight picked up the phone. Student Eight explained that "he has always accepted Lynch's sexual behavior as part of therapy. He said that Lynch had become like a 'grandfather figure' and had played a very important and long term role in his life"[36]—classic traumatic bonding. Case was promoted to director of Anglican schools in Queensland.

The Rev. John Litton Elliott, founder of the Church of England Boys' Society in his parish, as a layman befriended a family in the parish and between 1978 and 1981 molested their boys. In 1993 the parents of the now-adult boys learned of this abuse and reported it. Elliott confessed to Peter Hollingworth, Anglican archbishop of Brisbane, but Hollingworth merely sent him to a psychiatrist for evaluation, letting him function as a priest if he promised not to do it again, and told Elliott's wife to keep an eye on him—after all, it was only one boy one time (although the boy said he told Hollingworth the abuse was hundreds of times, that there were other victims,[37] and Hollingworth later referred to "both brothers" as abused). Hollingworth arranged for Elliott to meet the parents, who reported that "Elliott's attitude was all self pity. It was all 'poor me' and that he was sad that he would never see FG [their son] again. Another comment he made was that 'no harm was done.' At no time did he ask for forgiveness or express any kind of remorse."[38] Hollingworth also told the victim that "these matters were best handled internally, that there was a process that needed to be followed and that there was no need to involve any other parties in this process."[39] Other parties not to be notified included, of course, the police.

When the parents asked Hollingworth to dismiss Elliott as unfit, he refused "because at age sixty-three he (Elliott) would find it difficult to secure another job."[40] Hollingworth admitted that pedophiles were never cured, but he would not remove Elliott from his parish because the previous rector had left under a cloud and questions would be asked if Elliott left suddenly, and "it is better to upset one family than a whole parish." Was the echo of John 11:50 (Caiphas says of Jesus, "It is better that one man should die than that the whole people should perish") conscious or unconscious? Hollingworth later denied saying any of this.

In 1995 FG's brother, whom Elliott had also abused, faxed this letter to Hollingworth:

> I know that you know of John Elliott's activities and of my brother's case. WHAT I CAN'T WORK OUT IS WHY YOU SIR, WOULD HARBOUR A MAN WHO YOU KNOW HAS SEXUALLY ASSAULTED CHILDREN FOR YEARS. By letting him have a nice job in a quiet town away from the vicinity of his disgusting crimes. I do not see how a man who, it seems, has spent many of his waking hours for many years fantasizing about young boys and messing around with their minds could possibly be a fit person to hold the position of trust and responsibility in which you have placed him, a position that places him in the eyes of the congregation as someone who is a spiritual and moral example and guardian, society considers his type to be the lowest of the low as cold hearted devils. Why do you want to hold him up as a messenger of God?

The brother reminded Hollingworth that the damage that Elliott did continues:

> I am sure that John Elliott feels that a regrettable chapter of his life has closed, that by coming out with it as he did, that everything will be healing or be healed. I can imagine that by being in his current position, he can feel even better about himself that he is making up for his crimes (and they are not just sins Sir they are crimes) and that everything will be sweet. Perhaps you too believe this Sir and that is why you are happy for him to be a priest. Because it is best for him. Well guess what. Things are not that sweet for the boys and men who have been raped or manipulated by him. People like my brother may never get over it. My brother is not obsessed with revenge, but surely it is not too hard to see that when his attacker is so easily forgiven and kept under your wing my brother is denied the right to properly work through his feelings regarding his own guilt (or lack of) and his anger toward his aggressor. It seems to him that the rest of the world is more interested in the feelings of the Rector of Dalby.[41]

Whatever the rest of the world might think (and the writer is probably correct), Hollingworth certainly knew how to deal with the cries of the oppressed and to keep the focus on the real issue, Elliott's convenience: "He is now getting close to retirement and the disruption and upset that would be caused to the whole parish as well as to him and his family would be in nobody's best interests." After all, he said he was sorry—wasn't that enough?

Hollingworth tried to play the forgiveness card—"the Christian rule is one of forgiveness and reconciliation"—and warned the brother not to carry out his threat to send the letter to the newspapers: "I am not influenced by the last two lines of your fax, because that is in nobody's best interests and certainly not that of your family."[42] Bishop John Noble saw the insults in Hollingworth's reply and asked him not to send it, but Hollingworth was secure in his self-righteousness and sent the reply. The parents then contacted the police and the solicitors.

After Elliott retired, Hollingworth let him function as a fill-in priest, warning him, in a friendly fashion, to keep a low profile. After all, Elliott needed the money. Hollingworth congratulated Elliott (in phrases reminiscent of Cardinal Law's effusive letters to abusers): "Thank you for the work you did. I am sure it was valued by all."[43] Elliott pleaded guilty in 2002 to ten counts of sodomy with other boys and is in prison. He denied that Hollingworth was a friend but admitted that Hollingworth had set up a meeting between him and the family of a victim. Elliott whined that the media had made him out to be "a monster" merely because he molested boys, but his wife received telephone calls of support from all over Australia.[44] Hollingworth, with knowledge that Elliott was an abuser, had let him remain a priest. Hollingworth claimed he did not violate any policies in his handling of Elliott in 1993, because "none existed."[45] The Anglican committee that in 1995 wrote the policy protocols about handling cases of abuse had to fight the bishops for four years to have them released.

The housemaster of Toowoomba Preparatory School, Kevin George Guy, was accused of molesting girls, especially ones who had "blonde hair, blue eyes, dark skin."[46] The school ignored the complaints. Guy gassed himself the day he was to appear in court, and left a suicide note listing twenty girls he was "in love" with.[47] Headmaster Robert Brewster wrote to the parents that he and the staff could not believe that Guy had done anything wrong. He claimed that "the police have closed the case" and concluded, "I hope and pray that even his critics will be charitably disposed towards this young enthusiast who did so much that was good and positive for so many children in his care."[48] This is how one victim describes Guy's enthusiasm: "When I was naked one time he put his finger inside me trying to penetrate me and then when he saw he wasn't succeeding with that he would put his mouth in between my legs and then he would ask me if I had an orgasm" and "he would take my hand, my right hand and put it around his penis, he would make me feel it. He would ask me if it's big, if it's hard and it was and he would say, 'Rub your hand up and down,' he said, he would say, 'Don't be frightened if something wet happens' which it did."[49] One girl won $800,000 (Australian) in damages from the church.

A clinical psychologist and prominent Anglican, Michael James Crowley, wrote the 1998 report on pedophilia for the Tasmanian Anglican Church, *Not the Way of Christ*. He had started grooming a girl in 1972 when she was thirteen and molested her when she was fifteen and sixteen; he got her pregnant and arranged an abortion (he later pleaded guilty to this). He told all this to a Tasmanian Anglican priest, but the church saw no reason he should not write the report, and even after his guilty pleas, it insisted he was "still the best person"[50] to write the report. Who knows more about molestation than a molester? Hollingworth in February 2002 appointed the Rev. Ross McAuley, who had been accused of sexual abuse, to a committee investigating clerical sexual abuse.[51] McAuley later converted to Catholicism and with a hearty recommendation from Hollingworth (who believed in passing the trash) tried to become a Catholic priest, but has since disappeared.

Adults too were abused by Anglican priests. The Tasmanian Rev. Alan Arthur Farrell was convicted in 1995 of male rape. Farrell found a thirty-three-year-old invalid pensioner drunk and collapsed on the street. "Farrell took the man to his bedroom, tied his hands behind his back with a tie and proceeded to anally assault and rape him over a period of hours while plying him with more drink."[52] When Farrell was done he turned the man loose on the street with his hands still bound.

The Anglican bishops suspended Farrell, but were more understanding of Bishop George Browning. A woman was abused by her father when she was a child; she married but her husband turned out to be a homosexual. Distraught, she turned to the Rev. George Browning, "an Anglican pin-up boy" and "very charismatic."[53] He seduced her. Years later she confronted him; he confessed and resigned, but "a special Synod voted by an overwhelming majority to ask him to withdraw his resignation and resume his episcopate."[54] The woman, by contrast, "has endured much criticism in the media and through the Anglican community."[55]

The Rev. (later Bishop) Donald Shearman in 1955 began having sex with Beth Heinrich when she was fifteen years old and living in the Anglican St. John's Hostel in Forbes, of which he was warden. Heinrich said that, when Shearman's wife was away, he would lie in bed with her, reading a book about sex techniques and explaining, "This is what God wants it to be."[56]

Shearman expelled the girl from the hostel when she was seventeen for "promiscuity" and he confessed his abuse of her to his bishop, who let him continue in ministry. Over the years, he periodically promised Heinrich that he would leave his wife and six children and live with her, which he did for a period, until fetched home by Dean (later Bishop) Hurford, leaving Heinrich pregnant until she overdosed on sleeping pills and miscarried. Heinrich in 1995 wrote to several Anglican bishops about Shearman's behavior. Hollingworth became involved and found her story dubious. She continued to try to get an apology and that same year met with Hollingworth and Shearman, who claimed the girl had encouraged him. A few months later Hollingworth wrote to the victim and pointed out to her that Bishop Shearman and his wife "have very few financial resources,"[57] and that he fills in at various parishes. Hollingworth advised Shearman to "keep a low profile,"[58] which he did by officiating at Easter services in Brisbane Cathedral. The victim, remembering the parable of the unjust judge, kept pestering Hollingworth for justice. He fended her off with pleas for pity for poor old Shearman: "Your renewed complaint relates to someone who is now well into their seventies, who has sought to resolve the matter with you and exercise contrition in a Christian spirit. I am sorry that you cannot accept the efforts that he and we have made which does allow for a new start with a penitent heart."[59] There was no evidence of penitence. Shearman was finally defrocked in August 2004.

Hollingworth wrote a letter to her parents claiming that the girl "started" the relationship with the abuser.[60] The next day he publicly attacked the family. The *Herald Sun* wrote, "He makes claims this newspaper will not publish about the family of the child at the centre of the latest allegations. The Sunday *Herald Sun* believes the claims threaten the family's well-being and is withholding them."[61] On national television, Hollingworth suggested the woman was at fault, telling the public that in "my belief it was not sex abuse, there was no suggestion of rape or anything like that, quite the contrary. My information is that it was rather the other way around."[62] He realized that he had gone too far by saying this. He wrote to the victim, "What happened to you as a girl at the hostel was wrong and you were in no way responsible for it. I am deeply sorry for the words I used on *Australian Story* that suggested otherwise." Hollingworth refused to meet with her "because he was too busy"[63] and never expressed any sorrow to another victim of Shearman.

Rosemary Ann Jarmyn claimed that Hollingworth raped her when she was at a youth camp in the 1960s. Jarmyn had had a sad childhood; she claimed that she was molested in her foster homes.[64] Hollingworth denied raping her and claimed he was not in the area when the alleged rape occurred. Other witnesses, however, placed him there. The case was dismissed, because Jarmyn committed suicide. She was a disturbed woman, but mental disturbance can be caused by abuse and rape.

Appointed as governor-general (the queen's representative) of Australia in June 2001, Hollingworth had to resign in May 2003, while protesting the "misplaced and unwarranted allegations made against me"[65] and consoling himself with a pension of $184,000 a year, a paneled office in Melbourne's best office building at $100,000 a year, and business-class airplane tickets for himself and his wife for the rest of their lives.

Hollingworth exhibited all the failings of Catholic bishops: a total lack of sympathy to victims combined with a delicacy towards the slightest needs of abusers, attitudes shared by other Anglican clergy. The Rev. Tom Hall of Australia still claims Shearman and Hollingworth were the true victims, and explains, "There is a big difference between a little girl and a fifteen-year-old. One looks like a woman and the other looks like a little girl. It was also a different era back then."[66] In the mode of Dean Swift, Dr. Chris Goddard, director of the Child Abuse and Family research unit, thought Hollingworth should stay on as governor-general, whose role is to "encourage, articulate and represent those things which unite Australia as a nation" because Hollingworth indeed "encouraged, articulated, and represented" some of the less lovely aspects of Australian society: "our unwillingness to treat serious offenses against children as crimes; our inclination to protect and believe the perverted rather than their victims; our desire to blame the victim; and our repeated refusal to take child abuse and its terrible effects seriously."[67] However, these are not uniquely Australian—the United States and the Vatican share these attributes.

The Anglican Church in Australia decided to clean house. Bishop Aspinall in Brisbane "revoked six clergy licenses, suspended five other priests pending investigations, reported forty abuse complaints to police, and settled thirty-one claims via voluntary mediation."[68] Ian George, Anglican archbishop of Adelaide, admitted his failures: "We confess that there have been times when we have not acted with the compassion of God and we have met human suffering with too little concern."[69] Sydney archbishop Peter Jensen realized the folly of putting trust in men rather than God: "We shouldn't have got ourselves into this trouble, because our own Gospel tells us people are sinful and we should not put absolute trust in them. It also tells us that part of repentance is that you lose your ministry."[70] Jensen's remarks imply that clericalism is not just a Catholic disease. Roman Catholic clericalism cannot explain Anglican attitudes and failures, since these are liberal churches with a married clergy and extensive lay involvement in church governance.

## ANGLICANS — CANADA

Kingston is a beautiful town in Ontario, home of Queen's University and of the Anglican Cathedral of St. George which once had a renowned boys' choir. In 1974 the cathedral hired a new choirmaster, John Gallienne. Gallienne was an excellent musician, charming, popular, and most of all married, although some now remember that Gallienne "had been known as a molester of children in a previous parish."[71] Gallienne was a serial pedophile who molested several score, maybe several hundred, boys over sixteen years at the cathedral. He was a true pedophile and lost interest in the boys when their voices changed.

In 1976 Henrik Helmers quit the boys' choir and told his parents he had been molested by Gallienne. They did not know what to do. Their son pleaded with them not to go to the police, and they did not want to destroy Gallienne's reputation. Both the victim and his parents were caught in a traumatic bond with Gallienne. A few months later Henrik killed himself. His parents told the rector, the Rev. David Sinclair, and Gallienne, who were indifferent. With the only witness dead, not much could be done. The parents were assured the church would monitor Gallienne. It didn't. More rumors circulated and more reports were made. Gallienne molested boys in church, in his office, on trips, at summer camp, in their homes. "With access to a steady stream of new recruits, he constantly initiated eight- and nine-year-olds via masturbation, 'grooming' them, going as far with each one as he could, escalating his activities to oral sex, anal penetration, and group sex."[72] The parents adored Gallienne; he was so good with children. Suspicious parents were ostracized and driven from the church—by other parents.

Dean Grahame Baker, rector of the cathedral, had "a complacent, almost fatalist attitude towards child abuse"[73] because he was familiar with it from his youth in England; it was just "a fact of life in those days," Baker told reporters.[74] He admitted to the reporters that he himself had been approached by a man when he was twelve or thirteen. In 1985 he told parents of a victim of Gallienne, "That's how these geniuses are," and, "It happened to me, and I'm okay."[75] Baker kept "forgetting" that parents had complained to him and insisted on treating each incident as an isolated occurrence. Baker was also terrified of legal problems; at another church he had dismissed a choir director for molestation, and the choir director had sued him for wrongful dismissal. He feared Gallienne would do the same, and that Canadian courts would uphold the rights of molesters to molest undisturbed (a reasonable fear in a country that lowered the age of consent for homosexual intercourse to fourteen).

In 1985 Gallienne molested a boy, who told someone not affiliated with the church, an official at a summer choir camp, who went to the police. Gallienne confessed to one slip. The boy was frantic—he was hurting someone whom everyone loved. Gallienne showed apparent remorse and agreed to treatment. The cathedral reacted calmly; it was "just a one-time thing,"[76] said Dean Baker, although he had heard allegations before. Gallienne lied to the therapists he saw; he "did not disclose the full extent of his sexual problems to either of these psychiatrists and they took him at his word that his sexual involvement with boys had been limited in terms of the nature of the sexual behavior and in terms of the number of boys."[77] No attempt was made to investigate the situation; the therapists simply assumed that an admitted child molester would tell the truth. In fact, he had engaged in mutual masturbation, mutual oral-genital sex, and anal intercourse. The police did not follow up, nor did the Children's Aid Society, and Gallienne continued molesting boys for five more years. In 1985 Frances Harkness told Baker that Gallienne may have been molesting a friend of her children. Baker did nothing. Harkness concluded that "everyone involved has sought to protect the reputation of the cathedral. The protection of the children seems always to have been given a lower priority."[78]

In 1987 Tim Franks, a victim who had grown up, gave the police a statement about his molestation, which had ended only when he left the choir in 1978, but he asked them not to investigate his complaint; he also told his fiancée. More parents realized what had happened in the choir. In 1989 an inquiry at Mount Cashel in Newfoundland (see p. 75) revealed massive sexual abuse by Christian Brothers and obstruction of justice by almost everyone in the Newfoundland government who knew about the abuse. In September 1989 Franks, by this time a doctoral student at Harvard, committed suicide; John Gallienne led the choir for the funeral service. Only after the service did Franks's fiancée tell his parents that Gallienne had molested their son. The parents went public and were astonished at the general reaction: "It was as if the victims didn't matter. . . . The children were invisible. Everyone wanted to protect Gallienne."[79] David Hemmings, a friend of the Franks, with whom they had discussed their son's abuse and suicide, was organizing a new boys' school—with Gallienne as music director—and didn't want to jeopardize his investment.[80]

Nonetheless the police became involved and the Kingston *Whig-Standard* reported Gallienne's arrest and the two suicides. The members of St. George's were shocked, not at the abuse, but that the paper blamed Gallienne for the two suicides, "forgetting," according to the tenderhearted Mary E. Wyatt, "the very substantial contribution that he had made over the years to the Kingston musical scene."[81]

Gallienne eventually ended up in court. If he stood trial his victims could testify; he therefore pleaded guilty to twenty counts of sexual abuse so that they would not be heard. He took the victims' impact statements home and had a great time "laughing as he read aloud from the victim-impact statements, cheered on by his wife and her parents."[82] The head of education at the cathedral wrote to the court about Gallienne's "superb professionalism at all times." The head of the cathedral's subcommittee on youth wrote of Gallienne's "desire to do good and contribute to society." Another woman wrote, "Nothing in the world can ever damage the admiration and respect that I will always have for you." On United Church letterhead another member wrote that Gallienne was "imbued" with "Christian principles."[83]

Cathedral warden Janice Deakin explained that "no consistent records were kept. One can't expect ministers to transmit information from one set of wardens to another."[84] Child abuse apparently was not serious enough a matter to keep notes on. The cathedral refused to apologize. The cathedral did not like squealers: "A former church official screamed and swore at

Sandra Rowland for telling a reporter that she, Sandra, had informed the official about Gallienne's pedophilia in 1987."[85] The parents who wanted "systemic change" were told to "forgive and forget"; they then realized that "the victims have been silenced; now it's our turn to get lost. The church's only concern is protecting the hierarchy."[86] Phyllis Mitchell, Gallienne's mother-in-law,[87] wrote to a friend of his and asked, "The Greeks and Romans and Oscar Wilde did it, so what's wrong with sex with children?" Homosexuals aren't imprisoned anymore. "Pedophiles shouldn't be in prison. Most pedophiles aren't violent. I think society will change in regard to sex with children."[88]

The Anglican Church started developing guidelines to deal with sexual abuse. One guideline warned that "painful though it may be, confrontation and disclosure is the only helpful route in the long run."[89] Some parents of victims wanted the truth disclosed about what had happened and who had known about it over the years. Anglican officials did not want to know, and in 1992 announced that there would be no inquiry, but a convener to begin "reconciliation and healing." The victims, according to those parishioners who wanted to know the truth, "have been abandoned and betrayed by the church hierarchy and the congregation at large."[90] The cathedral discontinued the counseling offered by a social worker. The choirs at St. George's, which had 125 singers and a national reputation, are now down to twenty-five members.

Gallienne served a few years in jail, where his wife came for conjugal visits, "bringing lobster and white wine."[91] Although Bishop Peter Mason "has . . . banned Gallienne from any leadership positions within the church particularly those related to music and choirs,"[92] Gallienne has resurfaced, with the approval of the Anglican bishop of Ottawa, as a choir director at St. John's Church in Ottawa, where the website gushes, "We continue to be blessed with the talents of John Gallienne as assistant organist." St. John's describes itself as "an open and affirming congregation," with classes in gay and lesbian spirituality and an active "reintegration program for released sex offenders,"[93] which is trying to persuade the Ottawa synod to allow the blessing of same-sex unions. Its tolerance knows no bounds.

## EPISCOPALIANS — UNITED STATES

The Rev. William Edward Thompson was married, the father of four boys, assistant minister at St. Timothy's Church and headmaster of the church's school in Catonsville, Maryland. In 1988 his wife worked weekends at a hospital while her husband was entertaining boys in his bed. When she discovered homosexual pornography, Vaseline, a picture of her son's buttocks, and pictures of ten- to sixteen- year-old boys, one lying with his anus exposed, another with her husband's hand on his erect penis, she called the police. Thompson admitted the abuse, blamed his "compulsions" and was convicted of five counts of child abuse.[94]

A website, *reformation.com*, has dozens of cases of abuse by Episcopal priests. The former Rev. Donald Shissler had hundreds of pornographic pictures of twenty boys who were from eight to ten years old; he had assaulted numerous boys, including his own foster child.[95] The Rev. Robert K. Orr of Philadelphia, a divorced father of two, trafficked in child pornography on the Internet. His screen name was "xesyob"—"boysex" spelled backward. The pictures were of young boys having sex with each other and with grown men. Orr insisted he only looked and didn't touch, but he went to jail for possession of child pornography.[96]

Several seminarians at Nashotah House, a high-church Episcopal seminary, were charged with abusing children; Russell Martin (whose conviction was overturned),[97] Charles McCray, and Eugene Maxey.[98] Maxey was from Fort Worth and was sponsored by Bishop Clarence Pope. In 1986 a female seminarian, the Rev. Alice Morse, told the dean, Jack Knight, that Maxey was trying to seduce her son, and other students said that Maxey often had boys in his room. Knight dismissed the allegations as "innuendo" and said there was nothing he could do: "It is awkward for me because Bishop Pope . . . is a friend of mine, so I can't do anything." He told the students to stop gossiping about Maxey and to keep their children home. Maxey molested several sons of fellow seminarians, who alleged "everything from fondling to rape, sometimes accompanied by pornography displays and drug use."[99] Maxey got a very young-looking twenty-one-year-old man who was visiting Nashotah drunk and had sex with him—consensual, according to Maxey, nonconsensual according to the man. After they returned home his family reported it to their pastor, who contacted Bishop Pope and the Rev. Rex Perry, a close associate of Pope, and recommended that Maxey not be ordained. Pope instead arranged for Maxey's sponsorship to be transferred to Albany, New York. His final evaluation at the seminary noted Maxey's "talent for working with young people"[100] and Maxey was ordained for Albany, where he molested, according to his own admission, three boys. Maxey claimed to have been abused when he was a child.[101]

At the restrooms in a park in Dallas's White Rock Lake, the Rev. Rex Perry was arrested when he exposed himself and fondled an undercover officer.[102] Perry resigned his parish but obtained a position at a parish in Louisiana. As vice-president of the House of Deputies, the Rev. Wallace E. Frey, married with two children, was in the highest elective position of any priest in the Episcopal church. He fended off a resolution at the 1991 General Convention that would have allowed sexual relations only for married priests. He had a personal interest in the matter. Frey resigned, and his bishop wrote that "he has broken his ordination vows by being involved with sexual misconduct over a lengthy period of time with some male young adults and a teenager under his pastoral care."[103]

Episcopalian bishop David E. Johnson of Boston retired in early 1995. While his wife was out of town he committed suicide by shooting himself, it was claimed, with a rifle, which no one knew he owned.[104] He had cultivated a reputation as an enforcer of rules against sexual abuse but had been engaging in it himself with vulnerable women.[105] Margy Burroughs had been a victim of one priest, and she also represented two victims who complained about a priest to Johnson. Her experience was not good: "None of us could figure out why he kept fussing around and telling the women to just forget it. And then, lo and behold, he's just as guilty as the rest of them."[106] Despite the peculiar circumstances of the "suicide," and the rumors that he had been trading ordination for sexual favors, the *Boston Globe* dropped the story. It did not handle Cardinal Law so discreetly.

A story high in entertainment value is that of a widower, Rev. William Lloyd Andries of Brooklyn. He went to Brazil, fell in love with a hustler, Jairo Pereira, and brought him back to live at his rectory. Andries baptized Pereira, who in his first fervor insisted on a "commitment ceremony" with Andries (Andries admitted this). Long Island bishop Orris Walker heard of this union but decided that everyone involved was a consenting adult, so it was none of his business. The Brazilian, smelling money, then went to *Penthouse* with tales of orgies on the altar at St. Gabriel's church in which the participating priests wore cone bras and Marilyn Monroe wigs (this was not true and *Penthouse* had to retract the article). The Brazilian provided a photo of Andries wearing a jockstrap and turban but *Penthouse* discovered too late that these were not Episcopalian liturgical vestments. The investigating committee said there was no proof that Andries ever did anything so tasteless as having orgies in church, although they concluded that he had been an active homosexual with numerous partners, "some of whom were parishioners and one of whom might have been a minor."[107] The investigators were saddened that they could find no evidence that "those who knew of Andries's sexual behavior, including those who had authority over him, reprimanded him or even brought the inappropriateness of it to his attention."[108] Catholic bishops were not the only ones who thought that episcopal oversight meant that they should overlook outrageous behavior.

Nor is this attitude confined to the male clergy. After two and a half years of stories about child abuse in churches, the ultraliberal defender of gay rights, Rev. Wilifred Allen-Faiella of St. Stephen's Episcopal Church, Coconut Grove, Florida, knowingly let a convicted child molester, Steven Eddie Sypniewski, volunteer at the thrift shop next to the 300-student church school. Sypniewski was arrested in 1992. He had babysat an eight-year-old boy, and, the arrest affidavit continued, "while watching television in the living room, the subject approached the victim and told him he wanted him to remove his pants. The victim attempted to get away from the subject but was ultimately caught. The subject then removed the victim's pants and underwear. He then forced the victim to his hands and knees, as the subject knelt behind him. He then forcibly inserted his penis into the victim's rectum." Sypniewski confessed to this and was given ten years' probation. The Episcopal priestess gave him a key to the school and to the school bathroom. When parents discovered his record on the Internet and notified the school's principal, Carol Shabe, Shabe went to Allen-Faiella, who fired her. Allen-Faiella said, "I think it's being blown totally out of proportion," and anyway she had read "somewhere" that "he was not considered a criminal threat to the community."[109] Liberal female priests can demonstrate the same arrogance and disregard of children as the worst Catholic bishop.

The Rev. John Bennison is pastor of St. John's in Clayton, California. According to the local ABC station, which spoke with his first wife Maggie Thomson and his alleged victims, in the 1970s Bennison announced he wanted an open marriage. This involved having threesomes with thirteen-year-old girls. He tied one girl face down to a bed and forced himself on her; he paid for an abortion for one girl with church money. The Episcopal church learned all this in a 1993 investigation[110]; Bennison's father and brother are Episcopal bishops.[111] Bennison's congregation defends him, and says the priest has been open about "a consensual affair with a young woman." After Bishop Swing told him to resign or be removed, Bennison resigned.

Some reformers, such as the Voice of the Faithful, propose that the Catholic Church be remodeled along Episcopal lines to combat child abuse, but the Episcopal Church has handled abuse incidents as badly as the Catholic Church. There is a sexual underworld of Episcopal priests covering for one another; many priests, some of whom are married, have a taste for adolescent boys. Philip Jenkins, an Episcopalian, warned that "the Episcopal clergy has flourishing gay subcultures quite as active as those rumored in the Roman Church, only far more public."[112] No celibacy, no repression, in the Anglican churches, but sexual abuse occurs just the same and is mishandled just the same. Perhaps the incidence rates of different types of abuse differ, but I have noticed no effort on the part of the Episcopal Church to do its version of the John Jay survey, by which the Catholic Church made an attempt (however imperfect) to ascertain the number of abusers and victims since 1950.

## LIBERAL, EVANGELICAL AND CHARISMATIC FAILURES

The most famous pederast in American history is a man whose stories about boys made him a household word: Horatio Alger. In 1860 Alger became a Unitarian minister in Brewster, Massachusetts, on Cape Cod, where he developed a "special" ministry to boys. Rumors of this ministry came to the parish committee, which demanded an explanation. Alger admitted he had been imprudent and left town that night. The committee wrote to the secretary of the American Unitarian Association: "That Horatio Alger Jr. who has officiated as our minister for about fifteen months past has recently been charged with gross immorality and a most heinous crime, a crime of no less magnitude than the abominable and revolting crime of unnatural familiarity with *boys*, which is too revolting to think of in the most brutal of our race. . . ."[113] The committee thereby made sure that Alger would never serve as a Unitarian minister again; but that was all it did. The New York chapter of the North American Man-Boy Love Association is named after Alger.

Marie Fortune, a minister of the United Church of Christ, describes, using pseudonyms, the depredations of a narcissist in the First Church of a liberal mainline denomination in the suburbs of a small northern city. The First Church replaced a dull, stolid minister with the "young, flashy, dynamic"[114] "Peter Donovan," who was also "handsome, single, and thirty-six years old."[115] He had had to leave at least two, and maybe five, churches because of sexual misconduct, as First Church later discovered, but none of the other churches told the truth when asked for references. Donovan was divorced, but his denomination accepted divorce. He quickly set about revitalizing the First Church, but somehow the focus was always on him. His sermons were entertaining and he employed theatrics to keep the focus on himself.

He began collecting a harem among the women of the church, telling each one that it was necessary to keep the relationship secret for a while but promising to marry someday. A widow sought Donovan's help in dealing with her child who could not accept his father's death. Donovan used her vulnerability to initiate sex. She was dubious, but he reassured her "she should know that he would not suggest anything that was not for her well-being."[116] If seduction didn't work, Donovan raped. When the women accused Donovan to the church and to the denomination, they encountered walls of resistance. The women went to the president of the church, "Lawson," who told them "it would be handled internally and quietly with a minimum of commotion,"[117] but he did nothing except write a letter to them about "pastoral indiscretions" and admitted that "mistakes have been made" but there was "excellent leadership." Lawson promised these mistakes "will not be repeated in the future" and advised them to avoid confronting Donovan because it "would not result in any agreement" and would be "a traumatic experience for all concerned."[118] This church, like all churches, did not like conflict.

Lawson had not done nothing. He had spoken about rumors to Donovan, who admitted his "misbehavior" and promised to be "a good boy."[119] Donovan was in therapy and everything would be all right. After several years of inaction one woman went to the church district and also spoke to a county councilwoman. The district official promised to meet with the church council but instead met privately with Donovan to give him the chance to resign quietly. He refused. The district began looking at formal proceedings. It discovered that the procedures instructed that their first duty was "to clear the reputation of the pastor"[120] and nowhere did the procedures mention justice for victims. The vague procedures made the committee fear that Donovan would sue them. No individual church member, only church leaders, could bring charges. No indication was given that the local church should be informed of the charges. This liberal denomination had also removed any reference to clergy sexual misconduct from its policies lest any gay or lesbian be restricted.[121]

Donovan remained in control of the church and rallied his troops to support him and to attack the women he had abused. He told the hearing committee that the women were conspiring against him, that he was the victim. He threatened to take the church out of the denomination, so the district cut a deal with him and betrayed the women: he would resign but all files and lips would be sealed. The district wanted above all to avoid "embarrassment,"[122] and Donovan got what he wanted: "his reputation was being protected, while the needs of the women and First Church were abandoned."[123]

The women decided to leak the information to the press. One victim then found a message from Donovan on her voicemail: "I'm going to kill you."[124] The papers printed the story; the women felt bound to secrecy by the agreement, but Donovan vigorously defended himself as a victim of gossip. Many church members turned against the women as the source of all the trouble. When he gave his last sermon, "most of the overflow crowd gave him a standing ovation."[125] One victim was present; some church members screamed at her, "You should be stoned. How could you bring this disgrace on our church?"[126] The congregation chose not to believe the accusations against its pastor. The church and district refused to tell the congregation the facts; finally a victim did. Donovan left town and eventually married a nineteen-year-old girl whom he had begun dating when she was fifteen and a member of First Church's youth group.

Fortune identified three factors that allowed Donovan to abuse women. First, the church members' general ignorance of abuse by clergy; second, the failure of a congregational polity to recognize "the power of the pastoral role," and third, "the familial model of congregational life" that creates the possibility of incest and the dynamics of denial that accompany it.[127] This happened in a church with a weak denominational structure; the church could withdraw from the denomination and take its property. One church member said that "she almost wished at one point that the denomination had a bishop who would come to them and say what was what and what would be done about it."[128] The problems are not caused so much by governmental structures as by the flawed character of the people manning them: they want to avoid conflict, even at the cost of sacrificing the victim.

A pastor of the Evangelical Lutheran Church in America, Gerald Patrick Thomas Jr. went to seminary in 1993. In 1996 he worked as an intern near Lubbock, Texas, and befriended two Hispanic boys, ages thirteen and fourteen, to whom he gave tequila and showed pornography. The seminary found out, but Thomas cried and was forgiven. In his last year in seminary the supervisor of a parish afterschool program in which Thomas was working discovered that he was having two sixth-graders stay at his apartment on the weekends. She reported this to the seminary and banned Thomas from her church, but Thomas was ordained and sent to a congregation in Marshall, Texas, where he sought out troubled boys, plied them with gifts, cigarettes, and alcohol and introduced them to "child pornography, videotaped indecency, and sexual assault."[129] The Texas jury gave him 397 years in prison[130] (compare Canadian leniency to John Gallienne, above).

The Lutheran synod official who assigned Thomas to this parish, Earl Eliason, sent with him a letter congratulating the church for getting "a good, new pastor." Eliason had skeletons in his own closet; he had been arrested for indecent exposure in 1987, 1996, and 2003, and in a deposition admitted that he had exposed himself in public restrooms more than a hundred times.[131] The parents of the fourteen boys whom Thomas had molested sued the denomination, which reportedly settled for $40 million while not admitting it had done anything wrong. The local synod blamed everyone else in the denomination and refused to settle, but the jury awarded the nine plaintiffs $36 million. The judge confirmed the award.[132]

The Lutherans try to lessen their guilt by pointing out this is the only lawsuit based on molestation against their denomination, compared to the hundreds against the Catholic Church. But the Catholic Church is larger, and the mainline Protestant denominations have very few children to molest. The United Methodists, for example, have an average age of fifty-seven, and only 4.7% of their members are under age eighteen.[133] The 1998 census reports that 35.5% of Hispanics and 23.8% of non-Hispanic whites are under age eighteen. Thomas targeted Hispanic boys, whom I suspect were not raised as Lutherans. Liberal denominations do not provide as many targets for child molesters; they have a higher percentage of women, especially older women, than Catholic parishes, and therefore provide better targets for the narcissistic harem collectors that Marie Fortune described than for the pedophiles and pederasts found among Catholic clergy.

Evangelical churches, which are often independent, have problems with pastors and adult female members of the congregation. Sometimes the pastor is an evil predator; sometimes he is going through a crisis and falls once with a woman he is counseling. One congregation member committed adultery with her pastor, whose wife found out and told the church board. The church reacted in a familiar way: "In the beginning the leaders sought to preserve the secret. When this failed, they directed their energies to protecting the church's good name and the pastor's reputation. The members of the congregation saddled [the woman] with the blame and excused the pastor's conduct with the typical clichés"—"After all, even the pastor is human!"[134] The incidence of abuse in independent churches is impossible to determine. There is no denomination to report abuse to, there is no central office that keeps records, lawsuits can go after only the very limited assets of the local church, and the church may dissolve and all memory of abuse and abusers be lost by everyone except the lonely victim.

Evangelicals were silent during the revelation of sexual abuse in the Catholic Church. One would have expected a rousing denunciation of corrupt Romanism. In part Evangelicals kept quiet because they had come to see the Catholic Church as an ally against secularism and liberalism. The Rev. Jerry Falwell expressed astonishment that bishops would place abusive priests back into parishes where they had access to boys, but also criticized the media: "I believe the media is acting hypocritically in reporting on the controversy within the Catholic Church. The mainstream media has been typically critical of the leaders of the Boy Scouts of America for attempting to prevent similar situations from becoming pervasive in their organizations by banning homosexual Scout leaders."[135]

But conservative Protestants also remembered the proverb about glass houses, and remembered Jimmy Swaggart, who donned a wig to visit prostitutes and watch them while he masturbated, and Jim and Tammy Bakker, whose adultery and greed were eclipsed only by their tackiness. Even such squeaky-clean organizations as Focus on the Family had adulterous top officials. Memories of such embarrassing revelations induced an unusual silence among evangelicals about Catholic malfeasance.

Some of the worst cases have occurred among independent charismatic-Pentecostal churches. The excitement of the Spirit-filled revival sometimes spills over into sexual excitement, providing victims for the pedophile. Tony Leyva, independent pentecostal child prophet, claimed to have been molested when he was a small boy, and had an intense sexual interest in young teenage boys. When he gave them oral sex, he told them this "special way of loving each other" was for "true Christians like us."[136] All the actions of a prophet, no matter how strange, "were sacrosanct to the faithful Pentecostal." He warned his suspicious wife that "you're touching God's anointed if you say anything about me. Open your mouth and you'll be destroyed."[137] One boy told his parents, who went to an attorney who refused to take the case because the victim came from a "rough family" and Tony was from a "good family" and was "an outstandin' Christian preacher in the community, well known and well liked."[138] Tony toured the South with his Miracle Restoration Revival, raking in the cash and the boys, especially the throw-away boys from poor families. The police in dozens of towns ran him out of town, but they never arrested and prosecuted him. Tony was independent; he belonged to no denomination, and no one could even attempt to discipline him, until he was convicted in state court and pleaded guilty in federal court. After he was released from prison, he fled parole and was arrested in Haiti.[139]

Both six percent of Catholics and six percent of Protestants report that sexual abuse has occurred in their churches,[140] and in fact in 1999 most sexual abuse of children in Protestant churches was committed not by ministers but by laity: "42% of alleged child abusers were volunteers, about 25% were paid staff members [including clergy] and 25% were other children."[141]

## *Marriage and Sexual Abuse*

Sexual transgression in churches with married clergy tends to be adultery of male pastors with female laity, although molestation of minor males is not unknown. Married clergy have problems because it is hard to have two wives. "What wife hasn't been tempted to resent the Church, to be jealous of the time and energy it takes from her and the children?"[142] The demands of the ministry bring temptation. A troubled woman seeks out her minister for counseling and he, unlike her husband, is a good and compassionate listener. "Emotional bonding is often the first step toward infidelity, and nothing facilitates such bonding faster than an emotionally deprived woman and a compassionate pastor whose marriage and personal life are unfulfilling."[143] When the adulterous pastor is exposed, he loses his job, his home, and his circle of friends; his family is involved in his ruin. And this is the fate of a man who is sincere, but who succumbs to normal heterosexual temptations, who is neither a predator nor a monster.

Other ministers feel the sting that accompanies the ministry: laymen do not think a minister is much of a man because religion is an affair for women and children, not real men. Like inner-city adolescent boys, these insecure ministers seek to prove their masculinity by sexual conquests. "Clergy are not perceived as being in the intense, competitive, 'real' world of business. Engaging in affairs can confirm the clergy's sense of male identity."[144]

Marriage does not guard against adultery; it does not even guard against pedophilia and pederasty. Pedophilia is, properly speaking, a sexual interest in children before the age of puberty, and is, if anything, slightly more common among married men than among unmarried, perhaps because married men have more access to small children. Nor does it automatically protect against sexual interest in older children, as we have seen from the Anglican and Episcopal examples.

Ending celibacy would probably not reduce the number of homosexuals in the priesthood, perhaps not even the percentage of homosexuals. Why would married men flock to the Catholic priesthood? The ministry in liberal denominations (and the Catholic Church is more like the liberal, mainline churches than like the Southern Baptists) is not an attractive career for heterosexual men. It is underpaid, and it often subjects a man and his family to humiliating scrutiny. Even churches that have married clergy are unable to fill their pulpits.[145] Liberal Protestant churches may ordain more candidates than the Catholic Church does, but the ordinands cannot find suitable jobs to support families. Protestant churches cannot fill pulpits in small rural churches in dying areas. Why would a Catholic priest with a family want to move to central North Dakota? Richard Schoenherr, an advocate of a married clergy, imagined how marriage would affect appointments: "A parish wanting to hire a particular priest may be disappointed to hear the candidate say, 'Sorry, I must turn down this offer because my wife and I don't like the schools in your district.' A bishop must be more circumspect in making pastoral appointments. Not only educational opportunities but also job possibilities for wives will come into play."[146] Schoenherr did not see that for a church committed to the poor the prospect of family complications is an argument for a celibate clergy.

If continence and celibacy are impossible for heterosexuals, why are they possible for homosexuals? If heterosexual priests are to be allowed, in fact to be encouraged, to marry out of fear that they will become abusers, how is the substantial contingent of homosexual clergy to be treated? Are they to be allowed sexual partners, sending the message that sex outside of marriage is acceptable? Or will marriage be allowed to them? That is, will the Catholic Church, following the path the Episcopal Church has chosen, have to accept homosexually married priests, bishops, and eventually popes? Sister Jane Kelly, a courageous opponent of the abusive Bishop Ziemann, accepts this logic and desires a church "where Catholic priests can choose a life partner and marry, whether they are heterosexual or homosexual."[147]

It is highly unlikely that the Latin Church will accept priests in homosexual marriages, and only slightly less likely that it would allow priests to marry. Marriage might or might not increase the number of priests. It would certainly cause celibacy to vanish among the diocesan clergy. For some sociological reason, it seems to be impossible to have both married and celibate clerics in the same pastoral ministry. In Orthodox churches, by law or custom, priests in pastoral work must be married; celibate clergy are in monasteries or in the bishop's household. Since parish clergy are the ones with whom the laity have the most contact, celibacy tends to fade from the consciousness of the laity, and with it monasticism also tends to fade. Whatever underlying dynamic is present would be made more intense in the Latin Church, because the laity would assume, with some justification, as we have seen in the previous chapter, that unmarried clergy were homosexual.

## CHAPTER THIRTEEN

# CLERICAL ACCOMPLICES

Bishops and priests tolerated abuse and bear the greatest responsibility after the abusers themselves. Bishops were weak in dealing with abuse, a weakness which had its source in their nonconfrontational personalities, personalities which made them attractive to the Vatican as candidates for bishop. Abusers exploited bishops' desires to avoid confrontation and bad publicity. Priests almost always turned a blind eye to abuse going on in their rectories, because they knew the bishops did not want to know about it, and they would be marked as troublemakers for reporting it. Bishops likewise knew that the Vatican did not want to receive cases for involuntary laicization on grounds of sexual abuse. In addition to these personal failures, the Catholic Church suffered from a clericalism in both clergy and laity that led them to ignore any evidence of clerical failures. It also had structural weaknesses that abusers could exploit to escape punishment and to continue abusing.

### *The Bishops*

Some Catholic bishops themselves were directly involved in the abuse of minors or were sexually involved with men or women. Such bishops were not sensitive to the evils of sexual abuse, because they themselves were committing it, and they were also open to blackmail.

Two consecutive bishops of Palm Beach resigned. Bishop Keith Symons admitted he had abused five boys in Florida parishes.[1] Bishop Anthony O'Connell abused a student in a Missouri seminary in the 1970s. He may have been involved in a loose network of abusers.[2] Two abusive bishops in a row in Palm Beach may also not be a coincidence. Bishop Symons welcomed, over the protest of laity, the dissenting propagandists Robert Nugent and Jeannine Gramick (Gramick cannot admit that anything Paul Shanley has done might be criminally wrong).[3] After the revelation of Symons' abuse, priests of the diocese signed a letter supporting the bishop. By coincidence I knew from my college days a homosexual priest who had ended up in Palm Beach. He was charming and showed kindness to me, so I will not name him, but he was clearly a homosexual. The religious order he was in asked him to leave (apparently on other grounds) but he persuaded someone to ordain him and would pop up around the world in various bishops' entourages. Every time I tried to locate him, his previous parish disclaimed any knowledge that he had ever existed. By accident, a friend of mine ran into this priest at the West Palm Beach hospital where he was serving as chaplain. I sent him Christmas cards, but one year's came back marked "deceased." I immediately called, and no one at the hospital wanted to admit that he had ever known the priest. He had died in his mid-fifties, and probably (judging from the reaction of the people in Palm Beach) of AIDS. Again, he was charming and as far as I know not a predator, but why did he end up in Palm Beach?

Bishop Thomas L. Dupré fled Springfield, Massachusetts, hours after being confronted with allegations that he abused boys. He was indicted but escaped prosecution only because of the statute of limitations.[4] Joseph V. Sullivan, bishop of Baton Rouge from 1974 to 1982, and a hero to orthodox Catholics because of his doctrinal strictness, molested a teenage boy in 1975, according to diocesan admissions.[5] There are many other bishops against whom serious accusations have been made, although few accusations have been proved. In 1989 the first bishop was accused: Joseph Ferrario of Honolulu; the lawsuit against him was dismissed for lack of timeliness.[6] Archbishop Robert Sanchez of Santa Fe had to resign in 1993 because of his numerous affairs with young women, some of whom were just over the age of consent.[7] Robert H. Brom was accused by a seminarian of having pressured the seminarian into having sex when Brom was bishop of Duluth, Minnesota. The seminarian retracted the accusation only after receiving a financial settlement.[8] Bishop Joseph Hart was first accused in April 2002.[9] Bishop J. Kendrick Williams of Lexington, Kentucky, resigned in June 2002, shortly after being accused.[10]

The most recent allegations against a bishop concern the retired (in 1998) bishop of Sioux City, Iowa, Lawrence D. Soens. He was ordained in 1950 and served as principal of Regina High School in Iowa City in the Davenport diocese (see Chapter Two) from 1958 to 1967. There, according to seventy-nine former students, Soens became a sadistic reign of terror. Publicly he would engage in "purpling" (Soens admits to this,[11] but denies everything else). "Purpling" involved twisting a boy's nipples. Everyone knew about it. The seventy-five former students also allege that Soens had another practice in the privacy of his office. He would call in a boy for a talk, sit close to him, put his hand inside the boy's pants, and squeeze and torture the testicles and penis, all the while talking normally and smiling. The boys had heard rumors that something bad happened in Soen's office. But they had to go when he summoned them.

The more pious boys, like Michael Gould, had been taught that "priests are the direct hands of God the Almighty. He was taught that he would go to hell if he did not obey the priest." Gould therefore felt God's hands torturing his genitals. Gould knew that Soens wanted him to become sexually aroused, and responded by "biting the inside of my lip so hard that it bled" and then Gould "would basically disappear by letting my mind and head go away."[12] (This is dissociation; see p. 266.) Gould told his father, who did not believe him. Gould tried to flunk out of school to escape Soens. If a student resisted, Soens expelled him.[13] Nor were these incidents always private. Students reported that the school secretary on two occasions saw everything.[14]

The diocese of Davenport, according to a statement filed in court, had been told about Soen's actions. After Soens left Regina he served as rector of St. Ambrose Seminary from 1967 to 1975. D. Michl Uhde was there from 1968 to 1971, and said that "Bishop Lawrence Soens had inappropriate sexual contact with me" there.[15] Uhde said he met with Bishop O'Keefe of Davenport twelve times, and that O'Keefe took careful notes about the alleged abuse, but like all other reports of sexual abuse that were made to O'Keefe, they no longer exist (see p. 57). Soens was appointed bishop of Sioux City in 1983.

In April 2002, someone called Regina Education Center and made allegations against Bishop Soens. He said that he was a student at Regina in 1965–1966 and that Soens had engaged in "purpling" him. When Soens called the student in for a private disciplinary meeting, the student "felt Fr. Soen's finger run up and down his testicle from outside his pants." The Davenport diocese under Bishop Franklin conducted an investigation, and in the course of it a board member of Regina confirmed the "purpling" (also confirmed by Rev. Wally Helms) and also reported "that while principal of Regina, Fr. Soens called him into the office on more than one occasion pinched his testicles between the thumb and forefinger." The investigating committee concluded that "it is much more difficult to begin to assess whether any actions were sexual in any way rather than a disciplinary method," and that "the new Charter [for the Protection of Children and Young People] would not come into play because Bishop Soens is a bishop. However, in looking at the definition of sexual abuse in that Charter, we questioned whether any of this conduct described would be for the adult's gratification."[16] The committee did not think that pinching a boy's testicles or penis was in any way sexual. Bishop Soen's case was sent to the Congregation for Bishops at the Vatican, and there it languishes, year after year.

Bishop Rembert Weakland of Milwaukee,[17] Bishop G. Patrick Ziemann of Santa Rosa,[18] and Bishop James Rausch of Phoenix[19] were all involved in homosexual activity that made them hostile to teenage male victims of sexual abuse and hostile to accusers of priests who had been involved with male teenagers. Bishop Daniel L. Ryan of Springfield, Illinois, has been repeatedly accused by the watchdog group Roman Catholic Faithful of abuse and homosexual relationships. He was the subject of a domestic violence complaint by a male companion in July 2004.[20]

Archbishop Weakland is still a darling of Catholic liberals and is the type of bishop that would be elected if the activist American laity and clergy were able to choose bishops. He has tried to encourage acceptance of homosexual activity (in this matter he had a personal interest) and used nasty language about the victims of child abuse. A conservative Australian journal *AD2000* (in a spirit of fraternal charity Catholic conservatives keep an eye out for the faults of liberals, liberals for the faults of conservatives) commented on his 1992 invitation to Australia:

> Archbishop Weakland is a co-founder of the AIDS Resource Center of Wisconsin/Milwaukee AIDS Project (ARCW/MAP). His name has appeared on official letterhead and he has solicited funds—even donating archdiocesan funds to ARCW/MAP. A recent past-president of this organisation was known to have been a homosexual activist. The organisation distributes AIDS education brochures including instruction on "safe sex" which, apart from advocating condom usage, suggest "Watersports—urinating on each other," mutual masturbation, oral sex and other activities far too distasteful to list here. Additional literature distributed by ARCW/MAP carries advertisements for X-rated gay movies, gay baths and bars, pictures of gay strippers and a Gay Photo Calendar. In 1987, Weakland was asked by a group of lay Catholics to resign his position as co-chairman of the Board of Trustees of ARCW/MAP, but he declined to do so.[21]

Weakland supported pedophiliac dissenting priests:

> One of the several priests who celebrated Masses for Dignity-Milwaukee was Father James L. Arimond. Archbishop Weakland had supported Fr. Arimond against Catholics United for the Faith's 1987 criticisms of his dissenting teachings in a course of lectures, "Homosexuality and Its

> Impact on the Family," given at the archdiocesan Archbishop Cousins Catholic Center. Soon afterwards the Archbishop promoted Fr Arimond to the rank of parish pastor.

Arimond shortly thereafter pleaded no contest when tried for abuse.[22]

Weakland criticized and punished anyone who protested sexual predation by priests:

> In July 1983, a new "pastoral team" was appointed to a Milwaukee parish. When the priest-principal of the parish school (of 15 years) queried the team's immoral/homosexual activities they had him sacked. Three teachers then wrote a letter (signed by one of them) to Archbishop Weakland on the "improper conduct and scandal" of one of the new assistant "team" priests. The Archbishop's response was to threaten the letter's signatory with a libel suit.[23]

Soon afterwards all three teachers were pressured to resign. However, the team-priest in question, Fr. Dennis Pecore, was an abuser. He was convicted of abuse in 1987. While on probation for that conviction he molested his nephew and was again convicted in 1994.[24] Pecore cost the archdiocese about $795,000 in damages and legal costs.[25]

Less than a month later, Milwaukee's diocesan paper, the *Catholic Herald*, reported the archbishop's views on clerical pedophilia (May 26, 1988): "Not all adolescent victims are so innocent. Some can be sexually very active and aggressive and often quite streetwise. We frequently try such adolescents for crimes as adults at that age."[26]

The *Milwaukee Journal-Sentinel* cast a suspicious eye at its former pro-gay hero; it remembered:

> In 1988, Weakland drew a rebuke from one of Wisconsin's highest courts for his defensive response in 1984 to three teachers who blew the whistle to Weakland about sexual abuses by a Milwaukee priest, Father Dennis Pecore, then of Mother of Good Counsel Church, court records show.

> Weakland wrote to the teachers—who had reported their allegations in a letter to Weakland—that "any libelous material found in your letter will be scrutinized carefully by our lawyers."
>
> The Wisconsin Court of Appeals later chastised Weakland's response to the teachers as "abrupt" and "insensitive." In a 1994 interview with a *Milwaukee Journal* reporter, Weakland discussed his belief that true pedophilia among priests was rare. Instead, most of the priests who had trouble were attracted to teenage boys, he said—relationships he referred to as "affairs."
>
> "What happens so often in those cases is that they go on for a few years and then the boy gets a little older and the perpetrator loses interest," Weakland told a reporter. "That is when the squealing comes in and you have to deal with it."[27]

Weakland may well have remembered his former gay lover and feared squealing. Weakland had spent years in Rome as abbot primate of the Benedictines. In that capacity he associated with high officials in the Vatican curia. He then returned to the United States and had a homosexual affair. How likely is it that a man would have his first homosexual affair when he is in his fifties?

In 1993 Stephen J. Cook was suffering from AIDS and as part of his pain therapy underwent hypnosis. Under hypnosis he experiences a flood of memories about having sexual encounters with priests in the 1970s when Cook was in the Cincinnati minor seminary. One was the Rev. Ellis N. Harsham, who used to show seminarians pornographic movies of women having sex with a German shepherd.[28] The other priest, Cook would later allege in a suit filed in November 2003, was the future Cardinal Bernardin, who had also been independently accused of molesting a seminarian in Winona, Wisconsin.[29] Bernardin denied abusing Cook and drew widespread sympathy for his restraint in responding to his accuser. Harsham, although he had been removed from the seminary after admitting a sexual relationship with an adult seminarian, was working as a pastor at a university when the case was filed; he also denied abusing Cook.[30] Cook, as his

AIDS progressed, concluded that his memories recovered under hypnosis were unreliable, withdrew the suit against Bernardin, and was reconciled to Bernardin. However, the suit against Harsham went forward.

Some still have doubts about Bernardin's complete innocence.[31] Bernardin had lived in the Cathedral rectory in Charleston, South Carolina, with a molesting priest, Msgr. Frederick J. Hopwood,[32] but many if not most priests had inadvertently shared a residence with a molester at one time or another during their lives. Bernardin was, however, the Assistant Chancellor in Charleston while Hopwood was abusing, and later arranged for a top Chicago law firm, Meyer, Platt and Brown, the outside counsel for the Archdiocese of Chicago, to defend Hopwood.[33] The accusations by the Winona seminarian whom Bernardin was supposed to have molested were retracted only after the accuser received a $70,000 settlement.[34] Cook also received a settlement from the Archdiocese of Cincinnati for the alleged abuse by Harsham, who resigned from the priesthood.[35] Bernardin, who perhaps only wanted to make a conciliatory gesture to homosexuals who were alienated from the Church, asked the Windy City Gay Men's Chorus to sing at his wake, but this request only aroused further suspicions among those such as James Hitchcock, who had grave doubts about Bernardin's role in the sexual abuse crisis and in the liberalization of the Church.[36]

Most of the bishops were not directly involved in the abuse, but they tolerated it and covered it up. They have been like those bishops described by Catherine of Siena: "They are afraid of offending and making enemies—and all this because of self-love. Sometimes it's just that they would like to keep peace, and this, I tell you, is the worst cruelty one can inflict. If a sore is not cauterized or excised when necessary, but only ointment is applied, not only will it not heal, but it will infect the whole [body], often fatally. . . ."[37] A recent bishop of Munich, looking at such behavior in modern bishops, reflected, "The words of the Bible and of the Church Fathers rang in my ears, those sharp condemnations of shepherds who are like mute dogs; in order to avoid conflicts, they let the poison spread. Peace is not the first civic duty, and a bishop whose only concern is not to have any problems and to gloss over as many conflicts as possible is an image I find repulsive."[38] That bishop, Joseph Ratzinger, is now bishop of Rome, Pope Benedict XVI.

Bishops are chosen by diplomats in Rome because they are both orthodox and conflict-aversive; they are almost always "docile and diffident and make no waves."[39] The few erratic and obstreperous ones like Bishop Kurt Krenn of Sankt Pölten in Austria (see pp. 235–236) cause so much trouble that they make weak bishops look good by comparison.

The Vatican is staffed by diplomats; after Paul VI reorganized the curia, all congregations report to the secretary of state. Diplomacy is therefore the preferred way of dealing with problems, even within the Church. Diplomats hate confrontation; they think that all difficulties can be smoothed over with words, or if they can't be smoothed over, they can be ignored until they go away. The Vatican likes diplomatic types, conciliators, nonconfrontational types, team players, people who don't make waves.[40] The American episcopate is therefore staffed with them. Abusive priests know that their bishops are often cowards who want to avoid confrontation. Therefore abusers can play upon this weakness to get their way with children.

The molesters are sometimes weaklings like Geoghan, but more often they are arrested adolescents. They have an exaggerated adolescent masculinity that both women and adolescent boys find appealing. As arrested adolescents, the molesters are both obsessed with sex and narcissistic. They have also not made the difficult transition to an adult relationship with women.

Arrested adolescent abusers can be very aggressive and make a scene when they do not get their way. A bishop is usually chosen as a bishop because he hates confrontation, and if he takes effective action against a molester he will have confrontation on his hands, with the abuser, with the Vatican, and even with parishioners. The molester is a confidence artist and manipulates the weakness of the bishop. The bishop sometimes doesn't think homosexual activity with children is all that bad, not because he doesn't have children, but because he does not have the normal male's reaction and desire to protect boys from homosexual activity. A liberal bishop like Thomas O'Brien regarded such an attitude as "homophobia" and tolerated sex between boys and priests.[41] Such a bishop doesn't want confrontation; he therefore smoothes things over and tries to keep everyone happy. The parents can be lied to or threatened; the priest can be transferred to another parish, or for appearance's sake put into a treatment center. David Clohessy of SNAP (Survivors' Network of Those Abused by Priests) has been involved in exposing abuse for years; he has concluded that "we were led to the conclusion that what the bishops really lacked was courage. We're still looking for it."[42]

Bishops ignored victims as much as possible, and in this they followed the lead of Pope John Paul II (who to his death refused to meet with any victims). The Kulinas's son was molested in Phoenix: "Never once during the time that this was being reported to the church nor thereafter did the [C]hurch ever say that they were saddened or they were sorry."[43] Most bishops were not interested in protecting children. Archbishop Robert Sanchez of Santa Fe claimed that he made his decision to transfer pedophiles on the basis of his best knowledge. The attorney for the plaintiffs asked him: "But did you ever go to the library, call up a cardinal, get a book, read a magazine, do anything to develop an understanding from what literature or information there was about the consequences of childhood sexual abuse?" Sanchez replied, "No, sir, I did not make that effort."[44]

Bishops lied. The lying was continuous. The Catholic Church in the United States was, as the grand jury said of the archdiocese of Philadelphia, enveloped by a fog of "deceptions, half-truths, and rationalizations."[45] They were always promising parents that the abuser would have no contact with children, and then they put the abuser into a parish. Sanchez was asked under oath why he didn't report the sexual abuse of children to the police; he claimed, "I did not know it was a crime."[46] They lied to the treatment centers and psychologists by concealing information.

Some claim that a diplomat is a man who is hired to lie for his country; bishops seem to think they were consecrated to lie for the Church. Clerical culture, in my experience and in that of many others, is corrupted by endless lies. My wife and a friend met in the parking lot to see our then-pastor about a problem in the school. They flipped coins for who had to go first. My wife won. Her friend went in first to complain. After she left, my wife went in to voice the same complaint. The pastor's response: ""You are the first one ever to complain about this." That was the response given to parents who complained about molesting priests, even if the bishop had heard a dozen such complaints. The secretary of clergy in the Philadelphia archdiocese, Msgr. James Lyons, was frequently asked by victims whether they were "the only one." Lyons "lied and said they were the only one" when he knew they were not.[47] When asked under oath why he lied, Bishop McCormack responded, "I can't explain that."[48] Not only is this lying morally wrong, it destroys the fundamental role of the bishop as a preacher of the gospel. A bishop is consecrated and a successor of the apostles, who gave their lives to testify to the truth of the gospel of Jesus Christ. When a bishop lies, he destroys the value of his testimony to the Gospel.

Bishops often blamed the victims for their abuse. Shanley abused Gregory Ford beginning in 1983, when the boy was six. The boy and his parents sued Cardinal Law. Law responded through his lawyer that "the defendant says that the Plaintiffs were not in the exercise of due care, but rather the negligence of the Plaintiffs contributed to cause the injury or damage complained of. . . ." [49] Cardinal Law was blaming a six-year-old boy for the sexual abuse.

Bishops sometimes punished victims. Joseph Cerniglia was raped by a priest on Easter Sunday in Milwaukee; he sued unsuccessfully. Archbishop Weakland countersued and got a $4,000 judgment for court costs.[50] His mother gave Weakland's auxiliary bishop, Richard J. Sklba, her son's telephone number; Sklba did not call for four years. She finally asked Slkba at a meeting, "You never called my son. Is this a compassionate way to treat people who have suffered so much?"[51] The Nauheimer family of Westchester sued the Rev. Gennaro Gentile of the New York archdiocese for abuse and settled privately.[52] Msgr. Edward O'Donnell, personnel director for Cardinal O'Connor, "went to the pulpit of Holy Name of Mary and suggested to at least some of those in attendance that the case was without merit."[53] The archdiocese also raised in court papers the issue of the Nauheimer family finances and the fact that the father had been abused by a priest. The Rev. Thomas Quinn, director of communications for the Toledo diocese, was informed that Barbara Blaine, founder of SNAP, would speak in September 2002. His response: "Where do we place the bombs? And you can quote me on that."[54]

One of the few bishops to publicize the names of all priests against whom credible accusations had been made was Cardinal William Keeler, archbishop of Baltimore. The rationale behind this act, according to an archdiocesan spokesman, was that it was impossible to locate and contact individually all those who might have been abused as children. A public notification therefore was necessary. If parents had a son who suddenly had behaved very strangely after associating with one of these priests, the parent could now ask the adult son if something had happened. One of the priests of St. Matthew's parish, the parish in which I grew up, was on the list; one of our current neighbors, who also grew up in the parish, now suspects that her brother may have been a victim.

Keeler was widely criticized for publishing the list; I do not think that the purpose of publishing the list was made clear enough. Most saw it as Keeler's attempt to curry favor with the media. Almost all priests objected to it: they had an attitude of privilege, that a priest should not suffer any temporal consequences if he had done something wrong. Clericalism is deeply ingrained. Keeler's predecessor, Archbishop Borders, had also let priests do almost anything they wanted, depleting the endowment of the archdiocese in the process. Few bishops, even the ones who had promised to do so, followed Keeler's example, probably because Rome told them not to, as an inside source in the Baltimore archdiocese indicated to me.

## *Priests*

Priests almost always turned a blind eye to abuse. Msgr. Richard S. Sniezyk, who was left in charge of the Springfield diocese after Bishop Dupré disappeared, explained that the sexual abuse scandals in the United States were caused by "a belief among some priests in the 1960s, '70s, and '80s that sex with young men was acceptable." Sniezyk claimed that "no one thought much about it" and that "the whole atmosphere out there was, it was OK, it was OK to do,"[55] but now priests did not hold such permissive beliefs abut sex. Sniezyk's burst of candor (of which he quickly repented) shows that in some clerical circles sex with young men, in which category priests put any male over the age of puberty, was a harmless pastime. Even priests who did not engage in it did not feel any real harm was being done to the victims, and therefore they never confronted the evil.

Even if a decent priest warned about an erratic or dangerous priest, he was ignored. Father Gerard Creighton had a foul mouth, was in love with money, and was a gun nut.[56] A fellow priest, John J. McNally, who had to share a parish with Creighton, complained to Cardinal Medeiros about him. He then wrote to Medeiros,

> When I talked with you on the telephone a month ago, you asked me if I thought the solution was to shoot this man. Even though you were being facetious, you put your finger on a real concern. I already told you that he keeps a gun beside his bed and it is not unheard of for a man who is emotionally unstable to go berserk with a gun. Apart from shooting, however, it seems to be that, if the [C]hurch's administrative system has no means of dealing with a man of this type, then there is something lacking in the system."

McNally could not comprehend why everyone was being sacrificed to keep a maniac in the priesthood: "Why must we always place the immediate accommodation of the priest above the good of the [C]hurch? Why should so many people have to be abused and insulted and alienated from the [C]hurch, just so we can give this man a place to sleep? We seem to have our values confused."[57] Why indeed? Laziness, clericalism, administrative incompetence, or a fear of opening closets and revealing too many skeletons.

Bishops punished priests who broke the code of silence. The Rev. John Conley came home in 1997 to his rectory in Burlingame in the San Francisco archdiocese and discovered a very suspicious scene: his pastor, the Rev. James Aylward, "wrestling" with a fifteen-year-old boy. Conley spoke with Bishop McGrath about calling the police. McGrath asked him, "Are you sure you really want to do this? Prior to this we've always handled these things in-house."[58] Conley called the police but their investigation was inconclusive. The archdiocese transferred Aylward, who gave Conley a bad report for troublemaking. The archdiocese thereafter placed Conley on leave, said he "was in need of psychological therapy," "falsely informed other clergy and members of the archdiocese that he [Conley] had committed inappropriate conduct during church functions," and made him "undergo an inpatient evaluation of his mental state at a qualified therapeutic institution as a condition for his return to pastoral duties."[59] The archdiocese apparently thought that Conley must be crazy not to realize that teenage boys are the lawful prey of priests. The archdiocesean spokesman, Maurice Healy, claimed Conley was engaged in a "witch hunt" against the innocent Aylward.[60]

The boy sued and Aylward confessed to "a history of inappropriate touching of minor boys."[61] The boy received $750,000 from the San Francisco archdiocese for this "wrestling" and related activities by Aylward.[62] Conley also sued the archdiocese. He was a lawyer and a federal prosecutor (assistant U. S. attorney) before his ordination at age forty-nine, and knew that he was being punished for fulfilling his duty as a citizen to protect children. The archdiocese settled, gave him an undisclosed amount, a fully funded retirement at fifty-eight as a priest in good standing, and a two-bedroom apartment. Unfortunately Archbishop Levada of San Francisco, now the head of the Congregation for the Doctrine of the Faith and in charge of sexual abuse cases, didn't have to pay for this out of his personal assets. Conley also made the archdiocese issue this statement: "The archdiocese and Father Conley have agreed that Father Conley was right in what he did in reporting this incident to the police."[63] Levada didn't believe the statement that he had been forced to make. When asked in a deposition, "Based upon what [Conley] related to you [about] what he saw, would you have reported it to the police?" Levada answered, "I don't think so," and when asked again said, "I thought I said 'no' to that question."[64]

But most priests don't have the legal expertise or courage that Conley had, and are dependent upon bishops who want to keep abuse hidden.

## *The Vatican*

The Vatican—the pope and the curial officials he appoints—bears much responsibility for the sexual abuse of minors in the United States and throughout the world.[65] Some of the failures were caused by flawed policies which inadvertently allowed sexual abuse to flourish.[66] The Vatican created organizational conditions that allowed the abuse to go on with little or no correction. Some of the conditions grew up haphazardly as the Church was centralized.

By centralizing so much power in itself, the papacy has made it impossible for groups of bishops to discipline erring fellow bishops, made it impossible for bishops to discipline priests who are members of religious orders, and made it very difficult for bishops to discipline their own diocesan priests. This centralization does not even give the Church a unified administration. The Church is fragmented, because lines of administration extend upward to the papacy, but the papacy is unwilling or unable to exert strong disciplinary power. Horizontal communication is largely nonexistent. Bishops do not communicate very much with each other, nor do religious orders communicate with each other or with bishops.

The Vatican seems to follow the policy of divide and rule. The bishops are commanded to enforce laws against the lower clergy; the lower clergy then appeal to the Vatican, which protects them from the bishop's attempted enforcement. The lower clergy are then grateful to the Vatican and loyal to the pope. This may have made some sense when bishops were appointed not by the pope but by secular authorities, but it makes no sense when the bishops are appointed by the Vatican. Why does the Vatican appoint bishops and then not allow them to govern their clergy?

Bishops also exercise little or no oversight over religious orders. Orders are often set up on international lines. Their work, especially missionary work, may take them anywhere in the world; it therefore makes sense for them to report directly to the universal authority of the pope rather than to the dozens or hundreds of bishops in whose dioceses they happen to operate. But with such vast numbers to supervise, the pope gives no supervision. This works as long as religious priests are sincere and sane, but does not work when orders become corrupt or disordered.

The bishop has no direct authority over the religious priests in his diocese. These belong to orders that are independent and are ultimately responsible to the pope, not to a bishop. In Ireland Chris Moore investigated the pedophile Father Brendan Smyth, a Norbertine priest. Moore was surprised to discover: "It [the Norbertine order] appears to be entirely autonomous, answerable to no one within the Church—not to the bishop of the diocese, much less to the All Ireland Primate." Moore continues, "It is nothing short of amazing that it [the Catholic Church] tolerates religious orders where the Irish Church itself is not recognized as the authority. As we shall see, this is one of the factors which may have permitted the cover-up [of Smyth's pedophilia] to continue for as long as it did."[67]

This disorganization is further compounded by the divisions in the Church that began after Vatican II. The divisions obviously extend to the curia itself. One curial official says that homosexuals should not be ordained, another sees no problem with it. As the then Cardinal Ratzinger, now Pope Benedict XVI, recognized, there are two churches that uneasily coexist within the administrative framework of the Catholic Church; there are probably more than two, and they may be mutually incompatible, as they are in the Anglican Church in which evangelicals and high church coexist uneasily, but opponents of homosexual behavior and proponents of homosexual marriage are straining the Anglican communion to the breaking point.

The curia reports not directly to the pope, but to the secretary of state, a diplomat, who sees his role as mediating among various factions in the Church, as if they were sovereign nations. In the current setup of the curia under the secretary of state, the Holy See has become simply an administrative and diplomatic organ, which could function equally well if its doctrine were Zoroastrian or Confucian. If the purpose of the papal office is, however, to preserve the purity of the faith handed down from the apostles, the curial offices should report to the Congregation for the Doctrine of the Faith.

For centuries, the Vatican has issued various laws and then undermined bishops who tried to enforce them. As Henry Lea pointed out, in the Middle Ages the Vatican demanded celibacy of the clergy and then prevented bishops from enforcing celibacy: "not only did the claims of the papal chancery thus interfere with the execution of the law by its power of granting dispensations, but its appellate jurisdiction was constantly used to avert punishment from the worst offenders."[68] Lea blames the "centralization of all power in the papal court" which continues to the present and "the venality of the Roman officials" as chief obstacles to bishops who tried to reform the clergy. The Church as a whole was left without clear guidance because of the "uncertainty of this conflicting legislation, at times enforced and at times dispensed with by the supreme power." The wavering of the Vatican sent conflicting messages about clerical celibacy. At the Council of Trent, for example, the "archbishop of Sassari declared that more than half of the clerics in his diocese were exempt from his jurisdiction. How could the prohibitions against concubinary priests be made effective under these circumstances?"[69]

Pope Paul VI undermined the bishops who tried to enforce the teaching of *Humanae Vitae*. Bishops who tried to discipline sexually abusive clergy were also stymied and got the message—don't try to enforce discipline.[70] The American bishops learned "that the Vatican would not support them in maintaining discipline among priests and doctrinal integrity among theologians, even in order to safeguard what the Vatican believed to be basic moral truths, if the result were to be a public uproar."[71] Paul VI told the bishops that these priests should not be disciplined, that the force of truth was all that was necessary eventually to convince dissenters. (It wasn't.) Bishops were not especially inclined to engage in confrontation in any case, and Rome had sent a clear signal not to confront erring priests. When Shanley preached man-boy love and it was reported to the bishops of Boston, they did nothing because they knew that was what Rome wanted them to do: nothing.

In 1989 the American bishops asked the Vatican to give bishops the power to laicize abusive priests. The Vatican refused the request. Archbishop Agnolo explained that "canon law does not allow this power to be exercised by individual bishops."[72] If a bishop did try to discipline a sinning priest, he found that the priest could use appeals to Rome to tie up the process for years and to consume massive amounts of the bishop's time. It is a situation like that of tenured teachers in public schools. The rules allow a principal to fire a bad teacher, but that is all he can do. It will take all his time. It is better to "pass the trash": transfer the priest within the diocese, or palm him off on another diocese. Bishop Donald Wuerl of Pittsburgh was one of the few bishops willing to go to Rome in person to get rid of an abusive priest. He found the process lengthy, complicated, and time consuming. The other bishops didn't have the time, energy, or inclination to fight Rome. Why did Rome create such a process? Is this simply the natural tendency of any bureaucracy to elevate procedure over substance, or is it a policy to prevent, if at all possible, any priest from ever being removed involuntarily?

The Vatican also thought that the laity must be protected from the knowledge that priests were not perfect. In 1993 the Vatican thought that the main problem was not the abuse but the press: Pope John Paul II said that "it is unacceptable for moral evil to be treated as an occasion for sensationalism" because "harm is done to the fundamental right of individuals not to be easily exposed to the ridicule of public opinion."[73] That is, priests who molest children have a right to have their reputation protected and not to be exposed to public obloquy. Rev. Gianfranco Ghirlanda, dean of the canon law faculty at Gregorian University in Rome, wrote in the authoritative *Civiltà Cattolica* that "a priest who is reassigned to a new parish after being treated because of a history of sexual abuse should not have his 'good reputation' ruined by having his background revealed to the new parish."[74] The Vatican believes that clergy have the right to a good reputation, however undeserved.

The Vatican knew what was going on in the United States. It received complete dossiers with confessions of priest child molesters who were asking to be laicized. The pope or a high official reviews every case. No one in the Vatican, as far as is known, no pope, no cardinal, has ever expressed anything beyond generalities, has ever expressed any concern for particular victims or has ever inquired about their needs.

The bishops took the failure of the Vatican to criticize their handling of abuse cases as implicit approval of the way they were handling those cases: give the priest every chance, year after year, no matter how many children he molested, no matter how many families had their faith destroyed, no matter how many boys committed suicide. Archbishop Julián Herranz, a member of Opus Dei and the president of the Pontifical Council for the Interpretation of Legislative Texts, said that the financial settlements with victims were "unwarranted." He added "that requiring church leaders to report all abuse accusations to the civil authorities was unnecessary; he called the turning over of records on abusive priests by dozens of American bishops the result of 'an emotional wave of public clamor.'"[75] Everything the bishops did must be directed to one goal: preserving the clerical career.

## *Clericalism*

Any professional group tends to have an esprit de corps and to protect its reputation. Some drum out those who have disgraced the profession. Officer corps have colorful rituals for this; sometimes they give the disgraced officer a gun and leave him alone in a room—he knows what he is expected to do. But this group solidarity can sometimes lead a profession to protect its erring members without correcting them. Doctors don't like to turn in doctors who have committed malpractice; policemen are hesitant to turn in corrupt officers.

Institutions become self-perpetuating and forget their purpose in an attempt at self-preservation. Marie Fortune identifies this dynamic:

> Institutions also share a pattern of response to the misconduct of an authorized representative and to the public disclosure of that misconduct.

> An institution acts first on what it perceives to be its self-interest. Seldom does it identify its self-interest to be the same as the interest of the people it is supposed to serve. Thus it tries to protect itself by preventing disclosure of professional misconduct. It prefers instead to shoot the messenger, that is, to denigrate whoever had the courage to tell the secret.[76]

The pattern of response in a liberal Protestant church is much the same as in a Catholic diocese. Therefore, uniquely Catholic institutions and weaknesses cannot be blamed for sexual abuse. However, clericalism is stronger in the Catholic Church than in other churches because of the unique claims of the Catholic clergy.[77]

Too often the clergy view the laity as providing the clergy an opportunity to practice their métier. This is a common human failing. Among the French, the customer exists as a necessary evil whose only purpose is to allow the professional to practice his métier. This human folly is amusing in an elevator operator at the Eiffel Tower;[78] it is a calamity when it involves the Christian clergy.

To be afflicted by clericalism, a church must have a clergy, that is, a group within the church officially set apart to perform special functions, especially of government. Almost all Christian churches have something like a clergy; they may be Quaker clerks or Orthodox hierarchs, but someone has to begin and end worship and send out notices. Protestants tend to believe in the priesthood of all believers in the sense that every Christian can perform every sacramental function, but that for good order certain members are set aside and trained to perform these functions. Catholic and Orthodox believe that the fundamental structure of the Church is of divine origin: bishops are successors to the apostles in governing the Church, and priests are sharers in the ministry of bishops. Only a priest can confect (this is the technical term) the Eucharist or administer several of the sacraments.

The Catholic Church has developed an elaborate theology of the ordained ministry. Ordination is one of the seven sacraments, and it imprints an indelible character on the soul. Baptism also does this in a more fundamental manner. If someone is baptized, he cannot be rebaptized if he denies the faith and then returns to it. Similarly, a priest is not reordained if he leaves active ministry and returns to it, or even if he denies Christianity and then returns to it (as happened in the great persecutions in the Roman Empire).

This character imprinted on the soul enables the priest to administer the sacraments, especially to confect the Eucharist. Only an ordained priest may consecrate bread and wine, making them into the Body and Blood of Jesus Christ. The eucharistic action is the heart of the Church. In it the Church offers to the Father the sacrificed Son, the Lamb forever slain, and enters into the mystery of his death and resurrection. The Eucharist is completed when the faithful receive the Body and Blood and are transformed into the Body of Christ.

The fullness of the priesthood resides in the bishop; he alone can ordain new priests and bishops. Otherwise, a priest can perform all the other sacraments. All the non-sacramental functions of the priest flow from the centrality of the Eucharist. He preaches the word of God to prepare the faithful to receive the Eucharist. He absolves from sin so that a sinful laity may worthily receive the Eucharist. Because he must preach rightly and judge rightly, theology, both dogmatic and moral, was developed.

A priest is an *alter Christus*, another Christ. So is every Christian. "I live now, not I, but it is Christ who lives in me," should be said by every Christian. This was long forgotten in the emphasis on the importance of the ordained priesthood. The priest is more an *alter Christus* than a layman only because he is set apart as a minister of the sacraments, especially the Eucharist. The primary and true minister of the sacraments is Christ. The recipients of the sacrament do not have to worry about the state of the priest's soul when they receive the Eucharist and absolution because it is Christ who acts through the human minister, however imperfect and unworthy he is. Of course, a priest, like all Christians, is called to holiness, and because of his close association with the sacraments of salvation and his role as governor of the community, he should be an example of holiness to his flock. However, he remains subject to the same temptations as other

Christians and is a weak, fallible, sinful human being who is obliged to repent and to seek the mercy of God.

After he converted to Christianity, Constantine wished to honor the Church, and he began by granting the clergy special privileges and exemptions, especially exemption from taxation. The legal privileges of the clergy were a source of endless conflict in the Middle Ages. Once property was given to any church institution, it was out of the reach of taxes, and the Church could not be forced to give the property up. Kings were always scraping around for money and coveting church property. Henry VIII finally pounced, but he only did what every other king had been tempted to do. The persons of the clergy were also exempt from many laws. This was the source of the conflict between Henry II and Thomas à Becket, his counselor whom he made archbishop of Canterbury. The king wanted to punish criminous clerks, and Thomas insisted that they be punished by the Church alone. Until the eighteenth century, a criminal in England who could recite the Our Father in Latin had benefit of clergy and could not be executed.

The ordained priesthood was emphasized especially after the Council of Trent in reaction to Protestants who tended to think that all Christians (at least all male Christians) were equally priests, or who tended to deemphasize the sacraments. But the ordained priesthood makes sense only within the larger priesthood of all the faithful. When they are baptized, all Christians are made into priests, prophets, and kings. Every Christian must fulfill his destiny by offering his life and indeed his whole world to God in thanksgiving (Eucharist); the ordained priesthood was established to facilitate the laity in their basic task of Christian transformation. The ordained priesthood exists for the laity, not the other way around.

Even Protestants suffer from clericalism, but Catholics are especially susceptible to it. In response to Protestant attacks, the Roman Catholic Church in the Counter-Reformation exalted the office of priest and bishop and pope. The Church was seen mostly as a machine for validly administering the sacraments. Since the clergy were the primary administers of the sacraments, they were seen as "The Church." Later, in the eighteenth and nineteenth centuries, liberalism attacked the union of church and state, and the Roman Catholic Church developed an integralist strain, which insisted that the clergy should be involved in giving direction to the state. Lay Catholics were to carry out the orders of the clergy.

In responding to Protestantism, Catholicism has too often emphasized the effect of ordination in conforming a Christian to Christ and neglected the fundamental change that baptism works in a Christian. Contributing to this was a faulty theology of the states of perfection, a theology usually blamed on the Jesuits (especially by the Dominicans). The laity were given the impression that only those who had entered a religious order were called to observe the counsels of perfection—poverty, chastity, and obedience. The laity were not bound to seek sanctity, but only to keep the commandments. The laity were therefore second-class Christians, and members of religious orders were first-class Christians. Only priests and religious took Christianity seriously; the laity just escaped hell by avoiding mortal sin. Most priests are not members of religious orders, but the laity usually conflated religious and diocesan priests. Only church work was God's work; life in the world was a distraction from leading the Christian life. This misunderstanding was attacked by figures as diverse as Martin Luther and Josémaria Escriva, founder of Opus Dei.[79]

Clericalism in the modern world is "the erroneous belief that clerics form a special elite within the Church and that because of their powers as sacramental ministers, they are superior to the laity, are deserving of special and preferential treatment and finally, have a closer relationship to God."[80] One can accept the full and high view of the Catholic priesthood and not be a clericalist. Obviously ordination does not automatically make a priest a saint, any more than the greater sacrament of baptism automatically makes any Christian a saint. The ambiguity of the word "superior" is the source of much of the trouble. Because priests and bishops, who have the fullness of priesthood, are the ministers of the sacraments, they are also responsible for governing the sacramental order of the Church, which is essentially a sacramental reality. Since priests are the governors of the sacraments, they are, in this sense, and in this sense only, the superiors of the laity. No one in a religious order, such as the Dominicans or the Jesuits, thinks that the authorities of the order, the superiors, are superiors in any sense other than having governing authority. But those who possess governing authority are tempted to hide their mistakes so as not to call their authority into question.

Clericalism equates the Church and the clergy. The clergy are "really" the Church; the Christian, if he is serious, will be a priest or religious. The laity's job is to pray, pay, and obey. The clergy, in the clericalist mind, "are meant to be the active, dominant elite in the Church, and laymen the passive, subservient mass."[81] Priests are to be the experts in everything, and the Catholic bishops have taken it upon themselves to give their opinions on foreign policy, housing, the minimum wage, and a host of other issues which no doubt have moral dimensions, but in which Catholic laity, not clergy, are the real experts. This confusion of the secular and sacramental realms adds a further distortion to clericalism. The United States has not really fully experienced integralist clericalism because of the American separation of church and state, but such clericalism led to bitter anticlericalism in Catholic societies such as Spain, Italy, and Québec, and a rejection of Catholicism along with a rejection of the secular authority of the clergy.

In the poor immigrant Church in the United States, the clergy were often the only educated members, and were subjected to endless attacks by Know-Nothings and Nativists. The clergy provided a career path for poor Catholic boys who would otherwise have had no outlets for their abilities. Poor Catholics wanted their clergy to live well and be socially respected. The clergy internalized this exaltation and forgot the proverb about pride going before destruction. They began thinking of themselves as "The Church," and saw any attack on their prestige and position as an attack on Christianity and, indeed, on God. This fed both a group and an individual narcissism. The clergy saw everything, including child abuse, only in terms of possible consequences for itself. Individual child abusers often would have no feeling for the pain they caused their victims. They lived in a solipsistic world, but in this they mirrored the communal culture of the clergy which also lived in a form of group solipsism.

The laity were taught, or rather mistaught, that the priest was an *alter Christus* in that he was uniquely holy. The laity placed the priest on a pedestal and regarded him as above human weakness. Some priests enjoyed this adulation; a few grossly misused it. But the laity also derived a benefit from clericalism. If the métier of the priest was to be holy, then the layman did not have to worry about holiness—he left it to the priest. If the priest was by virtue of his ordination a shining example of holiness, the laity did not have to use ordinary human and supernatural prudence in dealing with priests. Such a situation is bad for the souls of priests, even if they are sincere.

At college I once walked into the cafeteria and saw two people I knew, a priest who taught at the college and a seminarian. They were sitting at a table and not talking. I walked over with my tray, set it down at the table, and cheerily greeted them both. The priest rose in a towering rage and thundered, "Never sit at a table with a priest without asking his permission!" He stormed off, leaving the seminarian and me in embarrassed silence. The priest was a religious vowed to poverty, chastity, and obedience, a theologian who served on a papal commission. I found out later that, according to common knowledge on campus, he was also an active homosexual who had collected a group of college students he liked to have sex with. He had an off-campus apartment, furnished with antiques and oriental rugs, that he used as his love nest. But he was ordained, and that made him better than everyone else, and mere laity were expected to grovel at his feet.

The laity have their own lives to live, their families to care for, and their work in the world to do. That is their Christian vocation. They do not want to sit on committees and share church government. They wish the clergy would govern the Church well. They will give advice when asked for, and they need to keep an eye on clerical affairs because the clergy are subject to individual and corporate temptations. A system of checks and balances is necessary in the Church. This is a minor (although important) role of the laity and should not distract the laity from its main task. The clergy should be largely self-governing, but lay involvement is necessary so that clerical self-respect does not turn into clerical arrogance, which inevitably leads to clerical malfeasance.

## *A Case of Benefit of Clergy*

The Rev. Michael Orsi of Camden, New Jersey, in 2003 offered a defense of old-fashioned clericalism. He saw no reason that criminal priests should be subject to the state, invoking Thomas à Becket's quarrel with Henry II: "There are numerous stories in every chancery office of recalcitrant clergy who have been released to their bishop by the police or district attorney with confidence that the problem would be handled for the benefit and satisfaction of all involved."[82] He admitted that the bishops "became negligent" but maintained that this procedure "helped maintain the integrity of the Church" and "protected the good name of the clergy in general."[83] Orsi claimed that "it has always been accepted that certain crimes should be addressed internally by the Church," and that efforts at reformation "with suspension and laicization as final penalties satisfied everyone."[84]

Orsi forthrightly defended "clerical privilege"[85] because the "clergy represents, at least theoretically, the best and most virtuous members of a community."[86] By turning over accusations of child molestation to the state, "the bishops have encouraged the state to further degrade society by diminishing its regard for religion *since the Church is often identified by its clergy*"[87] (emphasis added). Orsi disagreed with exemptions from the statute of limitations (although such statutes often serve to protect criminals who victimize children) and condemned Megan's Law (upheld by the Supreme Court). Orsi thought that bishops should have refused to hand over the names of accused priests and risked jail.[88]

Orsi's conception of the clerical status has little to do with the New Testament priesthood; it is instead a last relic of the Ancien Régime, in which members of society had unequal status before the law. Such inequality is always irritating, and is often used to protect privileged malefactors—and Orsi resents the loss of privilege. The atmosphere of clericalism is not good even for a sincere man. Power, privilege, and secrecy are not good for the soul, and neither is unearned deference.

What is Orsi defending? We shall examine the type of behavior that bishops found tolerable, and led them at most to transfer a priest from one parish to another. Terry McAteer's father became Catholic for political reasons, and linked up with the smooth operator, the Rev. Peter Keegan, who went by "Pete" and who let the father know that "the rules can be bent."[89] While running for mayor of San Francisco in 1967 the father died, and Keegan became his widow's escort at social and political events. Keegan also helped with the children. Keegan took Terry to Disneyland in 1967 and molested him. Terry reported that Keegan "was a big man, 6 feet tall and about 230 pounds. . . . I was what, 70 pounds? He used his weight to force me. If I resisted doing what he wanted, he would lay on top of me and push my face into the pillow."[91] Keegan turned the boy upside down, put his genitals in the boy's face, and then, as McAteer remembers, "put his penis into my mouth and ejaculated."[91] And all the time, McAteer said, Keegan was saying, "Father loves you," and, "Your mother is fine with this." McAteer reflected, "I was ten; it was 1967. At ten, you are so naive." Afterward, the priest cooed to him, "Let this be our secret, just between you and me."[92]

> The next day, going from ride to ride at Disneyland, he said, Keegan watched him like a hawk, not allowing him to phone home. "I think I was one of the first boys he molested. He was still scared of being exposed." That night, exhausted from the busy day, Terry fell asleep quickly. But at 5 a.m., the priest crept back into his bed. And this time he was much more violent, more brutal. McAteer refused to give in, but Keegan nearly suffocated him, and McAteer remembers that "his erect adult penis was forced into a small boy's anus. It was so painful I screamed while he struggled to get his penis into me. . . . I had ruptured a number of blood vessels in my anus."[93] "I was fighting to get away. There was blood all over the sheets. I'm in excruciating pain. My pajamas got ripped. Finally, I ran into the bathroom and locked the door."[94]

In 1994 McAteer read that Keegan had been accused of molesting other boys. "I came home in the afternoon, and Liz [his wife] handed me the *Chronicle* and said, 'You'd better sit down and read this.' I can remember her words. I picked up the front page, and there was a suit filed by three

Santa Rosa kids claiming that they had been molested by Peter Keegan. And the story said the diocese of Santa Rosa and the archdiocese of San Francisco denied any prior knowledge of any wrongdoing by Peter Keegan. Looking up at Liz, my first words were, 'They're lying.' She said, 'I know.'"[95]

In 1977, as a twenty-year-old history student at the University of California at Berkeley, Terry McAteer had taken a huge step. He said, "I finally realized the severity of what had happened to me. I put two and two together and understood why Father Keegan had been transferred from parish to parish. From St. Cecelia's to St. Vincent de Paul, to Epiphany, to Mary's Help Hospital. And so I went to the [C]hurch." Until then, he had never told a soul about what Father Pete Keegan did to him—not even his mother. McAteer asked Vincent Ring, his high-school history teacher at St. Ignatius and now a close and respected friend—as well as a priest—to help him approach the archdiocese of San Francisco. There, they spoke to the number two man in charge, Msgr. Patrick McGrath. "I bared my soul," said McAteer. "It was a pretty emotional day. It wasn't so much that I needed to get it off my chest, but that I just knew other boys were involved."[96]

McGrath promised to talk to Archbishop John Quinn and to get back to McAteer. Two weeks later came a letter saying that Keegan had just been transferred to a parish in Santa Rosa. "He wrote that while they were sorry about what had happened to me, they had no other knowledge of this and were taking no other action," said McAteer. "It was so unfair. I thought that they would do something about Father Keegan."[97]

But of course the bishop did nothing and in fact lied to McAteer. McAteer said that he since has learned that the Church knew about Keegan's sexually abusive behavior long before McAteer told them. "There had been multiple complaints. There was a police report in 1971. A parent had gone to the police. But in those days you didn't go and haul a priest into jail! The police would say, 'We'll let the archdiocese deal with this.' The [C]hurch had huge power in San Francisco."[98]

McAteer warned Keegan's new bishop, who again lied to him; McAteer wasn't deterred, however. He sent a letter to the bishop in Santa Rosa, warning him about his new priest: "And Bishop Hurley wrote me saying, 'thank you, but he's not in a parish where he'll have contact with children.' Of course, now we know that many, many of the boys he molested were in Santa Rosa."[99] Archbishop Quinn of San Francisco, after spending $2.4 million in legal costs in lawsuits with victims, recommended Keegan for a job at an orphanage in Tijuana, Mexico, where Keegan would be safe from American justice. He also gave him $900 a month.[100]

Keegan was asked by a reporter who went to see him in Mexico about the charges by Terry McAteer. The priest said Terry was a nice Catholic boy from a nice family, but he hadn't seen him for thirty years, and none of what he said was true. The reporter taped him during the day. "They showed him walking down the street, hand in hand with two little boys," said McAteer. "It was as repulsive as can be."[101] But Keegan could afford to be arrogant. He knew that in Mexico he was out of the reach of American courts for civil actions. And with a six-year statute of limitations in criminal cases, the priest may have thought he was protected from extradition. Clericalism makes priests think they are immune from punishment by the law, and evil priests will exploit that immunity to hurt children.

Although Orsi may have been temporarily disappointed when the Mexican police arrested Keegan on March 1, 2003, clerical immunity was vindicated nevertheless. The Supreme Court invalidated California's retroactive extension of the statute of limitations on child abuse, giving Keegan a get-out-of-jail-free card. The bishops had protected him from the law until he was out of reach of the justice of man.

## CHAPTER FOURTEEN

# LAY ACCOMPLICES

PHIL SAVIANO, a victim of the Rev. David Holley (see p. 252), noticed that "the silence from the pews was deafening" and asked "where [was] the Catholic laity when those notorious Massachusetts priests were sent off to prison in the early 1990s—Father Porter, Father Holley, Father Hanlon, Father Robert Kelly? What about Father Andrew Greeley's 1993 report in which he estimated that 2,000 to 4,000 Catholic priests had molested over 100,000 children."[1] The victims of the Rev. Louis Miller in Louisville wrote in an open letter: "We have not seen or heard the Catholics of Louisville being enraged over the behavior of their priests and bishops. We have not seen or heard the Catholics of Louisville calling for the resignation of the archbishop or asking that charges be filed. Yet many called for accountability of the corporate executives of Enron, WorldCom and Arthur Andersen."[2] The victims do not realize that in the Enron case money was involved, while the Miller case involved only the lives and souls of children.

### *Catholic Laity*

The laity have also bought into the poisonous clericalism that infects the Church. The "traditional" laity have participated in the corporate narcissism of Catholicism. They, like the bishops who protected abusers and neglected victims, embody what George Orwell called "nationalism," which he defined as "the habit of identifying oneself with a single nation or other unit, placing it beyond good or evil and recognizing no other duty than that of advancing its interests." The nationalist is hypersensitive: "the smallest slur upon his own unit, or any implied praise of a rival organization, fills him with uneasiness which he can only relieve by making some sharp retort."[3] The reaction of bishops and much of the Catholic laity to criticism has been to point to the faults of other organizations rather than to admit to and repent of their own faults. This religious nationalism or political Catholicism is one of the major roots of clericalism.

But this traditional clericalism has its counterpart among progressive laity who are willing to tolerate priests who abuse children (Paul Shanley is still defended by Gramick, see p. 170) and bishops who let that abuse go on, as long as the bishops are liberals (like Mahony and Weakland) or are charismatic and great entertainers. Many American Catholics consider entertainment to be the highest form of culture, to which everything else, including the innocence and lives of children, must be sacrificed.

The priest-abuser is often very successful and popular: "charismatic" is the word that recurs when people describe him. He gives people what they want. To older Catholics, he gives the pleasure of associating with a priest. To younger Catholics, he gives rock music and entertainment. In making the Mass more accessible to the laity after Vatican II, it was often converted into entertainment, and the laity want entertainment rather than the hard mysteries of death and resurrection and conversion and repentance. When the priest-abuser is exposed, the parishioners often rise to defend him and turn harshly on the accuser. They fear the loss of their star entertainer. They succumb to denial, the simple refusal to face unpleasant facts. And most of all, they do not want to experience the shame of belonging to an institution contaminated by the sexual abuse of children.

The laity therefore have often leapt to the defense of the abuser, not of his victims. "In almost every case, these charismatic abusers rally parishioners around them. That's just the standard M.O. of a child molester."[4]

The Rev. Gilbert Gauthé was like a rock star in rural Louisiana. One woman whose brother was abused says that, when she attended a high school reunion, a former classmate referred to the victims as "Gauthé's whores."[5] When the Rev. James Viall of St. Rose of Lima Church in Cleveland was removed after accusations, parishioners "jeered at diocesan administrators who urged compassion for victims."[6] The Rev. John Leonard of the Richmond diocese was sentenced to jail in 2004 for assaulting two teenage boys. This was the reaction of the laity: "Church members have supported him for the entire time and no support was seen more than when he left court and his congregation cheered for him."[7] How do the victims feel when they see the laity cheering on a rapist? When attorney Bruce Pasternack represented the victims of sexual abuse in New Mexico, the "attorneys, investigators and priests of the archdiocese of Santa Fe" called him "a Jew bastard,"[8] a "money-grubbing Jew, priest-hater, and Catholic basher."[9]

The laity are often far more sympathetic to the abusers than to their victims. The Rev. Timothy DeVenney of Dubuque, Iowa, was convicted of lascivious acts with a minor and assault with intent to commit sexual abuse, and was sentenced to ten years—although Marion Wettine, a parishioner, told the judge that DeVenney was "a very good administrator," and "maybe the young children will learn how to show some compassion"[10] instead of dragging DeVenney into court and seeking justice.

The Rev. Mark Lehman was "a handsome man who wore his hair over his shoulders and who some parishioners likened in appearance to Jesus Christ." He drew legions of supporters to the courtroom. During the 1991 trial, the atmosphere was hostile, said Laura Recker, a former Maricopa County, Arizona, deputy attorney who prosecuted the case. The priest's supporters taunted the victims' families and swore at her, she said: "The victims were being treated as if they were the bad people."[11] When Lehman was on trial (he was convicted) for molesting boys and girls, the pastor, Rev. Robert Skagen, showed up in the courtroom with parishioners to offer support to Lehman. Skagen had already written to the judge that he was certain Lehman would never offend again. The parishioners muttered at the victims—"travesty," "outrage," "lies." The parents who sued the diocese of Phoenix "got nasty letters saying they were ruthless liars peddling trumped-up accusations and exaggerated suffering for a little limelight and a lot of cash. They got harassing phone calls and anonymous death threats."[12] One of the girl victims spent her teen years in and out of psychiatric hospitals because of the abuse, and none of the victims remains a Catholic.

Bishop Howard Hubbard of Albany (who has his own troubles[13]) removed the Rev. Edward C. Pratt, a "charismatic leader," from his parish because of substantiated allegation of sexual misconduct with a minor. Patti Nichols was devastated: "Father Pratt is a wonderful, wonderful man. . . . I believe Father Pratt had paid his dues and moved on from his past. It's a shame the Catholic Church feels they have to go this far to make such an example." Parishioners wrote, "Please God, take good care of Father Pratt. We all love him,"[14] and wanted to send him special letters of support through a box in the church. In another parish, the priest replacing the abuser had to ask parishioners not to applaud the abusive priest at the end of Mass.

When he was eleven Mike Sullivan was sodomized by the Rev. James Porter. When Sullivan was in high school he sought counseling from a priest for the emotional damage that Porter had caused. That priest tried to molest Sullivan. The Catholic laity were not happy when Sullivan took his complaints to court: "Parishioners hounded my parents from their church during the publicity surrounding the Porter trials and lawsuits against the diocese, accusing their son of being a Church-basher or of just being in it for the money."[15] The laity blame not the abusers but the victims.

A priest I met around 1971, the Rev. Brian Cox, was arrested in Westminster, Maryland. I knew his parents, Richard and Shirley Cox, who helped me found the Charlottesville, Virginia, chapter of Birthright, an organization which helped pregnant women. Brian was in the Josephites at the time; he later switched to the archdiocese of Baltimore. His parents regarded him as otherworldly; I thought he was odd. He told a story (which he thought funny) of how he had had a home Mass and one of the participants had shared the host with her dog.

He became assistant pastor at St. John's in Westminster. A victim, Jeff Curran, admitted of Cox that "he has a naturally attractive personality, very outgoing. Everybody loved Father Brian."[16] Everybody loved Father Brian; he was a real entertainer, "a charismatic priest and extemporaneous preacher who used unconventional methods to involve his congregation in the Gospel.... He celebrated sunrise Mass on Easter with balloons tied to each pew. He walked newly baptized babies around the church to be applauded. And on more than one occasion, Cox ended Mass by dancing down the aisle or by playing a kazoo."[17] Parishioners never had to endure a dull moment when he said Mass.

When he was accused of abuse in 1995 and sent away for treatment, everyone turned on the victim: one letter writer to the local paper maintained that "more Father Brians are needed in this sad, hateful and so much jealous world.... Giving up his whole life for God is enough proof of his unselfishness. Come back, Father, nothing can compare to a bright tomorrow."[18] Marcie Wogan, the deputy state's attorney assigned to the case, saw nothing but sympathy for the priest, and anger toward the victim: "When my office was investigating this matter in 1995, there was a great deal of anger and hostility directed toward whoever the public perceived as the victim of Brian Cox, and that was very painful, I'm sure, for anyone who was in that position to experience."[19] The archdiocese of Baltimore protected him from the law: "Father Cox was never questioned, because when investigators from the state's attorney's office attempted to reach him, he went on sabbatical and the church would not disclose his whereabouts."[20]

Parish members still defend Father Brian: he was so interested in helping the poor; why are people bringing up things that happened twenty years ago? If he did anything, it was from simple exuberance. What in fact did he do with boys? He had oral sex with one boy in the rectory and in a parked car.[21] Curran recalls going to the pool with Cox as many as a dozen times over several months. After swimming, Cox would take Curran into the showers in the locker room, which were generally empty during the week, where he masturbated the youth on at least four occasions, Curran says.[22] And there were other victims.

The Rev. John Cornelius, a priest in Seattle, has been suspended. Everyone was so surprised; everyone loved him so much.

> Cornelius's involvement with teenage boys had been the stuff of whispers for years. But while there were rumors, there were few official church complaints. What most people saw were his dynamic preaching style, his championing of social causes and his ever-growing list of fans. In his eighteen years as pastor at Seattle's Immaculate Conception Church, and as chaplain for the Seattle Police Department, Cornelius counted among his friends some of the wealthiest and most powerful people in the city. Through their support, he drove new cars and lived in a big house along Lake Washington. He turned services into marathon events, infusing usually solemn ceremonies with energy and joy. Church membership swelled.[23]

When Joseph Coonan was a camp counselor twenty-seven years ago, Mark Bedard was twelve. Bedard alleges that Coonan molested him. Bedard, like many who were molested as children, was tormented by the memory and married late. He told a close friend at his bachelor party; the friend responded that he too had been molested by Coonan. Coonan had gone on to earn a degree in psychology, to teach, and to be ordained. Bedard went to the bishop of Worcester, Massachusetts, who removed Coonan pending an investigation.[24]

Bedard says fifteen others have alleged they were molested by Coonan. Two circumstances strongly suggest that the allegations are true. Their number: the state police have received fifteen complaints. The nature: Coonan has an unusual fascination with the excretory systems of boys:

> Mr. Bedard's allegations are similar to those of others who have come forward to say they remember Rev. Coonan as someone who wanted to be in their presence while they urinated or defecated.
>
> Mr. Bedard said the alleged sexual abuse happened during a camping trip, where Rev. Coonan urged a number of boys to urinate on trees, explaining that the scent would confuse the dogs that belonged to drug

> dealers. He said Rev. Coonan confided that he was working in conjunction with the police to thwart drug dealers.
>
> "He was very articulate. He could tell a story. He was interesting. He was like an Orson Welles type, that was his persona," Mr. Bedard said. "He talked a lot about a lot of different things, witchcraft, working for the police and helping them get rid of the drugs. He always encouraged all of the boys to express their sexuality by running naked and skinny dipping."
>
> It was during one of these camping trips, Mr. Bedard said, that Rev. Coonan "checked on me and sexually molested me. I have been for a long, long time embarrassed about this. I've questioned my saneness about this."[25]

Coonan's pop culture approach is present both in these alleged incidents of perverted conduct and in his style of preaching.

After Coonan's removal his parish exploded with support for him. His parishioners have put up hundreds of messages on a website (since deactivated). Here is a portrait of Coonan by his parishioners, and an inadvertent self-portrait by the parishioners (and their spelling):

> After moving to the Worcester area over ten years ago I could not find a Church that I felt comfortable joining. That is until I stepped into St. John's and listened to Father Coonan's untraditional and refreshing approach.
>
> He is a different kind of priest that captures everyones attention. I tell my friends about him and they think it is cool that he can combine a song and a poem that gives meaning to the weeks gospel.
>
> I only go to St. Johns because Fr. Coonan is a great speaker and plays very good music. I'll always support Fr. Coonan 100%.
>
> I, like so many of your parishoners at St John's, have experienced a renewed "faith" in our religion because of you and your ability to bring God to our level.

After a long absence from the church out of total boredom and a total lack of interesting spiritual guidance provided by many a parish priest Father Coonan was reccommended by a friend. After attending mass with Father Coonan I felt my spirit renewed and learned "Good Stuff" every week. I am really grateful for Father Coonan and his message it has given me a lot of hope.

He began each Mass with a declaration that "I am the greatest sinner among you", thanked all for their faith and their presence, and acknowledged that the members of the congregation were not all Saints. He acknowledged the presence of racial minorities, street people, alcoholics (drunk ones), the poverty stricken, the mentally compromised, and gays. He welcomed all for coming, being willing to listen to him, and for "trying".

I've seen you convey feeling through poetry, literature and music and sometimes the power of your meaning moves me to an unimaginable level. I think that a lot of people that "follow" a particular religion do so out of habit rather than belief because no one could ever make it understandable. You change all that by living in reality with "us" and by somehow, at the same time, really understanding what it means to follow Jesus and being able to express that in a way that any person can understand.

Father Coonan married us on October 21, 2000. When we first met with him in the rectory, we felt right at home with his Harley Davidson statue and Jerry Garcia dolls below the Bishop's picture.

After we had been dating a while, we started going to Mass together at her church — St. John's. I remember being blown away by this Jerry Garcia look-alike who played Grateful Dead tunes (could you even do that in church?) and preached as if Christ might come back tomorrow. He could "talk the talk" and explained the gospels better than any priest I'd ever heard.

Your masses are so funny and full of life. Most other masses said by other priests (excluding my great-great uncle, Msgr. Tinsley) are so dull they almost put me to sleep.

We all can't wait to see you up on the alter, tapping your foot while listening to the Grateful Dead.

We had found Father Joe Coonan. The rock music, the sermons, the "I am just like you" keep us all coming back week after week. Your message is for all of us. We miss you terribly and pray that you are well and will return to us very soon!

But, this week I remembered when Father Joe played "Big Yellow Taxi" by Joni Mitchell. In the song she sings "don't it always seem to go, that you don't know what you've got 'till its gone" I never knew what a special priest Father Coonan was until he was gone.

While I believe whole-heartedly that you are innocent, I believe that your admittedly sinful past is a testament to your own faith. Furthermore, your EMPATHY for other sinners, and people in pain has led to the enormous following that extends well beyond Worcester County. We're pullin' for ya, rock star!

You are human, mellow, and forgiving. Your words come from the heart, always inspired, never dull, and never from a written script. You are compassionate, yet realistic. You welcome all regardless of who or what they may be. You know sin and you know forgiveness.

The way you speak to me in your sermon is more than inspiring and hopeful, it gives me purpose and want to go out and be a better person. Please remember what you teach; to be strong when things go badly, being at the bottom of the circle won't last, and so much more than i can print. WE LOVE YOU FATHER JO!!!!

Coonan was a great entertainer—he brought God down to the level of his parishioners, who had found religion dull and no fun. Coonan made it fun. He preached pop psychology with an accompaniment of the Grateful Dead and with a veneer of Christianity—that is why they love him and want him back. Indeed, as Coonan preached, the abuser and his parishioners are like one another.

Coonan's bishop, Daniel P. Reilly, suspended him (following the new policy) as soon as an allegation was made. Bishops have not done that in the past, with terrible consequences. But the reaction of Coonan's parish shows why bishops have been so reluctant to remove priests. Abusers are frequently popular priests because they are good confidence artists who can identify and exploit the weaknesses of those they deal with.

Many Catholics find their religion boring and want to be entertained at Mass. The Catholic laity want Father Brian and Father Bob and Father William Romero, "a real Jerry Lewis type. He was fun"[26]—a type no one can take seriously.

Even after the endless publicity about the scandals, many laity continue to question and attack the victims. "Why did they wait so long?" and "They're in it just for the money," have been said in my presence. A liberal Catholic sitting next to me at an airport was holding forth on her theory that we were witnessing sexual McCarthyism, that after the end of the Cold War which had united Americans in opposing communism we now had identified new enemies, child molesters whom we could unite against. The child abuse scandals were a right-wing conspiracy to purge the Church of homosexuals and dissenters.

The laity have a positive will not to believe the facts. At the beginning of 2005, after thousands of stories about sexual abuse by priests had filled newspapers for three years, the parishioners of the Rev. Karl LeClaire in Phoenix continued to say he was innocent, that the victim was a liar and an extortioner, that "there's no doubt in my mind this didn't occur,"[27] and that his conviction was a "travesty of justice" *even after LeClair had pleaded guilty in open court* to "aggravated assault with sexual motive,"[28] to zeroing in on a fourteen-year-old-boy whose parents were going through a divorce, to driving "a wedge between the boy and his parents," to grooming the boy "by lavishing him with attention, gifts, and trips," and then to stripping down and giving the boy sensual massages on his genitals.[29] The parishioners "choose not to believe any of it,"[30] which I am afraid will be the response to the painful episodes I recount in this book. A too-common Catholic attitude is that if reality is painful, it is better to live in a dream world.

## *The Criminal Justice System*

The criminal justice system failed to protect the 12,000 reported (and the untold number of unreported) victims of abusive priests. Legislators in Massachusetts in 1983 exempted the Church from requirements to report sexual abuse. The Church was seen as an independent sphere which the state could not regulate. In fact, police sometimes favored abusers over victims. When Msgr. John P. Heaney was charged in 2003 with eight felony cases of molestation, "a deputy chief of the San Francisco Police Department and dozens of police officers appeared in court as an apparent show of support."[31]

The police have often failed to protect children. In 1975 officers of the Nashua, New Hampshire, police department came across the Rev. Paul Aube in a car on a dark road, giving oral sex to a teenage boy. Aube was even wearing his collar. Bishop Gendron later assured Aube, "I contacted the police chief in Nashua and I asked him to do me a favor and make sure there was no record of this in the files and he assured me that, you know, that would be taken care of."[32] The diocese was therefore able to lie to victims that they knew nothing about Aube until 1981, when a mother made an allegation. If the police had arrested Aube in 1975, and the prosecutor had done his job, all the boys who were molested after that might have been spared.

When the Rev. Leonardo Mateo arrived in Illinois from the Philippines he helped himself to American children. In 1983 parents complained to the police, who investigated, concluded a crime had been committed, and decided he should have counseling from a priest of the Joliet diocese. When years passed and more parents came forward to complain, Mateo fled the country. The diocese was supposed to notify the police of any more complaints. It didn't.[33]

Nahant, Massachusetts, police in 1977 spotted the Rev. Edward T. Kelley apparently engaged in a sex act with a teenage boy in a parked car. One officer knew the priest, but instead of arresting him, the police contacted Bishop Thomas V. Daily. Bishop Daily explained that the "archdiocese of Boston had a longtime understanding with local law enforcement officers that church officials rather than the police would 'take care of' priests implicated in sex abuse cases."[34] Daily came down and spoke with the Nahant chief of police. They "agreed the bishop would handle this."[35] Therefore, Kelley was neither arrested not charged, but there is no indication that Daily ever arranged for treatment.

Prosecutors are political animals with political ambitions. They want a good record of convictions, and they don't want to make enemies in high places who could thwart their political careers. For them, prosecuting priests was not a good career move. It was hard to get a conviction, and the laity would be mad at the prosecutor, as would the bishop. The only people who would be grateful were the victim and his family. Prosecutors can count potential votes. When the Rev. Maurice Blackwell was accused in Baltimore, the police forwarded the report to the state's attorney's office, which proceeded to "lose" it so they wouldn't have to prosecute a popular black priest on whose behalf Congressman Kweisi Mfume had spoken.

Attorneys for victims are anxious to conclude cases, to limit their costs, to get the victim something, and to receive their fees. When he was a child abuse prosecutor, Laurence Hardoon observed "once a predator, always a predator," but as the attorney for the victim of the Rev. Robert M. Burns, he agreed that Burns was no longer a threat to children. Burns then molested two more children.[36] Superior Court Judge Margot Botsford impounded the court file in the child rape case against the Rev. Richard O. Matte, a decision she later realized was wrong because it helped conceal the extent of the abuse.[37]

Bishop O'Brien in Phoenix "tried to persuade police, prosecutors and judges to downplay sex-related offenses involving church employees."[38] The Rev. Joseph Marcel Lessard was diagnosed as a "regressive pedophile" and was tried on felony charges of molesting a thirteen-year-old boy which could have led to a sentence of twenty-five years. O'Brien refused to cooperate with the police and wrote to Judge Michael D. Ryan, who reduced the charge from a felony to a misdemeanor, to the disappointment of the detective and probation officer involved.[39] When the Rev. George Bredemann was tried for numerous cases of molestation (he abused brothers who had been sent to him for counseling after they had been abused by someone else), O'Brien wrote to Judge Robert Hertzberg, "I do not believe that any purpose can be served by placing him in prison."[40] O'Brien suggested instead therapy and probation. The judge agreed, over the objections of the prosecutor. Bredemann violated parole and tried to flee to Brazil.

Even after the revelations and massive publicity began in January 2002, the criminal justice system and the Catholic hierarchy still show little interest in preventing abuse. In August 2002, Fernando Guido worked for the diocese of Orange County, California. He reports finding child pornography in a laptop that had been owned by Father Cesar Salazar. Guido turned the evidence over to the police, who investigated and then asked the Orange County district attorney to prosecute; the district attorney refused. Guido met with an official of the diocese, who admitted that Salazar had problems and was being restricted and treated. The district attorney still refused to do anything, and the one-year statute of limitations was running out. In July 2002 Guido went public and contacted the FBI. The district attorney tried to come up with an explanation of why he had let the statute of limitations run out and the diocese of Orange put Salazar on administrative leave. But the police still haven't gotten a search warrant to examine Salazar's computer, and neither the police nor the district attorney have ever contacted Guido.[41] The diocese and the district attorney do not want to know what is going on.

Ronald Justin Lasik beat and abused boys at Mount Cashel. The Canadian judge noted his lack of remorse and sentenced him to ten and a half years in prison, the longest sentence of any of the Mount Cashel abusers. But the federal parole board released him after three years, although it told Lasik that "you continue to deny your guilt and have failed to display victim empathy or remorse." Lasik was deported to the United States, where he lives in a Christian Brothers house in New York, a state where another abuser at Mount Cashel seminary, John Evangelist Murphy, was living. Murphy was convicted in 2004, but the Canadian judge declined to give him jail time; instead, the judge allowed him to go back to New York for twenty months of "house arrest," which includes driving around town and reading at Mass in St. Joseph's Church in Dolgeville, New York. Canadian prosecutors opposed the extradition of other accused abusers, Paul Raynham and Franciscan Gerald Chumik, from the United States to Canada for trial, for reasons they refuse to discuss.[42]

Authorities all over the world are unenthusiastic about prosecuting priests and religious for sexual abuse, as the *Dallas Morning News* has documented in a special report. Even suspicions of murder do not cause prosecutors to overcome their reluctance to indict priests. Richard Lavigne, the suspected murderer of the boy he abused (see pp. 186–188) was protected until the trail grew cold. John Feit was not prosecuted in 1960 when he was a suspect in a murder (see pp. 310–311).

Police have found new witnesses in the Feit case. Oblate of Mary Immaculate priest Joseph O'Brien, who was at a parish with Feit in 1960 when the murder occurred, has now revealed that Feit made incriminating statements. Dale Tacheny, who was a priest at a Trappist monastery at which Feit lived in 1963, also said that the abbot told him that Feit had killed a woman. Feit then talked with Tacheny and revealed details of the murder. Feit claimed he has "a sexual compulsion to attack women from behind." He attacked a woman (whom he did not name) whose confession he had heard in the rectory and "restrained the woman, kept her in the residence basement temporarily, hid her in another clergy residence until she suffocated with a bag over her head, and dumped the body in a canal on Easter Sunday night." Tacheny said that Feit "expressed no remorse" and said that his Oblate superiors have "helped him avoid a murder charge."[43]

Rene Guerra, the district attorney of Hidalgo County, where the murder occurred, still refuses to prosecute Feit and has threatened to prosecute the police if they release any information about the murder. Guerra dismisses O'Brien's testimony because he thinks that O'Brien has unspecified "problems." He disregards Tacheny's testimony because Tacheny has left the priesthood and therefore might have "an ax to grind" and might dislike the Church. Guerra says he will prosecute Feit only if there is DNA evidence or a "corroborated confession." In 1995 Guerra refused to prosecute another murder. Guerra says that "if John Feit did this, I hope he will atone for his sins," and he says of the victim, "I think if she died leaving that church after confession that she died in a state of grace and she should be in heaven, as I believe in God."[44] Guerra is obviously a devout Catholic, and perhaps he will not prosecute murder cases because he knows Texas executes murderers, contrary to the wishes of Pope John Paul II.

Stephen Galebach, an attorney who helped found VictimPower.org (see p. 624), blames the false doctrine of "church autonomy" for the mishandling of the scandals by the American justice system. The American courts consider the doctrine of churches outside their competence. But this deference has expanded to include the internal workings of a church, including criminal activity, but only if it is sexual. This deference can be seen "in prosecutors who are reluctant to indict church officials, in judges who soften pre-trial discovery requirements for churches, and in court decisions that order church documents produced in discovery to be sealed and kept secret." The courts created a "law-free" zone for sexual abuse, and the abusers took advantage of this to commit abuse with impunity.[45]

## *The Press*

The American press at one time was openly and vociferously anti-Catholic. It printed endless lies about the clergy. These scandals (it was a more innocent age) were about adult heterosexual relationships, mostly between priests and nuns, the tunnels between the rectory and the convent, and the sub-basement where the illegitimate babies were baptized, murdered, and buried. The Catholic Church organized the National Catholic Welfare Council to expose the lies, so that "tales of lascivious priests or nuns acquired the same ludicrous character as the notorious legends of Jews sacrificing Christian children on the Passover."[46] In addition to appeals to fairness (which did not get far), Catholic bishops organized boycotts against newspapers, and once their pocketbooks were touched, publishers became careful about printing lies. They also became extremely careful about printing unflattering truths about the Catholic Church, even such innocuous matters as priests getting stopped for driving under the influence. Raymond A. Schroth claims that Cardinal Cody of Chicago persuaded newspapers to kill the story of "a pedophile ring of priests in a neighboring state [Iowa? See Chapter Two] who were passing their victims from one to another."[47]

The press after the Second World War also had the very bad example of the Nazi-controlled press in Germany which in the 1930s led a campaign against the Catholic clergy as pedophiles. These lies were so pornographic that the Nazi women's organization protested against the newspaper coverage of the stories as an affront to public morality.[48]

Other bad experiences made the press leery about publicizing Catholic scandals. Some sexual scandals turned out to be hoaxes or exaggerations. The Satanic abuse scare was a repetition of the Salem witch trials. Accusations became more and more far fetched; investigators elicited stories from children by asking leading questions; and children gave investigators the stories they wanted to hear. Multiple personality disorders became fashionable; therapists convinced women that any problems they had must be due to incest because all fathers are incestuous. The *Wall Street Journal* has campaigned tirelessly against the injustice done to the Amirault family, who were falsely accused of abusing children in the day-care center they ran, and there were many other victims of a panic about day-care child abuse.[49] However, *Wall Street Journal* editor Dorothy Rabinowitz, desiring to play Voltaire defending the victims of legal hysteria, also sought to whitewash the convicted abuser Gordon MacRae (see pp. 183–185) by selectively citing data and by questioning the motives of the victims,[50] thereby supporting those who desired to minimize the reality of sexual abuse.

To complicate matters, it is extremely difficult to investigate allegations of sexual abuse of small children. Small children do not know what happened to them, and even normal children make only a vague distinction between fantasy and reality. The acts were done in secret and rarely leave physical evidence. A small child will often tell an investigator what he thinks the investigator wants to hear. Many innocent people were accused by overzealous and incompetent investigators. They reacted by forming forums such as Victims of Child Abuse Laws (VOCAL), which, however, also included those who did not think adult-child sex was necessarily wrong or damaging (see their featured speaker Leroy Schultz's comments, p. 442).[51]

When the scandals of real sexual abuse by priests first began to be published in the United States, they were treated as isolated cases and received mainly local attention. The press hesitated in breaking the scandal. The Newfoundland newspapers killed the 1970s story about the Mount Cashel abuse. Having been burned by dubious stories, the press was very slow in picking up true stories. Jason Berry tried to get the *New York Times*, the *Washington Post*, *Rolling Stone*, *Vanity Fair*, *The Nation*, and *Mother Jones* interested in the Gauthé story;[52] in the end only the *Times of Acadiana* was willing to publish it. When the *National Catholic Reporter* published the Gauthé story it was seen as part of a liberal, anti-Roman plot. Kos's story made little impact; Porter's story was not given national coverage. The *New York Times* showed a remarkable tenderness to Bruce Ritter even after his death. Other stories remained local, and were not followed up. It was not until Cardinal Law made the mistake of picking a fight with the *Boston Globe*, which also was able to use the Shanley documents, that the dam finally burst. But the stories had been out there, and could have been broken earlier, saving many children. The press does not have the legal responsibilities that bishops, police, and courts have, but it has a moral responsibility which only some papers fulfilled, like the courageous *Times of Acadiana*, which risked a church-led boycott to expose Gauthé.

Despite its initial hesitation to get involved, the press has been remarkably accurate in its coverage. The only distortions have been caused by an incomprehension of the structure and law of the Catholic Church. The general American ignorance about statistics also distorted the reportage. The press would say there were *x* number of abusers in a diocese over the past fifty years, and there were now *y* number of priests in the diocese. But that is, of course, comparing apples to oranges. The proper comparison would have been the number of abusers to the total number of priests who had served in that time period. But no one could give the press that number, because the dioceses had never calculated it.

The motives of the press are also suspect. It is not so much what was said as what was not said. The role of homosexuality in the scandals was rarely addressed. The similar scandals in Protestant churches were largely ignored because the decentralization of Protestantism makes research much harder. Even when stories demanded attention, they were ignored. David E. Johnson, the retired Episcopal Bishop of Massachusetts, committed suicide by shooting himself with a rifle. But no one knew he owned a gun, and it is hard to shoot yourself with a rifle (see p. 381). He was accused of affairs and sexual exploitation, and rumors circulated that he was exchanging ordination for sex. After three or four articles the story disappeared from the Boston newspapers. If a Catholic bishop had committed suicide under similar circumstances, the articles would have been in a hundred newspapers and gone on for months. The Episcopal story, however, sank like a stone. Not all clerical sins are equal.

Both the clergy and the laity failed the victims. The general human tendency to endure patiently the sufferings of other people was reinforced by clericalism in both the clergy and laity, a clericalism that affected even the criminal justice system. In addition to clericalism, there were other intellectual currents that contributed to the abuse, both new and old errors. It is to these that I shall now turn.

## CHAPTER FIFTEEN

# NEW ERRORS

No one was ever ruined by a book, according to the great moral theologian Jimmy Walker, who was also mayor of New York. This has been the line taken by bishops when Catholic laity complain about catechetical texts or theological speculations. However, human beings, although they do not need rationalizations to misbehave, are always looking for excuses for doing things that they really want to do, and will grasp at plausible arguments to justify their favorite immoral or illegal activity. Dissenting theologians should look at their own responsibility when offenders like Paul Shanley start applying theological speculations. Some theologians have persistently tried, with some success, to open Catholicism to the strong current in modern psychology that seeks to find adult-child sex, especially adult male-teenage male sex, a generally harmless, even beneficial, activity.

### *Sexual Liberation*

Alfred Kinsey began the modern march of folly. He was "an odd, creepy fellow" with his own "sexual demons,"[1] as John Leo of *US News and World Report* put it. Kinsey liked to masturbate while depriving himself of oxygen to intensify the orgasm and did things to his genitals that cannot be contemplated without shuddering. His methodology has been discredited by modern researchers. He reported in the infamous "Table 34" how long (to the second) it took male children—including infants—who were being masturbated to achieve orgasm. The Kinsey Institute claims these data are from the diary of a child molester; this is like using data from research at a Nazi death camp; it is "a moral horror, and neither Kinsey nor his patron, the Rockefeller Foundation, seemed to think that anything was amiss."[2] Kinsey made no attempt to locate and help the child victims.[3] Not that Kinsey thought they were victims; he claimed that "it is difficult to see why a child, except for its cultural conditioning, should be disturbed at having its genitalia touched…or disturbed at even more *specific* sexual contacts."[4] Kinsey's celebration of all types of sexual activity was taken up by *Playboy*, *Penthouse*, and *Hustler*, which featured Chester the Molester, and whose publisher, Larry Flynt, is, like Kinsey, a hero of the liberated left.

Sociologists discovered sexual liberation. Leroy Schultz, social work professor at the University of West Virginia, claimed that "sexual expression is a minor's right if it does not risk pregnancy"[5] and that adult-child sex and incest can be "voluntary consenting reciprocal sexual activities."[6] Calling the police creates "legal-process trauma." He dismissed concerns about the power differential in adult-child sex, and surveyed the "new attitudes and ideas" that have the potential to change the law about sexual activity, attitudes and ideas about "a sexual bill of rights for children," "sibling sexual activity that is positive," "boy-man sexual activities that may be either constrictive, nurturing or neutral, or adult-child incest activity that may be non-damaging."[7] In the absence of positive evidence of trauma, it should be assumed not to have occurred, because "sexual behavior between adult and child or between two minors is neither harmful or harmless always"[8] and can in fact have "one possibly positive or healthy result."[9]

John Money, who wrote that "a childhood sexual experience, such as being the partner of a relative or an older person, need not necessarily affect the child directly,"[10] also praised the Dutch sociologist Theo Sandfort's *Boys on Their Contacts with Men* as "a very important book, and a very positive one."[11] Sandfort asked a group of boys whether they experienced sexual relationships with men as positive. In twenty-four out of twenty-five cases, the answer was "a very emphatic yes."[12] The Netherlands is very enlightened about these matters: in 1987 "a Dutch television program designed for and produced by children had two little boys announcing they were going to talk about penises, whereupon they exposed their organs to the TV-cameras and played with them."[13] Sandfort was disgusted that in the 1980s the media tended to examine "only the negative side" of child-adult sex, and blames the "religious/ethical revival movement in North America."[14] The only negative feelings the boys had came from society, which "disapproved of sexual relations between children and adults."[15] Sandfort criticized feminists for saying that the power difference between the adult and child makes consensual sex impossible. After all, "in every kind of human interaction power and inequality play a role. This is true of adult interaction,"[16] and in any case the child, if he does not want sex, "can simply stay away."[17] Since no one can *demonstrate* harm to the boys, the adults should not be punished. A Dutch government committee found laws against adult-child sex to be "an unjust invasion of an individual's right to sexual self-determination"[18] and in effect adult-child sex, like euthanasia, has been legalized in the Netherlands. Minimal laws remain (a boy has to be twelve years old before an adult can legally have sex with him), but they are not enforced.[19] Incest is the next step in sexual liberation. The Dutch association of homosexuals, COC, "has been sympathetic to intergenerational contacts" including incest, and published another article, "Why Not Go to Bed with Your Son."[20]

Psychologists in the 1950s (and later) who favored sexual liberation minimized the extent of child molestation and the damage it caused; they believed the vast majority of sexual offenses against children are rather innocuous affairs best treated as "one of the minor and transient hazards of childhood."[21] Wardell Pomeroy, co-author of the Kinsey Report, claimed that "incest between...children and adults...can sometimes be beneficial."[22] Even incest is "not really that harmful and what harm there is comes from societal reaction."[23] It is a "myth," Richard Farson wrote in *Birthrights* (1974), "that adult-child sex usually forces physical violence and sexual activity on an unwilling child. That is not usually true. In many instances, the child is a willing participant."[24] Farson blamed public objection to adult-child sex for any difficulties the child feels: "The most ruinous situations are usually not the sexual activities involved in the act of molestation, but the community's response to the act when it has been discovered."[25] Farson, agreeing with Germaine Greer, thinks that objections to incest are baseless and that incest is a common and harmless activity. Farson proposes "all sex activity be decriminalized."[26] All, including incest. This is in a book published by a major, mainline publisher.

D. J. West, a psychiatrist who worked at the Cambridge University Institute of Criminology, claimed that "sexual stimulation of the young is not itself harmful" and that "psychiatric follow-up studies of individuals who, as children, have had sexual experiences with adults do not show any directly adverse effect upon later sexual development."[27]

In July 1998 the American Psychological Association published "A Meta-Analytic Examination of Assumed Properties of Child Sexual Abuse Using College Samples" by Bruce Rind of Temple University, Robert Bauserman of the University of Michigan, and Philip Tromovitch of the University of Pennsylvania. They surveyed a college population to see what effects were present in those who had been sexually abused as children. Their conclusion was that "the negative potential for CSA [child sexual abuse] for most individuals who experience it has been overstated"[28] and "the claim that CSA inevitably or usually produces harm is not justified."[29] They criticize the "indiscriminate use of this term [child sexual abuse] and related items such as victim and perpetrator."[30] The authors believe that a "willing encounter with positive reactions would be labeled simply adult-child sex."[31]

The researchers are convinced that boys especially are rarely harmed by adult-adolescent sex, which at most violates "social norms"[32] and is common in other societies. The authors of this study disclaim any implications for moral or legal attitudes to adult-child sex, but they are disingenuous. Bausermann wrote for the pro-pedophilia Dutch journal *Paidika*. Lack of harm to the child or adolescent could easily be used by courts to invalidate laws against all adult-child sex as irrational (as the Massachusetts Supreme Court did with laws allowing only man-woman marriage). Supreme Court

Justice Ruth Bader Ginsburg is already on record in 1977 as advocating the lowering of the age of consent to twelve.[33]

NAMBLA cheered the Rind article as "good news." Gay writers Andrew Sullivan and Jonathan Rauch criticized not the article, but the public reaction against it. As Mary Eberstadt noted, the furor caused by the publication of this article surprised psychologists, because many were moving in the same direction as the article, unlike the unenlightened public.[34]

Children needed to be introduced to sex as soon as possible, Brandeis University professor Abraham H. Maslow wrote in 1965:

> For instance, it always struck me as a very wise kind of thing that the lower-class Negroes did, as reported in one study, in Cleveland, Ohio. Among those Negroes the sexual life began at puberty. It was the custom for an older brother to get a friend in his own age grade to break in his little sister sexually when she came of a suitable age. And the same thing was done on the girl's side. A girl who had a younger brother coming into puberty would seek among her own girl friends for one who would take on the job of initiating the young boy into sex in a nice way. This seems extremely sensible and wise and could also serve highly therapeutic purposes in various other ways as well.[35]

Maslow was and remains very influential in humanistic psychology.

Homosexuality was declared to be not a disease by the American Psychiatric Association; this is extraordinary. It is like the American Medical Association declaring that cancer is not a disease. If a mental disease can be simply declared not to be a disease, it is not a disease like physical diseases. If something is called a mental disease it is largely because society finds it unacceptable. Society, however, changes, and what it finds acceptable and unacceptable also changes.

Homosexuality has been declared to be innate, and therefore it is wrong to condemn homosexuals for homosexual behavior. But other patterns of sexual desire are also innate. According to John Money, "Pedophilia and ephebophilia are no more a matter of voluntary choice than are left handedness or color blindness."[36] Homosexuals are told that God or Nature has made them what they are; they cannot and should not try to change, and therefore they cannot be condemned for their homosexual acts because their homosexuality is innate. Pedophiles and ephebophiles are told that God or Nature has made them what they are; by this logic no one should condemn them for their acts. In any case, adult-child sex does no necessary harm, according to the best liberal opinion.

Judith Levine published her *Harmful to Minors: The Perils of Protecting Children from Sex* in 2002 through the University of Minnesota Press. President Clinton's surgeon general, Jocelyn M. Elders, wrote the foreword, in which she denounces the "conservative political agenda that underlies many supposed 'child protection' efforts."[37] Levine holds that "even incest between siblings . . . is not ipso facto traumatic."[38] Levine requires sex with children to be *demonstrably* harmful before it should be restricted in any way.

William R. Stayton, a professor at Widener University (where he founded the human sexuality program), is an ordained minister of the American Baptist Church and a member of the American Psychological Association and SIECUS (Sexuality Information and Education Council of the United States). He has taught and worked at the University of Pennsylvania. A mainstream liberal, he wrote the article on pederasty for the Humboldt University online encyclopedia of sexuality. In the article he discusses the story of Jesus and the healing of the Roman officer's servant, who was, according to Stayton, the officer's catamite. Since pederastic relationships were so common and accepted in the ancient world of Jesus, it is likely that, as the story indicates, Jesus himself had no problem with the practice of pederasty. It was the homophobic Paul who first cast doubts on pederasty.

Stayton offers some cautions about pederasty. He states that

> in the context of our culture, it is *considered* [my emphasis] harmful and damaging to individual development. Indeed, in the context of our culture, this is often true. This illustrates how important cultural context is to understanding any particular sexual behavior. There seems to be

> nothing inherently harmful or damaging in sexual acts alone, but rather harmfulness and damage must be interpreted within the context of the way each particular behavior is seen in each culture and in terms of its long-range effects on the individual.[39]

That is, there is nothing inherently and universally wrong with man-boy sex. Our society does not like it, and therefore the participants are disturbed. But of course societies change, and SIECUS is one of the powerful engines that is trying to change American attitudes toward sex to conform to more enlightened European ones.

The pressure to legalize pedophilia continues. In November 2004 Glasgow University awarded a doctorate to Richard Yuill, who conducted research with victims and abusers, and said that his research "'challenges the assumption' that all sexual relationships between adults and children under the age of sixteen are inherently abusive." Yuill admits some victims thought they were hurt; others however "found positive experiences or at least what I'd call neutral." Nor did Yuill think his work was purely theoretical. He said that "the work could challenge the law" which prohibits sex between adults and children under sixteen.[40] Glasgow University defended Yuill's research, because "humans have a wide range of sexual tastes and can follow these in situations where they may be *regarded* [my emphasis] as immoral or illegal,"[41] but has restricted access to the thesis. Not everyone outside academia understands the innate relativism of all moral judgments.

## *Liberation Enters the Church*

Even in the 1950s many priests studied psychology. Priests frequently deal with disturbed people, and modern psychology seems to offer insights in how to help. Psychology tends to displace theology. Therefore, the Catholic clergy have been exposed to all the trends and fads of modern psychology, including the pernicious ones of sexual liberation. When psychologists were brought in to advise nuns about their rules or to advise bishops how to deal with sexual offenders, disaster has often been the result.

Joyce Milton, who had personal experience with the humanistic psychology movement of the 1970s and 1980s, has exposed its weaknesses in her *Road to Malpsychia* (a word-play on Maslow's *Road to Eupsychia*). Humanistic psychology "emphasized alienation from values based on the authority of revealed religion and a need for the individual to derive meaning through his search for identity and authenticity." Carl Rogers emphasized that "neither the Bible nor the prophets—neither Freud nor research—neither the revelations of God nor man—can take precedence over my own direct experience,"[42] that is, his "lived experience," a phrase that is always invoked by those who reject traditional Christian moral teaching. Presidents Higgins and Letson of St. Jerome's University note that only three percent of young people in England think that premarital sex is wrong and criticize "the Church's unwillingness to locate itself within the realm of lived experience,"[43] by which they mean the Church's unwillingness to accept the fallen reality that previous generations called "the world."

The teaching of Carl Rogers had a massive influence on the Catholic Church in the United States, from which it has never recovered.[44] For Rogers the therapist was only a facilitator (a word that still haunts Catholic meetings) who gave unqualified acceptance (unconditional love) to the client. Rogers, an unbeliever who had been formed in a strict but affectionate Protestant home, wanted everyone to explore and accept his deepest desires. Rogers's deepest desires were civilized and humane, but not everyone is like him. Rogers unwisely kept reassuring people that they should have no fear about "calling up and unleashing their hidden desires."[45] The Jesuits wanted to get in on the act. They consulted Rogers's associate William Coulson and discussed the new concept of the "third way between celibacy and marriage." Coulson asked what they meant. A Jesuit replied, "It means you don't have to marry the girl."[46]

Rogers and Coulson set up a massive group therapy program for the Immaculate Heart of Mary (IHM) nuns, who invited them in to help with the period of reflection that the Vatican Council had asked for. Coulson was a good Catholic. When he and Rogers got in touch with their inner selves, they discovered sensitive, enlightened consciences. When their patients were in the presence of Coulson and Rogers they too discovered sensitive consciences that gave good direction. But Coulson and Rogers trained facilitators who, they discovered, were unable to evoke such a conscience. Under these facilitators' direction, the nuns got in touch with their inner selves. What they discovered there was that they did not want to be nuns and they did want (at least some did) to be lesbians. The order disintegrated in a matter of months. Cardinal Manning became alarmed, and attempted to stop the collapse, but he only made it worse.[47]

Rogers and Coulson gave the same program at St. Anthony's Seminary. When the friars there looked into their inner selves and affirmed their deepest desires, a good proportion of them (about one-quarter) discovered that what they really wanted most of all was to have sex with fourteen-year-old boys, which they proceeded to do for the next twenty years. The encounter groups had convinced them to believe that "when people do what they deeply want to do, it isn't immoral."[48] The abuse had started before the encounter groups were formed, but after the encounter groups it vastly increased.

After complaints of abuse surfaced, the Franciscans who ran St. Anthony's Seminary commissioned an inquiry. The board discovered that twenty-five percent, eleven out of the forty-four friars at the seminary, had engaged in sex with the high school students there:

> There was a wide range of sexually abusive practices perpetrated on victims by the eleven priests: one of the eleven priests photographed young children nude; three of the eleven priests engaged in forms of uninvited sexual touching of non-genital areas, such as fondling of buttocks, rubbing backs, stomachs and thighs, palpating the lower abdomen, or embracing students; one of the eleven priests "disciplined" students by administering beatings to their naked buttocks in a manner that had clear sexual overtones; two of the eleven priests engaged in penetration of a student's anus with a finger or object; five of the eleven priests fondled students' genitalia; one of the eleven priests lay naked with an erection on top of a student; six of the eleven priests masturbated students; four of the eleven priests orally copulated students; one priest had a student

> engage in mutual masturbation with him and suggested that the student sodomize him (the student refused); one of the eleven priests had a student engage in mutual fellatio with him and sodomized him on numerous occasions.[49]

How could this have happened? Religious orders are realistic about human nature and over the centuries have therefore developed ways of minimizing temptations. But these safeguards were abandoned at St. Anthony's: "It must also be stated that within the system, over the years, many rules were broken: rules governing the conduct of guardians and teachers, and rules both explicit [canonical and constitutional law] and implicit in religious life."[50]

The seminary had changed. Rogers and Coulson had preached the new gospel of self-affirmation and disregard of external constraints. Rogers now blames himself for what happened at St. Anthony's:

> The Franciscans . . . were so enamored with our psychology that they introduced it to Saint Anthony's Seminary in Santa Barbara. Years later, eleven or twelve friars were accused of molesting thirty-four high school boys. I'm afraid that we planted the seeds and they carried the seeds to the next generation and they germinated.[51]

The "renewed" seminary of St. Anthony's opened itself to the world. A large number of laypeople from the town began attending services at the seminary, which had become exciting. "By 1968, Eucharistic services incorporated outdoor settings, electric guitars and drums, fluorescent vestments, pop art banners, and sculptures decorated with mod designs and slogans" such as, "Life is where the action is," and invitations to "Feel free (free, free, free, free) to be!"[52] Sister Corita (she of the felt banners) and Cesar Chavez (he of the grape boycott) were attracted to this liberated atmosphere. The rector of the seminary, Robert Van Handel, founded a boys' choir and molested the boys. The seminary closed in 1987 because of declining enrollment. In 1989 complaints against Van Handel led to the exposure of the abuse.[53] To whom could the boys have complained earlier?

The rector, Van Handel? He was abusing boys. The auxiliary bishop of Los Angeles, Ziemann, who was in charge of the Santa Barbara area? He was himself allegedly abusing boys (see pp. 217).[54]

The disasters do not seem to have chastened the authorities who caused them. Anita Caspary, who headed the IHM nuns when they collapsed, still blamed all the problems on Cardinal Manning.[55] She made no mention of the moral disorders that accompanied the psychological turmoil, and dismissed Coulson's change of heart as incomprehensible: "Why Coulson persists in denigrating Carl Rogers and insisting on the demise of a healthy and growing religious community are matters for speculation."[56]

When Christopher Dixon was an altar boy in Missouri, he went to confession face-to-face with the Rev. John Fischer (removed in 1993 for unrelated accusations). Fischer asked, "Would you like to kiss Jesus?" Priest and boy kissed and, according to Dixon, began a sexual relationship that lasted for years. Dixon went into a high school seminary and was troubled by this relationship. He asked the rector, Rev. (later Bishop) Anthony O'Connell, for advice. O'Connell had him undress completely and also stripped himself, and then they got into bed together. This went on for years. Dixon was ordained by O'Connell, and was assigned to teach in the seminary under another priest whom Dixon said had also abused him, the Rev. Manus Daly. This was too much for Dixon, and he went to the diocese. He was given a settlement and sworn to secrecy, secrecy that allowed O'Connell to become bishop of Palm Beach, succeeding Bishop Symons who had resigned after he was accused of child abuse. Dixon decided to go public, and O'Connell had to resign. He explained his actions with Dixon: "What I was trying to do was work with a youngster who has personal issues. We're talking about the late 70s. In Catholic theology there were different kinds of approaches."[57] Touching his naked body to the naked body of a fifteen-year-old boy was the approach that O'Connell took for several years. It was under the authority of the great theological experts Masters and Johnson, according to O'Connell.[58]

Therapists immediately said that what O'Connell did was unethical. But therapist Myriam Coppens, an assistant professor with the Psychiatry

Department at Oregon Health Sciences University, said it is possible O'Connell had good intentions, even though his actions may have been extremely harmful. 'I think he believes that what he did was innocent and furthermore meant to "help" the boy,' she said, saying that in fact the 1970s were an era of more experimental attitudes toward sexuality."[59] This in fact happened with some frequency at the time. The Rev. Ellwood "Bud" Kaiser, the "Hollywood Priest," became too close emotionally to an IHM nun, and suggested that she go into therapy. The therapist used sex play with her; they fell in love; he divorced his wife and married the nun. The therapist's actions were unethical and immoral, but "in the 1960s such procedures were not uncommon."[60] That therapy led therapists into such behavior might suggest that there is something wrong with the therapy. Perhaps Cardinal Manning's suspicions about the psychological treatment the entire IHM order was undergoing were justified.

Such folly was widespread in the Catholic Church and was encouraged and disseminated by bishops who were praised as progressive. Rembert Weakland sent his seminarians to a "Sexual Attitudes Reassessment Program." There the seminarians watched movies that "showcased on the big screen male and female masturbation, heterosexual and homosexual intercourse, and variations on oral sex."[61] Under Weakland's sponsorship the Rev. James Arimond (see pp. 397–398) gave workshops on homosexuality which preached that "when making a moral decision . . . ultimately it is the individual's conscience which must be his or her guide. A Catholic may in good conscience make a decision not in total agreement with [c]hurch teaching and still remain within the Church."[62] Arimond put his teaching into practice. He pleaded no-contest to a 1990 charge of sexually assaulting a teenage boy. Weakland, following his conscience, had an affair with an adult confidence artist, who extracted $450,000 in diocesan money from Weakland as hush money (see p. 399).

The spirit of Vatican II was widely seen as favoring sexual liberation. The respectable Catholic publisher Herder and Herder, after venturing into astrology, issued *The Sex Book: A Modern Pictorial Encyclopedia* "for young people with candid explanations and photographs of sexual behavior."[63]

The photographs were by Will McBride, who also provided similar photographs for *Show Me*, by St. Martin's Press. This book showed adults having various types of sex and children engaging in masturbation and intercourse: "The boy has seen—and we see through his eyes—his teenage brother and a barely pubescent girlfriend having intercourse," including "angles on intercourse no child will ever see, no matter how obliging his adolescent siblings, unless she is face up between the legs of the participants." They see "awesome adult-sized penises being masturbated and mouthed." The children are shown as "scared or worried about what they have just seen" and the reviewer wonders for whom the book is intended.[64]

After selling over 150,000 copies, *Show Me* was withdrawn by the publisher to avoid obscenity prosecution after the Supreme Court upheld New York's law against child pornography.[65] It has become a collector's item among pedophiles (listed on the Christopher Robin's Adult-Child Loving List), fetching up to $1,000 on amazon.com. Seabury Press joined in with *The Sex Atlas* by Erwin J. Haeberle, one of the authors of *The Sex Book*. As *Zieg Mal!* McBride's book has sold over 1,000,000 copies, and is used by church groups in Germany; it had a sequel, *Zieg Mal Mehr!* McBride's book *Boys* (available at Wal Mart) shows boys in various states of nudity.

## *Dissent*

Following Scripture's positive attitude to procreation, the Catholic Church teaches that a Christian should not have any sexual experiences, mental or physical, outside marriage, and that within marriage procreation is never to be excluded by a deliberate act. This is a hard saying for the human race, but the doctrine is clear, logical, and consistent with Scripture. The Church has always been merciful to the sins of the flesh, since the human sexual appetite is hard to keep within these strict boundaries.

However, after the Vatican Council, Catholic moral theologians began competing with one another to see how much of traditional teaching on sexuality they could reject. The Rev. Matthew Lamb, at that time a theologian at Boston College, claimed that

> No adequate diagnosis of the contributory causes of the Catholic priest scandals can overlook the role of dissent among theologians.... How many of the priests and bishops who have brought such suffering to minors and scandal to the public were encouraged by teachers and theologians to cut corners and dissent from the truth of Catholic faith and moral teaching? Many priests and future bishops read articles dissenting from Catholic sexual ethics in the 1960s and '70s. A climate of dissent was promoted by wholesale dissent from Catholic sexual ethics.[66]

The dissenters have denied any responsibility for anyone putting their theories into practice.

The Rev. Anthony Kosnick, seminary dean, headed a study group for the Catholic Theological Society of America, which published its findings in 1977. The study was full of blather about self-actualization, which was understood in psychological terms instead of the classical idea of virtue. The study, *Human Sexuality: New Directions in American Catholic Thought*, wanted "greater attention to the subjective elements in pastoral judgments."[67] Beginning in the 1960s the Catholic Church was flooded with ideas of self-affirmation. Ascetical discipline, the denial of the self in answer to the Master's command, "Take up your cross and follow me," was abandoned for the pleasures of self-actualization, for affirmation of self, for self-worship, a trend which continues unabated. The problem with self-affirmation is that every Christian is *simul justus et peccator*, the Old Adam and Christ. We remain fallen, and various heresies over the centuries try to make Christians forget this, with self-indulgence of sexual desires as the result. Sexual desires are strong and disorderly; every society has hedged sex with rules and taboos. When people are encouraged to jettison rules as inauthentic restraints on the real inner self, they discover a taste for a multiplicity of perversions, including pedophilia and pederasty.

For Kosnick, the validity of all moral judgments has to be established by the criteria of modern psychological research. The study asked the fatal question, "Is there any empirical data available which might support a claim that certain sexual expressions always and everywhere are detrimental to the full development of the human personality?"[68] The answer was *no*: "at this time the behavioral sciences have not identified any sexual expression that can be empirically demonstrated to be of itself, in a culture-free way, detrimental to full human existence."[69] Of course, society disapproves of many sexual practices, and "any activity of which one's society disapproves is a potential source of anxiety for one who engages in it." Society's views will eventually be changed to conform to what people want to do, so "until that day arrives, enlightened and well-integrated individuals might well free themselves of conflict by simply reflecting on the relativity of their society's sexual ethic and proceed discreetly with their sexual project."[70]

Priests and seminarians proceeded "discreetly with their sexual project." This meant that, after the Second Vatican Council, as seminary director Howard Bleichner admitted, "a degree of sexual acting out was tolerated that ten years before...was unthinkable."[71] The study was meant to influence behavior and did influence behavior. *Human Sexuality*

> was "received" by the CTSA, which also "arranged" for its publication "as a service to the membership of the Society and a wider public of interested persons"....The book has been widely used in seminaries. Seminarians and priests of the time who had a woman or a male lover on the side could, and did, cite *Human Sexuality* to reasonably claim that a very large part, if not the majority, of the academic theological establishment countenanced their behavior.[72]

The authors of the study discussed sexual expressions such as masturbation, premarital sex, and homosexuality, but they said their approach applied to "any sexual expression." "Any" includes rape, bestiality, and for our purpose, pedophilia and sex with teenage boys. These "expressions," according to the authors, who followed psychologists' opinion in this regard, have not been demonstrated as always harmful in and of themselves. It is only cultural taboos that create anxiety (see Paul Shanley's remarks, p. 161). Shanley was speaking in the mainstream of liberal American Catholic moral theology when he indicated there was nothing innately wrong with man-boy sex; only society's disapproval created the problems, and "enlightened and well-integrated individuals"—and who would not consider himself enlightened and well-integrated when he is adulated by liberal Boston for his advocacy of homosexuality?—can discreetly carry out their sexual projects.

No, the Catholic Theological Society did not identify pedophilia as a harmless activity, but it explicitly said that *no* sexual activity had yet been proved in itself to be harmful. Nor did the criteria give any objective guidance. Sex must be self-liberating, other-liberating, honest, faithful, socially responsible, life-serving, and joyous.[73] The traditional Christian teachings about sex outside of marriage are only rough guidelines, and "to the extent that they refer to concrete, physical actions (e. g., masturbation, sterilization, contraception, premarital sex) without specifying particular circumstances or intention, to that extent they cannot be regarded as universal and absolute moral norms."[74] The prohibition of sex with a child or teenage boy is not a universal and absolute moral norm.

These Catholic theologians were a little doubtful about swinging, "free sex [which] has become a popular pastime for many single, divorced, widowed and married people." Although it may look like "self-gratification," the authors are "open to the results of further research."[75] The theologians urged "caution" about adultery, threesomes, and mate-swapping, but were "open to further evidence from the empirical sciences" and pointed out that some are open to the possibility that "such an arrangement could uphold principles of true human growth and full integration."[76]

There was almost no sexual activity of which the authors disapproved. "Full development" understood in empirical psychological terms is their redefinition of virtue. Of adultery and group marriage, the authors at best can give a caution: they are not to be tolerated "at least in most cases,"[77] but the authors affirm that such sexual relationships "can be truly 'creative' and 'integrative' for all involved, and therefore morally acceptable."[78] The authors reject the extreme position which rejects "every deliberate experience of sexual pleasure outside the marriage context."[79] The evaluation of homosexual acts is surrounded by a fog, and the authors refuse to make any judgments.

These were not the opinions of fringe radicals, but of the Catholic Theological Society of America, of seminary deans and seminary professors both in the United States and Canada. The Rev. André Guindon, who taught moral theology at St. Paul's University in Canada until his death in 1993 and was dean of the faculty of theology there from 1978 to 1984, taught that an adult having sex with prepubescent children did little or no harm:

> It should be pointed out that most recent studies tend to disprove that lasting harm results from the pedophiliac contact itself. Rather the trauma comes from the familial panic which is the usual response to the incident. Nobody seems to care that children are exposed to violence, greed, social injustice, and family wars. But let a man kiss a young boy or touch his genitals—usually a meaningless gesture for the child, by the way—and the incident is blown up into a national tragedy. Many parents and citizens who pose as do-gooders should consider carefully whether they are not making a scapegoat out of the defenseless pedophile for their own sins.
>
> Equally traumatic for the "molested" child is often his appearance as a witness in court. Interrogation and cross examination are probably more damaging than the offense itself.[80]

Guindon is equally soft on pederasty: "According to all available statistics, the effects of pederasty, leaving aside very special cases of rape and brutality, are much less pronounced than is generally believed. The literature on the subject is rather non-alarmist."[81]

Not the molestation, but those who object to it harm the child. Note the quotation marks around "molested" that show that Guindon does not think that adult-child sex should be called molestation. The parents who persecute the poor pedophile are the evil people.

Guindon laments "the victimization of an adult homosexual by a teenager. The legal presumption, which aims at protecting minors, often plays somewhat harshly against the adult partner, for the seduction often comes from the younger partner, either consciously or unconsciously."[82]

The victims, as bishops frequently informed them, are themselves to blame for the molestation.

Rudy Kos studied at the Dallas seminary, which Michael Hartwig, rector and professor of moral theology, left to "marry" the head of the Gay Alliance. This seminary used the Guindon book *The Sexual Language*, from which these quotations are taken, as a moral theology textbook, according to Rev. Joseph Wilson who studied there.[83] The seminary invited Paul Shanley to speak. Shanley, who Cardinal Medeiros was told

> spoke of pedophilia (which is a non-coerced sexual manipulation of sexual organs including oral-genital sex between an adult and a child). He stated that the adult is not the seducer—the "kid" is the seducer and further the kid is not traumatized by the act per se, the kid is traumatized when the police and authorities "drag" the kid in for questioning.[84]

Father Wilson was at the Dallas seminary when Shanley lectured, and said, "I was sitting directly behind the then-bishop of Dallas, Thomas Tschoepe, who laughed and joked his way through a truly vile presentation."[85] As we have seen in Chapter Five, Tschoepe knew of and tolerated Rudy Kos's abuse of boys.

The bishops of the United States were fully aware that professors in their seminaries were teaching that sex with children and boys did no real harm, that it was only the fuss that unenlightened, pre-Vatican II parents created that harmed the children. Therefore the bishops did not turn the abusers over to the police and did little or nothing to help the victims—who had not been harmed, according to the advanced moral theology that was being taught in their seminaries. Msgr. Richard S. Sniezyk, interim leader of the Springfield, Massachusetts, diocese after Bishop Dupré disappeared, pointed to "a belief among some priests in the 1960s, '70s, and '80s that sex with young men was acceptable." Sniezyk claimed, "No one thought much about it" and that "the whole atmosphere out there was, it was OK, it was OK to do."[86] That is what was being taught in the seminaries.

And perhaps is still being taught. The bishops lied to parents and laity who complained about abuse and pernicious doctrines. Why should anyone believe the American bishops? At one seminary, André Guindon's *Sexual Language* is listed, without any explanation, as a recommended text for the course "Marriage and Human Sexuality."

The Vatican, chiefly Cardinal Ratzinger (now Benedict XVI) as head of the Congregation for the Doctrine of the Faith, occasionally tried to discipline priests who taught these horrors, and for his efforts was denounced by Catholic liberals as a Nazi and Grand Inquisitor. Nor is the Vatican blameless: the Vatican received a stream of complaints that bishops were allowing these doctrines to be taught to priests who then acted on those doctrines by having sex with minors, but not once has a bishop been removed for failure to exercise oversight over his seminary and clergy.

Guindon, "caught in the Roman dragnet,"[87] is still hailed as an example of an advanced moral thinker who was victimized by the Vatican. "The darling of the Catholic liberals in Canada," Guindon is praised on a website of the University of Montréal at Québec as a "figure d'une rare integrité, d'une subtile intelligence and d'une chaleureuse compassion." Douglas Letson, former president of St. Jerome's University at the University of Waterloo in Canada, refers to Guindon as "the only credible Catholic voice in a Canadian university with the potential to foster a meaningful dialogue within the Canadian community on sensitive issues of a sexual nature."[88] Letson and the current president of St. Jerome's, Michael W. Higgins, praise Guindon's "authentic orthodoxy" and his "wholly readable theological vision" and like him reject "infallible codes of obligation."[89] They do not see that Guindon's acceptance of pedophilia and pederasty might reveal a flaw in his method and attitude; or perhaps they agree with Guindon's assessment of pedophilia and pederasty. The attitude of many Catholic liberals is that the sexual revolution in the Church must go on, whatever the cost to children and adolescents. The return to moral absolutes and exceptionless norms might lessen child abuse, but it would also forbid fornication, adultery, homosexuality, and the other practices which the Catholic Theological Society was, and as far as I know, still remains open to as life-enhancing experiences.

Dissenters claim that there is absolutely no connection between dissent and the sexual scandals, but the dissenters wanted their ideas put into practice, and priests and seminarians obliged. If seminarians were taught the traditional doctrine, it was presented only as the "official teaching" while dissenting theologians were presented as "current theological thinking." The dissent reached into the very basis of ethics, and situation ethics became the solvent of all traditional teaching on moral absolutes. Paul Shanley explained to the confused young men who came to him for counseling the concept of "situation ethics" so that they would have sex with him. Samuel Johnson observed of a moral skeptic, "If he does really think that there is no distinction between virtue and vice, why, sir, when he leaves our houses let us count our spoons."

The *National Catholic Reporter* published an account by a priest who was sexually involved with a teenage boy. The priest wrote: "I read a book on situation ethics. The basic theme was that no act is objectively evil; its morality or immorality depends on the situation. I reasoned from this that all sex acts are basically good since God had created us sexual beings, or at least they were morally neutral. They are only evil if they harm someone (like rape or incest or infidelity)." There is nothing good or evil in itself; only the consequences make it so. Everyone is having sex in some way; it can't be wrong. "Then I read a statistic, reported in a newspaper, that ninety-nine percent of adolescents masturbated. I believed it and thought maybe I was strange. So, a period of sexual exploration began. It started with masturbation, and later I had several sexual encounters with classmates in the seminary. It was pleasurable."[90]

When the young priest, full of the latest moral theories, was ordained and sent off to a parish, he met a teenager, "Bill."

> I had known him a year or so when we first had sexual contact. It started gradually and built up to the real thing. He was sixteen then. I had suspected he was gay, and he was. He liked me and admired me. If he felt any shame, it was apparent to no one. We stayed friends and had sex off and on, but that was not the center of our relationship for either of us.

> I did not feel guilt at the time, or at least I deluded myself into thinking I actually was doing something good for Bill. I did not want him to live his youthful years suppressing his sexuality as I had done. I wanted him to feel liberated, like I thought I was. I wanted to be a positive role model.[91]

The priest decided that perhaps he should not continue such sexual encounters; he met a sympathetic woman and became close to her, but remained celibate. He became a pastor. Years later, Bill sued him and the diocese for these sexual activities. The bishop sent the priest for treatment; he was pronounced "cured" (of what? sexual desire? heresy?). He now wants to remain in ministry, and pleads against a zero-tolerance policy for sexual abuse.

Some theologians have focused especially on justifying homosexuality. The biblical passages against it have been explained away, and same-sex love held up as a model. The Rev. Paul Thomas, archivist of the archdiocese of Baltimore, wrote a series of articles that appeared first in the *Washington Blade* and then in the Baltimore *Catholic Review* on the supposed homoerotic relationship between David and Jonathan and between John and Jesus. Such analyses proved very useful to priests who had to deal with teenage boys who had irrational prejudices against homosexual behavior.

The Rev. Paul Aube tried to convince a fifteen-year-old boy that homosexual behavior was approved by the Bible: "[Aube] showed me several passages in the Bible that um supported a point of view that he was ah trying to, trying to I guess he was trying to convince me that um it was, it was an acceptable Godly thing for some type of ah sexual relationship between, well between myself and Father Aube."[92] Rudy Kos also used theological arguments on his victims. One boy who had homosexual feelings was sent to Kos for confession and counseling. Kos informed him of the latest theological thought on homosexuality. The victim recounted to the court that Kos told him:

> "Well, basically, there's only, like, nine passages in the Bible that refer to homosexuality, and that people"—he just went through this whole process of saying, you know, how it's really interesting how people pick and chose what they want to follow out of the Bible and that so much was lost in translation between different languages, that homosexuality was actually translated from mail [sic] prostitute and that mail [sic] prostitute means something totally different from homosexuality.
>
> He then took me through all of these passages in the Bible. And he—he showed me where it was written in the Bible about homosexuality and explained under what context it was used. And—and basically he was showing me examples of where there are two men who actually loved each other. And it said in the Bible something to the effect that they loved each other like a man and women [sic] love each other. And he is saying, "This is in the Bible. And God loved these people. There is nothing wrong with them. God doesn't hate them for being that way."[93]

Sexual liberation was taught in Catholic seminaries, with predictable results.

One underlying error is seeing the empirical finds of the psychological sciences as better grounds for morality than divine revelation, which is dismissed as arbitrary rules of behavior. Guindon criticized a "code morality" that held that God had decreed arbitrarily that some actions were evil; Guindon claimed to follow Thomas Aquinas's example by building a rational morality based on what was harmful and hurtful to man. He assumed, and this is one of his errors, that the human mind, specifically the human mind using the research techniques of mid-twentieth century psychology, could discover whether a sexual act did any harm. First of all, the time frame is too limited: some psychologists could not see any *immediate* psychological damage from adult-child sex; but they did not do a study over the lifetime of the victim. The tools of psychological research are inexact, and at best can determine variations from the common state of human life. But this state is fallen and therefore abnormal, and Christians are called to full human perfection. Only sanctity is truly normal, in that it fulfills what God wants the human person to be. Divine law prohibits actions because they are evil and damaging; but we may or may not be able to see the damage if we try to ascertain it by the very limited techniques of modern psychological research.

Sexual liberation was a strong wind blowing through the modern world when Pope John XXIII opened the windows of the Catholic Church to let in some fresh air. Pastoral considerations based upon the latest psychological fads led priests to permit previously forbidden sexual behavior. This was not good for the weak Christian. Conrad Baars, who recognized the problems that faulty "traditional" presentations of morality had created among Catholics, nevertheless rejected the new morality, which said in effect to a person struggling with moral difficulties: "You may ignore the teachings of the Magisterium. God's laws are too hard for you," that is, "You are not and never will be strong and good enough to adhere to these laws."[94]

Bad psychology and bad theology probably did not increase the number or activity of true pedophiles; these men live in a private hell with its own dynamics. But false doctrine did provide a justification for homosexual behavior, and the incidence of priests having sex with teenage boys increased markedly through the '70s and '80s. It then decreased. The number of priests fell rapidly; priests aged and had a lower sex drive; candidates for ordination were older and more mature; some of the worst offenders had been removed or put out to pasture. Even if the proportion of homosexuals in the clergy has increased, they have behaved better with teenage boys.

The toleration of the abuse raises deeper questions. Certainly some bishops were personally corrupt; a few were involved with teenage boys, more with adults. However, most bishops did not have this motive for tolerating abuse. They had nonconfrontational personalities, they were influenced by old-fashioned clericalism, they regarded priests as sacrament-producing machines whose personal abilities and integrity were irrelevant to their priesthood, and they were caught up in the new openness to the modern world that led them to lend an ear to bad advice from psychologists. They tolerated fashionable heresies and immorality among their priests, and the heresy contributed to the immorality. But the Church also suffered from older distortions and errors. These are more deeply rooted and are often regarded as "traditional," "authentic," "orthodox" Catholicism, and are therefore even more subtly dangerous than obvious dissent from Catholic teaching.

CHAPTER SIXTEEN

# OLD ERRORS

CONSERVATIVES OFTEN SAY that the answer to the sexual abuse crisis is simply "fidelity." But fidelity to what? To the Gospel? Or to the ethos of pre-Vatican II Catholicism, which produced some of the worst abusers in the rings of El Paso, Davenport, and Boston? The new errors discussed in the previous chapter would not have been productive of such evil unless older errors had prepared the way for them. Catholics (and to a large extent all western Christians) have suffered from spiritual distortions for centuries, distortions whose historical roots can be traced. First of all, Christians have misunderstood the role of the emotions; they have repressed anger that should be directed against evil. The repressed anger, instead, often motivated abusers to control victims. This misunderstanding of the role of the emotions in the spiritual life is built upon a deeper philosophical misunderstanding of what makes human actions good or bad: either their conformity to an objective created order or naked obedience to the arbitrary will of God. Stemming from this misunderstanding is a misunderstanding of the nature of sin and a consequent misunderstanding of repentance and forgiveness, a misunderstanding that made forgiveness a tool used by abusers to oppress the weak.

## *Repression of Emotions*

Researchers have attempted to differentiate between the personalities of sexually abusive priests and non-sexually abusive priests in a psychiatric institution by giving them the MMPI (Minnesota Multiphasic Personality Inventory). The only significant difference, and it was a major difference, was that the abusive priests scored very high on overcontrolled hostility: "Twice the number of priests scoring in the clinically significant range of the overcontrolled hostility measure were found in the hospitalized sexual abusive group...compared with the hospitalized non-abusing control group."[1] These priests had repressed (that is, refused to acknowledge or to feel) their anger to a far greater degree than the general population does. Either their personalities had led them to the clerical life, or clerical life had changed their personalities. They tended to be "passive, often assuming an overly compliant and obliging posture towards others—particularly those in authority."[2] They denied having any emotions of hostility, and therefore got along very well in the hierarchical institution of the Church, which values obedience and compliance above all.

Any institution tends to preserve itself by avoiding conflict, whether external or internal. In addition to this universal tendency, many Catholics have a false understanding of the nature and role of anger. It is seen as something negative, something that a Christian should not feel. Meekness, which is the virtue that moderates anger, is misunderstood as passivity. Moses angrily confronting Pharaoh was the meekest of men, because he moderated the plagues to allow Pharaoh time to repent. Meekness moderates anger so that it is in accord with reason; since most people suffer from an excess of anger, the virtue that *increases* anger in those who are deficient in it so that it is in accord with reason does not have a name. The abusive priests avoided expressing their anger; they had personalities inclined to "avoiding conflict, being unassertive, and lacking autonomy."[3] Such people make good, docile staff members of an institution; they do not rock the boat.

These priests feared rejection and abandonment; this fear created hostility which they felt to be wrong and un-Christian, and therefore they experienced guilt and shame. In order to preserve their sense of stability, they refused to admit to themselves that they were feeling this hostility. They feared that if they showed hostility to their superiors they would get into trouble. They sought refuge from conflicts with powerful people by "relating to people who do not threaten one's sense of stability and safety [that is, those who are smaller and weaker and possess less authority—young children and adolescents in the case of sexually abusing priests]."[4] Such priests felt no threat from these vulnerable victims. Anger is a powerful emotion, and if it is not felt and acknowledged (although not necessarily acted on) these priests "may experience a high degree of chronically overcontrolled anger and aggression which ultimately is acted upon through the sexual victimization of minors."[5]

Those who dealt with the bishops have consistently remarked that bishops have never expressed outrage or righteous anger,[6] even at the most horrendous cases of abuse and sacrilege such as abusing boys after getting them drunk on consecrated wine. Bishops seem to think that anger at sin is un-Christian. Gilbert Kilman, a child psychiatrist, commented, "What amazes me is the lack of outrage the [C]hurch feels when its good work is being harmed. So, if there is anything the [C]hurch needs to know, it needs to know how to be outraged."[7] Mark Serrano confronted Bishop Frank Rodimer, asking why he had let his priest-friend Peter Osinski[8] sleep with boys at Rodimer's beach house while Rodimer was in the next bedroom: "Where is your moral indignation?" Rodimer's answer was, "Then I don't get it. What do you want?"[9] What Serrano wanted Rodimer to do is to behave like a man with a heart, a heart that is outraged by evil. But Rodimer couldn't; his inability to feel outrage was a quality that helped make him a bishop. He would never get into fights, never rock the boat, never "divide" but only "unify." Rodimer could not understand why he should feel deep anger at evil, at the violation of the innocent, at oppression of the weak.

At one time Catholics tended to repress sexual feelings because they feared that acknowledging the existence of such feelings would lead to sin and hell. Fear, not reason, was used to control and direct desire. But fear itself must be directed by reason, and as a passion, fear is as likely to mislead people as sexual desire is. A general loosening of sexual behavior has relieved that problem of repression of sexual desire, although it has created others. The emotions that are now blocked are hatred and anger. Christians feel that they ought not to feel these emotions, that it is un-Christian to feel them. They secretly suspect that Jesus was being un-Christian in his attitude to the scribes and Pharisees when he was angry at them, that he was un-Christian when he drove the moneychangers out of the temple or declared that millstones (not vacations in treatment centers) were the way to treat child abusers.

Conrad Baars noticed this emotional deformation in the clergy in the mid-twentieth century. He recognized that there had been distortions in "traditional" Catholic spirituality. It had become too focused upon individual acts rather than on growth in virtue; it had emphasized sheer naked strength of will in a misunderstanding of Francisco Suarez's version of Thomas Aquinas's moral theology. In forgetting that growth in virtue was the goal of the Christian's moral life, it forgot that the emotions, all emotions, including anger and hate, are part of human nature and must be integrated into a virtuous life.[10] Baars had been imprisoned by the Nazis. He knew iniquity first hand and that there was something wrong with those who did not hate it: "A little reflection will make it clear that there is a big difference between the person who knows solely that something is evil and ought to be opposed, and the one who in addition also feels hate for that evil, is angry that it is corrupting or harming his fellow-men, and feels aroused to combat it courageously and vigorously."[11]

Wrath is a necessary and positive part of human nature: "Wrath is the strength to attack the repugnant; the power of anger is actually the power of resistance in the soul."[12] The lack of wrath against injustice is a deficiency: "One who does good with passion is more praiseworthy than one who is 'not entirely' afire for the good, even to the forces of the sensual realm."[13] Aquinas says that "lack of the passion of anger is also a vice" because a man who truly and forcefully rejects evil will be angry at it. The lack of anger makes the movement of the will against evil "lacking or weak." He quotes John Chrysostom: "He who is not angry, whereas he has cause to be, sins. For unreasonable patience is the hotbed of many vices, it fosters negligence, and incites not only the wicked but the good to do wrong."[14]

Josef Pieper observed the disappearance of the concept of just wrath in Catholic moral theology and spiritual life:

> The fact, however, that Thomas assigns to [just] wrath a positive relation to the virtue of fortitude has become largely unintelligible and unacceptable to present-day Christianity and its non-Christian critics. This lack of comprehension may be explained partly by the exclusion, from Christian ethics, of the component of passion (with its inevitably physical aspect) as something alien and incongruous—an exclusion due to a kind of intellectual stoicism—and partly by the fact that the explosive activity which reveals itself in wrath is naturally repugnant to good behavior regulated by "bourgeois" standards.[15]

Pieper's quote from Aquinas's commentary on John is relevant to both anger and forgiveness. Aquinas is commenting on the passage in which Jesus tells us to offer the other cheek:

> Holy Scripture must be understood in the light of what Christ and the saints have actually practiced. Christ did not offer the other cheek, nor Paul either. Thus to interpret the injunction of the Sermon on the Mount literally is to misunderstand it. This injunction signifies rather the readiness of the soul to bear, *if it be necessary*, such things and worse, without bitterness against the attacker. This readiness our Lord showed, when He gave up His body to be crucified. That response of the Lord was useful, therefore, for our instruction.[16]

The philosophical error that is at the root of this rejection of the passions is not stoicism so much as nominalism and a false concept of freedom which has become ingrained in Western Christianity.

The Rev. Kevin Culligan, a priest in his sixties, was angry when he was a teenager, but says, "Since then I have been uncomfortable with anger." He has been afraid of losing control of himself and doing something "I would later regret or have held against me." He feared becoming "irrational." But he saw a television program about a boy who had been abused by a priest when he was eight years old, and saw the arrogance of the church officials who dismissed the boy's cries for help. Culligan shouted at the TV set: "Those bastards! Look what they've done to the Church!" He felt the hot wrath of God in him against those who had made the Church a den of sexual predators. He reflected that "many current spiritualities regard strong emotion—fear, joy, anger, sadness, hope, pity—as 'obstacles to spiritual growth.'" But Jesus felt the full range of human emotions, including anger, and Culligan decided that "our emotions too—our rage as well as our compassion—are sacred" because they give us the energy needed to rebuild the Church and do God's work.[17]

One Irish bishop said the calm way everyone approached sexual abuse helped mislead him about the seriousness of the matter:

> "I think if it had come to me differently...if the parent had come roaring and shouting at me, it would have affected the response. It would have made me sit up more and be aware. The experience of having direct contact with a parent who was very angry and very upset would have alerted me more too. If someone had come thumping at the door outraged and making demands, which they are quite entitled to do, I would have learned a lot faster."[18]

As Gregory the Great said, "Reason opposes evil the more effectively when anger ministers at her side."[19]

The lack of aggressiveness among clerics has been noticed by psychologists. The National Conference of Catholic Bishops published a study that said "priests are often, by temperament and personality, anxious to establish harmony and to please. By theology and vocation they are concerned to be healers, reconcilers, and builders of the community."[20] Almost all psychological studies support this assessment: priests and seminarians are "unassertive, dislike violence . . . and have a high need for abasement (i.e., want to give in and avoid conflict)."[21] This dislike of conflict is present in other churches and their clergy as well. The presence of homosexuals in the clergy reinforces this aversion to conflict. Although homosexuals do not have a common set of personality traits, "there is one that tends to be shared by obligative homosexual males; as boys, they were not fighters. They avoided challenges to compete for dominance in the dominance hierarchy of boyhood."[22]

Diplomats rule in the Vatican, and diplomats dislike confrontation, anger, and hatred, because such emotions make diplomacy difficult. The Vatican has appointed the bishops, the bishops have trained the clergy. Therefore hatred of iniquity has been felt to be something that did not fit into the Christian life. The Catholic bishops had and have this lack of anger, and thereby betray a defect or weakness of the will in their rejection of child abuse. Pope John Paul II expressed sorrow but not anger at the mystery of evil that is child abuse, but he thereby demonstrated only part of the virtue of fortitude—Thomas Aquinas explained: "Whereas fortitude...has two parts, namely endurance and aggression, it employs anger, not in the act of endurance...but for the act of aggression...sorrow by its very nature gives way to the thing that hurts; though accidentally it helps in aggression...as being the cause of anger."[21] Sorrow at evil without anger at evil is a fault, a fault which the Catholic bishops have repeatedly fallen into in their handling of sexual abuse and which the late pope fell into when he tolerated the bishops' faults. Until just anger is directed at the bishops, until bishops (including the pope) feel just anger at their fellow bishops who have disgraced and failed their office, the state of sin in the Church continues.

## *Nominalism and Voluntarism*

Nominalism is a school of philosophy that holds that our ideas by which we classify things are arbitrary, mere names that do not correspond to anything in reality. Realists hold that the idea we have of "dog" corresponds to a real class of beings; nominalists say it is arbitrary, that we could divide up reality in any number of ways. In moral theology, nominalism says that actions are wrong because God forbids them. Realism maintains that God forbids certain actions because they are in themselves wrong and harmful to the good of the human person. Nominalists see morality as arbitrary and therefore in theory changeable. Realists see morality as simply an expression of reality, and therefore not changeable.

Augustine DiNoia of the International Theological Commission has argued that nominalism "let loose a catastrophe on the human race" because it separated morality from anthropology. DiNoia explained, "Imagine...a mother cooking dinner who spots her child eating cookies. The mother could say, 'Eating cookies is forbidden in this house,' appealing to her authority. Or she could say, 'If you eat those cookies, you'll spoil your appetite,' appealing to a truth about human nature." Nominalism is a morality of authority, rules, and prohibitions; Thomism (and patristic morality in general) is a morality of virtue based on the structure of human reality. DiNoia said of nominalism, "The prevalence of this kind of moral theology gave rise to the intolerable tensions experienced by many Catholics in the face of the moral teaching of *Humanae Vitae*—and eventually the entirety of Christian teaching about human sexuality—which seemed to impose an outdated moral obligation whose connection with the human good was either denied or dismissed, or more commonly, simply not apparent."[24]

Nominalism has a false idea of human freedom: for nominalism man is most free when he is indifferent to the alternatives placed before him, when he can choose one or the other with equal ease. This is the basis of the casuistry that dominated Catholic moral theology for centuries until about the 1960s. According to Romanus Cessario, "The casuist advanced the thesis that each person possesses the ability to remain radically indifferent or undetermined when confronted with a judgment of reason about a good to be pursued."[25] This is entirely different from being afire for the good, which Gregory the Great commended, or hungering and thirsting after justice, as Christ recommended. For the nominalist, moral life is based not on growth in virtue through a love of the good and a hatred of evil, but on obedience to the Divine Will, which is in essence arbitrary. For the casuists, and through them for modern Catholics, "moral commands replace moral objects as the way in which one comes to identify right from wrong,"[26] and the wrong is almost always identified with sexual wrongdoing.[27]

Voluntarism focuses on obedience to the Divine Will as the central aspect of morality. Voluntarists hold that what is morally right depends on what God arbitrarily wills. So if we are to know right from wrong, we must know what God wills with respect to the moral law. Since, however, God's will is (according to voluntarism) not determined by any reality, it would seem that human reason is powerless to ascertain what God wills with respect to the moral law. After all, if there is no reality that God consults in order to decide what to will regarding the moral law, there are certainly no reasons we can consult. Hence, if we are to know what morality requires, God has to tell us, either in Scripture or by granting us a special revelation.

If a person looks only to God's command rather than to the created good which the command is intended to preserve, he will be unaware of the harm that sin does in the creation. Psychologists told bishops, don't make a fuss when you are told that a priest has had sex with a child. No—or, at most, little—harm has been done to the child. It is no worse than being frightened by "a trip to the doctor, a ride on the airplane," because as Kinsey said, "It is difficult to understand why a child, except for its cultural conditioning, should be distressed at having its [note the depersonalized *its*] genitals touched."[28] The bishops adopted this attitude because they focused exclusively on the divine commands about sexuality rather than also looking at the created order which the commands are intended to foster and preserve. Sylvia Demarest, who represented victims of abuse, observed, "Never, never was there any effort to determine who the victims were, to offer assistance to them. The perpetrators never had to confront the harm they did to the victims. There was no indication that the bishops cared a whit about the victims."[29] Psychologists had told the bishops that the victims weren't harmed. The bishops believed this in part because of the impact of the nominalism that they had absorbed with their moral theology. The only harm the abusers had done was to themselves; they incurred guilt by disobeying a divine command. Once the abuser went to confession and through therapy tried to break his bad habit, there was nothing more to do.

The mistaken theory of voluntarism has immediate implications in the ordinary moral life of the Christian. Obedience is everything. Conrad Baars describes it as the attitude, "What counts is that you will the good and do it, no matter how you feel."[30] The Ignatian principle of *agere contra* was misapplied: Ignatius Loyola said that if you felt like giving up spiritual reading after a half hour rather than the prescribed hour, you should instead do it an hour and a half. This may be generally good advice in discipline, and sometimes it is necessary to act contrary to our emotions. But if in choosing the good and opposing evil, we always have to act contrary to our emotions, there is something wrong with us, because true virtue exists in a person in which the will and emotions are in harmony with reason. In fact the idea quickly spread among Christians that it was more virtuous to choose the good against one's emotions than to choose a good that one loved. Montaigne explored this idea, but rejected it when he remembered Socrates, the perfectly virtuous pagan.

With the Catholic Reformation, the Council of Trent, and the foundation of seminaries for priestly education in the 1500s, though nominalism as a philosophy had become obsolete, its voluntaristic or legalistic view of morality continued to have influence in the Church. This was partly due to the context of religious wars between Catholics and Protestants, which led the Catholic Church to emphasize strict obedience to moral rules as authoritative without much effort to show their source in the structure of reality, ultimately in the reality of God's triune personhood. But it was mostly due to the new emphasis on more frequent confession. Priests were trained to hear these confessions and used "manuals" of moral theology that listed moral rules and classification of sins. Because it reflected much pastoral experience, this legalism dominated moral theology until Leo XIII revived the theology of St. Thomas Aquinas in 1880, after which moral theology gradually began to be more centered on growth in the virtues culminating in the virtue of charity. Yet even now, many Catholics retain the manuals' legalistic view of Christian morality.

Russell Shaw's description of the prevalent legalism in the Catholic Church shows that it is a form of nominalism: "Legalism is essentially the view that specific moral norms are more or less like positive laws or rules—that is to say, they are legislative enactments that can be revised, suspended, or even taken off the books by a qualified lawgiver."[31] This is a widespread Catholic attitude: even in 2004, I heard Ralph McInerney (who as a Thomist knows better) referring to the Church's "ban" on artificial contraception; John Haas at the National Catholic Bioethics Center had to instruct his staff not to refer to immoral medical actions as "prohibited procedures." If actions are morally wrong, they are not wrong because the Church bans or prohibits them, but because they do not correspond to the structure of reality, a reality reflecting the nature of its Creator. However, Catholics have been imbued with legalism transmitted through casuistry from nominalism. Nominalism has shifted the focus of moral theology from happiness and the virtues that contribute to it to law and obligation: "there was near unanimity among ethicists, especially from the seventeenth century onward, that placed obligation at the center of morality."[32]

Nominalism and legalism are closely allied to clericalism, whether of the conservative or liberal variety. "Pastors and confessors imbued with legalism sometimes imagined that they had the power to dispense (or refuse to dispense) from a variety of moral obligations."[33] In the pastoral (that is, lax) approach, the priest told the inquiring layman to "follow your conscience." This is either a truism—"Do good and avoid evil"—or dangerously misleading: "Any decision is moral, as long as it is conscientious," or worst of all, "Your decision makes something right or wrong." The layman was left with the strong impression that the priest could give a person permission to act without reference to the moral law. When this advice led the layman to accept contraception or remarriage after divorce or abortion or homosexual behavior, the layman did not object. But the same approach was used to persuade teenage boys to have sex with the priest: "If Father says so," every Catholic had been propagandized to believe, "it can't be wrong." The law was full of loopholes, and a priest's job was to find them. The lack of emphasis upon the moral law as an expression of objective reality, and the consequent lack of a sense that virtue is the aim of human life, helped abusive priests to seduce teenagers.

If things are wrong because God forbids them, not because they harm the good of the human person, the only action that is necessary to make repentance complete is to seek the pardon of God. The sin has caused no harm to anyone except the sinner, because the only evil is his disobedience to a command of God. When God pardons this disobedience the *status quo ante* is restored. Sister Mary Ann Walsh, spokesman for the U.S. Conference of Catholic Bishops, revealed this attitude when she said, "Once this [pedophilia] was seen as a moral failing,...you could do penance and promise not to do it again."[34] But that is only part of the process if reality has been damaged.

Stephen J. Pope of Boston College observed that "the moral theology operative in the mid-twentieth century assumed that sexual sins from adultery to incest could be corrected by going to confession and reforming the will."[35] Confession removed the only real evil, disobedience to God, and restored the abuser to a state of grace. The abusive acts, like all human acts, were seen as isolated acts of will. The will chose wrongly, but could now choose rightly. The psychological force of habit was partially acknowledged; that is why the abusers were sent to psychologists to correct their bad behavior patterns. But the place of virtuous habits and good emotions was disregarded, because virtues had largely vanished from the casuistry that dominated Catholic moral theology.

If, however, actions are forbidden because they harm the human good, God's pardon of the guilt of the act of disobedience does not in itself restore the *status quo ante*. The harm that the sin has done in creation remains, even if the sinner has been restored to a right relationship with God. This, I think, is the main meaning of the Catholic teaching that the forgiveness of sins does not remove the temporal punishments due to sin. The consequences of the sin remain: the money of the robbery victim is still not in the hands of its rightful owner, the murder victim is still dead and his wife widowed and his children orphaned, the sexual abuse victim of a priest is still suffering from severe distortions of his sexual identity and feelings of being betrayed by the God-ordained messenger of salvation.

Feminist theologians have sometimes accused Christianity of being a religion of child abuse, in which the Father takes pleasure in the pain and death of his Son on the cross. This is a profound misunderstanding of biblical Christianity, but contains elements of truth about nominalistic, voluntaristic postmedieval Christianity. The abuser alternately terrorizes and reproves his victim. The victim starts to view the abuser as godlike (see p. 273) *because the abuser is behaving like the God of nominalism and voluntarism*. The emphasis on obedience to arbitrary commands as the essence of Christianity contributes to this. Protestantism is also the heir of medieval nominalism,[36] but the Catholic Church, with its casuistic moral theology and construction of a fine network of ever-changing (e.g., refraining from meat on Friday) rules that bind under pain of eternal death has deeply impressed this attitude on the laity. A priest is the closest thing to God, and an abusive priest is even more like God, who is always trying to trick and betray men into damnation, or alternatively freely and arbitrarily giving salvation to all, even to the unrepentant sinner.

This false image of God is useful to tyrants, and tyranny is always a temptation, even to those who hold legitimate authority. All power tends to corrupt and absolute power tends to corrupt absolutely, as Lord Acton said of the Catholic Church, but of course it applies to all authority. However, secular authorities do not claim to be able to punish even after death. The only honorable human attitude to such a tyrannical God is one of rebellion, but a rebellion that is doomed to defeat because this tyranny possesses an infinite and arbitrary power.

## *Obedience and Autocracy*

The errors of nominalism and voluntarism have become deeply ingrained in Catholicism not because of their compelling logic but because they buttress autocracy. Everyone in a position of authority, even fully legitimate and necessary authority, finds it convenient to demand absolute obedience from those subject to him. It is so easy to command, so hard to explain. This autocratic spirit attracts abusive personalities, and creates conditions in victims in which they are led into abuse by obedience to spiritual authority.

Romanus Cessario, summarizing Servais Pinckaers's analysis of casuistry, points out that "like nominalism, casuistry practically eschews the notion of final causality."[37] (The final cause is the end, *finis*, to which something tends.) "The absence of any reference to a final cause, exemplified by the omission of an adequate account of the New Testament Beatitudes and our final beatitude, implies that no effective final end exists for the human person, and, therefore, no end draws him or her." All human beings desire happiness; but in the casuistic system there is no goal of happiness, of beatitude, which draws human beings to it. "To fill the place of final causality, the casuists stressed obedience, which becomes the fundamental virtue of the casuist systems." A sense of duty replaces the natural desire for happiness, and "casuistic accounts wrench obedience from its place in the constellation of human virtues, rendering it virtually the sole denominator of the good. Consider some examples from mid-twentieth-century religious life." Cessario concludes, "When obedience serves as the architectonic virtue it easily occasions the exercise of an autocratic spirit by those in authority and a correlative servile spirit in those who serve under them."[38]

Cardinal Groër was the head of the Legion of Mary in Austria. Its handbook stressed "Gehorsam," obedience.[39] One monk observed that Groër made the members of the Legion into "Marionetten,"[40] puppets; another saw his adherents as practicing "kadavergehorsam,"[41] the "corpse-obedience" that Ignatius of Loyola held up as an ideal to the Jesuits. Udo Fischer, in responding to a disciplinary action by his abbot, reminded the abbot, "I have promised Christian, not military obedience."[42] Former monks of Göttweig wrote to their brothers who remained in the abbey that the controversy was not only about sexual abuse, but about "spiritual authority that was misused to create dependency, not to bring men to personal maturity, but to lead into inner lack of freedom and to manipulate them in their development."[43] Leo Pfister saw a connection between the "Marionettenhaftigkeit" (puppetry) of Groër's disciples and Groër's ever more obvious homosexual tendencies.[44] One observer of Groër suspected that family difficulties (father absence and mother dominance) were at the root of his personality problems. Groër, like many others, compensated through a "very strict spiritual-ideological system of rules,"[45] which was present in the Legion of Mary. This rigorous system attracted men with similar problems to the Legion, where he could prey on them.

Such an autocratic exercise of authority infantilizes the subject. He is not guided to a moral maturity in which he sees, loves, and pursues the good through the exercise of all the virtues, the foremost of which is charity, but instead follows arbitrary commands, the logic of which he cannot see. This infantilization prepares the ground for sexual abuse.

The abuser has a personality that finds pleasure in controlling others, usually to compensate for a sense that he is being controlled by unwanted and perverse sexual desires. He wants to be an autocrat, exercising total and arbitrary control over others. This control can extend to sexual abuse when the others, the victims, are vulnerable because of age, emotional confusion, or a conscience distorted by the idea that obedience is the supreme virtue.

## *Forgiveness*

An appellate judge in Illinois stated, "The following facts are true": When she was a teenager, Gina Trimble became the Rev. Raymond Kownacki's housekeeper after he told her parents that he would help her get a better education. He educated her in what it felt like to be raped. She got pregnant, and he induced an abortion. He had her drink quinine and then "entered her bedroom, removed Gina's slacks and underpants, inserted his entire hand into Gina's vagina and wrenched and squeezed her uterus." She passed out and later delivered a dead fetus.

She left him and told her parents. They visited Bishop Albert Zuroweste of Belleville, who "took no notes and showed little interest in Gina or her claims." After they left his office, the Rev. Dean J. Braun, Kownacki's successor at the parish, who had accompanied the Trimbles, told them "that Bishop Zuroweste would not discipline Father Kownacki and that Gina must forgive Father Kownacki and forget his physical and sexual abuse of her." To accomplish this, Braun performed a ceremony unknown to the Roman Rite: "He placed a ritualistic vestment on his shoulders, anointed Gina with oil, prayed over her in Latin, and while anointing her with oil, told her she must give up her anger and that she must forgive Father Kownacki and forget what he had done to her or her soul would die."[46]

This is an extreme but representative example of the misunderstanding and misuse of forgiveness. The demand that victims forgive their abusers is used to avoid the hard work of repentance and restitution: "The demand to forgive so that everyone will feel better, or the desire to minimize conflict in relationships, encourages 'forgiveness' that is too quick and, ultimately not redemptive."[47] Catholic and Protestant leaders find this misunderstanding of forgiveness a useful tool. "Church leaders often use forgiveness as a tool for settling abuse situations as quickly and easily as possible to avoid scandal, conflict, and disruption to institutional programs, to spare them from having to confront or oppose a powerful and threatening person, to avoid possible legal action, and to avoid having to face up to injustice and abuse in churches' own structures."[48] This desire to avoid conflict is strengthened by the predominantly female membership of the churches. Women have a stronger tendency than men to maintain relationships at any cost: they keep the family together, not only in hard times, but in cases of incest. They are frequently victims of abuse in churches, but are also the ones who do not want the abuse confronted lest it tear the Church apart.

Forgiveness has many stages. First of all, like any human act, it must be in accord with reality. Actions that are based on a false perception of reality are not good actions. The injured party must react in accord with reality. He must be angry at the real evil that has been done to him.[49] The reality of the sin and injustice must be recognized, not only in words, but in deeds. We speak of someone being in a false situation; the thief who verbally confesses his sin but refuses to return the money is living in a false situation. The offender must recognize the truth of his position in regard to the person he has offended. Then the offender must act on that position, by a repentance that includes acknowledging his offense to all hurt by it, by the acceptance of deserved punishment, and by the will to make restitution. Even though the injured party may have been desirous at all times of forgiving the offended, it is only at this point can forgiveness occur. As L. Gregory Jones explains, "The purpose of forgiveness is the restoration of communion, the reconciliation of brokenness."[50] Forgiveness ends in the renewal of a relationship. This renewal cannot occur without the repentance of the offender.

This is the structure of Christian forgiveness. Misunderstandings of forgiveness are based upon a misperception of what Christian charity is. God is love, *Deus caritas est*. But what type of love is charity? According to Thomas Aquinas, charity is friendship. Even if the universe were never created, God is love because he is trinitarian. The love within the Trinity is a love of friendship. God is also love in relation to his creatures. He offers this friendship to them, but friendship by its nature is reciprocal. A person can offer friendship, but friendship does not exist until the person to whom it is offered responds and offers friendship in return. Christian charity therefore must be distinguished from benevolence (modern "unconditional love"), which is wishing well to someone, desiring his good. Friendship includes benevolence, but it goes beyond benevolence in that (among other things) it is reciprocal. We can wish well to someone who does not wish well to us; we cannot be friends with someone who refuses to be our friend.

God therefore wills the good of all that He has created. He also offers the special gift of friendship to the rational creature He has created, man. Man, however, can refuse this gift of friendship by committing sin. To return to friendship the sinner must repent. It is a logical impossibility, a self-contradiction for God to restore the friendship without repentance. This repentance (itself a gift of God) effects a real change in the sinner, and he can receive the forgiveness offered him by God for the sake of the Passion of Christ and thereby restore the relationship of friendship. The forgiveness of sins therefore has a double cause; both must be present or forgiveness cannot exist: the Passion and repentance.

Jesus, like many rabbis, stressed the centrality and importance of forgiveness both between God and man and between man and man.

When we sin against God and we repent, He forgives us. Forgiveness is so important to Judaism that it teaches that "it is one of the seven things created even before the world was created."[51] But sin is not simply between man and God, but between man and man. God can forgive sin insofar as it offends him, but the one who is sinned against has to be the one to forgive the offense against him. The Mishnah says that "for transgressions between humans and the Omnipotent the Day of Atonement procures atonement, but for transgressions between one person and another, the Day of Atonement does not procure any atonement, until [the perpetrator] has appeased the victim."[52] Jesus referred to this teaching when He said, "If you are offering your gift at the altar, and there remember that your brother has something against you, leave your gift there before the altar and go; first be reconciled to your brother, and then come and offer your gift" (Mt 5:23).

We are told to forgive as God has forgiven us. God in turn forgives us as we forgive others. We should forgive others when they repent of their sin against us. We love our enemies because they are God's creatures and we therefore wish their good, which is that they repent of their sin and are restored to relationship with us, but we cannot forgive them and restore the relationship of charity (which is friendship) until they reciprocate. Paul asks Christians to be God's chosen ones, "forgiving each other; as the Lord has forgiven you, so you also must forgive" (Col 3:13). But God does not and cannot forgive without the repentance of the sinner. Similarly, we cannot forgive without the repentance of the one who has injured us. We can desire his good, which in this context is that he repent; we can be willing and eager to forgive, but we cannot forgive until the offender repents. "If your brother sins, rebuke him, and if he repents, forgive him; and if he sins against you seven times in the day, and turns to you seven times, and says, 'I repent,' you must forgive him" (Lk 17: 4).

For the offending party (or anyone else) to ask for forgiveness of an offense without repentance is the sin of presumption. In fact it is worse than presumption, because it is asking a mere mortal to do something that is unbecoming to God. It is the "cheap grace" that Dietrich Bonhoeffer denounced the Church for preaching—forgiveness without repentance.

Underlying this misunderstanding of forgiveness are nominalistic presuppositions. God is seen as declaring that a sinner is just, without making any real changes in him. Our only duty is to submit to God's will, which in this case is that the person who is in reality a sinner is to be regarded as just and is therefore saved. Forgiveness occurs without repentance, without a real change in the heart of the sinner. The sinner may then change as a response to this declaration, or he may not; he is still forgiven. Whether this represents the true Protestant position or a distortion of it is a matter of controversy between Catholics and Protestants. In any case, Catholics have adopted much the same attitude: A parishioner of the abusive priest Michael Allen was a little shocked when he confessed, but decided that "he really is a good priest. When this first came out, he admitted to it and everyone was just in shock—this is not the guy we know. But I think Catholics have been taught to go to confession, say they're sorry for their sins, be forgiven and life goes on. I think he's been punished enough."[53] (There was no punishment apart from the exposure.)

"Saying you're sorry" is only part of repentance. Allen never even did that to his victim David Prunty, who pointed out that "he never apologized to me. He only apologized publicly when he was cornered."[54] True repentance includes an acknowledgment in word and deed of the truth of the situation. To be truly repentant, the offender must not only acknowledge the truth of the situation, but also accept any punishment due him and will to make all the restitution that is possible.

The criminal crucified with Jesus told the criminal who mocked Jesus, "We indeed have been condemned justly, for we are getting what we deserve for our deeds" (Lk 23:41). His repentance allowed Jesus to tell him, "Truly I tell you, today you will be with me in Paradise" (Lk 23: 43). When Jesus announced that he would go to the house of the extortioner Zacchaeus, Zacchaeus received the gracious offer of forgiveness and repented: "Behold, Lord, the half of my goods I give to the poor; and if I have defrauded anyone of anything, I restore it fourfold" (Lk 19: 9). His repentance allowed Jesus to announce, "Today salvation has come to this house, since he also is a son of Abraham. For the Son of Man came to seek and to save the lost" (Lk 19: 9–10).

Any deliberate injury hurts us in two ways: the specific harm done by the injury, and the contempt which the offender shows us by injuring us. This contempt is often more painful to bear than the injury itself. When a person does us an injury he tells us: I am somebody, you are nobody; I am important, you are unimportant. This power differential has been noted in sexual abuse, but it is true of all cases of sin involving the injury of another. The attitude of the offender is false: all persons are of infinite worth, and no one can use another person as a mere tool to achieve his ends, whether it be sexual pleasure (abuse) or money (robbery). By hurting the victim, the offender has in fact become the victim's debtor and is below the victim. The victim is the creditor, the offender is the debtor in the commercial metaphor frequently used in the Bible. The offender must acknowledge the truth of this situation and seek to receive the forgiveness of this debt from the victim. Forgiveness flows down from God to the one who had sinned against Him, and from the human victim downward to the one who has offended him.

The offender must recognize that his offense has given the victim power over him; the positions are reversed. The offender who has regarded the victim as less important must now recognize that he is less important than the victim; he must humble himself before the victim and ask for forgiveness. This repentance, if sincere, must include a willingness to suffer punishment and a will to make restitution. A victim can then forgive the offender.

People sincerely repent, often in response to Christ's Passion.

> Olsen, one of Norway's most feared men, walked into the offices of *Dagbladet* [newspaper] and confessed to two bombings of Oslo's Blitz House, a self-styled "counterculture center" that is a gathering spot for young left-wing radicals. Olsen turned himself in to police late Saturday and claimed he would provide them with details that would prove he was responsible for the bombings. Olsen said that he had decided to confess after watching *The Passion of the Christ.*

Nor was Olsen the only one: "A Texas man recently confessed to murder and a Florida thief turned himself in after watching Gibson's film of the final hours of Christ's life."[55]

In regard to sexual abuse by a priest, the easiest error about forgiveness to confute is the confusion of forgiveness and restoration to office. No one has a right to a pastoral office, especially to the priesthood, as the Catholic Church tirelessly tells women. The ministry in all churches is fundamentally based upon God's call, discerned by the person called and ratified by the authorities of the community. No one has a right to be ordained. The suitability of the candidate for ordination must be discerned by the authorities, and this discernment must continue as long as the minister is holding office. Sometimes canon law is interpreted as meaning that a priest, once ordained, has an absolute right to a pastoral position, no matter how unsuitable he becomes for the office. If canon law says this, it needs to be rewritten, because it is against common sense and the good of the community that canon law is supposed to serve. The pope could change it in a moment, if it needs to be changed.

Few abusers have shown anything like true repentance. Since many of them are confidence artists, even protestations of sorrow must be carefully scrutinized to see whether they are sincere or manipulative. No clerical abuser has, to my knowledge, ever turned himself in to the police; only a handful approached their bishops before they were accused.

Forgiving a repentant abuser who has injured us is hard enough. How can he ever make restitution for a serious injury? "Even if physical scars can be healed, and that is not always possible, how can one erase the memories and horrors that afflict victims years and lifetimes after they have been attacked? Perhaps that is the true mystery of repentance and forgiveness, when it is properly earned. Perhaps that is why sincere repentance is so difficult to accomplish and forgiveness is so difficult to achieve."[56]

The logical connection between forgiveness and repentance cannot be broken. But must repentance precede the offer of forgiveness? Sometimes yes, but a common human and Christian instinct is to offer forgiveness to an offender who has been brought so low by outward circumstances, so humiliated, that he has "suffered enough." The victim feels that the outward circumstances now manifest the inward reality: the offender has been brought low, and can do no more evil. Then as a sheer act of grace, the victim, without denying the reality of the situation, can offer forgiveness. The victim, who has suffered a contemptuous injury, is manifestly not the one who is of lesser value, and can now offer forgiveness from a position of superiority. He can, without being asked, cancel the debt. It still, of course, must be received for forgiveness to achieve its purpose of reconciliation.

Thomas Blanchette says he was molested hundreds of times by the late Rev. Joseph E. Birmingham. As Birmingham lay dying, Blanchette sought him out. "I began with a litany of names I knew in Sudbury [Massachusetts] that he abused....With a sense of genuine righteousness, I told him that what you did to us, and to me specifically, was wrong and that you had no right to do that."[57]

Then Blanchette asked Birmingham to forgive him for the hatred and resentment that he held against the priest for nearly thirty years; he said Birmingham then dissolved into tears.

The process of forgiveness is described by an Australian abuse victim:

1. Recognition of the sin. Without recognition of sin by the sinner, there is no forgiveness.
2. Repentance of the sin. Without repentance by the sinner, and a firm intention to change, there is no forgiveness.
3. Recompense for the sin. In other words: payment, or punishment. Whatever word you use, there is clear evidence that God's forgiveness is dependent on someone paying the price for sin before forgiveness is possible.
4. Restitution for the sin. Sinners in the Bible who recognized their sin tried to restore the situation to a "pre-sin" state (e. g., Zacchaeus paying back four times what he stole). This was the action which authenticated their claim of repentance.[58]

To these I would add a fifth R that explains the purpose of the others:

5. Reconciliation of the sinner. Having fulfilled the first four stages, the abuser ceases to be an abuser: he becomes a new man, no longer an enemy, but a friend. The sinner cannot do this of his own power, but God will not, and indeed cannot, do it without the sinner's participation.

# CONCLUSION

BECAUSE OF THE UNIQUE CLAIMS of the Roman Catholic Church, its claim to be the mystical body of Christ, its claim that the papacy inherits the primacy of the apostle Peter and has immediate pastoral jurisdiction over every Christian, its claim that its priests transform bread and wine into the Body and Blood of Christ, its claim that its laws have the power to bind under pain of mortal sin and everlasting death, and its claim to be able to forgive or retain sins, it must be judged by its own high standards. No other church, not even the Orthodox churches, much less any secular institution such as the Boy Scouts or public schools, makes such extraordinary claims.

Court trials and newspaper reporters have established that over the past generation priests abused thousands, probably scores of thousands, of minors, mostly teenage boys, in the United States, and the abuse was tolerated by the Catholic Church. Children in other countries suffered in much the same way.

The Catholic bishops had the primary responsibility for maintaining discipline and therefore bear the primary responsibility for their failure to maintain discipline. They almost never acted effectively against abusers. Instead they tried to maintain the façade of the Church, a façade that became increasingly hollow. The bishops suffered from a clericalism that identified the Church with the clergy. The laity were unimportant except insofar as they provided the opportunity for clerical careers. The bishops "cared more for the steady stream of financial support from the laity and the reputation of the [C]hurch than for the ravaged and frightened souls of children."[1] The bishops wanted to keep the abuse quiet and out of the public eye, and the abusers were, of course, happy to cooperate so they could escape punishment and continue abusing.

Insofar as they are concerned with church discipline, bishops seem to feel that they have fulfilled their responsibilities by making sure that the sacraments are available to the laity and that they are administered according to the law of the Church, that is, validly. Cardinal Law disciplined Sister Jeanette Normandin for performing irregular baptisms, but he tolerated sexual abuse by priests.[2] In Austria, a publicized sacramental irregularity in which a deacon may have simulated Mass, seeming to do what only an ordained priest can do, caused greater controversy than homosexual behavior among the seminarians of St. Pölten.[3] To this mentality obedience to ritual law is more important than integrity of character.

In the Middle Ages, the popes had attempted to deal with clerics who practiced concubinage by telling the laity not to receive the sacraments from them, but this was unimaginable in the defensive world of the Counter-Reformation. Priests were the professionals of sanctity. The holiness (set-apartness) of their office was confused with personal sanctity and virtue. The laity were thereby relieved from acting responsibly as Christians—that was up to the clergy.

To be able to associate with the clergy was a high honor, and in the Counter-Reformation Church, this association allowed some of the priests' holiness to rub off on the sinful laity. Donors who financed the institutions and activities of the Catholic Church were rewarded by being allowed to associate with the clergy, an honor that they did not and do not want to jeopardize by raising awkward questions about clerical behavior and governance. Abusers were often successful as priests because they were able to evaluate the desires of the laity and manipulate them, whether the desires were for the "traditional" clericalism of privilege and pious, sentimental devotions, or more recently, for a false friendliness and a pop culture degradation of Christianity.

The Catholic Church, pope, Vatican officials, bishops, priests, laity have tolerated sexual abuse by priests, especially sexual abuse of teenage boys, as just one of the costs of doing business as usual. In the diocese of Venice, Florida, an administrator put abuse in perspective: "For each $10 put in the collection basket, less than 3 cents have been used for the cost of sexual abuse cases."[4] An enormous income from donations, landed wealth, and insurance have all protected the Catholic Church from any serious disruption in its finances, except perhaps in Boston, the only city in which contributions have fallen significantly.

Although forced by court judgments and settlements to make some efforts to purge the Catholic Church in the United States of abusers, this is not evidence of a sincere conversion of heart on the part of the bishops or the Vatican. The zero tolerance rule is confined to the United States; in other countries known abusers continue in ministry,[5] despite the statement of Pope John Paul II that "there is no place in the priesthood for those who would harm the young."[6]

Msgr. Ivan Rovira was accused of rape in 2002 in Brownsville, Texas; he admitted to some of the accusations. He moved across the Rio Grande to a Catholic university. Officials of the Brownsville diocese have assured everyone that Rovira is barred from public ministry, although Brownsville bishop Raymonda Peña has watched Rovira concelebrate Mass in Mexico as a new bishop was installed. Bishop Peña claimed he told the bishop of Matamoros about Rovira, but the Mexican bishop denied ever receiving any such information. A Brownsville diocesan official explained that Peña tried to get rid of Rovira, but "the Vatican denied it."[7] The Vatican, as is its custom, did not respond to inquiries.

The Rev. Manuel Fernández was removed by the Trenton diocese because of an accusation. Even though the diocesan website has the news article about the accusation, he remains a priest of the Trenton diocese. He moved to Spain and heads a parish there. When reporters asked the Spanish bishop, Luis Quinteiro Fiuza of Orense, for an explanation, the bishop responded,

"I am unaware of what right you have to send me those questions."[8] The bishop of Jackson, Mississippi, Joseph Latino, refuses to discuss why the Rev. Paul Madden remains in ministry even after he admitted abusing a thirteen-year-old boy. With Latino's permission, Madden transferred to the diocese of Chimbote, Peru. There are many other such instances.[9]

Many bishops seem to share Bishop Metzger's opinion that it is an old custom for priests to keep boys. The American Dominicans expelled the Rev. Cristobal Garcia (a member of one of the Philippines's richest families) in 1985; he had been giving young teenagers drugs in return for their acting out pornographic videos. The American police buried the complaint, and Garcia fled to his native diocese of Cebu in the Philippines. The diocese, although warned by the Dominicans, put him to work with children and made him a monsignor. Garcia, founder of the Society of the Angel of Peace, a male order, is also liturgical director for the diocese. He admits having sex with his accusers but blames them: one young teenager "not only seduced me, he also raped me," Garcia complained. Garcia questioned the American zero tolerance policy: "I wonder if some of it is a face-saving mechanism…or damage control. In the Third World, the damage is done. Too bad. Live with it."[10] That seems to be the attitude of many bishops and many Vatican officials: "Too bad. Live with it." Clerical arrogance remains untouched: the Vatican and many bishops refuse to answer questions.

The bishops looked at the late pope's actions as well as his words. John Paul to his death refused to meet with victims despite repeated requests through official channels. He publicly apologized for the errors of remote predecessors, but would not apologize for his own errors and the errors of the bishops he had appointed, errors in governing the Church that allowed the abuse to go on. He will almost certainly be canonized, but he will not be the only canonized saint (see St. Joseph Calasanctius, p. 19) to have tolerated the sexual abuse of children.

The numbers of abused children are impossible to determine, but reasonable estimates can be made. If about five percent of the priests in the United States are known to have abused minors in the past fifty years, then it can be assumed that about five percent of the total of 400,000 priests worldwide have abused, that there are about 20,000 *current* abusers. The number of victims per abuser is uncertain. Criminological studies suggest it may be an average of 150 (see pp. 239–243). Even using smaller multiples, it is almost certain there are hundreds of thousands of victims worldwide, perhaps even millions.[11] It is an evil on a scale that the Vatican might deign to notice. The Vatican might even consider this abuse in the light of what the prophets and the Gospels say about oppressing the weak and innocent and leading children astray. (Karen Liebreich never encountered a single mention of the Gospels in the Vatican archives that documented abuse in the Piarist order.)

Reforms in state and church are needed to end the sexual abuse of children, or at least to make it as rare and unacceptable as cannibalism.

## *The Statute of Limitations*

The chief secular reform needed is the abolition of the statute of limitations in all states for both civil and criminal actions stemming from sexual molestation. Many states already have no statute of limitations for felonies, and no state has a statute of limitations for murder. Because it often takes victims years or decades to confront the abuse and to speak about it publicly, the statute of limitations creates grave injustices.[12]

The Catholic Church in the United States opposes the reform or abolition of the statute of limitations, because it benefits from this grave injustice. The arguments the Church puts forward are intellectually dishonest. The church hierarchy claims that the passage of time makes it difficult for the hierarchy to prove itself innocent, but in our legal system there is a presumption of innocence. An accuser has to provide evidence to convince a court that the priest is guilty or that the Church is liable. The passage of time guarantees that memories will grow dim, documents be lost, and witnesses die, and therefore operates for the benefit of the one who is accused, not the accuser.

Laws should also be passed that make it a crime to endanger children. The law must clearly establish the criminal liability of churches and other organizations that allow child abuse to go on. The Philadelphia grand jury recognized the injustice that the statute of limitations created, an injustice compounded by the fact that Cardinal Bevilacqua, who has degrees in both civil and canon law, had organized the Philadelphia archdiocese as an unincorporated association, thereby escaping the provisions of the Pennsylvania criminal law that apply to corporations.[13]

This book has focused almost entirely on the sexual abuse of minors, but any sexual activity between a priest and someone under his pastoral care is also abusive. Priests, ministers, psychiatrists, lawyers, doctors, therapists, counselors, and similar professionals all deal with highly vulnerable people, and any sexual activity, even if both parties consent, is inherently abusive and a violation of professional ethics. It is not simply a matter of fornication or adultery, but a violation of office, which should normally result in removal from office. Catholic bishops have been forced by bad publicity to realize that sexual abuse of minors cannot be tolerated, but like B students, they cannot generalize and come to the conclusion that sexual abuse of adults also cannot be tolerated. When a college student struggling with extreme grief went to the Rev. Robert F. Moran (see p. 353) of St. Thomas Aquinas Church in West Lafayette, Indiana, for counseling, the priest began a sexual relationship with the young man and persuaded him to become a priest. This relationship lasted fifteen years. When the younger man went into therapy and realized he had been manipulated, he made a complaint to Bishop William L. Higi of Indianapolis, who claimed there was "no abuse" because the victim was nineteen years old when the sexual relationship started and was therefore a "consenting adult."[14]

## *Church Reforms*

In addition to the secular reforms, the Church must also consider several reforms in its handling of abusers, in church government, in the ordination of homosexuals, and perhaps in the celibacy of the priesthood. It must begin by engaging in a deep process of repentance.

## ZERO TOLERANCE AND CRIMINAL NETWORKS

From the evidence in this book and from evidence derived from court documents, it is certain that there are rings of abusers and almost certain that there is a loose network of abusers in the clergy of the Catholic Church in the United States. The ring of abusers in El Paso assembled from all over the United States. What drew them there? The ring of abusers in Davenport was homegrown, but extended to Chicago and to Tennessee. New England had a ring of abusers that was abetted by the corrupt House of Affirmation. The Rev. Francis P. Rogers of Philadelphia took a boy to his beach house and got the boy drunk. After passing out, the boy awoke, and "opening his eyes, he saw Fr. Rogers, three priests, and a seminarian looking at him. Two of the priests ejaculated on him while watching Fr. Rogers masturbate himself with one hand and caress [the victim's] penis with the other."[15]

Abusers form a network of unknown size, and the only way to disrupt it is to remove any priest who even once is discovered to have abused a minor, however distant in time the abuse may be. The abusers are confidence artists, and will pretend that the abuse was an isolated fall for which they are deeply repentant, and will appeal for Christian forgiveness. However, there is no way of knowing whether an abuser is an isolated individual or is part of a loose network, and therefore he must be removed, even if he gives signs of sincere repentance. The sincerity of the repentance is in any case impossible to judge, since the abuser is by definition a manipulative personality. He deceived his victim and can deceive a bishop or psychologist.

The Catholic Church is a worldwide institution, and more and more priests transfer from one country to another. Therefore, the zero-tolerance policy must be worldwide or it will not protect the children in any country. As it stands now, abusers in other countries can be allowed to continue in the ministry and come to the United States, and, as we have seen, priests who have abused in America can go to other countries and continue in ministry.

## CHURCH GOVERNANCE

Although the Catholic Church likes to give the impression that it is a highly organized, efficient body, it is in fact very complex and disorganized. Bishops theoretically have authority in their dioceses but this authority is severely limited. They have direct authority only over their own diocesan clergy, and this authority is constrained by canon law. Canon law protects priests from arbitrary actions by bishops, but it also makes it difficult for bishops to discipline erring priests. It is theoretically possible for a bishop to discipline a priest, but the obstacles that canon law places in the way are enormous. If a bishop has even one problem priest he can spend all his time disciplining and attending to canonical procedures and pleading with Roman courts about the priest rather than attending to all the other duties of his diocese.

As in civil law, the statute of limitations in canon law has to be abolished. In canon law, it is called "prescription." Although some Vatican officials think there is a natural right in justice to escape punishment if a criminal has been undetected for a number of years, Msgr. Charles Scicluna, promoter of justice for the Congregation for the Doctrine of the Faith under Cardinal Ratzinger, said that the current ten-year period of prescription is usually waived, because "experience has shown that a term of ten years is inadequate for these types of cases, and it would be desirable to return to the former system in which these delicts [grave offenses] were not subject to prescription at all."[16] The policy of waiving prescription should be formalized so that those who have committed grave crimes can be punished whenever sufficient evidence is brought forward.

Canon law needs to be reformed to guarantee that bishops have authority over all priests and religious who work in their dioceses, and to ensure that bishops are held accountable for any failure to supervise these priests. Not only the pope should be able to hold bishops accountable; other bishops should be able to act, as they did in the early Church, when a neighboring bishop starts creating problems for the Church.

## LAY PARTICIPATION IN GOVERNANCE

The fragmentation in the Church would almost certainly be made worse by lay participation in church government. If the laity shared governmental authority, the diffusion of power would also necessarily entail a diffusion of responsibility. There would be many more places to pass the buck. In any case, there is little reason to think that the laity would handle the scandals any better than the bishops did. Melinda Henneberger, who discovered that an abuser, the Rev. Mark Kurzendoerfer,[17] had witnessed her marriage and baptized her children, soon came to realize that "though lay involvement in abuse allegations is widely seen as one possible solution to the problem, many Catholics seem as willing as our church leaders have been to let this protected class of predators off the hook."[18] Confidence artists can exploit democratic structures with ease. The experience of congregational churches shows that similar dynamics of conflict avoidance are at work. The problem is a lack of fortitude, not just poor organization.

There is also a theological problem with laity having governmental authority in the Church: the Church is essentially a sacramental reality. The Eucharist is the heart of the Church, and the priests who confect the Eucharist are also its guardians and therefore have the responsibility to set the conditions for participation in the Eucharist. From this flow ecclesiology, moral theology, and canon law. This principle has often been compromised for political reasons over the centuries, and the Vatican is not about to give up a hard-won clerical independence of lay authority, especially since, in much of the Catholic world, lay authority could be manipulated by governments hostile to the Church and to Christianity.

With all these caveats, it is still possible to ensure wider lay participation in the government of the Church, while reserving ultimate authority and responsibility to the ordained. Even if the laity should not share in the direct government of the Church, they suffer if the Church is misgoverned, as it has been in the United States. To ensure that bishops carry out their responsibilities, episcopal government must be open to inspection by the laity. If a bishop cloaks his government in secrecy, it is usually because he is doing something he knows he should not be doing and that would not stand up to public scrutiny. The laity should certainly always be consulted on matters that concern them.

They should especially be informed about financial matters. Ordination does not grant competence in handling money. Most of the scandals have also involved financial malfeasance by abusers or by bishops paying for cover-ups. A promiscuous mingling of funds is often a sign that a promiscuous mingling of bodies has occurred. In many cases of abuse, abusers have stolen money from their parishes to buy gifts and trips for the victims, at first to groom them and then to ensure their silence.[19]

Parishes and dioceses should be fully audited once a year and the audits made public. A rule should be passed for the United States that if such an audit is not done, all donations and income of the parish or diocese automatically go to an escrow fund, over which the pastor or bishop has no control. A bill-paying service can use the escrow fund to pay utilities, salaries, payroll taxes, etc., until the audit is done. If Catholics had clear ideas of how money was being used, perhaps they would give more than they currently give, which is only at half the rate that Protestants give. When donors stop writing checks and instead require accountability for how their money is spent, the clergy will stop squandering it on personal and institutional follies.

The Internet has made it possible to keep track of who is really ordained, who is a priest in good standing, and where a priest is. Without this elementary knowledge, no one can effectively supervise a priest, and bishops (and the Vatican) do not have this knowledge easily available. When John O'Connor became bishop of Scranton in 1983, he set out to locate all his priests and to make sure they were properly assigned. I knew of a priest from the Scranton diocese who had gotten a job teaching at Catholic University and had made a very comfortable life for himself in Washington, and was not eager to go back to Pennsylvania. He was very nervous, but before O'Connor could finish this project, in 1984 he was made archbishop of New York, and the wheels of the ecclesiastical machinery he had set in motion ground to a halt, leaving the priest to enjoy the comforts of

Washington. His enjoyment was innocent, but not every priest simply wants to teach philosophy rather than baptize the children of coal miners. The laity should be able to determine the background of each priest with whom they come in contact.

At various times, priests and laity have chosen their bishops, in the same way that a religious order elects its superiors. Although this might not be possible under modern conditions because much of the Church is subject to pressure from hostile regimes, I can see no reason why the selection of bishops should not be a far more public matter than it is now. The secrecy surrounding the selection of bishops has created conditions in which priests known to be abusers and possibly even heretics and unbelievers (see pp. 232–233) have their names forwarded to Rome for consideration as bishops. A priest has no right to be appointed a bishop. The local church could be told that some priests on a list were being considered for appointment as bishops, and ask for any positive or negative information about them. Confidential investigations have not worked very well, and a more open process would keep out the worst candidates, and might even produce better ones. Similarly parishes should be consulted about their pastors. Parishioners, of course, have to be realistic: they may want a combination of the Curé of Ars, Fulton Sheen, and a super fundraiser, but they should not have to settle for a pederast, womanizer, or alcoholic.

## THE ORDINATION OF HOMOSEXUALS

Joaquin Navarro-Valls, Opus Dei member, psychiatrist, and John Paul II's press officer, made an ill-advised statement about homosexual priests: "people with these inclinations just cannot be ordained." By saying that homosexuals cannot be ordained, he is implying that homosexuality is an absolute impediment to ordination, and that the ceremony of ordination has no effect on a homosexual, any more than it would have on a woman or an unbaptized person. This was (I hope) a slip of the tongue—if only because it implies that there is an ontological category of human being, the homosexual, rather than a heterosexual with misdirected desires (which is the teaching of the Catholic Church). Navarro-Valls probably meant that homosexuals *should not* be ordained. Cardinal Bertone, secretary to the Congregation for the Doctrine of the Faith, said that "men with homosexual orientation should not be admitted to seminary life."[20] This directive was repeated with more authority by Pope Benedict XVI in 2005 (see p. 321).

Some suspect that barring homosexuals would mean a deep cut in the number of Catholic clergy. Mark Jordan, a gay Catholic theologian, thinks that the celibate Catholic priesthood has long been a haven for gays, that a priestly vocation is "a call to act out your manhood against social expectation, outside heterosexual marriage and in the company of other unmarried men."[21] The celibate Catholic priesthood has a larger percentage of gays than the general population—but the Anglican acceptance of married clergy has not lessened the number of homosexuals in their ranks.

One argument against the ordination of homosexuals is that celibacy means different things to a heterosexual and a homosexual. When he chooses celibacy, a heterosexual is giving up something good and lawful—Christian marriage and family—while a homosexual is renouncing something unlawful, because all sexual activity outside of marriage is unlawful. But celibacy is not so much an act of self-sacrifice as it is a call, and God can call men to celibacy from different backgrounds. Does the man who renounces vast wealth and becomes a monk have a true vocation, while the man who becomes a monk to escape destitution does not and cannot have a vocation? The vocation of the homosexual, like that of the poor man, may need greater scrutiny, but it could be a true vocation, as far as I can see. Celibacy is not simply a renunciation, but a positive way of life, just as monasticism is not simply a renunciation of the world, but a positive way of life.

Another argument is that a gay priest tends to think of himself as gay first and a priest second. Homosexuals tend to be even more obsessive about sex than other men. A heterosexual, when asked to identify himself, will almost never identify himself as a heterosexual. A homosexual will often identify himself as a homosexual, because his sexuality is obsessive. Their private temptations as homosexual priests become the center of their ministry. I have seen several examples of this. Whenever a homosexual priest becomes a pastor, the parish soon discovers that the central issue of the modern world is the acceptance of homosexuals. The bulletin has explanations about why the story of Sodom and Gomorrah has nothing to do with homosexuality, the gay and lesbian ministry becomes the biggest committee, felt rainbows proliferate around the church.

Once a profession becomes feminine or gay, it is extremely hard to make it attractive to heterosexual men. Even chaste homosexuals, if they project an explicitly gay image, create problems for the Church. Christianity in the Western world has long been seen as the proper sphere of women and children. It is a feminine sphere, and many men, especially young men, tend to keep their distance because they feel it is unmasculine. A gay clergy will distance men, especially young men, even more from Christianity.

Feminized heterosexuals don't help the image of the priesthood either. In fact, an effeminate heterosexual probably makes it more difficult to keep men connected to the Church than a masculine homosexual does (because very few people can imagine that a noticeably masculine man, like Gilbert Gauthé, could be homosexual). Gordon Thomas approvingly notes the lack of masculinity among priests: "Boys and young men with a feminine perception of themselves tended to be attracted to a vocation, and the long years of religious formation often reinforce this pattern. One survey of priests in 1994 revealed that only two out of every ten priests actually saw themselves as masculine, while four out of ten admitted to a strong feminine identification."[22] The psychiatrist William D. Perri thinks the androgyny of a male effeminate priest is an advantage, and writes approvingly of a priest who at an early age "liked doing stereotypically feminine things like ironing, washing the dishes and clothes, housekeeping, curling his grandmother's hair."[23]

A heavily homosexual clergy has also been a factor in the rejection of absolute norms of moral behavior. George Weigel blames the homosexuals who entered the seminary and priesthood while rejecting Catholic teaching on sexual morality both in theory and practice: "Men who adopted habits of intellectual deception in the seminary—pretending to accept church teachings which they really didn't believe and had no intention of teaching—are more likely to lead lives of deception in their sexual conduct."[24] Although both heterosexuals and homosexuals feel the yoke of the moral law, the yoke is heavier for homosexuals, since the law denies them any possibility of the types of sexual experience that they desire. Usually the homosexual pastor will not publicly contradict the official church teaching on moral sexual behavior, but will dance around it and undermine it. Not only does this not do gays any good, it also undermines the acceptance of Catholic sexual morality in the rest of the congregation. If homosexual behavior is implicitly acceptable, what else might be? Fornication? Adultery? Catholics are more accepting of extramarital sex than Evangelicals are, although both are influenced by American culture. Most of the arguments that have been used to justify homosexual behavior could also be applied to pedophilia or to sexual involvement with teenagers. God made pedophiles and pederasts with their desires; why should they be expected to be celibate? Certainly the interpretation that a Catholic can reject the moral teachings of the Church and remain a good Catholic does not help restrain appetites.

However, some homosexuals fully accept church teachings. Conservative Catholics do not like to recognize the existence of the orthodox homosexual priest. Young priests are more likely to be homosexual[25] and more likely to be orthodox[26] than priests ordained in the 1960s and 1970s, according to a *Los Angeles Times* survey. Are the two groups, the homosexuals and the orthodox, mutually exclusive? Anglicans have long known the Anglo-Catholic spike: homosexuals who do not want to engage in sexual activity and fear the consequences of giving into their desires. They therefore become ultra-rigid, and their ritualism is a defense against chaos. Some of the fussiness about ritual among young priests is not only silly, but may be a sign of something dangerous. A sane, balanced person is not always on guard against the slightest slip. And some "traditional" clerical culture has not been very masculine.

A mature man who has same-sex attraction, who recognizes it, who has a sincere desire to be chaste and celibate, and who is masculine in his attitudes and comportment, is no problem and in fact a great asset to the clergy. His experience of homosexual desire reminds him that he is a sinner, a reminder that all of us need. His awareness of the disorder within may well make him more acutely conscious of his need for God's grace. However, such cases are not what are causing difficulty in the Church. Homosexuals are, as they themselves recognize, more likely than heterosexuals to be dealing with adolescent sexual issues when they are adults, and are therefore more likely to seek out adolescent males as sexual partners. They are also likely to be more promiscuous than heterosexuals, and have more victims than a heterosexual would have. Even those who do not get involved with adolescents often distort their ministry. Their constant questioning of traditional Catholic teaching on sexual morality lessens the inhibitions of heterosexuals (who, as they fornicate, can say to themselves, "At least I am not gay") and may mislead those who are attracted to intergenerational sex. Nor do such priests confine their gayness to private behavior, but want everyone to focus upon the problems of homosexuals, as if *their* problems (as opposed to the problems of victims of poverty, drug addiction, war, and religious persecution) were the foremost challenge that Christianity faced today.

The Church should not automatically bar any man who has ever had some type of same sex attraction, but should be extremely cautious about ordaining them, both for their own good and the good of the Church as a whole.

One problem may be (although it needs further research) that homosexuality either by itself or in a environment that rejects it creates the anger and control issues that we have seen, issues that produce the worst types of abuse. Sexual desire, whether heterosexual or homosexual, seems like a minor component of the worst abuse. Something far worse than disorderly sexual desire leads men to corrupt and torture children, and this evil has not been identified by the Church and therefore cannot be purged from the Church. Control issues are scarcely absent from the hierarchy, whose arrogance led the abuse to fester so long.

Another problem is that sexual abuse victims sometimes suffer from identification with the aggressor and traumatic bonding. The sexual abuse itself creates a desire to be like the abuser. An abused boy may therefore want to be a priest precisely because he has been abused either before entering the seminary or in the seminary. He is at far greater risk of becoming an abuser himself, especially if he tries to convince himself that abuse is just a normal part of growing up. What has been done by a priest to him as a boy, he may well do to other boys when he becomes a priest. Although it seems like punishing the victim, anyone who has been sexually abused should receive the utmost scrutiny if he applies to the seminary. Probably the safer course is to bar anyone from the priesthood who has himself been abused by a priest. If the victim doesn't find the abuse disturbing, he may himself abuse. If he does find it disturbing, he may find it difficult to deal with people who have sexual difficulties.

## CENTRALIZATION

Over the centuries, the administration of the Church has become more and more centralized in Rome. In the first millennium the bishop of Rome would make final decisions on doctrinal matters, usually by ratifying a decision of a council, but administration was left up to bishops and local synods of bishops, who had the power to pass laws and to discipline bishops. In an attempt to reform the Church and to take church administration out of the hands of secular authorities, who even if they were Catholic, had their own agendas, the popes throughout the Middle Ages fought for the liberty of the Church, that is the right of the clergy to govern itself without lay interference. More recently, Pope Pius XII both centralized administration in Rome and developed a cult of the papal monarchy to raise the prestige of the papacy in its contest with the secular ideologies that bedeviled Europe after 1789.

Centralization has both pros and cons. It is easier to influence and intimidate a local church than the Vatican, as the Chinese Communists have discovered, so they have formed a nationalist, schismatic, subservient Catholic church. The myth has grown up that German Catholics were eager to oppose Hitler and that Pius XII sabotaged this by the concordat. This is simply not true, as will become clear when the papers of Dietrich von Hildebrand are published. German Catholics were seduced by Hitler even while Pius XII thought he was demonically possessed. A central administration in Rome can correct an erring local church, the same way a federal government in Washington passed anti-lynching laws to suppress an evil that local governments found tolerable. With few exceptions, bishops throughout the world have shown no great eagerness to discipline priests to end sexual abuse.

However, a central administration can also tolerate evils. What looms large in a local church may seem minor in Rome. This explains part of the failure of the popes and the Vatican in handling the cases of sexual abuse. As terrible as sexual abuse is, the popes and the Vatican in the twentieth century also had to deal with two world wars, concentration camps, mass starvation, and a triumphant atheistic ideology that threatened to eradicate all religion in half of the world. This does not excuse the failure of internal government in the matter of abusive clergy, but does place it in perspective.

## CELIBACY: A CONTROLLED EXPERIMENT

An easy way exists for the Catholic Church[27] to test the thesis that the requirement of celibacy for the clergy of the Latin Church is contributing both to a shortage of priests and to scandals. This could be done without any change to doctrine or even to discipline, by righting an injustice that has been done to the majority of Catholic Churches. At the beginning of the twentieth century, Irish bishops in the United States were horrified when they saw a married Catholic clergy ministering to Slavic immigrants, and complained to Rome that the laity would be "confused." In 1929 Pope Pius XI issued the decree *Cum data fuerit* which forbade the Eastern Churches in union with Rome to ordain married men outside their traditional homelands. Some Catholic parishes broke communion with Rome and entered the Orthodox Church so that they could keep their married clergy. Eastern Churches circumvented the decree by taking American seminarians back to Europe and ordaining them, and then loaning them back to America.

In Canada some Eastern Churches have decided on their own to end this charade. "David Motiuk, Winnipeg's Ukrainian Catholic auxiliary bishop, says that for at least five years, Canadian bishops have been ordaining married men in Canada without any negative response from Rome. The change of heart was signaled in 1990 when John Paul II approved a new code of canon law for the Eastern Churches that declared 'the state of married clerics...is to be held in honour.'"[28]

Although I strongly favor the Canadian policy and think it should be extended throughout the world, I doubt that a married clergy (even in the Latin Church) would significantly increase the availability of priests where they are needed. Married priests, if they have large families, cannot devote the time to their parishes that a celibate priest can. Nor would they want to live in the depopulating rural areas that have priestless churches. Big urban and suburban congregations have no clergy shortage. My parish could serve all its parishioners at one Mass, but schedules five weekend Masses for people's convenience. Tiny inner-city parishes are usually only a walk from one another and could be consolidated. The real problem is rural parishes, especially in the Midwest. But these regions are emptying of population, and have a hard time getting dentists and doctors and teachers and other professionals. A dispersed and declining population is hard to serve, and few priests with families would be willing to move to these dying areas. Catholic parishes have no resident pastor for the same reason that many Protestant churches have empty pulpits: the regions and towns are dying.

In the Third World, which is more and more the Catholic world, the problems are different. The married clergy of the Eastern Churches in union with Rome may be the solution to the lack of clergy. If it is, the Eastern Churches will flourish and will have an assured future. At present they are confined almost entirely to population groups that are dying out (Slavic) or are persecuted (Arab). Growth in the Third World will revitalize the Eastern Churches and assure that they will be around at the end of the Third Millennium, not as a tiny historical curiosity, but as "the second lung of Christendom," as Pope John Paul II called them. For historical reasons the Orthodox Churches have had only restricted missionary efforts; but the Western Churches, Catholic and Protestant, have been far more missionary, and they can help the Eastern Churches expand in the fertile fields of the Third World. Most Eastern Churches also have none of the historical baggage of imperialism that still burdens many Western efforts.

## *A Renewed Ethic*

These institutional reforms may do some good in the Church, but clearly the evil goes deeper and cannot be cured by passing a few laws. Some have yearned for a zealous reformer after the model of Pope Pius V, who used stringent means to deal with the corruption of the Church. It would be satisfying and is perhaps necessary that every abuser be removed and that bishops be held accountable and be removed from office when they have disgraced it. However, resorting only to discipline and obedience would reinforce the distorted moral attitudes that have contributed to the abuse and toleration of abuse. Obedience and discipline are necessary when there are gross violations of the law, as there have been in the modern Church, but the fact that the situation ever became so bad as to make the blunt instruments of obedience and law necessary shows that life in the Holy Spirit has grown weak in the Church. An exposure of sin is necessary, but it should lead not just to punishment, but to repentance.

The underlying problem is the ethical atmosphere of the Church, both Catholic and Protestant. Churches try to avoid internal conflict at almost any cost. Righteous anger is a forgotten concept, zeal is condemned as disruptive. Josef Pieper concludes his analysis of the place of anger in the virtuous life, "Only the combination of the intemperateness of lustfulness with the lazy inertia incapable of generating anger is the sign of complete and virtually hopeless degeneration. It appears whenever a caste, a people, or a whole civilization is ripe for its decline and fall."[29] An implicit nominalism colors the understanding of morality: moral laws, especially those about sex, are just rules; violating them does no real damage. There is nothing to get angry about, only at most a disobedience of God which He is always ready to forgive unconditionally. A confidence artist can easily manipulate this situation to get what he wants; if he is discovered, he will claim his victims have a duty to forgive him—and the bishops will concur.

The bishops fear bad publicity; they need to remember the fear of God, if in fact they believe in Him. "That there is a judgment, that there is justice, at least for the oppressed, for those who are unjustly treated, that is the real hope and in that sense good news. Those who belong to the oppressors and the workers of injustice are primarily the ones who feel threatened,"[30] as Cardinal Ratzinger reflected on the message of judgment in the New Testament. Until the pope meets with victims and apologizes, until any bishop complicit in the abuse offers to let victims decide whether he should resign, there is no repentance and there can be no forgiveness.

The bishops of the Roman Catholic Church still do not, as a body, see the serious wrong that they have perpetrated and, having satisfied the press, which is now turning its attentions elsewhere, want to ignore the situation. Only under public pressure did the bishops compose a charter for the protection of children; only under public pressure did they set up a national review board. The Vatican was obviously unhappy with both, and the bishops immediately started undermining the board they had set up. Governor Keating, who headed the board, was subject to personal attacks;[31] his successor, Judge Anne Burke, has denounced the bishops for their attempts to manipulate the board.[32] The bishops obviously feel they have done nothing wrong and do not understand why anyone is angry at them.

When asked in May 2004 about the responsibility of bishops for the scandal, Archbishop Daniel Pilarczyk said, "I think to say, lay it all at the door of the bishops, may be an understandable psychological stratagem. Whom do we blame? Blame the bishops. When you've got somebody to blame, you just feel better because you know it's their fault. Well, it's not that simple. We've got the psychological community, we've got the role of lawyers, we've got the role of the media. I think we have to be careful not to generalize. [People say] 'the bishops.' Which bishops? Are you talking about two or three here, two or three there, or did every bishop in the country mess up?"[33] The lawyers and the psychologists and the media, although they were complicit, did not transfer abusive priests from parish to parish, as, according to the *Dallas Morning News* survey, two-thirds of American bishops did.

Pilarczyk wants to continue evading the question of the responsibility of the bishops for the abuse. When asked about bishops who made terrible decisions and are still in office, he responded

> I would want to know who and how many and where. You can continue to say that forever if you want to. I think it's more just to say, what do we really know about what this bishop did? Where do we know that from? Do we know it from the daily paper, which is no friend of the bishop? Do we know exactly what he did? It seems to me that you don't want to simplify, you don't want to generalize, and you don't want to engage in what I call "presentism," meaning judging the behavior of the past by the criteria of the present.[34]

Being a bishop means never having to say you're sorry, because obviously you are never wrong. It is always someone else's fault.

Bishop Anthony O'Connell had to resign from Palm Beach when his abuse of seminarians was revealed. But he is ensconced in Mipkin Abbey and takes the Fifth Amendment when he is asked questions in the civil lawsuits against him.[35] He is still unwilling to accept the punishment that is his due. Even worse, his lawyers subject his victims to such withering questioning about every problem in their lives and in their families' lives that one of the victims attempted suicide.[36] The victims continue to be victimized, and O'Connell remains unrebuked by his fellow bishops or by the Vatican.

Bishop McCormack remains bishop of Manchester and continues to practice the arts of deception. His auxiliary bishop, Francis Christian, claimed that the attorney general's report was based "on what perpetrator priests said." This is not true. It was based on the archives of the diocese and any gaps in the report were caused by McCormack, who, in the judgment of the *Manchester Union Leader*, "deceived victims and investigators, and stonewalled the state's attempt to get information of the crimes." The paper concludes, "Honesty is not the policy of the Diocese of Manchester. . . . Even now the leadership of this diocese continues to damage the reputation of the [C]hurch by offering the public more lies and deception."[37]

The pope rewarded bishops who tolerated sexual abuse. Cardinal Law, having been forced from Boston by the exposure of his incompetence in dealing with sexual abuse, remains a cardinal and works in numerous Vatican offices, including the Congregation of Bishops and the Congregation for the Clergy.[38] John Paul II appointed him archpriest of St. Mary Major, an honorable sinecure that includes a palatial apartment and a comfortable salary. Law was given the honor of saying one of the public Masses after the death of John Paul II. If McCormack has to flee the United States to avoid prosecution, he can expect a similar welcome in Rome.

The boys and girls whose lives were destroyed were victimized not only by the abusers, but by all those who allowed the abuse to go on: by the bishops first of all, by fellow priests who turned a blind eye, by parishioners who wanted to hear no evil spoken of popular priests, by police officers who turned criminal priests over to bishops rather than to the courts, by judges who gave priests light sentences and sealed documents to hide patterns of abuse, by the newspapers which for so long were unwilling to print stories of abuse, by the Vatican and by the pope, who appointed the bishops who hated confronting abusive priests more than they hated child abuse, by the pope who gave every sign to the bishops that he wanted abusive priests to be given a second, third, fourth, tenth chance, by the pope who reviewed case files of abusers and never asked about the victims, by the pope who had time to meet with breakdancers but refused every request to meet with abuse victims.

One of the few bishops to demonstrate a grasp of the seriousness of the situation is the Anglican archbishop Phillip Aspinall of Brisbane, Australia. He told his clergy:

> . . . [W]e should not too quickly jump to the conclusion that dealing with this issue in the life of the [C]hurch is a distraction from the mission of God in the world, an irritating hindrance to the real work. The [C]hurch is called to make known the love of God in Christ for all people. This love is good news for the poor, freedom for those who are oppressed, liberty to those held captive. God's special concern to protect the vulner-

able and the defenseless is to shine through the life of the [C]hurch. So if it ever comes about that the weak or vulnerable are harmed by the actions of the [C]hurch it is a fundamental betrayal of the justice of God and the gospel of Christ. Dealing with this matter in the life of the [C]hurch, justly and with care for the most vulnerable, goes to the heart of God's mission. It is not a distraction from it.

. . . [T]he damage caused by sexual abuse never just goes away. It may be pushed down and hidden for a time but it festers away and eventually resurfaces often with the damage multiplied and the agony intensified. We've seen this in the lives of victims of abuse where the damage goes on wreaking havoc for decades, destroying the life of the individual concerned and distorting close relationships. The damage can even have impacts on successive generations. Many abusers have themselves been subjected to abuse. And what is true in the lives of individual victims is also true in the lives of institutions. In the [C]hurch abuse alleged to have occurred forty and fifty years ago is now resurfacing. We cannot simply say, "Leave it behind. It's all in the past. It happened a long time ago. Move on." The only way we can move on is if we face the hurtful reality of what has happened, extend care and support to those harmed and take steps to ensure as far as possible that it never happens again."[39]

Facing a hurtful reality which one or one's community has been responsible for is never easy. Germans tried to face up to their responsibility for Nazism, but have not succeeded. A German social psychologist discovered that two-thirds of the German families he interviewed had reconstructed their family memories so that they had become victims or opponents of Nazism.[40] Catholic bishops and the Vatican refuse to face their responsibility for abuse; they use every legal device to keep documents from the public, and have not set up a Truth and Reconciliation Commission such as South Africa set up to deal with the poisonous memories of apartheid.

Catholic bishops, to protect their assets, have opposed any retroactive extension of the statute of limitations.[41] The number of victims in the bishops' own files is over ten thousand; the real number is certainly many times that. What price can be placed on a ruined life? Many of the victims were vulnerable and the abuse pushed them over the edge into unemployability. If a person is made largely or completely unemployable because of drug or alcohol problems or inability to get along with authority figures (all common effects of abuse), he may lose forty years of work at $25,000 a year, in addition to the mental suffering and ruined marriages that result. The real liability of the Catholic Church may be in the tens of billions of dollars. This liability may not be legally enforceable because of the statute of limitations, but it is certainly a moral liability. Catholics have inherited the assets that previous generations built up, the churches, the real estate, the bank accounts. They have also inherited the liabilities, and should acknowledge them and make restitution—without which, the Church has taught since the beginning, there can be no forgiveness.

Forgiveness looks ultimately to reconciliation. Forgiveness is in the service of charity, which is the highest of all virtues, that which gives all virtues their ultimate meaning, and to which all virtues should lead. God offers sinners forgiveness, because He desires to be reconciled with them and restore friendship with them. He also wants sinners ultimately to be reconciled with one another.

This does not exclude vengeance. We rightly desire that the wicked perish; God also desires that. Yet simply condemning the wicked to hell does not destroy them. They cease to be enemies only when they are reconciled and become friends. Reconciliation is hard for victims to imagine when the abusers and those who facilitated them are still unrepentant. A long and painful process that must begin with seeing the truth of what has happened is necessary before forgiveness and reconciliation are even possible. If Christians cannot begin and carry through this process of truth-telling, repentance, and reconciliation to heal the wound in the Church that sexual abuse has made, what hope is there for the world that is embittered by war and genocide and terrorism?

# EPILOGUE

CARDINAL JOSEPH RATZINGER was elected pope on April 19, 2005. As the head of the Congregation for the Doctrine of the Faith, he had begun processing hundreds of abuse cases that were sent to Rome after 2002. No doubt the files he received were sanitized to some extent and did not contain the type of material I have presented in this book, but the facts of abuse were stark enough and undeniable.

On March 25, 2005, Cardinal Ratzinger gave the meditations on the Way of the Cross. At the ninth station, "Jesus falls for the third time," Cardinal Ratzinger said:

> Should we not also think of how much Christ suffers in his own Church? . . . How much filth there is in the Church, and even among those who in the priesthood ought to belong entirely to him! . . . The soiled garments and face of your Church throw us into confusion. Yet it is we ourselves who have soiled them! It is we who betray you time and time again, after all our lofty words and grand gestures.[1]

At the eighth station, "Jesus meets the women of Jerusalem who weep for him," Cardinal Ratzinger said of the words of Jesus, "Weep not for me, but for yourselves and your children":

> How are we to understand his words? Are they not directed at a piety which is purely sentimental, one which fails to lead to conversion and living faith? It is no use to lament the sufferings of this world if our life goes on as usual. And so the Lord warns us of the danger in which we find ourselves. He shows us both the seriousness of sin and the seriousness of judgment. Can it be that, despite all our expression of consternation in the face of evil and of innocent suffering, we are all too prepared to trivialize the mystery of evil? Have we accepted only the gentleness and love of God and Jesus, and quietly set aside the word of judgment? "How can God be so concerned with our weakness?" we say. "We are only human!" Yet as we contemplate the sufferings of the Son, we see more clearly the seriousness of sin, and how it needs to be fully atoned for if it is to be overcome. Before the image of the suffering Lord, evil can no longer be trivialized. To us too he says: "Do not weep for me, weep for yourselves…if they do this when the wood is green, what will happen when it is dry?"
>
> Lord, to the weeping women you spoke of repentance and the Day of Judgment, when all will stand before your face: before you, the Judge of the whole world. You call us to leave behind the trivialization of evil, which salves our consciences and allows us to carry on as before. You show us the seriousness of our responsibility, the danger of our being found guilty and without excuse on the Day of Judgment. Grant that we may not simply walk at your side, with nothing to offer other than compassionate words. Convert us and give us new life. [2]

As Pope Benedict XVI, Joseph Ratzinger confronts the mystery of evil in the Church, the voices that say "Father is only human," "It was less than one percent of priests," "The press is exaggerating it," "The boys will bounce back," "Why can't the victims forgive and forget?" The new pope has only a few years to act. If he severely disciplines bishops and priests he will be accused of violating collegiality and restoring the papal monarchy. If he only exhorts the bishops to do their duty he will be accused of shirking the issue and abandoning victims.

So far Benedict's record has been mixed. On the negative side, he has appointed William Levada, former archbishop of San Francisco, as his successor as head of the Congregation for the Doctrine of the Faith and therefore the person chiefly responsible for removing sexual abusers from the priesthood. Levada is compromised by the scandal (see p. 406). Benedict also appointed George H. Niederauer as archbishop of San Francisco. Niederauer was spiritual director at St. John's Seminary in Camarillo, California from 1974 to 1994, when the seminary produced a large number of abusers. Niederauer either noticed nothing wrong (in which case he is unobservant and therefore unqualified to be an overseer/*episcopos*) or saw the corruption and did not object to it.

But on the positive side, Ratzinger speeded up the trials of abusers, and as Pope Benedict XVI has taken two major steps.

## *Brother Gino*

The first concerns the notorious Gino Burresi. Until 1992 Burresi was a brother of the Oblates of the Virgin Mary. He was a great devoté of the apparition of Mary at Fatima, and he claimed to possess many supernatural abilities. He said he was a stigmatist, that the wounds of Christ had appeared on his body. He claimed to have the gift of knowledge, and to be able to see the secrets of men's souls. He claimed to have the odor of sanctity, the mysterious fragrance that surrounds the saints. In fact he was a fraud: an active homosexual who persuaded priests to reveal confessions to him so he could pretend to know people's secret sins and who had a large supply of perfume in his cell. In 1988 some of his followers went to their superiors and said that Gino had abused them. One wrote:

> Fr. Gino was kissing me, and at the same time he was saying wonderful, holy things: "Let yourself be touched by God. Loving is not a sin." I was confused and paralyzed. I knew that he was a stigmatist, someone who had direct contact with the Virgin Mary. So I felt that I was wrong, that he could not be like I thought he was, because if he had been that way

> God would not have chosen him as his minister on earth. I said to myself: Look at how evil and rotten I am, I see malice even in the affectionate embraces of a saint.[1]

His superiors sent him to a monastery in Austria and the accusation to the Vatican. But Burresi had friends in the Vatican, and the superiors who tried to discipline Burresi were themselves reprimanded. The superiors appealed to John Paul II with a list of the accusations against Burresi, but the pope denied their appeal.

Burresi left the Oblates in 1992 and founded his own order, the Servants of the Immaculate Heart of Mary. But Cardinal Ratzinger opened another investigation in 1997, and in 2002 issued a report with the accusations against Burresi : "violation of the seal of the confession, the illegitimate use against the penitent of confidential information revealed during confession, defamation, violation of the right to privacy, incitement to disobedience against superiors, false mysticism, and claims of apparitions, visions, and supernatural messages."[2] The report said that these actions were outside the statute of limitations, but that Burresi should be disciplined, lest his followers proclaim his innocence.

The first action that the newly-appointed Cardinal Levada took under the pontificate of Benedict XVI was a decree in May 2005 against Burresi. It specifies

- Burresi's faculties to hear confessions are revoked;
- He is definitively prohibited from providing spiritual direction;
- He is barred from preaching, as well as from celebrating the sacraments and sacramentals in public;
- He is barred from giving interviews, publishing and taking part in broadcasts that have anything to do with faith, morals, or supernatural phenomena.[3]

The supporters of Marcial Maciel Degollado began worrying.

## *Marcial Maciel Degollado*

Maciel was born in a devout Catholic family in Mexico and grew up during the time of the murderous anti-clerical persecution of the Church. His uncle will be canonized. Maciel entered two seminaries but was dismissed for unspecified reasons. Maciel then founded the Legionaries of Christ in Mexico and soon moved to Rome. In the 1950s, he was accused of drug usage and theft; he was removed as head of his order and a multi-year investigation was conducted. Maciel was exonerated and returned to his order.[4]

Beginning in the 1970s, former Legionaries began contacting Rome, accusing Maciel of molesting them when they were seminarians as young as 12. They said that Maciel told them that of course homosexuality was wrong, but that the Pope had given Maciel a dispensation from this law because of his health problems. The Legion has always cultivated obedience as a central virtue, and the victims said they complied and had sex with Maciel. This subtle argument is based upon an exaggeration of a dangerous strain of Catholic moral theology which holds that actions are not good or bad in themselves but only because God commands or forbid them, and that therefore naked obedience to the Divine Will is the ultimate and in fact only virtue.

The earlier accusations disappeared in the Vatican. There were problems both with the accusations against Maciel and the Legion's defense of him. The accusers (at least some of them) had sworn under oath in the 1950s that Maciel had done no wrong. They had perjured themselves—they later said they had done this because they had taken an oath never to speak ill of Maciel, but they had nonetheless perjured themselves. The testimony of a perjurer is ever after not reliable. One accuser recanted and said he had been pressured to make the accusation (this is not unusual; real victims often still feel a bond to their abuser and retract true accusations).

But the defense of Maciel by the Legion put forth was also questionable. Why had Maciel been thrown out of seminaries? Why had so many "calumnies" dogged his early career? One doctor who cleared Maciel of drug usage was an eye doctor who had been declared persona non grata by the

Vatican and who had lost his medical license. The letters that exonerated Maciel by a bishop Polidoro look like forgeries. And so on. The Vatican's hesitancy in making a judgment may therefore not be due to simple clericalism, but to an inability to sort through the facts of the case.

Maciel's order was very successful in getting vocations to the priesthood and in raising money. It attracted the attention of Pope John Paul II, who honored Maciel and praised him as "an efficacious guide to youth,"[5] and of Cardinal Angelo Sodano, the Secretary of State who favored Maciel.

But in 1998 a group of former Legionaries filed a canonical process accusing Maciel of absolving accomplices in sexual sin in confession. This is a grave sin and the penalty is excommunication. In 1999 Cardinal Ratzinger halted the investigation, and when asked publicly why displayed uncharacteristic petulance. The then-Cardinal Ratzinger became visibly upset when asked about the Maciel case by ABC News' Brian Ross in April 2002. "You do not ask such questions," he said and then slapped Ross's hand.[6]

But in the waning days of John Paul II's pontificate Ratzinger resumed the investigation. Ratzinger sent Msgr. Scicluna around the world to interview people. Scicluna gathered a steamer trunk of evidence against Maciel and the now Pope Benedict decided to act. When questioned about the investigation, the Legion denied it was going on, and produced an unsigned fax from the office of the Secretary of State (Sodano's section) denying that an investigation existed.[7]

In May 2006 the Vatican issued this statement:

> After having submitted the results of the investigation to attentive study, the Congregation for the Doctrine of the Faith, under the guidance of the new prefect, His Eminence Cardinal William Levada, has decided—taking into account both the advanced age of Rev. Maciel and his delicate health—to forgo a canonical process and to call the priest to a life reserved to prayer and penance, renouncing any public ministry.
>
> Independently of the person of the founder, the well-deserving apostolate of the Legionaries of Christ and of the association Regnum Christi is recognized with gratitude.[8]

Without a formal trial, the decision could not be definitive. The Vatican could not have a trial because Maciel was old and sick and might well die during a prolonged trial. He was old and sick because his allies had delayed the trial. They had delayed the trial because the Legion was one of the few bright spots in a disturbed Church and they did not want to hurt it. But Benedict would not let Maciel escape uncensured, and his decision paralleled the one about Burresi. Neither the Legion nor Maciel acknowledged any guilt in their response to the Vatican's decision.

Even a trial is not infallible. If Maciel had been found guilty and excommunicated, his followers could still think that he, like Joan of Arc, had been the victim of a bad decision, and that history would vindicate him. They are convinced that Maciel is the victim of a conspiracy to destroy him, but the motives for the conspiracy are unclear. Why would men from pious families, who had entered the Legion to serve God, later accuse Maciel of abusing them, even if they had become disillusioned and decided to leave the Legion. Would such a conspiracy be able to deceive Pope Benedict, who had every reason to want to think Maciel innocent?

If the Vatican is right, Maciel is the most successful confidence artist in the recent history of the Church. How could so many people, including John Paul II, have been taken in? What weakness in the Church led to such a massive failure of discernment, to a willed refusal to see the difference between a pious, zealous man and a child-abusing, money-grubbing charlatan?

Either Maciel is the victim of a generation-long, international conspiracy by former members of the Legionaries of Christ who are determined to defame and destroy him, a conspiracy which has deceived Pope Benedict XVI, or he is in fact guilty of at least some of the actions of which he has been accused. If he is guilty, a successful congregation of priests has been founded by a child molester. The Piarists were founded by Joseph Calasanctius, an austere man who decided to risk the safety of children rather than alienate the rich and influential family of the abuser Stefano Cherubini (see pp. 19–20). The Servants of the Immaculate Heart of Mary were founded by Gino Burresi, who by all accounts is far more corrupt and sleazy than Maciel has been accused of being even by his worst enemies. It is difficult for Catholics to understand that some of their organizations could have been founded by men who do not simply have faults, who are not simply ordinary sinners, but who are criminals. It is as if Judas had been the first Pope. Perhaps this shock will help Catholics to abandon their infantilized attitude toward authority, an attitude that ends either in mindless obedience or adolescent rebellion.

Benedict seeks to purify the Church of the filth that he saw in the cases of sexual abusers by letting all know that no one is immune from discipline, not even the founders of successful religious orders. Nicola Bux, a consulter of the Congregation of the Faith, speaking to a Mexican reporter, compared Maciel with Archbishop Milingo, who had married a Korean woman in a ceremony of the Unification Church (Moonies); but the accusations against Maciel are worse, "situationes contra natura," unnatural vice. Bux advised Maciel either to sue the accusers or to accept the Pope's decision, because "those who sin should pay." Bux said that Benedict wants a Church, "limpia, sin manchas," "pure, without stain."[9] The bishops of the world have not yet followed Benedict's lead, but he has given them an example to imitate.

# NOTES

For further documentation on cases, see BishopAccountability.org and podles.org. To report errors or omissions, please contact podles@podles.org.

## *Introduction*

1. The transcript of one court case in the Altoona-Johnstown diocese runs to almost 10,000 pages.
2. According to Joseph A. Varacalli, the "progressive modernizers" see the main source of the abuse in "an alleged outdated and self-serving oligarchy and hierarchical mode of Church government" while the "orthodox ecclesiasts" blame "a liberal Catholic social movement with a constitutive focus on sexual liberation" ("Dissecting the Anatomy of the Sexual Scandal," *Homiletic and Pastoral Review*, January 2004, pp. 45, 47). Both sides join in holding the bishops accountable for the abuse and cover-up.
3. Philip Jenkins, *Pedophiles and Priests: Anatomy of a Contemporary Crisis* (New York: Oxford University Press, 1996).
4. Jenkins however not only tries to correct the misapprehension that pedophilia is common among Catholic priests, but seems to minimize the violation of trust or the damage that teenagers suffer when a priest initiates a sexual liaison with them. See Philip Jenkins, *The New Anti-Catholicism: The Last Acceptable Prejudice* (New York: Oxford University Press, 2003), pp. 133–56.
5. Paul Likoudis, *Amchurch Comes Out: The U. S. Bishops, Pedophile Scandals and the Homosexual Agenda* (Petersburg, Illinois: Roman Catholic Faithful, Inc., 2002).
6. "Archdiocese of Baltimore List of Clergy Accused of Sexual Abuse," September 26, 2002, indicates that "in 1999, an individual alleged sexual abuse by Ross LaPorta in the 1960s. In 1999, LaPorta was retired and living out of state. LaPorta denied the allegations. His faculties to perform ministry were removed. LaPorta served at St. Matthew from 1951 to 1963...." The list was removed from the website of the archdiocese of Baltimore but is available at snapnetwork.org.
7. Anonymous, *A Woman in Berlin: Eight Weeks in a Conquered City: A Diary*, translated by Philip Boehm (New York: Henry Holt and Company, Metropolitan Books, 2005).
8. The most bizarre case associated with the sexual abuse crisis is that of the Rev. Gerald Robinson. On Holy Saturday morning, 1980, Sister Margaret Ann Pahl was murdered in the sacristy of the chapel of Mercy Hospital in Toledo, Ohio. Robinson was chaplain there.

The murderer strangled Pahl, placed an altar cloth over her, stabbed her around the heart in the pattern of an inverted cross, pulled her underwear down as if this bride of Christ had been raped, and anointed her head with her own blood in a parody of the sacrament of anointing. Robinson was the prime suspect, but the diocese interfered, and the case was dropped (James Ewinger, "Diocese Got Inside Data on Slaying Probe: Letter Reported Police Kept Quiet about Priest," *Cleveland Plain Dealer*, May 9, 2006).

In 2003, a woman told the review board of the Toledo diocese an unbelievable story: she had been abused in "Satanic ceremonies in which priests placed her in a coffin filled with cockroaches, forced her to ingest what she believed to be a human eyeball, and penetrated her with a snake" (David Yonke, "Priest Arrested in '80 Slaying Surfaced in Ritual-Abuse Claim," *Toledo Blade*, April 25, 2004, and "Dark Allegations Arise Amid Probe of Nun's Slaying," *Toledo Blade*, February 20, 2005). She said Robinson had abused her. The board thought she was delusory, and refused to act. A board member remembered Robinson's name in connection with the murder and went to the police; the diocese fired him for doing this. The police reexamined the forensic evidence. They realized that new computer techniques showed that the shape of the murder weapon on the bloody cloths matched the shape of the letter opener found on the desk in Robinson's locked apartment. Robinson was arrested, indicted, and in May 2006 convicted of second degree murder. His lawyer intends to appeal.

Other women had independently gone to victims' advocates with stories of Satanic abuse, stories so strange that even the advocates could not believe them. They named as the ringleader the Rev. Chet Warren. He had abused Barbara Blaine, the founder of SNAP, the Survivors Network of Those Abused by Priests (Bill Frogameni, "Abuse, Murder, in Troubled Toledo," *National Catholic Reporter*, February 17, 2006).

The police are investigating the abuse allegations, which were also the subject of a civil lawsuit against Robinson and the diocese. For the most complete account, see David Yorke, *Sin, Shame, and Secrets: The Murder of a Nun, the Conviction of a Priest, and the Cover-up in the Catholic Church* (New York: Continuum, 2006). These stories resemble the Satanic panic of the 1980s (see Jeffrey S. Victor's *Satanic Panic: The Creation of a Contemporary Legend* [Chicago: Open Court, 1993]), but in this case there is a body defiled by Satanic rituals. The presence of murdered infants in the stories may be explained by the abusers' connection with morgues (see p. 53–54).

Andrew Greeley claims he knows of a murder connected with a Chicago pedophile ring, but has declined to provide details (see Matt C. Abbott, "Attorney Challenges Renegade Priest-Author to Expose 'Ring of Pedophiles,'" *Renew America*, November 16, 2004).

9. John Cornwell, *The Pontiff in Winter: Triumph and Conflict in the Reign of John Paul II* (New York: Doubleday, 2004) p. 228. Randy Engel in *The Rite of Sodomy: Homosexuality in the Roman Catholic Church* (Export, Pennsylvania: New Engel Publishing, 2006) presents the extreme theory that a homosexual conspiracy, led in part by an actively homosexual Pope Paul VI, has infiltrated the Church. Even those who detect a strong homosexual element in the abuse would usually see it as the result of the interaction of cultural and psychological tendencies which produced like-minded individuals who, in turn, formed a loose network of enablers.

10. Joseph Cardinal Ratzinger (Pope Benedict XVI), *Salt of the Earth: The Church at the End of the Millennium,* translated by Adrian Walker (San Francisco: Ignatius Press, 1997), p. 24.
11. Jim Schaefer, Patricia Montemurri, and Alexa Capeloto, "Tom Paciorek Breaks Silence: Ex-Baseball Star: Priest Abused Me," *Detroit Free Press,* March 22, 2002.

## *1. The Rectory Boys of El Paso*

1. Benedicta Ward, translator, *The Sayings of the Desert Fathers: The Alphabetical Collection* (London: Mowbrays, 1975) p. 85.
2. Ibid., p. 101.
3. "Candela iugiter in eadem cella ardeat usque mane" (*S. Benedicti Regula,* XXII, http://www.intratext.com/IXT/LAT0011/_PN.HTM).
4. Peter Damian, *Letters 31-60,* translated by Owen J. Blum (Washington, D. C.: The Catholic University of America Press, 1990) p. 29.
5. See Thomas P. Doyle, A. W. Richard Sipe, and Patrick J. Wall, *Sex, Priests, and Secret Codes: The Catholic Church's 2,000-Year Paper Trail of Sexual Abuse* (Los Angeles: Vott Press, 2006). They discuss the legislation against clerical sodomy from the earliest times (see pp. 13ff).
6. Damian, *Letters 31-60,* p. 15.
7. For a further discussion, see Doyle et al., *Sex, Priests, and Secret Codes,* pp. 20–23
8. Stephen Haliczer, *Sexuality in the Confessional: A Sacrament Profaned* (New York: Oxford University Press, 1996) p. 107.
9. Doyle et al., *Sex, Priests, and Secret Codes.* The thesis of this book is that the early and medieval Church dealt publicly if not always effectively with abuse, but that after the Reformation the Church shrouded the subject in the darkest secrecy to protect its clergy from Protestant and secularist attacks.
10. Karen Liebreich, *Fallen Order: A History* (London: Atlantic Books, 2004) p. xxi.
11. Ibid., p. 77.
12. Ibid., p. 212.
13. Ibid., p. 213.
14. Ibid., p. 226.
15. Paul Wilkes, *Excellent Catholic Parishes: The Guide to Best Places and Practices* (New York: Paulist Press, 2001) p. 21.
16. M. Lilliana Owens, *Most Rev. Anthony Schuler, S. J., D.D., First Bishop of El Paso* (El Paso, Texas: Revista Catolica Press, 1953) p. 432.
17. Author interview with Gary Pineau, December 29, 2004.
18. Second Judicial District Court, County of Bernalillo, State of New Mexico, Gary Pineau, plaintiff, vs. Roman Catholic Church of the Diocese of El Paso, Texas, a corporation and The Estate of Monsignor Lawrence Gaynor, deceased, CV-95-0004434 (henceforth Pineau v. Gaynor).
19. *Pictorial History of St. Pius X Parish of El Paso,* pp. 17, 59.
20. At the Paraclete center at Jemez Springs Rev. Wilfred Savard encountered many graduates of All Hallows seminary in Dublin. It trained missionary priests. Savard

named them the "Clansmen" and noted that "many of these Clansmen seem to be sex perverts. They seem to pay one another for services rendered" (Notes dated 1958). However, most Paraclete priests at Jemez Springs, including Savard, were not told why priests were sent there.

21. Telegdy (died 1995) was accused of abusing a Boy Scout in Mystic, Iowa, around 1960. News release of the diocese of Davenport, January 18, 2005, available at www.davenport.org.
22. In a later rambling and somewhat incoherent confession Klister said this incident occurred in the late 1940s to early 1950, but Klister was a priest by then and presumably not living alone in an apartment.
23. County Court at Law Number 2, El Paso County, Texas, Casc 96-1670, John Doe I et al v. Catholic Diocese of El Paso et al (henceforth Doe v. El Paso). Exhibits to Plaintiffs' Response to Defendants' Motions for Summary Judgment—Submitted in Camera, U. S. Postal Inspection Case 675-1020470.
24. The description of the boy (blond, Swedish) and of the abuse bears marks of fantasy. The boy supposedly went to Vietnam and died there. Even if it was a fantasy, it showed Klister's tastes, and he undoubtedly abused boys in El Paso.
25. The former international head of the Society for the Propagation of the Faith, Msgr. Bernard Prince, was arrested in Canada on thirty-one charges of molesting twelve young males. Prince was "a personal friend of John Paul II" (Andrew Seymour, "Police Lay 15 New Charges against Ex-Vatican Official: Alleged Incidents Date to the 1960s, 1970s," *National Post*, April 25, 2006).
26. "Holy Family Church Golden Jubilee Honors Pioneer Missionaries, Laymen," *Deming Headlight*, January 6, 1956.
27. "Rev. O'Sullivan Host to Priests on Thanksgiving Day," *Deming Headlight*, December 4, 1958.
28. All quotations from "Mike" are taken from his affidavit in Doe v. El Paso.
29. All quotations from "Bob" are taken from his unsigned affidavit prepared for Doe v. El Paso.
30. Doe vs. Diocese, 96-1670, Exhibits to Plaintiffs' Response . . ., Exhibit 11, Affidavit of [———].
31. Investigative memorandum.
32. Author interview with the mother of a victim, January 20, 2005. Klister's former bishop in Superior, Albert Meyer, was archbishop of Chicago from 1958 to 1965. As a priest in Chicago, Edward M. Egan was Meyer's secretary. Egan then went to Bridgeport, Connecticut, where he mishandled abuse cases, and then became cardinal archbishop of New York. Egan was himself accused of abuse but the allegation was dismissed by a review board and by the Cook County state's attorney's office as totally unfounded (Daniel J. Wakin, "Egan Is Cleared of Allegation of Abuse," *New York Times*, December 28, 2002).
33. "Retired Priest Sentenced on Child-Porn Film Charge," *Albuquerque Journal*, February 17, 1990, p. 2G.
34. The Society collects and distributes funds for mission work. It therefore has contacts with many missionaries and bishops in poor countries who might be persuaded to take in a priest who needed to leave the United States suddenly and to disappear from the view of irate parents and suspicious police.
35. Pineau v. Gaynor.

36. Author interview with Gary Pineau, December 29, 2004.
37. See Elizabeth Hadin-Burrola, "Predator Priest Found to Be Living in Gallup," *Gallup Independent*, July 12, 2003. In an interview, MacArthur says that the catalyst for his sexual disorder was his graduate study in 1958 at the Catholic University of America. "An instructor there spoke about psychopaths. Fascinated, MacArthur began reading everything he could find about the amoral and asocial personality. 'I became a devil in the right sense of the word, without concept of punishment,' he said" (Jill Callison, "Bishop Didn't Out Abusive Priest," *Argus Leader*, June 22, 2003). MacArthur is clearly the anonymous priest-abuser who recounts his story in Chapter Three, "A Priest and His Father," in Patrick Fleming's, Sue Lauber-Fleming's, and Mark T. Matousek's *Broken Trust: Stories of Pain, Hope, and Healing from Clerical Abuse Survivors and Abusers* (New York: Crossroad Publishing Company, 2007, pp. 56-67).
38. Jill Callison, "Six Abuse Allegations Recorded," *Argus Leader*, May 23, 2003.
39. Callison, "Bishops Didn't Out Abusive Priest."
40. Darren Meritz, "El Paso Ex-Priest Arrested Again," *El Paso Times*, January 21, 2006.
41. He says he is repentant; there is no evidence he abused after leaving prison in 1981. He says he worked as a missionary in Africa and Mexico. After retiring, he lived in poverty in Gallup, New Mexico, and worked as a volunteer with the Missionaries of Charity and the Little Sisters of the Poor. He was arrested in January 2006 for the molestation of Judy DeLonga; the statute of limitations was suspended after he left Wisconsin.
42. Obituary, *Los Angeles Times*, April 17, 1986.
43. Tommy Fina-Olivas, "One in 20 Priests Accused of Abuse," *El Paso Times*, February 26, 2004.

## *2. Heart of Darkness in the Heartland: Davenport, Iowa*

1. Shirley Ragsdale, "Iowa's Priest-accusation Rate Trails Nation's: State's 2.6% Figure Is below the 4% for U.S.," *Des Moines Register*, February 28, 2004.
2. Murphy's full name is not identified in court records but the boy's description of where he molested them matches the assignment records of the Rev. James W. Murphy of the Memphis diocese. The SNAP Tennessee website, www.rememberthesurvivors.com, identifies James R. Murphy as the Father Murphy of the Davenport documents. Letters to the Nashville diocese asking whether the Father Murphy named in the Iowa court cases is the same as Father James W. Murphy have gone unanswered.
3. James N. Wells v. Father James Janssen and the Diocese of Davenport, Scott County District Court, Law 101220, Plaintiff's Statement of Disputed Facts in Resistance to Defendants' Motion for Summary Judgment, May 14, 2002 (Hence Wells v. Janssen). Exhibit 2. Letter of Marion L. Gibbons, C.M. to Most Rev. Ralph Lee Hayes, March 26, 1948. All newspaper accounts and documents relating to the Davenport, Iowa, abuse cases can be found on the website bishopaccountability.org.
4. Wells v. Janssen, Exhibit 1.
5. Wells v. Janssen, Exhibit 8. This however does not agree with the 1955 letter that indicated that Janssen "frequents" the Newton YMCA. The secretary indicated that "no record was made in the minutes"; it is possible that the YMCA was trying to

protect itself by backdating its action. However, something caused the 1953 transfer from Clinton.

6. Wells v. Janssen, Exhibit 9.
7. Wells v. Janssen, Exhibit 6.
8. Wells v. Janssen, Exhibit 3.
9. Wells v. Janssen, Exhibit 3.
10. Wells v. Janssen, Exhibit 5.
11. Wells v. Janssen, Exhibit 10.
12. Wells v. Janssen, Exhibit 34.
13. Wells v. Janssen, Exhibit 13.
14. Wells v. Janssen, Exhibit 16.
15. Wells v. Janssen, Exhibit 38.
16. Wells v. Janssen, Exhibit 13.
17. Wells v. Janssen, Exhibits 14 and 15.
18. Wells v. Janssen, Exhibit 38C.
19. Wells v. Janssen, Exhibit 38D.
20. Wells v. Janssen, Exhibit 17.
21. Wells v. Janssen, Exhibit 34.
22. Wells v. Janssen, Exhibits 34 and 38.
23. Wells v. Janssen, Exhibit 22.
24. Wells v. Janssen, Exhibit 23.
25. Wells v. Janssen, Exhibit 24.
26. Wells v. Janssen, Exhibit 25.
27. Wells v. Janssen, Exhibits 26 and 27.
28. Wells v. Janssen, Exhibit 28.
29. Wells v. Janssen, Exhibit 29.
30. Wells v. Janssen, Exhibit 30.
31. Wells v. Janssen, Exhibit 64.
32. Wells v. Janssen, Exhibit 1A.
33. Wells v. Janssen, Exhibit 1B.
34. Wells v. Janssen, Exhibits 1C and 1D.
35. Wells v. Janssen, Exhibit 32.
36. Wells v. Janssen, Exhibit 57.
37. Wells v. Janssen, Exhibit 32.
38. Wells v. Janssen, Exhibit 34.
39. Wells v. Janssen, Exhibits 58, 59, and 60.
40. Wells v. Janssen, Exhibit 20. Hayes wrote, "He confessed his guilt." Janssen wrote to Hayes, "Again I am sorry for those relapses into sin which I admitted to you at your home" (Exhibit 34).
41. Wells v. Janssen, Exhibit 38.
42. Wells v. Janssen, Exhibit 44.
43. Ibid.
44. Wells v. Janssen, Exhibit 38.
45. Wells v. Janssen, Exhibit 41. Rev. Raymond Leneweaver of Philadelphia organized a similar group, the "Philadelphia Rovers." He abused boys, usually by anal rape, "in the seminary swimming pool, in the ocean, in his rectory bedroom, at the church's summer camp, and in the church itself, in the sacristy behind the altar" (Court of

Common Pleas, First Judicial District of Pennsylvania, Criminal Trial Division, Misc. no. 03-00-239, Report of the Grand Jury, p. 104). Leneweaver repeatedly admitted his abuse to archdiocesan officials (p. 101) but suffered no consequences. He left the priesthood in 1980 to teach in the public schools. He was never charged with a crime because of the statute of limitations.

46. Wells v. Janssen, Exhibit 43.
47. Wells v. Janssen, Exhibit 43.
48. Wells v. Janssen, Exhibit 42.
49. John Doe III v. Father James Janssen, Father Francis Bass, Theodore Anthony Geerts, and the Diocese of Davenport, Iowa District Court for Scott County, Law No. 101428, Affidavit of John Doe III, Exhibit 51B.
50. Tim Townsend, "Pedophile Priest Lives near School," *St. Louis Post-Dispatch*, September 16, 2004.
51. Wells v. Janssen, Exhibit 38.
52. Wells v. Janssen, Exhibit 41.
53. John Doe I-A v. Father James Janssen and Diocese of Davenport, Iowa District Court for Clinton County, Law 29513, Plaintiff's Statement of Disputed Facts in Resistance to Defendant's Motion for Summary Judgment, August 23, 2004, Exhibit 1 (Hence Doe 1-A v. Janssen).
54. Quotes from the *Baltimore Catechism* are drawn from Wells v. Janssen, Exhibit 43.
55. Wells v. Janssen, Exhibit 36.
56. Doe 1-A v. Janssen, Exhibit 1.
57. Wells v. Janssen, Exhibit 45.
58. Wells v. Janssen, Exhibit 43.
59. Wells v. Janssen, Exhibit 38.
60. Wells v. Janssen, Exhibit 45.
61. Wells v. Janssen, Exhibit 32.
62. Wells v. Janssen, Exhibit 34.
63. Wells v. Janssen, Exhibit 43.
64. Wells v. Janssen, Exhibit 46.
65. Wells v. Janssen, Exhibit 10.
66. Wells v. Janssen, Exhibits 46, 10, 64.
67. When Bishop Franklin was later told of this as part of an abuse complaint, he observed, "It was not unusual for boys to go swimming in the nude back in those days." (Wells v. Janssen, Exhibit 39).
68. Wells v. Janssen, Exhibit 4.
69. Wells v. Janssen, Exhibit 36.
70. Wells v. Janssen, Exhibit 46.
71. Wells v. Janssen, Exhibit 39.
72. Wells v. Janssen, Exhibit 39.
73. Wells v. Janssen, Exhibit 44.
74. Lee Nelson, "From Saving Souls to Saving Lives: 78-year-old Retired Priest May Be World's Oldest Lifeguard," *Quad-City Times*, August 4, 2000.
75. Wells v. Janssen, Exhibit 41.
76. Ibid.
77. Wells v. Janssen, Exhibit 44.
78. Wells v. Janssen, Exhibit 43.

79. Wells v. Janssen, Exhibit 40.
80. Wells v. Janssen, Exhibit 43.
81. John Doe III v. Janssen, Exhibit 69. See Wells v. Janssen, Exhibit 43, para. 15 for the victim's own description of this incident.
82. Wells v. Janssen, Exhibit 43.
83. Wells v. Janssen, Exhibit 37.
84. Wells v. Janssen, Exhibit 43.
85. Wells v. Janssen, Exhibit 1.
86. John Doe III v. Janssen, Exhibit 49.
87. Wells v. Janssen, Exhibit 65.
88. Wells v. Janssen, Exhibit 40.
89. Wells v. Janssen, Exhibit 42.
90. Wells v. Janssen, Exhibit 34.
91. Wells v. Janssen, Exhibit 32.
92. Wells v. Janssen, Exhibit 28.
93. Wells v. Janssen, Exhibit 43.
94. Wells v. Janssen, Exhibit 41.
95. Wells v. Janssen, Exhibit 42.
96. Wells v. Janssen, Exhibit 43.
97. Ibid.
98. Ibid.
99. Shirley Ragsdale, "Iowa Church Officials for Years Hid Allegations of Sexual Abuse," *Des Moines Register*, May 25, 2004.
100. John Doe III v. Janssen, Exhibit 49.
101. Ibid.
102. John Doe III v. Janssen, Exhibit 48. See also Shirley Ragsdale, "Alleged Victim: I Told Church 6 Times," *Des Moines Register*, March 18, 2004.
103. Shirley Ragsdale, "Alleged Victim: I Told Church 6 Times: A Des Moines Man Says He Tried to Warn the Davenport Diocese about a Priest's Alleged Attempt to Molest Him," *Des Moines Register*, March 18, 2004.
104. Wells v. Janssen, Exhibit 32.
105. A February 25, 2004, press release of the Diocese of Davenport (available at www.davenportdiocese.org) indicated that "in 1989 Fr. James Leu was arrested for the sexual abuse of minors while he was assigned to St. Mary Church in Lone Tree, Iowa. Fr. Leu pleaded guilty and was sentenced to two years of incarceration in a state penal institution."
106. Michael Kasper, Robert Kasper, and Andre Kasper v. Father James Elmer Leu, Most Rev. Gerald O'Keefe et al., Iowa District Court in and for Johnson County, Law No. 53102 (hence Kasper v. Leu), Deposition of Bishop Gerald O'Keefe June 12, 1991, p. 50, ll. 8–11.
107. Kasper v. Leu, Deposition of Bishop Gerald O'Keefe, p. 19, ll. 17–22.
108. Kasper v. Leu, Deposition of Bishop Gerald O'Keefe, p. 19, l.23—p. 20, l. 4.
109. Kasper v. Leu, Deposition of Msgr. Michael J. Morrissey, p. 9, ll. 19 – p. 11, l. 16.
110. John Doe 1-A v. Janssen, Deposition of Msgr. Michael J. Morrissey, p. 175, l. 13.
111. John Doe 1-A v. Janssen, Deposition of Msgr. Michael J. Morrissey, p. 175, ll.14–20.
112. Kasper v. Leu, Deposition of Bishop Gerald O'Keefe, p. 178, ll.18–20.

113. Neither Denning nor Meyer have been accused of any misconduct.
114. Kasper v. Leu, Deposition of Bishop Gerald O'Keefe, p. 115, ll. 2–7.
115. John Doe III v. Janssen, Exhibit 2.
116. Wells v. Janssen, Exhibit 60.
117. John McCooley, "Priests Must Take Sex Abuse Classes: Diocese Has Not Seen Problem Here, " *Quad-City Times*, August 4, 1998.
118. Ruby Nancy, "Q[uad]-C[ity] Catholic Clergy Brace for Suspicion," *Quad-City Times*, April 18, 2002.
119. Todd Ruger, "Defrocked Priest Goes to Foster Parent Classes," *Quad-City Times*, October 6, 2004.
120. "Retired Priests," *Catholic Messenger*, December 4, 2003.
121. Wiebler was included in a settlement made by the Diocese of Davenport (News release, Diocese of Davenport, January 18, 2005).
122. For a detailed analysis of the omissions and misrepresentations in the diocese's supposed full confession see http://www.bishopaccountability.org/ia-davenport/franklin-report.htm.
123. In 1992 O'Keefe was himself sued for abuse, but the suit was dropped. Two women accused him of abusing them in the 1960s when he was auxiliary bishop in St. Paul, Minnesota. The accusations were based upon repressed memories recovered during therapy under the direction of a dubious therapist. See Jean Latz Griffin, "Specter of False Memories Can Taint Abuse Cases," *Chicago Tribune*, November 21, 1993. See also p. 267.
124. Griffin, "Specter of False Memories Can Taint Sex Cases."
125. Shirley Ragsdale, "Ex Diocesan Leader Accused of Child Abuse," *Des Moines Register*, July 30, 2005. A jury awarded D. Michael Uhde damages for abuse by Feeney. See Barb Arland-Fye, "Jury Rules against Diocese, Awards $1.5 Million to Abuse Claimant," *Catholic News Service*, September 19, 2006.
126. "The diocese reported that the Vatican decided that 'in the light of the fact that Bass is retired and advanced in age,' Franklin should oblige him to lead a life of prayer and penance, and to privately offer Holy Mass once a week for the remainder of his days in reparation for the crimes he has committed" (Todd Ruger, "Former Priest Settles Lawsuits," *Quad-City Times*, May 17, 2005).
127. Shirley Ragsdale, "Celibate Priest Faced Loneliness, Isolation," *Des Moines Register*, January 31, 2004.
128. Todd Ruger, "Defrocked Priest Goes to Foster Parent Classes," *Quad City Times*, October 6, 2004.
129. Shirley Ragsdale, "Parish Acts to Remove Pain Left by Abuse," *Des Moines Register*, January 24, 2004.
130. John Doe I-A v. Janssen, Plaintiff's Statement of Disputed Facts in Resistance to Defendant's Motion for Summary Judgment.
131. Todd Ruger, "Davenport Diocese Contends 1st Amendment Rights Have Been Violated," *Quad-City News*, April 28, 2004.
132. Green v. Janssen et al, Iowa District Court for Clinton County, LA 29990, Reply to Plaintiff's Memorandum in Opposition to the Diocese's Motion for Judgment on the Pleadings. The canon lawyer Thomas Doyle, in "Roman Catholic Clericalism, Religious Duress, and Clergy Sexual Abuse," contradicts these assertions: "The history of

Canon law reveals a consistent pattern of ecclesiastical legislation in which the Church accepted responsibility for the moral and spiritual welfare of its congregants and took great pains to enact laws that would protect them from harmful actions perpetrated by clerics" (*Pastoral Psychology*, Vol. 51, No. 3 [2003] p. 192).

133. "Remarks by Bishop Franklin," Thursday, September 30, 2004: on the diocesan website www.davenportdiocese.org. The other dioceses that have filed for bankruptcy because of claims resulting from sexual abuse are Portland (in Oregon), Seattle, Spokane, Tucson, and San Diego.
134. Erin Jordan, "Vicar Confessed in E-mail to Alleged Victim," *Des Moines Register*, March 20, 2004.
135. Todd Ruger, "Diocese Official Settles Abuse Lawsuit," *Quad City Times*, April 13, 2005.
136. Todd Ruger, "Victims: Diocese Finally Has Taken Responsibility," *Quad City Times*, October 29, 2004.
137. Todd Ruger, "Janssen Retracts Testimony," *Quad City Times*, May 6, 2005.
138. Barb Ickes, "Forgive Him, Father," *Quad City Times*, June 2, 2005.
139. Todd Ruger, "Former Priest Settles Lawsuits," *Quad City Times*, May 17, 2005. Bass said, "Given the number and nature of the claims and the extent of the evidence supporting them, I have concluded that it is not likely that I can prevail on the merits and that it is in my interest and the interest of all that these claims be resolved," and, "To Steven Davis and others I may have harmed, I apologize. I hope this statement will assist in the healing process."
140. Shirley Ragsdale, "Priest's Records Spark Questions: 8 Allege Davenport Clergyman Molested Them as Boys," *Des Moines Register*, February 15, 2004.
141. Wells v. Janssen, Exhibit 43.
142. Erin Jordan, "Parishes Skeptical of Abuse Allegations against Clergyman: Some Wonder Whether the Lawsuits Have Been Brought Forth for the Sake of Money," *Des Moines Register*, November 26, 2003.
143. Kay Luna, "Abuse Allegations Split Sugar Creek," *Quad-City Times*, October 4, 2003.
144. Ibid.
145. Wells v. Janssen, Exhibit 34.
146. Doe 1-A v. Janssen, Exhibit 7.
147. Peter Manseau, *Vows: The Story of a Priest, a Nun, and Their Son* (New York: Free Press, 2005) p. 47. William Manseau told his son Peter that "if you were to go and talk with a lot of priests, I think you'd find that when they were kids some priest in their parish had befriended them and had initiated them sexually. Or something close to it—like me" (p. 47). This book contains some astonishing surprises and should be read in its entirety.
148. Shirley Ragsdale, "Iowa Church Officials for Years Had Allegations of Sexual Abuse," *Des Moines Register*, May 25, 2004.

## *3. Distant Thunder*

1. Barry M. Coldrey wrote, "Until the mid-twentieth century, child welfare was essentially to protect society from the depredations of idle, disaffected, unemployed, pov-

erty-stricken children and young people" ("Mixture of Caring and Corruption: Church Orphanages and Industrial Schools," *Studies: An Irish Quarterly Review*, March 2000).

2. Sam Hughes, *Steering the Course: A Memoir* (Montréal: McGill-Queens University Press, 2000) p. 260.
3. Michael Harris, *Unholy Orders: Tragedy at Mount Cashel* (Markham, Ontario: Viking, 1990) p. 41.
4. Dereck O'Brien, *Suffer Little Children: An Autobiography of a Foster Child* (St. John's, Newfoundland: Breakwater, 1991) p. 102.
5. Ibid., p. 104.
6. Harris, *Unholy Orders*, p. 81.
7. Ibid., p. 86.
8. Ronda Bessner, *Institutional Child Abuse in Canada* (Law Commission of Canada, Fall 1998), available at www.lcc.gc.ca/en/themes/mr/ica/besrep/besrep_main.asp.
9. Harris, *Unholy Orders*, p. 98.
10. Brother D. F. Nash wrote to Brother G. G. McHugh: "At the most recent meeting, with Deputy Minister of Justice, Mr. McCarthy, the following points were raised....Brs Ted English and Gerry Ralph are not to return to the Province of Newfoundland....Brs. Kenny and Short are not to be reassigned to Mt. Cashel" (Philip Lee, "Kenny Hired as Teacher for Years after Mount Cashel Probe," *Sunday Express*, December 3, 1986, p. 2). Douglas Kenny was hired in 1979 by the Toronto Roman Catholic school board as a teacher, in 1986 he was made vice principal of Father Henry Carr Secondary School, and in 1986 vice principal of Michael Power-St. Joseph's school.
11. Harris, *Unholy Orders*, p. 129.
12. Ibid., p. 239.
13. Ibid., p. 238.
14. Ibid., p. 131.
15. Ibid., p. 239.
16. Ibid.
17. Ibid., p. 238.
18. Ibid., p. 241.
19. Brother Ralph: "The accused entered a guilty plea to ten counts of indecent assault and one count of gross indecency"; Brother Rooney: "The accused was found guilty of six out of ten sexual abuse charges and sentenced to six years in prison"; Brother Burke: "The accused was convicted of three counts of indecent assault and one count of assault of causing bodily harm." Burke appealed to the Supreme Court of Canada. "The S.C.C. allowed the appeal and quashed the convictions for indecent assault. The appeal regarding the conviction for assault causing bodily harm was dismissed and that decision was upheld." Brother Kenny: "The accused was found guilty on seven counts of indecent assault"; Brother French: "The accused was found guilty by a jury of three counts of assault on a male person and sentenced to a total of 18 months in jail." See Goldie M. Shea, "Institutional Child Abuse in Canada: Criminal Cases," October 1999, at Law Commission of Canada website. Brother Short was convicted and sentenced to "four years in jail for fondling boys" (Jonathan Wong, "Director Attended Violent School," *Vancouver Odyssey*, April 3, 1992).
20. For Hughes's account of this commission see "The Evil That Men Do," in *Steering the Course*, pp. 247–264.

21. Harris, *Unholy Orders*, p. 305.
22. Ibid.
23. Harris, *Unholy Orders*, p. 306.
24. Bill Roger, "Hypocrisy and the Holy Father," CBC Viewpoints, July 3, 2002.
25. Michael J. Higgins, "The Church Must Change: A Canadian Expert on the Vatican Examines the Sex Abuse Scandal," *Macleans*, May 13, 2002.
26. "Trying to Sue the Catholic Church," CBC News, March 25, 2004.
27. Phil Lee, "Rumors of Hickey's Deviance Abounded in the 1970s," *Sunday Express*, August 13, 1989, p. 1.
28. Roger, "Hypocrisy and the Holy Father."
29. Canadian Conference of Catholic Bishops, *From Pain to Hope: Report from the Ad Hoc Committee on Child Sexual Abuse* (Ottawa: Publication Service, Canadian Conference of Catholic Bishops, 1992) pp. 31–32.
30. Philip Lee, "Christian Brothers Condemn Statements of Nova Scotia Bishop," *Sunday Express*, August 13, 1989, p. 1.
31. See "Chapter Eight: Fatherly Treatment" in Harris, *Unholy Orders*, pp. 186–212.
32. Christie Blatchford, "Power Links the Two Father Rons," *Toronto Sun*, March 30, 1990.
33. See "Sins of the Father" at www.ufcw.net/articles/docs/sins_of_the_father.html.
34. Bonnie Belec, "Former Brother Arrested in New York," *St. John's Evening Telegram*, May 22, 1998.
35. Bonnie Belec, "Conditional Sentence 'Not Appropriate' for Former Christian Brother: Prosecutor," *St. John's Evening Telegram*, August 20, 1998.
36. Harris, *Unholy Orders*, p. 90.
37. Angela Piacenza, "Mt. Cashel Victims Wonder Why History Had to Repeat Itself," *Toronto Star*, May 25, 2002.
38. Jason Berry, *Lead Us Not into Temptation: Catholic Priests and the Sexual Abuse of Children* (Urbana, Illinois: University of Illinois Press, 2000) p. 40.
39. Evan Moore, "Judge's Intervention for Pedophile Raising Questions: Ex-priest Benefits from Free Legal Help, Special Treatment in Prison," *Houston Chronicle*, November 1, 1998.
40. Patrick Boyle, *Scout's Honor* (Rocklin, California: Prima Publishing, 1994) p. 252. Child abusers often claim to have been abused. From their testimony psychologists adduce that being molested is a risk factor for becoming a molester. But the honesty of abusers who have been caught cannot be assumed, and it is fair to wonder how many of these claims are lies and ploys to salvage some sympathy and get a reduced sentence.
41. Kathy Sawyer, "Priest's Child Molestation Case Traumatizes Catholic Community," *Washington Post*, June 9, 1985.
42. Alice Jackson Baughn, "A Victim's Story," *Time*, March 28, 2002.
43. Berry, *Lead Us Not into Temptation*, p. 36.
44. Ibid., p. 11.
45. Ibid., p. 12.
46. Ibid., p. 17.
47. Ibid., p. 18.
48. Ibid., p. 31.
49. Virginia de Leon, "Suit Alleges Childhood Sexual Abuse by Priest," *Spokane Spokes-*

*man Review*, March 13, 2003.

50. Dennis Domrzalski, "Therapist Is Sex Offender," *Albuquerque Tribune*, December 8, 1993, A1.
51. Berry, *Lead Us Not into Temptation*, p. 53.
52. Moore, "Judge's Intervention for Pedophile Raising Questions."
53. Berry, *Lead Us Not into Temptation*, p. 154.
54. Ibid.
55. Ibid., p. 142.
56. Ibid., pp. 167–168.
57. Brooks Egerton, "FBI Investigates Judge's Ties to Pedophile Priest: Jurist's Efforts to Get Ex-cleric Legal Help Defended," *Dallas Morning News*, December 23, 1997.
58. Eamonn O'Neill, "Sins of the Fathers," *The Scotsman*, April 6, 2002.
59. Michael Powell, "A Fall from Grace: When Ray Mouton Took on a Pedophile Priest as a Client, He Had No Idea How Much Was at Stake," *Washington Post*, August 4, 2002.
60. Ibid.
61. O'Neill, "Sins of the Fathers."
62. Egerton, "FBI Investigates Judge's Ties to Pedophile Priest."
63. Ibid. In Texas, Polk County prosecutor Lee Hon said he told the FBI that Judge Politz had never contacted him and that he had no evidence of interference. But he also said that the case had been marked by some unusual and troubling events. Louisiana corrections officials, he said, didn't comply with his office's two requests for Mr. Gauthé's prison file. Mr. Hon said he needed conviction records to prove that the defendant was a repeat offender subject to a stiffer sentence. "If you want to think there's something sinister about that, that's certainly an inference you could draw," Mr. Hon said. Assistant corrections secretary Johnny Creed said the requests may have gotten snagged in a processing backlog. "It's very unfortunate that this came out the way it did," Mr. Creed said. "I regret that bad."
64. Ibid.
65. Ibid.
66. Ibid.
67. Moore, "Judge's Intervention for Pedophile Raising Questions."

## *4. Storm Warnings*

1. Letter of Rev. Gerald Fitzgerald to Bishop Robert J. Dwyer, September 12, 1952. Reprinted in Thomas R. Doyle, A. W. Richard Sipe, and Patrick Wall, *Sex, Priests, and Secret Codes: The Catholic Church's 2,000-Year Paper Trail of Sexual Abuse* (Los Angeles: Volt Press, 2006), pp. 301–302.
2. Letter from Matthew F. Brady, bishop of Manchester to the Very Rev. Gerald Fitzgerald, September 23, 1957. New Hampshire Attorney General's Office documents from the diocese of Manchester (henceforth NHAGO) p. 5929.
3. Letter from Gerald Fitzgerald, Servant General to Matthew Brady, bishop of Manchester, September 26, 1957. NHAGO, pp. 5926–5927.
4. Ibid.

5. Letter from Matthew F. Brady, bishop of Manchester to George G. Rehring, bishop of Toledo, December 4, 1957. NHAGO, p. 5943. Brady also sent similar letters to numerous other bishops to whom Sullivan had applied.
6. Letter from Very Rev. Msgr. James P. Finucan, chancellor, diocese of La Crosse to Very Rev. Msgr. Thomas S. Hansberry, January 6, 1961. NHAGO, p. 6019.
7. Letter from Richard G. Meyer, archbishop of Milwaukee to Matthew Brady, bishop of Manchester, January 31, 1958. NHAGO, p. 5974.
8. Letter of John A. Lee to Ernest J. Primeau, bishop of Manchester, September 16, 1960 (NHAGO, p. 6008); letter of Ernest J. Primeau, bishop of Manchester, to John A. Lee, September 20, 1960 (NHAGO, p. 6007).
9. Letter of Gerald Fitzgerald, Servant General, to Ernest J. Primeau, bishop of Manchester, June 30, 1961. NHAGO, p. 6029.
10. Letter of Gerald Fitzgerald to Vincent J. Hynes, bishop of Norwich, May 7, 1963, reprinted in Doyle et. al., *Sex, Priests, and Secret Codes*, p. 303.
11. William C. Bier wrote: "The Mf (interest) scale [is] the one on which the seminary group manifests the most divergence from both the general test norms…and the scores of the other groups…. Mf is the masculine-feminine interest scale and is built upon the assumption that men and women have characteristic patterns of interest and that these interests may be interpreted as indices of masculine and feminine tendencies" ("A Comparative Study of a Seminary Group and Four Other Groups on the Minnesota Multiphasic Personality Inventory," *Studies in Psychology and Psychiatry*, Vol. 7, No. 3, [April 1948] pp. 60–61). This divergence may not be bad; seminarians may be showing up high on empathy, a feminine characteristic; but seminarians will still feel themselves (and be felt to be) different from most men and will therefore have an insecure sense of masculine identity.
12. Walter J. Coville, Paul F. D'Arcy, Thomas N. McCarthy, and John J. Rooney, *Assessment of Candidates for the Religious Life: Basic Psychological Issues and Problems* (Washington, D. C.: Center for Applied Research in the Apostolate, 1968) p. 28.
13. Eugene Kennedy and Victor J. Heckler, *The Catholic Priest in the United States: Psychological Investigations* (Washington, D. C.: United States Catholic Conference, 1972) p. 7.
14. Ibid., p. 9.
15. Ibid.
16. Ibid., p. 11.
17. Conrad W. Baars, *How to Treat and Prevent the Crisis in the Priesthood* (Chicago: Franciscan Herald Press, 1972) p. 11.
18. Conrad W. Baars, *The Role of the Church in the Causation, Treatment, and Prevention of the Crisis in the Priesthood*, available at inkster.com/interjustice/priesthoodcrisis.html" www32.brinkster.com/interjustice/priesthoodcrisis.html.
19. Roger Dobson and Maurice Chittenden, "Pope Given Priests 'Sex Time Bomb' Warning 30 Years Ago," *Sunday Times*, December 23, 2002.
20. This report is reprinted in Doyle et al, *Sex, Priests, and Secret Codes*, pp. 99–174. For the history of the inception and reception of the report, see ibid, pp. 88–98.
21. The *Executive Summary* is available at www.thelinkup.org/execsum.html; for excerpts see www.natcath.org/crisis/051702d.html. All quotations from the *Summary* are from these websites.

22. Quoted by Thomas C. Fox in "What They Knew in 1985," *National Catholic Reporter*, May 17, 2002.
23. Karen Dandurant, "1985 Report: Church Knew of Priest Abuse," www.seacoastonline.com, December 30, 2002.
24. Maria Panaritis, "Bishops Dismissed Warnings of Crisis," *Philadelphia Inquirer*, May 11, 2002.
25. In 2002 Mouton said, "When I decided to take the case, I destroyed my life, my family, my faith. I lost everything that I held dear" (Michael Powell, "A Fall from Grace: When Ray Mouton Took on a Pedophile Priest as a Client, He Had No Idea How Much Was at Stake," *Washington Post*, August 4, 2002).
26. Dr. Money told *Paidika: The Journal of Paedophilia* that "the vast majority of paedophiles who are put in jail have no business being in jail," and, "I would never report anybody who molested a child" (Judith Reisman and Dennis Jarrard, "Catholic Bishops Need Proper Counseling," *Washington Times*, September 1, 2002).
27. John Doe I, et al. vs. Rev. Rudolph Kos et al. (henceforth Doe vs. Kos), District Court of Dallas County, Texas, 93-05258-G, p. 3649, ll.16–17.
28. Doe vs. Kos, p. 4837, ll. 18–19.
29. BishopAccountability.org reports, "Peterson sent it to every bishop in the United States on December 9, 1985. Auxiliary bishops were not included in the distribution. Our copy is from the chancery archive of the Dallas diocese, and bears the curia stamp, indicating that it was received on December 27, 1985. Later updates to the package, sent to the bishops on August 27, 1986, were incorporated by the Dallas diocese into their copy, indicating that the *Guidelines* were not filed away and forgotten" (BishopAccountability.org, "Notes on the Peterson Guidelines").

## *5. The Gathering Storm*

1. Peter J. Wosh recounts Ritter's life and work in *Covenant House: Journey of a Faith-Based Charity* (Philadelphia: University of Pennsylvania Press, 2005). This book was commissioned by Covenant House (p. 10) and downplays as much as possible the sexual scandals. However, it places Ritter and Covenant House in the context of post-World War II Catholicism and gives insights into the dynamics of institutional development.
2. At the end of his life Ritter returned to using "John." See Tina Kelley, "In Quiet Fields, Father Ritter Found His Exile; After Scandal, Covenant House Founder Had a Simple, Solitary Life Upstate," *New York Times*, October 22, 1999.
3. Bruce Handy and Glynis Sweeney remembered, "My parents always said that Bruce was a nice Scottish name. But back in the '60s, Bruce was for some reason the jokey, archetypal name for male hairdressers and interior designers.... There was even a novelty song called 'Big Bad Bruce'...about a beautician who 'swished into town'" ("The Summer of Bruce," *Time*, August 18, 2002, p. 72).
4. Charles M. Sennott, *Broken Covenant* (Simon and Schuster, New York, 1992) pp. 60–61.
5. Bruce Ritter, *Covenant House: Lifeline to the Street* (Doubleday, New York, 1987) pp. 3–4.

6. See Sennott, *Broken Covenant*, p. 66.
7. Bruce Ritter, *Sometimes God Has a Kid's Face: The Story of America's Exploited Street Kids* (New York: Covenant House, 1988) pp. 6–7.
8. Sennott, *Broken Covenant*, p. 73.
9. Ibid., p. 74.
10. Ibid., p. 85.
11. Ibid., p. 76, p. 81.
12. Ibid., p. 91.
13. Russ Baker quoted a former employee of Covenant House that "a lot of kids in Toronto, especially in the early days, just missed the subway home and decided to use the facility.... A lot of them would turn their noses up when they were told they were to sleep on the floor" ("Breaking the Faith—A Close Look at Covenant House," *Village Voice*, Vol. 35, No. 12 [March 20, 1990]).
14. Ritter, *Covenant House*, p. 46.
15. Sennott, *Broken Covenant*, p. 177.
16. Ritter, *Covenant House*, p. 164.
17. Ibid., p. 68.
18. Ibid., p. 123.
19. Ibid., p. 182.
20. Ibid., p. 66.
21. M. A. Farber, "No Charges against Ritter on Finances," *New York Times*, March 1, 1990.
22. Kelley, "In Quiet Fields, Father Ritter Found His Exile."
23. Baker wrote, "Ritter's letters and accompanying photos suggested that his clients were teenaged, fresh faced blondes from Minnesota. 'The runaway poster child is not a blond kid with ringlets,' said Linda Glassman, Covenant House program director from 1987 to '89. 'It's a black or Latino person with a substance abuse problem. And that's not terribly marketable'" ("Breaking the Faith").
24. Ritter, *Sometimes God Has a Kid's Face*, p. 113.
25. Sennott, *Broken Covenant*, p. 171.
26. Howie Carr wrote, "Now it turns out that Fr. Shanley got his job at the Leo House through Dr. Frank Pilecki, the gay president of Westfield State who settled out of court with two male students he molested. Pilecki was a good buddy of Fr. Bruce Ritter, another 'street priest' who was molesting young boys before it became fashionable" ("Priest Scandal; Should He Stay or Go?; It Would Be Un-Law-ful to Remain, Your Eminence," *Boston Herald*, April 10, 2002)
27. Linda Matchan and Stephen Kurkjian, "Man Says Charge Made before Porter Was Priest," *Boston Globe*, October 23, 1992.
28. Ibid.
29. "Town Secret: The Case of James Porter," *Sunday Magazine*, *Boston Globe*, August 29, 1993.
30. Ibid.
31. Ibid.
32. Ibid.
33. In *The Church Impotent: The Feminization of Christianity* (Dallas: Spence Publishing Company, 1999), I examine the centuries-old male distrust of Christianity as a

religion suitable only for women and children, but which self-reliant, aggressive males do not need.

34. Michael Newton, *Father James Porter: Pedophile Priest*, www.crimelibrary.com/serial11/porter/2.htm.
35. Linda Matchan, Don Aucoin, and Stephen Kurkjian, "Anguished Cries Fell on Deaf Ears," *Boston Globe*, July 2, 1992. Edward B. Booth was pastor of St. Mary's until his retirement in 1969, when he was made monsignor. He died in 1972.
36. Ibid.
37. Luz Delgado, "Two Defend Coverage of Ex-priest," *Boston Globe*, May 25, 1992.
38. David Arnold, "Charges from the Past," *Boston Globe*, May 20, 1992.
39. Linda Matchan, "Ex-priest's Accusers Tell of the Damage," *Boston Globe*, June 8, 1992.
40. Walter V. Robinson, "For Father and Son, a Shared Anguish," *Boston Globe*, February 3, 2002.
41. Frank L. Fitzpatrick, *Isolation and Silence: A Male Survivor Speaks Out about Clergy Abuse*, Frank L. Fitzpatrick, /v3n1-firstperson.html" www.movingforward.org/v3n1-firstperson.html.
42. Matchan, Aucoin, and Kurkjian, "Anguished Cries Fell on Deaf Ears."
43. Jennifer Levitz, "Files Show RI Church Leaders Knew of Abuse for Decades," *Providence Journal*, May 17, 2002.
44. Dolores Kong, "6 More Allege Priest Abused Them in the '60s," *Boston Globe*, May 9, 1992.
45. Alison Bass, "30 More Allege Sex Abuse in 1960s by Priest," *Boston Globe*, May 12, 1992.
46. Matchan, Aucoin, and Kurkjian, "Anguished Cries Fell on Deaf Ears."
47. Chuck Haga and Paul McEnroe, "Porter Says Life as Pedophile Ended When He Left Priesthood," *Minneapolis Star Tribune*, June 6, 2002.
48. Linda Matchan and Stephen Kurkjian, "Porter Personnel Files Show What Church Knew," *Boston Globe*, October 21, 1992.
49. "Town Secret: The Case of James Porter."
50. Linda Matchan, "Diocese Allegedly Was Told of Abuse Man Says," *Boston Globe*, June 10, 1992.
51. Jack Sullivan, "Medeiros, Vatican Involved in Coverup," *Boston Herald*, May 16, 2002.
52. Ibid.
53. Linda Matchan and Stephen Kurkjian, "Despite Past, Jailed Priest Seeks 'Just One Chance,'" *Boston Globe*, July 14, 2002.
54. Newton, *Father James Porter: Pedophile Priest.*
55. Ibid.
56. Linda Matchan, "Former New Bedford Altar Boy Says Porter Raped Him in Church," *Boston Globe*, August 13, 1992. This boy said he saw Porter molest another boy at the church.
57. Linda Matchan, "Ex-priest's Accusers Tell of the Damage," *Boston Globe*, June 8, 1992.
58. Levitz, "Files Show RI Church Leaders Knew of Abuse for Decades."
59. Fox Butterfield and Jenny Hontz, "A Priest's Two Faces: Protector and Predator," *New York Times*, May 19, 2002.

60. Cathleen F. Crowley, "File: Church Ignored Sex Abuse," *Eagle-Tribune*, April 9, 2002.
61. Matchan and Kurkjian, "Despite Past, Jailed Priest Seeks 'Just One Chance.'"
62. Newton, *Father James Porter: Pedophile Priest*. Newton identifies William Foley as head of the Paracletes, but the head of the Paracletes from 1981 to 1987 was Michael E. Foley.
63. Matchan and Kurkjian, "Despite Past, Jailed Priest Seeks 'Just One Chance.'"
64. Linda Matchan and Stephen Kurkjian, "Porter Personnel Files Show What Church Knew."
65. Haga and McEnroe, "Porter Says Life as Pedophile Ended When He Left Priesthood."
66. Stephen Kurkjian, "Porter Got Minn[esota] Post with Help of Retreat Home," *Boston Globe*, July 25, 1992.
67. Linda Matchan, "Ex-priest Accused in Minnesota: Former Altar Boys Say Porter Abused Them," *Boston Globe*, July 14, 1992.
68. Haga and McEnroe, "Porter Says Life as Pedophile Ended When He Left Priesthood."
69. Matchan, "Ex-priest Accused in Minnesota."
70. John Ellement, "Victims Oppose Release of Porter," *Boston Globe*, April 6, 2004.
71. Matchan, "Ex-priest Accused in Minnesota."
72. Linda Matchan, "Porter's Leaving Was Urged in 1970; Psychologist Said He Shouldn't Be Priest," *Boston Globe*, January 19, 1993.
73. Ibid.
74. Matchan and Kurkjian, "Porter Personnel Files Show What Church Knew."
75. Linda Matchan and Stephen Kurkjian, "Church View on Porter Noted: Letter Said to Tell of 'Persistence in Evil," *Boston Globe*, October 29, 1992.
76. Ibid.
77. Jack Sullivan, "Medeiros, Vatican Involved in Coverup," *Boston Herald*, May 16, 2002.
78. Kurkjian, "Porter Said to Have Told Pope of Abuse."
79. Ibid.
80. Linda Matchan, "Thank God You Didn't Have to Live with Him," *Boston Globe*, June 5, 2002.
81. Linda Matchan, "Ex-priest's Abuse Haunts His Family."
82. Kathryn Marchocki, "Former Priest Revealed Assaults in '89; Porter Confessed Abuse to FBI Agents in Minn[esota] FBI Had Porter Confession in '89 Report," *Boston Herald*, October 22, 1992.
83. Fitzpatrick, *Isolation and Silence*.
84. Dennis Gaboury and Elinor Burkett, "The Secret of St. Mary's," *Rolling Stone*, November 11, 1993, p. 49.
85. Haga and McEnroe, "Porter Said His Life as Pedophile Ended When He Left Priesthood."
86. Matchan, "'Thank God You Didn't Have to Live with Him.'"
87. Steve Marantz, "Law Raps Ex-priest Coverage," *Boston Globe*, May 24, 1992.
88. Lynda Gorov, "Porter Says He Is Being Harassed," *Boston Globe*, September 9, 1992.
89. James L. Franklin, "Porter Says Church to Blame," *Boston Globe*, December 8, 1993.

90. Matchan and Kurkjian, "Despite Past, Jailed Priest Seeks 'Just One Chance.'"
91. Ibid.
92. Linda Matchan, "Alleged Victims of Porter Decry Elevation of Priest," *Boston Globe*, March 15, 1993. Similarly Cardinal Bevilacqua of Philadelphia made Father Caulfield a monsignor. The grand jury observed: "On this pastor who had silently ignored allegations of improper behavior by Fr. Bolesta for 10 months—while the priest continued to abuse numerous boys—Cardinal Bevilacqua chose to bestow an honor rather than a reprimand" (Court of Common Pleas, First Judicial District of Pennsylvania, Criminal Trial Division, Misc. no. 03-00-239, Report of the Grand Jury, p. 401).
93. Matchan, "'Thank God You Didn't Have to Live with Him.'"
94. Curt Brown, "Porter's Ex-wife Willing to Testify against Him," *New Bedford Standard-Times*, January 13, 2004.
95. Linda Matchan and Stephen Kurkjian, "Alleged Victims Urge Release of Porter Files," *Boston Globe*, October 22, 1992.
96. Brown, "Porter's Ex-wife Willing to Testify against Him."
97. Victoria Benning, "Porter's Alleged Abuse Victims Angry with Vatican," *Boston Globe*, October 25, 1992.
98. Jason Berry, *Vows of Silence: The Abuse of Power in the Papacy of John Paul II* (New York: Free Press, 2004), p. 238.
99. Ed Housewright, "Kos Said Diocese Had 'Forgiven' Him, Man Testifies: Witness Says Former Priest Never Revealed Issue but Thought Topic Was Serious," *Dallas Morning News*, July 11, 1997.
100. Ed Housewright, "Ex-priest's Siblings Tell of Sex Abuse," *Dallas Morning News*, May 17, 1997.
101. Ibid.
102. Ed Housewright, "Defense Psychiatrist in Kos Case Challenged: Diocese Rests; Arguments Set for Monday," *Dallas Morning News*, July 18, 1997.
103. Jim Schutze, "Diocese Defends Itself against Abuse Charges," *Houston Chronicle*, July 20, 1997.
104. Ed Housewright, "Man Tells of Abuse by Priest," *Dallas Morning News*, May 21, 1997.
105. "A Questionable History."
106. John Doe I, et al. vs. Rev. Rudolph Kos et al., District Court of Dallas County, Texas, 93-05258-G (henceforth Doe vs. Kos), p. 4357, ll.22–23.
107. Housewright, "Kos Said Diocese Had 'Forgiven' Him, Man Testifies."
108. Mark Wrolstad, "Msgr. Testifies Kos Would've Been Confronted," *Dallas Morning News*, June 11, 1997.
109. Joseph Wilson, "The Enemy Within: A Parish Priest Cautions His Would-be Defender," www.cwnews.com.
110. American Association of University Professors, "Albertus Magnus College," *Academe*, 2000.
111. Wilson, "The Enemy Within."
112. André Guindon, *The Sexual Language: An Essay in Moral Theology* (Ottawa: The University of Ottawa Press, 1977) p. 374. Guindon is still a hero to liberal Catholics in Canada (see p. 459).
113. Doe vs. Kos, p. 4364, l. 22.

114. Ed Housewright wrote, "Mr. Peebles and Mr. Hughes, who were defendants in the lawsuits, could not be reached for comment. The two of them and Mr. Kos all briefly worked together in 1981 and 1982 at All Saints Catholic Church in North Dallas." ("Abuse Suits Involving 2 Ex-Priests Settled: Agreement by Catholic Diocese Will Pay Out a Total of $5 Million in 4 Cases," *Dallas Morning News*, February 12, 1998).
115. The accusations against Hughes resulted in an out-of-court settlement by the diocese. Ed Housewright, "Abuse suits involving 2 ex-priests settled Agreement by Catholic diocese will pay out a total of $5 million in 4 cases," *Dallas Morning News*, February 12, 1998.
116. Ed Housewright, "Mother Says Church Ignored Girl's Sex Abuse," *Dallas Morning News*, June 27, 1997.
117. Brooks Egerton, "Justice's Aid Sought in Clergy-Abuse Dispute Local Judges' Suitability to Rule in Cases at Issue," *Dallas Morning News*, December 10, 1997.
117. Todd J. Gillman and Craig Flournoy, "Cleric OK'd Priest Transfer Despite Abuse Allegations," *Dallas Morning News*, August 9, 1994.
118. Brooks Egerton, "Removed Priests Go Uneasily into New Lives: Pedophile Left the Clergy and Became a Government Lawyer," *Dallas Morning News*, October 27, 2002.
119. Ibid.
120. Mark Wrolstad, "Man Says Diocese Hid Abuse by 2nd Priest," *Dallas Morning News*, June 14, 1997.
121. Egerton, "Removed Priests Go Uneasily into New Lives."
122. Ibid.
123. Memo, XI Robert Ray Peebles.
124. Egerton, "Removed Priests Go Uneasily into New Lives."
125. Ibid.
126. Ibid.
127. Housewright, "Kos Said Diocese Had 'Forgiven' Him, Man Testifies."
128. Christine Wicker, "Catholics Divided over Apology," *Dallas Morning News*, July 13, 1997.
129. Ed Housewright, "Priest Sought Bishop's Help in Kos Case: Church Official Wrote in 1986 He Felt Anxious about Boys' Visits," *Dallas Morning News*, May 28, 1997.
130. Ed Housewright, "Student, 23, Testifies He Got 'Runaround': Attorney for Diocese Admits Officials Slow in Response to Kos Accusations," *Dallas Morning News*, June 21, 1997.
131. Doe vs. Kos, p. 3097, l. 7.
132. Doe vs. Kos, p. 3087, ll. 4–11.
133. Doe vs. Kos, p. 3123, l. 10.
134. Doe vs. Kos, p. 4317, ll. 23–24.
135. Ed Housewright, "Victims Urge Others to Make Stand, Seek Aid," *Dallas Morning News*, July 25, 1997.
136. Ed Housewright, "Msgr. Cautioned in Kos Trial: Judge Close to Holding Ex-official in Contempt," *Dallas Morning News*, May 31, 1997.
137. Mark Wrolstad, "[Two] Men Testify Abuse by Kos Damaged Their Faith," *Dallas Morning News*, June 13, 1997.
138. Doe vs. Kos, p. 5057, ll. 19–20.
139. Doe vs. Kos, p. 5686, ll. 18–20.

140. Doe vs. Kos, p. 6130, ll. 8–16.
141. Doe vs. Kos, p. 6130, ll. 23–25.
142. Ed Housewright, "Ex-priest's Sleepovers No Secret," *Dallas Morning News*, May 24, 1997.
143. Doe vs. Kos, p. 4369, ll. 5–7.
144. Housewright, "Ex-priest's Sleepovers No Secret."
145. Housewright, "Priest Sought Bishop's Help in Kos Case."
146. Ibid.
147. Ed Housewright, "Bishop Stands by Decision," *Dallas Morning News*, July 3, 1997.
148. Housewright, "Msgr. Cautioned in Kos Trial."
149. Doe vs. Kos, p. 7638, ll. 17–21.
150. Ed Housewright, "He Cared about the Children," *Dallas Morning News*, July 26, 1997.
151. Ed Housewright, "Ex-official Says He Never Questioned Kos," *Dallas Morning News*, June 6, 1997.
152. Ed Housewright, "Dallas Bishop Testifies He Warned Kos," *Dallas Morning News*, July 2, 1997.
153. Ed Housewright, "Kos' Parish Wasn't Told Why He Left: 'Lie' Let Sexual Abuse Continue, Attorney Says," *Dallas Morning News*, May 30, 1997.
154. Mark Wrolstad, "Psychiatrist Says He Never Offered Assurances on Kos," *Dallas Morning News*, June 12, 1997.
155. Jan Jarboe Russell, "Fathers and Sins," *Texas Monthly*, June 2002.
156. Ed Housewright, "Doctor Tells of Sex-Abuse Damage in Kos Case; He Testifies Boys Suffered Stress Disorder; Diocese's Attorney Says Effects Overstated," *Dallas Morning News*, June 25, 1997.
157. Housewright, "He Cared about the Children."
158. Housewright, "Ex-official Says He Never Questioned Kos. "
159. Housewright, "Student, 23, Testifies He Got 'Runaround.'"
160. Wrolstad, "Psychiatrist Says He Never Offered Assurances on Kos."
161. Housewright, "Kos' Parish Wasn't Told Why He Left."
162. Housewright, "Kos Said Diocese Had 'Forgiven' Him, Man Testifies."
163. Ed Housewright, "[Two-hundred Thousand Dollars] Spent to Help Kos: Canon Law Cited in Aid after Sex Abuse of Boys," *Dallas Morning News*, July 1, 1997.
164. Ed Housewright, "Final Arguments in Kos Case: Catholic Officials' Liability Debated," *Dallas Morning News*, July 22, 1997.
165. "Showdown in Dallas," www.thelinkup.com/kos.html.
166. The judge told him, "Msgr., it is extremely important that you answer the questions asked. If you do not do so you will be in contempt of Court and we'll deal with that later" (Doe vs. Kos, p. 3562, ll. 22–25).
167. Doe vs. Kos, p. 4356, ll. 10–11.
168. Ed Housewright, "Parents of Abused Boys Share Blame in Kos Case, Ex-diocese Official Says," *Dallas Morning News*, August 8, 1997.
169. Ed Housewright and Brooks Egerton, "Former Bishop Who Didn't Testify in Kos Trial Still Active in Church," *Dallas Morning News*, August 1, 1997.
170. Ibid.
171. Rod Dreher, "Showdown in Dallas," *Catholic World News*, June 2003.
172. Michael Saul, "Kos Gets Life Term for Molesting Boys: Suspended Priest Eligible for

Parole in 15 Years; Notice of Appeal Filed," *Dallas Morning News*, April 2, 1998.

173. Brooks Egerton, "Priest Serves Despite Allegation: Leader of Dallas Cathedral Accused of Groping Man in '91," *Dallas Morning News*, November 11, 2002.
174. Dreher, "Showdown in Dallas"; Wicks Allison, "Why Won't the Bishop Go?" *D Magazine*, February 2003.
175. Paul Likoudis, "Diocese's Rotten Underbelly Exposed in Pedophile's Trial," *The Wanderer*, June 19, 1997, p. 7.
176. Michael J. Hartwig, *The Poetics of Intimacy and the Problem of Sexual Abstinence* (New York: Peter Lang, 2000) p. 2.
177. Ibid., p. 16.
178. Ibid., p. 268.

## *6. Hurricane Hits Boston*

1. But because of the statute of limitations none of the Philadelphia priests mentioned in this book have been prosecuted or even sued. David O'Reilly and Nancy Phillips wrote: "Because the allegations were old, priests couldn't be prosecuted because of a statute of limitations. And church officials couldn't be charged because of other gaps in state law" ("Grand Jury Harshly Criticizes Archdiocese for Hiding Clergy Sexual Abuse," *Philadelphia Inquirer*, September 21, 2005).
2. Jules Crittenden, "Records Depict Lonely, Immature, and Self-Deluded Priest," *Boston Herald*, January 27, 2002.
3. Ibid.
4. Michael Rezendes and *Globe* staff, "Church Allowed Abuse by Priest for Years," *Boston Globe*, January 6, 2002.
5. Crittenden, "Records Depict Lonely, Immature, and Self-Deluded Priest."
6. Rezendes, "Church Allowed Abuse by Priest for Years."
7. "The Geoghan Papers," *Boston Herald*, January 25, 2002.
8. Sacha Pfeiffer, "Letters Exhibit Gentle Approach toward Priest," *Boston Globe*, January 24, 2002.
9. The Investigative Staff of the *Boston Globe*, *Betrayal: The Crisis of the Catholic Church* (Boston: Little, Brown and Company 2002) p. 13.
10. "The Geoghan Papers," *Boston Herald*, January 25, 2002.
11. The niece had lost a child to crib death and needed time to recover.
12. "How America's Catholic Church Crucified Itself," *London Times*, March 13, 2005.
13. Rezendes, "Church Allowed Abuse by Priest for Years."
14. "How America's Catholic Church Crucified Itself."
15. Rezendes, "Church Allowed Abuse by Priest for Years."
16. *Betrayal*, p. 23.
17. "The Geoghan Papers."
18. Rezendes, "Church Allowed Abuse by Priest for Years."
19. Ibid.
20. *Betrayal*, p. 24.
21. Ibid., p. 208.
22. Michael Rezendes and Matt Carroll, "Doctors Who OK'd Geoghan Lacked Expertise, Review Shows," *Boston Globe*, January 16, 2002.

23. Pfeiffer, "Letters Exhibit Gentle Approach toward Priest."
24. *Betrayal*, pp. 214–215.
25. Ibid., p. 218.
26. Rezendes, "Church Allowed Abuse by Priest for Years."
27. Ibid.
28. Thomas Farragher, "Settlement Doesn't Heal Victims' Hearts," *Boston Globe*, September 20, 2002.
29. Michael Rezendes, "Memos Offer Split View of Priest," *Boston Globe*, January 24, 2002.
30. Rezendes, "Church Allowed Abuse by Priest for Years."
31. Rezendes, "Memos Offer Split View of Priest."
32. Ibid.
33. *Betrayal*, p. 223.
34. Rezendes, "Church Allowed Abuse by Priest for Years."
35. Sacha Pfeiffer and Matt Carroll, "Geoghan Shifted Real Estate to Trust," *Boston Globe*, January 14, 2002.
36. *Betrayal*, p. 225.
37. Crittenden, "Records Depict Lonely, Immature, and Self-Deluded Priest."
38. Stephen Kurkjian and Sacha Pfeiffer, "Police Probed Priest on Sex Abuse as Early as 1986," *Boston Globe*, January 25, 2002.
39. Globe Spotlight Team, "Documents Show Church Long Supported Geoghan," *Boston Globe*, January 24, 2002.
40. Kathleen Burge, "Man Testifies Geoghan Fondled Him," *Boston Globe*, January 17, 2002.
41. Marie Szaniszlo, "Geoghan Sentenced to 9–10 Years," *Boston Herald*, February 22, 2002.
42. Al Guart, "Perv Rev's Strangler a Hero in His Own Sick and Evil Mind," *New York Post*, August 31, 2003.
43. David Weber, "Druse's 1988 Murder Shows Parallels to Ex-priest's Slaying," *Boston Herald*, September 1, 2003.
44. "How America's Catholic Church Crucified Itself."
45. Guart, "Perv Rev's Strangler a Hero in His Own Sick and Evil Mind."
46. "How America's Catholic Church Crucified Itself."
47. Paul Schindler wrote, "In monitoring the unfolding sex abuse scandal, Erickson keeps in close touch with Daniel Shea, a gay attorney from Houston who has represented a number of sex abuse victims in central Massachusetts. Contacted about the Geoghan killing, Shea forwarded a copy of a subpoena that he served in July in a civil lawsuit alleging that George Rueger, an auxiliary bishop in the Worcester diocese, raped Sime J. Braio in 1964 when the accuser was 14. Shea explained that the subpoena, served on an official of the Boston archdiocese, clearly signaled his effort to link Rueger and Geoghan to a beach house in Scituate, a south shore suburb of Boston, where Braio alleges the abuse took place. The archdiocese succeeded in quashing the subpoena and Shea said his next move was to depose Geoghan directly on the matter, an option now foreclosed" ("Yet Another Victim: John J. Geoghan, Priest at Center of Catholic Scandal, Slain in Prison," *Gay City News*, 29 August–4 September 2003). Rueger denied the accusation and in late 2003 the suit was dropped (Richard Nangle, "Suit

against Auxiliary Bishop Rueger: Man Filed Rape Charge in 2002," *Worcester Telegram and Gazette*, November 21, 2003).

48. "Few tears are shed," *New York Newsday*, August 26, 2003.
49. Leon J. Podles, *The Church Impotent: The Feminization of Christianity* (Dallas: Spence Publishing Company, 1999) pp. 129–130.
50. Since the criminal and civil cases involve male victims, the documentation that has been supplied to the courts and therefore has been used in this book documents Shanley's abuse of males.
51. Thomas Farragher and Matt Carroll, "Bishop Often Sided with Priests in Abuse Cases: Records Show McCormack Brushed Aside Accusations," *Boston Globe*, January 26, 2003; Kevin Cullen, "No Consensus on Why Abuse Peaked in '60s," *Boston Globe*, February 27, 2004. O'Sullivan was convicted in 1984 in New Jersey of sodomizing a thirteen-year-old boy (Ralph Ranalli, "Priest Dismissed by Vatican, Given Probation in '84 Abuse Case," *Boston Globe*, July 30, 2005). A victim of Cotter, who is now deceased, received a settlement from the archdiocese of Boston in 1995 (Sacha Pfeiffer and Kathleen Burge, "Abuse Victims React with Relief, Reflection," *Boston Globe*, December 14, 2002). Lane was the object of six lawsuits which were all settled by the archdiocese of Boston in 2002 (Sacha Pfeiffer and Stephen Kurkjian, "Church Settled Six Suits vs. Priest: Kept Him in Post Despite Allegations," *Boston Globe*, January 2, 2005).
52. Jack Sullivan, "Shanley Said Ex-cardinal Abused Him as Seminarian," *Boston Herald*, April 9, 2002. The headline is misleading; it was a deceased, not an ex-cardinal, and it is not clear it happened in the seminary. Spellman's theatricality appealed to New York gays; he could wear a purple dress in public when everyone else was in the closet. In 1994 Shanley also told a psychiatrist that when he was twelve he was forced to have oral sex with a priest. See Fox Butterfield and Jenny Hontz, "A Priest's Two Faces: Protector and Predator," *New York Times*, May 19, 2002. Shanley's pastor at his childhood parish, St. Mark's, was Father Dunford, who according to Shanley's sister "singled out and mentored" her brother (Maureen Orth, "Communion," *Vanity Fair*, August 2002, p. 181). Unnamed clerical sources told Orth that "a deceased high-ranking member of the administration at St. John's Seminary was Shanley's abuser, and that the archdiocese's fear that Shanley would go public with the information was what allowed him to operate with impunity for 40 years" ("Communion," p. 186).
53. Sullivan wrote, "A former hockey star at Catholic Memorial High School, who has accused Msgr. Frederick Ryan of molesting him, claimed the late Humberto Cardinal Medeiros also made improper advances to him" ("Shanley Said Ex-Cardinal Abused Him as Seminarian"). An unsigned note found in Ryan's archdiocesan personnel file described him as "very dangerous" (Robin Washington, "Church Memo: Accused Priest Was 'Very Dangerous,'" *Boston Herald*, April 15, 2003); in 2006 Ryan was defrocked (Michael Levenson and Charles A. Radin, "[Eight] Clergymen Are Dismissed by the Vatican: Boston-area Clerics Accused of Sexually Abusing Children," *Boston Globe*, March 18, 2006).
54. "One of the most notorious, powerful, and sexually voracious homosexuals in the American Catholic Church's history . . . the archconservative Spellman was the epitome of the self-loathing, closeted, evil queen" (Michelangelo Signorile, "Cardinal Spellman's Dark Legacy," *New York Press*, April 30, 2002).

55. The affidavit misidentified the pastor as Msgr. Francis Sexton, who was the chancellor of the Boston archdiocese.
56. Butterfield and Hontz, "A Priest's Two Faces: Protector and Predator"
57. Ibid.
58. Gregory Ford et al v. Bernard Cardinal Law, et al, State of Massachusetts, Suffolk County, Superior Court Department, SUVC 2002-04551 T1 (henceforth Ford v. Law), Affidavit of John Doe.
59. Orth, "Communion," p. 119.
60. Ford v. Law, Affidavit of [—]. Names of victims are omitted unless they have spoken to the media and identified themselves.
61. Ralph Ranalli, "CEO Would Testify of Shanley Abuse, Diocese Neglect," *Boston Globe*, July 22, 2003.
62. Deposition of Cardinal Bernard Law, June 5, 2002, Suffolk County Superior Court, exhibit 23.
63. Ranalli, "CEO Would Testify of Shanley Abuse, Diocese Neglect."
64. Jean Dietz, "Priest Proposes Youth Work Centers," *Boston Globe*, December 28, 1968, n. p.
65. Orth, "Communion," p. 182.
66. Ibid., p. 183.
67. Linda Stark, "Dinner Set for Displaced Youth," *Boston Globe*, November 24, 1969.
68. Ford v. Law, Affidavit of [—].
69. Ibid.
70. Ibid.
71. Carolyn Kessel, "Hudson Priest Retires: Hudson Priest Was Accused Last Year of Decades-Old Abuse," *MetroWest Daily*, December 18, 2003. Curran denies the allegation.
72. Ford v. Law, Affidavit of [—].
73. Ibid.
74. Mary Meier, "Priest Has Advice for Parents of Gays," *Boston Globe*, May 6, 1975.
75. "[Six] Towns Reject House," *Boston Globe*, January 11, 1976.
76. Ford v. Law, Affidavit of [—].
77. Sacha Pfeiffer, "Famed 'Street Priest' Preyed upon Boys," *Boston Globe*, January 31, 2002.
78. *Betrayal*, pp. 232–233.
79. David France, *Our Fathers: The Secret Life of the Catholic Church in an Age of Scandal* (New York: Broadway Books, 2004) p. 398.
80. Tom Mashberg and Robin Washington, "Alleged Victim Links Priest to Man-Boy Sex Group," *Boston Herald*, April 7, 2002.
81. Michael Rezendes and Thomas Farragher, "Files Show Shanley Tried Blackmail," *Boston Globe*, April 26, 2002.
82. Elizabeth Mehren, "Papers Show Former Boston Priest Tried to Blackmail Cardinal," *Los Angeles Times*, April 27, 2002.
83. Sacha Pfeiffer, "Woman Says Church Ignored Her Outcries," *Boston Globe*, February 13, 2002.
84. Peter Gelzinis, "Shanley Case Opens a New Chapter in Horror Story," *Boston Herald*, April 9, 2002.

85. Enrique T. Rueda, *The Homosexual Network: Private Lives and Public Policy* (Old Greenwich, Connecticut: Devin Adair, 1982).
86. Ford v. Law, Affidavit of [—].
87. Tom Held and Mark Johnson, "Banks Says He Was Unaware of Shanley's Alleged Abusive History," *Milwaukee Journal-Sentinel*, November 22, 2002.
88. *Betrayal*, p. 244.
89. Eric Convey, "California Parish Rips Hub's Silence on Priest's Past," *Boston Herald*, April 9, 2002.
90. Felisa Cardona, "Man, 30, Plans to Sue Clergy Sex Abuse Figure," *San Bernardino County Sun*, December 16, 2002.
91. Nick Madigan, "Sent to California on Sick Leave, Boston Priest Bought Racy Gay Resort," *New York Times*, April 15, 2002.
92. Tascha Robertson, "Shanley Couldn't Outrun Past," *Boston Globe*, April 19, 2002.
93. Ibid.
94. Ibid.
95. Michael Rezendes, "Former Student Accuses Priest," *Boston Globe*, April 6, 2002.
96. "NH Bishop Closely Tied to Shanley Situation," *Manchester Union Leader*, April 9, 2002.
97. Tom Mashberg, "Priest Scandal: Records Show Church Coddles Problem Priests," *Boston Herald*, April 14, 2002.
98. Ibid.
99. Walter V. Robinson and Thomas Farragher, "Shanley's Record Long Ignored," *Boston Globe*, April 9, 2002.
100. Butterfield and Hontz, "A Priest's Two Faces: Protector and Predator."
101. Orth, "Communion," p. 185.
102. Ralph Ranalli, "Ex-churchleaders Said to Hide Data," *Boston Globe*, July 12, 2003.
103. Pilecki was indicted but found not guilty; his accusers filed a civil lawsuit and settled out of court with Pilecki (Michael Rezendes and Sacha Pfeiffer, "Defiant Letters: A Humbling Exit from Spotlight," *Boston Globe*, April 9, 2002).
104. Orth, "Communion," p. 185.
105. Jack Sullivan, "Pedophile Recruited Shanley to Church Inn," *Boston Herald*, April 9, 2002.
106. Orth, "Communion," p. 182.
107. Sullivan, "Pedophile Recruited Shanley to Church Inn."
108. Tom Mashberg and Eric Convey, "Church Judged Shanley 'Beyond Repair,'" *Boston Herald*, May 15, 2002.
109. "At no time were the nuns or staff of Leo House, who numbered about thirty-five, told of Shanley's negative psychiatric record" (Tom Mashberg and Eric Convey, "Church Judged Shanley 'Beyond Repair,'" *Boston Herald*, May 15, 2002).
110. *Betrayal*, p. 246.
111. Sullivan, "Pedophile Recruited Shanley to Church Inn."
112. Robertson, "Shanley Couldn't Outrun Past."
113. Sullivan, "Shanley Said Ex-cardinal Abused Him as Seminarian."
114. Christopher Cox and Robin Washington, "Shanley Visited Child-Sex Haven in Thailand," *Boston Herald*, May 7, 2002.

115. Robin Washington and Eric Convey, "Paquin, Shanley Defrocked amid Questions on Process," *Boston Herald*, May 7, 2004.
116. Walter V. Robinson and Michael Rezendes, "Abuse Scandal Far Deeper than Disclosed, Report Says," *Boston Globe*, July 24, 2003.

## 7. Scope of Destruction: New England

1. Sacha Pfeiffer, "He Invoked Religion for Sexual Acts," *Boston Globe*, December 4, 2002.
2. Gill Donovan, "Records Further Damage Boston Church's Credibility," *National Catholic Reporter*, December 13, 2002. Meffan was not the object of civil lawsuits or criminal prosecution. He was defrocked in 2002.
3. Michael Rezendes, "Bishop's Letter of Warning Ignored," *Boston Globe*, December 4, 2002.
4. Michael Rezendes, "The Life of a Violent South Shore Priest Is Detailed," *Boston Globe*, December 4, 2002.
5. Jules Crittenden, "Fearless Chaplain Alleged to Exhibit Violent Behavior," *Boston Globe*, December 4, 2002.
6. Donovan, "Records Further Damage Boston Church's Credibility." Forry has been defrocked but has not been the object of lawsuits or criminal prosecution.
7. Stephen Kurkjian and Walter W. Robinson, "A 'Classic Misuse of Power,'" *Boston Globe*, December 29, 2002.
8. Michael Rezendes and Stephen Kurkjian, "Cleric Had Two Children, Kept Status," *Boston Globe*, December 6, 2002.
9. He told a slightly different version to the children when he finally met them: Rita Perry invited him to spend the night with her. "After midnight, Foley told them, she became hysterical and questioned his love for her after he refused to spend the next day with her. Minutes later, she emerged from the bathroom with a bottle of pills, and asked Foley to help her get the top off. Foley said he took the bottle away from her and threw it under a sofa. But, the children said, the priest told them that when she became sick shortly after that, and then fainted, he realized that she had taken some pills while she was in the bathroom. Foley, the children said, acknowledged that he panicked after she collapsed and that he was unable to revive her. Then, he said, he grabbed his clothes, made an anonymous call to the Needham police emergency line and then fled the house" (Sacha Pfeiffer, "Records on 10 Clergy Released," *Boston Globe*, January 31, 2003).
10. Michael S. Rosenwald, "Children Fathered by Priest Settle Suit: Agreement Requires Law to Meet Family," *Boston Globe*, January 30, 2002.
11. Pfeiffer, "Records on 10 Clergy Released."
12. Eileen McNamara, "Priest Merely Fits the Mold," *Boston Globe*, December 12, 2002.
13. Ibid.
14. Katherine McQuaid, "NH Bishop: Had No Suspicion of Abuse," *Manchester Union Leader*, March 25, 2002.
15. Kathryn Marchocki, "Man Claiming Sex Abuse Says McCormack Knew of Incidents," *Manchester Union Leader*, March 26, 2003.

16. Bella English, "'I Wanted to Run,'" *Boston Globe*, May 15, 2002.
17. Ibid.
18. Eric Convey, "Cover-up Charges Made in Alleged Abuse Case," *Boston Herald*, April 5, 2002.
19. English, "'I Wanted to Run.'"
20. Letter of Patrick J. Kelly to the archdiocesan personnel office, January 17, 1970, at www.boston.com/globe/spotlight/abuse/documents/kelly_letter_011770.htm
21. Sacha Pfeiffer, "Dozens More Allege Abuse by Late Priest," *Boston Globe*, April 4, 2002.
22. AP, "Records: McCormack Reassured Parents While Priest in Therapy," *Portsmouth Herald*, December 19, 2002.
23. Michael Rezendes and Stephen Kurkjian, "Bishop Tells of Shielding Priests: McCormack Says Aide's Plea Ignored," *Boston Globe*, January 19, 2003.
24. Anita Perkins, "Therapists: Paquin Felt Victimized by Church, Too," *North Andover Eagle-Tribune*, June 5, 2002.
25. Kathie Neff Ragsdale, "Priest's Accusers Reveal Pattern of Wily Seduction," *North Andover Eagle-Tribune*, June 9, 2002.
26. Ibid.
27. Ibid.
28. Ibid.
29. Stephen Kurkjian, "Parent Alleges Deterring by Pastor," *Boston Globe*, April 23, 2002.
30. Stephen Kurkjian, "Records Show Law Reassigned Paquin after Settlements," *Boston Globe*, May 30, 2002.
31. Ibid.
32. Albert McKeon, "NH Church Files Highlight Alcohol's Role in Many Sex Abuse Cases," *New Hampshire Telegraph*, March 9, 2003.
33. See also the Investigative Staff of the *Boston Globe*, *Betrayal: The Crisis in the Catholic Church* (Boston: Little, Brown and Company, 2002) pp. 60–65.
34. Associated Press: "Malden Priest Sentenced for Child Rape," www.boston.com, December 31, 2002.
35. "Priest Pleads Guilty in Child Rape Case," www.thebostonchannel.com, December 31, 2002.
36. Ragsdale, "Priest's Accusers Reveal Pattern of Wily Seduction."
37. Tom Farmer, "Kids Detail Alleged Abuse by Middleton Youth Worker," *Boston Herald*, September 7, 2000.
38. Farah Stockman and Brian MacQuarrie, "'Guilty...Guilty' Reardon Admits to 75 Charges, Could Receive Life Sentence," *Boston Globe*, July 10, 2001.
39. David Talbot and Laurel L. Sweet, "Alleged Abuser 'Knew He Was Wrong,'" *Boston Herald*, June 22, 2000.
40. Stockman and MacQuarrie, "Guilty...Guilty' Reardon Admits to 75 Charges."
41. Farah Stockman, "Victims Confront Reardon, Prosecutors Seek 50–70 Year Term in Sex Abuse Case," *Boston Globe*, August 15, 2002.
42. Farah Stockman, "Reardon Was Suspected before Arrest," *Boston Globe*, February 10, 2002.
43. Tom Farmer and Tom Mashberg, "Report: Workers Pressured in Reardon Sex Case," *Boston Herald*, February 1, 2002.

44. Maggie Mulvihill, Tom Mashberg, and Eric Convey, "Forewarned—Worker: I Told Archdiocese about Reardon Months before Sex Arrest," *Boston Herald*, January 27, 2002.
45. Tom Farmer, "Explicit Lists Detail Alleged Molestations," *Boston Herald*, March 8, 2000.
46. Farmer, "Kids Detail Alleged Abuse by Middleton Youth Worker."
47. Farah Stockman, "In Middleton, Call for Forgiveness Meets Anger," *Boston Globe*, June 19, 2000.
48. Marie Szaniszlo, "Pastor granted leave from parish wracked by abuse case," *Boston Herald*, October 19, 2000.
49. Alan Burke, "'Singing Priest' Accused of Abuse," *Eagle-Tribune*, January 31, 2002.
50. Maggie Mulvihill, "It's a Crime: Law Aide Knew of Reardon," *Boston Herald*, April 24, 2002.
51. Stockman, "Reardon Was Suspected before Arrest."
52. Peter W. Heed, N. William Delker, James D. Rosenberg, *Report on the Investigation of the Diocese of Manchester*, March 3, 2003, p. 27 [henceforth *Manchester Report*].
53. Ibid.
54. Ibid.
55. Ibid.
56. Ibid.
57. J. M. Hirsch, "Once-abusive Priest Gives Evidence against the Church," *Boston Globe*, February 16, 2003.
58. Kathryn Marchocki, "Bishops Sought Immunity," *Manchester Union Leader*, March 13, 2003.
59. *Manchester Report*, p. 88.
60. Ibid., p. 98
61. Ibid., p. 131.
62. Ibid.
63. Ibid., p. 146.
64. Ibid., p. 147.
65. Ibid., p. 149.
66. Ibid., pp. 149–150.
67. Deibel works for the diocese of Sacramento as their point man for matters of sexual abuse.
68. *Manchester Report*, pp. 150–151.
69. Ibid., p. 153.
70. Ibid., p. 154.
71. Robin Washington, "NH Bishop Tells Parish about Priest's Affair with Teenager," *Boston Herald*, September 30, 2002.
72. Michael Rezendes and Stephen Kurkjian, "NH Report Lambastes Diocese on Priest Abuse," *Boston Globe*, March 4, 2003.
73. Adam Gorli, "Seeking Justice for 31 Years," *Hartford Courant*, April 6, 2003.
74. Andrea Estes, "Parishioners Find Allegations against Pastor Hard to Believe," *Boston Herald*, October 23, 1991.
75. Roselyn Tantraphol, "Boy's Death Follows Priest," *Hartford Courant*, August 8, 2002.

76. Associated Press, "Affidavit: Springfield Diocese Knew of Allegations against Lavigne in 1960s," *Providence Journal*, September 29, 2003.
77. Michelle Caruso, Andrea Estes, and David Weber, "Church Backs Priest as New Allegations Surface," *Boston Herald*, October 26, 1991.
78. Jason B. Johnson, "Former Altar Boys Testify against Priest's Release," *Boston Herald*, January 28, 1993.
79. Bill Zajac, "Court Papers Chilling, Inconclusive," *Springfield Republican*, August 8, 2004.
80. Kevin Cullen, "A Priest, a Boy, a Mystery," *Boston Globe*, December 14, 2003.
81. Andrea Estes and L. Kim Tan, "Church Leaders Knew That Priest Was Slay Suspect," *Boston Herald*, October 23, 1991.
82. Ibid.
83. Cullen, "A Priest, a Boy, a Mystery."
84. Editorial, "The Rev. Richard Lavigne Becomes Richard Lavigne," *Springfield Union-News*, December 18, 2002.
85. Cullen, "A Priest, a Boy, a Mystery."
86. Rev. Bill Pomerleau, "Father Scahill Deposition Details Interactions with Abuse Victims," iObserve, www.iobserve.org/rn1029a.html.
87. Bill Zajac, "Abuse Seen as Cause of Suicides," *Springfield Republican*, June 12, 2005.
88. Bill Zajac, "For Dupré, the Pressure Was Too Much," *Springfield Republican*, March 28, 2004.
89. Kevin Cullen, "Murder Probe Pressed against Ex-Priest: Lavigne House Searched Twice," *Boston Globe*, May 19, 2004.
90. Jonathan Finer, "Mass. Bishop Charged with Rape: No Trial Planned," *Washington Post*, September 28, 2004.
91. "Press Release from Greenberg Traurig Concerning Allegations of Abuse Regarding Bishop Thomas Dupré, Former Head of the Diocese of Springfield, Massachusetts, February 19, 2004," www.wwlp.com.
92. Bill Zajac, "Ex-Bishop Invokes 5th Amendment," *Springfield Republican*, July 9, 2004. The headline is misleading: Dupré remains a bishop, but he is no longer bishop of Springfield.
93. Johanna McGeary, "Can the Church Be Saved?" *Time*, April 1, 2002.
94. Elizabeth Hamilton and Eric Rich, "A Predator Blessed with Charm," *Hartford Courant*, September 15, 2002.
95. McGeary, "Can the Church Be Saved?"
96. Hamilton and Rich, "A Predator Blessed with Charm."
97. Associated Press, "Cardinal Encouraged Abuser to Stay," *Pioneer Press*, May 11, 2002.
98. Elizabeth Hamilton and Eric Rich, "Egan Protected Abusive Priests," *Hartford Courant*, March 17, 2002.
99. Hamilton and Rich, "A Predator Blessed with Charm."
100. Ibid.
101. Eric Rich and Elizabeth Hamilton, "Abusive Priest Found in Caribbean Hideaway," *Hartford Courant*, April 29, 2002.
102. McGeary, "Can the Church Be Saved?"
103. Rich and Hamilton, "Abusive Priest Found in Caribbean Hideaway."
104. Fourteen priests (including the ones named in this book) were covered by a global

settlement (AP: "Conn[ecticut] Archdiocese Reaches $22M Settlement," October 31, 2005). Because of the statute of limitations there were no criminal prosecutions.

105. Elizabeth Hamilton, "Egan Paid Accused Priest: Was It Hush Money or an Obligation?" *Hartford Courant,* May 18, 2002.
106. Daniel Tepfer, "Priest Sex Case Raises Doubts: Facts Appear to Contradict Firmness of Egan Policy," *Connecticut Post,* April 14, 2002. Coleman was included in the global settlement; he has vanished and is not the object of criminal prosecution.
107. Ibid.
108. Elizabeth Hamilton and Eric Rich, "Cardinal Egan under Fire," *Hartford Courant,* March 17, 2002.
109. For the Carr case, see Hamilton and Rich, "Egan Protected Abusive Priests."
110. Hamilton and Rich, "Egan Protected Abusive Priests."
111. Ibid.
112. Daniel Tepfer, "Lori's Apology Sparks Victims' Anger for Egan," *Connecticut Post,* October 19, 2003.
113. Paul Zielbauer, "After Accused Priest's Suicide, Shock and Second Thoughts," *New York Times,* May 18, 2002.
114. Daniel Tepfer, "Priest Sex Abuse Victims Confer," *Connecticut Post,* March 23, 2003.
115. Walter V. Robinson and Michael Rezendes, "Law Recalls Little on Abuse Case," *Boston Globe,* May 9, 2002.

## *8. Scope of Destruction: America and the World*

1. John Rivera, "Priest Who Killed Himself Was Accused of Child Molesting Boys," *Baltimore Sun,* August 30, 1993.
2. Archdiocese of Baltimore, "Archdiocese's List of Clergy Accused of Child Sexual Abuse," *Baltimore Sun,* September 26, 2002. This list contains the names of priests and brothers accused of abuse and brief summaries of the accusations.
3. Frank P. L. Somerville, "Priest Sued by Parents in Second Case," *Baltimore Sun,* October 27, 1988, p. 1D.
4. Allison Klein, "Former Teacher at City Parochial School Gets 5-Year Sentence for Molesting Girls," *Baltimore Sun,* August 27, 2002.
5. Jay Apperson, "Lawsuit Accuses Priest of Sexually Abusing Teen," *Baltimore Sun,* March 12, 1994.
6. Kate Shatzkin, "Appeals Court Ruling Erases Suit Alleging Sex Abuse by Priest," *Baltimore Sun,* August 21, 1996.
7. Janice D'Arcy, "Former Catholic School Student Claims Priest Sexually Abused Him," *Baltimore Sun,* January 21, 2005.
8. Jennifer McMenamin, "Priest Pleads Guilty to Abuse," *Baltimore Sun,* November 9, 2005.
9. Jim Haner, Gary Gately, and Jay Apperson, "Teacher Was Troubled as a Boy, Hapless as a Man," *Baltimore Sun,* January 4, 1994.
10. Jim Haner and Gary Gately, "Parents Say Complaints Led to Teacher's Transfer," *Baltimore Sun,* January 30, 1994.

11. State of Maryland, Circuit Court for Baltimore City, CL185737, Deposition of Steven Melnick. Melnick said he saw Merzbacher and Sister Eileen "through a keyhole" (p. 49) and that Merzbacher "had his pants down and he was doing her. She was laying on the table" (p. 52).
12. State of Maryland, Circuit Court for Baltimore City, CL185737, Deposition of Sharon Bruce, p. 48.
13. State of Maryland, Circuit Court for Baltimore City, CL185737, Deposition of Sharon Bruce, p. 71.
14. Affidavit of Gary R. Homberg, April 11, 1995, Appendix to Plaintiffs' Joint Response to Defendants' Motion for Summary Judgment, Circuit Court for Baltimore City, Case no. 94007053/CL174727. In 1974 the archdiocesan attorney wrote a letter to Merzbacher's attorney that the archdiocese had investigated the rumors about Merzbacher, cleared him, and fired the teacher (Homberg) who had spread the rumors. See Kate Shatzkin, "Sex Abuse Trial Again Delayed," *Baltimore Sun*, May 9, 1995, p. 1B.
15. Melody Simmons and Gary Gately, "Principal Denies Knowledge of Alleged Sexual Abuse," *Baltimore Sun*, January 12, 1994. The headline is not accurate; according to those who were there, Weisman said, "My conscience is clear" and did not explicitly deny knowledge of the abuse.
16. Kate Shatzkin, "Defense Rests in Sex Trial without Calling Teacher," *Baltimore Sun*, June 6, 1995.
17. Kate Shatzkin, "Merzbacher Convicted of Decades-Ago Rape," *Baltimore Sun*, June 9, 1995. The convictions all resulted from charges concerning the same victim.
18. Gail Gibson, "City Priest Pleads Guilty to Net Child Porn Charge," *Baltimore Sun*, July 17, 2002.
19. Ibid.
20. John Rivera, "[Two] More Allege Abuse by Priest," *Baltimore Sun*, May 22, 2002.
21. Baltimore City Police Department, Complaint No. 1HB203, August 9, 1993.
22. Michael Ollove, "Priest Suspended after Youth Alleged Sexual Misdeed Is Returned to Parish," *Baltimore Sun*, December 4, 1993.
23. Ibid.
24. William Cardinal Keeler, "Cardinal Explains Decision on Blackwell," *Baltimore Sun*, May 17, 2002.
25. Del Quentin Wilber and John Rivera, "Shooting Suspect Cites Priest's Abuse," *Baltimore Sun*, May 15, 2002.
26. Sarah Koenig, "Review Boards: Accountability or Rubberstamp," *Baltimore Sun*, May 17, 2002.
27. Mary Leonard, "Baltimore Panel Sharply Dissented on Priest's Return," *Boston Globe*, May 16, 2002.
28. Gail Gibson, "City Prosecutors Plan Search for 1998 Letters: Archdiocese Officials Wrote about Allegations of Abuse against Priest," *Baltimore Sun*, May 20, 2002.
29. Wilber and Rivera, "Shooting Suspect Cites Priest's Abuse."
30. Ibid.
31. John Rivera and Sarah Koenig, "Keeler Apologizes for Abuse by Priests," *Baltimore Sun*, May 17, 2002.
32. Allison Klein, "Stokes Found Not Guilty," *Baltimore Sun*, December 17, 2002.

33. Julie Bykowicz, "Case against Ex-Priest Dropped: State's Attorney Decides Not to Retry Blackwell on Sex Abuse Charges," *Baltimore Sun*, July 2, 2005.
34. Andrew Wolfson and Gregory A. Hall, "Report Says Priest Confessed Sex Abuse," *Louisville Courier-Journal*, July 24, 2002.
35. Peter Smith, "Priest Tells of Struggle with Pedophilia in Therapy Journal," *Louisville Courier-Journal*, February 12, 2003.
36. "Retired Priest Pleads Guilty in Abuse Cases as Trial About to Begin," Channel 3, Louisville, March 31, 2003 at www.wave3.com/Global/story.asp? S=1207103&nav=0RZFEvxy.
37. Smith, "Priest Tells of Struggle with Pedophilia in Therapy Journal." Williams has denied the allegations and there are no civil suits or criminal indictments against him.
38. Andrew Wolfson and Peter Smith, "Suit against Archdiocese Accuses Kelly of Perjury," *Louisville Courier-Journal*, July 6, 2002.
39. Peter Smith and Gregory A. Hall, "Pedophile Priest Says Abuse Was No Secret: Louis Miller Testifies Three Archbishops Knew about Molestation," *Louisville Courier-Journal*, May 23, 2003.
40. Andrew Wolfson, "In 2000, Kelly Wouldn't Say if Miller Had Been Previously Accused," *Louisville Courier-Journal*, June 23, 2002.
41. Peter Smith, "Kelly Knew of Abuse, Kept Priest in Post: Memos Show Creagh Admitted Molesting Boy," *Louisville Courier-Journal*, April 9, 2003.
42. Ibid.
43. Ibid.
44. Smith, "Priest Tells of Struggle with Pedophilia in Therapy Journal."
45. Paul McEnroe and Pam Louwagie, "Behind the Pine Curtain: Decades of Abuse and Secrecy at St. John's Abbey," *Minneapolis Star Tribune*, September 29, 2002.
46. "Problem Priests: The St. John's Solution: Shouldering the Burden," *St. Louis Post-Dispatch*, December 22, 2002.
47. McEnroe and Louwagie, "Behind the Pine Curtain."
48. Ibid.
49. Kelly Patricia O'Meara, "Sins of a Father: Sauna Kids' Abuse," *Insight Magazine*, September 16, 2003.
50. McEnroe and Louwagie, "Behind the Pine Curtain"
51. Patricia Lefevere, "Father Is 'Lion at the Gate' Pressing Case against Priest," *National Catholic Reporter*, December 27, 2002.
52. Gil Donovan, "Monks Investigated in Murder and Kidnap Cases," *National Catholic Reporter*, May 31, 2002.
53. McEnroe and Louwagie, "Behind the Pine Curtain."
54. Ibid.
55. Ibid.
56. Signed statement, August 26, 1992, St. John's Abuse Disclosure Project, www.abusedisclosureproject.com.
57. Pam Louwagie, "A Family's Faith Was Shaken after Their Sons Were Abused," *Minneapolis Star Tribune*, September 29, 2002.
58. Paul McEnroe, "A Broken Trust, a Sense of Shame," *Minneapolis Star Tribune*, September 29, 2002.
59. Signed statement, August 28, 1992, St. John's Abuse Disclosure Project.

60. Patricia Lefevere, "Scandal at the Abbey," *National Catholic Reporter*, December 13, 2002.
61. The abbey and the monks accused of abuse settled with their accusers (Paul McEnroe and Pam Louwagie, "Abuse Victims, Abbey Settle Claims: Compensation, Safeguards Are Part of Agreement," *Minneapolis Star Tribune*, September 27, 2002).
62. Warren Wolfe, "Abbey Promises Change; St. John's Apologized and Said an Outside Board and Other Measures Will Help Prevent More Sexual Abuse," *Minneapolis Star Tribune*, October 2, 2002.
63. For an overview of Trupia's career, see Berry and Renner's *Vows of Silence: The Abuse of Power in the Papacy of John Paul II* (New York: Free Press, 2004) pp. 234–35.
64. Nena Baker, "Catholic Church Hid Sexual Abuse in Tucson: Victims Say Tucson Settles Suit for $15 Million," *Arizona Republic*, February 10, 2002.
65. Ibid.
66. Stephenie Innes, "Life of Msgr. Trupia: A New Home in Maryland," *Arizona Daily Star*, February 9, 2003; Alan Cooperman, "For Dioceses, Legal Toll Quietly Rises," *Washington Post*, January 30, 2002.
67. Ron Russell, "Pedo-Homo Priests and Bishops Form Mahony's Network" *Los Angeles New Times*, June 13, 2002.
68. Michael Rezendes, "Ariz[ona] Abuse Case Names Bishop, Two Priests," *Boston Globe*, August 20, 2002; Stephanie Innes, "Man Seeks Cash from Archdiocese," *Arizona Star*, August 24, 2002; the victim's attorney claims to have compromising photographs of Rausch and the victim.
69. A. W. Richard Sipe, "View from the Eye of the Storm," LINKUP National Conference, Louisville, Kentucky, February 23, 2003.
70. Joseph A. Reaves and Kelly Ettenborough, "Inheriting a Legacy of Secrecy, Scandal," *Arizona Republic*, May 4, 2003.
71. Rezendes, "Ariz[ona] Abuse Case Names Bishops, 2 Priests."
72. Tim Steller and Stephanie Innes, "Bishop's Account on Priest Changed," *Arizona Daily Star*, February 12, 2002. In correcting his deposition (which is supposed to allow minor corrections of dates, spelling, and grammar), Moreno reversed the admission.
73. Rezendes, "Ariz[ona] Abuse Case Names Bishops, 2 Priests."
74. Michael Rezendes, "Bishop of Tucson Resigns: Criticized over Response to Allegations," *Boston Globe*, March 8, 2003.
75. At least after 1998 Fatooh was aware that Trupia was being sued for sexual abuse ("Church's Poor Choice," *Monterey Herald*, February 23, 2003).
76. Scott Simonson and Tom Beal, "Pope Defrocks Tucson Priests: Diocese Suspended Both; Same Penalty Sought for Two More," *Arizona Daily Star*, August 6, 2004.
77. Stephanie Innes, "No Cut Off Date for Tucson Stipend," *Arizona Daily News*, February 23, 2003.
78. Sheryl Kornman, "Vatican Defrocks 2 Former Tucson Priests," *Tucson Citizen*, April 5, 2004.
79. Joseph A. Reaves, "Diocese Downplays Abuse Scope: Case Shows Pattern of Suppression by Bishop," *Arizona Republic*, November 10, 2002.
80. Ibid.

81. Alan Scher Zagier, "Ex-Priest from Fort Myers Pleads Guilty to Arizona Sex Abuse," *Naples Daily News*, January 22, 2003.
82. Richard Ruelas, "Meeting the Bishop Makes Memories," *Arizona Republic*, December 9, 2002.
83. Joseph A. Reaves, "Officer Says O'Brien Hid Abuse by Priest When Lawman Was Boy," *Arizona Republic*, December 4, 2002.
84. Joseph A. Reaves, "Bishop Seeks Immunity in Abuse Cases," *Arizona Republic*, December 6, 2002.
85. Michael Lacey, "The Divine Sociopath: Why Isn't Bishop O'Brien in Jail," *Phoenix New Times*, April 15, 2004.
86. Ibid.
87. Ibid.
88. Joseph A. Reaves, "Ex-bishop Ordered Stonewall of Abuse Investigation," *Arizona Republic*, September 15, 2003.
89. Ibid.
90. Gary Grado, "Diocese Faces Another Lawsuit," *East Valley Tribune*, March 25, 2004.
91. Reaves, "Officer Says O'Brien Hid Abuse by Priest When Lawman Was Boy."
92. "Former Priest from Florida Sentenced for Sexual Abuse," *Fort Myers Herald Tribune*, March 5, 2003.
93. Joseph A. Reaves, "Bishop's Fall Slow, Painful," *Arizona Republic*, June 19, 2003.
94. Associated Press, "Bishop Spared Indictment in Deal," *Post and Courier*, June 3, 2002.
95. Reese Duncan and Susan Hogan, "Arizona Bishop Arrested in Hit-and-Run Death," *Dallas Morning News*, June 17, 2003; Brent Whiting and Shawn Day, "Victim Described as Big with Big Heart," *Arizona Republic*, June 17, 2003; Michael Chow, "Arrest Could Finish Arizona Bishop," *USA Today*, June 17, 2003; Joseph Reaves, "Bishop's Fall Slow, Painful," *Arizona Republic*, June 10, 2003.
96. Dale Hurd, "Bishop Accused of Hit and Run Resigns," *CBN News*, June 18, 2003.
97. Joseph A. Reaves, "O'Brien's Bid to Tally Travel Time Is Rejected," *Arizona Republic*, April 8, 2004.
98. Ron Russell, "Bishop Bad Boy," *SF Weekly*, March 19, 2003.
99. Russell, "Pedo-Homo Priests and Bishops Form Mahony's Network."
100. Sister Jane Kelly, *Taught to Believe the Unbelievable: A New Vision of Hope for the Catholic Church and Society* (New York: Writers Club Press / iUniverse, Inc., 2003) p. 18.
101. John Van der Zee, *Agony in the Garden: Sex, Lies, and Redemption for the Troubled Heart of the American Catholic Church* (New York: Thunder's Mouth Press / Nation Books, 2002) p. 15.
102. Russell, "Bishop Bad Boy."
103. AP, "Man Sues Former LA Bishop for 19 Years of Alleged Sex Abuse," *Berkeley Daily Planet*, July 8, 2002.
104. Derek J. Moore, "Santa Rosa Diocese Funds Land in Luxembourg," *Santa Rosa Press Democrat*, February 3, 2000.
105. Russell, "Mouth Wide Shut," *Los Angeles New Times*, April 18, 2002.
106. Ross Farrow, "Boy Wasn't Negligent in Sex Abuse Case, Stockton Diocese Attorney Says," *Lodi News-Sentinel*, August 16, 2003.

107. Ross Farrow, "Stockton Diocese Seeks Dismissal of Clergy Abuse Lawsuit," *Lodi News-Sentinel,* October 21, 2003.
108. Russell, "Mouth Wide Shut."
109. Don Lattin, "30 Million Awarded Men Molested by Family Priest," *San Francisco Chronicle,* July 17, 1998.
110. Russell, "Mouth Wide Shut."
111. Steve Lopez, "The Amazing 'Teflon Cardinal,'" *Los Angeles Times,* April 7, 2002.
112. Russell, "Mouth Wide Shut."
113. The Clergy Cases III, No. JCCP 4359, Deposition of Cardinal Roger Mahony Los Angeles California Tuesday, November 23, 2004 (henceforth 2004 Mahony Deposition)
114. The passage from the 1998 testimony is quoted in the deposition:
    Diepenbrock [attorney for the diocese]: "during a period of time you were the bishop of Stockton, were there any other priests that were involved in any kind of sexual misconduct with children?"
    Mahony: "Again, during my time, I cannot recall another case."
    Attorney: "Well, if there had been any other cases when you were the Bishop of Stockton, you certainly would have heard about it, wouldn't you?"
    Mahony: "Oh yes, but I can't recall another case."
    Attorney: "Were there any other cases?"
    Mahony: "Not that I know of."
    Attorney "This was the only one?"
    Mahony: "Yes."
    (2004 Mahony Deposition, p. 135, ll. 6-25, p. 136, 1–4.)
115. Jeffrey Anderson, "Mahony's Testimony in Sex Scandal Clashes with Earlier Statements and Reality," *Los Angeles Weekly,* December 16, 2004.
116. 2004 Mahony Deposition, p. 136, ll. 19–25.
117. Jeffrey M. Barker, "Perjury Charges Urged against Mahony," *Stockton Record,* December 18, 2004. O'Grady claimed in a filmed interview that Mahoney's lawyers promised him a pension in return for refusing to testify at the civil trial and thereby risking a citation for contempt of court (Amy Berg, *Deliver Us from Evil,* 2006).
118. Russell, "Pedo-Homo Priests and Bishops Form Mahony's Network."
119. William Lobdell and Jean O. Pasco, "Judging the Sins of the Father: Msgr. Michael Harris Lost His Priesthood over Sex-Abuse Claims, but the Former Orange County Principal's Aura Endures," *Los Angeles Times,* November 10, 2001.
120. Ibid.
121. Lobdell and Pasco, "Judging the Sins of the Father: Msgr. Michael Harris Lost His Priesthood over Sex-Abuse Claims, but the Former Orange County Principal's Aura Endures."
122. David France, "Gays and the Seminary," *Newsweek,* May 20, 2002.
123. Ron Russell, "Cardinal Coverup: Cardinal Roger Mahony Projected Himself as Leading a Charge to Clean up the Roman Catholic Sex Scandal," *Los Angeles New Times,* May 2, 2002.
124. The National Review Board for the Protection of Children and Young People observed that "in the 1970s and 1980s, in particular, there developed at certain seminaries a 'gay subculture,' and at these seminaries, according to several witnesses,

homosexual liaisons occurred among students or between students and teachers. Such subcultures existed or exist in certain dioceses and orders as well. The Board believes that the failure to take disciplinary action against such conduct contributed to an atmosphere in which sexual abuse of adolescent boys by priests was more likely" (*A Report on the Crisis in the Catholic Church in the United States* [Washington, D.C.: United States Conference of Catholic Bishops, 2004] p. 81).

125. "[Four] Cases Provide a Glimpse of How Archdiocese Responded: Abuser Received New Assignment after Counseling," *Los Angeles Times*, August 18, 2002.
126. Glenn F. Bunting, "Cardinal Mahony Kept Cleric's Abuse Secret for 16 Years," *Los Angeles Times*, May 16, 2002.
127. Jeffrey Anderson, "Behind the Robes: Pondering the Secrets Cardinal Mahony Might Hold about the Catholic Sex Scandal," *Los Angeles Weekly*, March 14, 2003.
128. Ibid.
129. "[Four] Cases Provide a Glimpse of How Archdiocese Responded."
130. Darcy Henton with David McCann, *Boys Don't Cry: The Struggle for Justice and Healing in Canada's Biggest Sex Abuse Scandal* (Toronto: McClellan and Stewart Inc., 1995) p. 3.
131. Ibid., p. 123.
132. Ibid.
133. Ibid., p. 140.
134. Ibid., p. 230.
135. Ibid., p. 186.
136. Mike Howell, "Ontario Premier Apologizes to Vancouver Man," *Vancouver Courier*, August 5, 2004.
137. See A. W. Richard Sipe, "Clergy Abuse in Ireland," in Anson Schupe, editor, *Wolves within the Fold: Religious Leadership and the Abuses of Power* (New Brunswick: Rutgers University Press, 1997) pp. 148–149.
138. Timothy Mitchell wrote, "Sociologist Pepe Rodríguez calculates that approximately 7 percent of Spain's priests have committed a serious act of sexual abuse with a child or adolescent (usually a boy)" (*Betrayal of Innocents: Desire, Power, and the Catholic Church in Spain* [Philadelphia: University of Pennsylvania Press, 1998] p. 31).
139. Chris Moore, *Betrayal of Trust: The Father Brendan Smyth Affair and the Catholic Church* (Marino / Mercier Press, 1995) p. 27.
140. Ibid., p. 35.
141. Ibid., p. 133.
142. Ibid., p. 44.
143. *The Ferns Report: Presented to the Minister for Health and Children*, October 2005.
144. Ibid., p. 161.
145. Ibid., p. 155.
146. Ibid., p. 86.
147. Kieron Wood, "Troubled Bishop Returns to Irish Diocese," *Catholic World News*, February 21, 1996.
148. *The Ferns Report*, p. 155.
149. Ibid.
150. Ibid., p. 156.
151. Ibid., p. 155.

152. Ibid., pp. 156–158
153. Ibid., p. 93.
154. Ibid., p. 99.
155. Ibid., p. 93.
156. Ibid., p. 92.
157. Ibid., p. 96.
158. Ibid., p. 93.
159. Ibid., p. 97.
160. Ibid., p. 159.
161. Ibid., p. 161.
162. Ibid., p. 158.
163. Ibid., p. 255.
164. Ibid., p. 254.
165. Kieron Woods, "Bishop Refutes Charges," *Catholic World News*, January 11, 2002.
166. *The Ferns Report*, p. 31.
167. Ibid., p. 97.
168. Ibid., p. 167.
169. Ibid., p. 169.
170. In Thailand Comiskey stayed at a hotel known for its prostitutes (Kevin Cullen, "Irish Bishop Quits over Priest Case," *Boston Globe*, April 2, 2002).
171. *The Ferns Report*, p. 220.
172. Ibid.
173. Patsy McGarry, "Ledwith Frontrunner for Bishop before Allegations," *Irish Times*, July 27, 2002. See *Ferns Report*, p. 101.
174. Patsy McGarry, "Church Silence That Hid 'Kernel of Evil' at Maynooth," *Irish Times*, June 6, 2002.
175. Patsy McGarry, "Maynooth Priest 'Humiliated' for Raising Concerns of Seminarians," *Irish Times*, June 5, 2002.
176. Patsy McGarry, "Ledwith's Name Submitted for Dublin Archbishop Post," *Irish Times*, January 13, 2003.
177. "About Us," www.ramtha.com/html/aboutus/faqs/school/gnostic-beliefs.stm.
178. "Ramtha School of Enlightenment," www.religiousmovements.lib.virginia.edu/nrms/Ramtha.html. This site has a history and analysis of Ramtha.
179. For an account in English see Jason Berry and Gerald Renner, *Vows of Silence: The Abuse of Power in the Papacy of John Paul II* (New York: Free Press, 2004) pp. 227–232.
180. Hubertus Czernin, *Das Buch Groër: Eine Kirchenchronik* (Vienna: Wieser Verlag, 1998) p. 20.
181. Ibid., p. 37.
182. Ibid., p. 54.
183. Ibid., p. 44. Also present were the prior of Göttweig, Father Berthold Goosens, and the prior of Maria Roggendorf, Father Clemens Reischl.
184. Karol Josef Gajewski wrote, "The 'Immorality' trials [of 1935] sought to destroy the reputation of Catholic religious, aimed in particular at those working in primary and secondary schools. Priests, monks, lay-brothers and nuns were accused of 'perverted and immoral' lifestyles—euphemisms for homosexuality and paedophilia" ("Nazi Policy and the Catholic Church," *Inside the Vatican*, November 1999).

185. At a press conference Schönborn, according to Czernin, said, "In diesem Sinne entschuldige ich mich hier für die pauschalen und unünberprüften Anschuldigungen, die ich in meiner ersten öfftentlichen Stellungnahme im Fernsehen gegen diejenigen erhoben habe, die den Herrn Kardinal beschuldigt haben" (*Das Buch Groër*, p. 103).
186. When he was at a meeting in Rome with the president of the Austrian Bishops' Conference the day before the convocation at which he became a cardinal, Schönborn learned that Groër was having a private audience with the pope. Schönborn had spoken with Groër a few days before and Groër had neglected to tell him of the meeting. Schönborn was "spürbar schwer verärgert" (Czernin, *Das Buch Groër*, p. 180).
187. "Religion Report," ABC radio Australia, February 4, 2003. Homosexual websites quote Humbertus Czernin of *Profil,* and author of *Das Buch Groër,* as claiming that Groër had sex with 2,000 seminarians, monks, and priests: "His sexual harassment began in the '50s, continued in the '60s, the '70s, the '80s and even in the '90s," Czernin said in dropping the latest bombshell. "The last case I know of was in 1996, when he was an old man and had already been kicked out as archbishop of Vienna but had returned to his monastery in Lower Austria" (www.lgcm.org.uk).
188. Pepe Rodríguez, *Pederastia en la Iglesia católica* (Barcelona: Ediciones B, 2002) p. 180.
189. Jane Perlez, "New Austrian Cardinal Apologizes for Predecessor's Sex Crimes," *New York Times*, April 20, 1998.
190. "Verordneter Rückzug," *Dialog*, May 1998: "Ich bitte Gott und die Menschen um Vergebung, wenn ich Schuld auf mich geladen habe."
191. Paul Jandl, "Schweigen und warten: Die österreichische Kirche erlebt neuerlich einen Skandal," *Neue Züricher Zeitung*, July 19, 2004.
192. William J. Kole, "Vienna Cardinal Accused of Pedophilia Dies," *Telegram*, March 25, 2003.
193. Krenn said, "Die Lügner sollen das Maul halten" (Reinhard Olt, "Schadensbegrenzung in St. Pölten," *Frankfurter Allgemeine Zeitung*, July 26, 2004).
194. "World Church News," *The Tablet*, June 1, 2002.
195. Ibid.
196. The Austrian bishops and the Polish bishops had agreed to screen candidates for their seminaries for psychological problems, including active homosexuality. Krenn refused to participate in this program, and his seminary increased from four to fifty seminarians as candidates rejected in Austria and Poland came to him.
197. Irene Brockner and Peter Meyr, "Kinderporno: Priesteranwärter entlarvt," *Der Standard*, July 15, 2004. The German is: "Das geht die Bischofskonferenz einen Dreck an."
198. Paul Jandl wrote, "St. Pöltnerer Schüler sollen von Seminaristen sexual bedrängt worden sein" ("Schweigen und warten").
199. Schüller said of the Vatican's delay: "Damit falle der Vatikan der Ortskirche in den Rücken" ("Vatikan wartet and schweigt," *Der Standard*, July 15, 2004).
200. John Tagliabue, "Priests and Sex: Europe Has Problems, but Not Like America's. Maybe," *New York Times*, April 21, 2002. Jason Berry, *Vows of Silence: The Abuse of Power in the Papacy of John Paul II* (New York: Free Press, 2004) pp. 279–80.
201. "Polish Archbishop 'Molested Students,'" BBC News, February 23, 2002; John L.

Allen Jr., "Polish Prelate Accused of Sexual Abuse," *National Catholic Reporter*, March 15, 2002; "Sins of the Fathers," *Warsaw Voice*, March 3, 2002.

202. Marian Tankiewicz, "Im Schatten des Domes: Vatikan bekämpft Skandal, nicht sexuelle Gewalt gegen Kinder: Erzbischof Paetz vom Papst zurückgetreten," *Junge Welt*, April 2, 2004.

203. "Polen: Klerus-Skandal um sexuellen Missbrauch," *Der Standard*, February 25, 2002. Gabriele Lesser wrote, "Der gesuchte 'Spion im Vatikan' sei ein Pole, schrieb damals Jerzy Urban, der letzte kommunistische Regierungssprecher Polens. In seinem Wochenblatt *Nie* (Nein) enthüllte er auch den Namen: 'Erzbischof P.'—für jedermann erkennbar der gerade erst zum Erzbischof von Posen ernannte Juliusz Paetz" ("Popenzoff in Polen: Ist der Erzbischof von Posen ein Sexualstraftäter? Eine Kommission des Vatikans untersucht den Fall," *Die Tageszeitung*, February 25, 2002).

## *9. Victims*

1. John Jay College of Criminal Justice, *The Nature and Scope of Sexual Abuse of Minors by Catholic Priests and Deacons in the United States 1950-2000* (Washington, D.C., United States Conference of Catholic Bishops, 2004) [Henceforth the *John Jay Report*], p. 154. The forensic psychiatrist William H. Reid wrote that "careful studies have indicated…that child molesters commit an average of sixty offences for every incident that comes to public attention" (from *The Psychiatric Times*, April 1988, quoted by A. W. Richard Sipe, *Sex, Priests, and Power: Anatomy of a Crisis* [New York: Brunner/Mazel, 1995] p. 24). A recent Connecticut study used a random telephone survey and discovered that "26 percent of women and 10 percent of men had experienced at least one sexual assault. Only 15 percent of those people had reported the assault to the police" (Sherry Fisher, "Social Worker Researcher Reports Findings on Sexual Abuse of Children,' *University of Connecticut Advance*, September 22, 2003).
2. David Finkelhor, *Sexually Victimized Children* (New York: Free Press, 1979) p. 136-137. Finkelhor found 8.6 percent of men had been victimized as children (p. 53).
3. *John Jay Report*, p. 4; United States Conference of Catholic Bishops [USCCB], "Cara 2005 Survey of Allegations and Costs Released as Part of "Charter' Implementation Report," March 30, 2006. There seems to be a gap for 2003; the number of victims who made allegations during that year is not reported.
4. *John Jay Report*, p. 26; USCCB, "Cara 2005 Survey of Allegations and Costs Released as Part of 'Charter' Implementation Report."
5. *John Jay Report*, p. 28.
6. *John Jay Report*, p. 4.
7. See the table at http://www.bishop-accountability.org/usccb/natureandscope/regiontable.htm. There are discrepancies in various reports that may be caused by how abusers are counted. Some tabulators included religious priests and priests not incardinated in the diocese but who were serving in the diocese. The dioceses naturally used criteria that would minimize the numbers and percentages of abusers, but the wide divergence among dioceses are still clear.
8. In 2005 A. W. Richard Sipe testified that "several Catholic dioceses in the United States reveal that over 10 percent of active priests have been sexually involved with

minors. In 1995 10 percent of the priests in the Belleville, Illinois Diocese were identified as abusers of minors. The Boston Archdiocese acknowledges that 7.6 percent of its priests have been abusers (with new revelations that figure is approaching 10 percent); New Hampshire, 8.2 percent; 24 percent of all the priests active in the diocese of Tucson, Arizona in 1986 were abusers of minors; in 1992 56 of 710 priests in the Archdiocese of Los Angeles were abusers, a jurisdiction that admits 244 of its priests abused minors." Sipe Report III.

9. *John Jay Report*, p. 6.
10. *John Jay Report*, p. 69.
11. *John Jay Report*, p. 68; "the majority of victims are males between the ages of 11-17. . . . The average age . . . increased over time (*John Jay Report*, p. 70).
12. David Finkelhor, *Sexually Victimized Children* (New York, The Free Press, 1979). The percentage for boys especially may be low, because boys often consider only homosexual abuse to be abuse. Other researchers have found ranges from 2.5% to 33%. See Matthew Parynik Mendel, *The Male Survivor: The Impact of Sexual Abuse* (Thousand Oaks: Sage Publications, 1995) p. 41. A useful survey of estimates of child sexual abuse can be found in the *John Jay Report*, pp. 154-162.
13. David Finkelhor, *Sexually Abused Children* (New York: Free Pres, 1979) p.138.
14. Kurt Freund and Robin J. Watson wrote that "the mean number of victims of nonincestuous sex offenders against female children was 9.8, while that of such offenders against male children was 150.2" ("The Proportions of Heterosexual and Homosexual Pedophiles Among Sex Offenders against Children: An Exploratory Study," *Journal of Sex and Marital Therapy*, Vol. 18, No. 1 (Spring 1992) p. 35). See also Gene G. Abel, J. V. Becker, M. S. Mittelman, J. Cunningham-Rathner, J. L. Rouleau, and W. D. Murphy, W. D. (1987), "Self-reported sex crimes of nonincarcerated paraphiliacs," *Journal of Interpersonal Violence*, (2) 1987, 3 - 25. A typical pedophile, John Boone, was convicted of abusing "more than 142 boys at Polacca Day School on the Hope Reservation in Arizona" (Susan Landon, "Sex Abuse Bill Deficient, Indians Say," *Albuquerque Journal*, May 31, 1990, p. 30).
15. *John Jay Report*, p. 54.
16. Stephen Rossetti, "The Mark of Cain: Reintegrating Pedophiles," *America*, Vol. 173, No. 6, September 9, 1995.
17. Scott Wescott, "Rebuilding Trust, Part 2: What Becomes of Abusive Priests?" *Erie Times-News*, June 30, 2003. Plante, A. W. Richard Sipe and others think that the average priest abuser has fewer victims than the average pedophile, who often has several hundred victims (see above).
18. Paul J. Isely, "Child Sex Abuse and the Catholic Church: An Historical and Contemporary Review," *Pastoral Psychology*, Vol. 43, No. 4 (1997) pp. 293-294. Isely disagrees with many of Rossetti's characterizations of sexual abuse by priests. See also Jan Hindman, "Research disputes assumptions about child molesters," *National District Attorneys Association Bulletin*, *7*(4), 1, 3. Hindman compared paroled male sexual offenders against children in two periods. In the second period, the patients were told that they would have to submit to a polygraph test and if their self-reports were contradicted they would be returned to jail. In the period before the polygraph, the average number of victims was 1.5; afterwards, it was 9.0.
19. Finkelhor, *Sexually Abused Children*, p. 138.

20. David Crary, "Parents Deceived by Priests," *Worcester Telegram and Gazette*, April 29, 2002.
21. Joshua Robin, "Other Brother Shares Story: Says Priest Abuse Still Haunts Him," *Newsday*, March 16, 2002.
22. Michel Dorais, *Don't Tell: The Sexual Abuse of Boys* (Montreal & Kingston: McGill-Queens University Press, 2002) p. 28.
23. "Alleged Victims Say the Incidents Altered Lives: Comprehensive Look at Lawsuits against Diocese Shows Many Similarities," *Louisville Courier-Journal*, Priest Abuse Project, available at www.courier-journal.com.
24. Maureen Hayden, "Long Wait Is Over: Victim Feels Relief over 27-year Hurt," *Evansville Courier and Press*, May 7, 2002.
25. Ibid.
26. Allen confessed his abuse from the pulpit; he received a standing ovation. He was not the object of any civil or criminal action (Maureen Hayden, "Priest Confesses His Sin to Church: Rev. Allen Gets Ovation, Will Stay on as Pastor," *Evansville Courier and Press*, May 6, 2002). Allen was last reported in Kuwait (Philip Elliot, "It's Hard to Keep Tabs on Abusive Priests," *Evansville Courier and Press*, March 21, 2004).
27. Nancy Meersman, "Four Men Allege Sex Abuse at Camp Fatima," *Manchester Union Leader*, May 29, 2002. Osgood was named in a lawsuit which was settled in 2002 (Pat Grossmith, "Allegations Revealed in Lawsuit Settled vs. Manchester Diocese," *Manchester Union Leader*, October 12, 2002).
28. Linda Matchan, "Town Secret," *Boston Globe*, August 29, 1993.
29. Stephen Kurkjian and Linda Matchan, "Other Abuse by Porter Alleged in NM," *Boston Globe*, July 24, 1992.
30. Gloria I. Wang, "Church Members Rally Support for Clergymen at St. Mary's," *Los Gatos Weekly Times*, April 3, 2002.
31. In 2002 Burke pleaded guilty to abuse and was sentenced to two years in prison (Glenn F. Bunting, "Jesuits Settle Case with Abused Men," *Los Angeles Times*, September 5, 2002).
32. Connor was convicted in 2002 and served six months of home detention (Barbara Whitaker, "Jesuits to Pay $7.5 Million to Men Who Contended Abuse," *New York Times*, September 6, 2002).
33. Lane was accused of raping boys at the Alpha Omega House, a facility for disturbed youth; he was not criminally prosecuted, but lawsuits against him were settled (Sacha Pfeiffer and Stephen Kurkjian, "Church Settled Six Suits vs. Priest," *Boston Globe*, January 27, 2002.
34. Tourigney was sued and the case was settled in 1995 ("Scores of Priests Involved in Sex Abuse Cases: Settlements Kept Scope of Issue out of Public Eye," *Boston Globe*, January 31, 2002).
35. Beaulieu was a Brother of the Sacred Heart; the suit against him was settled in 2003 (Andrew Wolfe, "Siblings Settle BG Suit," *Worcester Telegraph and Gazette*, August 29, 2003). Dowd is deceased ("Four Men Allege Sex Abuse at Camp Fatima," *Manchester Union Leader*, May 29, 2002).
36. Rachelle Cohen, "NH Tales of Horror by a Lakeside," *Boston Herald*, March 6, 2002.
37. Leslie Bennetts, "Unholy Alliances," *Vanity Fair*, December 1991, p. 228.
38. Kerry Fater and Jo Ann Mullaney, "The Lived Experience of Adult Male Survivors

Who Allege Childhood Sexual Abuse by Clergy," *Issues in Mental Health Nursing*, Vol. 21 (2000) p. 287.

39. Eric G. Mart, "Victims of Abuse by Priests: Some Preliminary Observations," *Pastoral Psychology*, Vol. 52, No. 6 (July 2004) p. 467.
40. Court of Common Pleas, First Judicial District of Pennsylvania, Criminal Trial Division, Misc. no. 03-00-239, Report of the Grand Jury, p. 14 (henceforth Philadelphia Grand Jury).
41. Ibid., p. 82.
42. Ibid., p. 81.
43. Ibid., p. 181.
44. Richard B. Gartner, *Betrayed as Boys: Psychodynamic Treatment of Sexually Abused Men* (New York: The Guilford Press, 1999) pp. 208–209.
45. Hawke Fracassa, "Ex-priest Says It Was '2-way Thing': Former Metro Cleric, 82, Said He Had Relationships with Boys for Years," *Detroit News*, August 28, 2002.
46. Ronald Hansen and Kim Kozlowski, "[Four] Ex-priests Charged: 15 Elude Prosecution," *Detroit News*, August 28, 2002. Burkholder was convicted (Ben Schmitt, "Priest Convicted of Sex Abuse," *Detroit Free Press*, November 2, 2002).
47. Walter H. Bera in Australia noticed that victims often are "youths who come from families who are very devout believers in their faith and their minister. These families encourage and willingly hand over their sons for mentoring, religious education, and counseling to the priest or minister, who is often charismatic, beloved, and thereby of high status within their church community. Their deep faith contributes to their vulnerability" ("Clergy Sexual Abuse and Male Survivors," in John C. Gonsiorek, editor, *Breach of Trust: Sexual Exploitation by Health Care Professionals and Clergy* [Thousand Oaks, California: Sage Publications, 1995] p. 93).
48. Mart, "Victims of Abuse by Priests," p. 469.
49. Jim Parker, *Raped in the House of God: The Murder of My Soul and Its Lifetime Effects* (New York: iUniverse, Inc., 2004) p. 3.
50. Joseph A. Reaves, "Family Reveals Pain of Sex Abuse: Faith Has Been Kept at a Huge Cost," *Arizona Republic*, December 4, 2002.
51. Crary, "Parents Deceived by Priests."
52. Carl M. Cannon, "Victims of 'Fathers' Lose Religious Faith," *San Jose Mercury*, December 30, 1987, p. 13A.
53. "Saving Hearts and Minds," *San Francisco Examiner*, July 2, 2002.
54. Mart, "Victims of Abuse by Priests," p. 469.
55. One victim of Cardinal Groër described the result of confessing masturbation to him (addressing Groër): "Instead of helping me out of this circular problem, during one confession you took my hand and led it to your penis. With this you whispered in my ear, that God also loves this part of the body" (Hubertus Czernin, *Das Buch Groër: Eine Kirchenchronik* [Vienna: Wieser Verlag, 1998] p. 193).
56. Letter from (name blacked out) to Bishop Leo E. O'Neil, New Hampshire Attorney General's documents, p. 94.
57. Ibid, p. 111. See also p. 241.
58. See Leon J. Podles, *The Church Impotent: The Feminization of Christianity* (Dallas: Spence Publishing, 1999) pp. 102–108.
59. Letter to Bishop O'Neil, p. 95.

60. Sacha Pfeiffer, "He Invoked Religion for Sexual Acts," *Boston Globe*, December 4, 2002.
61. CNN *Insight*: "Catholic Church Rocked by Scandal," aired April 5, 2002.
62. "'I Couldn't Live with Myself': Ex-baseball Star Says Priest Molested Him," abcNEWS.com, Kissimmee, Florida, March 28, 2002.
63. Jim Schaefer, Patricia Montemurri, and Alexa Capeloto, "Tom Paciorek Breaks Silence: Ex-baseball Star: Priest Molested Me," *Detroit Free Press*, March 22, 2002.
64. Ibid.
65. "Church in Crisis: Rev. Louis E. Miller," *Louisville Courier-Journal*, Priest Abuse Project.
66. Ibid.
67. Holley in 1993 pleaded guilty in New Mexico to molesting eight boys and was sentenced to 55 to 275 years in prison; his requests for parole have been denied (Kathleen Shaw, "Rev. Holley Stays in Prison: New Mexico Board Denies Parole for Worcester Priest," *Worcester Telegram and Gazette*, September 18, 2004).
68. Paul Logan, "Later in Life, Ex-altar Boy Recalls Sexual Abuse," *Albuquerque Journal*, April 21, 2002.
69. Al Winn, "Theologians Address Sex Abuse," *Pennsylvania Patriot-News*, September 24, 2003.
70. Jason Berry, "Survivors Connect to Heal, Raise Voices," *National Catholic Reporter*, November 8, 2002.
71. Sheelagh Wegman, "Children Do Not Forget Abuse Says Brisbane Report Author," *The Melbourne Anglican*, August 2002.
72. Mart, "Victims of Abuse by Priests," p. 465.
73. Alan Scher Zagier, "A Priest's Betrayal: A Generation Later, St. Ann Graduates Struggle with Legacy of Abuse," *Naples Daily News*, June 23, 2002.
74. Romero and the diocese were sued and the case was settled (Janine A. Zeitlin, "Cases against Ex-Naples Priest Settled for $1.5 Million," *Naples Daily News*, March 5, 2002).
75. Alan Scher Zagier, "Former Naples, Cape Coral Priests Sued on Sex Abuse Charges by Ex-orphan Ward," *Naples Daily News*, January 23, 2004.
76. Neil Fleming was sued in Miami; the case is pending (Zagier, "Former Naples, Cape Coral Priests Sued on Sex Abuse Charges").
77. Rob Hiaasen, "Priest Abused Him, Says Former Altar Boy," *Baltimore Sun*, April 23, 1995.
78. Debbi Wilgoren, "Two Priests Plead Guilty to Sexually Abusing Boys," *Washington Post*, August 5, 1995.
79. Philadelphia Grand Jury, p. 118.
80. Ibid., p. 119.
81. Ibid., p. 179.
82. Shauris was one of the priests whom Mark D. Barry promised not to sue as part of the settlement of a sexual abuse lawsuit (Richard Nangle and Kathleen A. Shaw, "Priests Named in Sex Abuse Settlement," *Worcester Telegram and Gazette*, February 26, 2002). He is on leave from the priesthood; George Shea received $10,000 from the Worcester diocese as part of a settlement after he accused Shauris and another priest of abuse (Kathleen A. Shaw, "Vatican Decided Not to Defrock Retired Monsignor Battista," *Worcester Telegram and Gazette*, March 10, 2006). There are no criminal

actions against him. Shauris has continued his career as a composer of church music and leader of the Shauris Chorale in Worcester.

83. Kathleen Shaw, "Man Accuses Teacher-Priest of Molestation," *Worcester Telegram and Gazette*, March 27, 2002. The settlement between Mark Barry and Thomas Kane in the 1993 lawsuit provided that Barry would not sue Shauris, who also was not involved in a criminal prosecution (Nangle and Shaw, "Priests Named in Sex Abuse Settlement").
84. Dianne Williamson, "Telling on Priests Not Easy," *Worcester Telegram and Gazette*, March 17, 2002.
85. "Cries for Help Ignored," *Newsday*, March 26, 2002. Vollmer was named in two pending lawsuits against the diocese of Rockville Centre (Jerry Burke, "Three from WH Church Sue over Abuse," *Long Island Herald*, April 24, 2002). He has not been criminally charged.
86. Vollmer was named in lawsuits against the diocese of Rockville Centre (Rita Ciolli, "[Thirty-Four] Sue Diocese for Priest Sex Abuse," *Newsday*, April 15, 2003). Vollmer was suspended from the priesthood and his current whereabouts are unknown. He is not the object of a criminal action.
87. Chuck Haga and Paul McEnroe, "July 19, 1992: Porter Says Life as Pedophile Ended When He Left Priesthood; but His Victims Cannot Forgive or Forget," *Minneapolis Star Tribune*, June 6, 2002.
88. Dorais, *Don't Tell*, p. 69.
89. Bennetts, "Unholy Alliances."
90. The archdiocese wrote to the district attorney: "This action on the part of the Archdiocese should therefore not be considered by your office as in any way seeking the initiation of criminal charges with respect to the material or any activities of Dr. Cinel in relation thereto" (Jon Weiner, "The Porn Prof on Trial: Sex, Lies, and Tenure," *The Nation*, November 8, 1993). Cinel admitted having sex with his accusers but said they were all over seventeen, the age of consent in Louisiana. Cinel was never charged with abuse. He was charged with trafficking in child pornography and was acquitted. Cinel was fired from his professorship at CUNY after his past was discovered, and his scholarly books, which used evidence he had fabricated, were examined (Sebastian Ficera, "The Disturbing Case of Dino Cinel," History News Network, April 28, 2003).
91. Chris Moore, *Betrayal of Trust: The Father Brendan Smyth Affair and the Catholic Church* (Dublin, 1995) p. 133.
92. Ibid.
93. Ibid.
94. Quoted in Barry M. Coldrey, *Religious Life without Integrity: The Sexual Abuse Crisis in the Catholic Church* (Thornbury, Australia: Tamanaraik Press, n. d.) p. 44.
95. Meg Kissinger, "Making Peace with Past: Betrayed and Scarred as a Child by a Parish Priest, a Sexual Abuse Victim Looks Back on His Life," *Milwaukee Journal Sentinel*, April 13, 2002.
96. Edgerton did not sue but received $52,500 from the archdiocese of Milwaukee. Nichols is deceased (Meg Kissinger, "Archdiocese to Pay Abuse Victim: Two Funds Established for Milwaukee Man's College, Living Expenses," *Milwaukee Journal Sentinel*, January 21, 2004).

97. Andrew Wolfson, "Ex-principal Says Priest Given Jobs Despite Sex Claim," *Louisville Courier-Journal,* July 14, 2002.
98. St. John's Abuse Disclosure Project, signed statement of August 26, 1992. Tarlton was included in the settlement with St. John's Abbey (see p. 209). He was not criminally charged.
99. Glenn Gastal, et al. v. Archbishop Philip M. Hannan, et al. 15th Judicial District Court, Parish of Vermilion, State of Louisiana, 84-48175-A. Deposition of Scott Anthony Gastal August 5, 1985, p. 45, 11. 11–21.
100. Philadelphia Grand Jury, p. 107.
101. Gary Bergeron, *Don't Call Me a Victim: Faith, Hope and Sexual Abuse in the Catholic Church* (Lowell, Massachusetts: Arc Angel Publishing, 2005) p. 225.
102. David France, *Our Fathers: The Secret Life of the Catholic Church in an Age of Scandal* (New York: Broadway Books, 2004) p. 332.
103. Michael Newton, "Father James Porter: Pedophile Priest," www.crimelibrary.com/serial11/porter/
104. Archdiocese of Boston, Gerard Creighton personnel file, 2-426 to 2-429.
105. Philadelphia Grand Jury, p. 328.
106. Ibid., p. 331.
107. Ibid., p. 335.
108. Newton, "Father James Porter."
109. Robin Washington, "Some Priests Allegedly Abused Confession Info," *Boston Herald,* July 1, 2002.
110. "Sex Abuse Scandal Emerges," abclocal.go.com, July 12, 2003.
111. Peter Smith, "Five More Lawsuits Say Priest Molested Boys; Men Accuse Louisville Archdiocese of Failing to Report Years of Abuse," *Louisville Courier-Journal,* May 5, 2002.
112. Elizabeth Hamilton and Eric Rich, "Egan Protected Abusive Priests," *Hartford Courant,* March 17, 2002.
113. Philadelphia Grand Jury, p. 322.
114. Kathleen A. Shaw, "Rape by Priest Alleged in Latest Suit," *Worcester Telegram and Gazette,* May 14, 2002.
115. In the 1970s Kelley had told Cardinal Medeiros of his sexual interest in young girls. Kelley pleaded guilty to child rape (Kathleen A. Shaw, "Tape Says Kelley Confided in Medeiros," *Worcester Telegram and Gazette,* August 15, 2003).
116. Philadelphia Grand Jury, p. 130.
117. Ibid., p. 135.
118. Malcolm Gay, "Immaculate Deception: Some Dirty Little Secrets Followed Archbishop Raymond Burke from Wisconsin to St. Louis," *Riverfront Times,* August 25, 2004. Garthwaite was not prosecuted.
119. Zagier, "A Priest's Betrayal."
120. "Former Altar Boy Files Lawsuit against Suburban Priest," NBC5.com, December 4, 2003. Bishop Imesch transferred Lenczycki out of town in 1985 when the allegations began. Lenczycki was convicted of abuse and jailed (Megan Riechgott, "Ill[inois] Seeks to Commit Sex Offender," *Syracuse Post-Standard,* April 11, 2002).
121. Frank Bruni and Elinor Burkett, *A Gospel of Shame: Children, Sexual Abuse, and the Catholic Church* (New York: HarperCollins Publishers, Perennial, 2002) p. 33.

122. Michael Rezendes and Sacha Pfeiffer, "New Files Show Cardinal Acting on Seven Abuse Cases," *Boston Globe*, December 10, 2002. The Archdiocese of Boston was sued because of Conte's abuse; it settled out of court for $195,000. Conte admitted sharing a bed with the boy but denied sexually abusing him. Conte does not seem to have been the object of criminal prosecution. He was defrocked in 2005.
123. Dennis O'Brien, "Arundel Couple's Lawsuit Alleges Priest Molested Son," *Baltimore Sun*, March 22, 1988, p. B3.
124. Dennis Gaboury and Elinor Burkett, "The Secret of St. Mary's," *Rolling Stone*, November 11, 1993, p. 49.
125. Jennifer Jacobs, "Priest Abuse Victim Pleads for Full Disclosure," *Syracuse Post-Standard*, January 17, 2004; Renee K. Gadoua, "Accuser Calls Report a 'Baby Step,'" *Syracuse Post-Standard*, January 7, 2004. Bailey describes his abuse and the effects it had on him and his family in Charles L. Bailey, Jr., *The Shadow of the Cross: The True Account of My Childhood Sexual and Ritual Abuse at the Hands of a Roman Catholic Priest* (New York: iUniverse, Inc., 2006).
126. David Crary, "Priests' Victims Feel Great Sense of Betrayal," *Telegram*, February 24, 2002.
127. Haga and McEnroe, "Porter Says Life as Pedophile Ended When He Left Priesthood."
128. Clark was convicted of molestation in 1988 and again in 2003 (Peter Smith, "Priest Sentenced for Sexual Abuse," *Louisville Courier-Journal*, August 14, 2003).
129. Andrew Wolfson, "Priest to Go on Trial in Sex-Abuse Case: Clark Was Convicted in 1988 of Molesting Two Boys in Bullitt," *Louisville Courier-Journal*, June 23, 2003.
130. Investigator Anthony Fowler interview with (name blacked out—but on p. 7284 identified as "Robert Langlois Interview"). September 18, 2002, NHAG p. 7292.
131. "Alleged Victims Say the Incidents Altered Lives: Comprehensive Look at Lawsuits against Diocese Shows Many Similarities," *Louisville Courier-Journal*, Priest Abuse Project.
132. Ibid.
133. "Church in Crisis: Rev. Louis E. Miller," *Louisville Courier-Journal*.
134. "Church in Crisis: Rev. Daniel C. Clark," *Louisville Courier-Journal*.
135. "Church in Crisis: Rev. Arthur L. Wood," *Louisville Courier-Journal*. Wood (deceased 1983) was named by thirty-nine plaintiffs in a lawsuit that the Archdiocese of Louisville settled (Peter Smith and Andrew Wolfson, "Louisville Attorney Sues the Vatican," *Louisville Courier-Journal*, June 6, 2004).
136. Gaboury and Burkett, "The Secret of St. Mary's," p. 49.
137. William C. Holmes and Gail B. Slap, "Sexual Abuse of Boys: Definition, Prevalence, Correlates, Sequelae, and Management," *Journal of the American Medical Association*, Vol. 280, No. 21 (December 2, 1998) p. 1858.
138. Gaboury and Burkett, "The Secret of St. Mary's," p. 49.
139. Linda Matchan, "Ex-priest's Victims Tell of the Damage," *Boston Globe*, June 8, 1992.
140. Richard B. Gartner, *Betrayed as Boys: Psychodynamic Treatment of Sexually Abused Men* (New York: The Guilford Press, 1999) p. 30.
141. Patrick J. Carnes, *The Betrayal Bond: Breaking Free of Exploitative Relationships* (Deerfield, Florida: Health Communications, Inc., 1997) p. 15.
142. Philadelphia Grand Jury, p. 180.
143. Richard B. Gartner discusses the concept of dissociation in a nonacademic way in

*Beyond Betrayal: Taking Charge of Your Life after Boyhood Sexual Abuse* (Hoboken, New Jersey: John Wiley and Sons, 2005) pp. 54–72. He gives a simple definition: "*Dissociation* is the opposite of *association*. It means to sever or disconnect one set of mental concepts from other sets" (p. 54).

144. Mic Hunter, *Abused Boys: The Neglected Victims of Sexual Abuse* (New York: Fawcett Books, 1990) p. 61. See also pp. 66–69.
145. John N. Briere, *Child Abuse Trauma: Theory and Treatment of the Lasting Effects* (Newbury Park, California: Sage Publications, Inc., 1992) p. 36.
146. "'I Couldn't Live with Myself,'" abcNEWS.com, Kissimmee, Florida.
147. Logan, "Later in Life, Ex-altar Boy Recalls Sexual Abuse."
148. Czernin, *Das Buch Groër*, p. 74.
149. See Briere, *Child Abuse Trauma*, pp. 39–40. Some doubt that memories of sexual abuse can be repressed. But according to one study, "After seventeen years, 38 percent of women whose hospital records show they had been abused as children remembered neither the abuse nor the medical treatment they had received for it" (Donnel B. Stearn, "Discussion: Dissociation and Constructivism," in Richard B. Gartner, editor, *Memories of Sexual Betrayal: Truth, Fantasy, Repression, and Dissociation* [Northvale, New Jersey: Jason Aronson Inc., 1997], p. 77).
150. www.whitehousedrugpolicy.gov/publications/factsht/rohypnol/
151. Philadelphia Grand Jury, p. 206.
152. Ibid., p. 184.
153. Frank L. Fitzpatrick, "Isolation and Silence: A Male Survivor Speaks Out about Clergy Abuse," www.movingforward.org/v3nl-firstperson.html.
154. Ibid.
155. The Report of the Working Party of the British Psychological Society, "Recovered Memories," in *The Recovered Memory / False Memory Debate*, edited by Kathy Pezdek and William P. Banks (San Diego: Academic Press, 1996) p. 381.
156. Mendel, *The Male Survivor*, p. 75.
157. Ibid., p. 76.
158. Richard Nangle, "New Circles of Tragedy Follow Sexual Abuse," *Worcester Telegram and Gazette*, March 10, 2002.
159. Gill Donovan, "Priest Says He Also Was a Victim of Clerical Abuse," *National Catholic Reporter*, January 17, 2003. Hands was convicted and jailed; Ribaudo, who has not been the object of civil or criminal actions, denied abusing Hands, but indirectly confirmed he was "Priest O" in the Rockville Centre Grand Jury Report (Rita Colli, "Monsignor Denies Abuse Allegations: Defends Himself in 'Open Letter' to Friends," *Newsday*, March 12, 2003).
160. Gaboury and Burkett, "The Secret of St. Mary's," p. 87.
161. Philadelphia Grand Jury, p. 158.
162. Freda Briggs and Russell M. F. Hawkins, "A Comparison of the Childhood Experiences of Convicted Male Child Molesters and Men Who Were Sexually Abused in Childhood and Claimed to Be Nonoffenders," *Child Abuse and Neglect*, Vol. 20, No. 3, p. 230.
163. Ibid., p. 232.
164. Cannon, "Victims of 'Fathers.'"
165. Hiaasen, "Priest Abused Him, Says Former Altar Boy."
166. Jay Lindsay, "Change Is Little Comfort to Some," *Worcester Telegram and Gazette*,

December 15, 2002.

167. "Alleged Victims Say the Incidents Altered Lives," *Louisville Courier-Journal*, Priest Abuse Project.
168. Cannon, "Victims of 'Fathers,'" p. 13A.
169. "'I Couldn't Live with Myself,'" abcNEWS.com, Kissimmee, Florida.
170. Jim Schaefer and Alexa Capeloto, "Stories of Broken Victims Lie Behind Catholic Summit," *Detroit Free Press*, April 23, 1992.
171. Luz Delgado, "Two Defend Coverage of Ex-priest: Porter Accusers Say It Helped Them Cope," *Boston Globe,* May 25, 1992.
172. Linda Matchan, "Town Secret," *Boston Globe*, August 29, 1993.
173. Judith Lewis Herman, *Trauma and Recovery* (New York: Basic Books, 1992, 1997) pp. 38–39, 238.
174. Carnes, *The Betrayal Bond*, p. 35. For a full account of this and similar incidents, see Dee L. R. Graham, with Edna I. Rawlings and Roberta K. Rigsby, *Loving to Survive: Sexual Terror, Men's Violence, and Women's Lives* (New Yor: New York University Press, 1994), pp. 1–19.
175. Ibid., p. 29.
176. Herman, *Trauma and Recovery*, p. 92.
177. Thomas Doyle calls this religious duress. See his "Roman Catholic Clericalism, Religious Duress, and Clergy Sexual Abuse," *Pastoral Psychology*, Vol. 51, No. 32, (January 2003) especially pp. 222–227.
178. Graham, *Loving to Survive*, p. 273.
179. Briggs and Hawkins, "A Comparison of the Childhood Experiences of Convicted Male Child Molesters and Men Who Were Sexually Abused in Childhood and Claimed to Be Nonoffenders," p. 222.
180. Ibid., p. 227.
181. Ibid., p. 230.
182. Ibid.
183. Ibid., p. 227.
184. Ibid., p. 226.
185. Shirilla was sued in Michigan in 1997 (AP, "Priest's Statement Permits Abuse Case Despite Time Lag," March 4, 1997). He was removed from the priesthood in March 2002, after Paciorek's accusations, and died in 2004.
186. Schaefer, Montemurri, and Capeloto, "Tom Paciorek Breaks Silence."
187. Ibid.
188. Bea O'Quinn Dewberry, "Bishop Dupré Accusers Tell Lurid Tale," *Springfield Republican*, February 20, 2004.
189. Quoted in Kenneth Jost, "Child Sexual Abuse in the Catholic Church: An Overview" in Louise I. Gerdes, *Child Sexual Abuse in the Catholic Church* (San Diego: Greenhaven Press, 2003) p. 17.
190. But in one study of women who had been abused as children, "only 7.5% of the women had reported the abuse to any investigative authority" (Shirley Jülich, "Stockholm Syndrome and Child Sexual Abuse," *Journal of Child Sexual Abuse*, Vol. 14 [3] 2005, p. 108.
191. Jülich writes, "Those survivors who had been subjected to ongoing contact with sexually abusive members within their family or social network . . . seem to be

emotionally bonded to the offender, and this appeared to contribute significantly to their reluctance to criminally report" ("Stockholm Syndrome," p. 109).

192. Gartner, *Betrayed as Boys*, p. 30.
193. Dorais, *Don't Tell*, p. 4.
194. Ibid., p. 18.
195. Mendel, *The Male Survivor*, p. 19.
196. Philadelphia Grand Jury, p. 26.
197. A survey by the gay magazine *Advocate* showed that 21 percent of the respondents had been sexually abused before they were sixteen. See Dorais, *Don't Tell*, p. 18.
198. Mendel, *The Male Survivor*, p. 118.
199. Edward O. Laumann, John H. Gagnon, Robert T. Michael, and Stuart Michaels, *The Social Organization of Sexuality: Sexual Practices in the United States* (Chicago, University of Chicago Press, 1994) p. 344. This study is of boys who were molested prior to age thirteen; the study did not ask the same question about adolescent molestation.
200. John N. Briere wrote that "homosexual men who were sexually abused by males may be convinced that their sexual orientation somehow caused them to be abused by men, or that their abuse caused them to be homosexual—conclusions that can lead to feelings of guilt, shame, and self betrayal" (*Child Sexual Abuse*, p. 157).
201. Julie Bindel, "Gay Men Need to Talk Straight about Paedophila," *The Guardian*, March 3, 2001.
202. Letter of Robert F. Miailovich, "Perspectives on Shanley," *National Catholic Reporter*, February 4, 2005.
203. Thomas Farragher, "Through Kansas Parishes, a Trail of Suicides," *Boston Globe*, July 18, 2002.
204. John Rivera, "Victims Share Stories of Abuse by Priests," *Baltimore Sun*, June 13, 2002.
205. "Alleged Victims Say the Incidents Altered Lives: Comprehensive Look at Lawsuits against Diocese Shows Many Similarities," *Louisville Courier-Journal*, Priest Abuse Project.
206. James Hanley in a deposition said he had admitted the abuse to Bishop Frank Rodimer. Because of the statute of limitations, Hanley was not prosecuted, but Rodimer had settled with Serrano for $350,000 in 1987 (Eugene Mulero, "Ex-Priest: Rodimer Knew about Sexual Abuse; Court Papers Say Bishop Persuaded Victim to Keep Quiet," *Daily Record* [New Jersey], August 27, 2004).
207. Berry, "Survivors Connect to Heal, Raise Voices."
208. Michael Paulson, "Lessons Unlearned: Church Struggle Pains L[ouisian]a region Stung by Abuse in '80s," *Boston Globe*, June 12, 2002.
209. Mart, "Victims of Abuse by Priests," p. 478.
210. Alice Jackson Baughn, "A Victim's Story," *Time*, November 1, 2002.
211. Letter to Bishop O'Neil, p. 102.
212. Herman, *Trauma and Recovery*, p. 113.
213. Bill Zajac, "Abuse Seen as Cause of Suicides," *Springfield Republican*, June 12, 2005.
214. Farragher, "Through Kansas Parishes, a Trail of Suicides." Other studies show rates of suicide among abused males that are "1.5 to 14 times higher" than among nonabused males. See William C. Holmes and Gail B. Slap, "Sexual Abuse of Boys: Definition, Prevalence, Correlates, Sequelae, and Management," *Journal of the American Medical Association*, Vol. 280, No. 21 (December 2, 1998) p. 1858.

215. Scott Shane, "A Personal Tragedy Shows a Crisis within the Church," *Baltimore Sun*, September 5, 1993.
216. Dorais, *Don't Tell*, p. 68.
217. Ibid., p. 85.
218. Philadelphia Grand Jury, p. 322.
219. Delores King, "[Six] More Allege Priest Abused Them in 60s," *Boston Globe*, May 9, 1992.
220. Don Lattin, "Diocese Sued by Siblings," *San Francisco Chronicle*, December 11, 2003.
221. Farragher, "Through Kansas Parishes, a Trail of Suicides."
222. Ibid.
223. Ibid.
224. Tom Mashberg, "Son's Suicide Leaves a Void in Mom's Life," *Boston Herald*, September 20, 2002.
225. Dana Hertneky, "Hervey County Priest Released from Prison," KSN News, April 4, 2006.
226. Stephen Kurkjian and Walter V. Robinson, "Suit Ties Boy's Death to Abuse by Priest," *Boston Globe*, April 11, 2002.
227. Bella English, "'He Was so Angry, Upset, and Ashamed. I Know It Affected His Whole Life," *Boston Globe*, September 18, 2002.
228. Bella English and Don Aucoin, "How Can One Rejoice? Catholics at One Canton Parish Have Begun to Heal, but the Scars of Broken Trust Linger," *Boston Globe*, December 17, 2002.
229. There is no indication that Frost has been the subject of civil lawsuits or criminal prosecution.
230. Bella English, "Kevin McDonough Died of a Drug Overdose Last Year," *Boston Globe*, September 18, 2002.
231. Cannon, "Victims of 'Fathers,'" p. 13A.
232. Ibid.
233. Stephanie Saul, "Alleged Sex Victim Dies; Was Lead Plaintiff in Planned Suit Accusing Priest of Abuse," *Newsday*, September 25, 2003.
234. His identifier in Peter W. Heed, Attorney General, N. William Delkar, Senior Assistant Attorney General, James D. Rosenberg, Assistant Attorney General, "Report on the Investigation of the Diocese of Manchester," (Concord, New Hampshire, March 3, 2002) p. 130ff.
235. Interview of J. McLaughlin of the Keene Police Department with (name blacked out), July 30, 1993, (hence cited as McLaughlin Interview) NHAG documents, p. 10537.
236. Ibid., p. 10536.
237. Ibid., p. 10537.
238. Ibid., p. 10541.
239. McLaughlin Interview, p. 10541.

## 10. Abusers and Their Treatment

1. Adele Meyer writes, "The sex offender no longer is viewed as a criminal whose behavior is 'sinful' or 'bad' and who chooses to act in deviant ways that ultimately are under

his control. Rather, he is seen as ill and in need of medical intervention" (*Sex Offenders: Approaches to Understanding and Management* [Holmes Beach, Florida: Learning Publications, Inc, 1988] p. 79).

2. Fred S. Berlin points out that "*in our society* [my emphasis] to have a pedophilic sexual orientation can create both psychological burdens and impairments" ("When Is a Difference a Disorder?" in "Peer Commentaries on Green [2002] and Schmidt [2002]," *Archives of Sexual Behavior*, Vol. 31, No. 6 [December 2002] p. 480). Vern L. Bullough stated that the pedophile must adapt to new social standards: "rather than demonize the pedophile for what he thinks is his natural inclination, we have to emphasize that what was normative in the past is no longer the case" ("Pedophilia and Sexual Harassment: Do They Have Similarities?" in "Peer Commentaries on Green [2002] and Schmidt [2002]" p. 481).
3. Sigmund Freud, *Introductory Lectures on Psychoanalysis* (London: Allen and Unwin, 1952) p. 266.
4. Robert L. Spitzer and Jerome C. Wakefield, "Why Pedophilia Is a Disorder of Sexual Attraction—At Least Sometimes," in "Peer Commentaries on Green (2002) and Schmidt (2002)," p. 499.
5. Berlin, "When Is a Difference a Disorder?" p. 479.
6. Michael C. Seto wrote in defense of defining pedophilia as sexual interest in prepubertal children: "From a Darwinian perspective, a preference for sexually immature, non-reproductive persons is anomalous, while a preference for sexually mature, potentially reproductive persons, even if they are below the socially or legally prescribed age of availability, is not" ("Precisely Defining Pedophilia" in "Peer Commentaries on Green [2002] and Schmidt [2002]," p. 498).
7. Richard Green pointed out that Seto's comment on pedophilia, "from a Darwinian perspective, a preference for a sexually immature, non-reproductive person is anomalous" would also make homosexuality "anomalous" and a mental disorder ("Rejoinder," *Archives of Sexual Behavior*, Vol. 31, No. 6 [December 2002] p. 505).
8. Ibid.
9. Richard Green, "Is Pedophilia a Mental Disorder?" *Archives of Sexual Behavior*, Vol. 31, No. 6 (December 2002) pp. 467–468.
10. K. Freund and R. Costell, "The Structure of Erotic Preference in the Nondeviant Male," *Behavioral Research and Therapy*, Vol. 8 (1970) pp. 15–20.
11. John Bierne and Marsh Runty, "University Males' Sexual Interest in Children: Predicting Potential Indices for Pedophilia in a Nondeviant Sample," *Child Abuse and Neglect*, Vol. 13 (1989) p. 65. Because of the odium in which pedophilia is usually held, these percentages are probably understatements. They are also much higher than the percentage of men who are homosexual (see p. 332).
12. See Richard Green, "Is Pedophilia a Mental Disorder?" pp. 479–480.
13. George A. Gaither wrote that "clinical evidence suggests that, similar to homosexual or heterosexual orientation, a pedophilic sexual orientation typically begins by early adolescence, tends to be lifelong, and is resistant to change ("Pedophilia as a Sexual Orientation" in "Peer Commentaries on Green [2002] and Schmidt [2002]," p. 485).
14. www.clem.mscd.edu/~norwoodm/drapetomania.htm.
15. Frederick Suppe, "Classifying Sexual Disorder: *The Diagnostic and Statistical Manual*

of the American Psychiatric Association," *Journal of Homosexuality*, Vol. 9, p. 26.

16. Julia A. Erickson, "Understanding Pedophilia" in "Peer Commentary on Green (2002) and Schmidt (2002)," p. 483.
17. Philip Lee, "Convicted Newfoundland Priest Holds High Position in Toronto," *Sunday Express*, November 19, 1989, p. 3. For more about Kelly, see "Fatherly Treatment" in Michael Harris's *Unholy Orders: Tragedy at Mount Cashel* (Markham, Ontario: Viking, 2000) pp. 186–212.
18. This approach to morality has difficulty in dealing either morally or legally with cases in which adults consent to acts that harm them. These acts range from prostitution to anonymous, unprotected bathhouse sex to cannibalism. In 2002, Armin Miewes of Germany met a fellow homosexual and cannibal on the Internet. With the victim's consent Miewes killed and ate the victim. Miewes was convicted only of assisting suicide, which is still illegal in Germany.
19. Gunter Schmidt admitted that this condemnation of adult-child sex based on lack of full, informed consent between equals "does not apply to all ages and all cultures but instead to a very limited social and temporal spectrum: the late modern, postfeminist industrial societies of the West" ("Reply: Is There Nothing Special about Adult-Child Sex?" *Archives of Sexual Behavior*, Vol. 31, No. 6 [December 2002], p. 509). But of course this society is not static, and presumably can rapidly change into one in which adult-child sex is allowed, as pedophiles and pederasts hope.
20. Richard C. Friedman holds that "the fact that trauma may occur as a result of inequalities that are inherent in sexual activity between adults and children is an important reason that the acts are...morally unacceptable. The notion that such activity must necessarily be injurious in every case is not necessary in order to reach this conclusion" ("Pedophilia: Morality and Psychopathology" in "Peer Commentaries on Green [2002] and Schmidt [2002]," p. 484).
21. Gary Richard Schoener, "Historical Overview" in John C. Gonsiorek, editor, *Breach of Trust: Sexual Exploitation by Health Care Professionals and Clergy* (Thousand Oaks, California: Sage Publications, 1995) p. 5.
22. Nanette K. Gartrell, Nancy Milliken, William H. Goodson III, Sue Thierman, and Bernard Lo, "Physician-Patient Sexual Contact, Prevalence and Problems" in Gonsiorek, *Breach of Trust*, p. 24.
23. Joel Friedman and Marcia Mobilia Boumil, *Betrayal of Trust: Sex and Power in Personal Relationship* (Westport, Connecticut: Praeger, 1995) p. xi.
24. Dr. Leon Hoffman, "The Priest Scandal Isn't Just about Sex: Violation of Trust and Abuse of Authority Are Keys to Pedophilia," *Newsday*, April 14, 2002.
25. Anthony Storr, *Feet of Clay: Saints, Sinners and Madmen: A Study of Gurus* (New York: Free Press, 1997) p. 97.
26. Kenneth S. Pope, Barbara G. Tabachnick, and Patricia Keith-Spiege, "Sexual Attraction to Clients: The Human Therapist and the (Sometimes) Inhuman Training System," www.kspope.com/sexiss/research5.php#copy.
27. Nils C. Friberg and Mark R. Laaser, *Before the Fall: Preventing Pastoral Sexual Abuse* (Collegeville, Minnesota: Liturgical Press, 1998) p. vii.
28. Stephen J. Grenz and Roy D. Bell, *Betrayal of Trust: Confronting and Preventing Clergy Sexual Misconduct* (Grand Rapids, Michigan: Baker Books, 2001) p. 25.
29. Marie Fortune, "Is Nothing Sacred? When Sex Invades the Pastoral Relationship," in

Gonsiorek, *Breach of Trust*, p. 31.

30. James S. Evinger and Dorothea L. Yoder, "Sexual Abuse, Forgiveness, and Justice: A Journey in Faith" in Marie M. Fortune and Joretta L. Marshall, *Forgiveness and Abuse: Jewish and Christian Reflections* (New York: Haworth Pastoral Press, 2002) p. 73.
31. John C. Gonsiorek, "Assessment for Rehabilitation of Exploitative Health Care Professionals and Clergy," in John C. Gonsiorek, editor, *Breach of Trust: Sexual Exploitation by Health Care Professionals and Clergy* (Thousand Oaks, California: Sage Publications, 1995) p. 151.
32. Storr, *Feet of Clay*, pp. xiv–xv.
33. Ibid.
34. Ibid., pp. xiv–xv.
35. Letter of Paul Aube to Bishop Leo E. O'Neil, September 18, 1993, documents released by New Hampshire Attorney General's Office (henceforth NHAGO) p. 2875.
36. Ibid., p. 57.
37. Ibid.
38. Interview of New Hampshire Attorney General's Office with Paul Aube, August 14, 2002, NHAGO, p. 4804.
39. Ibid., p. 4806.
40. Ibid., p. 4812.
41. Ibid., p. 6513.
42. Ibid., p. 4814.
43. Ibid., p. 4836.
44. Ibid.
45. Ibid., pp. 4873–4874.
46. Ibid., p. 4874.
47. Ibid., p. 4875.
48. Ibid., p. 4855.
49. Ibid., p. 4865.
50. Investigator Anthony Fowler interview with (name blacked out—but on p. 7284 identified as "Robert Langlois Interview"), September 18, 2002, NHAGO, p. 7288.
51. A word on terminology: the literature is not consistent in its use of words. Sometimes psychopathology and sociopathology are used interchangeably to name the condition of a person who has no conscience, but I am distinguishing them. Psychopathology is the broader term, indicating an illness of the psyche or mind; sociopathology is the narrower term, indicating a person whose conscience is far less sensitive than the normal person's. Empathy is the ability to understand the emotions that another person is feeling; it is the broader term. Sympathy is the ability to feel the pain that another person is feeling; it is the narrower term. Some psychologists use them in the opposite way, so caveat lector.
52. Charles A. Weisberger, "Survey of a Psychological Screening Program in a Clerical Order," in Vincent V. Herr, Magda B. Arnold, Charles A. Weisberger, and Paul F. D'Arcy, *Screening Candidates for the Priesthood and Religious Life* (Chicago: Loyola University Press, 1964) p. 121.
53. Charles A. Weisberger, quoted in William D. Perri, *A Radical Challenge for the Priesthood Today: Can It Survive?* (Mystic, Connecticut: Twenty-Third Publications, 1996) p. 55.

54. Vincent V. Herr, "Selecting Seminarians," in Herr, Arnold, Weisberger, and D'Arcy, p. 96.
55. Perri, p. 54.
56. Ashbel S. Green, "A Priest's Confession: Three Decades after Father Thomas Loughlin Abused Dozens of Boys, the Once Powerful Priest Returned This Week to Face His Victims," *The Oregonian*, March 13, 2005. Laughlin was convicted of abuse and jailed (Gordon Oliver, "Sex Abuse Sparks Program," *National Catholic Reporter*, September 23, 1983).
57. An excellent discussion of narcissism using the Aristotelian concept of the Golden Mean is Michael H. Stone's "Normal Narcissism," in *Disorders of Narcissism: Diagnostic, Clinical, and Empirical Implications*, edited by Elsa F. Ronningstam (Northvale, New Jersey: Jason Aronson, Inc., 2000) pp. 7–28.
58. Ibid., p. 15.
59. Otto F. Kernberg, "Pathological Narcissism and Narcissistic Personality Disorder: Theoretical Background and Diagnostic Classification," in *Disorders of Narcissism*, p. 35.
60. Arnold M. Cooper, "Further Developments in the Clinical Diagnosis of Narcissistic Personality Disorder," in *Disorders of Narcissism*, pp. 58–60.
61. Theodore Millon, "DSM Narcissistic Personality Disorder: Historical Reflections and Future Directions," in *Disorders of Narcissism*, p. 92.
62. Sam Vaknin, *Malignant Self Love: Narcissism Revisited* (Prague: Narcissus Publications, 2002) p. 19.
63. Ibid., pp. 19–20.
64. Arlene B. Brewster, "Clergy Sexual Misconduct: The Affair Everyone Remembers," *Pastoral Psychology*, Vol. 44, No. 6 (1996) p. 354. Narcissism is a big problem among religious workers: "The reality is that individuals with a narcissistic pattern are attracted to ministries, particularly high-visibility ministries and positions of leadership. Furthermore, narcissistic ministers are becoming increasingly common in religious organizations, including parishes, religious communities of men and women, and in diocesan and other ecclesial offices" (Leo Sperry, *Sex, Priestly Ministry, and the Church* [Collegeville, Minnesota: Liturgical Press, 2003] pp. 88–89).
65. Joseph Cardinal Ratzinger (Pope Benedict XVI), *Salt of the Earth: The Church at the End of the Millennium*, translated by Adrian Walker (San Francisco, Ignatius Press, 1997) p. 176.
66. Sperry, p. 99.
67. Brewster, "Clergy Sexual Misconduct," p. 355.
68. Donald Cozzens, *Sacred Silence: Denial and the Crisis in the Church* (Collegeville, Minnesota: Liturgical Press, 2002) p. 105.
69. Storr, p. 211.
70. Sperry, p. 95.
71. Richard N. Ostling, "Vatican, U. S. Bishops May Be at Odds," Associated Press, May 22, 2002.
72. Court of Common Pleas, First Judicial District of Pennsylvania, Criminal Trial Division, Misc. no. 03-00-239, Report of the Grand Jury, p.300. Henceforth Philadelphia Grand Jury.
73. Amy Hammel-Zabin, *Conversations with a Pedophile: In the Interest of Our Children* (Fort Lee, New Jersey: Barricade Press, 2003) p. 33.

74. Ibid., p. 35.
75. Ibid.
76. Ibid.
77. Ibid., pp. 35–36.
78. Ibid., p. 68.
79. Ibid., p. 69.
80. Ibid., p. 136.
81. Ibid., p. 114.
82. Ibid., p. 131.
83. G. T. Blanshard, "Sexually Abusive Clergymen: A Conceptual Framework for Intervention and Recovery," *Pastoral Psychology*, vol. 39 (1991) p. xxx.
84. Curtis Bryant, "Psychological Treatment of Priest Sex Offenders," in Thomas G. Plante, editor, *Bless Me Father for I Have Sinned: Perspectives on Sexual Abuse Committed by Roman Catholic Priests* (Westport, Connecticut: Praeger, 1998) p. 94.
85. Letter of Francis J. Schenk, Bishop of Duluth, "To Any Catholic Bishop," January 28, 1966.
86. Curtis Bryant observed that "priests, steeped in ritual, scrupulously follow ritual in their sexual escapades" ("Psychological Treatment of Priest Sex Offenders," in Plante, *Bless Me Father*, p. 95). But all pedophiles tend to be ritualistic.
87. Stephen J. Rossetti, *A Tragic Grace: The Catholic Church and Child Sexual Abuse* (Collegeville, Minnesota: The Liturgical Press, 1996) p. 74.
88. A. W. Richard Sipe, *Sex, Priests and Power: Anatomy of a Crisis* (New York: Brunner / Mazel Publishers, 1995) p. 12.
89. Ryan E. Melsky wrote, "By identifying with their aggressors, assuming their attributes, and imitating their aggression, crime victims cognitively transform themselves from the people threatened into those making the threat. This mental transformation allows the victim to achieve some feeling of strength in an otherwise humiliating situation" (*CPI Newsletter* at www.crisisprevention.com).
90. Paul J. Iseley, "Sexual Abuse and the Catholic Church: An Historical and Contemporary Review," *Pastoral Psychology*, Vol. 45, No. 4 (1997) p. 294.
91. *John Jay Report*, p. 45. The report continues with a caution: "unless a priest self-disclosed his own prior abuse or it had been specifically raised as an issue, there might not have been an indication of abuse in Church files."
92. Thomas Szasz, "The Psychiatrist as Accomplice," *Washington Times*, April 28, 2002.
93. Matt Carroll, "Director of Milton Rehabilitation Center Faces Abuse Charges," *Boston Globe*, July 19, 2002. No civil suits or criminal charges against Beale or Kelley resulted.
94. Sacha Pfeiffer, "Treatment Center for Priest Called Site of Abuse," *Boston Globe*, March 20, 2002.
95. John Allan Loftus and Robert J. Canargom, "Treating the Clergy," *Annals of Sex Research*, Vol. 6 (1993) p. 300.
96. Canice Connors, "Rebuilding Trust: Clergy Sexual Abuse," *Church*, Summer 1993.
97. Barry Werth, "Fathers' Helper: How the Church Used Psychiatry to Care for—and Protect—Abusive Priests," *New Yorker*, June 9, 2003.
98. Eric Rich and Elizabeth Hamilton, "Doctors: Church Used Us," *Hartford Courant*, March 24, 2002.

99. Ibid.
100. Werth, "Fathers' Helper."
101. Ibid.
102. Ibid.
103. Jay Nelson, "Mysteries Remain a Decade after NM Priest Scandals," *Albuquerque Tribune*, May 8, 2002.
104. Dennis Domrzalski, "Priest Told Bishops in the '60s That Paraclete Had Problems," *Albuquerque Tribune*, May 15, 1993, A8.
105. Eileen Welsome, "Church Knew of Porter's 'Boy Trouble,'" *Albuquerque Tribune*, January 7, 1993, A1.
106. Nancy Plevin, "Therapist Says He Warned Church: He Said He Told Paraclete to Keep Priests from Kids," *Albuquerque Tribune*, February 19, 1993, A3.
107. Eileen Welsome, "Founder Didn't Want Molesters at Paraclete," *Albuquerque Tribune*, April 2, 1993, pp. A 1–9.
108. Ibid., p. A 9.
109. Eileen Welsome, "Island Exile for Priests Once Proposed," *Albuquerque Tribune*, March 12, 1993, p. A1.
110. Eileen Welsome, "'Program' Sent Molesters into Churches, Lawsuit Says," *Albuquerque Tribune*, March 3, 1993, p. xxx.
111. Welsome, "Island Exile for Priests Once Proposed," A7.
112. John A. Hardon, S.J., *A Prophet for the Priesthood: A Spiritual Autobiography of Father Gerald M. C. Fitzgerald* (Bardstown, Kentucky: Eternal Life, 1998) p. 148.
113. Letter from Rev. Peter Lechner, s. P to author, March 13, 2004.
114. Ron Russell, "Camp Ped," *Los Angeles New Times*, August 15, 2002.
115. Welsome, "Island Exile for Priests Once Proposed."
116. Reese Dunklin, "Convicted Priest Helped Abusers Stay in Ministry," *Dallas Morning News*, July 13, 2002.
117. Brooks Egerton, "DA Refuses to Pursue Ex-priest: 1960 Murder Case Remains Unresolved Despite New Witnesses," *Dallas Morning News*, November 20, 2004.
118. "Convicted Priest Helped Abusers Stay in Ministry: After Assault, He Supervised Clerics at Treatment Center," *Dallas Morning News*, July 13, 2002.
119. Howard Chua-Eoan, "After the Fall," *Time*, May 9, 1994.
120. Elinor Burkett and Frank Bruni, *A Gospel of Shame: Children, Sexual Abuse, and the Catholic Church* (New York: Viking, 1993) p. 196.
121. Eileen Welsome, "Treatment Center Chucks Priest Files," *Albuquerque Tribune*, January 8, 1993, A1.
122. Kane's account of the founding of The House of Affirmation omits any mention of Baars. See Thomas A. Kane, *The Healing Touch of Affirmation* (Whitinsville, Massachusetts: Affirmation Books, 1976) pp. 92–93.
123. Conrad W. Baars, *Feeling and Healing Your Emotions* (Gainesville, Florida: Bridge-Logos, 1979) p. 235.
124. Paul Della Valle wrote: "When the story of Kane's alleged fiscal misdeeds first broke in the *Telegram & Gazette* in September 1987, Kane owned an inn in Islesboro, Maine (he sold that for $650,000 before the settlement), a farm in Islesboro (he sold that to actress Kirstie Alley this spring), three condominiums in Boston in total worth more than $200,000, two condos in Florida worth more than $120,000, a home in

Whitinsville worth $98,700 and at least several other properties in this and other states. Kane also had a major interest in trusts that owned a condominium building at 398 Marlboro St., Boston, valued in 1987 at $720,000, and in properties on St. Stephen Street and Symphony Road, Boston, then with a total value of more than $700,000" ("[Five] Years Later, Rev. T. Kane Teaches Ethics: House of Affirmation Scandal," *Worcester Sunday Telegram*, June 21, 1992).

125. Robin Washington, "Experts See Psych Text as Priest Abuse Primer," *Boston Herald*, February 13, 2002.
126. Jeanne Pugh, "Counseling Program for Catholic Clergy Faces Uncertain Future," *St. Petersburg Times*, September 26, 1987.
127. Kathleen A. Shaw, "Priest May Have Lied about Ph.D.," *Worcester Telegram and Gazette*, February 10, 2002.
128. George B. Griffin, "Bishop Places Rev. Kane on Leave: Priest Subject of Claim of Sex Abuse," *Worcester Telegram and Gazette*, April 24, 1993.
129. Kathleen A. Shaw, "Suit Claims Priests Ran Sex Ring," *Worcester Telegram and Gazette*, July 24, 2002. Blizard was found innocent of assault and battery on August 14, 2004 ("Worcester DA John Conte, 0; Worcester Clergy, 2," www.conte2006.com, August 30, 2004). In 1988 Frobas had been convicted in Missouri and jailed for molestation; he was indicted in Massachusetts for molestation but died before trial ("Frobas Case 'Painfully Common,'" *Worcester Telegram and Gazette*, March 12, 2003).
130. Ibid. Placa is "Priest F" of the Rockville Centre grand jury report.
131. Teczar was convicted in Texas of giving alcohol to a minor who said Teczar then abused him (AP, "Documents Detail Suspicion of Priest's Abuse," *Paris* [Texas] *News*, June 5, 2005). He lost a civil suit in Massachusetts (Kathleen A. Shaw, "Jury Rules Teczar Committed Abuse," *Worcester Telegram and Gazette*, October 4, 2002). Apart from the Worcester settlement, no other suits or charges have been filed against Shauris and Riordan.
132. Kathleen A. Shaw and Richard Nangle, "Accused Priest in Mexico," *Worcester Telegram and Gazette*, February 7, 2002.
133. Richard Nangle, "Priest's Name Removed from Site," *Worcester Telegram and Gazette*, February 13, 2002.
134. Robin Washington, "'Missing' Priest Still Gets Church Checks," *Boston Herald*, February 12, 2002.
135. For more information on the House of Affirmation, see Jason Berry, *Lead Us Not into Temptation: Catholic Priests and the Sexual Abuse of Children* (Urbana, Illinois: University of Illinois Press, 2000) p. 239.
136. Berry, *Lead Us Not into Temptation*, p. 239.
137. For more on Michael Peterson's problems, see Berry, *Lead Us Not into Temptation*, pp. 39, 56–59.
138. Ibid., p. 241.
139. Leslie Payne, "Salt for Their Wounds," *Catholic World Report*, February 1997.
140. BostonHerald.com, "Trail of Abuse: Rev. Paul J. Mahan."
141. Tom Mashberg, "Court Papers Show Law Told Pedophile Priest 'Untreatable,'" *Boston Herald*, August 23, 2002.
142. Payne, "Salt for Their Wounds."

143. Stephen J. Rossetti, *A Tragic Grace: The Catholic Church and Child Sexual Abuse* (Collegeville: Liturgical Press, 1996) p. xx.
144. Michael Paulson, "Possible Law Successor Decries Secrecy," *Boston Globe*, March 29, 2003.
145. Stephen J. Rossetti, "The Catholic Church and Child Sex Abuse," *America*, April 22, 2002, p. 9.
146. Isely, "Sexual Abuse and the Church," p. 291.
147. Ellen Barry, "Priest Treatment Unfolds in Costly, Secretive World," *Boston Globe*, April 3, 2002.
148. Deposition of Ned Cassem, M.D., at Greenberg Traurig, May 20–21, 2003, p. 38. The deposition and other documents pertaining to Cassem can be found at www.parcc.org.
149. Robin Washington, "Shrink-Priest Blasted Clergy, Victim without Meeting Them," *Boston Herald*, May 8, 2003.
150. Associated Press, "Psychiatrist Blasts Boston Archdiocese," *Tacoma New Tribune*, September 7, 2003.
151. Tom Mashberg, Eric Convey, and Robin Washington, "MGH Psychiatrists Being Investigated in Priest Abuse Scandal," *Boston Herald*, September 6, 2003.
152. Foster was eventually exonerated and the suit against him was dropped (Walter V. Robinson, "Church Clears Foster of Abuse: Monsignor to Regain Job as Canon Lawyer," *Boston Globe*, September 12, 2002).
153. Affidavit of Ned Cassem in the case of Paul R. Edwards v. Michael Smith Foster and the Archdiocese of Boston, available at www.parcc.org.
154. Letter from Ned Cassem to Sean Connor, October 17, 2002, available at www.parcc.org.
155. The grand jury concluded that "he and his aides made a mockery of evaluations and therapy to avoid reaching these diagnoses," Philadelphia Grand Jury, p. 45.
156. Ibid., p. 46.
157. Andrew Greeley, "Both Sides Wrong on Church Abuse," *Chicago Sun-Times*, March 12, 2004.

## *11. Abusers and Homosexuality*

1. Available at www.vatican.va.
2. "In the 1970s, as roughly one hundred Americans left the priesthood every month, most of them to marry, the proportions of homosexuals among men remaining in the ministry escalated. By the mid-eighties, the cultural dynamics of a gay world took hold in rectories, religious orders, and many seminaries" (Jason Berry, *Vows of Silence: The Abuse of Power in the Papacy of John Paul II* [New York: Free Press, 2004] p. 33).
3. Howard P. Bleichner, *View from the Altar: Reflections on the Rapidly Changing Catholic Priesthood* (New York: Crossroad Publishing Company, 2004) p. 40.
4. Eric Convey, "Priest Scandal: Issue of Gay Priests a Recurring Theme in Sex Scandal," *Boston Herald*, April 24, 2002.
5. Donald Cozzens, *The Changing Face of the Priesthood: A Reflection on the Priest's Crisis of Soul* (Collegeville, Minnesota: Liturgical Press, 2000) p. 100.

6. George Weigel, *The Courage to Be Catholic: Crisis, Reform and the Future of the Church* (New York: Basic Books, 2002) p. 150.
7. The University of San Diego is run by the Jesuits. The homosexual Jesuit Patrick M. Arnold wrote *Warriors, Wildmen and Kings: Masculine Spirituality and the Bible* (New York: Crossroad, 1991). He taught at the University of San Diego and died of AIDS (Judy L. Thomas, "Seminary Taught Spirituality, Liturgy and Latin—Sexuality Was Taboo," *Kansas City Star*, January 30, 2000).
8. Jason Berry, "Survivors Connect to Heal, Raise Voices," *National Catholic Reporter*, November 8, 2002.
9. Ibid.
10. Tim Ryland, "The Cost of Blowing the Whistle: Diocese Settles with Former Seminarian," *San Diego News Notes*, December 1995.
11. Michael S. Rose, *Goodbye! Good Men: How Catholic Seminaries Turned away Two Generations of Vocations from the Priesthood* (Cincinnati: Aquinas Publishing Ltd., 2002). See especially Chapter 4, "The Gay Subculture."
12. The peculiarities of this cardinal are an open secret and are known to the Vatican (a friend of mine reported him). Paul E. Dinter, one-time chaplain at Columbia University, also knows this prelate: "One now prominent churchman, as a young bishop, would invite groups of student priests to his country place. When they arrived, he would assign each a guest bed but would invariably run one short. The last guy, the bishop's pick, would be told, 'Well, I guess you get to sleep with your bishop,' to the nervous laughter of the group" (*The Other Side of the Altar: One Man's Life in the Catholic Priesthood* [New York: Farrar, Straus and Giroux, 2003] pp. 72–73). This bishop explained to the Vatican that he has adopted the European custom of sharing a bed, and uptight Americans insisted on misunderstanding a perfectly innocent custom.
13. Christopher Schiavone, with Janice Page, "Broken Vows: A Former Catholic Priest Speaks Out about Secrecy, Scandal, and Being Gay in the Church," *Boston Globe*, December 8, 2002.
14. Leonard Greene and John Lehmann, "Critics See 'Gay Bullying' at Seminaries," *New York Post*, March 23, 2002.
15. Hanna Rosin, "At Seminary, Unease over Gay Priests," *Washington Post*, July 21, 2003.
16. Annabel Miller, "This Endangered Species," *The Tablet*, April 24, 1999.
17. Paul Valley, "Catholic Church Alarmed that Priesthood Is Becoming a 'Gay Profession,'" *Independent*, May 1, 2001.
18. David France, *Our Fathers: The Secret Life of the Catholic Church in an Age of Scandal* (New York: Broadway Books, 2004).
19. Stephanie Barry, "Accused Clergy Had Influential Posts," *Springfield Republican*, March 1, 2004. Huller and Welch are deceased; Bishop Dupré removed Meehan, Lavelle, and Kennedy from the ministry; Welch, Kennedy, Meehan, and Lavelle were included in a settlement with the diocese of Springfield (Bill Zajac, "Eighteen Priests Named in Settlement," *Springfield Republican*, August 17, 2004).
20. Bill Zajac, "Priest, Bishop at Odds," *Springfield Republican*, October 29, 2003.
21. Patrick McGee, "Ex-bishop Doesn't Regret Hiring Priests," *Dallas-Fort Worth Star-Telegram*, July 9, 2002.

22. Chuck Colbert, "Rome's No Doesn't Stop Mass at New Ways Conference; Ministry Marks 25 Years of Service to Gays, Lesbians," *National Catholic Reporter*, March 22, 2002. Colbert, a reporter for the *National Catholic Reporter*, disrupted a Mass when the celebrant criticized same-sex marriage and has announced his intention to marry his long-term male partner.
23. Allyson Smith, "Confab Pushes Homosexuality in Church," WorldNetDaily.com, March 17, 2002.
24. Cozzens, p. 99.
25. Eugene Kennedy, *The Unhealed Wound: The Church and Human Sexuality* (New York: St. Martin's Press, 2001) p. 136.
26. Cozzens, p. 107. He shares the perception "that the priesthood is or is becoming a gay profession."
27. Peter McDonough, Peter and Eugene C. Bianchi, *Passionate Uncertainty: Inside the American Jesuits* (Berkeley: University of California Press, 2002) p. 261.
28. Larry B. Stammer, "The Times Poll: 15% Identify as Gay or 'On Homosexual Side,'" *Los Angeles Times*, October 20, 2002. A survey of Canadian seminarians in 1995 indicated that 19 percent were homosexual or bisexual (Martin Rogers, *Who's in the Seminary? Roman Catholic Seminarians Today* [Toronto: Novalis, 1996] p. 30).
29. Andrew Greeley, "Bishops Paralyzed over Heavily Gay Priesthood," *National Catholic Reporter*, November 10, 1989.
30. Andrew Greeley, *Priests: A Calling in Crisis* (Chicago: University of Chicago Press, 2004), p. 27.
31. Ibid., p. 39.
32. Ibid., p. 41.
33. Donald Cozzens describes a similar process; see Cozzens, p. 108.
34. Pete Sherman, "A Higher Calling," *Illinois Times*, December 12–18, 2002.
35. Pete Sherman, "Defender of the Faith," *Illinois Times*, June 19, 2003.
36. Sherman, "A Higher Calling."
37. Letter of P. Jesús Torres, undersecretary, Congregation for Institutes of Apostolic Life and Societies of Apostolic Life, July 11, 2002; Letter of Very Rev. David F. Wright, O. P., socius for the prior provincial, Dominican Province of St. Albert the Great, January 21, 2003.
38. Jason Berry, *Lead Us Not into Temptation: Catholic Priests and the Sexual Abuse of Children* (Urbana: University of Illinois Press, 2000) p. 167.
39. Ibid., p. 225.
40. Jim Schutze, "The Gay Priest Thing: The Conference of Bishops Ignored 'The Elephant in the Sacristy,'" *Dallas Observer*, June 20, 2002.
41. Ibid.
42. Ibid.
43. Stephen Rossetti, "The Catholic Church and Child Sexual Abuse," *America*, April 22, 2002.
44. Greeley, p. 115.
45. Donald L. Boisvert and Robert E. Goss, *Gay Catholic Priests and Clerical Sexual Misconduct: Breaking the Silence* (New York: Harrington Park Press, 2005) p. 3. The gay essayists in this book betray a fundamental dishonesty because they harp on the fact that gays are not disproportionately molesters of small children, while ignoring

the fact that the victims of Catholic priests were mostly pubescent and postpubescent boys who were the objects of homosexual actions by priests who often considered themselves as homosexual.

46. The *John Jay Report* reviews the literature and concludes that females were more likely than the males to disclose such information (p. 156).
47. The National Review Board for the Protection of Children and Young People, *A Report on the Crisis in the Catholic Church in the United States*, 2002, p. 8.
48. Louise Haggett, *The Bingo Report: Mandatory Celibacy and Clergy Sexual Abuse* (Freeport, Maine: Center for the Study of Religious Issues, 2005) p. 104.
49. Paul J. Isely and Peter Isely, "The Sexual Abuse of Male Children by Church Personnel: Intervention and Prevention," *Pastoral Psychology*, Vol. 39, No. 2 (1990) p. 86.
50. Haggett, p. 118.
51. Detailed instructions to the media to avoid making "the erroneous correlation between a gay sexual orientation and child sexual abuse" are given in *Subtle Demoting: The Media, Homosexuality and the Priest Sexual Abuse Scandal* by Glenda M. Russell and Nancy H. Kelly (Amherst, Massachusetts: Institute for Gay and Lesbian Strategic Studies, 2003).
52. Louise Cervine, president of Dignity/USA, a Catholic gay organization, claimed the abuse "has nothing to do with sexual orientation," in Peter Freiberg, "Mass Confusion," *The Advocate*, April 30, 2002.
53. Haggett, p. 118.
54. Michael Paulson and Thomas Farragher, "Priest Abuse Cases Focus on Adolescents," *Boston Globe*, May 17, 2002. Thomas Plante and Courtney Daniels concur: "The vast majority of priests who sexually abuse children abuse post-pubescent adolescent boys rather than latency-age children or young girls" ("The Sexual Abuse Crisis in the Roman Catholic Church: What Psychologists and Counselors Should Know," *Pastoral Psychology*, Vol. 52, No. 5 [2002] p. 384).
55. Robert Kumpel, "Hear No Evil: Not the Answer to Priest Scandal," *San Diego News Notes*, May 2003.
56. Gerald D. Coleman writes, "Sexual involvement with postpubescent adolescents is not currently considered a diagnosable psychiatric disorder" ("Clergy Sexual Abuse and Homosexuality," in Thomas G. Plante, editor, *Sin against the Innocents: Sexual Abuse by Priests and the Role of the Catholic Church* [Westport, Connecticut: Praeger, 2004] p. 75).
57. Alan P. Bell and Martin S. Weinberg, *Homosexualities: A Study of Diversity among Men and Women* (New York: Simon and Schuster, 1978) p. 308.
58. Ibid., p. 312.
59. Edward O. Laumann, John H. Gagnon, Robert T. Michael, and Stuart Michaels, *The Social Organization of Sexuality: Sexual Practices in the United States* (Chicago: University of Chicago Press, 1994) p. 315.
60. Stephen Ellington and Kirby Schroeder, "Race and the Construction of Same-Sex Markets in Four Chicago Neighborhoods" in Edward O. Laumann, Stephen Ellington, Jenna Mahay, Anthony Paik, and Yoosik Youm, editors, *The Sexual Organization of the City* (Chicago: University of Chicago Press, 2002) p. 107.
61. Only 2.8 percent of men identify themselves as homosexual or bisexual. See Laumann, Gagnon, Michael, and Michaels, p. 293. These researchers refute Kinsey: see "The

Myth of 10 Percent and the Kinsey Research," pp. 287–290.

62. W. D. Erickson, N. H. Walbek, and R. K. Seely wrote: "Eighty-six percent of offenders against males describe themselves as homosexual or bisexual" ("Behavior Patterns of Child Molesters," *Archives of Sexual Behavior*, Vol. 17, No. 1 [1988] p. 82).
63. Studies may overstate the proportion of homosexually oriented true pedophiles, because they are often based on legal statistics, which do not segregate minors into pre- and post-pubescent categories. That is, men who have sexual relations with teenage boys (and girls) are included in this category, because they are legally pedophiles, although they are not in the psychological category of pedophiles.
64. Steve Baldwin, "Child Molestation and the Homosexual Movement," *Regent University Law Review*, Vol. 14, no. 2 (2001–2002) p. 268.
65. Kurt Freund and Robin J. Watson, "The Proportions of Heterosexual and Homosexual Pedophiles among Sex Offenders against Children: An Exploratory Study," *Journal of Sex and Marital Therapy*, Vol. 18, No. 1 [Spring 1992] p. 35.
66. Ibid., p. 40. See the discussion of this in Robert A. J. Gagnon's "Immoralism, Homosexual Unhealth, and Scripture," available at www.robgagnon.net.
67. Ibid., p. 41. For further citations, see Peter Sprigg and Timothy Dailey, editors, *Getting It Straight: What Research Shows about Homosexuality* (Washington, D.C.: Family Research Council, 2004) pp. 121–142.
68. Ibid., p. 34.
69. Joseph A. Reaves, "Pedophile Priest Released by Judge," *Arizona Republic*, November 14, 2003.
70. Bell and Weinberg, p. 311.
71. For the rejection of NAMBLA by many gays in the 1990s, see Mike Echols, *Brother Tony's Boys: The Largest Case of Child Prostitution in U. S. History* (Amherst, NY: Prometheus Books, 1996) pp. 347–348. See also Gagnon's "Immoralism, Homosexual Unhealth, and Scripture." For an account of the varying relationships of homosexual and pedophile liberation groups, see David Thorstad's "Man/Boy Love and the American Gay Movement," in Theo Sandfort, Edward Brongersma, and Alex van Naerssen, editors, *Male Intergenerational Intimacy: Historical, Socio-Psychological, and Legal Perspectives* (New York: Harrington Park Press, 1991), pp. 251–274.
72. Thane Burnett, "Prof Says He's a Hooker: Ryerson Educator Moonlights as Hustler," *Toronto Sun*, November 25, 1995.
73. Chris Bearchell, Rick Bebout, and Alexander Wilson, "Another Look," *Issue*, Vol. 51 (March / April 1979).
74. Judy Steed, *Our Little Secret: Confronting Child Sexual Abuse in Canada* (Toronto: Vintage, Random House of Canada) p. 57–58.
75. Gudrun Schultz, "Canada Legalizes 'Sex Clubs'—'14-year-olds Will Be Exploited," www.lifesitenews.com, December 21, 2005.
76. Joyce Howard Price, "Predator Priests," *Washington Times*, April 16, 2002.
77. Sprigg and Dailey, p. 136. See pp. 134–138 for more evidence of gay-pedophilia connections.
78. Mary Eberstadt, "'Pedophilia Chic' Reconsidered," *Weekly Standard*, January 1, 2001.
79. Quoted by Julie Bindel, "Gay Men Need to Talk Straight about Paedophila," *The Guardian*, March 3, 2001.

80. Karla Jay and Allen Young, *The Gay Report: Lesbians and Gay Men Speak Out about Sexual Experiences and Lifestyles* (New York: Summit Books, 1977) p. 97.
81. Ibid., p. 98.
82. Ibid., p. 99.
83. Ibid.
84. Ibid., p. 98.
85. Ibid.
86. Ibid., p. 281.
87. Ibid., p. 277.
88. Ibid., pp. 279–280.
89. Hanna Rosin, "Chickenhawk," *New Republic*, May 8, 1995.
90. Camille Paglia, "The Purity of Allen Ginsberg's Boy-Love," www.salon.com, April 15, 1997.
91. Toby Johnson, "Priestly Pedophilia," *White Crane: A Journal of Gay Men's Spirituality*, No. 55.
92. For examples see Judith A. Reisman, "Crafting Bi/Homosexual Youth," *Regent University Law Review*, especially pp. 295–301.
93. Andrea Dworkin, *Woman Hating* (New York: Penguin, Plume, 1974) pp. 190, 191–192.
94. Philip Jenkins, *The New Anti-Catholicism: The Last Acceptable Prejudice* (New York: Oxford University Press, 2003) p. 149; Eric Lax, "A Joyful Portrait of the Author and Friend, Mainly about Lindsay Anderson," *Los Angeles Times*, October 4, 2000.
95. The website www.2violent.com describes Polanski's crime: "He became embroiled in a scandal surrounding rape charges involving him and a 13-year-old girl, Samantha Geimer, daughter of an actress. Polanski was initially charged with rape, suspicion of sodomy, child molestation and furnishing dangerous drugs to a minor; however these charges were eventually reduced to statutory rape at the request of the victim's mother. According to reports, his fame gained him the trust of her mother to host the young model at his home for a photo session. Her mother hoped he would help her daughter into show business. After convincing her to get into his hot-tub, the victim alleged he drugged her with quaaludes and alcohol, and then proceeded to have nonconsensual intercourse with her. The sister of the girl heard her reporting the fact of sexual intercourse to her friend over the phone. When her mother reported the incident to the police, he fled the United States but returned later to face the charges. On February 1, 1978, after pleading guilty to the charges, Polanski skipped bail and fled to France."
96. Sigmund Freud wrote, "A strong libidinal fixation to the narcissistic type of object-choice is to be included in the predisposition to manifest homosexuality" (*Introductory Lectures on Psychoanalysis,* translated by James Strachey [New York: W. W. Norton and Company, 1977] p. 530).
97. Zebulun A. Silverthorne and Vernon L. Quincy discovered that "men who preferred male partners preferred younger partners than those who preferred female partners" ("Sexual Partner Age Preference of Homosexual and Heterosexual Men and Women" *Archives of Sexual Behavior*, Vol. 29, No. 1 [2000] p. 74).
98. Philip Guichard, "I Hate Older Men," *The Village Voice*, June 21–27, 2000.

99. Michael Lacey, "The Divine Sociopath: Why Isn't Bishop O'Brien in Jail," *Phoenix New Times*, April 15, 2002.
100. See www.jeffcovey.net/personal/dan/
101. Homosexuality probably has many etiologies, but this type of immature homosexuality seems to stem from an incomplete masculine development. The human body has a basically feminine template, which is masculinized in the womb by a combination of genes and hormones. A boy grows inside a woman, and then is nursed and cared for by a woman. His closest emotional bond is with a woman, but he soon realizes that he is not and should not be like the person in the world he loves most. He has to break that bond and differentiate himself from the feminine so that he can accept the challenges of life and reconnect to the feminine, taking a wife and begetting children, and providing for and protecting a woman and her children. But some men never get this far on their life journey.
102. Report of Suffolk County Supreme Court, Special Grand Jury, May 2, 2002, released January 17, 2003, pp. 6–7.
103. *John Jay Report*, p. 69.
104. Ibid., p. 54.
105. A twenty- to thirty-year lag between an incident of abuse and the reporting of that incident is common and the delay may affect the shape of the bell curve.
106. Professional opinion is divided about why this drop occurred and how much of the drop is real as opposed to a reflection of factors such as changes in definitions, reporting, and investigation by the states (*John Jay Report*, p. 156). See also David Finkelhor and Lisa M. Jones, "Explanations for the Decline in Child Sexual Abuse Cases," *Juvenile Justice Bulletin*, January 2004.
107. The *John Jay Report* indicated, "Every published empirical study on the disclosure of child sexual abuse indicates a high percentage of those child sexual abuse victims who report their abuse to authorities delay disclosure of their abuse" (p. 172).
108. Court of Common Pleas, First Judicial District of Pennsylvania, Criminal Trial Division, Misc. no. 03-00-239, Report of the Grand Jury , p. 164.
109. The fear of emotional chaos that leads some homosexuals to the priesthood, religious life, and the liturgy may also lead others to a life in the arts. Homosexuals seem to be over-represented in the arts, perhaps because they find art a way of structuring their lives and fending off chaos.
110. Brooks Egerton and David Levinthal, "Ex-Catholic Worker Sentenced for Rape," *Dallas Morning News*, April 12, 2003.
111. Gill Donovan, "Priest-Liturgist Arrested for Sex Abuse in 1970s," *National Catholic Reporter*, July 13, 2001. Martin pleaded guilty but received unsupervised pre-sentence probation (Cathleen Fasani, "Priest Who Worked Here Need Not Register as Sex Offender," *Chicago Sun-Times*, March 7, 2003).
112. Dave Rogers, "Priest Charged with Sexual Assault: Judge Orders Psychiatric Examination of Former High-Ranking Church Official," *Ottawa Citizen*, April 9, 2005. When he was arraigned, he was told he must not communicate with the alleged victims; "he started giggling."
113. Lisa Black, "Priest Named as Abuser Leaves Post," *Chicago Tribune*, August 7, 2002.
114. "Ottawa Priest Accused of Sexual Abuse," CBC.CA News, August 9, 2002; "Action

on sexually abusive priests comes only after media exposure: Ottawa Catholic university attracts sexually abusive professors," www.lifesite.net, August 12, 2002. Huels admitted the abuse but does not seem to be the object of civil or criminal action (Lisa Black, "Priest Named as Abuser Leaves Post," *Chicago Tribune*, August 7, 2002). In 1974 Glendinning pleaded guilty to abuse (Peter Geigen-Miller, "Brother's Abuse Termed as Bad as Priest's," *London* [Canada] *Free Press*, October 28, 2003).

115. David Finkelhor, *Sexually Victimized Children* (New York: Free Press, 1979) p. 82.
116. In Baltimore the gay-friendly parish of St. Sebastian is run by the Rev. David B. G. Flaherty, a priest of the United Reform Catholic Church International. He studied at St. Mary's Seminary in Baltimore until 1998 and then went to study liturgy at Catholic University.
117. France, p. 473.
118. Bishop Joseph Gerry of Portland, Maine, and his auxiliary bishop Michael R. Cote were "slow to discipline three priests involved with a pornographic website" (St. Sebastian's Angels) but Cote as bishop of Norwich was swift to remove the Rev. Justinian B. Rweyemamu because of poor homilies and mismanagement of a private charity, because, Cote explained, "It is sometimes necessary to do so in order to maintain the high standards to which we must all hold our priests today" (Tom Breen, "Norwich Bishop Called Lenient in Maine Case," *Journal Inquirer*, March 3, 2005).
119. Finkelhor, p. 75. See "What Is Masculinity?" in this author's book, *The Church Impotent: The Feminization of Christianity* (Dallas: Spence Publishing, 1999).
120. Eugen Drewermann, *Kleriker:Psychogramm eines Ideals* (Munich: Deutscher Taschenbuch Verlag, 1991) p. 589.
121. As boys grow up in Spain, most reject the feminine world of which religion is a part. Timothy Mitchell wrote, "Many boys were allowed and even encouraged to dress up as priests and pretend to say mass. But with the onset of puberty and peer-bonding with male cousins and friends, the erstwhile little angel learned to mock feminine piety, and indeed to reject anything that might seem 'sissy'" (Timothy Mitchell, *Betrayal of Innocents: Desire, Power, and the Catholic Church in Spain* [Philadelphia: University of Pennsylvania Press, 1998] p. 43).
122. William C. Bier, "A Comparative Study of a Seminary Group and Four Other Groups on the Minnesota Multiphasic Personality Inventory," *Studies in Psychology and Psychiatry*, Vol. 7, No. 3 (April 1948) p. 30.
123. Drewermann, p. 589.
124. Stephen J. Rossetti, "The Catholic Church and Child Sexual Abuse," *America*, April 22, 2002.
125. Brooks Egerton and Ed Housewright, "Kos's Belongings Stored in a Dallas-area Attic: Boxes' Caretaker Says Son among Those Abused," *Dallas Morning News*, July 24, 1997.
126. Alice Jackson Baugh, "A Victim's Story," *Time*, March 24, 2002.
127. "Scott Simon Interviews Father Steve Rossetti on the Problems with the Priesthood," National Institute for the Renewal of the Priesthood, www.jknirp.com.
128. Paul R. Dorecki, *The Clergy Sexual Abuse Crisis: Reform and Renewal in the Catholic Community* (Washington, D.C.: Georgetown University Press, 2004) p. 16.
129. Alistair Bell, "He Was Acting as if He Was Getting Revenge on God," *The Age*, May 21, 2006.

130. Jason Berry, *Vows of Silence: The Abuse of Power in the Papacy of John Paul II* (New York: Free Press, 2004) p. 145.
131. Richard D. Walton and Linda Graham Caleca, "Trusting Young Victims, All Easy Prey," *Indianapolis Star*, February 16, 1997, p. 10.
132. Richard D. Walton and Linda Graham Caleca, "Abuse of the Collar," *Indianapolis Star*, February 18, 1997.
133. Ibid., pp. 1, 4, 5. Neither Voss, Moran, or Mahalic are the objects of criminal or civil actions. Voss is in Haiti.
134. A. W. Richard Sipe, *Sex, Priests, and Power: Anatomy of a Crisis* (New York: Brunner/Mazel Publishers, 1995) p. 12.
135. Eugen Drewermann observed: "Auch sehr viel später noch ergeben sich im Leben homosexueller Priester daher bevorzugt Liebesbeziehungen zu Jungen oder Jugendlichen, die gerade dem Alter entsprechen, in denen seinerzeit die ersten 'Erfahrungen' der Liebe gemacht wurden...." (Drewermann, p. 598).
136. A. W. Richard Sipe, "Problem of Prevention," in Thomas G. Plante, editor, *Bless Me Father for I Have Sinned: Perspectives on Sexual Abuse Committed by Roman Catholic Priests* (Westport, Connecticut: Praeger, 1998) p. 124.

## *12. Abusers and Celibacy*

1. Quoted by Eugen Drewermann, *Kleriker: Psychogramm eines Ideals* (Munich: Deutscher Taschenbuch Verlag, 1991) p. 746.
2. Henry C. Lea, *A History of Sacerdotal Celibacy in the Christian Church* (Honolulu: University Press of the Pacific, 2003) p. 423.
3. Louise Haggett, *The Bingo Report: Mandatory Celibacy and Clergy Sexual Abuse* (Freeport, Maine: Center for the Study of Religious Issues, 2005) p. 170.
4. Gerald T. Blanchard discusses the similarities between clergy abuse and incest in "Sexually Abusive Clergymen: A Conceptual Framework for Intervention and Recovery," *Pastoral Psychology*, Vol. 39, No. 4 (1991) pp. 237–246.
5. The council of Elvira deposed from office clerics who did not refrain from intercourse with their wives. See James A. Brundage, *Law, Sex, and Christian Society in Medieval Europe* (Chicago: University of Chicago Press, 1987) p. 69–70.
6. Ibid., pp. 64–68.
7. Catholics recognized the problem. Brundage wrote that at the Council of Trent "the Duke of Bavaria's representative, for example, declared publicly during the Council that a recent visitation had shown that ninety-six or ninety-seven Bavarian priests out of a hundred had concubines or clandestine wives" (Brundage, p. 568).
8. Roland Bainton, *Erasmus of Christendom* (New York: Crossroad, 1982) p. 49.
9. Donald Cozzens, *Sacred Silence: Denial and the Crisis in the Church* (Collegeville, Minnesota: Liturgical Press, 2002) p. 126.
10. Andrew M. Greeley, *Priests: A Calling in Crisis* (Chicago: University of Chicago Press: 2004) p. 115.
11. Priests and male religious constitute about .15% of the population of Ireland (50% male, median age 33) but are responsible for 3.2 % of the reported cases of child sexual abuse. As in the United States, the abuse is predominantly homosexual. 5.8%

of abused boys reported their abuser to be a member of the clergy, but only 1.4% of abused girls. See Helen Goode, Hannah McGee, and Ciarán O'Boyle, *Time to Listen: Confronting Child Sexual Abuse by Catholic Clergy in Ireland* (Dublin: The Liffey Press, 2002), pp. 18, 241–242.

12. Freda Briggs and Russell M. F. Hawkins, "A Comparison of the Childhood Experiences of Convicted Male Child Molesters and Men Who Were Sexually Abused in Childhood and Claimed to be Nonoffenders," *Child Abuse and Neglect*, Vol. 20, No. 3, p. 225.
13. Josef Dirnbeck, *Reibebaum Krenn: Vom Papstfrühstuck zu den "Bubendummheiten,"* (Wien-Klosterneuberg: Edition Va Bene, 2004) p. 152.
14. Quoted in Kenneth Jost, "Child Sexual Abuse in the Catholic Church: An Overview" in Louise I. Gerdes, *Child Sexual Abuse in the Catholic Church* (San Diego: Greenhaven Press, 2003) p. 18.
15. This differs from Andrew Greeley's claim, based on sociological research, that 82 percent of priests are celibate (Greeley, p. 40). Much hinges on the definition of celibacy. If a celibate is one who is not married, almost all priests are celibate; if a celibate is one who refrains from all sexual activity after promising to be celibate, far fewer are celibate.
16. A. W. Richard Sipe, *Celibacy in Crisis: A Secret World Revisited* (New York: Brunner-Routledge, 2003) pp. 50–51.
17. Karol Jackowski, *The Silence We Keep: A Nun's View of the Catholic Priest Scandal* (New York: Harmony Books, 2004) p. 16.
18. Marie M. Fortune, *Is Nothing Sacred? The Story of a Pastor, the Women He Sexually Abused and the Congregation He Nearly Destroyed* (Cleveland: United Church Press, 1999) p. 147.
19. Philip Jenkins notes that "no evidence indicates that Catholic or celibate clergy are more (or less) involved than their non-celibate counterparts" (*The New Anti-Catholicism: The Last Acceptable Prejudice* [New York: Oxford University Press, 2003] p. 142).
20. Heather Ewart, "ABC Online 7:30 report," at www.abc.net.au/7:30/content/s849496.htm.
21. Ibid.
22. Ibid.
23. Ibid.
24. Heather Ewart, "Cover-up Left Pedophile to Prey on Vic Altar Boys," ABC Australia, May 8, 2003.
25. Jeremy Roberts and Carol Altmann, "Crusading against an Unholy Scourge," *The Weekend Australian*, November 29, 2003.
26. Carol Altmann and Thea Williams, "Archbishop Faces His Own Ghosts," *The Australian*, May 22, 2003.
27. Catherine Anderson, "Boy-Sex Guilty Pleas," *Hobart Mercury*, April 24, 1999.
28. Colin James and Ellen Whinnett, "Boy-Sex Ring in Tassie, Claims Priest," *Hobart Mercury*, May 22, 2003. The people who bought Brandenburg's house after his suicide discovered "200 photographs of boys," pictures of conquests which he showed to his victims (Colin James, "Trophy Album of Two Hundred Abused Boys," *Adelaide Advertiser*, May 24, 2005).

29. Ellen Whinnett, "Pedophile Priest Faces the Music: Guilty Plea Brings Victim Relief," *Hobart Mercury*, November 19, 2003.
30. Ellen Whinnett, "Priest Admits Sordid Life of Sexual Abuse," *Hobart Mercury*, November 19, 2003.
31. Report of the Board of Inquiry into Past Handling of Complaints of Sexual Abuse in the Anglican Church Diocese of Brisbane (May 2003) pp. 32, 214–215. (Henceforth the "Report of the Board of Inquiry.")
32. Ibid., p. 32, 220.
33. Ibid., p. 32.
34. Ibid., p. 281.
35. Ibid., p. 283.
36. Ibid., p. 291.
37. Ibid., p. 409.
38. Ibid., p. 382.
39. Ibid., p. 383.
40. Ibid., p. 392.
41. Ibid., pp. 396–397.
42. Ibid., p. 398.
43. Jamie Walker, "Only the Lonely: Hollingworth at the Brink," *The Weekend Australian*, May 10, 2003.
44. Jasmin Lill, "Jailed Priest Denied Friendship with G-G," *Hobart Mercury*, May 19, 2003.
45. Leisa Scott, "Anglican Abuse Protocol Came Only after the Event: The Hollingworth Crisis," *The Australian*, May 13, 2003.
46. Report of the Board of Inquiry, p. 68.
47. Ashleigh Wilson, "Monsters Who Preyed on Children: Hollingworth under Fire," *The Australian*, May 2, 2003.
48. Report of the Board of Inquiry, p. 105.
49. Ibid., p. 77.
50. Carol Altmann, "Pedophile Wrote the Book on Abuse," *The Australian*, July 29, 2003.
51. Ellen Whinnett, "Bacon Backs Sex Probe," *Hobart Mercury*, April 28, 2003.
52. Bruce Montgomery, "Priest Sentenced to Eight Years' Jail for 'Violent' Rape," *The Australian*, July 11, 1995.
53. Jonathan Este, "Bishop Betrayed Victim of Child Abuse," *The Australian*, January 2000.
54. Ibid.
55. Ibid.
56. "Former G-G Snubbed Sex Claims, Woman Says," *Sydney Morning Herald*, March 7, 2005.
57. Report of the Board of Inquiry, p. 315.
58. Ibid., p. 322.
59. Ibid., p. 324.
60. Darrell Giles and Chris Taylor, "Anger at G-G Letter," *Australia Sunday Times*, May 25, 2003.
61. Gerald McManus, "Hollingworth Lashes Out," *Sunday Herald Sun*, May 25, 2003.

62. Rafael Epstein, "Dr. Hollingworth on *Australian Story,*" *ABC Online*, www.abc.net.au/am/s484774.htm.
63. "G-G Hit by New Abuse Claims," *The Age*, May 3, 2002.
64. Peter Gregory and Andrew Stevenson, "Death of Accuser Seals Fate of Rape Case against G-G," *Sydney Morning Herald*, May 24, 2003.
65. "Hollingworth Quits," *The Advertiser*, May 25, 2002.
66. Greg Roberts, "No Ending the Affair," *The Australian*, March 12, 2005.
67. Chris Goddard, "A Role Fit for Hollingworth," *The Age*, May 6, 2002.
68. "Kids Treated as Objects: Archbishop," *The Age*, June 28, 2003.
69. Steve Larkin, "Anglican Archbishop Apologizes," *Courier Mail*, May 29, 2003.
70. Barney Zwartz, "Anglican Leaders See Silver Lining," *Courier Mail*, May 27, 2002.
71. Lee Huddleston, "Churches Defend the Indefensible," *Kingston Whig-Standard*, May 21, 2002.
72. Judy Steed, *Our Little Secret: Confronting Sexual Abuse in Canada* (Toronto: Vintage Canada, 1995) p. 9.
73. Paulette Peirol and Michael Den Tandt, "'Suffer the Children': Dean Baker Confesses: 'I Was Told of Abuse 14 Years Ago,'" *Kingston Whig-Standard*, May 16, 1992.
74. Paulette Peirol and Michael Den Tandt, "Questions and Answers," *Kingston Whig-Standard*, May 16, 1992.
75. Ibid.
76. Steed, p. 16.
77. "Court Documents Examine Reasons for Gallienne's Pedophilia, Likely Prognosis," *Kingston Whig-Standard*, January 21, 1991.
78. Jeff Outhit and Carol Toller, "Woman Says She Reported Alleged Sex Abuse at Cathedral 5 Years Ago," *Kingston Whig-Standard*, March 15, 1990.
79. Steed, pp. 21–22.
80. Ibid., pp. 21–22, 26.
81. Ibid., p. 26.
82. Ibid., p. 28.
83. Ibid.
84. Ibid., p. 32.
85. Ibid., p. 33.
86. Ibid.
87. Ibid., p. 58.
88. Ibid., p. 35.
89. Jeff Outhit, "Kingston Abuse Prompts New Anglican Rules," *Kingston Whig-Standard*, November 15, 1990.
90. Michael Den Tandt, "St. George's Rules Out Inquiry," *Kingston Whig-Standard*, February 10, 1992.
91. Steed, p. 28.
92. Jeff Outhit, "Former Choirmaster a Free Man Today," *Kingston Whig-Standard*, October 2, 1996.
93. See Don Butler, "Band of Angels Strive to Save Reviled Outcasts," *Ottawa Citizen*, May 22, 2004. The program, which purports to monitor sex offenders, would be more convincing if Gallienne were working as a dishwasher rather than disobeying his bishop's order which forbade him to work as a church organist.

94. State of Maryland, Circuit Court for Baltimore City, #18835804.
95. Howard Pankratz, "Ex-Priest Sentenced: Shissler Gets 24 Years to Life for Raping Boys; More Cases Feared," *Denver Post*, October 18, 2002.
96. Matt Stearns, "Trial of Wyncote Priest Begins," *Philadelphia Inquirer*, March 5, 1999; Meredith Fischer, "Jail Sentence Upheld for Priest Convicted in Child-Porn Case," *Philadelphia Inquirer*, August 19, 1999.
97. Martin, who denied the abuse, was initially convicted but his conviction was overturned by a federal appeals court on the grounds that the prosecutor should not have told the jury to disregard character witnesses ("Federal Appeals Court Throws out Child Molestation Conviction," *Duluth News Tribune*, September 21, 2005).
98. McCray and Maxey were both convicted of abuse (Jessica McBride, "Priest Denies Sexually Assaulting Boy," *Milwaukee Journal-Sentinel*, June 22, 1995).
99. Brooks Egerton, "Man Ordained Despite Abuse Allegations; Episcopal Seminaries' Ex-dean Says Evidence Was Lacking," *Dallas Morning News*, October 5, 1997.
100. Ibid.
101. Ibid.
102. Midge Hill and Cameron Harper, "11 News at 6," KTVT, Dallas, May 15, 1996. Perry, "pastor at the city's second-largest Episcopal church for six years, was fined $500 and given twelve months of deferred adjudication, a form of probation, for the Class A misdemeanor. If he successfully completes his probation, no conviction will appear on his record" (Christine Wicker, "Lewdness Charge Leads to Pastor's Resignation," *Dallas Morning News*, May 15, 1996).
103. Dennis Hevesi, "Episcopal Priest Resigns amid Sex-Abuse Charges," *New York Times*, October 7, 1992.
104. Tim Cornell, "Mystified Colleagues Saw No Signals," *Boston Herald*, January 17, 1995.
105. James L. Franklin, "Misconduct Is Disclosed: Diocese Reveals Sexual Exploitation by Bishop Who Committed Suicide," *Boston Globe*: January 27, 1995.
106. Doug Fraser, "A Church Acts Swiftly on Abuse Claim," *Cape Cod Times*, December 30, 2002.
107. "Sexual Conduct Charges Long Island Report: Some Confirmed, Others Disputed," *The Living Church*, June 29, 1997.
108. Ibid.
109. Tristram Korten, "The Principal, the Pedophile, His Pastor, Her Parish: Exclusive Private School Finds Itself in Turmoil after Parents Revolt," *Miami New Times*, November 4, 2004.
110. Don Noyes, "Priest Can't Escape History of Sexual Misconduct," abc7news.com.
111. Davis Virtue, "California: Sex Abuse Victims Warn Episcopal Leadership about Abusive Priest," virtueonline.org, May 10, 2006.
112. Philip Jenkins, "The Celibacy Requirement for Priests Does Not Contribute to Child Sexual Abuse," in Louise I. Gerdes, *Child Sexual Abuse in the Catholic Church* (San Diego: Greenhaven Press, 2003) p. 34.
113. Edwin P. Hoyt, *Horatio's Boys: The Life and Works of Horatio Alger, Jr.* (Radnor, Pennsylvania: Chilton Book Company, 1974) pp. 5–6.
114. Marie M. Fortune, *Is Nothing Sacred? The Story of A Pastor, The Women He Sexually Abused, and the Congregation He Nearly Destroyed* (Cleveland: United Church Press, 1999) p. 6.

115. Ibid., p. 5.
116. Ibid., p. 20.
117. Ibid., p. 49.
118. Ibid., p. 50.
119. Ibid., p. 51.
120. Ibid., p. 64.
121. Ibid., pp. 100–101.
122. Ibid., p. 76.
123. Ibid., p. 77.
124. Ibid., p. 79.
125. Ibid., p. 82.
126. Ibid., p. 83.
127. Ibid., p. 99.
128. Ibid., p. 97.
129. Associated Press, "Selection of Jury Starts in Lutheran Assault Case," *Houston Chronicle*, April 6, 2004.
130. Bobby Ross Jr., "Lutheran Officials Accused of Allowing Molester to Join Clergy," *San Diego Union-Tribune*, April 6, 2004.
131. Associated Press, "Judge Denies Lutheran Synod Request to Exclude Evidence," *Houston Chronicle*, April 8, 2004.
132. Bobby Ross Jr., "Jury Finds Lutheran Synod Negligent in Abuse Case," *Tacoma News-Tribune*, April 22, 2004.
133. Pamela Crosby, "Churches Join Project to Gauge 'Pulse' of Young Adults," www.wfn.org/2004/04/msg00035.html.
134. Stephen J. Grenz and Roy D. Bell, *Betrayal of Trust: Confronting and Preventing Clergy Sexual Misconduct* (Grand Rapids, Michigan: Baker Books, 2001) p. 26.
135. Carl Limbacher, "Falwell Blasts Catholic Church for Not Defrocking Abusive Priests," www.newsmax.com, April 25, 2002.
136. Mike Echols, *Brother Tony's Boys: The Largest Case of Child Prostitution in U. S. History* (Amherst, NY: Prometheus Books, 1996) p. 43.
137. Ibid., pp. 44, 45.
138. Ibid., p. 60.
139. AP, "Evangelist in Child Prostitution Ring Gets 20 Years," *New York Times*, March 29, 1989; AP, "Haitian Cops Capture U.S. Child Molester," *Washington Times*, August 30, 2003.
140. Andrew M. Greeley, "Anti-Catholicism Is Alive, Well," *Intelligencer*, April 14, 2002.
141. Richard Foot, "Catholic Clergy Far from Only Abusers: U.S. Survey," *National Post*, April 12, 2002.
142. Richard Exley, *Perils of Power: Immorality in the Ministry* (Tulsa, Oklahoma: Honor / Harrison House, Inc., 1988) p. 37.
143. Ibid., p. 39.
144. Arlene B. Brewster, "Clergy Sexual Misconduct: The Affair Everyone Remembers," *Pastoral Psychology*, Vol. 44, No. 6, 1966, p. 355.
145. *Touchstone: A Journal of Mere Christianity* reported that "the ELCA [Evangelical Lutheran Church in America] Board of Pensions predicts that 6,000 pastors will retire in the next 15 years, and that at the current rate of ordination the church will

have one-fourth to one-third fewer pastors than it has now" (May 2005, p. 53).

146. Richard A. Schoenherr, *Goodbye Father: The Celibate Male Priesthood and the Future of the Catholic Church* (New York: Oxford University Press, 2002) p. 213.
147. Sister Jane Kelly, *Taught to Believe the Unbelievable: A New Vision of Hope for the Catholic Church and Society* (New York: Writers Club Press / iUniverse, Inc., 2003) p. 119.

## *13. Clerical Accomplices*

1. "A Roman Catholic Bishop in Florida Resigns, Admitting He Molested 5 Boys," *New York Times*, June 3, 1998.
2. Laurie Goodstein, "Catholic Bishop in Florida Quits, Admitting Sex Abuse in the '70s," *New York Times*, March 9, 2002. "Mr. Dixon [the victim] said he had gone to Father O'Connell to confide that he had been abused by two other clergymen: the Rev. John Fischer, who was his parish priest and head of the Catholic elementray school he had attended, and the Rev. Manus Daly, the dean of students at the seminary."
3. Gramick claims to have read all the documents pertaining to Shanley ("Gramick Responds to Orth," *National Catholic Reporter*, February 18, 2005) and refers to the offense of Shanley by his niece, "Furthermore, her uncle told her he had never raped a child or forced anyone to engage in sexual acts, and he would not lie to her." ("Finding Empathy for Shanley: Nun Says Christian Response Goes Beyond Innocence or Guilt," *National Catholic Reporter*, January 14, 2005) and calls into question the motives of Shanley's accusers.
4. "Baton Rouge Diocese Settles Sex Abuse Claim Involving Late Bishop, Will Rename High School," *Charleston* [West Virginia] *Gazette*, November 11, 2004.
5. Ibid.
6. Ron Russell, "Camp Ped: Long after Roman Catholic Leaders Knew Pedo-Priests Couldn't Be Cured, Cardinal Roger Mahony Kept Packing Off His Worst Offenders to a Notorious New Mexico Rehab Center," *Los Angeles New Times*, August 15, 2002. An internal church investigation exonerated Ferrario.
7. Demetria Martinez, "Sanchez Asks Pope's Permission to Resign," *National Catholic Reporter*, April 2, 1993.
8. Stephen Kurkjian and Michael Rezendes, "Settlement in Minn[esota] and Retraction Cited," *Boston Globe*, March 22, 2002.
9. Tom Morton, "Former Wyo[ming] Bishop Sued for Sex Abuse,"*Casper Star-Tribune*, January 24, 2004. The suit is pending.
10. "Kentucky Bishop Resigns Amid Abuse Allegations," CNN.com, June 12, 2002.
11. Michael Gould vs. Bishop Lawrence D. Soens et al, Iowa District Court for Scott County, Law No. 104526, Plaintiff's Statement of Disputed Facts in Resistance to Defendant Iowa City Regina High School's Motion for Summary Judgment (henceforth Gould v. Soens), Exhibit 19.
12. Gould v. Soens, Exhibit 1.
13. Gould v. Soens, Exhibits 5, 11, 15.
14. Gould v. Soens, Exhibit 15, 17.
15. Gould v. Soens, Exhibit 27.

16. Gould v. Soens, Exhibit 26.
17. John W. Fountain, "Retired Bishop Offers Apology for 'Sinfulness,'" *New York Times*, June 1, 2002; "1980 Letter from Weakland to Marcoux," *Milwaukee Journal Sentinel*, May 2, 2002. Weakland wrote to his lover that his mother warned "me that I should not put down on paper what I would not want the whole world to read."
18. See p. 217.
19. See p. 219.
20. Paul Likoudis, "Former Bishop Involved in Domestic Dispute," *The Wanderer*, October 21, 2004.
21. "Why Is Archbishop Weakland Invited to Australia?" *AD2000* Vol. 5 No. 9 (October 1992).
22. Arimond was "convicted of fourth-degree sexual assault on a teenage boy in 1990" (Tom Heinen, "List of 43 Abusive Priests Released: Dolan Names Only Diocesan Clergy in Long-awaited Move," *Milwaukee Journal-Sentinel*, July 10, 2004).
23. "Why Is Archbishop Weakland Invited to Australia?"
24. Tom Heinen and John Diedrich, "Priest Faces Four Counts in Sex Assault of Child: Man Who Left Wisconsin Years Ago Arrested in New Jersey," *Milwaukee Journal-Sentinel*, June 4, 2004.
25. Margaret Joughin, "The Weakland File, Part 1," *Christian Order*, August/September 1996.
26. "Why Is Archbishop Weakland Invited to Australia?"
27. Dave Umhoeffer, "Weakland's views take on new meaning after scandal," *Milwaukee Journal-Sentinel*, May 25, 2002.
28. Jason Berry, *Vows of Silence: the Abuse of Power in the Papacy of John Paul II* (New York: Free Press, 2004) p. 112–13.
29. Ibid., p. 114–21.
30. Berry, Vows of Silence, p. 113.
31. Sipe, commenting on Bernardin's assertion that "I am sixty-five years old, and I have always lived a chaste and celibate life," said, "I knew that the statement was not unassailably true. Years before, several priests who were associates of Bernardin prior to his move to Chicago revealed that they had 'partied' together; they talked about their visits to the Josephinum to socialize with seminarians" ("View from the Eye of the Storm," The Linkup National Conference, Louisville, Kentucky, February 23, 2003). In a private communication to the author, Sipe reported that others consulted him about Bernadin's alleged sexual activities.
32. Hopwood was accused of abusing hundreds of boys, pleaded guilty to one charge, and received a suspended sentence and probation (Christina Lee Knauss, "Study Lists Sex Abuse Cases in S.C.: Diocese Leader Pledges to Renew Our Commitment to Protect Children," *Columbia State*, February 28, 2004; Margaret N. O'Shea, "Guilty Plea Ends Priest Abuse Case: Deal Pre-empts More Charges," *Columbia State*, March 22, 1994).
33. Paul Likoudis, *Amchurch Comes Out: The U. S. Bishops, Pedophile Scandals and the Homosexual Agenda* (Petersburg, Illinois: Roman Catholic Faithful, 2002) p.138.
34. Berry, *Vows of Silence*, pp. 121. Stephen Kurkjian and Michael Rezendes reported that "According to [Bishop] Vlazny, the former seminarian accused other top prelates, including the late Chicago Cardinal Joseph Bernardin, of coercing seminarians at

Immaculate Heart of Mary Seminary in Winona, Wisconsin, into having sex." Vlazny continued that "he did not place much credibility in the accuracy of the charges against Brom and the others 'because they were too bizarre to be believed'" ("Settlement in Minn. and Retraction cited," *Boston Globe*, March 22, 2002). But see the case of the Rev. Gerald Robinson of Toledo, Ohio, who was convicted of the ritualistic murder of a nun and accused of participating in Satanic rituals involving sexual abuse (pp. 521–522, note 8).

35. "Archdiocese Settles Sex Lawsuit," *New York Times*, April 19, 1994.
36. James Hitchcock, "Cardinal Bernardin's Legacy," *Catholic World News*, January 7, 2002. Bernardin, for example, when he was in Cincinnati, placed three accused abusers together in at Our Lady of Victory parish: Lawrence R. Strittmatter, Thomas F. Feldhaus, and David J. Kelley (see assignment records, BishopAccountability.org)
37. Quoted by Donald Cozzens in *Sacred Silence: Denial and the Crisis in the Church* (Collegeville, Minnesota: Liturgical Press, 2002) p. 11.
38. Joseph Cardinal Ratzinger (Pope Benedict XVI), *Salt of the Earth: The Church at the End of the Millennium*, translated by Adrian Walker (San Francisco, Ignatius Press, 1997) p. 82.
39. Andrew M. Greeley, *Priests: A Calling in Crisis* (Chicago: University of Chicago Press, 2004) p. 131.
40. John L. Allen, Jr. has observed the Vatican's obsession with maintaining a *bella figura* and the consequent desire to avoid confrontation. See *All the Pope's Men: The Inside Story of How the Vatican Really Thinks* (New York, Doubleday, 2004) pp. 100–103.
41. Then-attorney (and now Phoenix district attorney) Andrew Peyton Thomas wrote that O'Brien warned a priest who reported molestation that he "should get beyond his obsession with 'gay pedophile priests'" ("When Relativism Becomes Theology," *National Review Online*, February 23, 2004).
42. Susan Hogan, "Survivors of Abuse Priests Struggled for Credibility," *Dallas Morning News*, June 10, 2002.
43. "Family Reveals Pain of Sex Abuse: Faith Has Been Kept at a Huge Cost," *Arizona Republic*, December 4, 2002.
44. Deposition of Bishop Robert Sanchez, Second Judicial District Court, County of Bernalillo, State of New Mexico, cases CV-91-11688 et al, January 12–15, 1994, p. 373 (henceforth "Sanchez Deposition").
45. Court of Common Pleas, First Judicial District of Pennsylvania, Criminal Trial Division, Misc. no. 03-00-239, Report of the Grand Jury , p. 177 (henceforth "Philadelphia Grand Jury").
46. Sanchez Deposition, p. 686.
47. Philadelphia Grand Jury, p. 41.
48. Michael Rezendes and Stephen Kurkjian, "Bishop Tells of Shielding Priests: McCormack Says Aide's Plea Ignored," *Boston Globe*, January 9, 2003.
49. Walter V. Robinson, "An Alleged Victim Is Called Negligent: Term Is Ascribed to Law in Lawyer's Response to Suit," *Boston Globe*, April 29, 2002.
50. Tom Kertscher and Marie Rohde, "Archdiocese Fought Hard in Court: Church Added Victims, but Records Show It also Sought Legal Costs," *Milwaukee Journal-Sentinel*, April 4, 2002.

51. Jodi Wilgoren, "At Forum, Victims of Clergy Plead and Vent," *New York Times,* October 24, 2002.
52. Gentile was not criminally charged; he was suspended from the priesthood in 2002 and named in the Westchester Grand Jury Report (Noreen O'Donnell, "New York Grand Jury Says Church Lied to Victims of Abuse," *Journal News*, June 19, 2002). Gentile also wrote a children's Christmas book, *Mouse in the Manger.*
53. Alison Leigh Cowan, "A Secret Settlement, but Little Solace for Family in Lawsuit against Priest," *New York Times*, March 24, 2002.
54. Michael D. Sallah and David Yonke, "Shame, Sin and Secrets," *Toledo Blade*, December 3, 2002.
55. John McElhenny, "Msgr. Says Harm of Abuse Wasn't Recognized," *Boston Globe*, February 23, 2004.
56. The suit against Creighton was dismissed because of the statute of limitations (Greg Frost, "Massachusetts Top Court Throws out Clergy Sex Case," Reuters, May 1, 2003). He is not the object of criminal charges.
57. Letter of Rev. John C. McNally to Humberto Cardinal Medeiros, May 18, 1973, Archdiocese of Boston, Gerard Creighton personnel file, 2-122 to 2-123. Creighton is a prominent figure in Peter Manseau's *Vows: The Story of a Priest, a Nun, and Their Son.*
58. Ron Russell, "Settling Things Quietly," *SF Weekly*, January 14, 2004.
59. Elizabeth Fernandez, "Burlingame Whistleblower Priest Sues S.F. Diocese," *San Francisco Chronicle*, November 2, 2000.
60. Teresa Malcolm and Patricia Lefevere, "Priest May Sue Church, California Court Rules," *National Catholic Reporter*, January 12, 2002.
61. Fernandez, "Burlingame Whistleblower Priest Sues S.F. Diocese."
62. Ibid.
63. Russell, "Settling Things Quietly."
64. Ibid.
65. For an account of how the Vatican obstructed attempts to discipline priests, see Jason Berry, *Vows of Silence: the Abuse of Power in the Papacy of John Paul II* (New York: Free Press, 2004) pp. 99–104.
66. Some of these are discussed by the National Review Board for the Protection of Children and Young People in *A Report on the Crisis in the Catholic Church in the United States* (Washington, D.C.: United States Conference of Catholic Bishops, 2004) pp. 101–04.
67. Chris Moore, *Betrayal of Trust: The Father Brendan Smyth Affair and the Catholic Church* (Dublin: Marino Books, Mercier Press, 1995) p. 26.
68. Henry C. Lea, *History of Sacerdotal Celibacy in the Christian Church* (Honolulu: University Press of the Pacific, 2003) p. 398.
69. Stephen Haliczer, *Sexuality in the Confessional: A Sacrament Profaned* (New York: Oxford University Press, 1996) p. 153.
70. Allen, pp. 234–235.
71. George Weigel, *The Courage to Be Catholic: Crisis, Reform, and the Renewal of the Church* (New York: Basic Books, 2002) p. 71.
72. Stephen J. Rossetti, *A Tragic Grace: The Catholic Church and Child Sexual Abuse* (Collegeville, Minnesota: Liturgical Press, 1996) p. 17.

73. "Pope Expresses 'Deep Pain' in Letter to Bishops on Scandal," *The Wanderer*, July 1, 1993, pp. A1, A7.
74. Laura Goodstein, "A Vatican Lawyer Says That Bishops Should Not Reveal Abuse Claims," *New York Times*, May 18, 2002.
75. Ibid.
76. Marie M. Fortune, *Is Nothing Sacred? The Story of a Pastor, the Women He Sexually Abused, and the Congregation He Nearly Destroyed* (Cleveland: United Church Press, 1999) p. xiv.
77. For a further discussion of clericalism and its relation to sexual abuse see Thomas Doyle, "Roman Catholic Clericalism, Religious Duress, and Clergy Sexual Abuse," *Pastoral Psychology*, Vol. 51, No. 3 (January 2003), pp. 209–218.
78. See "Trouble at the Tower" in Adam Gopnik, *Paris to the Moon* (New York: Random House, 2000) pp. 123ff.
79. Jose L. Sequieros Tizon writes, "The Weberian logic of Opus Dei, offering a model of leaving pastoral work to the priests and other activities to professional laymen, contributed in a decisive way to economic modernization and the undermining of clerical power in favor of lay people." ("The Demographic Transition of the Catholic Priesthood and the End of Clericalism in Spain," *Sociology of Religion*, March 22, 1998.)
80. Doyle, "Roman Catholic Clericalism, Religious Duress, and Clergy Sexual Abuse," p. 209.
81. Russell Shaw, *To Hunt, to Shoot, to Entertain: Clericalism and the Catholic Laity* (San Francisco: Ignatius Press, 1993) p. 13.
82. Michael P. Orsi, "Bishops Sacrifice Accommodations, Privileges and Rights: Everybody Loses," *Homiletic and Pastoral Review*, Vol. 103, No. 5 (February 2002), p. 67.
83. Ibid., p. 67.
84. Ibid., p. 68.
85. Ibid.
86. Ibid., p. 69.
87. Ibid.
88. Ibid., p. 70.
89. J. H. Handlin, *Survivors of Predator Priests* (Irving, Texas: Tapestry Press, 2005) p. 28.
90. Richard Somerville, "Witness for the Prosecution," *Western Nevada County Union*, March 5, 2003.
91. Handlin, p. 34.
92. Somerville, "Witness for the Prosecution."
93. Handlin, p. 37.
94. Somerville, "Witness for the Prosecution."
95. Richard Somerville, "'They're Lying,' Said McAteer of Church Leaders," *Western Nevada County Union*, March 7, 2003.
96. Richard Somerville, "McAteer Hits a Wall of Denial," *Western Nevada County Union*, March 6, 2003.
97. Ibid.
98. Ibid.
99. Ibid.

100. Evelyn Zappia, "Joseph Sullivan: A San Francisco Catholic Life," *Catholic San Francisco*, March 14, 2003.
101. Somerville, "'They're Lying,' Said McAteer of Church Leaders."

## *14. Lay Accomplices*

1. Margery Eagan, "One Survivor Tells a Tale of Triumph," *Boston Herald*, October 17, 2002. John R. Hanlon is serving a life sentence for rape (Cathy Lynn Grossman and Anthony DeBarros, "Facts of Abuse Crisis at Odds with Perception," *USA Today*, November 11, 2002). Robert Kelley pleaded guilty to abuse (Matt O'Brien, "Priest Guilty in 1980s Rape of Tewksbury Girl," *Lowell Sun*, August 16, 2003).
2. Phil Resch, Geoffrey Schilling, Andrew Corcoran, Dr. Boz Tabler, Dr. John Robertson, Jim Corcoran, Tim Baker, Michael Clark, Thomas Hulsewede, Martha Weinert, Richard Clark, Dr. Jim Jewell, and Mark Talley, "'He Cornered Us and Abused Us," *Louisville Courier-Journal*, April 6, 2003.
3. George Orwell, "Notes on Nationalism," *Essays* (New York: Alfred A. Knopf, 2002) pp. 865, 866, 870.
4. Patricia Montemurri, "Priest Gets Probation in Molestation: Rev. Olszewski, 70, Was Found Guilty on 4 Counts," *Detroit Free Press*, January 31, 2003.
5. Anthony DePalma, "Church Scandal Resurrects Old Hurts in Louisiana Bayou," *New York Times*, March 17, 2002.
6. Rachel Zoll, "Catholic Bishops' Strategy to Oust Abusive Priests May Be Unraveling," *Boston Globe*, September 14, 2002. Accusers said Viall's abuse started in 1955. Viall was suspended from the priesthood but he is not the object of criminal investigation and there is no record of the results of any lawsuit.
7. "Father Leonard Sentenced," WRIC, April 1, 2004.
8. Frank Bruni and Elinor Burkett, *A Gospel of Shame: Children, Sexual Abuse, and the Catholic Church* (New York: Viking, 1993) p. 128.
9. Ibid., p. 126.
10. Kathleen Sweeney, "Priest to Serve 10-year Sentence," *Telegraph Herald*, April 5, 1997.
11. Nena Baker, "Diocese Aid to Priest Angers Phoenix Victim," *Arizona Republic*, April 25, 2002.
12. Bruni and Burkett, pp. 117–18.
13. Daniel J. Wakin, "Albany Bishop Denies Sexual Abuse Claim," *New York Times*, February 6, 2004. Hubbard hired an investigator who exonerated him.
14. Deborah Martinez, "Parishioners Torn over the Dismissal of Pastors," *Times Union*, July 1, 2002. Pratt, the former vice chancellor of the Albany diocese, is not the object of civil action or criminal prosecution.
15. Letter from Mike Sullivan in *Boston College Magazine*, Summer 2002.
16. John Rivera, "At Outset, Privileged Trips with His Priest: 22 Years Later, Man Tells Authorities about Abuse," *Baltimore Sun*, May 23, 2002.
17. Jennifer McMenamin and Athima Chansanchai, "Sad Parishioners Recall Cox's Kindness," *Baltimore Sun*, May 24, 2002.

18. John Rivera, "Carroll Priest Arrested in 1980 Abuse," *Baltimore Sun*, May 23, 2002.
19. Ibid.
20. Ibid.
21. Rivera, "Carroll Priest Arrested in 1980 Abuse."
22. Rivera, "At Outset, Privileged Trips with His Priest."
23. Ray Rivera and Janet I. Tu, "Rev. Cornelius, 'I Have Failed,'" *Seattle Times*, May 25, 2002. Cornelius, who has been defrocked, has apologized in a general way for failings but has not admitted to abuse. He is the defendant in a pending civil lawsuit (Janet I. Tu, "Seattle Archdiocese Removed as Defendant in Sex-Abuse Case," *Seattle Times*, February 15, 2005).
24. Richard Nangle and Kathleen A. Shaw, "Accusers, Backers Know Different Man," *Worcester Telegram and Telegraph*, August 22, 2002. Coonan is appealing his suspension from the priesthood. The alleged abuse is outside the statute of limitations, but Coonan in April 2006 was charged with choking his mother and assaulting his sister with whom he shares an apartment (Dianne Williamson, "Farewell, Father Coonan," *Worcester Telegram and Gazette*, April 4, 2006).
25. Nangle and Shaw, "Accusers, Backers Know Different Man."
26. Alan Scher Zagier, "A Priest's Betrayal: A Generation Later, St. Ann Graduates Struggle with a Legacy of Abuse," *Naples Daily News*, June 23, 2002.
27. Jim Walsh, "Priest Given 1 Year in Jail," *Arizona Republic*, January 29, 2005.
28. Ibid.
29. Mary K. Reinhart, "Abused Boy Not Alone in Being Used," *East Valley Tribune*, January 29, 2005.
30. Ibid.
31. J. H. Handlin, *Survivors of Predator Priests* (Irving, Texas: Tapestry Press, 2005) p. 145. Charges against Heaney were dismissed when the U.S. Supreme Court overturned California's retroactive extension of the statute of limitations (Jason van Derbeken and Henry K. Lee, "Accused Abusers Freed in Bay Area: 16, Including Ex-Priests, Released after Court Ruling," *San Francisco Chronicle*, June 28, 2003).
32. Interview with Paul Aube by Investigator Anthony Fowler, August 14, 2002, New Hampshire Attorney General, p. 4857.
33. Allison Hantschel, "Ex-diocese Priest May Yet Be Prosecuted—if he can be found," *Daily Southtown*, August 30, 2002.
34. Tom Mashberg, "Hub Ex-vicar: Police Gave Church Leeway on Abuse," *Boston Herald*, October 29, 2002.
35. Tom Mashberg, "Records: Archdiocese Official Intervened in Abuse Case," *Boston Herald*, October 28, 2002.
36. Eileen McNamara, "Courts Must End Secrecy," *Boston Globe*, February 27, 2002.
37. Walter V. Robinson and Sacha Pfeiffer, "Boston Priest Abuse Cases Were Sealed by Judges," *Boston Globe*, February 16, 2002. The diocese settled with Matte's accusers and removed him from the priesthood in 1993.
38. Joseph A. Reaves, "Diocese Downplays Abuse Scope: Cases Show Pattern of Suppression by Bishop," *Arizona Republic*, November 10, 2002.
39. Ibid.
40. Ibid.

41. Gustavo Arellano, "No Vow of Silence Here: Fernando Guido Wants to Talk, but Investigators Don't Wan to to Listen," *Orange County Weekly*, December 25, 2003.
42. Brooks Egerton and Reese Dunklin, "Taking Cover under the Red, White and Blue: Canada Lets 4 Accused of Child Molestation Call U.S. Home," *Dallas Morning News*, December 6, 2004.
43. Brooks Egerton, "DA Refuses to Pursue Ex-priest: 1960 Murder Remains Unsolved Despite New Witnesses," *Dallas Morning News*, November 20, 2004.
44. Ibid.
45. Stephen H. Galebach, "Catholic Clerical Abuse and the Role of the Court System," *Washington Post*, March 14, 2004.
46. Philip Jenkins, "Creating a Culture of Clergy Deviance," in Amson Shupe, editor, *Wolves within the Fold: Religious Leadership and the Abuses of Power* (New Brunswick: Rutgers University Press, 1997) p. 121.
47. Raymond A. Schroth, "Failed Lives, Lost Faith and Aching Hearts," *National Catholic Reporter*, March 15, 2002.
48. Jenkins, "Creating a Culture of Clergy Deviance," p. 127.
49. See Dorothy Rabinowitz, *No Crueler Tyrannies: Accusation, False Witness, and Other Terrors of Our Time* (New York: Wall Street Journal Press, 2003).
50. Dorothy Rabinowitz, "A Priest's Story," *Wall Street Journal*, April 27, 2005, p. A14.
51. David Hechler, *The Battle and the Backlash* (Lexington, Massachusetts: D. C. Heath and Company, Lexington Books, 1988) pp. 123–127.
52. Carl M. Cannon, "The Priest Scandal: How Old News Became a National Story...and Why It Took so Long," *American Journalism Review*, May 2002.

## *15. New Errors*

1. John Leo, "A Look at Kinsey," www.townhall.com, November 15, 2004.
2. Ibid.
3. See Judith A. Reisman and Edward W. Eichel, *Kinsey, Sex and Fraud: The Indoctrination of a People* (Lafayette, Louisiana: Lochinvar-Huntington House Publication, 1990) pp. 34–40. Reisman has been attacked for exaggeration, but the facts of Kinsey's use of data from pedophiles, of his deliberate use of a skewed sample of prisoners, and of his own personal perversion are not contested.
4. Ibid., p. 204.
5. Leroy H. Schultz, "Child Sexual Abuse in Historical Perspective" in J. R. Conte and D. A. Shore, editors, *Social Work and Child Sexual Abuse* (New York: Haworth Press, 1982) pp. 28–29.
6. Ibid., p. 28.
7. Ibid., p. 30.
8. Leroy G. Schultz, "Diagnosis and Treatment—Introduction," in Leroy G. Schultz, editor, *The Sexual Victimology of Youth* (Springfield, Illinois: Charles C. Thomas, Publisher, 1980) p. 40.
9. Ibid., p. 41.
10. "Attacking the Last Taboo," *Time*, April 15, 1980.

11. John Money, "Introduction" in Theo Sandfort, *Boys on Their Contacts with Men: A Study of Sexually Expressed Friendships* (Elmhurst, New York: Global Academic Publishers, 1987) p. 6.
12. Ibid., p. 8.
13. Ibid., p. 15.
14. Ibid., p. 23.
15. Ibid., p. 84.
16. Ibid., p. 90.
17. Ibid., p. 91.
18. Ibid., p. 124.
19. Ibid., p. 122.
20. Ibid., p. 21.
21. David Finkelhor, *Sexually Victimized Children* (New York: The Free Press, 1979) p. 31.
22. "Attacking the Last Taboo." Pomeroy also sought to normalize bestiality. He wrote in a book for children, "I have known cases of farm boys who have had a loving sexual relationship with an animal and who felt good about their behavior until they got to college, where they learned for the first time that what they had done was 'abnormal.' Then they were upset" (*Boys and Sex* [New York: Delacorte Press, 1981] pp. 171–172).
23. Finkelhor, p. 15.
24. Richard Farson, *Birthrights: A Bill of Rights for Children* (New York: Macmillan Publishing Co., Inc., 1974) pp. 146–147.
25. Ibid., pp. 147–148.
26. Ibid., p. 153.
27. D. J. West, *Homosexuality* (Hammondsworth: Penguin Books, 1960) p. 79.
28. Bruce Rind, Robert Bauserman, and Philip Tromovitch, "A Meta-Analytic Examination of Assumed Properties of Child Sexual Abuse Using College Samples," *Psychological Bulletin of the American Psychological Association*, July 1998, p. 42.
29. Ibid., p. 44.
30. Ibid., p. 22.
31. Ibid., p. 46.
32. Ibid., p. 23.
33. Ginsburg coauthored "Sex Bias in the U. S. Code," Report for the U. S. Commission on Civil Rights, April 1977, which proposes this. See Frank V. York and Robert H. Knight, "Homosexual Behavior and Pedophilia," available at www.US2000.org/cfmc/pedophilia.pdf, p. 7. Some have attempted to defend Ginsburg. Timothy Noah claims Ginsburg merely approved of a statute that, among other things, lowered the age of consent to twelve, and did not state that she approved of lowering the age of consent to twelve ("Lindsay Graham's Smear, Part II," *Slate*, September 29, 2005). At the very least, Ginsburg did not object to lowering the age of consent to twelve.
34. Eberstadt, "'Pedophilia Chic' Reconsidered," *Weekly Standard*, Vol. 6 Issue 16, January 1, 2001.
35. Abraham H. Maslow, *Eupsychian Management: A Journal* (Homewood, Illinois: Richard R. Irwin, Inc., and The Dorsey Press, 1965) p. 167.
36. Sandfort, p. 6.

37. Judith Levine, *Harmful to Minors: The Perils of Protecting Children from Sex* (Minneapolis: University of Minnesota Press, 2002) p. x.
38. Ibid., p. 57.
39. William R. Stayton, "Pederasty in Ancient and Early Christian History," www2.hu-berlin.de/sexology/GESUND/ARCHIV/SEN/CH20.HTM.
40. Phil Baty, "Fury over PhD for Child-Sex Research," *Times Higher Education Supplement*, December 6, 2004.
41. Olga Wojtas, "Academic Freedom versus the Last Taboo," *Times Higher Education Supplement*, November 23, 2001.
42. Quoted in Joyce Milton, *The Road to Malpsychia: Humanistic Psychology and Its Discontents* (San Francisco: Encounter Books, 2002) p. 135.
43. Michael W. Higgins and Douglas R. Letson, *Power and Peril: The Catholic Church at the Crossroads* (Toronto: HarperCollins Publishers Ltd., 2002) p. 228.
44. Howard P. Bleichner discusses the catastrophic effects of humanist psychology. See *View from the Altar: Reflections on the Rapidly Changing Catholic Priesthood* (New York: Crossroad Publishing Company, 2004) pp. 33–34.
45. Milton, p. 135.
46. Ibid.
47. See Rosemary Curb and Nancy Manahan, *Lesbian Nuns: Breaking the Silence* (New York: Warner Books, 1985), pp. 3–14.
48. Milton, p. 135.
49. Independent Board of Inquiry Regarding St. Anthony's Seminary, Santa Barbara, California, Findings.
50. Ibid.
51. George Neumayr, "Liberal Catholicism's Just Desserts," *The American Prowler*, March 1, 2002.
52. Elizabeth Pullen, "An Advocacy Group for Victims of Clerical Sex Abuse," in Anson Shupe, editor, *Wolves within the Fold: Religious Leadership and Abuses of Power* (New Brunswick: Rutgers University Press, 1998) p. 70.
53. "Van Handel was convicted of child abuse in 1994, sentenced to eight years in prison and now lives in Santa Cruz as a registered sex offender" (Fred Alvarez, "Two Brothers' Suit Accuses Priests of Molestation," *Los Angeles Times*, December 30, 2004).
54. "Lawsuit Accuses Bishop of Sex Abuse; Church: A Former Altar Boy Alleges Molestation When the Cleric Served in Huntington Park," *Los Angeles Times*, July 6, 2002.
55. For the history of the crisis, see Ann Carey, *Sisters in Crisis: The Tragic Unraveling of Women's Religious Communities* (Huntington, Indiana: Our Sunday Visitor Publishing Division, 1997) pp. 184–210.
56. Anita M. Caspery, *Witness to Integrity: The Crisis of the Immaculate Heart Community of California* (Collegeville, Minnesota: Liturgical Press, 2003) p. 241.
57. "Breaking Silence: Former Priest Describes Alleged Abuse by Florida Bishop," *ABC News*, March 22, 2002. Fischer had denied abusing Dixon, but "in a secret agreement, the Jefferson City diocese gave Dixon $125,000 with the promise that he not pursue any further claims against the diocese and the priests [Fischer and Daly]" (Dawn Fallik, "Ex-Seminarian's Charges Lead to Removal of Priest," *St. Louis Post-Dispatch*, March 8, 2002). Fischer and Daly have not been the objects of criminal prosecution.

58. William F. Buckley Jr., "The Writhings of Bishop O'Connell: The Pope Must Rue Those Who Corrupt the Young," *National Review*, March 12, 2002.
59. "Questionable Defense: Mental Health Experts Doubt Bishop's Explanation," ABC News, March 22, 2002.
60. Ellwood E. Keiser, *Hollywood Priest* (New York: Doubleday, 1991) p. 169.
61. Michael S. Rose, *Goodbye! Good Men: How Catholic Seminaries Turned away Two Generations of Vocations from the Priesthood* (Cincinnati: Aquinas Publishing Ltd., 2002) p. 285.
62. Ibid.
63. Henry Raymint, "Herder and Herder Books Undergo a Vast Change," *New York Times*, May 27, 1971.
64. Linda Wolfe, "The Birds and the Bees Were Never Like This," *New York Times*, July 17, 1975.
65. Edwin McDowell, "Picture Book on Sex Withdrawn," *New York Times*, September 19, 1982.
66. Michael Paulson, "Church Meets Dissenting Voices with Silence," *Boston Globe*, September 16, 2002.
67. Anthony Kosnick, William Carroll, Agnes Cunningham, Ronald Modras, and James Schulte, *Human Sexuality: New Directions in American Catholic Thought* (New York: Paulist Press, 1977) p. 52.
68. Ibid., p. 55.
69. Ibid., p. 59.
70. Ibid., p. 56.
71. Howard P. Bleichner, *View from the Altar: Reflections on the Rapidly Changing Catholic Priesthood* (New York: Crossroad Publishing Company, 2004) p. 40.
72. Richard John Neuhaus, "Scandal Time (Continued)," *First Things*, June/July 2002.
73. Kosnick et al., pp. 92–93.
74. Ibid., p. 97.
75. Ibid., pp. 147–148.
76. Ibid., pp. 148–149.
77. Ibid., p. 150.
78. Ibid., p. 151.
79. Ibid., p. 164.
80. André Guindon, *The Sexual Language: An Essay in Moral Theology* (Ottawa: University of Ottawa Press, 1976) p. 374.
81. Ibid., p. 315.
82. Ibid., p. 375.
83. Joseph Wilson, "The Enemy Within: A Parish Priest Cautions His Would-be Defenders," www.cwnews.com
84. *Boston Globe* Staff, *Betrayal: The Crisis of the Catholic Church* (Boston: Little, Brown, and Company, 2002) pp. 232–233.
85. Wilson, "The Enemy Within."
86. John McElhenny, "Msgr. Says Harm of Abuse Wasn't Recognized," *Boston Globe*, February 23, 2004.
87. Michael W. Higgins, and Douglas R. Letson, *Power and Peril: The Catholic Church at the Crossroads* (Toronto: HarperCollins Publishers Ltd, 2002) p. 232.

88. Douglas Letson, "Catholic Universities in the Modern World," *The Tablet*, October 2, 2001.
89. Higgins and Letson, p. 233.
90. "Sex Offense: One Part of His Story," *National Catholic Reporter*, June 7, 2002.
91. Ibid.
92. Investigator Anthony Fowler, December 16, 2002 Interview with Anonymous (name blacked out), p. 10,851, New Hampshire Attorney General's Office documents.
93. John Doe I, et al. vs. Rev. Rudolph Kos et al., District Court of Dallas County, Texas, 93-05258-G, p. 5904, ll. 2025, p. 5905, l. 1–14.
94. Anna A. Terruwe and Conrad Baars, *Psychic Wholeness and Healing: Using All the Powers of the Human Psyche* (New York: Alba House, 1981) pp. 253–54.

## *16. Old Errors*

1. Thomas G. Plante, Gerdenio Manuel, and Curtis Bryant, "Personality and Cognitive Functioning among Hospitalized Sexually Offending Roman Catholic Priests," *Pastoral Psychology*, Vol. 45, No. 2, 1996, p. 135.
2. Ibid., p. 136.
3. Ibid.,
4. Ibid., p.137. Adele Meyer stated that "anger is energy and, like any other form of energy, it eventually seeks release, sometimes in convoluted, indirect, and inappropriate ways" (*Sex Offenders: Approaches to Understanding and Management* [Holmes Beach, Florida: Learning Publications, Inc., 1988] p. 20).
5. Plante, Manuel, and Bryant, "Personality and Cognitive Functioning," p.137.
6. The National Review Board for the Protection of Children and Young People observed that "the lack of expressions of outrage by bishops—both at the time they first learned of the abhorrent acts of some priests and in dealing with the crisis publicly—is troubling. The Board has seen no letters condemning the men who have engaged in such conduct" (*A Report on the Crisis in the Catholic Church in the United States* [Washington, D.C.: United States Conference of Catholic Bishops, 2004] p. 94).
7. David Kiefer, "Saving Minds and Hearts," *San Francisco Examiner*, July 2, 2002.
8. Osinski is serving a ten-year sentence for abusing a minor (Patricia Lefevere, "Bishop to Reimburse Diocese $250,000 for Abuse Settlement," *National Catholic Reporter*, June 21, 2002).
9. Jason Berry, "Survivors Connect to Heal, Raise Voices," *National Catholic Reporter*, November 8, 2002.
10. Servais Pinckaers saw the source of this error in the nominalist conception of the liberty of indifference: "Because of its pretension to be the unique source of the moral act, liberty ought to refuse all direct participation of the other faculties of man, of the emotions and the bodily especially, in the moral decision" (Servais Pinckaers, O.P., "La nature de la moralité: Morale casuistique et morale thomiste," in *Saint Thomas D'Aquin: Somme Theologique: Les Actes Humaines II* [Paris: Les editions du Cerf, 1997] p. 226, author's translation).

11. Conrad Baars, *Feeling and Healing Your Emotions* (Gainesville, Florida: Bridge-Logos, 1979, 2003), p. 77.
12. Josef Pieper, *The Four Cardinal Virtues* (Notre Dame, Indiana: University of Notre Dame Press, 2003) p. 193.
13. Ibid., p. 194.
14. *Summa Theologica*, IIa-IIae, Q. 158, Art. 8. (Westminster, Maryland: Christian Classics, 1981).
15. Pieper, p. 130.
16. Pieper, p. 132.
17. Kevin Culligan, "Sacred Rage and Rebuilding the Church: Jesus Shows Us How Emotions Can Move Us to Action," *National Catholic Reporter*, September 13, 2002.
18. Helen Goode, Hannah McGee, and Ciarán O'Boyle, *Time to Listen: Confronting Child Sexual Abuse by Catholic Clergy in Ireland* (Dublin: The Liffey Press, 2002) p. 171.
19. Pieper, p. 194.
20. Quoted by William D. Perri, *A Radical Challenge for Priesthood Today: Can It Survive* (Mystic, Connecticut: Twenty-Third Publications, 1996) p. 75.
21. Ibid.
22. John Money and Anke A. Ehrhardt, *Man & Woman, Boy & Girl: The Differentiation and Dimorphism of Gender Identity from Conception to Maturity* (Baltimore: Johns Hopkins University Press, 1972) p. 234.
23. *Summa Theologica*, IIa-IIae, Q. 123, Art. 10.
24. John Allen, "The Word from Rome," *National Catholic Reporter*, December 5, 2003.
25. Romanus Cessario, O.P., *Introduction to Moral Theology* (Washington, D.C.: The Catholic University of America Press, 2001) pp. 229–230.
26. Ibid., p. 231.
27. Pinckaers sees the nominalist conception of the liberty of indifference as the source of the Catholic tendency to identify sin with sexual sin, because desire tends to negate liberty. See "La nature de la moralité," p. 227.
28. Alfred C. Kinsey, *Sexual Behavior in the Human Female* (Philadelphia: Saunders, 1953) p. 121.
29. Fred Tasker, "Burgeoning Scandal Spotlights Flaws in the Therapy Given to Priests," *Miami Herald*, April 14, 2002.
30. Baars, p. 74.
31. Russell Shaw, *To Hunt, to Shoot, to Entertain: Clericalism and the Catholic Laity* (San Francisco: Ignatius Press, 1993) p. 25.
32. Servais Pinckaers, O.P., *The Sources of Christian Ethics,* translated by Sr. Mary Thomas Noble, O.P. (1985. Washington, D.C.: Catholic University of America Press, 1995) p. 252.
33. Shaw, p. 26.
34. Tasker, "Burgeoning Scandal Spotlights Flaws in the Therapy Given to Priests."
35. Stephen J. Pope, "The Catholic Church's Response Is Inadequate" in Louise I. Gerdes, *Child Sexual Abuse in the Catholic Church* (San Diego: Greenhaven Press, 2003), p. 50.
36. See Louis Bouyer's *The Spirit and Forms of Protestantism,* translated A. V. Littledale (Princeton: Sceptre Press, 2001) pp. 184–198. Bouyer recognized that the God of

nominalism is "a monster repugnant both to common sense and to moral feeling" (p. 197).

37. See Pinckaers, "La nature de la moralité," pp. 215–276.
38. Cessario, p. 237.
39. Humbertus Czernin, *Das Buch Groër: Eine Kirchenchronik* (Vienna: Wieser Verlag, 1998) p. 16.
40. Ibid., p. 42.
41. Ibid., p. 146.
42. Ibid., p. 158.
43. Ibid., p. 159.
44. Ibid., p. 173.
45. Ibid., p. 181.
46. State of Illinois, 5th District, June 1, 1999, No. 5-97-0900 Parks v. Kownacki. The Illinois Supreme Court dismissed the suit because it had been filed outside the statute of limitations, but Kownacki is the object of other unresolved lawsuits by boys who say he had abused them. He has not been criminally charged.
47. Marie M. Fortune and Joretta L. Marshall, *Forgiveness and Abuse: Jewish and Christian Reflections* (New York: Haworth Pastoral Press, 2002) p. 2.
48. Peter Horsfield, "Forgiving Abuse—An Ethical Critique" in Fortune and Marshall, p. 58.
49. Anger at evil is especially important in cases of sexual abuse. Those who do not react violently to the sexual abuse done to them may in turn abuse others. See Australian study, p. 274.
50. L. Gregory Jones, *Embodying Forgiveness: A Theological Study* (Grand Rapids, Michigan: William B. Eerdmans Publishing Company, 1995) p. 5.
51. Rabbi Mark Dratch, "Forgiving the Unforgivable? Jewish Insights into Repentance and Forgiveness," in Fortune and Marshall, p. 8.
52. Ibid., p. 11.
53. Jessica Wehrman, "Gettelfinger Makes a Stand: Local Bishop Was One of the Few to Vote against Revised Abuse Policies," *Evansville Courier & Press*, November 14, 2002.
54. Ibid.
55. Karin Bøhm-Pedersen, "Confessed after Seeing 'Passion,'" *Aftenposten*, March 29, 2004.
56. Dratch, "Forgiving the Unforgivable?" p. 21.
57. Sacha Pfeiffer and Thomas Farragher, "Suit Names Archdiocese, N.H. Bishop," *Boston Globe*, March 24, 2002.
58. http://www.pip.com.au/~chenderson/forgive.htm. She goes on to discuss:

    *Forgive and forget:* We are often told to "forgive and forget", and we assume it is Scriptural. It isn't. The phrase "forgive and forget" comes from Shakespeare's *King Lear*. While God may forget, at no time does God require humans to do so. In fact, requiring victims of abuse to forget is the worst thing possible. It is the exact opposite of the healing process. Healing requires integration, not repression, of the memories.

    *Forgiveness and trust:* Forgiveness is often confused with trust. This confusion ignores the fact that forgiveness is about past events, while trust is about the future. Even when a perpetrator has truly repented, it is still the only responsible course to ensure that they are kept out of situations that may cause temptation.

*Forgiveness and punishment:* Many believe that forgiveness and punishment are opposites—that forgiveness negates the need for punishment. This is not so. The opposite of forgiveness is revenge. Punishment, on the other hand, is society's means of enforcing moral standards and the offender's personal responsibility.

*Forgiveness and reconciliation:* Often victims are expected to be reconciled to the offender, especially after they claim to have forgiven. Forgiveness, however, only says that there is no continuing bitterness. It does not, and cannot necessarily, mean that the relationship can be restored, as if the abuse had never happened. Sins may be forgiven, but their consequences may be permanent. Letting go of the past does not mean altering it.

*Repentance and remorse:* Remorse is not repentance, although is often mistaken for it. Remorse focuses on the possible consequences of discovery for the offender, rather than focusing on recognition and restitution. Repentance is about taking responsibility; remorse is about avoiding it.

## *Conclusion*

1. Shirley Ragsdale, "Iowa Church Officials for Years Hid Allegations of Sexual Abuse," *Des Moines Register*, May 25, 2004.
2. Jane Lampman, "Man at the Center of Catholics' Maelstrom," *Christian Science Monitor*, March 22, 2002.
3. Michael J. Miller, "Extreme Liturgical Abuse," *Catholic World News*, April 2005.
4. Alan Scher Zagier, "Diocese of Venice Abuse Settlements Top $1.5 Million," *Naples Daily News*, June 12, 2002.
5. John L. Allen, Jr. reports that "the May 13 bulletin of Adista, an Italian Catholic news agency . . . documents the cases of 32 priests in Italy accused of sexual abuse from 2000 to 2006 alone. These are not 'allegations' in the sense of mere rumor, but cases in which criminal procedures are either pending or have been brought to resolution, which is how the names and details became public. . . .

   "Perhaps most startling for American sensibilities is the fact that, according to the Adista report, at least five of these priests are still in active ministry, in four cases after having been convicted criminally of acts of sexual abuse with minors.

   "For the sake of clarity, it should be noted that the 'one-strike' policy under which a priest is permanently removed from ministry for even one act of sexual abuse pertains only to the United States, and does not apply in other parts of the world, where bishops enjoy greater discretion.

   "Adista quotes a May 21, 2002, statement from the secretary general of the Italian bishops' conference, Msgr. Giuseppe Betori, who said that the phenonmenon of clerical sexual abuse in Italy is 'such a small reality that it does not merit specific attention . . . more than that reserved for other social categories.' For that reason, Betori said, 'the Permanent Council of the Conference has never spoken about cases of pedophilia, the conference has no list in this regard, we do not have any cases in evidence nor a procedure for monitoring [them]" ("The Word from Rome," *National Catholic Reporter*, May 12, 2006).

6. Melinda Hennenberger, "Scandals in the Church: The Overview: Pope Offers Apology to Victims of Sex Abuse by Priests," *New York Times*, April 24, 2002.
7. Brooks Egerton and Brendan M. Case, "Priest Thwarts U.S. Bishops' Abuse Policy by Crossing River: Rovira, Accused of Rape in Texas, Finds 'Different Set of Rules' in Mexico," *Dallas Morning News*, March 15, 2005.
8. Brendan M. Case, Brooks Egerton, and Reese Dunklin, "Too Much Tolerance? Even as U.S. Catholic Leaders Tout Their Tougher Child Abuse Policy, Some Have Allowed Fallen Priests to Start over Abroad, and Some Haven't Even Asked the Vatican to Expel Them," *Dallas Morning News*, March 15, 2005.
9. Ibid.
10. Brooks Egerton, "Priest Accused of Rapes Finds Prominence: Filipino Church Leaders Welcome Garcia Despite Incidents with Altar Boys," *Dallas Morning News*, March 15, 2005.
11. See the conservative estimates in Louise Haggett, *The Bingo Report: Mandatory Celibacy and Clergy Sex Abuse* (Freeport, Maine: Center for the Study of Religious Issues, 2005) p. 188.
12. Shirley Jülich sees a version of the Stockholm Syndrome as creating a bond between victims and abusers, a bond which delays reporting of abuse. It is not until the bond is broken that victims can report, and "for many victims this could be some years after the sexual abuse has ceased." Jülich concludes that "the introduction of any statute of limitations could disadvantage victims of child sexual abuse" ("Stockholm Syndrome and Child Sexual Abuse," *Journal of Child Sexual Abuse*, Vol. 14 [3], 2005, p. 128).
13. Court of Common Pleas, First Judicial District of Pennsylvania, Criminal Trial Division, Misc. no. 03-00-239, Report of the Grand Jury, p.7 (henceforth Philadelphia Grand Jury). See pp. 68–76 of this report for recommended changes in Pennsylvania law.
14. Linda Graham Caleca and Richard D. Walton, "Faith Betrayed," *Indianapolis Star*, February 16, 1997, p. A9.
15. Philadelphia Grand Jury, p. 291.
16. John L. Allen, Jr., "Vatican Prosecutor Weighs in on Sex Abuse: Article Calls for End to Statute of Limitations in Abuse Cases," *National Catholic Reporter*, February 4, 2005.
17. "Prosecutor Byron Overton said the Rev. Mark Kurzendoerfer, 47, committed a crime, but the statute of limitations on the actions has expired" (Dave Hosick, "Kurzendoerfer Won't Face Charges," *Evansville Courier and Press*, June 12, 2002).
18. Melinda Henneberger, "My Priest, the Child Molester: Why Was the Congregation So Quick to Forgive Him?" www.slate.com. She sees the dynamics of incest at work: "Just as in families, where sexual abuse is often denied and victims blamed, church communities that have trusted and leaned on these men are deeply, viscerally reluctant to believe allegations against them."
19. See Associated Press, "Ousted Priest Also Stole," October 30, 2004; Michelle Nicolosi, "Cases around Country Show Theft-Abuse Link: Alleged Victims Say They Often Received Lavish Gifts from Priests," *Seattle Post-Intelligencer*, October 30, 2004; Nicolosi, "Few Safeguards Made It Easy to Skim from the Collection," *Seattle Post-Intelligencer*, October 30, 2004; Gregg M. Miliote, "Diocese Sues Priest on Embezzlement Charge," *Fall River Herald News*, March 5, 2005. In this last case, the

diocese of Fall River claims that Father Bernard Kelly stole $1.2 million from two parishes. At one he had as a roommate his friend Paul Nolin, who has been accused of child rape and murder.

20. Mark Dowd, "Gays in the Priesthood," *The Tablet*, May 5, 2001.
21. Mark D. Jordan, "Summit at the Vatican: The Forbidden Question," *Newsday*, April 28, 2002.
22. William D. Perri, *A Radical Challenge for Priesthood Today: Can It Survive?* (Mystic, Connecticut: Twenty-Third Publications, 1996) p. 75.
23. Ibid., p. 80.
24. George Weigel, "Self-Deception Key to Priest Scandal," *Newsday*, April 29, 2002.
25. Larry B. Stammer wrote, "But among those younger priests—those ordained twenty years or less—the figure was 23%." ("The Times Poll: 15% Identify as Gay or 'On Homosexual Side,'" *Los Angeles Times*, October 20, 2002).
26. Teresa Watanabe, "The Times Poll: Young Priests Hold Old Values: Their Views Are Often at Odds with Liberal Reform of Vatican II in 1960s," *Los Angeles Times*, October 21, 2002.
27. I have used "Catholic Church" largely as a synonym for the Latin Church, but this is misleading. Twenty-four Churches are in communion with the Pope, and twenty-three of them allow married clergy. Only the Latin (or Western Church) requires celibacy of its priests (although not of its deacons), with very few exceptions (Protestant clergy who have converted). The other twenty-three churches have had married clergy since their foundations, and at least since the Council of Trullo priests have been allowed to have marital relations with their wives.
28. Bob Harvey, "Married to God, and Family: Alone in the West, Ottawa's Ukrainian Catholic Seminary Trains Married Men for the Priesthood," *Ottawa Citizen*, October 26, 2003.
29. Josef Pieper, *The Four Cardinal Virtues* (Notre Dame, Indiana: University of Notre Dame Press, 2003) p. 197.
30. Joseph Cardinal Ratzinger (Pope Benedict XVI), *Salt of the Earth: The Church at the End of the Millennium*, translated by Adrian Walker (San Francisco: Ignatius Press, 1997) p. 185.
31. Frank Keating was shown a letter that the vicar general of the Diocese of Kansas City wrote to his counterpart in Chicago. "The letter alleged that I didn't attend Mass. But that wasn't all. It also charged that I kept a mistress whom the priest-author mentioned by name. Every word was a lie" (Frank Keating, "The Last Straw: Quitting the Bishops' Review Board," *Crisis*, October 2003).
32. Genevieve Abdo, "Bishops, Lay Panel at Odds," *Chicago Tribune*, May 12, 2004.
33. John L. Allen Jr., "Interview with Archbishop Daniel Pilarczyk," *National Catholic Reporter*, May 11, 2004.
34. Ibid.
35. Dennis Coday, "Former Seminarians Want Alma Mater Investigated: Faculty Accused of Sexual Abuse," *National Catholic Reporter*, May 14, 2004.
36. John Lantingua wrote, "Mike Wegs...said church lawyers questioned him so aggressively last year during a deposition session about O'Connell's sexual relationship with him and his painful family past that he attempted suicide and was hospitalized for weeks" ("Accuser Decries Bishop's 'Plantation' Life" *Palm Beach Post*, May 17, 2004).

37. "Bishop Spin: Christian Discredits Church Again," *Manchester Union Leader*, May 30, 2004.
38. The others are the Congregation for Eastern Churches, the Congregation for Divine Worship and the Discipline of the Sacraments, Congregation for the Evangelization of Peoples, the Congregation for Consecrated Life and the Societies of Apostolic Life, Congregation for Catholic Education, the Council for the Family.
39. Report of the Board of Inquiry into Past Handling of Complaints of Sexual Abuse in the Anglican Church Diocese of Brisbane (May 2003) pp. 57–58.
40. Martin Keller, "Das Ganze Leben is eine Erfindung," *Die Zeit*, November 4, 2005.
41. Martin DeAgostino, "Bill Extends Time to File Sex-Abuse Lawsuit: Dioceses Claim Proposal 'Punitive, Vindictive,'" *South Bend Tribune*, January 28, 2004; Justin McIntosh, "Child Abuse Disclosure Law Backed," *Marietta Times*, May 9, 2005; Andy Newman, "Court Rejects Abuse Claims Citing Church," *New York Times*, February 22, 2006; T. R. Reid, "Catholic Leaders Fight Legislation on Suits: States Consider Easing Statutes of Limitations," *Washington Post*, April 1, 2006; "Colorado, Ohio Bishops' Fight on Child Sex Abuse Measures Successful," *Catholic News Service*, April 17, 2006.

## *Epilogue*

1. www.vatican.va/news_services/liturgy/2005/via_crucis/en/station_08.html
2. www.vatican.va/news_services/liturgy/2005/via_crucis/en/station_09.html
3. Sandro Magister, "The First Sentence from Prefect Levada Makes the Legion Tremble," *Espresso*, July 28, 2005.
4. Ibid.
5. John L. Allen, Jr., "The Word from Rome," *National Catholic Reporter*, July 22, 2005.
6. For the evidence about Maciel, see Jason Berry, *Vows of Silence: the Abuse of Power in the Papacy of John Paul II* (New York: Free Press, 2004).
7. John L. Allen, Jr., "Vatican Restricts Ministry of Legionaries Order Founder," *National Catholic Reporter*, May 19, 2006.
8. Maddy Sauer, "Tough Call for Pope on Sex Abuse Case," ABC News, May 18, 2006.
9. John L. Allen, Jr., "Legion's News Traced to Vatican Ally," *National Catholic Reporter*, June 3, 2005.
10. Cindy Wooden, "Vatican Says Legionaries' Founder Cannot Exercise Ministry Publicly," Catholic News Service, May 19, 2006.
11. "Maciel debe acatar resolucíon: Nicola Bux," *Milenio*, June 7, 2006.

# BOOKS CITED


Allen, Jr., John L. *All the Pope's Men: The Inside Story of How the Vatican Really Thinks.* New York: Doubleday, 2004

Allen, Jr., John L. *Opus Dei.* New York: Doubleday, 2005.

Baars, Conrad W. *Feeling and Healing Your Emotions.* Gainesville, Florida: Bridge-Logos, 1979, 2002.

Baars, Conrad W. *How to Treat and Prevent the Crisis in the Priesthood.* Chicago: Franciscan Herald Press, 1972.

Bailey, Jr., Charles L. *The Shadow of the Cross: The True Account of My Childhood Sexual and Ritual Abuse at the Hands of a Roman Catholic Priest.* New York: iUniverse, Inc., 2006.

Bainton, Roland. *Erasmus of Christendom.* 1969. New York: Crossroad, 1982.

Bell, Alan P. and Martin S. Weinberg. *Homosexualities: A Study of Diversity among Men and Women.* New York: Simon and Schuster, 1978.

Benyei, Candace R. *Understanding Clergy Misconduct in Religious Systems: Scapegoating, Family Secrets, and the Abuse of Power.* New York: Haworth Pastoral Press, 1998.

Bergeron, Gary. *Don't Call Me a Victim: Faith, Hope, and Sexual Abuse in the Catholic Church.* Lowell, Massachusetts: Arc Angel Publishing, 2005.

Berry, Jason. *Lead Us Not into Temptation: Catholic Priests and the Sexual Abuse of Children.* Urbana: University of Illinois Press, 2000.

Berry, Jason and Gerald Renner. *Vows of Silence: The Abuse of Power in the Papacy of John Paul II.* New York: Free Press, 2004.

Bleichner, Howard P. *View from the Altar: Reflections on the Rapidly Changing Catholic Priesthood.* New York: Crossroad Publishing Company, 2004.

Boisvert, Donald L. and Robert E. Goss. *Gay Catholic Priests and Clerical Sexual Misconduct: Breaking the Silence.* New York: Harrington Park Press, 2005.

Boston Globe Staff. *Betrayal: The Crisis of the Catholic Church*. Boston: Little, Brown, and Company, 2002.

Bouyer, Louis. *The Spirit and Forms of Protestantism*. Translated by A. V. Littledale. 1956. Princeton: Sceptre Press, 2001.

Boyle, Patrick. *Scout's Honor*. Rocklin, California: Prima Publishing, 1994.

Briere, John N. *Child Sexual Trauma: Theory and Treatment of Its Lasting Effects*. Newbury Park, California: Sage Publications, 1992.

Brundage, James A. *Law, Sex, and Christian Society in Medieval Europe*. Chicago: University of Chicago Press, 1987.

Bruni, Frank and Elinor Burkett. *A Gospel of Shame: Children, Sexual Abuse, and the Catholic Church*. New York: Viking, 1993.

Canadian Conference of Catholic Bishops. *From Pain to Hope: Report from the Ad Hoc Committee on Child Sexual Abuse*. Ottawa: Publication Service, Canadian Conference of Catholic Bishops, 1992.

Carey, Ann. *Sisters in Crisis: The Tragic Unraveling of Women's Religious Communities*. Huntingdon, Indiana: Our Sunday Visitor Publishing Division, 1997.

Carnes, Patrick J. *The Betrayal Bind: Breaking Free of Exploitative Relationships*. Deerfield, Florida: Health Communications, Inc., 1997.

Caspery, Anita M. *Witness to Integrity: The Crisis of the Immaculate Heart Community of California*. Collegeville, Minnesota: Liturgical Press, 2002.

Cessario, Romanus. *Introduction to Moral Theology*. Washington, D. C.: The Catholic University of America Press, 2001.

Coldrey, Barry M. *Religious Life without Integrity: The Sexual Abuse Crisis in the Catholic Church*. Thornbury, Australia: Tamanaraik Press, n.d.

Conte, J. R., and D. A. Shore, editors. *Social Work and Child Sexual Abuse*. New York: Haworth Press, 1982.

Cornwell, John. *The Pontiff in Winter: Triumph and Conflict in the Reign of John Paul II*. New York: Doubleday, 2004.

Coville, Walter J., Paul F. D'Arcy, Thomas N. McCarthy, and John J. Rooney. *Assessment of Candidates for the Religious Life: Basic Psychological Issues and Problems*. Washington, D. C.: Center for Applied Research in the Apostolate, 1968.

Cozzens, Donald. *The Changing Face of the Priesthood: A Reflection on the Priest's Crisis of Soul*. Collegeville, Minnesota: Liturgical Press, 2000.

Cozzens, Donald. *Sacred Silence: Denial and the Crisis in the Church*. Collegeville, Minnesota: Liturgical Press, 2002.

Curb, Rosemary and Nancy Manahan. *Lesbian Nuns: Breaking Silence*. New York: Warner Books, 1985.

Czernin, Hubertus. *Das Buch Groër: Eine Kirchenchronik*. Vienna: Wieser Verlag, 1998.

Damian, Peter. *Letters 31–60*. Translated by Owen J. Blum. Washington, D. C.: The Catholic University of America Press, 1990.

Dinter, Paul E. *The Other Side of the Altar: One Man's Life in the Catholic Priesthood*. New York: Farrar, Straus and Giroux, 2003.

Dirnbeck, Josef. *Reibebaum Krenn: Vom Pabstfrühstuck zu den "Bubendummheiten."* Vienna-Klosterneuberg: Edition Va Bene, 2004.

Dorais, Michel. *Don't Tell: The Sexual Abuse of Boys*. Montréal and Kingston: McGill-Queens University Press, 2002.

Dorecki, Paul R. *The Clergy Sexual Abuse Crisis: Reform and Renewal in the Catholic Community*. Washington, D.C.: Georgetown University Press, 2004.

Doyle, Thomas P., A. W. Richard Sipe, and Patrick J. Wall. *Sex, Priests, and Secret Codes: The Catholic Church's 2,000-Year Paper Trail of Sexual Abuse*. Los Angeles: Volt Press, 2002.

Drewermann, Eugen. *Kleriker: Psychogramm eines Ideals*. 1989. Munich: Deutscher Taschenbuch Verlag, 1991.

Dworkin, Andrea. *Woman Hating*. New York: Penguin Books, 1974.

Echols, Mike. *Brother Tony's Boys: The Largest Case of Child Prostitution in U. S. History*. Amherst, New York: Prometheus Books, 1996.

Engel, Randy. *The Rite of Sodomy: Homosexuality and the Roman Catholic Church*. Export, Pennsylvania: New Engel Publishing, 2006.

Exley, Richard. *Perils of Power: Immorality in the Ministry*. Tulsa: Honor / Harrison House, Inc., 1988.

Farson, Richard. *Birthright: A Bill of Rights for Children*. New York: Macmillan Publishing Co., Inc., 1974.

Finkelhor, David. *Sexually Victimized Children*. New York: Free Press, 1979.

Fleming, Patrick, Sue Lauber-Fleming, and Mark T. Matousek. *Broken Trust: Stories of Pain, Hope, and Healing from Clerical Abuse Survivors and Abusers*. New York: Crossroad Publishing Company, 2007.

Fortune, Marie M. *Is Nothing Sacred? The Story of a Pastor, the Women He Sexually Abused, and the Congregation He Nearly Destroyed.* Cleveland: United Church Press, 1999.

Fortune, Marie M., and Joretta L. Marshall. *Forgiveness and Abuse: Jewish and Christian Reflections.* New York: Haworth Pastoral Press, 2002.

France, David. *Our Fathers: The Secret Life of the Catholic Church in an Age of Scandal.* New York: Broadway Books, 2004.

Freud, Sigmund. *Introductory Lectures on Psychoanalysis.* Translated by James Strachey. New York: W. W. Norton and Company, 1977.

Friberg, Nils C., and Mark R. Laaser. *Before the Fall: Preventing Pastoral Sexual Abuse.* Collegeville, Minnesota: The Liturgical Press, 1998.

Friedman, Joel, and Marcia Mobilia Boumil. *Betrayal of Trust: Sex and Power in Personal Relationships.* Westport, Connecticut: Praeger, 1995.

Gartner, Richard B. *Betrayed as Boys: Psychodynamic Treatment of Sexually Abused Men.* New York: The Guilford Press, 1999.

Gartner, Richard B. *Beyond Betrayal: Taking Charge of Your Life after Boyhood Sexual Abuse.* Hoboken, New Jersey: John Wiley and Sons, 2005.

Gartner, Richard B., editor. *Memories of Sexual Betrayal: Truth, Fantasy, Repression, and Dissociation.* Northvale, New Jersey: Jason Aronson, Inc., 1997.

Gerdes, Louise I. *Child Sexual Abuse in the Catholic Church.* San Diego: Greenhaven Press, 2003.

Gonsiorek, John C. *Breach of Trust: Sexual Exploitation by Health Care Professionals and Clergy.* Thousand Oaks, California: Sage Publications, 1995.

Goode, Helen, Hannah McGee, and Ciarán O'Boyle. *Time to Listen: Confronting Child Sexual Abuse by Catholic Clergy in Ireland.* Dublin: The Liffey Press, 2002.

Graham, Dee L. R. with Edna I. Rawlings and Roberta K. Rigsby. *Loving to Survive: Sexual Terror, Men's Violence, and Women's Lives.* New York: New York University Press, 1994.

Greeley, Andrew M. *Priests: A Calling in Crisis.* Chicago: University of Chicago Press, 2004.

Grenz, Stephen J., and Roy D. Bell. *Betrayal of Trust: Confronting and Preventing Clergy Sexual Misconduct.* Grand Rapids, Michigan: Baker Books, 2002.

Guindon, André. *The Sexual Language: An Essay in Moral Theology.* Ottawa: University of Ottawa Press, 1976.

Haggett, Louise. *The Bingo Report: Mandatory Celibacy and Clergy Sexual Abuse.* Freeport, Maine: Center for the Study of Religious Issues, 2005.

Haliczer, Stephen. *Sexuality in the Confessional: A Sacrament Profaned.* New York: Oxford University Press, 1996.

Hammel-Zabin, Amy. *Conversations with a Pedophile: In the Interest of Our Children.* Fort Lee, New Jersey: Barricade Books, 2003.

Handlin, J. H. *Survivors of Predator Priests.* Irving, Texas: Tapestry Press, 2005.

Hardon, John A. *A Prophet for the Priesthood: A Spiritual Autobiography of Father Gerald M. C. Fitzgerald.* Bardstown, Kentucky: Eternal Life, 1998.

Harris, Michael. *Unholy Orders: Tragedy at Mount Cashel.* Markham, Ontario: Viking, 1990.

Hechler, David. *The Battle and the Backlash.* Lexington, Massachusetts: D. C. Heath and Company, Lexington Books, 1998.

Henton, David, with David McCann. *Boys Don't Cry: The Struggle for Justice and Healing in Canada's Biggest Sex Abuse Scandal.* Toronto: McClellan and Stewart, Inc., 1995.

Herman, Judith Lewis. *Trauma and Recovery.* New York: Basic Books, 1992, 1997.

Herr, Vincent V., Magda B. Arnold, Charles A. Weisberger, and Paul F. D'Arcy. *Screening Candidates for the Priesthood and Religious Life.* Chicago: Loyola University Press, 1962, 1964.

Higgins, Michael W., and Douglas R. Letson. *Power and Peril: The Catholic Church at the Crossroads.* Toronto: HarperCollins Publishers Ltd., 2002.

Hoyt, Edwin P. *Horatio's Boys: The Life and Works of Horatio Alger, Jr.* Radnor, Pennsylvania: Chilton Book Company, 1974.

Hughes, Sam. *Steering the Course: A Memoir.* Montréal: McGill-Queens University Press, 2002.

Hunter, Mic. *Abused Boys: The Neglected Victims of Sexual Abuse.* New York: Fawcett Books, 1990.

Jackowski, Karol. *The Silence We Keep: A Nun's View of the Catholic Priest Scandal.* New York: Harmony Books, 2004.

Jay, Karla, and Allen Young. *The Gay Report: Lesbians and Gay Men Speak out about Sexual Experiences and Lifestyles.* New York: Summit Books, 1977.

Jenkins, Philip. *The New Anti-Catholicism: The Last Acceptable Prejudice.* New York: Oxford University Press, 2003.

Jenkins, Philip. *Pedophiles and Priests: Anatomy of a Contemporary Crisis.* New York: Oxford University Press, 1996.

John Jay College of Criminal Justice. *The Nature and Scope of Sexual Abuse of Minors by Catholic Priests and Deacons in the United States, 1950–2002.* Washington, D.C.: The United States Conference of Catholic Bishops, 2004.

Jones, L. Gregory. *Embodying Forgiveness: A Theological Study.* Grand Rapids, Michigan: William B. Eerdmans Publishing Company, 1995.

Kane, Thomas A. *The Healing Touch of Affirmation.* Whitinsville, Massachusetts: Affirmation Books, 1976.

Kelly, Sister Jane. *Taught to Believe the Unbelievable: A New Vision of Hope for the Catholic Church and Society.* New York: Writers Club Press / iUniverse, Inc., 2002.

Kennedy, Eugene. *The Unhealed Wound: The Church and Human Sexuality.* New York: St. Martin's Press, 2001.

Kennedy, Eugene and Victor J. Heckler. *The Catholic Priest in the United States: Psychological Investigations.* Washington, D. C.: United States Catholic Conference, 1972.

Kieser, Ellwood E. *Hollywood Priest.* New York: Doubleday, 1991.

Kinsey, Alfred C. *Sexual Behavior in the Human Female.* Philadelphia: Saunders, 1953.

Kosnick, Anthony, William Carroll, Agnes Cunningham, Ronald Modras, and James Schulte. *Human Sexuality: New Direction in Catholic Thought.* New York: Paulist Press, 1977.

Laumann, Edward O., John H. Gagnon, Robert T. Michael, and Stuart Michaels. *The Social Organization of Sexuality: Sexual Practices in the United States.* Chicago: University of Chicago Press, 1994.

Lea, Henry C. *A History of Sacerdotal Celibacy in the Christian Church, Vol. I.* 1907. Honolulu: University Press of the Pacific, 2003.

Levine, Judith. *Harmful to Minors: The Perils of Protecting Children from Sex.* Minneapolis: University of Minnesota Press, 2002.

Liebreich, Karen. *Fallen Order: A History.* London: Atlantic Books, 2004.

Likoudis, Paul. *Amchurch Comes Out: The U. S. Bishops, Pedophile Scandals and the Homosexual Agenda.* Petersburg, Illinois: Roman Catholic Faithful, Inc., 2002.

Manseau, Peter. *Vows: The Story of a Priest, a Nun, and Their Son.* New York: Free Press, 2005.

Martínez de Velasco, José. *Los documentos secretos de los Legionarios de Cristo.* Barcelona: Ediciones B, 2004.

Maslow, Abraham H. *Eupsychian Management: A Journal.* Homewood, Illinois: Richard D. Irvin, Inc., and the Dorsey Press, 1965.

McDonough, Peter, and Eugene C. Bianci. *Passionate Uncertainty: Inside the American Jesuits.* Berkeley: University of California Press, 2002.

Mendel, Matthew Parynik. *The Male Survivor: The Impact of Sexual Abuse.* Thousand Oaks, California: Sage Publications, 1995.

Meyer, Adele. *Sex Offenders: Approaches to Understanding and Management.* Holmes Beach, Florida: Learning Publications, Inc., 1998.

Milton, Joyce. *The Road to Malpsychia: Humanistic Psychology and Our Discontents.* San Francisco: Encounter Books, 2002.

Mitchell, Timothy. *Betrayal of Innocents: Desire, Power, and the Catholic Church in Spain.* Philadelphia: University of Pennsylvania Press, 1998.

Money, John, and Anke A. Ehrhardt. *Man and Woman, Boy and Girl: The Differentiation and Dimorphism of Gender Identity from Conception to Maturity.* Baltimore: Johns Hopkins University Press, 1972.

Moore, Chris. *Betrayal of Trust: The Father Brendan Smyth Affair and the Catholic Church.* Dublin: Merino Press, 1995

National Review Board for the Protection of Children and Young People. *A Report on the Crisis in the Catholic Church in the United States.* Washington, D.C.: The United States Conference of Catholic Bishops, 2004.

O'Brien, Dereck. *Suffer Little Children: An Autobiography of a Foster Child.* St. John's, Newfoundland: Breakwater, 1991.

O'Connor, Alison. *A Message from Heaven: The Life and Crimes of Father Sean Fortune.* Dingle, Ireland: Brandon, Mount Eagle Publications, 2000.

Owens, M. Lilliana. *Most Rev. Anthony Schuler, S.J., D.D., First Bishop of El Paso.* El Paso, Texas: Revista Catolica Press, 1953.

Parker, Jim. *Raped in the House of God: The Murder of My Soul and Its Lifetime Effects.* New York: iUniverse, Inc., 2004.

Perri, William D. *A Radical Challenge for Priesthood Today: Can It Survive?* Mystic, Connecticut: Twenty-Third Publications, 1996.

Pexdek, Kathy, and William P. Banks, editors. *The Recovered Memory / False Memory Debate.* San Diego: The Academic Press, 1996.

*Pictorial History of St. Pius X Parish of El Paso.*

Pieper, Josef. *The Four Cardinal Virtues*. 1954. Notre Dame, Indiana: University of Notre Dame Press, 2003.

Pinckaers, Servais. *The Sources of Christian Ethics*, translated by Sr. Mary Thomas Noble, O. P., 1985. Washington, D. C.: The Catholic University of America Press, 1995.

Pinckaers, Servais, translator. *Saint Thomas D'Aquin: Somme Théologique: les Actes Humaines II*. Paris: les editions du Cerf, 1997.

Plante, Thomas G. *Bless Me Father For I Have Sinned: Perspectives on Sexual Abuse Committed by Roman Catholic Priests*. Westport, Connecticut: Praeger, 1998.

Plante, Thomas G., editor. *Sin against the Innocents: Sexual Abuse by Priests and the Role of the Catholic Church*. Westport, Connecticut: Praeger, 2004.

Podles, Leon J. *The Church Impotent: The Feminization of Christianity*. Dallas: Spence Publishing Company, 1999.

Rabinowitz, Dorothy. *No Crueler Tyrannies: Accusation, False Witness, and Other Terrors of Our Time*. New York: Wall Street Journal Press, 2003.

Ratzinger, Cardinal Joseph (Pope Benedict XVI). *Salt of the Earth: The Church at the End of the Millennium*, translated by Adrian Walker. San Francisco: Ignatius Press, 1997.

Reisman, Judith A., and Edward W. Eichel. *Kinsey, Sex and Fraud: The Indoctrination of a People*. Lafayette, Louisiana: Lochinvar – Huntington House Publication, 1990.

*Report of the Archdiocesan Commission of Enquiry into the Sexual Abuse of Children by Members of the Clergy*. St. John's, Newfoundland: Archdiocese of St. John's, 1990.

*Report of the Board of Inquiry into Handling Past Complaints of Sexual Abuse in the Anglican Church Diocese of Brisbane*. May 2003.

Ritter, Bruce. *Covenant House: Lifeline to the Street*. New York: Doubleday, 1987.

Ritter, Bruce. *Sometimes God Has a Kid's Face: The Story of America's Exploited Street Kids*. New York: Covenant House, 1988.

Rodríguez, Pepe. *Pederastia en la Iglesia católica*. Barcelona: Ediciones B, 2002.

Rogers, Martin. *Who's in the Seminary? Roman Catholic Seminarians Today*. Toronto: Novalis, 1996.

Ronningham, Elsa F., editor. *Disorders of Narcissism: Diagnostic, Clinical, and Empirical Implications*. Northvale, New Jersey: Jason Aronson, Inc., 2000.

Rose, Michael S. *Goodbye! Good Men: How Catholic Seminaries Turned Away Two Generations of Vocations from the Priesthood*. Cincinnati: Aquinas Publications, Ltd., 2002.

Rossetti, Stephen J. *A Tragic Grace: The Catholic Church and Child Sexual Abuse.* Collegeville, Minnesota: Liturgical Press, 1996.

Rueda, Enrique T. *The Homosexual Network: Private Lives and Public Policy.* Old Greenwich, Connecticut: Devin Adair, 1982.

Russell, Glenda M., and Nancy H. Kelly. *Subtle Demoting: The Media, Homosexuality, and the Priest Abuse Scandal.* Amherst, Massachusetts: Institute for Gay and Lesbian Strategic Studies, 2003.

Sandfort, Theo. *Boys on Their Contacts with Men: A Study of Sexually Expressed Friendships.* Elmhurst, New York: Global Academic Publishers, 1987.

Sandfort, Theo, Edward Brongersma, and Alex van Naerssen, editors. *Male Intergenerational Intimacy: Historical, Socio-Psychological, and Legal Perspectives.* New York, Harrington Park Press, 1991.

Schoenherr, Richard A. *Goodbye Father: The Celibate Male Priesthood and the Future of the Catholic Church.* New York: Oxford University Press, 2002.

Sennott, Charles M. *Broken Covenant.* New York: Simon and Schuster, 1992.

Schultz, Leroy G., editor. *The Sexual Victimology of Youth.* Springfield, Illinois: Charles C. Thomas, Publisher, 1980.

Shaw, Russell. *To Hunt, to Shoot, to Entertain: Clericalism and the Catholic Laity.* San Francisco: Ignatius Press, 1993.

Shupe, Amson, editor. *Wolves within the Fold: Religious Leadership and the Abuses of Power.* New Brunswick, New Jersey: Rutgers University Press, 1997.

Sipe, A. W. Richard. *Celibacy in Crisis: A Secret World Revisited.* New York: Brunner / Mazel Publishers, 2003.

Sipe, A. W. Richard. *Sex, Priests, and Power: Anatomy of a Crisis.* New York: Brunner / Mazel Publishers, 1995.

Sperry, Leo. *Sex, Priestly Ministry and the Church.* Collegeville, Minnesota: Liturgical Press, 2003.

Sprigg, Peter, and Timothy Dailey, editors. *Getting It Straight: What Research Shows about Homosexuality.* Washington, D. C.: Family Research Council, 2004.

Steed, Judy. *Our Little Secret: Confronting Child Abuse in Canada.* Toronto: Vintage, Random House of Canada, 1995.

Storr, Anthony. *Feet of Clay: Saints, Sinners and Madmen: A Study of Gurus.* New York: Free Press, 1997.

Terruwe, Ann A., and Conrad W. Baars. *Psychic Wholeness and Healing: Using All the Powers of the Human Psyche.* New York: Alba House, 1981.

Thigpen, Paul, editor. *Shaken by Scandals: Catholics Speak Out about Priests' Sexual Abuse*. Ann Arbor, Michigan: Charis, Servant Publications, 2002.

Thomas Aquinas. *Summa Theologica, Complete English Translation in Five Volumes*, translated by the English Dominican Province. Benzinger Bros., 1911, 1948. Westminster, Maryland: Christian Classics.

Vaknin, Sam. *Malignant Self Love: Narcissism Revisited*. Prague: Narcissus Publications, 2002.

Van der Zee, John. *Agony in the Garden: Sex, Lies, and Redemption for the Troubled Heart of the American Catholic Church*. New York: Thunder Mouth's Press / Nation Books, 2002.

Victor, Jeffrey S. *Satanic Panic: The Creation of a Contemporary Legend*. Chicago: Open Court, 1993.

Ward, Benedicta, translator. *The Sayings of the Desert Fathers: The Alphabetical Collection*. London: Mowbrays, 1975.

Weigel, George. *The Courage to Be Catholic: Crisis, Reform and the Future of the Church*. New York: Basic Books, 2002.

West, D. J. *Homosexuality*. Hammondsworth, England: Penguin Books, 1960.

Wilkes, Paul. *Excellent Catholic Parishes: The Guide to Best Places and Practices*. New York: Paulist Press, 2001.

Wosh, Peter J. *Covenant House: Journey of a Faith-Based Charity*. Philadelphia: University of Pennsylvania Press, 2005.

Yonke, David. *Sin, Shame, and Secrets: The Murder of a Nun, the Conviction of a Priest, and the Cover-up in the Catholic Church*. New York: Continuum, 2006.

# RESOURCES

## BishopAccountability.org

When court orders forced the archdiocese of Boston to release its personnel files on abusive priests, a small group of Bostonians realized that it was important for everyone to have access to these documents. They began posting them on line so that anyone could see how the bishops had handled reports of abuse. This was to hold the bishops accountable (whence the name) for their governance of the Church, a governance which affects not only Catholics but society as a whole, which had to deal with the human wreckage that abuse creates.

The enormous number of documents required organization to make them useful, and bishop accountability set out become a public electronic archive of all court papers and newspaper articles on abuse. It has begun on the material available in the United States, and will expand first to other English-speaking countries and then to the world.

This will enable anyone who is interested to know the facts about the abuse crisis.

The organization does not of itself propound any analysis of the causes of the crisis or how to end abuse, but seeks to provide the information without which any response is only emotional rather than rational and effective.

# VictimPower.org

VictimPower.org is a website that allows anyone to report a crime anonymously and to respond to requests for further information in complete anonymity.

Unlike confidential tip lines, Victimpower.org sets up an anonymous two-way communication between law enforcement and the victim, allowing the victim to tell his story fully and find out what law enforcement will do with his information. It also allows law enforcement to ask follow-up questions, to communicate back to the victim on the importance of his report, and to ascertain the legitimacy of his charges.

The VictimPower web site completely protects the victim's anonymity from computer hackers and overzealous prosecutors. No identifying information is kept by the site or by the web hosting service. What does not exist cannot be hacked and cannot be subpoenaed.

The creators of VictimPower are united by a desire to help victims by connecting them to law enforcement and other authorities in a way that protects victims and witnesses, while holding accountable those in positions of authority. Our hope is that enhanced accountability will make the schools, neighborhoods, workplaces, and churches of our land into safer places for the next generation.

## *Frequently Asked Questions*
## *(from the VictimPower website)*

Q: What types of crime can be reported via VictimPower.org?

A: Any type. VictimPower is especially useful for victims and witnesses who have a particular need for anonymity and security while they learn about the relevant law enforcement authorities and make their decision about whether to come forward in person to those authorities. This is often the case for victims of sexual abuse and harassment, as well as any other offense where there is a risk of adverse consequences for a victim or witness who reports a violation of law by the offender.

Q: What types of authorities can receive reports of crimes or violations of law via VictimPower?

A: Police, prosecutors, and responsible persons in private organizations can all receive reports. Even if VictimPower's database does not include an e-mail address, fax number, or other contact information for a particular authority, you can fill in the contact information and VictimPower staff will forward your report and your questions to that authority. Please note that we retain discretion over whether to forward individual reports.

## SNAP

### *www.snapnetwork.org*

The Survivors Network of those Abused by Priests (SNAP) is a volunteer self-help organization of survivors of clergy sexual abuse and their supporters. We work to end the cycle of abuse in two ways:

- By supporting one another in personal healing;
- By pursuing justice and institutional change by holding individual perpetrators responsible and the church accountable.

Our most powerful tool is the light of truth. Through our stories and our actions, we bring healing and justice. Specifically, we:

- Reach out to survivors, their families, and supporters;
- Build mechanisms to support our life-long journey of personal healing including individual contact, peer counseling, support groups, written and web-based information and materials;
- Work through education and persuasion to change the structure and culture of abuse in the church and society at large.

SNAP has national and regional offices and local support groups that can be contacted through the website.

# ACKNOWLEDGMENTS

MY FIRST THANKS GO TO ALL the reporters who worked on the sexual abuse scandal; without their work this book would not have been possible. Their reporting was a great help to the victims who wanted the truth proclaimed and recognized. I would like to thank Charles Eby for his assistance in researching this book and Terry McKiernan of BishopAccountability.org for his endless work in putting documents online. I am grateful to Father Tom Doyle, Richard Sipe, and Jason Berry for their example of decades-long dedication to helping victims of abuse, and to them and to all those who assisted in reading and correcting the manuscript. All errors are my responsibility.

Special thanks belong to the lawyers who represented victims and brought the facts to light. The lawyers took big chances, had their reputations attacked, and themselves went through emotional grinders. Without the lawyers there would have been no reforms and abuse would be still destroying numberless victims. Timothy Lytton tells this story in his forthcoming *Holding Bishops Accountable: How Lawsuits Helped the Catholic Church Confront Clergy Sexual Abuse.*

I am grateful to Dr. Richard Perlmutter for his assistance in helping me deal with my own emotional reactions to the horrors I uncovered in my research, and to my wife and children for their support and patience in dealing with a husband and father who was not always in the best mood during the years I worked on this book.

My thanks to Sam Torode for his design and layout of the book.

I thank all those who helped me with their sympathy and prayers. After the sorrows of this life, I pray that we may all merrily meet in heaven.

# INDEX

*Notes are referenced by the letter* n *and the note number following the page number*